Third Edition

Programming in C++

Nell Dale
University of Texas, Austin

Chip Weems
University of Massachusetts, Amherst

JONES AND BARTLETT PUBLISHERS

Sudbury, Massachusetts

BOSTON   TORONTO   LONDON   SINGAPORE

World Headquarters
Jones and Bartlett Publishers
40 Tall Pine Drive
Sudbury, MA 01776
978-443-5000
info@jbpub.com
www.jbpub.com

Jones and Bartlett Publishers
Canada
2406 Nikanna Road
Mississauga, ON L5C 2W6
CANADA

Jones and Bartlett Publishers
International
Barb House, Barb Mews
London W6 7PA
UK

ISBN 0-7637-3234-6

Library of Congress Cataloging-in-Publication Data

Dale, Nell B.
  Programming in C++ / Nell Dale, Chip Weems.
    p. cm.
  Includes bibliographical references and index.
  ISBN 0-7637-3234-6 (pbk.)
  1. C++ (Computer program language)   I. Weems, Chip.   II. Title.
  QA76.73.C153D35 2004
  005.13'3—dc22

                              2004013772

Production Credits

Chief Executive Officer: Clayton Jones
Chief Operating Officer: Don W. Jones, Jr.
President, Higher Education and Professional Publishing: Robert W. Holland, Jr.
V.P., Design and Production: Anne Spencer
V.P., Manufacturing and Inventory Control: Therese Bräuer
Acquisitions Editor: Stephen Solomon
Production Manager: Amy Rose
Marketing Manager: Matthew Bennett
Editorial Assistant: Deborah Arrand
Production Assistant: Caroline Senay
Text Design: Anne Spencer
Cover Design: Kristin E. Ohlin
Manufacturing and Inventory Coordinator: Amy Bacus
Composition: Northeast Compositors, Inc.
Printing and Binding: Courier Westford
Cover Printing: John Pow Company

Printed in the United States of America
08 07 06 05 04   10 9 8 7 6 5 4 3 2 1

To Al, my husband and best friend, and to our children and our children's children.

N.D.

To Lisa, Charlie, and Abby with love.

C.W.

To quote Mephistopheles, one of the chief devils, and tempter of Faust,

> *...My friend, I shall be pedagogic,*
> *And say you ought to start with Logic...*
> *...Days will be spent to let you know*
> *That what you once did at one blow,*
> *Like eating and drinking so easy and free,*
> *Can only be done with One, Two, Three.*
> *Yet the web of thought has no such creases*
> *And is more like a weaver's masterpieces;*
> *One step, a thousand threads arise,*
> *Hither and thither shoots each shuttle,*
> *The threads flow on, unseen and subtle,*
> *Each blow effects a thousand ties.*
> *The philosopher comes with analysis*
> *And proves it had to be like this;*
> *The first was so, the second so,*
> *And hence the third and fourth was so,*
> *And were not the first and second here,*
> *Then the third and fourth could never appear.*
> *That is what all the students believe,*
> *But they have never learned to weave.*

J. W. von Goeth, *Faust*, Walter Kaufman trans., New York, 1963, 199.

As you study this book, do not let the logic of algorithms bind your imagination, but rather make it your tool for weaving masterpieces of thought.

Preface

The first two editions of *Programming in C++* have provided a straight-forward, no-frills introduction to C++. Throughout the successive editions of this book, one thing has not changed: our commitment to the student. As always, our efforts are directed toward making the sometimes difficult concepts of computer science more accessible to all students.

This edition of *Programming in C++* continues to reflect our philosophy that topics once considered too advanced can be taught in the first course. For example, we address metalanguages explicitly as the formal means of specifying programming language syntax. We discuss modular design in terms of abstract steps, concrete steps, functional equivalence, and functional cohesion. Preconditions and postconditions are used in the context of the algorithm walk-through, in the development of testing strategies, and as interface documentation for user-written functions. Data abstraction and abstract data types (ADTs) are explained in conjunction with the C++ class mechanism, creating a natural lead-in to object-oriented programming.

ISO/ANSI-standard C++ is used throughout the book, including relevant portions of the new C++ standard library.

Changes to the Third Edition

The third edition does not introduce additional C++ syntax nor change the order of the content. What we have done is completely revamp the goals, the case studies, and the exercises. In addition, beginning with Chapter 13, the language of the material has become more object oriented.

Goals The chapter goals have been reorganized to reflect two aspects of learning: knowledge and skills. Thus, the goals are divided into two sections. The first lists the knowledge goals, phrased in terms of what the student should know after reading the chapter. The second lists what the student should be able to do after reading the chapter.

Programming Examples Each chapter has a completely new programming example. Programming examples that begin with a problem statement and end with a tested program have been the hallmark of our books. In this edition, we have added screen shots of the output for each of the examples.

All of the exercises are new in this edition. The number of exercises has been expanded by between twenty and thirty percent. All of the programming problems are new.

Object-Oriented Language The List ADT in Chapter 13 has been changed by removing the Print operation and introducing an iterator pair, Reset and GetNextItem. This change provides better encapsulation. The list does not need to know anything about the items that it contains. The list simply returns objects to the client program, which should know what the objects are. The flaw in this design is pointed out in Chapter 14: The Delete and BinSearch operations use the relational operators, limiting the type of item to built-in types. In this chapter, the relational operators are replaced by operations LessThan and Equal; the documentation states that ItemType must implement these operations. The concepts of action responsibilities and knowledge responsibilities also are discussed. Each class is independently tested, stressing the importance of testing.

C++ and Object-Oriented Programming

Some educators reject the C family of languages (C, C++, Java) as too permissive and too conducive to writing cryptic, unreadable programs. Our experience does not support this view, *provided that the use of language features is modeled appropriately*. The fact that the C family permits a terse, compact programming style cannot be labeled simply as "good" or "bad". Almost any programming language can be used to write in a style that is too terse and clever to be easily understood. The C family indeed may be used in this manner more often than are other languages, but we have found that with careful instruction in software engineering, and a programming style that is straightforward, disciplined, and free of intricate language features, students can learn to use C++ to produce clear, readable code.

It must be emphasized that although we use C++ as a vehicle for teaching computer science concepts, the book is not a language manual and does not attempt to cover all of C++. Certain language features—templates, operator overloading, default arguments, run-time type information, and mechanisms for advanced forms of inheritance, to name a few—are omitted in an effort not to overwhelm the beginning student with too much, too fast.

There are diverse opinions about when to introduce the topic of object-oriented programming (OOP). Some educators advocate an immersion in OOP from the very beginning, whereas others (for whom this book is intended) favor a more heterogeneous approach, in which both functional decomposition and object-oriented design are presented as design tools. The chapter organization of *Programming in C++* reflects a transitional approach to OOP. Although we provide an early preview of object-oriented design in Chapter 4, we delay a focused discussion until Chapter 14, after students have acquired a firm grounding in algorithm design, control abstraction, and data abstraction with classes.

Synopsis

Chapter 1 is designed to create a comfortable rapport between students and the subject. The basics of hardware and software are presented, and problem-solving techniques are introduced and reinforced in a problem-solving case study.

Instead of overwhelming the student right away with the various numeric types available in C++, Chapter 2 concentrates on only two types: `char` and `string`. (For the latter, we use the ISO/ANSI string class provided by the standard library.) With fewer data types to keep track of, students can focus on overall program structure and get an earlier start on creating and running a simple program. Chapter 3 follows with a discussion of the C++ numeric types and proceeds with material on arithmetic expressions, function calls, and output. Unlike many books that detail *all* of the C++ data types and *all* of the C++ operators at once, these two chapters focus on only the `int`, `float`, `char`, and `string` types, and the basic arithmetic operators. Details of the other data types, and the more elaborate C++ operators, are postponed until Chapter 10.

Functional decomposition and object-oriented design methodologies are a major focus of Chapter 4, and the discussion is written with a healthy degree of formalism. The treatment of object-oriented design this early in the book is more superficial than that of functional decomposition. However, students gain the perspective early that there are two—not just one—design methodologies in widespread use and that each serves a specific purpose. Object-oriented design is covered in depth in Chapter 14. Chapter 4 also covers input and file I/O. The early introduction of files permits the assignment of programming problems that require the use of sample data files.

Students learn to recognize functions in Chapters 1 and 2, and they learn to use standard library functions in Chapter 3. Chapter 4 reinforces the basic concepts of function calls, argument passing, and function libraries. Chapter 4 also relates functions to the implementation of modular designs, and begins the discussion of interface design that is essential to writing proper functions.

Chapter 5 begins with Boolean data, but its main purpose is to introduce the concept of flow of control. Selection, using If-Then and If-Then-Else structures, is used to demonstrate the distinction between physical ordering of statements and logical ordering. We also develop the concept of nested control structures. Chapter 5 concludes with a lengthy Testing and Debugging section that expands on the modular design discussion by introducing preconditions and postconditions. The algorithm walk-through and code walk-through are introduced as means of preventing errors, and the execution trace is used to find errors that may have made it into the code.

Chapter 6 is devoted to loop control strategies and looping operations using the syntax of the While statement. Rather than introducing multiple syntactical structures, our approach is to teach the concepts of looping using only the While statement. However, because many instructors have told us that they prefer to show students the syntax for all of C++'s looping statements at once, the discussion of For and Do-While statements in Chapter 9 can be covered after Chapter 6.

By Chapter 7, students are already comfortable with breaking problems into modules and using library functions, and they are receptive to the idea of writing their own functions. Thus Chapter 7 focuses on passing arguments by value and covers flow of control in function calls, arguments and parameters, local variables, and interface design. Coverage of interface design includes preconditions and postconditions in the interface documentation, control abstraction, encapsulation, and physical versus conceptual hiding of an implementation. Chapter 8 expands the discussion to include reference parameters, scope and lifetime, stubs and drivers, and more on interface design, including side effects.

Chapter 9 covers the remaining "ice cream and cake" control structures in C++ (Switch, Do-While, and For), along with the Break and Continue statements. These structures are useful but not necessary. Chapter 9 is a natural ending point for the first quarter of a two-quarter introductory course sequence.

Chapter 10 begins the transition between the control structures orientation of the first part of the book and the abstract data type orientation of the second part. We examine the built-in simple data types in terms of the set of values represented by each type and the allowable operations on those values. We introduce additional C++ operators and discuss at length the problems of floating-point representation and precision. User-defined simple types, user-written header files, and type coercion are among the other topics covered in this chapter.

We begin Chapter 11 with a discussion of simple versus structured data types. We introduce the record (struct in C++) as a heterogeneous data structure, describe the syntax for accessing its components, and demonstrate how to combine record types into a hierarchical record structure. From this base, we proceed to the concept of data abstraction and give a precise definition to the notion of an ADT, emphasizing the separation of specification from implementation. The C++ class mechanism is introduced as a programming language representation of an ADT. The concepts of encapsulation, information hiding, and public and private class members are stressed. We describe the separate compilation of program files, and students learn the technique of placing a class's declaration and implementation into two separate files: the specification (.h) file and the implementation (.cpp) file.

In Chapter 12, the array is introduced as a homogeneous data structure whose components are accessed by position rather than by name. One-dimensional arrays are examined in depth, including arrays of structs and arrays of class objects. Material on multidimensional arrays completes the discussion.

Chapter 13 integrates the material from Chapters 11 and 12 by defining the list as an ADT. Because we have already introduced classes and arrays, we can clearly distinguish between arrays and lists from the beginning. The array is a built-in, fixed-size data structure. The list is a user-defined, variable-size structure, represented in this chapter as a length variable and an array of items bound together in a class object. The elements in the list are those elements in the array from position 0 through position *length* 2 1. In this chapter, we design C++ classes for unsorted and sorted list ADTs, and we code the list algorithms as class member functions. Finally, we examine C strings in order to give students some insight into how a higher-level abstraction (a string as a list of characters) might be implemented in terms of a lower-level abstraction (a null-terminated char array).

Chapter 14 extends the concepts of data abstraction and C++ classes to an exploration of object-oriented software development. Object-oriented design, introduced briefly in Chapter 4, is revisited in greater depth. Students learn to distinguish between inheritance and composition relationships during the design phase, and C++'s derived classes are used to implement inheritance. This chapter also introduces C++ virtual functions, which support polymorphism in the form of run-time binding of operations to objects.

Chapter 15 concludes the text with coverage of recursion. There is no consensus as to the best place to introduce this subject. We believe that it is better to wait until at least the second semester to cover it. However, we have included this material for those instructors who have requested it. We suggest the following prerequisite reading for the topics in Chapter 15:

Section(s)	Topic	Prerequisite
15.1–15.3	Recursion with simple variables	Chapter 8
15.4	Recursion with arrays	Chapter 12

Additional Features

Goals As described earlier, each chapter begins with a list of goals for the student, broken into two categories: knowledge goals and skill goals. They are reinforced and tested in the end-of-chapter exercises.

Programming Examples Problem solving is demonstrated through examples. In each example, we present a problem and use problem-solving techniques to develop a manual solution. Then we code the algorithm in C++. We show sample test data and output and follow up with a discussion of what is involved in thoroughly testing the program.

Testing and Debugging Testing and debugging sections follow the programming examples in each chapter and consider in depth the implications of the chapter material with regard to thorough testing of programs. These sections conclude with a list of testing and debugging hints.

Quick Checks At the end of each chapter are questions that test the student's recall of major points associated with the chapter goals. Upon reading each question, the student immediately should know the answer, which he or she can then verify by glancing at the answers at the end of the section. The page number on which the concept is discussed appears at the end of each question so that the student can review the material in the event of an incorrect response.

Exam Preparation Exercises These questions help the student prepare for tests. The questions usually have objective answers and are designed to be answerable with a few minutes of work. Answers to selected questions are given in the back of the book, and the remaining questions are answered in the *Instructor's Guide.*

Programming Warm-Up Exercises This section provides the student with experience in writing C++ code fragments. The student can practice the syntactic constructs in each chapter without the burden of writing a complete program. Solutions to selected questions from each chapter appear in the back of the book; the remaining solutions can be found in the *Instructor's Guide.*

Programming Problems These exercises, drawn from a wide range of disciplines, require the student to design solutions and write complete programs.

Programming Example Follow-Up Much of modern programming practice involves reading and modifying existing code. These exercises give the student an opportunity to strengthen this critical skill by answering questions about the example code or by making changes to it. All of the solutions to these exercises are in the *Instructor's Guide,* rather than the text, allowing the instructor the flexibility of assigning them as programming problems.

Supplements

Instructor's Guide and Test Bank The *Instructor's Guide* features chapter-by-chapter teaching notes, answers to the balance of the exercises, and a compilation of exam questions with answers. The *Instructor's Guide,* included on the *Instructor's ToolKit,* is available to adopters on request from Jones and Bartlett.

Instructor's ToolKit The *Instructor's ToolKit* is a powerful teaching tool available to adopters upon request from the publisher. It contains an electronic version of the *Instructor's Guide,* a computerized test bank, PowerPoint lecture presentations, and the complete programs from the text.

Programs The programs contain the source code for all of the complete programs that are found within the textbook. They are available on the *Instructor's ToolKit,* and also as a free download for instructors and students from the publisher's website (http://computerscience.jbpub.com/cs_resources.cfm). The programs from all of the programming examples, plus complete programs that appear in the chapter bodies, are included. (Fragments or snippets of program code are not included nor are the solutions to the chapter-ending "Programming Problems.") The program files can be viewed or edited using any standard text editor, but a C++ compiler must be used in order to compile and run the programs. The publisher offers compilers bundled with this text at a substantial discount.

Companion Website This website (www.problemsolvingcpp.jbpub.com) features the complete programs from the text.

A Laboratory Course in C++, Fourth Edition Written by Nell Dale, this lab manual follows the organization of this edition of the text. The lab manual is designed to allow the instructor maximum flexibility and may be used in both open and closed laboratory settings. Each chapter contains three types of activities: Prelab, Inlab, and Postlab. Each lesson is broken into exercises that thoroughly demonstrate the concepts covered in the corresponding chapter. The programs, program shells (partial programs), and data files that accompany the lab manual can be found on the website for this book (www.problemsolvingcpp.jbpub.com).

Acknowledgments

We would like to thank the many individuals who have helped us in the preparation of this third edition. We are indebted to the members of the faculties of the Computer Science Departments at the University of Texas at Austin and the University of Massachusetts at Amherst.

We extend special thanks to Jeff Brumfield for developing the syntax template metalanguage and allowing us to use it in the text.

For their many helpful suggestions, we thank the lecturers, teaching assistants, consultants, and student proctors who run the courses for which this book was written, as well as the students themselves.

We are grateful to the following people who took the time to offer their comments on potential changes for previous editions: Trudee Bremer, Illinois Central College; Mira Carlson, Northeastern Illinois University; Kevin Daimi, University of Detroit, Mercy; Bruce Elenbogen, University of Michigan, Dearborn; Sandria Kerr, Winston-Salem State University; Alicia Kime, Fairmont State College; Shahadat Kowuser, University of Texas, Pan America; Bruce Maxim, University of Michigan, Dearborn; William McQuain, Virginia Tech; Xiannong Meng, University of Texas, Pan America; William Minervini, Broward University; Janet Remen, Washtenaw Community College; Viviana Sandor, Oakland University; Mehdi Setareh, Virginia Tech; Katy Snyder, University of Detroit, Mercy; Tom Steiner, University of Michigan, Dearborn; John Weaver, West Chester University; Charles Welty, University of Southern Maine; Cheer-Sun Yang, West Chester University.

We also thank Mike and Sigrid Wile, along with the many people at Jones and Bartlett who contributed so much, especially Stephen Solomon and Anne Spencer. Our special thanks go to Amy Rose, our Production Manager, whose skills and genial nature turn hard work into pleasure.

Anyone who has ever written a book—or is related to someone who has—can appreciate the amount of time involved in such a project. To our families—all of the Dale clan and the extended Dale family (too numerous to name), and to Lisa, Charlie, and Abby—thanks for your tremendous support and indulgence.

N.D.
C.W.

CONTENTS

4   Program Input and the Software Design Process   109

10 Simple Data Types: Built-In and User-Defined   347

12 Arrays 457

13 Array-Based Lists   511

Overview of Programming and Problem Solving

Knowledge Goals

Goals

- *To understand what a computer program is.*
- *To understand what an algorithm is.*
- *To learn what a high-level programming language is.*
- *To understand the compilation and execution processes.*
- *To learn what the major components of a computer are and how they work together.*

Skill Goals

To be able to:

- *List the basic stages involved in writing a computer program.*
- *Describe what a compiler is and what it does.*
- *Distinguish between hardware and software.*
- *Choose an appropriate problem-solving method for developing an algorithmic solution to a problem.*

1.1 Overview of Programming

Much of human behavior and thought is characterized by logical sequences. Since infancy, you have been learning how to act, how to do things. And you have learned to expect certain behavior from other people.

On a broader scale, mathematics never could have been developed without logical sequences of steps for solving problems and proving theorems. Mass production never would have worked without operations taking place in a certain order. Our whole civilization is based on the order of things and actions.

We create order, both consciously and unconsciously, through a process we call programming. This book is concerned with the programming of one of our tools, the computer.

Just as a concert program lists the order in which the players perform pieces, a computer program lists the sequence of steps the computer performs. From now on, when we use the words *programming* and *program*, we mean computer programming and *computer program*.

com•put•er \kəm-'pyüt-ər\ *n. often attrib* (1646): one that computes; *specif*: a programmable electronic device that can store, retrieve, and process data*

Programming Planning or scheduling the performance of a task or an event.

Computer A programmable device that can store, retrieve, and process data.

Computer program A sequence of instructions to be performed by a computer.

Computer programming The process of planning a sequence of steps for a computer to follow.

The computer allows us to do tasks more efficiently, quickly, and accurately than we could by hand—if we could do them by hand at all. In order to use this powerful tool, we must specify what we want done and the order in which we want it done. We do this through programming.

How Do We Write a Program?

To write a program, we must go through a two-phase process: *problem solving* and *implementation* (see Figure 1–1).

Problem-Solving Phase

1. *Analysis and specification.* Understand (define) the problem and what the solution must do.

2. *General solution (algorithm).* Develop a logical sequence of steps that solves the problem.

3. *Verify.* Follow the steps exactly to see if the solution really does solve the problem.

---

*By permission. From *Merriam-Webster's Collegiate Dictionary*, Tenth Edition. © 1994 by Merriam-Webster Inc.

PROBLEM-SOLVING PHASE

IMPLEMENTATION PHASE

Analysis
and
specification

General solution
(algorithm)

Verify

Concrete solution
(program)

Test

MAINTENANCE PHASE

Figure 1–1 *Programming Process*

Implementation Phase

1. *Concrete solution (program).* Translate the algorithm into a programming language.
2. *Test.* Have the computer follow the instructions. Then manually check the results. If you find errors, analyze the program and the algorithm to determine the source of the errors, and then make corrections.

Once a program has been written, it enters a third phase: *maintenance.*

Maintenance Phase

1. *Use.* Use the program.
2. *Maintain.* Modify the program to meet changing requirements or to correct any errors that show up in using it.

The programmer begins the programming process by analyzing the problem and developing a general solution called an **algorithm.** Understanding and analyzing a problem take up much more time than Figure 1–1 implies. They are the heart of the programming process.

Algorithm   A step-by-step procedure for solving a problem in a finite amount of time.

If our definitions of a computer program and an algorithm look similar, it is because all programs are algorithms. A program is simply an algorithm that has been written for a computer.

An algorithm is a verbal or written description of a logical sequence of actions. We use algorithms every day. Recipes, instructions, and directions are all examples of algorithms that are not programs.

When you start your car, you follow a step-by-step procedure. The algorithm might look something like this:

1. Insert the key.
2. Make sure the transmission is in Park (or Neutral).
3. Depress the gas pedal.
4. Turn the key to the start position.
5. If the engine starts within six seconds, release the key to the ignition position.
6. If the engine doesn't start in six seconds, release the key and gas pedal, wait ten seconds, and repeat Steps 3 through 6, but not more than five times.
7. If the car doesn't start, call the garage.

Without the phrase "but not more than five times" in Step 6, you could be trying to start the car forever. Why? Because if something is wrong with the car, repeating Steps 3 through 6 over and over again will not start it. This kind of never-ending situation is called an *infinite loop*. If we leave the phrase "but not more than five times" out of Step 6, the procedure does not fit our definition of an algorithm. An algorithm must terminate in a finite amount of time for all possible conditions.

Suppose a programmer needs an algorithm to determine an employee's weekly wages. The algorithm reflects what would be done by hand:

1. Look up the employee's pay rate.
2. Determine the number of hours worked during the week.
3. If the number of hours worked is less than or equal to 40, multiply the number of hours by the pay rate to calculate regular wages.
4. If the number of hours worked is greater than 40, multiply 40 by the pay rate to calculate regular wages, and then multiply the difference between the number of hours worked and 40 by $1\frac{1}{2}$ times the pay rate to calculate overtime wages.
5. Add the regular wages to the overtime wages (if any) to determine total wages for the week.

The steps the computer follows are often the same steps you would use to do the calculations by hand.

After developing a general solution, the programmer tests the algorithm, walking through each step mentally or manually. If the algorithm doesn't work, the programmer repeats the problem-solving process, analyzing the problem again and coming up with another algorithm. Often the second algorithm is just a variation of the first. When the programmer is satisfied with the algorithm, he or she translates it into a **programming language**. We use the C++ programming language in this book.

> **Programming language**   A set of rules, symbols, and special words used to construct a computer program.

A programming language is a simplified form of English (with math symbols) that adheres to a strict set of grammatical rules. English is far too complicated a language for today's computers to follow. Programming languages, because they limit vocabulary and grammar, are much simpler.

Although a programming language is simple in form, it is not always easy to use. Try giving someone directions to the nearest airport using a vocabulary of no more than 45 words, and you'll begin to see the problem. Programming forces you to write very simple, exact instructions.

Translating an algorithm into a programming language is called *coding* the algorithm. The product of that translation—the program—is tested by running (*executing*) it on the computer. If the program fails to produce the desired results, the programmer must *debug* it—that is, determine what is wrong and then modify the program, or even the algorithm, to fix it. The combination of coding and testing an algorithm is called *implementation*.

Some people try to speed up the programming process by going directly from the problem definition to coding the program (see Figure 1–2). A shortcut here is very tempting and at first seems to save a lot of time. However, for many reasons that will become obvious to you as you read this book, this kind of shortcut actually takes *more* time and effort. Developing a general solution before you write a program helps you manage the problem, keep your thoughts straight, and avoid mistakes. If you don't take the time at the beginning to think out and polish your algorithm, you'll spend a lot of extra time debugging and revising your program. So think first and code later! The sooner you start coding, the longer it takes to write a program that works.

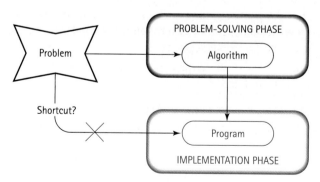

Figure 1–2   *Programming Shortcut?*

> **Documentation** The written text and comments that make a program easier for others to understand, use, and modify.
>
> **Information** Any knowledge that can be communicated.
>
> **Data** Information in a form a computer can use.

In addition to solving the problem, implementing the algorithm, and maintaining the program, documentation is an important part of the programming process. Documentation includes written explanations of the problem being solved and the organization of the solution, comments embedded within the program itself, and user manuals that describe how to use the program. Most programs are worked on by many different people over a long period of time. Each of those people must be able to read and understand your code.

After you write a program, you must give the computer the information or data necessary to solve the problem. **Information** is any knowledge that can be communicated, including abstract ideas and concepts such as "the earth is round." **Data** is information in a form the computer can use—for example, numbers and letters.

1.2   What Is a Programming Language?

In the computer, all data, whatever its form, is stored and used in binary codes, strings of 1s and 0s. Instructions and data are stored together in the computer's memory using these binary codes. If you were to look at the binary codes representing instructions and data in memory, you could not tell the difference between them; they are distinguished only by the manner in which the computer uses them. It is thus possible for the computer to process its own instructions as a form of data.

> **Machine language** The language, made up of binary-coded instructions, that is used directly by the computer.
>
> **Compiler** A program that translates a high-level language into machine code.

When computers were first developed, the only programming language available was the primitive instruction set built into each machine, the **machine language**, or *machine code*. For example:

Instruction Name	Machine Language Form
Add	100101
Subtract	010011

Computer scientists have developed high-level programming languages that are easier to use than machine code because they are closer to English and other natural languages (see Figure 1–3).

A program called a **compiler** translates programs written in certain high-level languages (C++, Pascal, FORTRAN, COBOL, Java, and Ada, for example) into machine language. If you write a program in a high-level language, you can run it on any computer that has the appropriate compiler. This is possible because most high-level languages are

Figure 1–3 *Levels of Abstraction*

standardized, which means that an official description of the language exists.*

A program in a high-level language is called a **source program**. To the compiler, a source program is just input data. It translates the source program into a machine language program called an **object program** (see

Source program A program written in a high-level programming language.

Object program The machine language version of a source program.

Some programming languages–LISP, Prolog, and many versions of BASIC, for example–are translated by an *interpreter* rather than a compiler. The difference between a compiler and an interpreter is outside of the scope of this textbook, which focuses only on compiled languages.

Figure 1-4). Some compilers also output a *listing*—a copy of the program with error messages and other information inserted.

A benefit of standardized high-level languages is that they allow you to write *portable* (or *machine-independent*) code. As Figure 1-4 emphasizes, a single C++ program can be used on different machines, whereas a program written in machine language is not portable from one computer to another.

It is important to understand that compilation and execution are two distinct processes. During compilation, the computer runs the compiler program. During execution, the object program is loaded into the computer's memory unit, replacing the compiler program. The computer then runs the object program, doing whatever the program instructs it to do (see Figure 1-5).

The instructions in a programming language reflect the operations a computer can perform. A computer can:

- transfer data from one place to another.
- input data from an input device (a keyboard or mouse, for example) and output data to an output device (a screen, for example).
- store data into and retrieve data from its memory and secondary storage.
- compare two data values for equality or inequality.
- perform arithmetic operations.

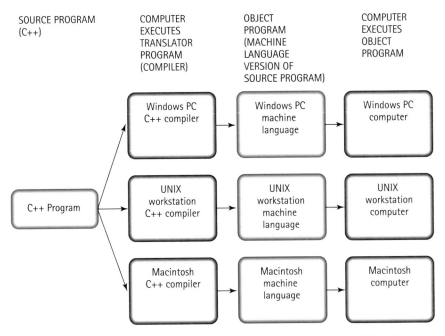

Figure 1-4 *High-Level Programming Languages Allow Programs to Be Compiled on Different Systems*

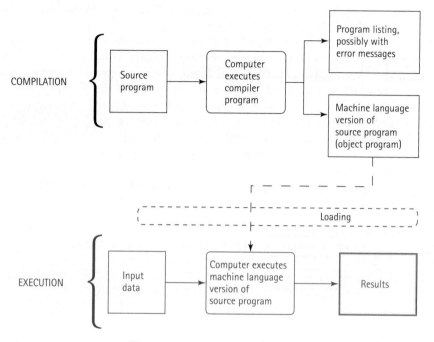

Figure 1–5 *Compilation and Execution*

Programming languages require that we use certain *control structures* to express algorithms as programs. There are four basic ways of structuring statements (instructions) in most programming languages: sequentially, conditionally, repetitively, and with subprograms (see Figure 1–6). A *sequence* is a series of statements that are executed one after another. *Selection*, the conditional control structure, executes different statements depending on certain conditions. The repetitive control structure, the *loop*, repeats statements while certain conditions are met. The *subprogram* allows us to structure a program by breaking it into smaller units.

Imagine you're driving a car. Going down a straight stretch of road is like following a sequence of instructions. When you come to a fork in the road, you must decide which way to go and then take one or the other branch of the fork. This is what the computer does when it encounters a selection control structure (sometimes called a *branch* or *decision*) in a program. Sometimes you have to go around the block several times to find a place to park. The computer does the same sort of thing when it encounters a loop in a program.

A subprogram is a process that consists of multiple steps. Every day, for example, you follow a procedure to get from home to work. It makes sense, then, for someone to give you directions to a meeting by saying, "Go to the office, then go four blocks west" without specifying all the steps you have to take to get to the office. Subprograms allow us to write parts of our programs separately and then assemble them into final form. They can greatly simplify the task of writing large programs.

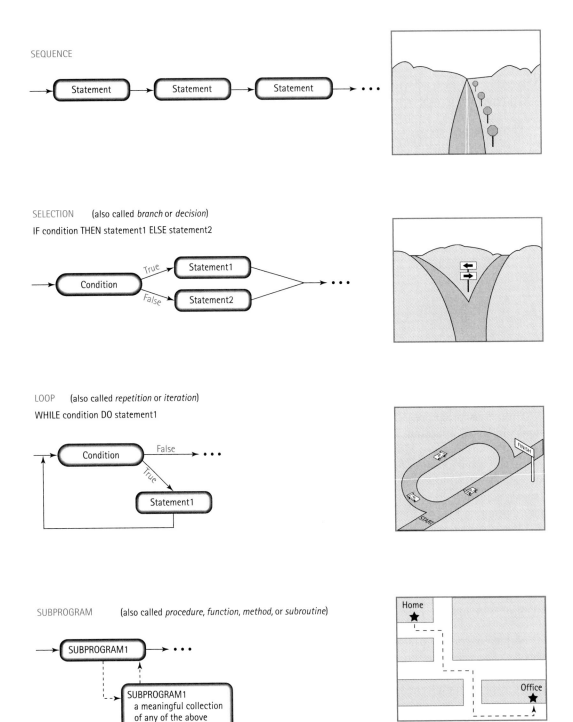

SEQUENCE

SELECTION   (also called *branch* or *decision*)

IF condition THEN statement1 ELSE statement2

LOOP   (also called *repetition* or *iteration*)

WHILE condition DO statement1

SUBPROGRAM   (also called *procedure*, *function*, *method*, or *subroutine*)

Figure 1–6   *Basic Control Structures of Programming Languages*

1.3   What Is a Computer?

You can learn how to write programs without knowing much about computers. But if you know something about the parts of a computer, you can better understand the effect of each instruction in a programming language.

Most computers have six basic components: the memory unit, the arithmetic/logic unit, the control unit, input devices, output devices, and auxiliary storage devices. Figure 1–7 is a stylized diagram of the basic components of a computer.

The **memory unit** is an ordered sequence of storage cells, each capable of holding a piece of data. Each memory cell has a distinct address to which we refer in order to store data into it or retrieve data from it. These storage cells are called *memory cells*, or *memory locations*.* The memory unit holds data

| **Memory unit**   Internal data storage in a computer. |

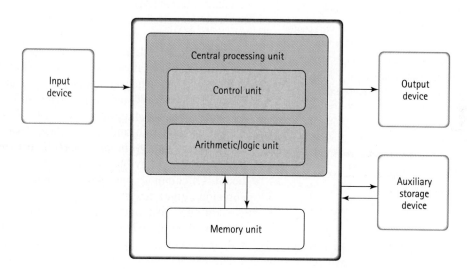

Figure 1–7   *Basic Components of a Computer*

---

*The memory unit is also referred to as RAM, an acronym for random-access memory (so called because we can access any location at random).

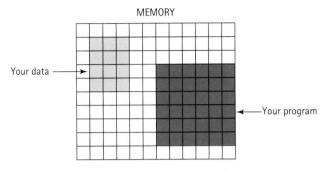

Figure 1–8   *Memory*

(input data or the product of computation) and instructions (programs), as shown in Figure 1–8.

The part of the computer that follows instructions is called the **central processing unit (CPU)**. The CPU usually has two components. The **arithmetic/logic unit (ALU)** performs arithmetic operations (addition, subtraction, multiplication, and division) and logical operations (comparing two values). The **control unit** controls the actions of the other components so that program instructions are executed in the correct order.

For us to use computers, there must be some way of getting data into and out of them. **Input/output (I/O) devices** accept data to be processed (input) and present data values that have been processed (output). A keyboard is a common input device. A display screen is a common output device.

For the most part, computers simply move and combine data in memory. The many types of computers differ primarily in the size of their memories, the speed with which data can be recalled, the efficiency with which data can be moved or combined, and limitations on I/O devices.

When a program is executing, the computer proceeds through a series of steps, the *fetch-execute cycle:*

1. The control unit retrieves (*fetches*) the next coded instruction from memory.

2. The instruction is translated into control signals.

Central processing unit (CPU)   The part of the computer that executes the instructions (program) stored in memory; made up of the arithmetic/logic unit and the control unit.

Arithmetic/logic unit (ALU)   The component of the central processing unit that performs arithmetic and logical operations.

Control unit   The component of the central processing unit that controls the actions of the other components so that instructions (the program) are executed in the correct sequence.

Input/output (I/O) devices   The parts of the computer that accept data to be processed (input) and present the results of that processing (output).

3. The control signals tell the appropriate unit (arithmetic/logic unit, memory, I/O device) to perform (execute) the instruction.

4. The sequence repeats from Step 1.

> **Peripheral device** An input, output, or auxiliary storage device attached to a computer.
>
> **Auxiliary storage device** A device that stores data in encoded form outside the computer's main memory.
>
> **Hardware** The physical components of a computer.
>
> **Software** Computer programs; the set of all programs available on a computer.
>
> **Interface** A connecting link at a shared boundary that allows independent systems to meet and act on or communicate with each other.
>
> **Operating system** A set of programs that manages all of the computer's resources.
>
> **Editor** An interactive program used to create and modify source programs or data.

Computers can have a wide variety of peripheral devices attached to them. An auxiliary storage device, or *secondary storage device*, holds coded data for the computer until we actually want to use the data. Instead of inputting data every time, we can input it once and have the computer store it onto an auxiliary storage device. Typical auxiliary storage devices are disk drives and magnetic tape drives. A *disk drive* is a cross between a compact disc player and a tape recorder. It uses a thin disk made out of magnetic material. A read/write head (similar to the record/playback head in a tape recorder) travels across the spinning disk, retrieving or recording data. A *magnetic tape drive* is like a tape recorder and is most often used to *back up* (make a copy of) the data on a disk in case the disk is ever damaged.

Together, all of these physical components are known as hardware. The programs that allow the hardware to operate are called software. Hardware usually is fixed in design; software is easily changed. In fact, the ease with which software can be manipulated is what makes the computer such a versatile, powerful tool.

In addition to the programs that we write or purchase, there are programs in the computer that are designed to simplify the user/computer interface, making it easier for us to use the machine.

The set of programs that simplify the user/computer interface and improve the efficiency of processing is called *system software*. It includes the compiler as well as the operating system and the editor (see Figure 1–9). The operating system manages all of the computer's resources. It can input programs, call the compiler, execute object programs, and carry out any other system commands. The editor is an interactive program used to create and modify source programs or data.

Although solitary (*stand-alone*) computers are often used in private homes and small businesses, it is very common for many computers to be connected together, forming a *network*. A *local area network* (*LAN*) is one in which the computers are connected by wires and must be reasonably close together, as in a single office building. In a *wide area network* (*WAN*) or *long-haul network*, the computers can be far apart geographically and communicate through phone lines, fiber optic cable, and other media. The most well-known long-haul network is the Internet, which was originally devised as

Figure 1–9   *User/Computer Interface*

a means for universities, businesses, and government agencies to exchange research information. The Internet exploded in popularity with the establishment of the World Wide Web, a system of linked Internet computers that support specially formatted documents (*Web pages*) that contain text, graphics, audio, and video.

1.4 Problem-Solving Techniques

You solve problems every day, often unaware of the process you are going through. In a learning environment, you usually are given most of the information you need: a clear statement of the problem, the necessary input, and the required output. In real life, the process is not always so simple. You often have to define the problem yourself and then decide what information you have to work with and what the results should be.

After you understand and analyze a problem, you must come up with a solution—an algorithm. Most of your experience with algorithms is in the context of *following* them. You follow a recipe, play a game, assemble a toy, take medicine. In the problem-solving phase of computer programming, you will be *designing* algorithms, not following them. This means you must be conscious of the strategies you use to solve problems in order to apply them to programming problems.

Ask Questions

If you are given a task orally, you ask questions—When? Why? Where?—until you understand exactly what you have to do. If your instructions are written, you might put question marks in the margin, underline a word or a sentence, or in some other way indicate that the task is not clear. Your questions may be answered by a later paragraph, or you might have to discuss them with the person who gave you the task.

These are some of the questions you might ask in the context of programming:

- With what do I have to work—that is, what is my data?
- What do the data items look like?
- How much data is there?
- How will I know when I have processed all the data?
- What should my output look like?
- How many times is the process going to be repeated?
- What special error conditions might come up?

Look for Things That Are Familiar

Never reinvent the wheel. If a solution exists, use it. If you've solved the same or a similar problem before, just repeat your solution. In programming, certain problems occur again and again in different guises. A good programmer immediately recognizes a subtask he or she has solved before and plugs in the solution. For example, finding the daily high and low temperatures is really the same problem as finding the highest and lowest grades on a test. You want the largest and smallest values in a set of numbers (see Figure 1-10).

Solve by Analogy

Often a problem reminds you of a similar problem you have seen before. You may find solving the problem at hand easier if you remember how you solved the other problem. In other words, draw an analogy between the two problems. As you work your way through the new problem, you come across things that are different than they were in the old problem, but usually these are just details that you can deal with one at a time.

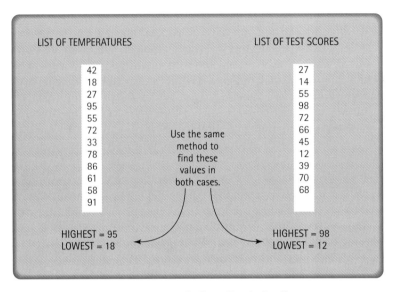

Figure 1–10 *Look for Things That Are Familiar*

Analogy is really just a broader application of the strategy of looking for things that are familiar. When you are trying to find an algorithm for solving a problem, don't limit yourself to computer-oriented solutions. Step back and try to get a larger view of the problem. Don't worry if your analogy doesn't match perfectly—the only reason for using an analogy is that it gives you a place to start (see Figure 1–11). The best programmers are people who have broad experience solving all kinds of problems.

Means-Ends Analysis

Often the beginning state and the ending state are given; the problem is to define a set of actions that can be used to get from one to the other. Suppose you want to go from Boston, Massachusetts, to Austin, Texas. You know the beginning state (you are in Boston) and the ending state (you want to be in Austin). The problem is how to get from one to the other. In this example, you have lots of choices. You can fly, walk, hitchhike, ride a bike, or whatever. The method you choose depends on your circumstances. If you're in a hurry, you'll probably decide to fly.

Once you've narrowed down the set of actions, you have to work out the details. It may help to establish intermediate goals that are easier to meet than the overall goal. Let's say there is a really cheap, direct flight to Austin out of Newark, New Jersey. You might decide to divide the trip into legs: Boston to Newark and then Newark to Austin. Your intermediate goal is to get from Boston to Newark. Now you only have to examine the means of meeting that intermediate goal (see Figure 1–12).

A library catalog system can give insight into how to organize a parts inventory.

Figure 1–11   *Analogy*

The overall strategy of means-ends analysis is to define the ends and then to analyze your means of getting between them. The process translates easily to computer programming. You begin by writing down what the input is and what the output should be. Then you consider the actions a computer can perform and choose a sequence of actions that can transform the data into the results.

Divide and Conquer

We often break up large problems into smaller units that are easier to handle. Cleaning the whole house may seem overwhelming; cleaning the rooms one at a time seems much more manageable. The same principle applies to programming. We break up a large problem into smaller pieces that we can solve individually (see Figure 1-13). In fact, the functional decomposition and object-oriented methodologies, which we describe in Chapter 4, are based on the principle of divide and conquer.

Start: Boston **Goal:** Austin	**Means:** *Fly*, walk, hitchhike, bike, drive, sail, bus
Start: Boston **Goal:** Austin	**Revised Means:** Fly to Chicago and then Austin; *fly to Newark and then Austin;* fly to Atlanta and then Austin
Start: Boston **Intermediate Goal:** Newark **Goal:** Austin	**Means to Intermediate Goal:** *Commuter flight*, walk, hitchhike, bike, drive, sail, bus
Solution: Take commuter flight to Newark and then catch cheap flight to Austin	

Figure 1–12   *Means-Ends Analysis*

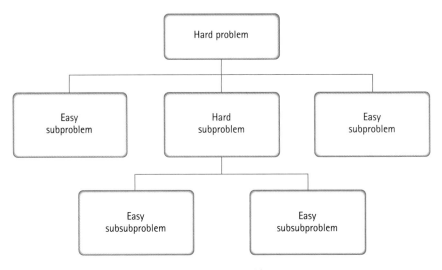

Figure 1–13   *Divide and Conquer*

The Building-Block Approach

Another way of attacking a large problem is to see if any solutions for smaller pieces of the problem exist. It may be possible to put some of these solutions together end-to-end to solve most of the big problem. This strategy is just a combination of the look-for-familiar-things and divide-and-conquer approaches. You look at the big problem and see that it can be divided into smaller problems for which solutions already exist. Solving the big problem is just a matter of putting the existing solutions together, like mortaring together blocks to form a wall (see Figure 1–14).

Merging Solutions

Another way to combine existing solutions is to merge them on a step-by-step basis. For example, to compute the average of a list of values, we must both sum and count the values. If we already have separate solutions for summing values and for counting values, we can combine them. But if we first do the summing and then do the counting, we have to read the list twice. We can save steps if we merge these two solutions: Read a value and then add it to the running total and add 1 to our count before going on to the next value. Whenever the solutions to subproblems duplicate steps, think about merging them instead of joining them end-to-end.

Figure 1–14   *Building-Block Approach*

Mental Blocks: The Fear of Starting

Writers are all too familiar with the experience of staring at a blank page, not knowing where to begin. Programmers have the same difficulty when they first tackle a big problem. They look at the problem and it seems overwhelming.

Remember that you always have a way to begin solving any problem: Write it down on paper in your own words so that you understand it. Once you paraphrase the problem, you can focus on each of the subparts individually instead of trying to tackle the entire problem at once. This process gives you a clearer picture of the overall problem. It helps you see pieces of the problem that look familiar or that are analogous to other problems you have solved, and it pinpoints areas where something is unclear, where you need more information.

As you write down a problem, you tend to group things together into small, understandable chunks, which may be natural places to split the problem up—to divide and conquer. Your description of the problem may collect all of the information about data and results into one place for easy reference. Then you can see the beginning and ending states necessary for means-ends analysis.

Most mental blocks are caused by not really understanding the problem. Rewriting the problem in your own words is a good way to focus on the subparts of the problem, one at a time, and to understand what is required for a solution.

Algorithmic Problem Solving

Coming up with a step-by-step procedure for solving a particular problem is not always a cut-and-dried process. In fact, it is usually a trial-and-error process requiring several attempts and refinements. We test each attempt to see if it really solves the problem. If it does, fine. If it doesn't, we try again. Solving any nontrivial problem typically requires a combination of the techniques we've described.

Remember that the computer can only do certain things (see p. 18). Your primary concern, then, is how to make the computer transform, manipulate, calculate, or process the input data to produce the desired output. If you keep in mind the allowable instructions in your programming language, you won't design an algorithm that is difficult or impossible to code.

Summary

Computer programming is the process of planning a sequence of steps for a computer to follow. It involves a problem-solving phase and an implementation phase. After analyzing a problem, we develop and test a general solution (algorithm). This general solution becomes a concrete solution—our program—when we write it in a high-level programming language. The sequence of instructions that makes up our program is then compiled into machine code, the language the computer uses. After correcting any errors ("bugs") that show up during testing, our program is ready to use.

Once we begin to use the program, it enters the maintenance phase. Maintenance involves correcting any errors discovered while the program is being used and changing the program to reflect changes in the user's requirements.

Data and instructions are represented as binary numbers (numbers consisting of just 1s and 0s) in electronic computers. The process of converting data and instructions into a form usable by the computer is called coding.

A programming language reflects the range of operations a computer can perform. The basic control structures in a programming language—sequence, selection, loop, and subprogram—are based on these fundamental operations. In this text, you will learn to write programs in the high-level programming language called C++.

Computers are composed of six basic parts: the memory unit, the arithmetic/logic unit, the control unit, input and output devices, and auxiliary storage devices. The arithmetic/logic unit and control unit together are called the central processing unit. The physical parts of the computer are called hardware. The programs that are executed by the computer are called software.

System software is a set of programs designed to simplify the user/computer interface. It includes the compiler, the operating system, and the editor.

We've said that problem solving is an integral part of the programming process. Although you may have little experience programming computers, you have lots of experience solving problems. The key is to stop and think about the strategies you use to solve problems, and then to use those strategies to devise workable algorithms. Among those strategies are asking questions, looking for things that are familiar, solving by analogy, applying means-ends analysis, dividing the problem into subproblems, using existing solutions to small problems to solve a larger problem, merging solutions, and paraphrasing the problem in order to overcome a mental block.

The computer is used widely today in science, engineering, business, government, medicine, consumer goods, and the arts. Learning to program in C++ can help you use this powerful tool effectively.

Quick Check

The Quick Check is intended to help you decide if you've met the goals set forth at the beginning of each chapter. If you understand the material in the chapter, the answer to each question should be fairly obvious. After reading a question, check your response against the answers listed at the end of the Quick Check. If you don't know an answer or don't understand the answer that's provided, turn to the page(s) listed at the end of the question to review the material.

1. What do we call a sequence of instructions that is executed by a computer? (p. 2)
2. How does an algorithm differ from a computer program? (pp. 3–4)
3. How does a programming language differ from a human language? (p. 5)
4. What is the input and output of a compiler? (pp. 6–9)
5. What do we call the combination of the Control Unit and the Arithmetic/Logic Unit? (pp. 11–12)
6. What are the three phases of the software life cycle? (pp. 2–3)
7. Which of the following tools translates a C++ program into machine language: editor, operating system, compiler, or loader? (pp. 6–9)
8. What is the general term that we use to refer to the physical components of the computer? (p. 13)
9. When would you use the building-block approach to solve a problem? (pp. 18–19)

Answers
1. A computer program.   2. An algorithm can be written in any language, to be carried out by a person or a processor of any kind. A program is written in a programming language, for execution by a computer.   3. A programming language has a very small vocabulary of words and symbols, and a very precise set of rules that specify the form of valid language constructs (syntax) and the actions that result when a construct is executed by the computer (semantics).   4. The compiler inputs a source program written in a high-level language, and outputs an equivalent program in machine language. Some compilers also output a listing, which is a copy of the source program with error messages inserted.   5. The central processing unit. 6. Problem-solving, implementation, maintenance.   7. Compiler.   8. Hardware.   9. When you see that a problem can be divided into pieces that may correspond to subproblems for which solutions are already known.

Exam Preparation Exercises

1. Match the following terms to their definitions, given below:
   a. Programming
   b. Computer

    c. Algorithm
    d. Computer program
    e. Programming language
    f. Documentation
    g. Information
    h. Data

      i. A programmable device that can store, retrieve, and process data.
     ii. Information in a form a computer can use.
    iii. A sequence of instructions to be performed by a computer.
    iv. A set of rules, symbols, and special words used to construct a computer program.
     v. Planning or scheduling the performance of a task or event.
    vi. Any knowledge that can be communicated.
   vii. The written text and comments that make a program easier for others to understand, use, and modify.
  viii. A step-by-step procedure for solving a problem in a finite amount of time.

2. List the three steps in the problem-solving phase of the software life cycle.
3. List steps in the implementation phase of the software life cycle.
4. If testing uncovers an error, what step in the software life cycle does the programmer return to?
5. Explain why the following series of steps isn't an algorithm, and then rewrite the steps to make a valid algorithm:

Wake up.
Go to school.
Come home.
Go to sleep.
Repeat from first step.

6. Match the following terms with their definitions, given below.
    a. Machine language
    b. Compiler
    c. Source program
    d. Object program

      i. A program that translates a high-level language into machine code.
     ii. The machine language version of a source program.
    iii. The language, made up of binary coded instructions, that is used directly by the computer.
    iv. A program written in a high-level programming language.

7. What is the advantage of writing a program in a standardized programming language?
8. What does the control unit do?
9. The editor is a peripheral device. True or false?
10. Memory (RAM) is a peripheral device. True or false?

11. Match the problem-solving strategies to the descriptions following.
    a. Ask questions.
    b. Look for things that are familiar.
    c. Solve by analogy.
    d. Means-ends analysis.
    e. Divide and conquer.
    f. Building-block approach.
    g. Merging solutions.

       i. Break up the problem into more manageable pieces.
      ii. Gather more information to help you discover a solution.
     iii. Identify aspects of the problem that are similar to a problem in a different domain.
     iv. Combine the steps in two or more different algorithms.
      v. Identify aspects of the problem that you've solved before.
     vi. Join existing problem solutions together.
    vii. Look at the input, output, and available operations and find a sequence of operations that transform the input into the output.

Programming Warm-Up Exercises

1. In the following algorithm for making black-and-white photographs, identify the steps that are branches (selection), loops, or references to subalgorithms defined elsewhere.
   a. Mix developer according to instructions on package.
   b. Pour developer into tray.
   c. Mix stop bath according to instructions on package.
   d. Pour stop bath into tray.
   e. Mix fixer according to instructions on package.
   f. Pour fixer into tray.
   g. Turn off white lights and turn on safelight.
   h. Place negative in enlarger and turn on.
   i. Adjust size of image and focus, and then turn off enlarger.
   j. Remove one piece of printing paper from paper safe and place in enlarging easel.
   k. Turn enlarger on for thirty seconds and then off.
   l. Place paper in developer for 1 minute, stop bath for 30 seconds, and fixer for 1 minute.
   m. Turn on white lights and inspect the first print, and then turn off white lights.
   n1. If first print is too light:
       Remove one piece of paper from paper safe, place on easel, and expose for 60 seconds to create a too-dark print. Then place in developer for 1 minute, stop bath for 30 seconds, and fixer for 1 minute.

n2. If first print is too dark:
Remove one piece of paper from paper safe, place on easel, and expose for 15 seconds to create a too-light print. Then place in developer for 1 minute, stop bath for 30 seconds, and fixer for 1 minute.

n3. If first print is about right:
Remove one piece of paper from paper safe, place on easel, and expose for 60 seconds to create a too-dark print. Then place in developer for 1 minute, stop bath for 30 seconds, and fixer for 1 minute. Remove one piece of paper from paper safe, place on easel, and expose for 15 seconds to create a too-light print. Then place in developer for 1 minute, stop bath for 30 seconds, and fixer for 1 minute.

o. Analyze too-light and too-dark prints to estimate base exposure time, and then identify highlights and shadows that require less or more exposure and estimate the necessary time for each area.

p. Remove one piece of paper from paper safe, place on easel, and expose for base exposure time, covering shadow areas for estimated time, and then cover entire print except for highlight areas, which are further exposed as estimated. Then place print in developer for 1 minute, stop bath for 30 seconds, and fixer for 1 minute.

q. Analyze print from step p and adjust estimates of times as appropriate.

r. Repeat steps p and q until a print is obtained with the desired exposure.

s. Document exposure times that result in desired print.

t. Remove one piece of paper from paper safe, place on easel, and expose according to documentation from step s. Then place in developer for 1 minute, stop bath for 30 seconds, and fixer for 4 minutes. Place print in print washer.

u. Repeat step t to create as many prints as needed.

v. Wash all prints for 1 hour.

w. Place prints in print dryer.

2. Write an algorithm for brushing teeth. The instructions must be very simple and exact because the person who will follow them has never done this before, and takes every word literally.

3. Identify the steps in your solution to Exercise 2 that are branches, loops, and references to subalgorithms defined elsewhere.

4. Change the algorithm in Exercise 1 so that 10 properly exposed prints are created each time it is executed.

C++ Syntax and Semantics, and the Program Development Process

Knowledge Goals

- To understand how a C++ program is composed of one or more subprograms (functions).
- To know what a metalanguage is, and how it is used.
- To understand the concept of a data type.

Skill Goals

To be able to:

- Read syntax templates in order to understand the formal rules governing C++ programs.
- Create and recognize legal C++ identifiers.
- Declare named constants and variables of type `char` and `string`.
- Distinguish reserved words in C++ from user-defined identifiers.
- Assign values to variables.
- Construct simple string expressions made up of constants, variables, and the concatenation operator.
- Construct a statement that writes to an output stream.
- Determine what is printed by a given output statement.
- Use comments to clarify your programs.
- Construct simple C++ programs.

2.1 The Elements of C++ Programs

In Chapter 1, we said that subprograms allow us to write parts of our program separately and then assemble them into final form. In C++, all subprograms are referred to as functions, and a C++ program is a collection of one or more functions.

Each function performs some particular task, and collectively they all cooperate to solve the entire problem.

Function A subprogram in C++.

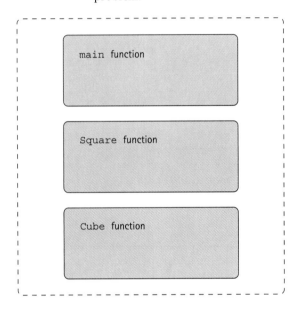

Every C++ program must have a function named main. Execution of the program always begins with the main function. You can think of main as the master and the other functions as the servants. When main wants the function Square to perform a task, main *calls* (or *invokes*) Square. When the Square function completes execution of its statements, it obediently returns control to the master, main, so the master can continue executing.

Let's look at an example of a C++ program with three functions: main, Square, and Cube. Don't be too concerned with the details in the program—just observe its overall look and structure.

```
#include <iostream>

using namespace std;

int Square( int );
int Cube( int );
```

```
int main()
{
    cout << "The square of 27 is " << Square(27) << endl;
    cout << "and the cube of 27 is " << Cube(27) << endl;
    return 0;
}

int Square( int n )
{
    return n * n;
}

int Cube( int n )
{
    return n * n * n;
}
```

In each of the three functions, the left brace ({) and right brace (}) mark the beginning and end of the statements to be executed. Statements appearing between the braces are known as the *body* of the function.

Execution of a program always begins with the first statement of the main function. In our program, the first statement is

```
cout << "The square of 27 is " << Square(27) << endl;
```

This is an output statement that causes information to be printed on the computer's display screen. You will learn how to construct output statements like this later in the chapter. Briefly, this statement prints two items. The first is the message

```
The square of 27 is
```

The second to be printed is the value obtained by calling (invoking) the Square function, with the value 27 as the number to be squared. As the servant, the Square function performs its task of squaring the number and sending the computed result (729) back to its *caller*, the main function. Now main can continue executing by printing the value 729 and proceeding to its next statement.

In a similar fashion, the second statement in main prints the message

```
and the cube of 27 is
```

and then invokes the Cube function and prints the result, 19683. The complete output produced by executing this program is, therefore,

```
The square of 27 is 729
and the cube of 27 is 19683
```

Both `Square` and `Cube` are examples of *value-returning functions*. A value-returning function returns a single value to its caller. The word `int` at the beginning of the first line of the `Square` function

```
int Square( int n )
```

states that the function returns an integer value.

Now look at the `main` function again. You'll see that the first line of the function is

```
int main()
```

The word `int` indicates that `main` is a value-returning function that should return an integer value. And it does. After printing the square and cube of 27, `main` executes the statement

```
return 0;
```

to return the value 0 to its caller. But who calls the `main` function? The answer is: the computer's operating system.

When you work with C++ programs, the operating system is considered to be the caller of the `main` function. The operating system expects `main` to return a value when `main` finishes executing. By convention, a return value of 0 means everything went OK. A return value of anything else (typically 1, 2, ...) means something went wrong. In this book we always conclude the execution of `main` by returning the value 0.

We have looked only briefly at the overall picture of what a C++ program looks like—a collection of one or more functions, including `main`. We have also mentioned what is special about the `main` function—it is a required function, execution begins there, and it returns a value to the operating system. Now it's time to begin looking at the details of the C++ language.

Syntax and Semantics

A programming language is a set of rules, symbols, and special words used to construct a program. There are rules for both **syntax** (grammar) and **semantics** (meaning).

Syntax is a formal set of rules that defines exactly what combinations of letters, numbers, and symbols can be used in a programming language. There is no room for ambiguity in the syntax of a programming language because the computer can't think; it doesn't "know what we mean." To avoid ambiguity, syntax rules themselves must be written in a very simple, precise, formal language called a **metalanguage**.

Syntax The formal rules governing how valid instructions are written in a programming language.

Semantics The set of rules that determines the meaning of instructions written in a programming language.

Metalanguage A language that is used to write the syntax rules for another language.

Syntax rules are the blueprints we use to build instructions in a program. They allow us to take the elements of a programming language—the basic building blocks of the language—and assemble them into *constructs*, syntactically correct structures. If our program violates any of the rules of the language—by misspelling a crucial word or leaving out an important comma, for instance—the program is said to have *syntax errors* and cannot compile correctly until we fix them.

Metalanguages

Metalanguage is the word *language* with the prefix *meta-*, which means "beyond" or "more comprehensive." A metalanguage is a language that goes beyond a normal language by allowing us to speak precisely about that language. It is a language for talking about languages. One of the oldest computer-oriented metalanguages is *Backus-Naur Form* (*BNF*), which is named for John Backus and Peter Naur, who developed it in 1960. BNF syntax definitions are written out using letters, numbers, and special symbols. For example, an *identifier* (a name for something in a program) in C++ must be at least one letter or underscore (_), which may or may not be followed by additional letters, underscores, or digits. The BNF definition of an identifier in C++ is as follows.

```
<Identifier> ::= <Nondigit> | <Nondigit> <NondigitOrDigitSequence>
<NondigitOrDigitSequence> ::= <NondigitOrDigit> | <NondigitOrDigit> <NondigitOrDigitSequence>
<NondigitOrDigit> ::= <Nondigit> | <Digit>
<Nondigit> ::= _ | A | B | C | D | E | F | G | H | I | J | K | L | M | N | O | P | Q | R | S | T | U | V | W | X | Y | Z |
               a | b | c | d | e | f | g | h | i | j | k | l | m | n | o | p | q | r | s | t | u | v | w | x | y | z
<Digit> ::= 0 | 1 | 2 | 3 | 4 | 5 | 6 | 7 | 8 | 9
```

Where the symbol ::= is read "is defined as," the symbol | means "or," the symbols < and > are used to enclose words called *nonterminal symbols* (symbols that still need to be defined), and everything else is called a *terminal symbol*.

The first line of the definition reads as follows: "An identifier is defined as either a nondigit or a nondigit followed by a nondigit-or-digit sequence." This line contains nonterminal symbols that must be defined. In the second line, the nonterminal symbol NondigitOrDigitSequence is defined as either a NondigitOrDigit or a NondigitOrDigit followed by another NondigitOrDigitSequence. The self-reference in the definition is a roundabout way of saying that a NondigitOrDigitSequence can be a series of one or more nondigits or digits. The third line defines NondigitOrDigit to be either a Nondigit or a Digit. In the fourth and last lines, we finally encounter terminal symbols, which define Nondigit to be an underscore or any upper- or lowercase letter and Digit as any one of the numeric symbols 0 through 9.

BNF is an extremely simple language, but that simplicity leads to syntax definitions that can be long and difficult to read. In this text, we introduce another metalanguage, called a *syntax template*. Syntax templates show at a glance the form a C++ construct takes.

One final note: Metalanguages only show how to write instructions that the compiler can translate. They do not define what those instructions do (their semantics). Formal languages for defining the semantics of a programming language exist, but they are beyond the scope of this text. Throughout this book, we describe the semantics of C++ in English.

Syntax Templates

In this book, we write the syntax rules for C++ using *syntax templates*. A syntax template is a generic example of the C++ construct being defined. Graphic conventions show which portions are optional and which can be repeated. A boldface word or symbol is a literal word or symbol in the C++ language. A nonboldface word can be replaced by another template. A curly brace is used to indicate a list of items, from which one item can be chosen.

Let's look at an example. This template defines an identifier in C++:

Identifier

The shading indicates a part of the definition that is optional. The three dots (...) mean that the preceding symbol or shaded block can be repeated. Thus, an identifier in C++ must begin with a letter or underscore and is optionally followed by one or more letters, underscores, or digits.

Remember that a word not in boldface type can be replaced with another template. These are the templates for Letter and Digit:

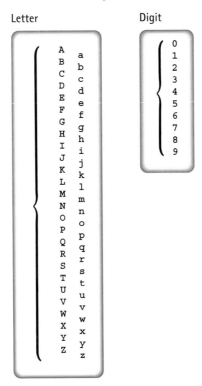

In these templates, the braces again indicate lists of items from which any one item can be chosen. So a letter can be any one of the upper- or lowercase letters, and a digit can be any of the numeric characters 0 through 9.

Now let's look at the syntax template for the C++ `main` function:

MainFunction

```
int main()
{
    Statement
      ⋮
}
```

The `main` function begins with the word `int`, followed by the word `main` and then left and right parentheses. This first line of the function is the *heading*. After the heading, the left brace signals the start of the statements in the function (its body). The shading and the three dots indicate that the function body consists of zero or more statements. (In this diagram we have placed the three dots vertically to suggest that statements usually are arranged vertically, one above the next.) Finally, the right brace indicates the end of the function.

In principle, the syntax template allows the function body to have no statements at all. In practice, however, the body should include a Return statement because the word `int` in the function heading states that `main` returns an integer value. Thus, the shortest C++ program is

```
int main()
{
    return 0;
}
```

As you might guess, this program does absolutely nothing useful when executed!

As we introduce C++ language constructs throughout the book, we use syntax templates to display the proper syntax. At the publisher's Web site, you will find these syntax templates gathered into one central location.*

When you finish this chapter, you should know enough about the syntax and semantics of statements in C++ to write simple programs. But before we can talk about writing statements, we must look at how names are written in C++ and at some of the elements of a program.

---

*The publisher's Web site is `www.problemsolvingcpp.jbpub.com`

Naming Program Elements: Identifiers

Identifiers are used in C++ to name things–things such as subprograms and places in the computer's memory. Identifiers are made up of letters (A–Z, a–z), digits (0–9), and the underscore character (_), but must begin with a letter or underscore.

> **Identifier** A name associated with a function or data object and used to refer to that function or data object.

Remember that an identifier *must* start with a letter or underscore:

Identifier

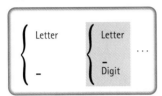

(Identifiers beginning with an underscore have special meanings in some C++ systems, so it is best to begin an identifier with a letter.)

Here are some examples of valid identifiers:

```
sum_of_squares   J9   box_22A   GetData   Bin3D4   count
```

And here are some examples of invalid identifiers and the reasons why they are invalid:

Invalid Identifier	Explanation
40Hours	Identifiers cannot begin with a digit.
Get Data	Blanks are not allowed in identifiers.
box-22	The hyphen (–) is a math symbol (minus) in C++.
cost_in_$	Special symbols such as $ are not allowed.
int	The word int is predefined in the C++ language.

> **Reserved word** A word that has special meaning in C++; it cannot be used as a programmer-defined identifier.

The last identifier in the table, int, is an example of a reserved word. Reserved words are words that have specific uses in C++; you cannot use them as programmer-defined identifiers. Appendix A lists all of the reserved words in C++.

Using Meaningful, Readable Identifiers

The names we use to refer to things in our programs are totally meaningless to the computer. The computer behaves in the same way whether we call the value 3.14159265 pi or cake, as long as we always call it the same thing. However, it is much easier for somebody to figure out how a program works if the names we choose for elements actually tell something about them. Whenever you have to make up a name for something in a program, try to pick one that is meaningful to a person reading the program.

C++ is a *case-sensitive* language. Uppercase letters are different from lowercase letters. The identifiers

PRINTTOPPORTION   printtopportion   pRiNtToPpOrTiOn   PrintTopPortion

are four distinct names and are not interchangeable in any way. As you can see, the last of these forms is the easiest to read. In this book, we use combinations of uppercase letters, lowercase letters, and underscores in identifiers. We explain our conventions for choosing between uppercase and lowercase as we proceed through this chapter.

Now that we've seen how to write identifiers, we look at some of the things that C++ allows us to name.

Data and Data Types

A computer program operates on data (stored internally in memory, stored externally on disk or tape, or input from a device such as a keyboard, scanner, or electrical sensor) and produces output. In C++, each piece of data must be of a specific **data type**. The data type determines how the data is represented in the computer and the kinds of processing the computer can perform on it.

> **Data type** A specific set of data values, along with a set of operations on those values.

Some types of data are used so frequently that C++ defines them for us. Examples of these *standard* (or *built-in*) *types* are int (for working with integer numbers), float (for working with real numbers having decimal points), and char (for working with character data).

Additionally, C++ allows programmers to define their own data types—*programmer-defined* (or *user-defined*) *types*. Beginning in Chapter 10, we show you how to define your own data types.

In this chapter, we focus on two data types—one for representing data consisting of a single character, the other for representing strings of characters. In the next chapter, we examine the numeric types (such as int and float) in detail.

Data Storage

Where does a program get the data it needs to operate? Data is stored in the computer's memory. Remember that memory is divided into a large number of separate locations or cells, each of which can hold a piece of data. Each memory location has a unique address to which we refer when we store or retrieve data.

Of course, the actual address of each location in memory is a binary number in a machine language code. In C++ we use identifiers to name memory locations; the compiler then translates them into binary for us. This is one of the advantages of a high-level programming language: It frees us from having to keep track of the numeric addresses of the memory locations in which our data and instructions are stored.

The `char` Data Type

The built-in type `char` describes data consisting of one alphanumeric character—a letter, a digit, or a special symbol:

```
'A'    'a'    '8'    '2'    '+'    '-'    '$'    '?'    '*'    ' '
```

Each machine uses a particular *character set*, the set of alphanumeric characters it can represent. (See Appendix D for some sample character sets.) Notice that each character is enclosed in single quotes (apostrophes). The C++ compiler needs the quotes to differentiate, say, between the character data '8' and the integer value 8 because the two are stored differently inside the machine. Notice also that the blank, ' ', is a valid character.*

You wouldn't want to add the character 'A' to the character 'B' or subtract the character '3' from the character '8', but you might want to compare character values. Each character set has a *collating sequence*, a predefined ordering of all the characters. Although this sequence varies from one character set to another, 'A' always compares less than 'B', 'B' less than 'C', and so forth. And '1' compares less than '2', '2' less than '3', and so on.

The `string` Data Type

Whereas a value of type `char` is limited to a single character, a *string* is a sequence of characters, such as a word, name, or sentence, enclosed in double quotes. For example, the following are strings in C++:

```
"Problem Solving"    "C++"    "Programming and "    " . "
```

---

*Most programming languages use ASCII (the American Standard Code for Information Interchange) to represent the English alphabet and other symbols. Each ASCII character is stored in a single byte of memory.

A newer character set called Unicode includes the larger alphabets of many international human languages. A single Unicode character occupies two bytes of memory. C++ provides the data type `wchar_t` (for "wide character") to accommodate larger character sets such as Unicode. In C++, the notation `L'`*something*`'` denotes a value of type `wchar_t`, where the *something* depends on the particular wide character set being used. We do not examine wide characters any further in this book.

A string must be typed entirely on one line. For example, the string

```
"This string is invalid because it
is typed on more than one line."
```

is not valid because it is split across two lines. In this situation, the C++ compiler issues an error message at the first line. The message may say something like "UNTERMIN-ATED STRING," depending on the particular compiler.

The quotes are not considered to be part of the string but are simply there to distinguish the string from other parts of a C++ program. For example, `"amount"` (in double quotes) is the character string made up of the letters *a, m, o, u, n,* and *t* in that order. On the other hand, `amount` (without the quotes) is an identifier, perhaps the name of a place in memory. The symbols `"12345"` represent a string made up of the characters *1, 2, 3, 4,* and *5* in that order. If we write `12345` without the quotes, it is an integer quantity that can be used in calculations.

A string containing no characters is called the *null string* (or *empty string*). We write the null string using two double quotes with nothing (not even spaces) between them:

```
""
```

The null string is not equivalent to a string of spaces; it is a special string that contains no characters.

To work with string data, this book uses a data type named `string`. This data type is not part of the C++ language (that is, it is not a built-in type). Rather, `string` is a programmer-defined type that is supplied by the C++ *standard library*, a large collection of prewritten functions and data types that any C++ programmer can use. Operations on `string` data include comparing the values of strings, searching a string for a particular character, and joining one string to another. We look at some of these operations later in this chapter and cover additional operations in subsequent chapters.

Naming Elements: Declarations

Identifiers can be used to name both constants and variables. In other words, an identifier can be the name of a memory location whose contents are not allowed to change or it can be the name of a memory location whose contents can change.

How do we tell the computer what an identifier represents? By using a *declaration*, a statement that associates a name (an identifier) with a description of an element in a

> **Declaration**   A statement that associates an identifier with a data object, a function, or a data type so that the programmer can refer to that item by name.

C++ program (just as a dictionary definition associates a name with a description of the thing being named). In a declaration, we name an identifier and what it represents. For example, the declaration

```
int year;
```

announces that `year` is the name of a variable whose contents are of type `int`. When we declare a variable, the compiler picks a location in memory to be associated with the identifier. We don't have to know the actual address of the memory location because the computer automatically keeps track of it for us.

In C++, each identifier can represent just one thing (except under special circumstances, which we talk about in Chapters 7 and 8). Every identifier you use in a program must be different from all others.

Constants and variables are collectively called *data objects*. Both data objects and the actual instructions in a program are stored in various memory locations. You have seen that a group of instructions—a function—can be given a name. A name also can be associated with a programmer-defined data type.

In C++, you must declare every identifier before it is used. This allows the compiler to verify that the use of the identifier is consistent with what it was declared to be. If you declare an identifier to be a constant and later try to change its value, the compiler detects this inconsistency and issues an error message.

There is a different form of declaration statement for each kind of data object, function, or data type in C++. The forms of declarations for variables and constants are introduced here; others are covered in later chapters.

Variables While a program is executing, different values may be stored in the same memory location at different times. This kind of memory location is called a **variable**, and its content is the *variable value*. The symbolic name that we associate with a memory location is the *variable name* or *variable identifier* (see Figure 2–1). In practice, we often refer to the variable name more briefly as the *variable*.

> **Variable** A location in memory, referenced by an identifier, that contains a data value that can be changed.

Declaring a variable means specifying both its name and its data type. This tells the compiler to associate a name with a memory location whose contents are of a specific type (for example, `char` or `string`). The following statement declares `myChar` to be a variable of type `char`:

```
char myChar;
```

In C++, a variable can contain a data value only of the type specified in its declaration. Because of the above declaration, the variable `myChar` can contain *only* a char

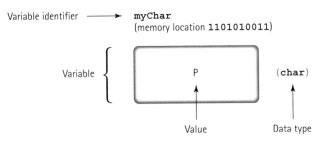

Figure 2–1 *Variable*

value. If the C++ compiler comes across an instruction that tries to store a `float` value into `myChar`, it generates extra instructions to convert the `float` value to the proper type. In Chapter 3, we examine how such type conversions take place.

Here's the syntax template for a variable declaration:

VariableDeclaration

```
DataType Identifier , Identifier . . . ;
```

where DataType is the name of a data type such as `char` or `string`. Notice that a variable declaration always ends with a semicolon.

From the syntax template, you can see that it is possible to declare several variables in one statement:

```
char letter, middleInitial, ch;
```

Here, all three variables are declared to be `char` variables. Our preference, though, is to declare each variable with a separate statement:

```
char letter;
char middleInitial;
char ch;
```

With this form it is easier, when modifying a program, to add new variables to the list or delete ones you no longer want.

Declaring each variable with a separate statement also allows you to attach comments to the right of each declaration, as shown here:

```
float payRate;      // Employee's pay rate
float hours;        // Hours worked
float wages;        // Wages earned
int   empNum;       // Employee ID number
```

These declarations tell the compiler to reserve memory space for three `float` variables—`payRate`, `hours`, and `wages`—and one `int` variable, `empNum`. The comments explain to someone reading the program what each variable represents.

Now that we've seen how to declare variables in C++, let's look at how to declare constants.

Constants   All single characters (enclosed in single quotes) and strings (enclosed in double quotes) are constants.

```
'A'    '@'    "Howdy boys"    "Please enter an employee number:"
```

Literal value   Any constant value written in a program.

Named constant (symbolic constant)   A location in memory, referenced by an identifier, that contains a data value that cannot be changed.

In C++ as in mathematics, a constant is something whose value never changes. When we use the actual value of a constant in a program, we are using a literal value (or *literal*).

An alternative to the literal constant is the named constant (or symbolic constant), which is introduced in a declaration statement. A named constant is just another way of representing a literal value. Instead of using the literal value in an instruction, we give it a name in a declaration statement, then use that name in the instruction. For example, we can write an instruction that prints the title of this book using the literal string `"Programming and Problem Solving with C++"`. Or we can declare a named constant called `BOOK_TITLE` that equals the same string and then use the constant name in the instruction. That is, we can use either

`"Programming and Problem Solving with C++"`

or

`BOOK_TITLE`

in the instruction.

Using the literal value of a constant may seem easier than giving it a name and then referring to it by that name. But, in fact, named constants make a program easier to read because they make the meaning of literal constants clearer. Named constants also make it easier to change a program later on.

This is the syntax template for a constant declaration:

ConstantDeclaration

```
const DataType Identifier = LiteralValue;
```

Notice that the reserved word `const` begins the declaration, and an equal sign (=) appears between the identifier and the literal value.

The following are examples of constant declarations:

```
const string STARS = "********";
const char   BLANK = ' ';
const string BOOK_TITLE = "Programming in C++";
const string MESSAGE = "Error condition";
```

As we have done above, many C++ programmers capitalize the entire identifier of a named constant and separate the English words with an underscore. The idea is to let the reader quickly distinguish between variable names and constant names when they appear in the middle of a program.

It's a good idea to add comments to constant declarations as well as variable declarations. We describe in comments what each constant represents:

```
const float MAX_HOURS = 40.0;    // Maximum normal work hours
const float OVERTIME = 1.5;      // Overtime pay rate factor
```

Capitalization of Identifiers

Programmers often use capitalization as a quick visual clue to what an identifier represents. Different programmers adopt different conventions for using uppercase letters and lowercase letters. Some people use only lowercase letters, separating the English words in an identifier with the underscore character:

```
pay_rate    emp_num   pay_file
```

The conventions we use in this book are as follows:

- For identifiers representing variables, we begin with a lowercase letter and capitalize each successive English word.

  ```
  lengthInYards   middleInitial   hours
  ```

- Names of programmer-written functions and programmer-defined data types (which we examine later in the book) are capitalized in the same manner as variable names except that they begin with capital letters.

  ```
  CalcPay(payRate, hours, wages)   Cube(27)   MyDataType
  ```

  Capitalizing the first letter allows a person reading the program to tell at a glance that an identifier represents a function name or data type rather than a variable. However, we cannot use this capitalization convention everywhere. C++ expects every program to have a function named main—all in lowercase letters—so we cannot name it Main. Nor can we use Char for the built-in data type char. C++ reserved words use all lowercase letters, as do most of the identifiers declared in the standard library (such as string).

- For identifiers representing named constants, we capitalize every letter and use underscores to separate the English words.

  ```
  BOOK_TITLE   OVERTIME   MAX_LENGTH
  ```

  This convention, widely used by C++ programmers, is an immediate signal that BOOK_TITLE is a named constant and not a variable, a function, or a data type.

These conventions are only that—conventions. C++ does not require this particular style of capitalizing identifiers. You may wish to capitalize in a different fashion. But whatever system you use, it is essential that you use a consistent style throughout your program. A person reading your program will be confused or misled if you use a random style of capitalization

Taking Action: Executable Statements

Up to this point, we've looked at ways of declaring data objects in a program. Now we turn our attention to ways of acting, or performing operations, on data.

Assignment The value of a variable can be set or changed through an **assignment statement**. For example,

```
lastName = "Lincoln";
```

assigns the string value `"Lincoln"` to the variable `lastName` (that is, it stores the sequence of characters "Lincoln" into the memory associated with the variable named `lastName`).

The semantics (meaning) of the assignment operator (=) is "store"; the value of the **expression** is *stored* into the variable. Any previous value in the variable is destroyed and replaced by the value of the expression.

Only one variable can be on the left-hand side of an assignment statement. An assignment statement is *not* like a math equation (*x* + *y* = *z* + 4); the expression (what is on the right-hand side of the assignment operator) is **evaluated**, and the resulting value is stored into the single variable on the left of the assignment operator. A variable keeps its assigned value until another statement stores a new value into it.

> **Assignment statement**   A statement that stores the value of an expression into a variable.
>
> **Expression**   An arrangement of identifiers, literals, and operators that can be evaluated to compute a value of a given type.
>
> **Evaluate**   To compute a new value by performing a specified set of operations on given values.

Given the declarations

```
string firstName;
string middleName;
string lastName;
string title;
char   middleInitial;
char   letter;
```

the following assignment statements are valid:

```
firstName = "Abraham";
middleName = firstName;
middleName = "";
lastName = "Lincoln";
title = "President";
middleInitial = ' ';
letter = middleInitial;
```

However, these assignments are not valid:

Invalid Assignment Statement	Reason
`middleInitial = "A.";`	`middleInitial` is of type `char`; `"A."` is a string.
`letter = firstName;`	`letter` is of type `char`; `firstName` is of type `string`.
`firstName = Thomas;`	`Thomas` is an undeclared identifier.
`"Edison" = lastName;`	Only a variable can appear to the left of `=`.
`lastName = ;`	The expression to the right of `=` is missing.

String Expressions   Although we can't perform arithmetic on strings, the `string` data type provides a special string operation, called *concatenation*, that uses the + operator. The result of concatenating (joining) two strings is a new string containing the characters from both strings. For example, given the statements

```
string bookTitle;
string phrase1;
string phrase2;

phrase1 = "Programming and ";
phrase2 = "Problem Solving";
```

we could write

```
bookTitle = phrase1 + phrase2;
```

This statement retrieves the value of `phrase1` from memory and concatenates the value of `phrase2` to form a new, temporary string containing the characters

```
"Programming and Problem Solving"
```

This temporary string (which is of type `string`) is then assigned to (stored into) `book-Title`.

The order of the strings in the expression determines how they appear in the resulting string. If we instead write

```
bookTitle = phrase2 + phrase1;
```

then `bookTitle` contains

```
"Problem SolvingProgramming and "
```

Concatenation works with named `string` constants, literal strings, and `char` data as well as with `string` variables. The only restriction is that at least one of the operands of the + operator *must* be a `string` variable or named constant (so you cannot use expressions like `"Hi"` + `"there"` or `'A'` + `'B'`). For example, if we have declared the following constants:

```
const string WORD1 = "rogramming";
const string WORD5 = "C++";
```

then we could write the following assignment statement to store the title of this book into the variable `bookTitle`:

```
bookTitle = 'P' + WORD1 + " in " + WORD5;
```

As a result, `bookTitle` contains the string

```
"Programming in C++"
```

The preceding example demonstrates how we can combine identifiers, `char` data, and literal strings in a concatenation expression. Of course, if we simply want to assign the complete string to `bookTitle`, we can do so directly:

```
bookTitle = "Programming in C++";
```

But occasionally we encounter a situation in which we want to add some characters to an existing string value. Suppose that `bookTitle` already contains `"Programming"` and that we wish to complete the title. We could use a statement of the form

```
bookTitle = bookTitle + " in C++";
```

Such a statement retrieves the value of `bookTitle` from memory, concatenates the string `" in C++"` to form a new string, and then stores the new string back into `bookTitle`. The new string replaces the old value of `bookTitle` (which is destroyed).

Keep in mind that concatenation works only with values of type `string`. Even though an arithmetic plus sign is used for the operation, we cannot concatenate values of numeric data types, such as `int` and `float`, with strings.

Output   In C++ we write out the values of variables and expressions by using a special variable named `cout` (pronounced "see-out") along with the *insertion operator* (<<):

```
cout << "Hello";
```

This statement displays the characters Hello on the *standard output device*, usually the display screen.

The variable cout is predefined in C++ systems to denote an *output stream*. You can think of an output stream as an endless sequence of characters going to an output device. In the case of cout, the output stream goes to the standard output device.

The insertion operator << (often pronounced as "put to") takes two operands. Its left-hand operand is a stream expression (in the simplest case, just a stream variable such as cout). Its right-hand operand is an expression, which could be as simple as a literal string:

```
cout << "The title is ";
cout << bookTitle + ", 2nd Edition";
```

The insertion operator converts its right-hand operand to a sequence of characters and inserts them into (or, more precisely, appends them to) the output stream. Notice how the << points in the direction the data is going—*from* the expression written on the right *to* the output stream on the left.

You can use the << operator several times in a single output statement. Each occurrence appends the next data item to the output stream. For example, we can write the preceding two output statements as

```
cout << "The title is " << bookTitle + ", 2nd Edition";
```

If bookTitle contains "American History", both versions produce the same output:

```
The title is American History, 2nd Edition
```

The following output statements yield the output shown. These examples assume that the char variable ch contains the value '2', the string variable firstName contains "Marie", and the string variable lastName contains "Curie".

Statement	What Is Printed (□ means blank)
cout << ch;	2
cout << "ch = " << ch;	ch□=□2
cout << firstName + " " + lastName;	Marie□Curie
cout << firstName << lastName;	MarieCurie
cout << firstName << ' ' << lastName;	Marie□Curie
cout << "ERROR MESSAGE";	ERROR□MESSAGE
cout << "Error=" << ch;	Error=2

An output statement prints literal strings exactly as they appear. To let the computer know that you want to print a literal string—not a named constant or variable—you must remember to use double quotes to enclose the string. If you don't put quotes around a string, you'll probably get an error message (such as "UNDECLARED IDENTI-FIER") from the C++ compiler. If you want to print a string that includes a double quote, you must type a backslash (\) character and a double quote, with no space between them, in the string. For example, to print the characters

```
Al "Butch" Jones
```

the output statement looks like this:

```
cout << "Al \"Butch\" Jones";
```

Normally, successive output statements cause the output to continue along the same line of the display screen. The sequence

```
cout << "Hi";
cout << "there";
```

writes the following to the screen, all on the same line:

```
Hithere
```

To print the two words on separate lines, we can do this:

```
cout << "Hi" << endl;
cout << "there" << endl;
```

The output from these statements is

```
Hi
there
```

The identifier endl (meaning "end line") is a special C++ feature called a *manipulator*. We discuss manipulators in the next chapter. For now, the important thing to note is that endl lets you finish an output line and go on to the next line whenever you wish.

Beyond Minimalism: Adding Comments to a Program

All you need to create a working program is the correct combination of declarations and executable statements. The compiler ignores comments, but they are of enormous help to anyone who must read the program. Comments can appear anywhere in a program except in the middle of an identifier, a reserved word, or a literal constant.

C++ comments come in two forms. The first is any sequence of characters enclosed by the /* */ pair. The compiler ignores anything within the pair. Here's an example:

```
string idNumber;     /* Identification number of the aircraft */
```

The second, and more common, form begins with two slashes (//) and extends to the end of that line of the program:

```
string idNumber;    // Identification number of the aircraft
```

The compiler ignores anything after the two slashes.

Writing fully commented programs is good programming style. A comment should appear at the beginning of a program to explain what the program does:

```
// This program computes the weight and balance of a Beechcraft
// Starship-1 airplane, given the amount of fuel, number of
// passengers, and weight of luggage in fore and aft storage.
// It assumes that there are two pilots and a standard complement
// of equipment, and that passengers weigh 170 pounds each
```

Another good place for comments is in constant and variable declarations, where the comments explain how each identifier is used. In addition, comments should introduce each major step in a long program and should explain anything that is unusual or difficult to read (for example, a lengthy formula).

It is important to make your comments concise and to arrange them in the program so that they are easy to see and it is clear what they refer to. If comments are too long or crowd the statements in the program, they make the program more difficult to read—just the opposite of what you intended!

2.2 Program Construction

We have looked at basic elements of C++ programs: identifiers, declarations, variables, constants, expressions, statements, and comments. Now let's see how to collect these elements into a program. As you saw earlier, C++ programs are made up of functions, one of which must be named main. A program also can have declarations that lie outside of any function. The syntax template for a program looks like this:

Program

```
Declaration
    ⋮
FunctionDefinition
FunctionDefinition
    ⋮
```

A function definition consists of the function heading and its body, which is delimited by left and right braces:

FunctionDefinition

```
Heading
{
    Statement
        ⋮
}
```

Here's an example of a program with just one function, the main function:

```cpp
//************************************************************************
// PrintName program
// This program prints a name in two different formats
//************************************************************************
#include <iostream>
#include <string>

using namespace std;

const string FIRST = "Herman";    // Person's first name
const string LAST = "Smith";      // Person's last name
const char   MIDDLE = 'G';        // Person's middle initial

int main()
{
    string firstLast;    // Name in first-last format
    string lastFirst;    // Name in last-first format

    firstLast = FIRST + " " + LAST;
    cout << "Name in first-last format is " << firstLast << endl;

    lastFirst = LAST + ", " + FIRST + ", ";
    cout << "Name in last-first-initial format is ";
    cout << lastFirst << MIDDLE << '.' << endl;

    return 0;
}
```

The program begins with a comment that explains what the program does. Immediately after the comment, the following lines appear:

```cpp
#include <iostream>
#include <string>

using namespace std;
```

The #include lines instruct the C++ system to insert into our program the contents of the files named iostream and string. The first file contains information that C++ needs in order to output values to a stream such as cout. The second file contains information about the programmer-defined data type string. We discuss the purpose of these #include lines and the using statement a little later in the chapter.

Next comes a declaration section in which we define the constants FIRST, LAST, and MIDDLE. Comments explain how each identifier is used. The rest of the program is the function definition for our main function. The first line is the function heading: the reserved word int, the name of the function, and then opening and closing parentheses. (The parentheses inform the compiler that main is the name of a function, not a variable or named constant.) The body of the function includes the declarations of two variables, firstLast and lastFirst, followed by a list of executable statements. The compiler translates these executable statements into machine language instructions. During the execution phase of the program, these are the instructions that are executed.

Our main function finishes by returning 0 as the function value:

```
return 0;
```

Remember that main returns an integer value to the operating system when it completes execution. This integer value is called the *exit status*. On most computer systems, you return an exit status of 0 to indicate successful completion of the program; otherwise, you return a nonzero value.

Notice how we use spacing in the PrintName program to make it easy for someone to read. We use blank lines to separate statements into related groups, and we indent the entire body of the main function. The compiler doesn't require us to format the program this way; we do so only to make it more readable. We have more to say in the next chapter about formatting a program.

Blocks (Compound Statements)

The body of a function is an example of a *block* (or *compound statement*). This is the syntax template for a block:

Block

A block is just a sequence of zero or more statements enclosed (delimited) by a { } pair. Now we can thus redefine a function definition as a heading followed by a block. In later chapters when we learn how to write functions other than main, we define the syntax of Heading in detail. In the case of the main function, Heading is simply

```
int main()
```

Here is the syntax template for a statement, limited to the C++ statements discussed in this chapter:

Statement

```
{
    NullStatement
    Declaration
    AssignmentStatement
    OutputStatement
    Block
```

A statement can be empty (the *null statement*). The null statement is just a semicolon (;). It does absolutely nothing at execution time; execution just proceeds to the next statement. It is not used often.

As the syntax template shows, a statement also can be a declaration, an executable statement, or even a block. The latter means that you can use an entire block wherever a single statement is allowed. In later chapters in which we introduce the syntax for branching and looping structures, this fact is very important.

We use blocks often, especially as parts of other statements. Leaving out a { } pair can dramatically change the meaning as well as the execution of a program. This is why we always indent the statements inside a block—the indentation makes a block easy to spot in a long, complicated program.

Notice in the syntax templates for the block and the statement that there is no mention of semicolons. Yet the PrintName program contains many semicolons. If you look back at the templates for constant declaration, variable declaration, assignment statement, and output statement, you can see that a semicolon is required at the end of each kind of statement. However, the syntax template for the block shows no semicolon after the right brace. The rule for using semicolons in C++, then, is quite simple: Terminate each statement *except* a compound statement (block) with a semicolon.

One more thing about blocks and statements: According to the syntax template for a statement, a declaration is officially considered to be a statement. A declaration, therefore, can appear wherever an executable statement can. In a block, we can mix declarations and executable statements if we wish:

```
{
    char ch;
    ch = 'A';
    cout << ch;
    string str;
    str = "Hello";
    cout << str;
}
```

It's far more common, though, for programmers to group the declarations together before the start of the executable statements:

```
{
    char    ch;
    string str;

    ch = 'A';
    cout << ch;
    str = "Hello";
    cout << str;
}
```

The C++ Preprocessor

Imagine that you are the C++ compiler. You are presented with the following program. You are to check it for syntax errors and, if there are no syntax errors, you are to translate it into machine language code.

```
//***********************************
// This program prints Happy Birthday
//***********************************

int main()
{
    cout << "Happy Birthday" << endl;
    return 0;
}
```

You, the compiler, recognize the identifier int as a C++ reserved word and the identifier main as the name of a required function. But what about the identifiers cout and endl? The programmer has not declared them as variables or named constants, and they are not reserved words. You have no choice but to issue an error message and give up.

To fix this program, the first thing we must do is insert a line near the top that says

```
#include <iostream>
```

just as we did in the PrintName program (as well as in the sample program at the beginning of this chapter).

The line says to insert the contents of a file named iostream into the program. This file contains declarations of cout, endl, and other items needed to perform stream input and output. The #include line is not handled by the C++ compiler but by a program known as the *preprocessor*.

The preprocessor concept is fundamental to C++. The preprocessor is a program that acts as a filter during the compilation phase. Your source program passes through the preprocessor on its way to the compiler (see Figure 2–2).

Figure 2-2   C++ Preprocessor

A line beginning with a pound sign (#) is not considered to be a C++ language statement (and thus is not terminated by a semicolon). It is called a *preprocessor directive*. The preprocessor expands an #include directive by physically inserting the contents of the named file into your source program. A file whose name appears in an #include directive is called a *header file*. Header files contain constant, variable, data type, and function declarations needed by a program.

In the directives

```
#include <iostream>
#include <string>
```

the angle brackets < > are required. They tell the preprocessor to look for the files in the standard *include directory*—a location in the computer system that contains all the header files that are related to the C++ standard library. The file iostream contains declarations of input/output facilities, and the file string contains declarations about the string data type. In Chapter 3, we make use of standard header files other than iostream and string.

An Introduction to Namespaces

In our Happy Birthday program, even if we add the preprocessor directive #include <iostream>, the program will not compile. The compiler *still* doesn't recognize the identifiers cout and endl. The problem is that the header file iostream (and, in fact, every standard header file) declares all of its identifiers to be in a *namespace* called std:

```
namespace std
{
    :   Declarations of variables, data types, and so forth
}
```

An identifier declared within a namespace block can be accessed directly only by statements within that block. To access an identifier that is "hidden" inside a namespace, the programmer has several options. We describe two options here. Chapter 8 describes namespaces in more detail.

The first option is to use a *qualified name* for the identifier. A qualified name consists of the name of the namespace, then the : : operator (the *scope resolution operator*), and then the desired identifier:

```
std::cout
```

With this approach, our program looks like the following:

```
#include <iostream>

int main()
{
    std::cout << "Happy Birthday" << std::endl;
    return 0;
}
```

Notice that both `cout` and `endl` must be qualified.

The second option is to use a statement called a *using directive:*

```
using namespace std;
```

When we place this statement near the top of the program before the `main` function, we make *all* the identifiers in the `std` namespace accessible to our program without having to qualify them:

```
#include <iostream>

using namespace std;

int main()
{
    cout << "Happy Birthday" << endl;
    return 0;
}
```

This second option is the one we used in the PrintName program and the sample program at the beginning of the chapter. In many of the following chapters, we continue to use this method. However, in Chapter 8 we discuss why it is not advisable to use the method in large programs.

2.3 More About Output

We can control both the horizontal and vertical spacing of our output to make it more appealing (and understandable). Let's look first at vertical spacing.

Creating Blank Lines

We control vertical spacing by using the `endl` manipulator in an output statement. You have seen that a sequence of output statements continues to write characters across the current line until an `endl` terminates the line. Here are some examples:

Statements	Output Produced*
`cout << "Hi there, ";`	
`cout << "Lois Lane. " << endl;`	Hi there, Lois Lane.
`cout << "Have you seen ";`	
`cout << "Clark Kent?" << endl;`	Have you seen Clark Kent?
`cout << "Hi there, " << endl;`	Hi there,
`cout << "Lois Lane. " << endl;`	Lois Lane.
`cout << "Have you seen " << endl;`	Have you seen
`cout << "Clark Kent?" << endl;`	Clark Kent?
`cout << "Hi there, " << endl;`	Hi there,
`cout << "Lois Lane. ";`	
`cout << "Have you seen " << endl;`	Lois Lane. Have you seen
`cout << "Clark Kent?" << endl;`	Clark Kent?

*The output lines are shown next to the output statement that ends each of them. There are no blank lines in the actual output from these statements.

What do you think the following statements print out?

```
cout << "Hi there, " << endl;
cout << endl;
cout << "Lois Lane." << endl;
```

The first output statement causes the words *Hi there,* to be printed; the `endl` causes the screen cursor to go to the next line. The next statement prints nothing but goes on to the next line. The third statement prints the words *Lois Lane.* and terminates the line. The resulting output is the three lines

```
Hi there,

Lois Lane.
```

Whenever you use an `endl` immediately after another `endl`, a blank line is produced. As you might guess, three consecutive uses of `endl` produce two blank lines, four consecutive uses produce three blank lines, and so forth.

Note that we have a great deal of flexibility in how we write an output statement in a C++ program. We could combine the three preceding statements into two statements:

```
cout << "Hi there, " << endl << endl;
cout << "Lois Lane." << endl;
```

In fact, we could do it all in one statement. One possibility is

```
cout << "Hi there, " << endl << endl << "Lois Lane." << endl;
```

Here's another:

```
cout << "Hi there, " << endl << endl
     << "Lois Lane." << endl;
```

The last example shows that you can spread a single C++ statement onto more than one line of the program. The compiler treats the semicolon, not the physical end of a line, as the end of a statement.

Inserting Blanks Within a Line

To control the horizontal spacing of the output, one technique is to send extra blank characters to the output stream. (Remember that the blank character, generated by pressing the spacebar on a keyboard, is a perfectly valid character in C++.)

For example, to produce this output:

```
  *   *   *   *   *   *   *   *   *

*   *   *   *   *   *   *   *   *   *

  *   *   *   *   *   *   *   *   *
```

you would use these statements:

```
cout << "  *   *   *   *   *   *   *   *   *" << endl << endl;
cout << "*   *   *   *   *   *   *   *   *   *" << endl << endl;
cout << "  *   *   *   *   *   *   *   *   *" << endl;
```

All of the blanks and asterisks are enclosed in double quotes, so they print literally as they are written in the program. The extra `endl` manipulators give you the blank lines between the rows of asterisks.

If you want blanks to be printed, you *must* enclose them in quotes. The statement

```
cout << '*' <<                                        '*';
```

produces the output

```
**
```

Despite all of the blanks we included in the output statement, the asterisks print side by side because the blanks are not enclosed by quotes.

Programming Example

Printing a Chessboard

PROBLEM Your college is hosting a chess tournament, and the people running the tournament want to record the final positions of the pieces in each game on a sheet of paper with a chessboard preprinted on it. Your job is to write a program to preprint these pieces of paper. The chessboard is an eight-by-eight pattern of squares that alternate between black and white, with the upper left square being white. You need to print out squares of light characters (spaces) and dark characters (such as *) in this pattern to form the chessboard.

DISCUSSION You could simply type up a program consisting of a series of output statements with alternating patterns of blanks and asterisks. But the organizers aren't sure exactly what they want the chessboard to look like, and you decide it would be safer to write the program in a manner that allows the design of the chessboard to be modified easily.

It is easy to make a changeable chessboard if the design is built up using string variables. You can begin by defining string constants for rows of characters that make up the black and white areas. Then you can concatenate these to form variables containing the alternating patterns of black and white that are repeated to print a row of chessboard squares. For example, suppose your initial design for the chessboard looks like this:

```
            * * * * * * *         * * * * * * *         * * * * * * *         * * * * * * *
            * * * * * * *         * * * * * * *         * * * * * * *         * * * * * * *
            * * * * * * *         * * * * * * *         * * * * * * *         * * * * * * *
            * * * * * * *         * * * * * * *         * * * * * * *         * * * * * * *
            * * * * * * *         * * * * * * *         * * * * * * *         * * * * * * *
    * * * * * * *         * * * * * * *         * * * * * * *         * * * * * * *
    * * * * * * *         * * * * * * *         * * * * * * *         * * * * * * *
    * * * * * * *         * * * * * * *         * * * * * * *         * * * * * * *
    * * * * * * *         * * * * * * *         * * * * * * *         * * * * * * *
    * * * * * * *         * * * * * * *         * * * * * * *         * * * * * * *
            * * * * * * *         * * * * * * *         * * * * * * *         * * * * * * *
            * * * * * * *         * * * * * * *         * * * * * * *         * * * * * * *
            * * * * * * *         * * * * * * *         * * * * * * *         * * * * * * *
            * * * * * * *         * * * * * * *         * * * * * * *         * * * * * * *
            * * * * * * *         * * * * * * *         * * * * * * *         * * * * * * *
    * * * * * * *         * * * * * * *         * * * * * * *         * * * * * * *
    * * * * * * *         * * * * * * *         * * * * * * *         * * * * * * *
    * * * * * * *         * * * * * * *         * * * * * * *         * * * * * * *
    * * * * * * *         * * * * * * *         * * * * * * *         * * * * * * *
    * * * * * * *         * * * * * * *         * * * * * * *         * * * * * * *
            * * * * * * *         * * * * * * *         * * * * * * *         * * * * * * *
            * * * * * * *         * * * * * * *         * * * * * * *         * * * * * * *
            * * * * * * *         * * * * * * *         * * * * * * *         * * * * * * *
            * * * * * * *         * * * * * * *         * * * * * * *         * * * * * * *
            * * * * * * *         * * * * * * *         * * * * * * *         * * * * * * *
    * * * * * * *         * * * * * * *         * * * * * * *         * * * * * * *
    * * * * * * *         * * * * * * *         * * * * * * *         * * * * * * *
    * * * * * * *         * * * * * * *         * * * * * * *         * * * * * * *
    * * * * * * *         * * * * * * *         * * * * * * *         * * * * * * *
    * * * * * * *         * * * * * * *         * * * * * * *         * * * * * * *
            * * * * * * *         * * * * * * *         * * * * * * *         * * * * * * *
            * * * * * * *         * * * * * * *         * * * * * * *         * * * * * * *
            * * * * * * *         * * * * * * *         * * * * * * *         * * * * * * *
            * * * * * * *         * * * * * * *         * * * * * * *         * * * * * * *
            * * * * * * *         * * * * * * *         * * * * * * *         * * * * * * *
    * * * * * * *         * * * * * * *         * * * * * * *         * * * * * * *
    * * * * * * *         * * * * * * *         * * * * * * *         * * * * * * *
    * * * * * * *         * * * * * * *         * * * * * * *         * * * * * * *
    * * * * * * *         * * * * * * *         * * * * * * *         * * * * * * *
    * * * * * * *         * * * * * * *         * * * * * * *         * * * * * * *
```

You can begin by defining constants for WHITE and BLACK that contain eight blanks and eight asterisks respectively, and then concatenate these together into variables that follow the patterns

```
WHITE + BLACK + WHITE + BLACK + WHITE + BLACK + WHITE + BLACK
```

and

```
BLACK + WHITE + BLACK + WHITE + BLACK + WHITE + BLACK + WHITE
```

that can then be printed with cout statements the appropriate number of times in order to create the chessboard.

From this discussion we know that there are two constants and two variables, as summarized in the following tables:

Constants

Name	Value	Function
BLACK	"********"	Characters forming one line of a black square
WHITE	" "	Characters forming one line of a white square

Variables

Name	Data Type	Description
whiteRow	string	A row beginning with a white square
blackRow	string	A row beginning with a black square

If we look carefully at the chessboard, the algorithm jumps out at us. We need to output five whiteRows, five blackRows, five whiteRows, five blackRows, five whiteRows, five blackRows, five whiteRows, and five blackRows. We can summarize this in our algorithm to output the five whiteRows and five blackRows four times.

```
Repeat four times
    Output five whiteRows
    Output five blackRows
```

```
//*****************************************************************
// Chessboard program
// This program prints a chessboard pattern that is built up from
// basic strings of white and black characters.
//*****************************************************************
```

```cpp
#include <iostream>
#include <string>
using namespace std;

const string BLACK = "*********";  // Define a line of a black square
const string WHITE = "         ";  // Define a line of a white square

int main ()
{
    string whiteRow;                  // A row beginning with a white square
    string blackRow;                  // A row beginning with a black square

    // Create a white-black row by concatenating the basic strings
    whiteRow = WHITE + BLACK + WHITE + BLACK +
               WHITE + BLACK + WHITE + BLACK;
    // Create a black-white row by concatenating the basic strings
    blackRow = BLACK + WHITE + BLACK + WHITE +
               BLACK + WHITE + BLACK + WHITE;

    // Print five white-black rows
    cout << whiteRow << endl;
    cout << whiteRow << endl;
    cout << whiteRow << endl;
    cout << whiteRow << endl;
    cout << whiteRow << endl;

    // Print five black-white rows
    cout << blackRow << endl;
    cout << blackRow << endl;
    cout << blackRow << endl;
    cout << blackRow << endl;
    cout << blackRow << endl;

    // Print five white-black rows
    cout << whiteRow << endl;
    cout << whiteRow << endl;
    cout << whiteRow << endl;
    cout << whiteRow << endl;
    cout << whiteRow << endl;

    // Print five black-white rows
    cout << blackRow << endl;
    cout << blackRow << endl;
    cout << blackRow << endl;
```

```
        cout << blackRow << endl;
        cout << blackRow << endl;

        // Print five white-black rows
        cout << whiteRow << endl;
        cout << whiteRow << endl;
        cout << whiteRow << endl;
        cout << whiteRow << endl;
        cout << whiteRow << endl;

        // Print five black-white rows
        cout << blackRow << endl;
        cout << blackRow << endl;
        cout << blackRow << endl;
        cout << blackRow << endl;
        cout << blackRow << endl;

        // Print five white-black rows
        cout << whiteRow << endl;
        cout << whiteRow << endl;
        cout << whiteRow << endl;
        cout << whiteRow << endl;
        cout << whiteRow << endl;

        // Print five black-white rows
        cout << blackRow << endl;
        cout << blackRow << endl;
        cout << blackRow << endl;
        cout << blackRow << endl;
        cout << blackRow << endl;

        return 0;
    }
```

There are eight blocks of five lines that look alike. In Chapter 6, we introduce a looping statement that allows us to shorten this program considerably.

After you show the printout from this program to the organizers of the tournament, they suggest that the board would look better with the "#" character instead of "*" filling the black squares. You cheerfully agree to make this change because you know that the only difference in the program is that the value of the constant BLACK becomes "########".

Testing and Debugging

1. Every identifier that isn't a C++ reserved word must be declared. If you use a name that hasn't been declared—either by your own declaration statements or by including a header file—you get an error message.

2. If you try to declare an identifier that is the same as a reserved word in C++, you get an error message from the compiler. See Appendix A for a list of reserved words.

3. C++ is a case-sensitive language. Two identifiers that are capitalized differently are treated as two different identifiers. The word `main` and all C++ reserved words use only lowercase letters.

4. To use identifiers from the standard library, such as `cout` and `string`, you must either (a) give a qualified name such as `std::cout` or (b) put a `using` directive near the top of your program:

   ```
   using namespace std;
   ```

5. Check for mismatched quotes in `char` and string literals. Each `char` literal begins and ends with an apostrophe (single quote). Each string literal begins and ends with a double quote.

6. Be sure to use only the apostrophe (') to enclose `char` literals. Most keyboards also have a reverse apostrophe (`), which is easily confused with the apostrophe. If you use the reverse apostrophe, the compiler issues an error message.

7. To use a double quote within a literal string, use the two symbols \" in a row. If you use just a double quote, it ends the string, and the compiler then sees the remainder of the string as an error.

8. In an assignment statement, be sure that the identifier to the left of = is a variable and not a named constant.

9. In assigning a value to a `string` variable, the expression to the right of = must be a `string` expression, a literal string, or a `char`.

10. In a concatenation expression, at least one of the two operands of + must be of type `string`. For example, the operands cannot both be literal strings or `char` values.*

11. Make sure your statements end in semicolons (except compound statements, which do not have a semicolon after the right brace).

---

*The invalid concatenation expression `"Hi" + "there"` results in a syntax error message such as `"INVALID POINTER ADDITION."` The topic of pointers is not covered in this book.

Summary

The syntax (grammar) of the C++ language is defined by a metalanguage. In this text, we use a form of metalanguage called syntax templates. We describe the semantics (meaning) of C++ statements in English.

Identifiers are used in C++ to name things. Some identifiers, called reserved words, have predefined meanings in the language; others are created by the programmer. The identifiers you invent are restricted to those *not* reserved by the C++ language. Reserved words are listed in Appendix A.

Identifiers are associated with memory locations by declarations. A declaration may give a name to a location whose value does not change (a constant) or to one whose value can change (a variable). Every constant and variable has an associated data type. C++ provides many built-in data types, the most common of which are int, float, and char. Additionally, C++ permits programmer-defined types such as the string type from the standard library.

The assignment operator is used to change the value of a variable by assigning it the value of an expression. At execution time, the expression is evaluated and the result is stored into the variable. With the string type, the plus sign (+) is an operator that concatenates two strings. A string expression can concatenate any number of strings to form a new string value.

Program output is accomplished by means of the output stream variable cout, along with the insertion operator (<<). Each insertion operation sends output data to the standard output device. When an endl manipulator appears instead of a data item, the computer terminates the current output line and goes on to the next line.

Output should be clear, understandable, and neatly arranged. Messages in the output should describe the significance of values. Blank lines (produced by successive uses of the endl manipulator) and blank spaces within lines help to organize the output and improve its appearance.

A C++ program is a collection of one or more function definitions (and optionally some declarations outside of any function). One of the functions *must* be named main. Execution of a program always begins with the main function. Collectively, the functions all cooperate to produce the desired results.

Quick Check

1. What is the name of the one function that every C++ program must have? (p. 26)
2. What is the purpose of a metalanguage? (pp. 28–29)
3. What is a data type? (p. 33)
4. Use the following syntax template to decide if the string "C++ 4th edition" is a valid "Sentence." (pp. 30–31)

Sentence

5. Which of the following are valid C++ identifiers? (p. 32)

   ```
   Hello    Bob    4th-edition    C++    maximum    all_4_one
   ```

6. The only difference between a variable declaration and a constant declaration is that the reserved word `const` precedes the declaration. True or false? (pp. 35–38)
7. The reserved words listed in Appendix A cannot be used as identifiers. True or false? (p. 32)
8. Write a statement to assign the letter "A" to the `char` variable `initial`. (pp. 40–41)
9. What value is stored in the variable `name` by the following statement? (pp. 41–42)

   ```
   name = "Alexander" + " Q. " + "Smith";
   ```

10. Write a statement that sends the value in variable `name` to the stream `cout`. (pp. 42–44)
11. What is printed by the following statement, given the value assigned to `name` in Exercise 10? (pp. 42–44)

    ```
    cout << name << " Jr." << endl;
    ```

12. What are the two ways to write comments in C++? (pp. 44–45)
13. Fill in the blanks in the following statements, which appear at the beginning of a program. (pp. 49–51)

    ```
    #include <_____>
    #include <_____>

    using namespace _____;
    ```

Answers
1. `main`   2. To provide a language for expressing the syntax rules of a programming language.
3. A specific set of values, together with a set of operations that can be applied to those values.
4. No. According to the template, a Sentence must end in a period, exclamation point, or question mark.   5. `Hello`, `Bob`, `maximum`, and `all_4_one` are the valid C++ identifiers.   6. False. The constant declaration also assigns a literal value to the identifier.   7. True. Identifiers must differ from reserved words.   8. `initial = 'A';`   9. `Alexander Q. Smith`   10. `cout << name;`   11. The string `Alexander Q. Smith Jr.` is output and then successive output will appear on the next line.   12. Between the delimiters /* and */, or following // to the end of the line.
13. `#include <iostream>`
    `#include <string>`

    `using namespace std;`

Exam Preparation Exercises

1. Mark the following identifiers as either valid or invalid.

		Valid	Invalid
a.	`theDog`	_____	_____
b.	`all-In-One`	_____	_____
c.	`const`	_____	_____
d.	`recycling`	_____	_____
e.	`DVD_ROM`	_____	_____
f.	`elizabeth_the_2nd`	_____	_____
g.	`2morrow`	_____	_____
h.	`page#`	_____	_____

2. Match the following terms with the definitions given below.
   a. Function
   b. Syntax
   c. Semantics
   d. Metalanguage
   e. Identifier
   f. Data type
   g. Variable
   h. Named constant
   i. Literal
   j. Expression
      i. An identifier referring to a value that can be changed.
      ii. A specific set of values, along with operations that can be applied to those values.
      iii. A value that appears in a program.
      iv. The set of rules that determines the meaning of instructions written in a programming language.
      v. A language that is used to write the rules for another language.
      vi. A subprogram in C++.
      vii. A name that is used to refer to a function or data object.
      viii. An arrangement of identifiers, literals, and operators that can be evaluated.
      ix. The formal rules governing how valid instructions are written in a programming language.
      x. An identifier referring to a value that cannot be changed.
3. A reserved word is a named constant that is predefined in C++. True or false?
4. What is wrong with the following syntax template for a C++ identifier?

```
{
  Letter
  Digit     ...
  -
}
```

5. A `char` literal can be enclosed either in single or double quotes. True or false?
6. The null string represents a string containing no characters. True or false?
7. Concatenation only works with a `char` value when its other operand is a string value. True or false?
8. What is output by the following statement?

```
cout << "Four score and" << endl << "seven years ago"
     << "our fathers" << endl
     << "brought forth on this" << endl
     << "continent a new nation..." << endl
```

9. Given these assignments to string variables:

```
string1 = "Bjarne Stroustrup";
string2 = "C";
string3 = "programming language";
string4 = "++ because it is a successor to the ";
string5 = " named his new ";
```

What is the value of the following expression?

```
string1 + string5 + string3 + " " + string2 + string4 + string2
+ " " + string3 + "."
```

10. How do we insert a double quote into a string?
11. What danger is associated with the use of the `/*` and `*/` form of comment, and is avoided by use of the `//` comment form?
12. What are the limitations associated with the `//` form of comment?
13. What is the name of the `<<` operator, and how might we pronounce it in reading a line of code that contains it?
14. Can we concatenate `endl` with a string in an expression? Explain.
15. What does the `#include` preprocessor directive do?
16. If you do not include the line

```
using namespace std;
```

at the start of a program, how must you change the following output statement to work correctly?

```
cout << "Hello everybody!" << endl;
```

17. What is the name of the C++ construct that begins with `{` and ends with `}`?
18. How do you write a string that is too long to fit on a single line?
19. Reorder the following lines to make a working program.

```
{
}
#include <iostream>
```

```
const string TITLE = "Dr.";
cout << "Hello " + TITLE + " Stroustrup!";
int main()
#include <string>
return 0;
using namespace std;
```

Programming Warm-Up Exercises

1. Write an output statement that prints today's date and then goes to the next line.
2. Write a single output statement that outputs the following three lines:

```
He said, "How is that possible?"
She replied, "Using manipulators."
"Of course!" he exclaimed.
```

3. Write declarations for the following:
   a. A named constant, called ANSWER, of type string with the value "True"
   b. A char variable with the name middleInitial
   c. A string variable with the name courseTitle
   d. A named char constant, called PERCENT, with the value '%'
4. Change the three declarations in the printName program on page 46 so that it prints your name.
5. Given the following declarations:

```
const string PART1 = "Pro";
const string PART2 = "gramming";
const string PART3 = "in C++";
```

   write an output statement that prints the title of this book, using only the cout stream, the stream insertion operator, and the above named constants.
6. Write an expression that results in a string containing the title of this book, using only the concatenation operator and the declarations of Exercise 5.
7. Write C++ output statements to print the following exactly as shown here (a portion of the text found on page iv of this book, relating the action of a weaver's loom to the complexity of human thought). You should write one output statement for each line of text.

```
Yet the web of thought has no such creases
And is more like a weaver's masterpieces;
One step a thousand threads arise,
Hither and thither shoots each shuttle,
The threads flow on unseen and subtle,
Each blow effects a thousand ties.
```

8. Fill in the missing lines in the following program, which outputs:

```
Rev. H.G. Jones
```

_____

_____

_____

```
const string TITLE = "Rev. ";
const char FIRST = 'H';
const char MID 'G';
```

_____

_____

```
{
    cout << TITLE << FIRST << DOT << MID << DOT << " Jones";
```

_____

9. Enter and run the following program. Be sure to type it exactly as it appears here, but substitute your name and the date as indicated.

```cpp
//*************************************************************
// Program entry and compilation exercise
// Your name goes here
// Today's date goes here
//*************************************************************

#include <iostream>
#include <string>

using namespace std;

const string STARS35 = "***********************************";
const char   STAR = '*';
const string BLANKS33 = "                                 ";
const string MSG = "Welcome to C++ Programming!";
const string BLANKS3 = "   ";

int main()
{
    cout << STARS35 << endl << STAR << BLANKS33 << STAR << endl;
    cout << STAR << BLANKS3 << MSG << BLANKS3 << STAR << endl;
    cout << STAR << BLANKS33 << STAR << endl << STARS35 << endl;
}
```

Programming Problems

1. Write a program that prints out your course schedule for a single week. Here's an example of the output for one day:

```
Monday  9:00 Computer Science 101
Monday 11:00 Physics 201
Monday  2:00 Dance 153
```

Use named string constants wherever possible to avoid retyping any words or numbers. Be sure to include appropriate comments in your code, choose meaningful identifiers, and use indentation as we do with the programs in this chapter.

2. Write a program that prints out all six permutations of the ordering of the following three lines. Declare a named constant for each line and write an output statement for each permutation. Be sure to include appropriate comments in your code, choose meaningful identifiers, and use indentation as we do with the programs in this chapter.

```
I saw the big brown bear.
The big brown bear saw me.
Oh! What a frightening experience!
```

3. Write a program that displays a checkerboard pattern made of stars and blanks, as shown below. A checkerboard is eight squares by eight squares. This will be easier if you first declare two named string constants representing the two different row patterns. Be sure to include appropriate comments in your code, choose meaningful identifiers, and use indentation as we do with the programs in this chapter.

```
  *  *  *  *
*  *  *  *
  *  *  *  *
*  *  *  *
  *  *  *  *
*  *  *  *
  *  *  *  *
*  *  *  *
```

4. Write a program that prints out business cards for yourself. A card should include your name, address, phone number(s), and email. You also can make up a company name and put that on the card if you wish. To save paper, the program should print eight cards per page, arranged in two columns of four cards. Thus, to reduce typing, you should declare a named string constant for each line of the card, and then write output statements to print the eight cards using those constants. Be sure to include appropriate comments in your code, choose meaningful identifiers, and use indentation as we do with the programs in this chapter.

Programming Example Follow-Up

1. What change would you have to make to the Chessboard program to cause the black squares to be printed with the "%" character instead of "*"?

2. How would you change the Chessboard program to print periods in the white squares instead of blanks?

3. How would the Chessboard program change if you wanted to reverse the colors (that is, make black squares white and vice versa) without changing the constant declarations or the values of `whiteRow` and `blackRow`?

4. Change the Chessboard program so that the squares are 10 characters wide by 8 rows high.

5. The organizers of the chess tournament find it difficult to write in the black squares of the printed chessboard. They want you to change the program so that the black squares have a blank space in their center that is four characters wide and two lines high. (*Hint:* You may have to define another string constant.)

6. How many characters are stored in each of the string variables in the Chessboard program?

Numeric Types, Expressions, and Output

Knowledge Goals

- To understand implicit type coercion and explicit type conversion.
- To recognize and understand the purpose of function arguments.
- To learn and use additional operations associated with the `string` type.
- To learn how to format program statements in a clear and readable fashion.

Skill Goals

To be able to:

- Declare named constants and variables of type `int` and `float`.
- Construct simple arithmetic expressions.
- Evaluate simple arithmetic expressions.
- Construct and evaluate expressions that contain multiple arithmetic operations.
- Call (invoke) a value-returning function.
- Use C++ library functions in expressions.
- Call (invoke) a void function (one that does not return a function value).
- Use C++ manipulators to format output.

In Chapter 2, we examined enough C++ syntax to be able to construct simple programs using assignment and output. In this chapter we continue to write programs that use assignment and output, but we concentrate on additional built-in data types: int and float.

3.1 Numeric Data Types

You already are familiar with the basic concepts of integer and real numbers in math. However, as used on a computer, the corresponding data types have certain limitations, which we now consider.

Integral Types

The data types char, short, int, and long are known as integral types (or integer types) because they refer to integer values—whole numbers with no fractional part. (We postpone talking about the remaining integral type, bool, until Chapter 5.)

In C++, the simplest form of integer value is a sequence of one or more digits:

```
22    16    1    498    0    4600
```

Commas are not allowed.

A minus sign preceding an integer value makes the integer negative:

```
-378   -912
```

The data types char, short, int, and long are intended to represent different sizes of integers, from smaller (fewer bits) to larger (more bits). The sizes are machine dependent (that is, they may vary from machine to machine). For one particular machine, we might picture the sizes this way:

char memory cell
short memory cell
int memory cell
long memory cell

On another machine, the size of an int might be the same as the size of a long. In general, the more bits there are in the memory cell, the larger the integer value that can be stored.

Although we used the char type in Chapter 2 to store character data such as 'A', there are reasons why C++ classifies char as an integral type. Chapter 10 discusses the reasons.

int is by far the most common data type for manipulating integer data. You nearly always use int for manipulating integer values, but sometimes you have to use long if your program requires values larger than the maximum int value. (On personal computers, ints commonly range from -2147483648 through +2147483647.) If your program tries to compute a value larger than your machine's maximum value, the result is *integer overflow*. Some machines give you an error message when overflow occurs, but others don't.

Floating-Point Types

Floating-point types (or floating types), the second major category of simple types in C++, are used to represent real numbers. Floating-point numbers have an integer part and a fractional part, with a decimal point in between. Either the integer part or the fractional part, but not both, may be missing. Here are some examples:

```
18.0    127.54    0.57    4.    193145.8523    .8
```

Just as the integral types in C++ come in different sizes (char, short, int, and long), so do the floating-point types. In increasing order of size, the floating-point types are float, double (meaning double precision), and long double. Again, the exact sizes are machine dependent. Each larger size potentially gives us a wider range of values and more precision (the number of significant digits in the number), but at the expense of more memory space to hold the number.

Floating-point values also can have an exponent, as in scientific notation. (In scientific notation, a number is written as a value multiplied by 10 to some power.) Instead of writing 3.504×10^{12}, in C++ we write 3.504E12. The E means exponent of base 10. The number preceding the letter E doesn't need to include a decimal point. Here are some examples of floating-point numbers in scientific notation:

```
1.74536E-12    3.652442E4    7E20
```

Most programs don't need the double and long double types. The float type usually provides sufficient precision and range of values for floating-point numbers. Most personal computers provide float values with a precision of six or seven significant digits and a maximum value of about 3.4E+38. We use floating-point values to represent money and interest rate in the programming example at the end of the chapter.

We talk more about floating-point numbers in Chapter 10. But there is one more thing you should know about them now. Computers cannot always represent floating-point numbers exactly. You learned in Chapter 1 that the computer stores all data in binary (base-2) form. Many floating-point values can only be approximated in the binary number system. Don't be surprised if your program prints out the number 4.8 as 4.7999998. In most cases, slight inaccuracies in the rightmost fractional digits are to be expected and are not the result of programmer error.

3.2 Declarations for Numeric Types

Just as with the types char and string, we can declare named constants and variables of type int and float. Such declarations use the same syntax as before, except that the literals and the names of the data types are different.

Named Constant Declarations

In the case of named constant declarations, the literal values in the declarations are numeric instead of being characters in single or double quotes. For example, here are some constant declarations that define values of type `int` and `float`. For comparison, declarations of `char` and `string` values are included.

```
const float  PI = 3.14159;
const float  E = 2.71828;
const int    MAX_SCORE = 100;
const int    MIN_SCORE = -100;
const char   LETTER = 'W';
const string NAME = "Elizabeth";
```

Although character and string literals are put in quotes, literal integers and floating-point numbers are not, because there is no chance of confusing them with identifiers. Why? Because identifiers must start with a letter or underscore, and numbers must start with a digit or sign.

Using Named Constants Instead of Literals

It's a good idea to use named constants instead of literals. In addition to making your program more readable, named constants can make your program easier to modify. Suppose you wrote a program last year to compute taxes. In several places you used the literal 0.05, which was the sales tax rate at the time. Now the rate has gone up to 0.06. To change your program, you must locate every literal 0.05 and change it to 0.06. And if 0.05 is used for some other reason—to compute deductions, for example—you need to look at each place where it is used, figure out what it is used for, and then decide whether to change it.

The process is much simpler if you use a named constant. Instead of using a literal constant, suppose you had declared a named constant, TAX_RATE, with a value of 0.05. To change your program, you would simply change the declaration, setting TAX_RATE equal to 0.06. This one modification changes all of the tax rate computations without affecting the other places where 0.05 is used.

C++ allows us to declare constants with different names but the same value. If a value has different meanings in different parts of a program, it makes sense to declare and use a constant with an appropriate name for each meaning.

Named constants also are reliable; they protect us from mistakes. If you mistype the name PI as PO, the C++ compiler tells you that the name PO has not been declared. On the other hand, even though we recognize that the number 3.14149 is a mistyped version of pi (3.14159), the number is perfectly acceptable to the compiler. It won't warn us that anything is wrong.

Variable Declarations

We declare numeric variables the same way in which we declare `char` and `string` variables, except that we use the names of numeric types. The following are valid variable declarations:

```
int     studentCount;    // Number of students
int     sumOfScores;     // Sum of their scores
float   average;         // Average of the scores
char    grade;           // Student's letter grade
string  stuName;         // Student's name
```

Given the declarations

```
int    num;
int    alpha;
float  rate;
char   ch;
```

the following are appropriate assignment statements:

Variable	Expression
alpha =	2856;
rate =	0.36;
ch =	'B';
num =	alpha;

In each of these assignment statements, the data type of the expression matches the data type of the variable to which it is assigned. Later in the chapter we see what happens if the data types do not match.

3.3 Simple Arithmetic Expressions

Now that we have looked at declaration and assignment, we consider how to calculate with values of numeric types. Calculations are performed with expressions. We first look at simple expressions that involve at most one operator so that we may examine each operator in detail. Then, we move on to compound expressions that combine multiple operations.

Arithmetic Operators

Expressions are made up of constants, variables, and operators. The following are all valid expressions:

```
alpha + 2      rate - 6.0      4 - alpha      rate      alpha * num
```

The operators allowed in an expression depend on the data types of the constants and variables in the expression. The *arithmetic operators* are

+	Unary plus
-	Unary minus
+	Addition
-	Subtraction
*	Multiplication

/ $\left\{\begin{array}{l}\text{Floating-point division (floating-point result)}\\ \text{Integer division (no fractional part)}\end{array}\right.$

%   Modulus (remainder from integer division)

The first two operators are **unary operators**—they take just one operand. The remaining five are **binary operators**, taking two operands. Unary plus and minus are used as follows:

> Unary operator   An operator that has just one operand.
>
> Binary operator   An operator that has two operands.

```
-54    +259.65    -rate
```

Programmers rarely use the unary plus. Without any sign, a numeric constant is assumed to be positive anyway.

You may not be familiar with integer division and modulus (%). Let's look at them more closely. Note that % is used only with integers. When you divide one integer by another, you get an integer quotient and a remainder. Integer division gives only the integer quotient, and % gives only the remainder. (If either operand is negative, the sign of the remainder may vary from one C++ compiler to another.)

$$
\begin{array}{cc}
3 \leftarrow 6/2 & 3 \leftarrow 7/2 \\
2\overline{)6} & 2\overline{)7} \\
\underline{6} & \underline{6} \\
0 \leftarrow 6\%2 & 1 \leftarrow 7\%2
\end{array}
$$

In contrast, floating-point division yields a floating-point result. The expression

```
7.0 / 2.0
```

yields the value 3.5.

Here are some expressions using arithmetic operators and their values:

Expression	Value
3 + 6	9
3.4 - 6.1	–2.7
2 * 3	6
8 / 2	4
8.0 / 2.0	4.0
8 / 8	1
8 / 9	0
8 / 7	1
8 % 8	0
8 % 9	8
8 % 7	1
0 % 7	0
5 % 2.3	error (both operands must be integers)

Be careful with division and modulus. The expressions `7.0 / 0.0`, `7 / 0`, and `7 % 0` all produce errors. The computer cannot divide by zero.

Because variables are allowed in expressions, the following are valid assignments:

```
alpha = num + 6;
alpha = num / 2;
num = alpha * 2;
num = 6 % alpha;
alpha = alpha + 1;
num = num + alpha;
```

As we saw with assignment statements involving `string` expressions, the same variable can appear on both sides of the assignment operator. In the case of

```
num = num + alpha;
```

the value in `num` and the value in `alpha` are added together, and then the sum of the two values is stored back into `num`, replacing the previous value stored there. This example shows the difference between mathematical equality and assignment. The mathematical equality

$$num = num + alpha$$

is true only when *alpha* equals 0. The assignment statement

```
num = num + alpha;
```

is valid for *any* value of `alpha`.

Here's a simple program that uses arithmetic expressions:

```
//*****************************************************************
// FreezeBoil program
// This program computes the midpoint between
// the freezing and boiling points of water
//*****************************************************************
#include <iostream>

using namespace std;

const float FREEZE_PT = 32.0;    // Freezing point of water
const float BOIL_PT = 212.0;     // Boiling point of water

int main()
{
    float avgTemp;                  // Holds the result of averaging
                                    //   FREEZE_PT and BOIL_PT

    cout << "Water freezes at " << FREEZE_PT << endl;
    cout << " and boils at " << BOIL_PT << " degrees." << endl;

    avgTemp = FREEZE_PT + BOIL_PT;
    avgTemp = avgTemp / 2.0;

    cout << "Halfway between is ";
    cout << avgTemp << " degrees." << endl;

    return 0;
}
```

The program begins with a comment that explains what the program does. Next comes a declaration section where we define the constants FREEZE_PT and BOIL_PT. The body of the main function includes a declaration of the variable avgTemp and then a sequence of executable statements. These statements print a message, add FREEZE_PT and BOIL_PT, divide the sum by 2, and finally print the result.

Increment and Decrement Operators

In addition to the arithmetic operators, C++ provides *increment* and *decrement* *operators*:

++   Increment
--   Decrement

These are unary operators that take a single variable name as an operand. For integer and floating-point operands, the effect is to add 1 to (or subtract 1 from) the operand. If `num` currently contains the value 8, the statement

```
num++;
```

causes `num` to contain 9. You can achieve the same effect by writing the assignment statement

```
num = num + 1;
```

but C++ programmers typically prefer the increment operator. This is how the C++ language got its name: C++ is an enhanced ["incremented"] version of the C language.)

The ++ and - - operators can be either *prefix* operators

```
++num;
```

or postfix operators

```
num++;
```

Both of these statements behave in exactly the same way; they add 1 to whatever is in `num`. The choice between the two is a matter of personal preference.

C++ allows the use of ++ and - - in the middle of a larger expression:

```
alpha = num++ * 3;
```

In this case, the postfix form of ++ does *not* give the same result as the prefix form. In Chapter 10, we explain the ++ and - - operators in detail. In the meantime, you should use them only to increment or decrement a variable as a separate, stand-alone statement.

3.4 Compound Arithmetic Expressions

The expressions we've used so far have contained at most a single arithmetic operator. We also have been careful not to mix integer and floating-point values in the same expression. Now we look at more complicated expressions—ones that are composed of several operators and ones that contain mixed data types.

Precedence Rules

Arithmetic expressions can be made up of many constants, variables, operators, and parentheses. In what order are the operations performed? For example, in the assignment statement

```
avgTemp = FREEZE_PT + BOIL_PT / 2.0;
```

is `FREEZE_PT + BOIL_PT` calculated first or is `BOIL_PT / 2.0` calculated first?

The basic arithmetic operators (unary +, unary -, + for addition, - for subtraction, * for multiplication, / for division, and % for modulus) are ordered the same way mathematical operators are, according to *precedence rules*:

Highest precedence level:	Unary + Unary -
Middle level:	* / %
Lowest level:	+ -

Because division has higher precedence than addition, the expression in the example above is implicitly parenthesized as

```
FREEZE_PT + (BOIL_PT / 2.0)
```

That is, we first divide BOIL_PT by 2.0 and then add FREEZE_PT to the result.

You can change the order of evaluation by using parentheses. In the statement

```
avgTemp = (FREEZE_PT + BOIL_PT) / 2.0;
```

FREEZE_PT and BOIL_PT are added first, and then their sum is divided by 2.0. We evaluate subexpressions in parentheses first and then follow the precedence of the operators.

When an arithmetic expression has several binary operators with the same precedence, their *grouping order* (or *associativity*) is from left to right. The expression

```
int1 - int2 + int3
```

means (int1 - int2) + int3, not int1 - (int2 + int3). As another example, we would use the expression

```
(float1 + float2) / float1 * 3.0
```

to evaluate the expression in parentheses first, then divide the sum by float1, and multiply the result by 3.0. Below are some more examples.

Expression	Value
10 / 2 * 3	15
10 % 3 - 4 / 2	-1
5.0 * 2.0 / 4.0 * 2.0	5.0
5.0 * 2.0 / (4.0 * 2.0)	1.25
5.0 + 2.0 / (4.0 * 2.0)	5.25

In C++, all unary operators (such as unary + and unary -) have right-to-left associativity. Though this fact may seem strange at first, it turns out to be the natural grouping order. For example, - + x means - (+ x) rather than the meaningless (- +) x.

Type Coercion and Type Casting

Integer values and floating-point values are stored differently inside a computer's memory. The pattern of bits that represents the constant 2 does not look at all like the pattern of bits representing the constant 2.0. What happens if we mix integer and floating-point values together in an assignment statement or an arithmetic expression? Let's look first at assignment statements.

Assignment Statements If you make the declarations

```
int   someInt;
float someFloat;
```

then `someInt` can hold *only* integer values, and `someFloat` can hold *only* floating-point values. The assignment statement

```
someFloat = 12;
```

appears to store the integer value 12 into `someFloat`. But the computer refuses to store anything other than a `float` value into `someFloat`. The compiler inserts extra instructions that first convert 12 into 12.0 and then store 12.0 into `someFloat`. This implicit (automatic) conversion of a value from one data type to another is known as **type coercion**.

> **Type coercion** The implicit (automatic) conversion of a value from one data type to another.

The statement

```
someInt = 4.8;
```

also causes type coercion. When a floating-point value is assigned to an `int` variable, the fractional part is truncated (cut off). As a result, `someInt` is assigned the value 4.

With both of the assignment statements above, the program would be less confusing for someone to read if we avoided mixing data types:

```
someFloat = 12.0;
someInt = 4;
```

More often, it is not just constants but entire expressions that are involved in type coercion. Storing the result of an `int` expression into a `float` variable generally doesn't cause loss of information; a whole number such as 24 can be represented in floating-point form as 24.0. However, storing the result of a floating-point expression into an `int` variable can cause loss of information because the fractional part is truncated. It is easy to overlook the assignment of a floating-point expression to an `int` variable when we try to discover why our program is producing the wrong answers.

To make our programs as clear (and error free) as possible, we can use explicit **type casting** (or **type conversion**). A C++ *cast operation* consists of a data type name and then, within parentheses, the expression to be converted:

> **Type casting** The explicit conversion of a value from one data type to another; also called type conversion.

```
someFloat = float(3 * someInt + 2);
someInt = int(5.2 / someFloat - anotherFloat);
```

Both of the statements

```
someInt = someFloat + 8.2;
someInt = int(someFloat + 8.2);
```

produce identical results. The only difference is in clarity. With the cast operation, it is perfectly clear to the programmer and to others reading the program that the mixing of types is intentional, not an oversight. Countless errors have resulted from unintentional mixing of types.

Note that there is a nice way to round off rather than truncate a floating-point value before storing it into an `int` variable. Here is the way to do it:

```
someInt = int(someFloat + 0.5);
```

With pencil and paper, see for yourself what gets stored into `someInt` when `someFloat` contains 4.7. Now try it again, assuming `someFloat` contains 4.2. (This technique of rounding by adding 0.5 assumes that `someFloat` is a positive number.)

Arithmetic Expressions   So far we have been talking about mixing data types across the assignment operator (=). It's also possible to mix data types within an expression:

```
someInt * someFloat
4.8 + someInt - 3
```

> **Mixed type expression** An expression that contains operands of different data types; also called mixed mode expression.

Such expressions are called **mixed type** (or **mixed mode**) **expressions**.

Whenever an integer value and a floating-point value are joined by an operator, implicit type coercion occurs as follows.

1. The integer value is temporarily coerced to a floating-point value.

2. The operation is performed.

3. The result is a floating-point value.

Let's examine how the machine evaluates the expression 4.8 + someInt - 3, where someInt contains the value 2. First, the operands of the + operator have mixed types, so the value of someInt is coerced to 2.0. (This conversion is only temporary; it does not affect the value that is stored in someInt.) The addition takes place, yielding a value of 6.8. Next, the subtraction (-) operator joins a floating-point value (6.8) and an integer value (3). The value 3 is coerced to 3.0, the subtraction takes place, and the result is the floating-point value 3.8.

Just as with assignment statements, you can use explicit type casts within expressions to lessen the risk of errors. Writing expressions such as

```
float(someInt) * someFloat
4.8 + float(someInt - 3)
```

makes it clear what your intentions are.

Explicit type casts are not only valuable for program clarity, but also are mandatory in some cases for correct programming. Given the declarations

```
int    sum;
int    count;
float  average;
```

suppose that sum and count currently contain 60 and 80, respectively. If sum represents the sum of a group of integer values and count represents the number of values, let's find the average value:

```
average = sum / count;      // Wrong
```

Unfortunately, this statement stores the value 0.0 into average. Here's why. The expression to the right of the assignment operator is not a mixed type expression. Both operands of the / operator are of type int, so integer division is performed. 60 divided by 80 yields the integer value 0. Next, the machine implicitly coerces 0 to the value 0.0 before storing it into average. The way to find the average correctly, as well as clearly, is this:

```
average = float(sum) / float(count);
```

This statement gives us floating-point division instead of integer division. As a result, the value 0.75 is stored into average.

As a final remark about type coercion and type conversion, you may have noticed that we have concentrated only on the int and float types. It is also possible to stir char values, short values, and double values into the pot. The results can be confusing and unexpected. In Chapter 10, we return to the topic with a more detailed discussion. In the meantime, you should avoid mixing values of these types within an expression.

3.5   Function Calls and Library Functions

Value-Returning Functions

At the beginning of Chapter 2, we showed a program consisting of three functions: `main`, `Square`, and `Cube`. Here is a portion of the program:

```
int main()
{
    cout << "The square of 27 is " << Square(27) << endl;
    cout << "and the cube of 27 is " << Cube(27) << endl;
    return 0;
}

int Square( int n )
{
    return n * n;
}

int Cube( int n )
{
    return n * n * n;
}
```

We said that all three functions are value-returning functions. `Square` returns to its caller a value—the square of the number sent to it. `Cube` returns a value—the cube of the number sent to it. And `main` returns to the operating system a value—the program's exit status.

Let's focus for a moment on the `Cube` function. The `main` function contains a statement

```
cout << " and the cube of 27 is " << Cube(27) << endl;
```

In this statement, the master (`main`) causes the servant (`Cube`) to compute the cube of 27 and give the result back to `main`. The sequence of symbols

```
Cube(27)
```

is a **function call** or **function invocation**. The computer temporarily puts the `main` function on hold and starts the `Cube` function running. When `Cube` has finished doing its work, the computer goes back to `main` and picks up where it left off.

Function call (function invocation)   The mechanism that transfers control to a function.

In the above function call, the number 27 is known as an *argument* (or *actual parameter*). Arguments make it possible for the same function to work on many different values. For example, we can write statements like these:

```
cout << Cube(4);
cout << Cube(16);
```

Here's the syntax template for a function call:

FunctionCall

FunctionName (ArgumentList)

The **argument list** is a way for functions to communicate with each other. Some functions, like `Square` and `Cube`, have a single argument in the argument list. Other functions, like `main`, have no arguments in the list. And some functions have two, three, or more arguments in the argument list, separated by commas.

> **Argument list**   A mechanism by which functions communicate with each other.

Value-returning functions are used in expressions in much the same way that variables and constants are. The value computed by a function simply takes its place in the expression. For example, the statement

```
someInt = Cube(2) * 10;
```

stores the value 80 into `someInt`. First the `Cube` function is executed to compute the cube of 2, which is 8. The value 8—now available for use in the rest of the expression—is multiplied by 10. Note that a function call has higher precedence than multiplication, which makes sense if you consider that the function result must be available before the multiplication takes place.

Here are several facts about value-returning functions:

- The function call is used within an expression; it does not appear as a separate statement.
- The function computes a value (*result*) that is then available for use in the expression.
- The function returns exactly one result—no more, no less.

The `Cube` function expects to be given (or *passed*) an argument of type `int`. What happens if the caller passes a `float` argument? The answer is that the compiler applies implicit type coercion. The function call `Cube(6.9)` computes the cube of 6, not 6.9.

Although we have been using literal constants as arguments to `Cube`, the argument could just as easily be a variable or named constant. In fact, the argument to a value-returning function can be any expression of the appropriate type. In the statement

```
alpha = Cube(int1 * int1 + int2 * int2);
```

the expression in the argument list is evaluated first, and only its result is passed to the function. For example, if `int1` contains 3 and `int2` contains 5, the above function call passes 34 as the argument to `Cube`.

An expression in a function's argument list can even include calls to functions. For example, we could use the `Square` function to rewrite the above assignment statement as follows:

```
alpha = Cube(Square(int1) + Square(int2));
```

Library Functions

Certain computations, such as taking square roots or finding the absolute value of a number, are very common in programs. To help make the programmer's life easier, every C++ system includes a standard library—a large collection of prewritten functions, data types, and other items that any C++ programmer may use. Here is a very small sample:

Header File	Function	Argument Type(s)	Result Type	Result (Value Returned)
`<cstdlib>`	`abs(i)`	`int`	`int`	Absolute value of i
`<cmath>`	`cos(x)`	`float`	`float`	Cosine of x (x is in radians)
`<cmath>`	`fabs(x)`	`float`	`float`	Absolute value of x
`<cstdlib>`	`labs(j)`	`long`	`long`	Absolute value of j
`<cmath>`	`pow(x, y)`	`float`	`float`	x raised to the power y (if x = 0.0, y must be positive; if x ≤ 0.0, y must be a whole number)
`<cmath>`	`sin(x)`	`float`	`float`	Sine of x (x is in radians)
`<cmath>`	`sqrt(x)`	`float`	`float`	Square root of x (x ≥ 0.0)

Technically, the entries in the table marked `float` should all say `double`. These library functions perform their work using double-precision floating-point values. But because of type coercion, the functions work just as you would like them to when you pass `float` values to them.

Using a library function is easy. First, you place an `#include` directive near the top of your program, specifying the appropriate header file. This directive ensures that the C++ preprocessor inserts declarations into your program that give the compiler some information about the function. Then, whenever you want to use the function, you just make a function call.* Here's an example:

```
#include <iostream>
#include <cmath>        // For sqrt() and fabs()
```

---

*Some systems require you to specify a particular compiler option if you use the math functions. For example, with some versions of UNIX, you must add the option `-lm` when compiling your program.

```
using namespace std;
   ⋮
float alpha;
float beta;
   ⋮
alpha = sqrt(7.3 + fabs(beta));
```

Remember from Chapter 2 that all identifiers in the standard library are in the namespace `std`. If we omit the `using` directive from the above code, we must use qualified names for the library functions (`std::sqrt`, `std::fabs`, and so forth).

The C++ standard library provides dozens of functions for you to use. Appendix C lists a much larger selection than we have presented here. You should glance briefly at this appendix now, keeping in mind that much of the terminology and C++ language notation will make sense only after you have read further into the book.

Void Functions

In this chapter, the only kind of function that we have looked at is the value-returning function. C++ provides another kind of function as well. For example, the following definition for function `CalcPay` begins with the word `void` instead of a data type like `int` or `float`:

```
void CalcPay( ...  )
{
   ⋮
}
```

`CalcPay` is an example of a function that doesn't return a function value to its caller. Instead, it just performs some action and then quits. We refer to a function like this as a *non-value-returning function*, a *void-returning function*, or, most briefly, a **void function**. In some programming languages, a void function is known as a **procedure**.

> **Void function (procedure)**   A function that does not return a function value to its caller and is invoked as a separate statement.
>
> **Value-returning function**   A function that returns a single value to its caller and is invoked from within an expression.

Void functions are invoked differently from **value-returning functions**. With a value-returning function, the function call appears in an expression. With a void function, the function call is a separate, stand-alone statement. For example:

```
DoThis(x, y, z);
DoThat();
```

For the next few chapters, we won't be writing our own functions (except `main`). Instead, we'll be concentrating on how to use existing functions, including functions for performing stream input and output. Some of these functions are value-returning functions; others are void functions. Again, we emphasize the difference in how you invoke these two kinds of functions: A call to a value-returning function occurs in an expression, whereas a call to a void function occurs as a separate statement.

3.6 Formatting the Output

To format a program's output means to control how it appears visually on the screen or on a printer. If the variables i, j, and k contain the values 15, 2, and 6, respectively, the statement

```
cout << "Results: " << i << j << k;
```

outputs the stream of characters

```
Results: 1526
```

Without spacing between the numbers, this output is difficult to interpret.

To separate the output values, you could print a single blank (as a char constant) between the numbers:

```
cout << "Results: " << i << ' ' << j << ' ' << k;
```

This statement produces the output

```
Results: 15 2 6
```

If you want even more spacing between items, you can use literal strings containing blanks, as we discussed in Chapter 2:

```
cout << "Results: " << i << "    " << j << "    " << k;
```

Here, the resulting output is

```
Results: 15    2    6
```

Another way to control the horizontal spacing of the output is to use *manipulators*. For some time now, we have been using the endl manipulator to terminate an output line. In C++, a manipulator is a rather curious thing that behaves like a function but travels in the disguise of a data object. Like a function, a manipulator causes some action to occur. But like a data object, a manipulator can appear in the midst of a series of insertion operations:

```
cout << someInt << endl << someFloat;
```

Manipulators are used only in input and output statements.

The C++ standard library supplies many manipulators, but for now we look at only five of them: endl, setw, fixed, showpoint, and setprecision. The endl, fixed, and showpoint manipulators come "for free" when we #include the header file iostream to perform I/O. The other two manipulators, setw and setprecision, require that we also #include the header file iomanip:

```
#include <iostream>
#include <iomanip>
```

```
using namespace std;
   ⋮
cout << setw(5) << someInt;
```

The manipulator setw—meaning "set width"—lets us control how many character positions the next data item should occupy when it is output. (setw is only for formatting numbers and strings, not char data.) The argument to setw is an integer expression called the *fieldwidth specification*; the group of character positions is called the *field*. The next data item to be output is printed *right-justified* (filled with blanks on the left to fill up the field).

Let's look at an example. Assuming two int variables have been assigned values as follows:

```
ans = 33;
num = 7132;
```

then the following output statements produce the output shown to their right.

Statement	Output (□ means blank)

1. `cout << setw(4) << ans`
`    << setw(5) << num`
`    << setw(4) << "Hi";`
	□□33□7132□□Hi
	‾4‾ ‾‾5‾‾ ‾‾4‾‾

2. `cout << setw(2) << ans`
`    << setw(4) << num`
`    << setw(2) << "Hi";`
	337132Hi
	‾2‾ ‾4‾ ‾2‾

3. `cout << setw(6) << ans`
`    << setw(3) << "Hi"`
`    << setw(5) << num;`
	□□□□33□Hi□7132
	‾‾‾6‾‾‾ ‾3‾ ‾‾5‾‾

4. `cout << setw(7) << "Hi"` `    << setw(4) << num;`	□□□□□Hi7132 ‾‾‾‾7‾‾‾ ‾‾4‾‾
5. `cout << setw(1) << ans` `    << setw(5) << num;`	33□7132 ↑ 5 Field automatically expands to fit the two-digit value

In (1), each value is specified to occupy enough positions so that there is at least one space separating them. In (2), the values all run together because the fieldwidth specified for each value is just large enough to hold the value. This output obviously is not very readable. It's better to make the fieldwidth larger than the minimum size required so that some space is left between values. In (3), there are extra blanks for readability; in (4), there are not. In (5), the fieldwidth is not large enough for the value in ans, so it automatically expands to make room for all of the digits.

Setting the fieldwidth is a one-time action. It holds only for the very next item to be output. After this output, the fieldwidth resets to 0, meaning "extend the field to exactly as many positions as are needed." In the statement

```
cout << "Hi" << setw(5) << ans << num;
```

the fieldwidth resets to 0 after ans is output. As a result, we get the output

```
Hi    337132
```

You can specify a fieldwidth for floating-point values just as for integer values. But you must remember to allow for the decimal point when you specify the number of character positions. The value 4.85 requires four output positions, not three. If x contains the value 4.85, the statement

```
cout << setw(4) << x << endl
     << setw(6) << x << endl
     << setw(3) << x << endl;
```

produces the output

```
4.85
  4.85
4.85
```

In the third line, a fieldwidth of 3 isn't sufficient, so the field automatically expands to accommodate the number.

There are several other issues related to output of floating-point numbers. First, large floating-point values are printed in scientific (E) notation. The value 123456789.5 may print on some systems as

```
1.23457E+08
```

You can use the manipulator named fixed to force all subsequent floating-point output to appear in decimal form rather than scientific notation:

```
cout << fixed << 3.8 * x;
```

Second, if the number is a whole number, C++ doesn't print a decimal point. The value 95.0 prints as

To force decimal points to be displayed in subsequent floating-point output, even for whole numbers, you can use the manipulator `showpoint`:

```
cout << showpoint << floatVar;
```

Third, you often would like to control the number of *decimal places* (digits to the right of the decimal point) that are displayed. If your program is supposed to print the 5% sales tax on a certain amount, the statement

```
cout << "Tax is $" << price * 0.05;
```

may output

```
Tax is $17.7435
```

Here, you clearly would prefer to display the result to two decimal places. To do so, use the `setprecision` manipulator as follows:

```
cout << fixed << setprecision(2) << "Tax is $" << price * 0.05;
```

Provided that `fixed` has already been specified, the argument to `setprecision` specifies the desired number of decimal places. Unlike `setw`, which applies only to the very next item printed, the value sent to `setprecision` remains in effect for all subsequent output (until you change it with another call to `setprecision`). Here are some examples of using `setprecision` in conjunction with `setw`:

Value of x	Statement	Output (▯ means blank)
	`cout << fixed;`	
310.0	`cout << setw(10)`	
	`     << setprecision(2) << x;`	`▯▯▯▯310.00`
310.0	`cout << setw(10)`	
	`     << setprecision(5) << x;`	`▯310.00000`
310.0	`cout << setw(7)`	
	`     << setprecision(5) << x;`	`310.00000` (expands to nine positions)
4.827	`cout << setw(6)`	
	`     << setprecision(2) << x;`	`▯▯4.83` (last displayed digit is rounded off)
4.827	`cout << setw(6)`	
	`     << setprecision(1) << x;`	`▯▯▯4.8` (last displayed digit is rounded off)

Again, the total number of print positions is expanded if the fieldwidth specified by `setw` is too narrow. However, the number of positions for fractional digits is controlled entirely by the argument to `setprecision`.

The following table summarizes the manipulators we have discussed in this section. Manipulators without arguments are available through the header file `iostream`. Those with arguments require the header file `iomanip`.

Header File	Manipulator	Argument Type	Effect
`<iostream>`	`endl`	None	Terminates the current output line
`<iostream>`	`showpoint`	None	Forces display of decimal point in floating-point output
`<iostream>`	`fixed`	None	Suppresses scientific notation in floating-point output
`<iomanip>`	`setw(n)`	int	Sets fieldwidth to n*
`<iomanip>`	`setprecision(n)`	int	Sets floating-point precision to n digits

*`setw` is only for numbers and strings, not `char` data. Also, `setw` applies only to the very next output item, after which the fieldwidth is reset to 0 (meaning "use only as many positions as are needed").

Program Formatting

As far as the compiler is concerned, C++ statements are *free format*. However, it is extremely important that your programs be readable, both for your sake and for the sake of anyone else who has to examine them.

When you write an outline for an English paper, you follow certain rules of indentation to make it readable. Similar rules make your programs easier to read.

Take a look at the following program for computing the cost per square foot of a house. Although it compiles and runs correctly, it does not conform to any formatting standards.

```
// HouseCost program
// This program computes the cost per square foot of
    // living space for a house, given the dimensions of
// the house, the number of stories, the size of the
// nonliving space, and the total cost less land
#include <iostream>
#include <iomanip>// For setw() and setprecision()
using namespace
std;
```

(continued) ▼

Program Formatting

```
const float WIDTH = 30.0; // Width of the house
    const float LENGTH = 40.0; // Length of the house
const float STORIES = 2.5; // Number of full stories
const float NON_LIVING_SPACE = 825.0;// Garage, closets, etc.

const float PRICE = 150000.0; // Selling price less land
int main() { float grossFootage;// Total square footage
    float livingFootage;         // Living area
float costPerFoot;      // Cost/foot of living area
   cout << fixed << showpoint;    // Set up floating-pt.
//   output format

grossFootage = LENGTH * WIDTH * STORIES; livingFootage =
grossFootage - NON_LIVING_SPACE; costPerFoot = PRICE /
livingFootage; cout << "Cost per square foot is "
<< setw(6) << setprecision(2) << costPerFoot << endl;
return 0; }
```

Now look at the same program with proper formatting:

```
//****************************************************************
// HouseCost program
// This program computes the cost per square foot of
// living space for a house, given the dimensions of
// the house, the number of stories, the size of the
// nonliving space, and the total cost less land
//****************************************************************
#include <iostream>
#include <iomanip>     // For setw() and setprecision()

using namespace std;

const float WIDTH = 30.0;              // Width of the house
const float LENGTH = 40.0;             // Length of the house
const float STORIES = 2.5;             // Number of full stories
const float NON_LIVING_SPACE = 825.0;  // Garage, closets, etc.
const float PRICE = 150000.0;          // Selling price less land

int main()
{
    float grossFootage;        // Total square footage
    float livingFootage;       // Living area
    float costPerFoot;         // Cost/foot of living area
    cout << fixed << showpoint;            // Set up floating-pt.
                                           //    output format

    grossFootage = LENGTH * WIDTH * STORIES;
    livingFootage = grossFootage - NON_LIVING_SPACE;
    costPerFoot = PRICE / livingFootage;
```

(continued) ▼

> *Program Formatting*
>
> ```
>     cout << "Cost per square foot is "
>         << setw(6) << setprecision(2) << costPerFoot << endl;
>     return 0;
> }
> ```
>
> Need we say more?
>   Appendix E talks about programming style. Use it as a guide when you are writing programs.

3.7 Additional `string` Operations

Now that we have introduced numeric types and function calls, we can take advantage of additional features of the `string` data type. In this section, we introduce four functions that operate on strings: `length`, `size`, `find`, and `substr`.

The `length` and `size` Functions

The `length` function, when applied to a `string` variable, returns an unsigned integer value that equals the number of characters currently in the string. If `myName` is a `string` variable, a call to the `length` function looks like this:

```
myName.length()
```

You specify the name of a `string` variable (here, `myName`), then a dot (period), and then the function name and argument list. The `length` function requires no arguments to be passed to it, but you still must use parentheses to signify an empty argument list. Also, `length` is a value-returning function, so the function call must appear within an expression:

```
string firstName;
string fullName;

firstName = "Alexandra";
cout << firstName.length() << endl;        // Prints 9
fullName = firstName + " Jones";
cout << fullName.length() << endl;         // Prints 15
```

Perhaps you are wondering about the syntax in a function call like

```
firstName.length()
```

This expression uses a C++ notation called *dot notation*. There is a dot (period) between the variable name `firstName` and the function name `length`. Certain programmer-defined data types, such as `string`, have functions that are tightly associated with them, and dot notation is required in the function calls. If you forget to use dot notation, writing the function call as

```
length()
```

you get a compile-time error message, something like "UNDECLARED IDENTIFIER." The compiler thinks you are trying to call an ordinary function named `length`, not the `length` function associated with the `string` type. In Chapter 4, we discuss the meaning behind dot notation.

Some people refer to the length of a string as its *size*. To accommodate both terms, the `string` type provides a function named `size`. Both `firstName.size()` and `firstName.length()` return the same value.

We said that the `length` function returns an unsigned integer value. If we want to save the result into a variable `len`, as in

```
len = firstName.length();
```

then what should we declare the data type of `len` to be? To keep us from having to guess whether `unsigned int` or `unsigned long` is correct for the particular compiler we're working with, the `string` type defines a data type `size_type` for us to use:

```
string firstName;
string::size_type len;

firstName = "Alexandra";
len = firstName.length();
```

Notice that we must use the qualified name `string::size_type` (just as we do with identifiers in namespaces) because the definition of `size_type` is otherwise hidden inside the definition of the `string` type.

Before leaving the `length` and `size` functions, we should make a remark about capitalization of identifiers. In the guidelines given in Chapter 2, we said that in this book we begin the names of programmer-defined functions and data types with uppercase letters. We follow this convention when we write our own functions and data types in later chapters. However, we have no control over the capitalization of items supplied by the C++ standard library. Identifiers in the standard library generally use all-lowercase letters.

The find **Function**

The find function searches a string to find the first occurrence of a particular substring and returns an unsigned integer value (of type string:: size_type) giving the result of the search. The substring, passed as an argument to the function, can be a literal string or a string expression. If str1 and str2 are of type string, the following are valid function calls:

```
str1.find("the")        str1.find(str2)        str1.find(str2 + "abc")
```

In each case above, str1 is searched to see if the specified substring can be found within it. If so, the function returns the position in str1 where the match begins. (Positions are numbered starting at 0, so the first character in a string is in position 0, the second is in position 1, and so on.) For a successful search, the match must be exact, including identical capitalization. If the substring could not be found, the function returns the special value string::npos, a named constant meaning "not a position within the string."

Given the code segment

```
string phrase;
string::size_type position;

phrase = "The dog and the cat";
```

the statement

```
position = phrase.find("the");
```

assigns to position the value 12, whereas the statement

```
position = phrase.find("rat");
```

assigns to position the value string::npos, because there was no match.

The argument to the find function can also be a char value. In this case, find searches for the first occurrence of that character within the string and returns its position (or string::npos, if the character was not found). For example, the code segment

```
string theString;

theString = "Abracadabra";
cout << theString.find('a');
```

outputs the value 3, which is the position of the first occurrence of a lowercase *a* in theString.

Below are some more examples of calls to the find function, assuming the following code segment has been executed:

```
string str1;
string str2;
```

```
str1 = "Programming and Problem Solving";
str2 = "gram";
```

Function Call	Value Returned by Function
`str1.find("and")`	12
`str1.find("Programming")`	0
`str2.find("and")`	`string::npos`
`str1.find("Pro")`	0
`str1.find("ro" + str2)`	1
`str1.find("Pr" + str2)`	`string::npos`
`str1.find(' ')`	11

Notice in the fourth example that there are two copies of the substring "Pro" in str1, but find returns only the position of the first copy. Also notice that the copies can be either separate words or parts of words—find merely tries to match the sequence of characters given in the argument list. The final example demonstrates that the argument can be as simple as a single character, even a single blank.

The substr Function

The substr function returns a particular substring of a string. Assuming myString is of type string, here is a sample function call:

```
myString.substr(5, 20)
```

The first argument is an integer that specifies a position within the string, and the second is an integer that specifies the length of the desired substring. The function returns the piece of the string that starts with the specified position and continues for the number of characters given by the second argument. Note that substr doesn't change myString; it returns a new, temporary string value that is a copy of a portion of the string. Following are some examples, assuming the statement

```
myString = "Programming and Problem Solving";
```

has been executed.

Function Call	String Contained in Value Returned by Function
`myString.substr(0, 7)`	`"Program"`
`myString.substr(7, 8)`	`"ming and"`
`myString.substr(10, 0)`	`""`
`myString.substr(24, 40)`	`"Solving"`
`myString.substr(40, 24)`	None. Program terminates with an execution error message.

In the third example, specifying a length of 0 produces the null string as the result. The fourth example shows what happens if the second argument specifies more characters than are present after the starting position: substr returns the characters from the starting position to the end of the string. The last example illustrates that the first argument, the position, must not be beyond the end of the string.

Because substr returns a value of type string, you can use it with the concatenation operator (+) to copy pieces of strings and join them together to form new strings. The find and length functions can be useful in determining the location and end of a piece of a string to be passed to substr as arguments.

Here is a program that uses several of the string operations:

```cpp
//*********************************************************************
// StringOps program
// This program demonstrates several string operations
//*********************************************************************
#include <iostream>
#include <string>        // For string type

using namespace std;

int main()
{
    string fullName;
    string name;
    string::size_type startPos;

    fullName = "Jonathan Alexander Peterson";
    startPos = fullName.find("Peterson");
    name = "Mr. " + fullName.substr(startPos, 8);
    cout << name << endl;
    return 0;
}
```

This program outputs Mr. Peterson when it is executed. First it stores a string into the variable fullName, and then it uses find to locate the start of the name Peterson within the string. Next, it builds a new string by concatenating the literal "Mr. " with the characters Peterson, which are copied from the original string. Last, it prints out the new string. As we see in later chapters, string operations are an important aspect of many computer programs.

The following table summarizes the string operations we have looked at in this chapter.

Function Call (s is of type string)	Argument Type(s)	Result Type	Result (Value Returned)
s.length() s.size()	None	string::size_type	Number of characters in the string
s.find(arg)	string, literal string, or char	string::size_type	Starting position in s where arg was found; if not found, result is string::npos
s.substr(pos,len)	string::size_type	string	Substring of at most len characters, starting at position pos of s. If len is too large, it means "to the end" of string s. If pos is too large, execution of the program is terminated.*

*Technically, if pos is too large, the program generates what is called an *out-of-range exception*—the program simply terminates with a message such as "ABNORMAL PROGRAM TERMINATION."

Programming Example

Mortgage Payment Calculator

PROBLEM Your parents are thinking about refinancing their mortgage, and have asked you to help them with the calculations. Now that you're learning C++, you realize that you can save yourself a lot of calculator button-pressing by writing a program to do the calculations automatically.

DISCUSSION There are often three obvious steps in almost any problem of this type:

1. Get the data.
2. Compute the results.
3. Output the results.

The data we need in this problem are the amount of money to borrow, the number of years for the loan, and the interest rate. From these three values, the monthly payment can be calculated. Although you could solve this problem for your parents using paper and pencil, you might as well write a program to solve it. You can make the data values constants now and later; when you learn how to input values, you can rewrite the program.

After a chat with your parents, you find that they still owe $50,000 on the house and have exactly 7 years worth of payments to go. The latest quote from their credit union is for an interest rate of 5.24 with no closing costs.

Define Constants

> Set LOAN_AMOUNT = 50000.00
> Set NUMBER_OF_YEARS = 7
> Set INTEREST_RATE = 0.0524

Here is the formula for determining payments, using compound interest.

$$\frac{\text{Amount} * (1 + \text{Monthly Interest})^{\text{number of payments}} * \text{Monthly Interest}}{(1 + \text{Monthly Interest})^{\text{number of payments}} - 1}$$

The C++ `<cmath>` header file contains the power function. Before you actually enter the values in the formula, two intermediate values need to be calculated: monthly interest rate and number of payments.

Calculate Values

> Set monthlyInterest to YEARLY_INTEREST divided by 12
> Set numberOfPayments to NUMBER_OF_YEARS times 12
> Set payment to (LOAN_AMOUNT * pow(monthlyInterest+1,
>   numberOfPayments) * monthlyInterest) /
>   (pow(monthlyInterest+1, numberOfPayments) – 1)

Now all that is left is to print out the answer in a clear, concise format. Let's use a precision of 2 for the floating point values and a fixed format.

Output Results

> Print "For a loan amount of "LOAN_AMOUNT " with an interest rate of "
>   YEARLY_INTEREST " and a " NUMBER_OF_YEARS " year mortgage, "
> Print "your monthly payments are $" payment "."

From the algorithm we can create tables of constants and variables to help us write the declarations for the program. We do not show these here.

```
//*******************************************************************
// Mortgage Payment Calculator program
// This program determines the monthly payments on a mortgage given
// the loan amount, the yearly interest, and the number of years.
//*******************************************************************

#include <iostream>                        // Access cout
```

```cpp
#include <cmath>                          // Access power function
#include <iomanip>                        // Access manipulators
using namespace std;

const float LOAN_AMOUNT = 50000.00;       // Amount of the loan
const float YEARLY_INTEREST = 0.0524;     // Yearly interest rate
const int NUMBER_OF_YEARS = 7;            // Number of years

int main()
{
    // local variables
    float monthlyInterest;                // Monthly interest rate
    int numberOfPayments;                 // Total number of payments
    float payment;                        // Monthly payment

    // Calculate values
    monthlyInterest = YEARLY_INTEREST / 12;
    numberOfPayments = NUMBER_OF_YEARS * 12;
    payment = (LOAN_AMOUNT *
               pow(monthlyInterest + 1, numberOfPayments)
               * monthlyInterest)/( pow(monthlyInterest + 1,
               numberOfPayments) - 1 );

    // Output results
    cout << fixed << setprecision(2) << "For a loan amount of "
         << LOAN_AMOUNT  << " with an interest rate of "
         << YEARLY_INTEREST << " and a " << NUMBER_OF_YEARS
         << " year mortgage, " << endl;
    cout << " your monthly payments are $" << payment
         << "." << endl;
    return 0;
}
```

Here is a screen shot of the output.

```
========================= mortgage.out.out =========================
For a loan amount of 50000.00 with an interest rate of 0.05 and a 7 year mortgage,
your monthly payments are $712.35.
```

Something looks strange about the output: The interest should be 0.0524, not 0.05. The decision to use a precision of 2 was correct for dollars and cents, but not for interest rates, which are rarely whole percentages. You are asked to make this correction in Follow-Up Exercise 1.

Testing and Debugging

1. An `int` constant other than 0 should not start with a zero. If it starts with a zero, it is an octal (base–8) number.

2. Watch out for integer division. The expression `47 / 100` yields 0, the integer quotient. This is one of the major sources of wrong output in C++ programs.

3. When using the `/` and `%` operators, remember that division by zero is not allowed.

4. Double-check every expression according to the precedence rules to be sure that the operations are performed in the desired order.

5. Avoid mixing integer and floating-point values in expressions. If you must mix them, consider using explicit type casts to reduce the chance of mistakes.

6. For each assignment statement, check that the expression result has the same data type as the variable to the left of the assignment operator (=). If not, consider using an explicit type cast for clarity and safety. And remember that storing a floating-point value into an `int` variable truncates the fractional part.

7. For every library function you use in your program, be sure to `#include` the appropriate header file.

8. Examine each call to a library function to see that you have the right number of arguments and that the data types of the arguments are correct.

9. With the `string` type, positions of characters within a string are numbered starting at 0, not 1.

10. If the cause of an error in a program is not obvious, leave the computer and study a printed listing. Change your program only after you understand the source of the error.

Summary

C++ provides several built-in numeric data types, of which the most commonly used are `int` and `float`. The integral types are based on the mathematical integers, but the computer limits the range of integer values that can be represented. The floating-point types are based on the mathematical notion of real numbers. As with integers, the computer limits the range of floating-point numbers that can be represented. Also, it limits the number of digits of precision in floating-point values. We can write literals of type `float` in several forms, including scientific (E) notation.

Much of the computation of a program is performed in arithmetic expressions. Expressions can contain more than one operator. The order in which the operations are performed is determined by precedence rules. In arithmetic expressions, multiplication, division, and modulus are performed first, then addition and subtraction. Multiple binary (two-operand) operations of the same precedence are grouped from left to right. You can use parentheses to override the precedence rules.

Expressions may include function calls. C++ supports two kinds of functions: value-returning functions and void functions. A value-returning function is called by writing its name and argument list as part of an expression. A void function is called by writing its name and argument list as a complete C++ statement.

The C++ standard library is an integral part of every C++ system. The library contains many prewritten data types, functions, and other items that any programmer can use. These items are accessed by using #include directives to the C++ preprocessor, which inserts the appropriate header files into the program.

In output statements, the setw, showpoint, fixed, and setprecision manipulators control the appearance of values in the output. These manipulators do not affect the values actually stored in memory, only their appearance when displayed on the output device.

Not only should the output produced by a program be easy to read, but the format of the program itself should be clear and readable. C++ is a free-format language. A consistent style that uses indentation, blank lines, and spaces within lines helps you (and other programmers) understand and work with your programs.

Quick Check

1. What happens to the fractional portion of a floating-point number when it is converted to an integer type? (pp. 79–80)
2. Where do arguments appear, and what is their purpose? (pp. 82–84)
3. What is the value of the following expression, given that the string variable quickCheck contains the string "My friend I shall be pedagogic"? (pp. 92–97)

   quickCheck.substr(10, 20) + " " + quickCheck.substr(0, 9) + "."

4. Neatly formatting a program makes it easier to find errors. True or false? (pp. 90–92)
5. How does the declaration of named constants and variables of type int and float differ from declarations of named constants and variables of type string? (pp. 71–73)
6. How would you write an expression that gives the remainder of dividing integer1 by integer2? (pp. 73–75)
7. If integer1 contains 37 and integer2 contains 7, what is the result of the expression in exercise 6? (pp. 73–75)
8. What is the result of the following expression? (pp. 77–79)

   27 + 8 * 6 - 44 % 5

9. Write an expression that computes the square root of 17.5. (pp. 82–85)
10. How does a call to a void function differ from a call to a value-returning function? (pp. 85–86)
11. Which stream manipulator would you use to set the output precision for floating-point values? (pp. 86–90)

Answers

1. The fractional part is truncated.   2. They appear in the call to a function, between parentheses, and are used to pass data to or from a function.   3. "I shall be pedagogic My friend."   4. True.
5. The declarations are exactly the same, except that we use the reserved word `int` or `float` instead of `string`, and we assign a numerical value to the constant rather than a string value.
6. `integer1 % integer2`   7. 37 % 7 = 2   8. 27 + (8 * 6) – (44 % 5) = 27 + 48 – 4 = 71
9. `sqrt(17.5)`   10. A void function call appears as a separate statement rather than being part of an expression.   11. `setprecision`

Exam Preparation Exercises

1. What are the four integral types in C++? List them in order of size, from smallest to largest.
2. What is the result if the computer tries to calculate a value that is larger than the maximum integer allowed for a given integral type?
3. In a floating-point value, what does it mean when the letter E appears as part of a number?
4. Label each of the following as an integer or floating-point declaration, and whether it is a constant or a variable declaration.

	integer / floating	constant / variable
a. `const int tracksOnDisk = 17;`	_____	_____
b. `float timeOfTrack;`	_____	_____
c. `const float maxTimeOnDisk = 74.0;`	_____	_____
d. `short tracksLeft;`	_____	_____
e. `float timeLeft;`	_____	_____
f. `long samplesInTrack;`	_____	_____
g. `const double sampleRate = 262144.5;`	_____	_____

5. What are the two meanings of the / operator?
6. What is the result of each of the following expressions?
   a. `27 + 8 / 5 - 7`
   b. `27.0 + 8.0 / 5.0 - 7.0`
   c. `25 % 7 + 9.0`
   d. `17++`
   e. `int(15.0 + 12.0 * 2.2 - 3 * 7)`
   f. `23--`
   g. `18 / 1.0`
7. List the following operators in the order of highest precedence to lowest precedence. If a set of operators has the same precedence, write them enclosed in square brackets within the ordered list.

   ```
   *     +     %     /     -     unary -     ()
   ```

8. The increment and decrement operators can either precede or follow their operand. True or false?

9. Match the following terms to the definitions given below.
   a. Unary operator
   b. Binary operator
   c. Type coercion
   d. Type casting
   e. Mixed type expression
   f. Argument list
   g. Void function

   i. A computation involving both floating-point and integer values.
   ii. An operator with two operands.
   iii. A function that is called as a separate statement.
   iv. Explicitly changing a value of one type into another.
   v. The values that appear between the parentheses in a function call.
   vi. An operator with just one operand.
   vii. Implicitly changing a value of one type into another.

10. The statement

    ```
    count = count + 1;
    ```

    is equivalent to what C++ operator?

11. How do you write a C++ cast operation?

12. Is main a value-returning or a void function?

13. Show precisely what the following statement outputs.

    ```
    cout << setw(6) << showpoint << setprecision(2) << 215.0;
    ```

14. The prefix and postfix forms of the increment operator (++) always behave the same way. We can use them interchangeably anywhere in C++ code. True or false? Explain your answer.

15. What data type do we use to declare a variable to hold the result of applying the length function to a string?

16. Given that the string variables str1 and str2 contain

    ```
    "you ought to start with logic"
    ```

    and

    ```
    "ou"
    ```

    respectively, what is the result of each of the following expressions?
    a. str1.length()
    b. str1.find(str2)
    c. str1.substr(4, 25)
    d. str1.substr(4, 25).find(str2)
    e. str1.substr.(str1.find("logic"), 3)

  f. `str1.substr(24, 5).find(str2.substr(0,1))`

  g. `str1.find("end")`

17. What does the manipulator `fixed` do?

Programming Warm-Up Exercises

1. Write an expression to convert a time stored in the `int` variables `hours`, `minutes`, and `seconds` into the number of seconds represented by the time. For example, if `hours` contains 2, `minutes` contains 20, and `seconds` contains 12, then the result of your expression should be 8412.

2. Given an `int` variable `days` that contains a number of days,

  a. Write an expression that gives the number of whole weeks corresponding to `days`. For example, if `days` contains 23, then the number of whole weeks is 3.

  b. Write an expression that gives the number of days remaining after taking the whole weeks out of the value in `days`. For example, if `days` contains 23, then the number of days remaining after 3 whole weeks is 2.

3. Given `int` variables called `dollars`, `quarters`, `dimes`, `nickels`, and `pennies`, write an expression that computes the total amount of the money represented in the variables. The result should be an integer value representing the number of pennies in the total.

4. Given the same variables as in Exercise 3, compute the total but store it in a floating-point variable so that the integral part is dollars and the fractional part is cents.

5. Write an assignment statement that adds 3 to the value in `int` variable `count`.

6. Write expressions that implement the following formulas.

  a. $3X + Y$

  b. $A^2 + 2B + C$

  c. $\left(\dfrac{A + B}{C - D}\right) \times \left(\dfrac{X}{Y}\right)$

  d. $\dfrac{\left(\dfrac{A^2 + 2B + C}{D}\right)}{XY}$

  e. $\sqrt{|A - B|}$

  f. $X^{-\cos(Y)}$

7. Write a series of assignment statements that find the first three positions of the string `"and"` in a `string` variable `sentence`. The positions should be stored in `int` variables called `first`, `second`, and `third`. You may declare additional variables if necessary. The contents of `sentence` should remain unchanged.

8. Write an assignment statement to find the first blank in a `string` variable called `name`. Store the result plus one in the `int` variable `startOfMiddle`.

9. Write an output statement that prints the value in `float` variable `money` in eight spaces on the line, with a leading $ sign, and two digits of decimal precision.

10. Write an output statement that prints the value in `double` variable `distance` in fifteen spaces on a line with five digits of decimal precision.

11. If you include the header file `climits` in a program, the constants `INT_MAX` and `INT_MIN` are provided, which give the highest and lowest int values that can be represented. Write the include statement for this file, and an output statement that displays the two values, identified with appropriate labels.

12. Complete the following C++ program. The program should compute and output the Celsius value corresponding to the given Fahrenheit value.

```
//************************************************
// Celsius program
// This program outputs the Celsius temperature
// corresponding to a given Fahrenheit temperature
//************************************************

#include <iostream>

using namespace std;

int main()
{
    const float fahrenheit = 72.0;
```

Programming Problems

1. Write a C++ program that computes and outputs the volume of a cone, given the diameter of its base and its height. The formula for computing the cone's volume is:

$$\frac{1}{3}\pi \times Radius^2 \times Height$$

Be sure to use proper formatting and appropriate comments in your code. The output should be clearly labeled.

2. Write a C++ program that computes the mean and standard deviation of a set of four integer values. The mean is the sum of the four values divided by 4, and the formula for the standard deviation is:

$$s = \sqrt{\frac{\sum_{i=1}^{n}(x_i - \bar{x})^2}{n-1}}$$

Where $n = 4$, x_i refers to each of the four values, and $\bar{x}$ is the mean. Note that although the individual values are integers, the results are floating-point values.

Be sure to use proper formatting and appropriate comments in your code. The output should be clearly labeled and neatly formatted.

3. The factorial of a number *n* (written *n!*) is the number times the factorial of itself minus one. This self-referential definition is easiest to understand through an example. The factorial of 2 is 2 * 1. The factorial of 3 is 3 * 2 * 1. The factorial of 4 is 4 * 3 * 2 * 1, and so on. Factorials grow very large, very quickly. An approximation to the factorial for larger values is given by Stirling's formula, which is:

$$n! = e^{-n} n^n \sqrt{2\pi n}$$

The `exp` function in the `<cmath>` header file gives the value of *e* raised to given power (see Appendix C.5). We've already discussed all of the other functions that are needed to write this formula. Write a C++ program that computes the factorial of 15 both directly and with Stirling's formula, and outputs both results, together with their difference. You will need to use the `double` type for this computation. Be sure to use proper formatting and appropriate comments in your code. The output should be clearly labeled and neatly formatted.

4. The number of permutations of a set of *n* items take *r* at a time is given by the formula:

$$\frac{n!}{r!(n-r)!}$$

Where *n!* is the factorial of *n*. (See Programming Problem 3 for a discussion of ways to compute the factorial.) If there are 18 people in your class and you want to divide the class into programming teams of 3 members, you can compute the number of different teams that can be arranged using the above formula. Write a C++ program that determines the number of potential team arrangements. You will need to use the double type for this computation. Be sure to use proper formatting and appropriate comments in your code. The output should be labeled clearly and formatted neatly.

5. Write a C++ program that takes a string containing a full name, and outputs each part of the name separately. The name should be in the form of first, middle, and last name separated from each other by a single space. For example, if the name string contains

"John Jacob Schmidt"

then the program would output:

```
First name: John
Middle name: Jacob
Last name: Schmidt
```

6. Extend Programming Problem 5 to output the length of each name. This problem can be solved using a combination of the string operations presented in this

chapter. Be sure to use proper formatting and appropriate comments in your code. The output should be clearly labeled and neatly formatted.

Programming Example Follow-Up

1. Change the output statements so that the interest rate prints to 4 decimal places, but the dollar amounts remain at 2 decimal places.
2. The program assumes that the number of years left on the old mortgage is an even multiple of 12. Change the program so that the constant is the number of months left, not the number of years.
3. We usually speak of interest rates as percentages. Rewrite the program so that the interest rate is set as a percentage; that is, 5.24 rather than 0.0524.
4. The calculation of `monthlyInterest + 1` is made twice. Rewrite the program making this calculation only once. In your judgment, which version of the program is better? Justify your answer.

Program Input and the Software Design Process

Knowledge Goals

- *To understand the value of appropriate prompting messages for interactive programs.*
- *To know when noninteractive input/output is appropriate and how it differs from interactive input/output.*
- *To understand the basic principles of object-oriented design.*

Skill Goals

To be able to:

- *Construct input statements to read values into a program.*
- *Determine the contents of variables assigned values by input statements.*
- *Write programs that use data files for input and output.*
- *Apply the functional decomposition methodology to solve a simple problem.*

A program needs data on which to operate. We have been writing all of the data values in the program itself, in literal and named constants. If this were the only way we could enter data, we would have to rewrite a program each time we wanted to apply it to a different set of values. In this chapter, we look at ways of entering data into a program while it is running.

Once we know how to input data, process the data, and output the results, we can begin to think about designing more complicated programs. We have talked about general problem-solving strategies and writing simple programs. For a simple problem, it's easy to choose a strategy, write the algorithm, and code the program. But as problems become more complex, we have to use a more organized approach. In the second part of this chapter, we look at two general methodologies for developing software: object-oriented design and functional decomposition.

4.1 Getting Data into Programs

One of the biggest advantages of computers is that a program can be used with many different sets of data. To do so, we must keep the data separate from the program until the program is executed. Then instructions in the program copy values from the data set into variables in the program. After storing these values into the variables, the program can perform calculations with them.

The process of placing values from an outside data set into variables in a program is called *input*. In widely used terminology, the computer is said to *read* outside data into the variables. The data for the program can come from an input device or from a file on an auxiliary storage device. We look at file input later in this chapter; here we consider the *standard input device*, the keyboard.

Input Streams and the Extraction Operator (>>)

The concept of a stream is fundamental to input and output in C++. As we stated in Chapter 3, you can think of an output stream as an endless sequence of characters going from your program to an output device. Likewise, think of an *input stream* as an endless sequence of characters coming into your program from an input device.

To use stream I/O, you must use the preprocessor directive

```
#include <iostream>
```

The header file `iostream` contains, among other things, the definitions of two data types: `istream` and `ostream`. These are data types representing input streams and output streams, respectively. The header file also contains declarations that look like this:

```
istream cin;
ostream cout;
```

The first declaration says that `cin` (pronounced "see-in") is a variable of type `istream`. The second says that `cout` (pronounced "see-out") is a variable of type `ostream`. Furthermore, `cin` is associated with the standard input device (the keyboard), and `cout` is associated with the standard output device (usually the display screen).

As you have already seen, you can output values to `cout` by using the insertion operator (`<<`), which is sometimes pronounced "put to":

```
cout << 3 * price;
```

In a similar fashion, you can input data from `cin` by using the *extraction operator* (`>>`), sometimes pronounced "get from":

```
cin >> cost;
```

When the computer executes this statement, it inputs the next number you type on the keyboard (425, for example) and stores it into the variable `cost`.

The extraction operator `>>` takes two operands. Its left-hand operand is a stream expression (in the simplest case, just the variable `cin`). Its right-hand operand is a variable into which we store the input data.

You can use the `>>` operator several times in a single input statement. Each occurrence extracts (inputs) the next data item from the input stream. For example, there is no difference between the statement

```
cin >> length >> width;
```

and the pair of statements

```
cin >> length;
cin >> width;
```

Using a sequence of extractions in one statement is a convenience for the programmer.

When you are new to C++, you may get the extraction operator (`>>`) and the insertion operator (`<<`) reversed. Here is an easy way to remember which one is which: Always begin the statement with either `cin` or `cout`, and use the operator that points in the direction in which the data is going. The statement

```
cout << someInt;
```

sends data from the variable `someInt` *to* the output stream. The statement

```
cin >> someInt;
```

sends data from the input stream *to* the variable `someInt`.

Unlike the items specified in an output statement, which can be constants, variables, or complicated expressions, the items specified in an input statement can *only* be variable names. Why? Because an input statement indicates where input data values should be stored. Only variable names refer to memory locations where we can store values while a program is running.

When you enter input data at the keyboard, you must be sure that each data value is appropriate for the data type of the variable in the input statement.

Data Type of Variable in an >> Operation	Valid Input Data
char	A single printable character other than a blank
int	An int literal constant, optionally preceded by a sign
float	An int or float literal constant (possibly in scientific, E, notation), optionally preceded by a sign

Notice that when you input a number into a float variable, the input value doesn't have to have a decimal point. The integer value is automatically coerced to a float value. Any other mismatches, such as trying to input a float value into an int variable or a char value into a float variable, can lead to unexpected and sometimes serious results. Later in this chapter we discuss what might happen.

When looking for the next input value in the stream, the >> operator skips any leading *whitespace characters*. Whitespace characters are blanks and certain nonprintable characters such as the character that marks the end of a line. (We talk about this end-of-line character in the next section.) After skipping any whitespace characters, the >> operator proceeds to extract the desired data value from the input stream. If this data value is a char value, input stops as soon as a single character is input. If the data value is int or float, input of the number stops at the first character that is inappropriate for the data type, such as a whitespace character. Here are some examples, where i, j, and k are int variables, ch is a char variable, and x is a float variable:

Statement	Data	Contents After Input
1. cin >> i;	32	i = 32
2. cin >> i >> j;	4 60	i = 4, j = 60
3. cin >> i >> ch >> x;	25 A 16.9	i = 25, ch = 'A', x = 16.9
4. cin >> i >> ch >> x;	25	
	A	
	16.9	i = 25, ch = 'A', x = 16.9
5. cin >> i >> ch >> x;	25A16.9	i = 25, ch = 'A', x = 16.9
6. cin >> i >> j >> x;	12 8	i = 12, j = 8
		(Computer waits for a third number)
7. cin >> i >> x;	46 32.4 15	i = 46, x = 32.4
		(15 is held for later input)

Examples (1) and (2) are straightforward examples of integer input. Example (3) shows that you do not use quotes around character data values when they are input. Example (4) demonstrates how the process of skipping whitespace characters includes going on to the next line of input if necessary. Example (5) shows that the first character encountered that is inappropriate for a numeric data type ends the number. Input for the variable i stops at the input character A, after which the A is stored into ch, and then input for x stops at the end of the input line. Example (6) shows that if you are at the keyboard and haven't entered enough values to satisfy the input statement, the computer waits for more data. Example (7) shows that if more values are entered than there are variables in the input statement, the extra values remain waiting in the input stream until they can be read by the next input statement. If there are extra values left when the program ends, the computer disregards them.

The Reading Marker and the Newline Character

To help explain stream input in more detail, we introduce the concept of the *reading marker*. The reading marker works like a bookmark, but instead of marking a place in a book, it keeps track of the point in the input stream where the computer should continue reading. The reading marker indicates the next character waiting to be read. The extraction operator >> leaves the reading marker on the character following the last piece of data that was input.

Each input line has an invisible end-of-line character (the *newline character*) that tells the computer where one line ends and the next begins. To find the next input value, the >> operator crosses line boundaries (newline characters) if it has to.

Where does the newline character come from? What is it? The answer to the first question is easy. When you are working at a keyboard, you generate a newline character yourself each time you hit the Return or Enter key. Your program also generates a newline character when it uses the endl manipulator in an output statement. The endl manipulator outputs a newline, telling the screen cursor to go to the next line. The answer to the second question varies from computer system to computer system. The newline character is a nonprintable control character that the system recognizes as meaning the end of a line, whether it's an input line or an output line.

In a C++ program, you can refer directly to the newline character by using the two symbols \n, a backslash and an n with no space between them. Although \n consists of two symbols, it refers to a single character—the newline character. Just as you can store the letter *A* into a char variable ch like this:

```
ch = 'A';
```

so you can store the newline character into a variable:

```
ch = '\n';
```

You also can put the newline character into a string, just as you can any printable character:

```
cout << "Hello\n";
```

This last statement has exactly the same effect as the statement

```
cout << "Hello" << endl;
```

But back to our discussion of input. Let's look at some examples using the reading marker and the newline character. In the following table, i is an int variable, ch is a char variable, and x is a float variable. The input statements produce the results shown. The part of the input stream printed in color is what has been extracted by input statements. The reading marker, denoted by the shaded block, indicates the next character waiting to be read. The \n denotes the newline character produced by striking the Return or Enter key.

Statements	Contents After Input	Marker Position in the Input Stream
1.		25 A 16.9\n
cin >> i;	i = 25	25 A 16.9\n
cin >> ch;	ch = 'A'	25 A 16.9\n
cin >> x;	x = 16.9	25 A 16.9\n
2.		25\n A\n 16.9\n
cin >> i;	i = 25	25\n A\n 16.9\n
cin >> ch;	ch = 'A'	25\n A\n 16.9\n
cin >> x;	x = 16.9	25\n A\n 16.9\n
3.		25A16.9\n
cin >> i;	i = 25	25A16.9\n
cin >> ch;	ch = 'A'	25A16.9\n
cin >> x;	x = 16.9	25A16.9\n

Reading Character Data with the get Function

As we have discussed, the >> operator skips any leading whitespace characters in the input stream. Suppose that ch1 and ch2 are char variables and the program executes the statement

```
cin >> ch1 >> ch2;
```

If the input stream consists of

```
R 1
```

then the extraction operator stores 'R' into `ch1`, skips the blank, and stores '1' into `ch2`. (Note that the `char` value '1' is not the same as the `int` value 1. The two are stored completely differently in a computer's memory. The extraction operator interprets the same data in different ways, depending on the data type of the variable that's being filled.)

What if we had wanted to input *three* characters from the input line: the R, the blank, and the 1? With the extraction operator, it's not possible. Whitespace characters such as blanks are skipped over.

The `istream` data type provides a second way in which to read character data, in addition to the `>>` operator. You can use the `get` function, which inputs the very next character in the input stream without skipping any whitespace characters. A function call looks like this:

```
cin.get(someChar);
```

You give the name of an `istream` variable (here, `cin`), then a dot (period), and then the function name and argument list. Notice that the call to `get` uses the syntax for calling a void function, not a value-returning function. The function call is a complete statement; it is not part of a larger expression.

The effect of the above function call is to input the next character waiting in the stream—even if it is a whitespace character like a blank—and store it into the variable `someChar`. The argument to the `get` function *must* be a variable.

Using the `get` function, we now can input all three characters of the input line

```
R 1
```

We can use three consecutive calls to the `get` function:

```
cin.get(ch1);
cin.get(ch2);
cin.get(ch3);
```

or we can do it this way:

```
cin >> ch1;
cin.get(ch2);
cin >> ch3;
```

The first version is probably a bit clearer for someone to read and understand.

Here are some more examples of character input using both the `>>` operator and the `get` function. `ch1`, `ch2`, and `ch3` are all `char` variables.

Statements	Contents After Input	Marker Position in the Input Stream
1.		A B\n CD\n
cin >> ch1;	ch1 = 'A'	A B\n CD\n
cin >> ch2;	ch2 = 'B'	A B\n CD\n
cin >> ch3;	ch3 = 'C'	A B\n CD\n
2.		A B\n CD\n
cin.get(ch1);	ch1 = 'A'	A B\n CD\n
cin.get(ch2);	ch2 = ' '	A B\n CD\n
cin.get(ch3);	ch3 = 'B'	A B\n CD\n
3.		A B\n CD\n
cin >> ch1;	ch1 = 'A'	A B\n CD\n
cin >> ch2;	ch2 = 'B'	A B\n CD\n
cin.get(ch3);	ch3 = '\n'	A B\n CD\n

Skipping Characters with the ignore Function

Most of us have a specialized tool lying in a kitchen drawer or in a toolbox. It gathers dust and cobwebs because we almost never use it. But when we suddenly need it, we're glad we have it. The ignore function associated with the istream type is like this specialized tool. You rarely have occasion to use ignore; but when you need it, you're glad it's available.

The ignore function is used to skip (read and discard) characters in the input stream. It is a function with two arguments, called like this:

```
cin.ignore(200, '\n');
```

The first argument is an int expression; the second, a char value. This particular function call tells the computer to skip the next 200 input characters *or* to skip characters until a newline character is read, whichever comes first.

Here are some examples that use a char variable ch and three int variables, i, j, and k:

Statements	Contents After Input	Marker Position in the Input Stream
1.		957 34 1235\n 128 96\n
`cin >> i >> j;`	i = 957, j = 34	957 34█ 1235\n 128 96\n
`cin.ignore(100, '\n');`		957 34 1235\n 128 96\n
`cin >> k;`	k = 128	957 34 1235\n 128█96\n

2.
`cin >> ch;`
`cin.ignore(100, 'B');`
`cin >> i;`
	
	ch = 'A'
	
	i = 16
		A 22 B 16 C 19\n
		A█22 B 16 C 19\n
		A 22 B█16 C 19\n
		A 22 B 16█C 19\n

3.
`cin.ignore(2, '\n');`
`cin >> ch;`
	
	ch = 'C'
		ABCDEF\n
		ABCDEF\n
		ABCDEF\n

Example (1) shows the most common use of the `ignore` function, which is to skip the rest of the data on the current input line. Example (2) demonstrates the use of a character other than '\n' as the second argument. We skip over all input characters until a *B* has been found, then read the next input number into `i`. In both (1) and (2), we are focusing on the second argument to the `ignore` function, and we arbitrarily choose any large number, such as 100, for the first argument. In (3), we change our focus and concentrate on the first argument. Our intention is to skip the next two input characters on the current line.

Reading String Data

To input a character string into a `string` variable, we have two options. The first is to use the extraction operator (>>). When reading input characters into a `string` variable, the >> operator skips any leading whitespace characters such as blanks and newlines. It then reads successive characters into the variable, stopping at the first *trailing* whitespace character (which is not consumed, but remains as the first character waiting in the input stream). For example, assume we have the following code:

```
string firstName;
string lastName;

cin >> firstName >> lastName;
```

If the input stream initially looks like this (where ⬚ denotes a blank):

⬚⬚Mary⬚Smith⬚⬚⬚18

then our input statement stores the four characters `Mary` into `firstName`, stores the five characters `Smith` into `lastName`, and leaves the input stream as

⬚⬚⬚18

Although the `>>` operator is widely used for string input, it has a potential drawback: it cannot be used to input a string that has blanks within it. (Remember that it stops reading as soon as it encounters a whitespace character.) This fact leads us to the second option for performing string input: the `getline` function. A call to this function looks like this:

```
getline(cin, myString);
```

The function call, which does not use dot notation, requires two arguments. The first is an input stream variable (here, `cin`) and the second is a `string` variable. The `getline` function does not skip leading whitespace characters and continues until it reaches the newline character `'\n'`. That is, `getline` reads and stores an entire input line, embedded blanks and all. Note that with `getline`, the newline character is consumed (but is not stored into the string variable). Given the code segment

```
string inputStr;
```

```
getline(cin, inputStr);
```

and the input line

⬚⬚Mary⬚Smith⬚⬚⬚18

the result of the call to `getline` is that all 17 characters on the input line (including blanks) are stored into `inputStr`, and the reading marker is positioned at the beginning of the next input line.

4.2 Interactive Input/Output

An interactive program is one in which the user communicates directly with the computer. Many of the programs that we write are interactive. There is a certain "etiquette" involved in writing interactive programs that has to do with instructions for the user to follow.

To get data into an interactive program, we begin with *input prompts*, printed messages that explain what the user should enter. Without these messages, the user has no idea what data values to type. In many cases, a program also should print out all of the data values typed in so that the user can verify that they were entered correctly. Printing out the input values is called *echo printing*. Here's a program showing the proper use of prompts:

```cpp
//*********************************************************************
// Prompts program
// This program demonstrates the use of input prompts
//*********************************************************************
#include <iostream>
#include <iomanip>    // For setprecision()

using namespace std;

int main()
{
    int   partNumber;
    int   quantity;
    float unitPrice;
    float totalPrice;

    cout << fixed << showpoint            // Set up floating-pt.
         << setprecision(2);              //    output format

    cout << "Enter the part number:" << endl;       // Prompt
    cin >> partNumber;

    cout << "Enter the quantity of this part ordered:" // Prompt
         << endl;
    cin >> quantity;

    cout << "Enter the unit price for this part:"     // Prompt
         << endl;
    cin >> unitPrice;

    totalPrice = quantity * unitPrice;
    cout << "Part " << partNumber                     // Echo print
         << ", quantity " << quantity
         << ", at $ " << unitPrice << " each" << endl;
    cout << "totals $ " << totalPrice << endl;
    return 0;
}
```

Here is the program's output, with the user's input shown in color:

```
Enter the part number:
4671
Enter the quantity of this part ordered:
10
Enter the unit price for this part:
27.25
Part 4671, quantity 10, at $ 27.25 each
totals $ 272.50
```

The amount of information you should put into your prompts depends on who is going to be using a program. If you are writing a program for people who are not familiar with computers, your messages should be more detailed. For example, "Type a four-digit part number, then press the key marked Enter." If the program is going to be used frequently by the same people, you might shorten the prompts: "Enter PN" and "Enter Qty." If the program is for very experienced users, you can prompt for several values at once and have them type all of the values on one input line:

```
Enter PN, Qty, Unit Price:
4176 10 27.25
```

In programs that use large amounts of data, this method saves the user keystrokes and time. However, it also makes it easier for the user to enter values in the wrong order.

Prompts are not the only way in which programs interact with users. It can be helpful to have a program print out some general instructions at the beginning ("Press Enter after typing each data value. Enter a negative number when done."). When data is not entered in the correct form, a message that indicates the problem should be printed. For users who haven't worked much with computers, it's important that these messages be informative and "friendly." The message

```
ILLEGAL DATA VALUES!!!!!!!
```

is likely to upset an inexperienced user. Moreover, it doesn't offer any constructive information. A much better message would be

```
That is not a valid part number.
Part numbers must be no more than four digits long.
Please reenter the number in its proper form:
```

In Chapter 5, we introduce the statements that allow us to test for erroneous data.

4.3 Noninteractive Input/Output

Although we tend to use examples of interactive I/O in this text, many programs are written using noninteractive I/O. A common example of noninteractive I/O on large computer systems is batch processing. In batch processing, the user and the computer do not interact while the program is running. This method is most effective when a program is going to input or output large amounts of data. An example of batch processing is a program that inputs a file containing semester grades for thousands of students and prints grade reports to be mailed out.

When a program must read in many data values, the usual practice is to prepare them ahead of time, storing them into a disk file. This allows the user to go back and make changes or corrections to the data as necessary before running the program. When a program is designed to print lots of data, the output can be sent directly to a high-speed printer or another disk file. After the program has been run, the user can examine the data at leisure. In the next section, we discuss input and output with disk files.

Programs designed for noninteractive I/O do not print prompting messages for input. It is a good idea, however, to echo print each data value that is read. Echo printing allows the person reading the output to verify that the input values were prepared correctly. Because noninteractive programs tend to print large amounts of data, their output often is in the form of a table—columns with descriptive headings.

Most C++ programs are written for interactive use. But the flexibility of the language allows you to write noninteractive programs as well. The biggest difference is in the input/output requirements. Noninteractive programs are generally more rigid about the organization and format of the input and output data.

4.4 File Input and Output

In everything we've done so far, we've assumed that the input to our programs comes from the keyboard and that the output from our programs goes to the screen. We look now at input/output from and to files.

Files

A file is a named area in secondary storage that holds a collection of information (for example, the program code we have typed into the editor). The information in a file usually is stored on an auxiliary storage device, such as a disk. Our programs can read data from a file in the same way they read data from the keyboard, and they can write output to a disk file in the same way they write output to the screen.

Why would we want a program to read data from a file instead of the keyboard? If a program is going to read a large quantity of data, it is easier to enter the data into a file with an editor than to enter it while the program is running. With the editor, we can go back and correct mistakes. Also, we do not have to enter the data all at once; we can take a break and come back later. And if we want to rerun the program, having the data stored in a file allows us to do so without retyping the data.

Why would we want the output from a program to be written to a disk file? The contents of a file can be displayed on a screen or printed. This gives us the option of looking at the output over and over again without having to rerun the program. Also, the output stored in a file can be read into another program as input.

Using Files

If we want a program to use file I/O, we have to do four things:

1. Request the preprocessor to include the header file `fstream`.
2. Use declaration statements to declare the file streams we are going to use.
3. Prepare each file for reading or writing by using a function named `open`.
4. Specify the name of the file stream in each input or output statement.

Including the Header File `fstream`   Suppose we want Chapter 3's Mortgage program (p. 98) to read data from a file and to write its output to a file. The first thing we must do is use the preprocessor directive

```
#include <fstream>
```

Through the header file `fstream`, the C++ standard library defines two data types, `ifstream` and `ofstream` (standing for *input file stream* and *output file stream*). Consistent with the general idea of streams in C++, the `ifstream` data type represents a stream of characters coming from an input file, and `ofstream` represents a stream of characters going to an output file.

All of the `istream` operations you have learned about—the extraction operator (>>), the `get` function, and the `ignore` function—are also valid for the `ifstream` type. And all of the `ostream` operations, such as the insertion operator (<<) and the `endl`, `setw`, and `setprecision` manipulators, apply also to the `ofstream` type. To these basic operations, the `ifstream` and `ofstream` types add some more operations designed specifically for file I/O.

Declaring File Streams   In a program, you declare stream variables the same way that you declare any variable—you specify the data type and then the variable name:

```
int       someInt;
float     someFloat;
ifstream  inFile;
ofstream  outFile;
```

(You don't have to declare the stream variables `cin` and `cout`. The header file `iostream` already does this for you.)

For our Mortgage program, let's name the input and output file streams `inData` and `outData`. We declare them like this:

```
ifstream inData;      // Holds loan amount, interest, and length
ofstream outData;     // Holds input values and monthly payments
```

Note that the `ifstream` type is for input files only, and the `ofstream` type is for output files only. With these data types, you cannot read from and write to the same file.

Opening Files The third thing we have to do is prepare each file for reading or writing, an act called *opening a file.* Opening a file causes the computer's operating system to perform certain actions that allow us to proceed with file I/O.

In our example, we want to read from the file stream inData and write to the file stream outData. We open the relevant files by using these statements:

```
inData.open("loan.in");
outData.open("loan.out");
```

Both of these statements are function calls. In each function call, the argument is a literal string enclosed by quotes. The first statement is a call to a function named open, which is associated with the ifstream data type. The second is a call to another function (also named open) associated with the ofstream data type. As we have seen earlier, we use dot notation (as in inData.open) to call certain library functions that are tightly associated with data types.

Exactly what does an open function do? First, it associates a stream variable used in your program with a physical file on disk. Our first function call creates a connection between the stream variable inData and the actual disk file, named loan.in. (Names of file streams must be identifiers; they are variables in your program. But some computer systems do not use this syntax for file names on disk. For example, many systems allow or even require a dot within a file name.) Similarly, the second function call associates the stream variable outData with the disk file loan.out. Associating a program's name for a file (outData) with the actual name for the file (loan.out) is much the same as associating a program's name for the standard output device (cout) with the actual device (the screen).

The next thing the open function does depends on whether the file is an input file or an output file. With an input file, the open function sets the file's reading marker to the first piece of data in the file. (Each input file has its own reading marker.)

With an output file, the open function checks to see whether the file already exists. If the file doesn't exist, open creates a new, empty file for you. If the file already exists, open erases the old contents of the file. Then the writing marker is set at the beginning of the empty file (see Figure 4–1). As output proceeds, each successive output operation advances the writing marker to add data to the end of the file.

Figure 4–1 *The Effect of Opening a File*

Because the reason for opening files is to *prepare* the files for reading or writing, you must open the files before using any input or output statements that refer to the files. In a program, it's a good idea to open files right away to be sure that the files are prepared before the program attempts any file I/O.

```
    ⋮

int main()
{

    ⋮     } Declarations

    // Open the files

    inData.open("loan.in");
    outData.open("loan.out");
     ⋮
}
```

In addition to the open function, the ifstream and ofstream types have a close function associated with each. This function has no arguments and may be used as follows.

```
ifstream inFile;

inFile.open("mydata.dat");   // Open the file
 ⋮                           // Read and process the file data
inFile.close();              // Close the file
 ⋮
```

Closing a file causes the operating system to perform certain wrap-up activities on the disk and to break the connection between the stream variable and the disk file.

Should you always call the close function when you're finished reading or writing a file? In some programming languages, it's extremely important that you remember to do so. In C++, however, a file is automatically closed when program control leaves the block (compound statement) in which the stream variable is declared. (Until we get to Chapter 7, this block is the body of the main function.) When control leaves this block, a special function associated with each of ifstream and ofstream called a *destructor* is implicitly executed, and this destructor function closes the file for you. Consequently, you don't often see C++ programs explicitly calling the close function. On the other hand, many programmers like to make it a regular habit to call the close function explicitly, and you may wish to do so yourself.

Specifying File Streams in Input/Output Statements   There is just one more thing we have to do in order to use files. As we said earlier, all istream operations also are valid for the `ifstream` type, and all `ostream` operations are valid for the `ofstream` type. So, to read from or write to a file, all we need to do in our input and output statements is substitute the appropriate file stream variable for `cin` or `cout`. In our Mortgage program, we would use a statement like

```
inData >> loanAmount >> yearlyInterest >> numberOfYears;
```

to instruct the computer to read data from the file `inData`. Similarly, all of the output statements that write to the file `outData` would specify `outData`, not `cout`, as the destination:

```
outData << fixed << setprecision(2) << "For a loan amount of "
        << loanAmount
        << " with an interest rate of " << setprecision(4)
        << yearlyInterest  << " and a "
        << numberOfYears << " year mortgage, " << endl;
outData << fixed << setprecision(2)
        << "your monthly payments are $" << payment
        << "." << endl;
```

What is nice about C++ stream I/O is that we have a uniform syntax for performing I/O operations, regardless of whether we're working with the keyboard and screen, with files, or with other I/O devices.

An Example Program Using Files

The reworked Mortgage program is shown below. Now it reads its input from the file `inData` and writes its output to the file `outData`. Compare this program with the original version on page 98 and notice that named constants have disappeared because the data are now input at execution time. Notice also that to set up the floating-point output format, the `fixed` and `setprecision` manipulators are applied to the `outData` stream variable, not to `cout`.

```
//***************************************************************
// Mortgage Payment Calculator program
// This program determines the monthly payments on a mortgage given
// the loan amount, the yearly interest rate, and the number of
// years.
//***************************************************************

#include <fstream>
#include <cmath>
#include <iomanip>
```

```cpp
using namespace std;

#include <fstream>
#include <cmath>
#include <iomanip>

using namespace std;

int main()
{

    // Input variables
    float loanAmount;
    float yearlyInterest;
    int numberOfYears;
    ofstream outData;
    ifstream inData;

    // Local variables
    float monthlyInterest;
    int numberOfPayments;
    float payment;

    inData.open("loan.in");
    outData.open("loan.out");

    // Read values from the file
    inData >> loanAmount >> yearlyInterest >> numberOfYears;

    // Calculate values
    monthlyInterest = yearlyInterest * 0.01 / 12;
    numberOfPayments = numberOfYears * 12;
    payment = (loanAmount
                * pow(1 + monthlyInterest, numberOfPayments)
                *  monthlyInterest)
                /(pow(1 + monthlyInterest, numberOfPayments) - 1 );

    // Output results
    outData << fixed << setprecision(2) << "For a loan amount of "
            << loanAmount
            << " with an interest rate of " << setprecision(4)
            << yearlyInterest  << " and a "
            << numberOfYears << " year mortgage, " << endl;
    outData << fixed << setprecision(2)
            << "your monthly payments are $" << payment
```

```
            << "." << endl;

      inData.close();
      outData.close();
      return 0;
}
```

Before running the program, you would use the editor to create and save a file `loan.in` to serve as input. The contents of the file might look like this:

```
50000.00 0.05 5
```

In writing the new Mortgage program, what happens if you mistakenly specify `cout` instead of `outData` in one of the output statements? Nothing disastrous; the output of that one statement merely goes to the screen instead of the output file. And what if, by mistake, you specify `cin` instead of `inData` in the input statement? The consequences are not as pleasant. When you run the program, the computer will appear to go dead (to *hang*). Here's the reason: Execution reaches the input statement and the computer waits for you to enter the data from the keyboard. But you don't know that the computer is waiting. There's no message on the screen prompting you for input, and you are assuming (wrongly) that the program is getting its input from a data file. So the computer waits, and you wait, and the computer waits, and you wait. Every programmer at one time or another has had the experience of thinking the computer has hung, when, in fact, it is working just fine, silently waiting for keyboard input.

Run-Time Input of File Names

Until now, our examples of opening a file for input have included code similar to the following:

```
ifstream inFile;

inFile.open("datafile.dat");
   ⋮
```

The `open` function associated with the `ifstream` data type requires an argument that specifies the name of the actual data file on disk. By using a literal string, as in the example above, the file name is fixed at compile time. Therefore, the program works only for this one particular disk file.

We often want to make a program more flexible by allowing the file name to be determined at *run time*. A common technique is to prompt the user for the name of the file, read the user's response into a variable, and pass the variable as an argument to the `open` function. In principle, the following code should accomplish what we want. Unfortunately, the compiler does not allow it.

```
ifstream inFile;
string   fileName;

cout << "Enter the input file name: ";
cin >> fileName;
inFile.open(fileName);                    // Compile-time error
```

The problem is that the `open` function does not expect an argument of type `string`. Instead, it expects a C *string*. A C string (so named because it originated in the C language, the forerunner of C++) is a limited form of string. A literal string, such as `"datafile.dat"`, happens to be a C string and thus is acceptable as an argument to the `open` function.

To make the above code work correctly, we need to convert a `string` variable to a C string. The `string` data type provides a value-returning function named `c_str` that is applied to a `string` variable as follows:

```
fileName.c_str()
```

This function returns the C string that is equivalent to the one contained in the `fileName` variable. (The original string contained in `fileName` is not changed by the function call.) The primary purpose of the `c_str` function is to allow programmers to call library functions that expect C strings, not `string` strings, as arguments.

Using the `c_str` function, we can code the run-time input of a file name as follows:

```
ifstream inFile;
string   fileName;

cout << "Enter the input file name: ";
cin >> fileName;
inFile.open(fileName.c_str());
```

4.5 Input Failure

When a program inputs data from the keyboard or an input file, things can go wrong. Let's suppose that we're executing a program. It prompts us to enter an integer value, but we absentmindedly type some letters of the alphabet. The input operation fails because of the invalid data. In C++ terminology, the `cin` stream has entered the *fail state*. Once a stream has entered the fail state, any further I/O operations using that stream are considered to be null operations—that is, they have no effect at all. Unfortunately for us, *the computer does not halt the program or give any error message.* The computer just continues executing the program, silently ignoring each additional attempt to use that stream.

Invalid data is the most common reason for input failure. When your program inputs an `int` value, it is expecting to find only digits in the input stream, possibly preceded by a plus or minus sign. If there is a decimal point somewhere within the digits, does the input operation fail? Not necessarily; it depends on where the reading marker is. Let's look at an example.

Assume that a program has `int` variables i, j, and k, whose contents are currently 10, 20, and 30, respectively. The program now executes the following two statements:

```
cin >> i >> j >> k;
cout << "i: " << i << "  j: " << j << "  k: " << k;
```

If we type these characters for the input data:

```
1234.56 7 89
```

then the program produces this output:

```
i: 1234   j: 20   k: 30
```

Let's see why.

Remember that when reading `int` or `float` data, the extraction operator >> stops reading at the first character that is inappropriate for the data type (whitespace or otherwise). In our example, the input operation for i succeeds. The computer extracts the first four characters from the input stream and stores the integer value 1234 into i. The reading marker is now on the decimal point:

```
1234.56 7 89
```

The next input operation (for j) fails; an `int` value cannot begin with a decimal point. The `cin` stream is now in the fail state, and the current value of j (20) remains unchanged. The third input operation (for k) is ignored, as are all the rest of the statements in our program that read from `cin`.

Another way to make a stream enter the fail state is to try to open an input file that doesn't exist. Suppose that you have a data file on your disk named `myfile.dat`. In your program you have the following statements:

```
ifstream inFile;
```

```
inFile.open("myfil.dat");
inFile >> i >> j >> k;
```

In the call to the `open` function, you misspelled the name of your disk file. At run time, the attempt to open the file fails, so the stream `inFile` enters the fail state. The next three input operations (for i, j, and k) are null operations. Without issuing any error message, the program proceeds to use the (unknown) contents of i, j, and k in calculations. The results of these calculations are certain to be puzzling.

The point of this discussion is not to make you nervous about I/O but to make you aware. The Testing and Debugging section at the end of this chapter offers suggestions for avoiding input failure, and Chapters 5 and 6 introduce program statements that let you test the state of a stream.

4.6 Software Design Methodologies

Over the last two chapters and the first part of this one, we have introduced elements of the C++ language that let us input data, perform calculations, and output results. The programs we wrote were short and straightforward because the problems to be solved were simple. We are ready to write programs for more complicated problems, but first we need to step back and look at the overall process of programming.

As you learned in Chapter 1, the programming process consists of a problem-solving phase and an implementation phase. The problem-solving phase includes *analysis* (analyzing and understanding the problem to be solved) and *design* (designing a solution to the problem). Given a complex problem—one that results in a 10,000-line program, for example—it's simply not reasonable to skip the design process and go directly to writing C++ code. What we need is a systematic way of designing a solution to a problem, no matter how complicated the problem is.

In the remainder of this chapter, we describe two important methodologies for designing solutions to more complex problems: *functional decomposition* and *object-oriented design*. These methodologies help you create solutions that can be easily implemented as C++ programs. The resulting programs are readable, understandable, and easy to debug and modify.

One software design methodology that is in widespread use is known as **object-oriented design** (OOD). C++ evolved from the C language primarily to facilitate the use of the OOD methodology. In the next two sections, we present the essential concepts of OOD; we expand our treatment of the approach later in the book. OOD is often used in conjunction with the other methodology that we discuss in this chapter, **functional decomposition**.

Object-oriented design A technique for developing software in which the solution is expressed in terms of objects—self-contained entities composed of data and operations on that data.

Functional decomposition A technique for developing software in which the problem is divided into more easily handled subproblems, the solutions of which create a solution to the overall problem.

OOD focuses on entities (*objects*) consisting of data and operations on the data. In OOD, we solve a problem by identifying the components that make up a solution and identifying how those components interact with each other through operations on the data that they contain. The result is a design for a set of objects that can be assembled to form a solution to a problem. In contrast, functional decomposition views the solution to a problem as a task to be accomplished. It focuses on the sequence of operations that are required to complete the task. When the problem requires a sequence of steps that is long or complex, we divide it into subproblems that are easier to solve.

The choice of which methodology we use depends on the problem at hand. For example, a large problem might involve several sequential phases of processing, such as gathering data and verifying its correctness with noninteractive processing, analyzing the data interactively, and printing reports noninteractively at the conclusion of the analysis. This process has a natural functional decomposition. Each of the phases, however, may best be solved by a set of objects that represent the data and the operations that can be applied to it. Some of the individual operations may be sufficiently complex that they require further decomposition, either into a sequence of operations or into another set of objects.

If you look at a problem and see that it is natural to think about it in terms of a collection of component parts, then you should use OOD to solve it. For example, a banking problem may require a `checkingAccount` object with associated operations `OpenAccount`, `WriteCheck`, `MakeDeposit`, and `IsOverdrawn`. The `checkingAccount` object consists of not only data (the account number and current balance, for example) but also these operations, all bound together into one unit.

On the other hand, if you find that it is natural to think of the solution to the problem as a series of steps, then you should use functional decomposition. For example, when computing some statistical measures on a large set of real numbers, it is natural to decompose the problem into a sequence of steps that read a value, perform calculations, and then repeat the sequence. The C++ language and the standard library supply all of the operations that we need, and we simply write a sequence of those operations to solve the problem.

4.7 What Are Objects?

Let's take a closer look at what objects are and how they work before we examine OOD further. We said earlier that an object is a collection of data together with associated operations. Several programming languages, called *object-oriented programming languages*, have been created specifically to support OOD. Examples are C++, Java, Smalltalk, CLOS, Eiffel, and Object-Pascal. In these languages, a *class* is a programmer-defined data type from which objects are created. Although we did not say it at the time, we have been using classes and objects to perform input and output in C++. `cin` is an object of a data type (class) named `istream`, and `cout` is an object of a class `ostream`. As we explained earlier, the header file `iostream` defines the classes `istream` and `ostream` and also declares `cin` and `cout` to be objects of those classes:

```
istream cin;
ostream cout;
```

Similarly, the header file `fstream` defines classes `ifstream` and `ofstream`, from which you can declare your own input file stream and output file stream objects.

Another example you have seen already is `string`—a programmer-defined class from which you create objects by using declarations such as

```
string lastName;
```

In Figure 4–2, we picture the `cin` and `lastName` objects as entities that have a private part and a public part. The private part includes data and functions that the user cannot access and doesn't need to know about in order to use the object. The public

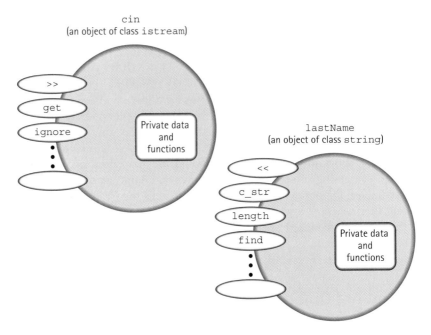

Figure 4–2 *Objects and Their Operations*

part, shown as ovals in the side of the object, represents the object's *interface*. The interface consists of operations that are available to programmers wishing to use the object. In C++, public operations are written as functions and are known as *member functions*. Except for operations using symbols such as << and >>, a member function is invoked by giving the name of the class object, then a dot, and then the function name and argument list:

```
cin.ignore(100, '\n');
cin.get(someChar);
cin >> someInt;
len = lastName.length();
pos = lastName.find('A');
```

4.8 Object-Oriented Design

The first step in OOD is to identify the major objects in the problem, together with their associated operations. The final problem solution is ultimately expressed in terms of these objects and operations.

OOD leads to programs that are collections of objects. Each object is responsible for one part of the entire solution, and the objects communicate by accessing each other's member functions. There are many libraries of prewritten classes, including the C++ standard library. In many cases, it is possible to browse through a library, choose classes you need for a problem, and assemble them to form a substantial portion of your program. Putting existing pieces together in this fashion is an excellent example of the building-block approach we discussed in Chapter 1.

When there isn't a suitable class available in a library, it is necessary to define a new class. We see how this is done in Chapter 11. The design of a new class begins with the specification of its interface. We must decide what operations are needed on the outside of the class to make its objects useful. Once the interface is defined, we can design the implementation of the class, including all of its private members.

It is quite common to discover a class in a library that is almost right for your purpose but is missing some key feature. OOD addresses this situation with a concept called *inheritance*, which allows you to adapt an existing class to meet your particular needs. You can use inheritance to add features to a class without having to inspect and modify its source code.

To summarize the OOD process: We identify the major components of a problem solution and how they interact. We then look in the available libraries for classes that correspond to the components. When we find a class that is almost right, we can use inheritance to adapt it. When we can't find a class that corresponds to a component, we must design a new class. Our design specifies the interface for the class, and we then implement the interface with public and private members as necessary. OOD isn't always used in isolation. Functional decomposition may be used in designing member functions within a class or in coordinating the interactions of objects.

4.9   Functional Decomposition

The second design technique we use is functional decomposition. In functional decomposition, we work from the abstract (a list of the major steps in our solution) to the particular (algorithmic steps that can be translated directly into C++ code). You can also think of this as working from a high-level solution, leaving the details of implementation unspecified, down to a fully detailed solution.

The easiest way to solve a problem is to give it to someone else and say, "Solve this problem." This is the most abstract level of a problem solution: a single-statement solution that encompasses the entire problem without specifying any of the details of implementation. It's at this point that we programmers are called in. Our job is to turn the abstract solution into a concrete solution, a program.

If the solution clearly involves a series of major steps, we break it down (decompose it) into pieces. In the process, we move to a lower level of abstraction—that is, some of the implementation details (but not too many) are now specified. Each of the major steps becomes an independent subproblem that we can work on separately. In a very large project, one person (the *chief architect or team leader*) formulates the subproblems and then gives them to other members of the programming team, saying, "Solve this problem." In the case of a small project, we give the subproblems to ourselves. Then we choose one subproblem at a time to solve. We may break the chosen subproblem into another series of steps that, in turn, become smaller subproblems. Or we may identify components that are naturally represented as objects. The process continues until each subproblem cannot be divided further or has an obvious solution.

Why do we work this way? Why not simply write out all of the details? Because it is much easier to focus on one problem at a time. For example, suppose you are working on part of a program to output certain values and discover that you need a complex formula to calculate an appropriate fieldwidth for printing one of the values. Calculating fieldwidths is not the purpose of this part of the program. If you shift your focus to the calculation, you are likely to forget some detail of the overall output process. What you do is write down an abstract step—"Calculate the fieldwidth required"—and go on with the problem at hand. Once you've written the major steps, you can go back to solving the step that does the calculation.

By subdividing the problem, you create a hierarchical structure called a *tree structure*. Each level of the tree is a complete solution to the problem that is less abstract (more detailed) than the level above it. Figure 4–3 shows a generic solution tree for a

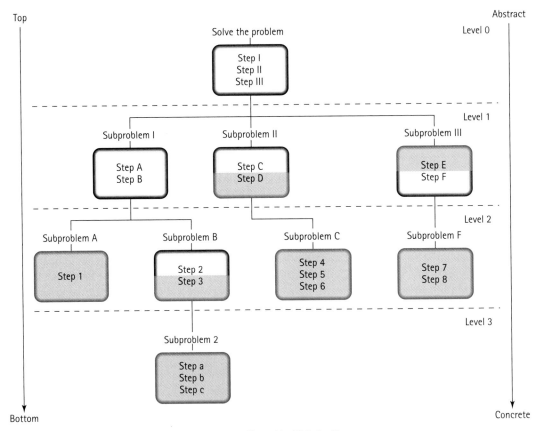

Figure 4–3   *Hierarchical Solution Tree*

problem. Steps that are shaded have enough implementation details to be translated directly into C++ statements. These are **concrete steps**. Those that are not shaded are **abstract steps**; they reappear as subproblems in the next level down. Each box in the figure represents a **module**. Modules are the basic building blocks in a functional decomposition. The diagram in Figure 4–3 is also called a *module structure chart*.

> **Concrete step**   A step for which the implementation details are fully specified.
>
> **Abstract step**   A step for which some implementation details remain unspecified.
>
> **Module**   A self-contained collection of steps that solves a problem or subproblem; can contain both concrete and abstract steps.

Like OOD, functional decomposition uses the divide-and-conquer approach to problem solving. Both techniques break up large problems into smaller units that are easier to handle. The difference is that in OOD the units are objects, whereas the units in functional decomposition are modules representing algorithms.

Modules

A module begins life as an abstract step in the next-higher level of the solution tree. It is completed when it solves a given subproblem—that is, when it specifies a series of steps that does the same thing as the higher-level abstract step.

In a properly written module, the only steps that directly address the given subproblem are concrete steps; abstract steps are used for significant new subproblems. The idea is that each module should do just one thing and do it well. Knowing which details to make concrete and which to leave abstract is a matter of experience, circumstance, and personal style. For example, you might decide to include a fieldwidth calculation in a printing module if there isn't so much detail in the rest of the module that it becomes confusing. On the other hand, if the calculation is performed several times, it makes sense to write it as a separate module and just refer to it each time you need it.

Writing Modules   Here's one approach to writing modules:

1. Think about how you would solve the subproblem by hand.
2. Begin writing down the major steps.
3. If a step is simple enough that you can see how to implement it directly in C++, it is at the concrete level; it doesn't need any further refinement.
4. If you have to think about implementing a step as a series of smaller steps or as several C++ statements, it is still at an abstract level.
5. If you are trying to write a series of steps and start to feel overwhelmed by details, you probably are bypassing one or more levels of abstraction. Stand back and look for pieces that you can write as more abstract steps.

As you work your way down the solution tree, you make a series of design decisions. If a decision proves awkward or wrong (and many times it does!), you can backtrack (go back up the tree to a higher-level module) and try something else. You don't have to scrap your whole design—only the small part you are working on.

Pseudocode   You'll find it easier to implement a design if you write the steps in pseudocode. *Pseudocode* is a mixture of English statements and C++-like control structures that can be translated easily into C++. (We've been using pseudocode in the algorithms in the Programming Examples.) When a concrete step is written in pseudocode, it should be possible to rewrite it directly as a C++ statement in a program.

Documentation

As you create your functional decomposition or object-oriented design, you are developing documentation for your program. *Documentation* includes the written problem specifications, design, development history, and actual code of a program.

Good documentation helps other programmers read and understand a program and is invaluable when software is being debugged and modified (maintained). If you haven't looked at your program for six months and need to change it, you'll be happy that you documented it well. Of course, if someone else has to use and modify your program, documentation is indispensable.

Documentation is both external and internal to the program. External documentation includes the specifications, the development history, and the design documents. Internal documentation includes the program format and self–documenting code—meaningful identifiers and comments. You can use the pseudocode from the design process as comments in your programs.

Self-documenting code   Program code containing meaningful identifiers as well as judiciously used clarifying comments.

This kind of documentation may be sufficient for someone reading or maintaining your programs. However, if a program is going to be used by people who are not programmers, you must provide a user's manual as well.

Be sure to keep documentation up-to-date. Indicate any changes you make in a program in all of the pertinent documentation. Use self-documenting code to make your programs more readable.

Programming Example

Display a Name in Multiple Formats

PROBLEM You are beginning to work on a problem that needs to output names in several formats along with the corresponding social security number. As a start, you decide to write a short C++ program that inputs a social security number and a single name and displays it in the different formats so you can be certain that all of your string expressions are correct.

INPUT The social security number and a name in three parts, on file `name.dat`, each separated by one or more white space characters.

OUTPUT The name is to be written in four different formats on file `name.out`:

1. First name, middle name, last name, social security number
2. Last name, first name, middle name, social security number
3. Last name, first name, middle initial, social security number
4. First name, middle initial, last name

DISCUSSION You easily could just type the social security number and the name in the four formats as string literals in the code, but the purpose of this exercise is to develop and test the string expressions that you need for the larger problem. The problem statement doesn't say in which order the parts of the name are entered on the file, but it does say that they are separated by white space. You assume that they are in first name, middle name or initial, and last name order. Because the data are on a file, you don't need to prompt for the values. Once you have the social security number and the name, you just write them out in the various formats.

ASSUMPTION Name is in first, middle, and last order on the file.

Main Module	Level 0

> Open files
> Get social security number
> Get name
> Write data in proper formats
> Close files

Open Files	Level 1

> inData.open("name.dat")
> outData.open("name.out")

The "Get social security number" step can be directly implemented by reading into the string variable. Thus, it doesn't require expansion at Level 1 of our design.

Get Name

Get first name
Get middle name or initial
Get last name

Is there a problem reading the middle name if an initial is in the file rather than a middle name? Not really. You just assume that a middle name is entered and extract the initial from the middle name when you need it for the third and fourth formats. If the initial was entered for the middle name, then the second and third output forms will be the same. What about punctuation in the output? If the last name comes first, it should be followed by a comma, and the middle initial should be followed by a period. Thus, if the initial is entered rather than the middle name, it must be followed by a period. This must be added to the assumptions.

ASSUMPTION Name is in first, middle, and last order, and a period must follow the middle initial if it is entered instead of a middle name.

Write Data in Proper Formats

Write first name, blank, middle name, blank, last name, blank, social
    security number
Write last name, comma, blank first name, blank, middle name, blank,
    social security number
Write last name, comma, blank, first name, blank, middle initial, period,
    blank, social security number
Write first name, blank, middle initial, period, blank, last name

The only thing left to define is the middle initial. We can use the `substr` method to access the first character in the middle name.

Middle Initial   **Level 2**

Set initial to middleName.substr(0, 1) + period

Close Files

inData.close()
outData.close()

Module Structure Chart

```
//**********************************************************************
// Format Names program
// This program reads in a social security number, a first name, a
// middle name or initial, and a last name from file inData.
// The name is written to file outData in three formats:
//      1. First name, middle name, last name, and social security
//         number.
//      2. Last name, first name, middle name, and social
//         security number
//      3. Last name, first name, middle initial, and social security
//         number
//      4. First name, middle initial, last name
//**********************************************************************

#include <fstream>                          // Access ofstream
#include <string>                           // Access string

using namespace std;

int main()
{
    // Declare and open files
    ifstream inData;
    ofstream outData;
    inData.open("name.dat");
    outData.open("name.out");

    // Declare variables
    string socialNum;                       // Social security number
    string firstName;                       // First name
    string lastName;                        // Last name
```

```
string middleName;                    // Middle name
string initial;                       // Middle initial

// Read in data from file inData
inData >> socialNum >> firstName >> middleName >> lastName;

// Access middle initial and append a period
initial = middleName.substr(0, 1) + '.';

// Output information in required formats
outData << firstName << ' ' << middleName << ' ' << lastName
        << ' ' << socialNum << endl;
outData << lastName << ", " << firstName << ' ' << middleName
        << ' ' << socialNum  << endl;
outData << lastName << ", " << firstName << ' ' << initial
        << ' ' << socialNum  << endl;
outData << firstName << ' ' << initial << ' ' << lastName;

// Close files
inData.close();
outData.close();
return 0;
}
```

Here are sample input and output files.

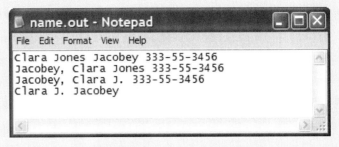

Testing and Debugging

An important part of implementing a program is testing it (checking the results). From here on, these Testing and Debugging sections offer tips on how to test your programs and what to do if a program doesn't work the way you expect it to work. But don't wait until you've found a bug to read the Testing and Debugging sections. It's much easier to prevent bugs than to fix them.

When testing programs that input data values from a file, it's possible for input operations to fail. And when input fails in C++, the computer doesn't issue a warning message or terminate the program. The program simply continues executing, ignoring any further input operations on that file. The two most common reasons for input failure are invalid data and the *end-of-file error*.

An end-of-file error occurs when the program has read all of the input data available in the file and needs more data to fill the variables in its input statements. It might be that the data file simply was not prepared properly. Perhaps it contains fewer data items than the program requires. Or perhaps the format of the input data is wrong. Leaving out whitespace between numeric values is guaranteed to cause trouble. For example, we may want a data file to contain three integer values—25, 16, and 42. Look what happens with this data:

```
2516   42
```

and this code:

```
inFile >> i >> j >> k;
```

The first two input operations use up the data in the file, leaving the third with no data to read. The stream `inFile` enters the fail state, so `k` isn't assigned a new value and the computer quietly continues executing at the next statement in the program.

If the data file is prepared correctly and there is still an end-of-file error, the problem is in the program logic. For some reason, the program is attempting too many input operations. It could be a simple oversight such as specifying too many variables in a particular input statement. It could be a misuse of the `ignore` function, causing values to be skipped inadvertently. Or it could be a serious flaw in the algorithm. You should check all of these possibilities.

The other major source of input failure, invalid data, has several possible causes. The most common is an error in the preparation or entry of the data. Numeric and character data mixed inappropriately in the input can cause the input stream to fail if it is supposed to read a numeric value but the reading marker is positioned at a character that isn't allowed in the number. Another cause is using the wrong variable name (which happens to be of the wrong data type) in an input statement. Declaring a variable to be of the wrong data type is a variation on the problem. Last, leaving out a variable (or including an extra one) in an input statement can cause the reading marker to end up positioned on the wrong type of data.

Another oversight, one that doesn't cause input failure but causes programmer frustration, is to use `cin` or `cout` in an I/O statement when you meant to specify a file stream. If you mistakenly use `cin` instead of an input file stream, the program stops and waits for input from the keyboard. If you mistakenly use `cout` instead of an output file stream, you get unexpected output on the screen.

By giving you a framework that can help you organize and keep track of the details involved in designing and implementing a program, functional decomposition (and, later, object-oriented design) should help you avoid many of these errors in the first place.

Testing and Debugging Hints

1. Input and output statements always begin with the name of a stream object, and the `>>` and `<<` operators point in the direction in which the data is going. The statement

   ```
   cout << n;
   ```

   sends data *to* the output stream `cout`, and the statement

   ```
   cin >> n;
   ```

   sends data *to* the variable `n`.

2. When a program inputs from or outputs to a file, be sure each I/O statement from or to the file uses the name of the file stream, not `cin` or `cout`.

3. The `open` function associated with an `ifstream` or `ofstream` object requires a C string as an argument. The argument cannot be a `string` object. At this point in the book, the argument can only be (a) a literal string or (b) the C string returned by the function call `myString.c_str()`, where `myString` is of type `string`.

4. When you open a data file for input, make sure that the argument to the `open` function supplies the correct name of the file as it exists on disk.

5. When reading a character string into a `string` object, the `>>` operator stops at, *but does not consume*, the first trailing whitespace character.

6. Be sure that each input statement specifies the correct number of variables and that each of those variables is of the correct data type.

7. If your input data is mixed (character and numeric values), be sure to deal with intervening blanks.

8. Echo print the input data to verify that each value is where it belongs and is in the proper format. (This is crucial, because an input failure in C++ doesn't produce an error message or terminate the program.)

Summary

Programs operate on data. If data and programs are kept separate, the same program can be run with different sets of input data.

The extraction operator (>>) inputs data from the keyboard or a file, storing the data into the variable specified as its right-hand operand. The extraction operator skips any leading whitespace characters to find the next data value in the input stream. The get function does not skip leading whitespace characters; it inputs the very next character and stores it into the char variable specified in its argument list. Both the >> operator and the get function leave the reading marker positioned at the next character to be read. The next input operation begins reading at the point indicated by the marker.

The newline character (denoted by \n in a C++ program) marks the end of a data line. You create a newline character each time you press the Return or Enter key. Your program generates a newline each time you use the endl manipulator or explicitly output the \n character. Newline is a control character; it does not print. It controls the movement of the screen cursor or the position of a line on a printer.

Interactive programs prompt the user for each data entry and directly inform the user of results and errors. Designing interactive dialogue is an exercise in the art of communication.

Noninteractive input/output allows data to be prepared before a program is run and allows the program to run again with the same data in the event that a problem crops up during processing.

Data files often are used for noninteractive processing and to permit the output from one program to be used as input to another program. To use these files, you must do four things: (1) include the header file fstream, (2) declare the file streams along with your other variable declarations, (3) prepare the files for reading or writing by calling the open function, and (4) specify the name of the file stream in each input or output statement that uses it.

Object-oriented design produces a problem solution by focusing on objects and their associated operations. The first step is to identify the major objects in the problem and choose appropriate operations on those objects. An object is an instance of a data type called a class. The result of the design process is a program consisting of self-contained objects that manage their own data and communicate by invoking each other's operations.

Functional decomposition begins with an abstract solution that then is divided into major steps. Each step becomes a subproblem that is analyzed and subdivided further. A concrete step is one that can be translated directly into C++; those steps that need more refining are abstract steps. A module is a collection of concrete and abstract steps that solves a subproblem.

Careful attention to program design, program formatting, and documentation produces highly structured and readable programs.

Quick Check

1. Why do we need to use prompts for interactive I/O? (pp. 118–120)
2. What conditions would you look for in a problem to decide whether interactive or noninteractive input is appropriate? (pp. 120–121)
3. What is the first step in the object-oriented design process? (pp. 132–133)
4. Write an input statement that reads three integer values into variables a, b, and c. (pp. 110–112)
5. If an input line contains

   ```
   Jones, Walker Thomas
   ```

   what will be the values in the `string` variables `first`, `middle`, and `last` when the following statement is executed? (pp. 117–118)

   ```
   cin >> first >> middle >> last;
   ```

6. After including the header file `fstream`, and declaring a file stream, what is the next step in using a file I/O? (pp. 123–124)
7. What characterizes a concrete step in a functional decomposition design? (pp. 133–135)

Answers

1. To tell the user how and when to enter values as input.   2. The amount of data to be input, and whether the data can be prepared for entry before the program is run.   3. To identify the major objects in the problem.   4. `cin >> a >> b >> c;`
5. `first = "Jones,"`
   `middle = "Walker"`
   `last = "Thomas"`
6. Preparing the file for reading or writing with the `open` function.   7. It is a step that can be implemented directly in a programming language.

Exam Preparation Exercises

1. The statement

   ```
   cin >> maximum >> minimum;
   ```

   is equivalent to the two statements:

   ```
   cin >> minimum;
   cin >> maximum;
   ```

   True or false?
2. What is wrong with each of the following statements?
   a. `cin << score;`
   b. `cout >> maximum;`
   c. `cin >> "Enter data";`
   d. `cin.ignore('Y', 35);`
   e. `getLine(someString, cin);`

3. If input data are entered as follows

```
10    20
30    40
50    60
70    80
```

and the input statements that read it are

```
cin >> a >> b >> c;
cin >> d >> e >> f;
cin >> a >> b;
```

what are the contents of the variables a, b, c, d, e, and f after the statements have executed?

4. If input data are entered as follows:

```
10    20    30    40    50    60
10    20    30    40    50    60
10    20    30    40    50    60
70    80
```

and the input statements that read it are:

```
cin >> a >> b >> c;
cin.ignore(100, '\n');
cin.get(ch1);
cin >> d >> e >> f;
cin.ignore(100, '\n');
cin.ignore(100, '\n');
cin >> a >> b;
```

What are the contents of the variables a, b, c, d, e, and f after the statements have executed?

5. Given the input data

```
January 25, 2005
```

and the input statement

```
cin >> string1 >> string2;
```

   a. What is contained in each of the string variables after the statement is executed?
   b. Where is the reading marker after the statement is executed?

6. Given the input data

```
January 25, 2005
```

and the input statement

```
getline(cin, string1);
```

  a. What is contained in the string variable after the statement is executed?

  b. Where is the reading marker after the statement is executed?

7. Given the input data

```
January 25, 2005
```

and the input statement (where the type of each variable is given by its name)

```
cin >> string1 >> int1 >> char1 >> string2;
```

  a. What is contained in each of the variables after the statement is executed?

  b. Where is the reading marker after the statement is executed?

8. If the reading marker is on the newline character at the end of a line, and you call the `get` function, what value does it return in its argument?

9. What do the two arguments to the `ignore` function specify?

10. You are writing a program that inputs a date in the form of mm/dd/yyyy.

  a. Write the output statement to prompt an inexperienced user to enter a date.

  b. Write the output statement to prompt an experienced user to input a date.

11. What are the four steps necessary to use a file for input or output?

12. What are the two file stream data types discussed in this chapter?

13. What is the purpose of the following statements?

```
ifstream inFile;
inFile.open("datafile.dat");
```

14. Correct the following code segment so that it opens the file whose name is entered via the input statement.

```
ifstream inData;
string name;

cout << "Enter the name of the file: ");
cin >> name;
infile.open(name);
```

15. What happens when an input operation is performed on a file that is in the fail state?

16. When you try to open a file that doesn't exist, C++ outputs an error message and terminates execution of the program. True or false?

17. Just opening an input file stream cannot cause it to enter the fail state. True or false?

18. You're writing a program for a rental car company that keeps track of vehicles. What are the major objects in this problem?

19. What C++ construct is used to implement an object?

20. Which of the following are member functions of the `istream` class?

  a. `>>`

  b. `ignore`

  c. `get`

d. getline

e. cin

21. The open function is a member of both the ifstream and the ofstream classes. True or false?

Programming Warm-Up Exercises

1. Write a C++ input statement that reads three integer values into variables int1, int2, and int3, in that order.

2. Write a prompting output statement and then an input statement that reads a name into three string variables: first, middle, and last. The name is to be entered in the format: first middle last.

3. Write a prompting output statement and then an input statement that reads a name into a single string variable, name. The name is to be entered on one line, in the format: first middle last.

4. Write the statements necessary to prompt for and input three floating point values, and then output their average. For this exercise, assume that the user has no prior experience with computers and thus needs very detailed instructions. To help avoid errors, the user should enter each value separately.

5. Write the statements necessary to prompt for and input three floating point values, and then output their average. For this exercise, assume that the user has plenty of experience with computers and thus needs minimal instructions. The user should enter all three values on one line.

6. Write the declarations and input statements necessary to read each of the following sets of data values into variables of the appropriate types. You choose the names of the variables. In some cases, there are punctuation marks or special symbols that must be skipped.

a. 100 A 98.6

b. February 23 March 19

c. 19, 25, 103.876

d. A a B b

e. $56.45

7. Write a single input statement that reads the following lines of data into the variables streetNum, street1, street2, town, state, and zip.

782 Maple Avenue
Blithe, CO 56103

8. Write the statements necessary to prepare a file called "temperatures.dat" for reading as an ifstream called temps.

9. The file "temperatures.dat" contains a list of six temperatures, arranged one per line. Assuming that the file has already been prepared for reading, as described in Exercise 8, write the statements to read in the data from the file and print out the average temperature. You will also need to declare the necessary float variables to accomplish this task.

10. Fill in the blanks in the following program:

```
#include <iostream>
#include _____

using namespace std;

_____ inData;
_____ outData;
const float PI = 3.14159265;
float radius;
float circumference;
float area;

int main()
{
        _____("indata.dat");
        _____("outdata.dat");
        _____ >> radius;
    circumference = radius * 2 * PI;
    area = radius * radius * PI;
    cout << "For the first circle, the circumference is "
        << circumference << " and the area is " << area << endl;
        _____ << radius << " " << circumference << " " << area
            << endl;
        _____ >> radius;
    circumference = radius * 2 * PI;
    area = radius * radius * PI;
    cout << "For the second circle, the circumference is "
        << circumference << " and the area is " << area << endl;
        _____ << radius << " " << circumference << " " << area
            << endl;
    return 0;
}
```

11. Modify the program in Exercise 10 so that it allows the user to enter the name of the output file instead of having the program use "outdata.dat".

12. The file stream inFile contains two integer values. Write an input statement that will cause it to enter the fail state.

13. Write a code segment that prompts the user for a file name, reads the file name into a string called filename, and then opens the file stream userFile using the supplied name.

14. Use functional decomposition to write an algorithm for writing and mailing a business letter.

15. What are the objects in the problem described in Exercise 14?

Programming Problems

1. Write an interactive C++ program that inputs a name from the user in the format of:

```
last, first middle
```

The program then should output the name in the format of:

```
first middle last
```

The program will have to use string operations to remove the comma from the end of the last name. Be sure to use proper formatting and appropriate comments in your code. The input should have an appropriate prompt, and the output should be labeled clearly and formatted neatly.

2. Write an interactive C++ program that inputs a series of 12 temperatures from the user. It should write out on file "tempdata.dat" each temperature and the difference between the current temperature and the one preceding it. The difference is not output for the first temperature that is input. At the end of the program, the average temperature should be displayed for the user via cout. For example, given the following input data:

```
34.5 38.6 42.4 46.8 51.3 63.1 60.2 55.9 60.3 56.7 50.3 42.2
```

File tempdata.dat would contain:

```
34.5
38.6    4.1
42.4    3.8
46.8    4.4
51.3    4.5
63.1    11.8
60.2    -2.9
55.9    -4.3
60.3    4.4
56.7    -3.6
50.3    -6.4
42.2    -8.1
```

Be sure to use proper formatting and appropriate comments in your code. The input should have appropriate prompts, and the output should be labeled clearly and formatted neatly.

3. Write an interactive C++ program that computes and outputs the mean and standard deviation of a set of four integer values that are input by the user. (If you did Programming Problem 2 in Chapter 3, then you can reuse much of that

code here.) The mean is the sum of the four values divided by 4, and the formula for the standard deviation is

$$s = \sqrt{\frac{\sum_{i=1}^{n}(x_i - \bar{x})^2}{n-1}}$$

where $n = 4$, x_i refers to each of the four values, and $\bar{x}$ is the mean. Note that although the individual values are integers, the results are floating-point values. Be sure to use proper formatting and appropriate comments in your code. Provide appropriate prompts to the user. The output should be labeled clearly and formatted neatly.

4. Write a C++ program that reads data from a file whose name is input by the user, and that outputs the first word following each of the first three commas in the file. For example, if the file contains the text of this problem, then the program would output:

```
and
if
then
```

Assume that a comma appears within at least every 200 characters in the file. Be sure to use proper formatting and appropriate comments in your code. Provide appropriate prompts to the user. The output should be labeled clearly and formatted neatly.

5. Write a C++ program that allows the user to enter the percentage of the moon's face that appears illuminated, and that outputs the surface area of that portion of the moon. The formula for the surface area of a segment of a sphere is

$$S = 2R^2\theta$$

where R is the radius of the sphere (the moon's radius is 1738.3 km), and θ is the angle of the wedge in radians. There are 2π radians in a circle, so the hemisphere of the moon that we see accounts for at most π radians. Thus, if the user enters 100% (full moon), the angle of the wedge is π and the formula can be evaluated as follows.

$$S = 2 \times 1738.3^2 \times 3.14159 = 18985818.672 \text{ square kilometers}$$

If the user enters 50% (first or last quarter), then the angle of the wedge is $\pi \times 0.5$, and so on. Be sure to use proper formatting and appropriate comments in your code. Provide appropriate prompts to the user. The output should be labeled clearly and formatted neatly (limit the decimal precision to three places as in the example above).

Programming Example Follow-Up

1. Replace Clara Jones Jacobey's information with your own name as input to the Format Names program.
2. Change this program so that the social security number is written on a line by itself with the various name formats indented five spaces on the next four lines.
3. Change the program so that the name of the input file is read from the keyboard.
4. Change the program so that the names of both the input file and the output file are read from the keyboard.
5. In Chapter 3, the example program was a mortgage payment calculator where the data were stored as constants. Rewrite that program so that the information is input from the keyboard.

Conditions, Logical Expressions, and Selection Control Structures

Knowledge Goals

- To understand how the Boolean operators work.
- To understand the flow of control in a branching statement.
- To understand the flow of control in a nested branching statement.
- To know what preconditions and postconditions are.

Skill Goals

To be able to:

- Construct a simple logical (Boolean) expression to evaluate a given condition.
- Construct a complex logical expression to evaluate a given condition.
- Construct an If-Then-Else statement to perform a specific task.
- Construct an If-Then statement to perform a specific task.
- Construct a set of nested If statements to perform a specific task.
- Trace the execution of a C++ program.
- Test and debug a C++ program.

So far, the statements in our programs have been executed in their physical order. But what if we want the computer to execute the statements in some other order? Suppose we want to check the validity of input data and then perform a calculation *or* print an error message, not both. To do so, we must be able to ask a question and then, based on the answer, choose one or another course of action.

The If statement allows us to execute statements in an order that is different from their physical order. We can ask a question with it and do one thing if the answer is yes (true) or another if the answer is no (false). In the first part of this chapter, we deal with asking questions; in the second part, we deal with the If statement itself.

5.1 Flow of Control

The order in which statements are executed in a program is called the flow of control. In a sense, the computer is under the control of one statement at a time. When a statement has been executed, control is turned over to the next statement (like a baton being passed in a relay race).

Flow of control is normally sequential (see Figure 5–1). That is, when one statement is finished executing, control passes to the next statement in the program. When we want the flow of control to be nonsequential, we use control structures, special statements that transfer control to a statement other than the one that physically comes next. Control structures are so important that we focus on them in the remainder of this chapter and in the next four chapters.

> **Flow of control** The order in which the computer executes statements in a program.
>
> **Control structure** A statement used to alter the normally sequential flow of control.

Figure 5–1 *Sequential Control*

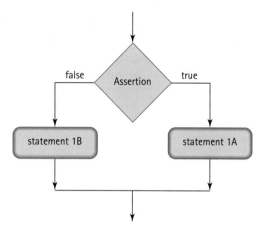

Figure 5-2   *Selection (Branching) Control Structure*

Selection

We use a selection (or branching) control structure when we want the computer to choose between alternative actions. We make an assertion, a claim that is either true or false. If the assertion is true, the computer executes one statement. If it is false, it executes another (see Figure 5–2).

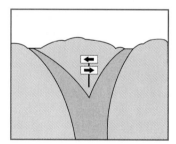

Suppose the computer must decide whether a year is a leap year. It does this by testing the assertion that the year is not divisible by 4. If the assertion is true, the computer follows the instructions to indicate that the year is not a leap year. If the assertion is false, the computer goes on to check the exceptions to the general rule. Before we examine selection control structures in C++, let's look closely at how we get the computer to make decisions.

5.2   Conditions and Logical Expressions

To ask a question in C++, we state it as an assertion. If the assertion we make is true, the answer to the question is yes. If the statement is not true, the answer to the question is no. The computer *evaluates* the assertion, checking it against some internal condition (the values stored in certain variables, for instance) to see whether it is true or false.

The `bool` Data Type

In C++, the `bool` data type is a built-in type consisting of just two values, the constants `true` and `false`. The reserved word `bool` is short for Boolean (pronounced 'BOOL-e-un).* Boolean data is used for testing conditions in a program so that the computer can make decisions (with a selection control structure).

We declare variables of type `bool` the same way we declare variables of other types, that is, by writing the name of the data type and then an identifier:

```
bool dataOK;     // True if the input data is valid
bool done;       // True if the process is done
bool taxable;    // True if the item has sales tax
```

Each variable of type `bool` can contain one of two values: `true` or `false`. It's important to understand right from the beginning that `true` and `false` are not variable names and they are not strings. They are special constants in C++ and, in fact, are reserved words.

Logical Expressions

In programming languages, assertions take the form of *logical expressions* (also called *Boolean expressions*). Just as an arithmetic expression is made up of numeric values and operations, a logical expression is made up of logical values and operations. Every logical expression has one of two values: true or false.

Here are some examples of logical expressions:

- A Boolean variable or constant
- An expression followed by a relational operator followed by an expression
- A logical expression followed by a logical operator followed by a logical expression

Let's look at each of these in detail.

Boolean Variables and Constants As we have seen, a Boolean variable is a variable declared to be of type `bool`, and it can contain either the value `true` or the value `false`. For example, if `dataOK` is a Boolean variable, then

```
dataOK = true;
```

is a valid assignment statement.

---

*The word *Boolean* is a tribute to George Boole, a nineteenth-century English mathematician who described a system of logic using variables with just two values, True and False.

Relational Operators   Another way of assigning a value to a Boolean variable is to set it equal to the result of comparing two expressions with a *relational operator*. Relational operators test a relationship between two values.

Let's look at an example. In the following program fragment, lessThan is a Boolean variable and i and j are int variables:

```
cin >> i >> j;
lessThan = (i < j);   // Compare i and j with the "less than"
                      // relational operator, and assign the
                      // truth value to lessThan
```

By comparing two values, we assert that a relationship (like "less than") exists between them. If the relationship does exist, the assertion is true; if not, it is false. These are the relationships we can test for in C++:

Operator	Relationship Tested
==	Equal to
!=	Not equal to
>	Greater than
<	Less than
>=	Greater than or equal to
<=	Less than or equal to

An expression followed by a relational operator followed by an expression is called a *relational expression*. The result of a relational expression is of type bool. For example, if x is 5 and y is 10, the following expressions all have the value true:

```
x != y
y > x
x < y
y >= x
x <= y
```

If x is the character 'M' and y is 'R', the values of the expressions are still true because the relational operator <, used with letters, means "comes before in the alphabet," or, more properly, "comes before in the collating sequence of the character set." For example, in the widely used ASCII character set, all of the uppercase letters are in alphabetical order, as are the lowercase letters, but all of the uppercase letters come before the lowercase letters. So

```
'M' < 'R'
```

and

```
'm' < 'r'
```

have the value `true`, but

```
'm' < 'R'
```

has the value `false`.

Of course, we have to be careful about the data types of things we compare. The safest approach is to always compare `ints` with `ints`, `floats` with `floats`, `chars` with `chars`, and so on. If you mix data types in a comparison, implicit type coercion takes place just as in arithmetic expressions. If an `int` value and a `float` value are compared, the computer temporarily coerces the `int` value to its `float` equivalent before making the comparison. As with arithmetic expressions, it's wise to use explicit type casting to make your intentions known:

```
someFloat >= float(someInt)
```

If you compare a `bool` value with a numeric value (probably by mistake), the value `false` is temporarily coerced to the number 0, and `true` is coerced to 1. Therefore, if `boolVar` is a `bool` variable, the expression

```
boolVar < 5
```

yields `true` because 0 and 1 both are less than 5.

Until you learn more about the `char` type in Chapter 10, be careful to compare `char` values only with other `char` values. For example, the comparisons

```
'0' < '9'
```

and

```
0 < 9
```

are appropriate, but

```
'0' < 9
```

generates an implicit type coercion and a result that probably isn't what you expect.

We can use relational operators not only to compare variables or constants, but also to compare the values of arithmetic expressions. In the following table, we compare the results of adding 3 to x and multiplying y by 10 for different values of x and y.

Value of x	Value of y	Expression	Result
12	2	x + 3 <= y * 10	true
20	2	x + 3 <= y * 10	false
7	1	x + 3 != y * 10	false
17	2	x + 3 == y * 10	true
100	5	x + 3 > y * 10	true

Caution: It's easy to confuse the assignment operator (=) and the == relational operator. These two operators have very different effects in a program. Some people pronounce the relational operator as "equals-equals" to remind themselves of the difference.

Comparing Strings   The `string` class is designed such that you can compare strings using the relational operators. Syntactically, the operands of a relational operator can either be two `string` objects, as in

```
myString < yourString
```

or a `string` object and a C string:

```
myString >= "Johnson"
```

However, the operands cannot both be C strings.

Comparison of strings follows the collating sequence of the machine's character set (ASCII, for instance). When the computer tests a relationship between two strings, it begins with the first character of each, compares them according to the collating sequence, and if they are the same repeats the comparison with the next character in each string. The character-by-character test proceeds until either a mismatch is found or the final characters have been compared and are equal. If all their characters are equal, then the two strings are equal. If a mismatch is found, then the string with the character that comes before the other is the "lesser" string.

For example, given the statements

```
string word1;
string word2;

word1 = "Tremendous";
word2 = "Small";
```

the relational expressions in the following table have the indicated values.

Expression	Value	Reason
word1 == word2	false	They are unequal in the first character.
word1 > word2	true	'T' comes after 'S' in the collating sequence.
word1 < "Tremble"	false	Fifth characters don't match, and 'b' comes before 'e'.
word2 == "Small"	true	They are equal.
"cat" < "dog"	Unpredictable	The operands cannot both be C strings.*

*The expression is syntactically legal in C++ but results in a *pointer* comparison, not a string comparison.

In most cases, the ordering of strings corresponds to alphabetical ordering. But when strings have mixed-case letters, we can get nonalphabetical results. For example, in a phone book we expect to see Macauley before MacPherson, but the ASCII collating sequence places all uppercase letters before the lowercase letters, so the string "MacPherson" compares as less than "Macauley". To compare strings for strict alphabetical ordering, all the characters must be in the same case.

If two strings with different lengths are compared and the comparison is equal up to the end of the shorter string, then the shorter string compares as less than the longer string. For example, if word2 contains "Small", the expression

```
word2 < "Smaller"
```

yields true, because the strings are equal up to their fifth character position (the end of the string on the left), and the string on the right is longer.

Logical Operators   In mathematics, the *logical* (or *Boolean*) *operators* AND, OR, and NOT take logical expressions as operands. C++ uses special symbols for the logical operators: && (for AND), || (for OR), and ! (for NOT). By combining relational operators with logical operators, we can make more complex assertions. For example, suppose we want to determine whether a final score is greater than 90 *and* a midterm score is greater than 70. In C++, we would write the expression this way:

```
finalScore > 90 && midtermScore > 70
```

The AND operation (&&) requires both relationships to be true in order for the overall result to be true. If either or both of the relationships are false, the entire result is false.

The OR operation (||) takes two logical expressions and combines them. If *either* or *both* are true, the result is true. Both values must be false for the result to be false. Now we can determine whether the midterm grade is an A *or* the final grade is an A. If either the midterm grade or the final grade equals A, the assertion is true. In C++, we write the expression like this:

```
midtermGrade == 'A' || finalGrade == 'A'
```

The && and || operators always appear between two expressions; they are binary (two-operand) operators. The NOT operator (!) is a unary (one-operand) operator. It precedes a single logical expression and gives its opposite as the result. If (grade == 'A') is false, then !(grade == 'A') is true. NOT gives us a convenient way of reversing the meaning of an assertion. For example,

```
!(hours > 40)
```

is the equivalent of

```
hours <= 40
```

In some contexts, the first form is clearer; in others, the second makes more sense.

The following pairs of expressions are equivalent:

Expression	Equivalent Expression
`!(a == b)`	`a != b`
`!(a == b || a == c)`	`a != b && a != c`
`!(a == b && c > d)`	`a != b || c <= d`

Take a close look at these expressions to be sure you understand why they are equivalent. Try evaluating them with some values for a, b, c, and d. Notice the pattern: The expression on the left is just the one to its right with ! added and the relational and logical operators reversed (for example, == instead of != and || instead of &&). Remember this pattern. It allows you to rewrite expressions in the simplest form.*

Logical operators can be applied to the results of comparisons. They also can be applied directly to variables of type bool. For example, instead of writing

```
isElector = (age >= 18 && district == 23);
```

to assign a value to the Boolean variable isElector, we could use two intermediate Boolean variables, isVoter and isConstituent:

```
isVoter = (age >= 18);
isConstituent = (district == 23);
isElector = isVoter && isConstituent;
```

The two tables below summarize the results of applying && and || to a pair of logical expressions (represented here by Boolean variables x and y).

Value of x	Value of y	Value of x && y
true	true	true
true	false	false
false	true	false
false	false	false

Value of x	Value of y	Value of x || y
true	true	true
true	false	true
false	true	true
false	false	false

---

*In Boolean algebra, the pattern is formalized by a theorem called *DeMorgan's law.*

The following table summarizes the results of applying the ! operator to a logical expression (represented by Boolean variable x).

Value of x	Value of !x
true	false
false	true

Technically, the C++ operators !, &&, and || are not required to have logical expressions as operands. Their operands can be of any simple data type, even floating-point types. Throughout this text we apply the logical operators *only* to logical expressions, not to arithmetic expressions.

Caution: It's easy to confuse the logical operators && and || with two other C++ operators, & and |. We don't discuss the & and | operators here, but we'll tell you that they are used for manipulating individual bits within a memory cell—a role quite different from that of the logical operators. If you accidentally use & instead of &&, or | instead of ||, you won't get an error message from the compiler, but your program probably will compute wrong answers. Some programmers pronounce && as "and-and" and || as "or-or" to avoid making mistakes.

Short-Circuit Evaluation   Consider the logical expression

```
i == 1 && j > 2
```

C++ uses short-circuit (or conditional) evaluation of logical expressions. Evaluation proceeds from left to right, and the computer stops evaluating subexpressions as soon as possible—that is, as soon as it knows the value of the entire expression. How can the computer know if a lengthy logical expression yields true or false if it doesn't examine all the subexpressions? Let's look first at the AND operation.

Short-circuit (conditional) evaluation   Evaluation of a logical expression in left-to-right order with evaluation stopping as soon as the final truth value can be determined.

An AND operation yields the value true only if both of its operands are true. In the expression above, suppose that the value of i happens to be 95. The first subexpression yields false, so it isn't necessary even to look at the second subexpression. The computer stops evaluation and produces the final result of false.

With the OR operation, the left-to-right evaluation stops as soon as a subexpression yielding true is found. Remember that an OR produces a result of true if either one or both of its operands are true. Given this expression:

```
c <= d || e == f
```

if the first subexpression is `true`, evaluation stops and the entire result is `true`. The computer doesn't waste time with an unnecessary evaluation of the second subexpression.

Precedence of Operators

In Chapter 3, we discussed the rules of precedence, the rules that govern the evaluation of complex arithmetic expressions. C++'s rules of precedence also govern relational and logical operators. Here's a list showing the order of precedence for the arithmetic, relational, and logical operators (with the assignment operator thrown in as well):

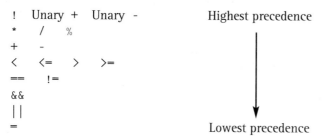

`!` Unary `+` Unary `-`	Highest precedence
`*` `/` `%`	
`+` `-`	
`<` `<=` `>` `>=`	
`==` `!=`	
`&&`	
`||`	
`=`	Lowest precedence

Operators on the same line in the list have the same precedence. If an expression contains several operators with the same precedence, most of the operators group (or *associate*) from left to right. For example, the expression

```
a / b * c
```

means (a / b) * c, not a / (b * c). However, the unary operators (!, unary +, unary -) group from right to left. Although you'd never have occasion to use this expression:

```
!!badData
```

the meaning of it is `!(!badData)` rather than the meaningless `(!!)badData`. Appendix B, "Precedence of Operators," lists the order of precedence for all operators in C++.

Parentheses are used to override the order of evaluation in an expression. If you're not sure whether parentheses are necessary, use them anyway. The compiler disregards unnecessary parentheses. So if they clarify an expression, use them.

One final comment about parentheses: C++, like other programming languages, requires that parentheses always be used in pairs. Whenever you write a complicated expression, take a minute to go through and pair up all of the opening parentheses with their closing counterparts.

Changing English Statements into Logical Expressions

In most cases, you can write a logical expression directly from an English statement or mathematical term in an algorithm. But you have to watch out for some tricky situations. Consider the logical expression:

```
midtermGrade == 'A' || finalGrade == 'A'
```

In English, you would be tempted to write this expression: "Midterm grade or final grade equals A." In C++, you can't write the expression as you would in English. That is,

```
midtermGrade || finalGrade == 'A'
```

won't work because the || operator is connecting a char value (midtermGrade) and a logical expression (finalGrade == 'A'). The two operands of || should be logical expressions.

Similarly "*i* equals either 3 or 4" must be written as

```
i == 3 || i == 4
```

In math books, you might see a notation like this:

$$12 < y < 24$$

which means "*y* is between 12 and 24." This expression is legal in C++ but gives an unexpected result. First, the relation $12 < y$ is evaluated, giving the result true or false. The computer then coerces this result to 1 or 0 in order to compare it with the number 24. Because both 1 and 0 are less than 24, the result is always true. To write this expression correctly in C++, you must write:

```
12 < y && y < 24
```

Relational Operators with Floating-Point Types

So far, we've talked only about comparing int, char, and string values. Here we look at float values.

Do not compare floating-point numbers for equality. Because small errors in the rightmost decimal places are likely to arise when calculations are performed on floating-point numbers, two float values rarely are exactly equal. For example, consider the following code that uses two float variables named oneThird and x:

```
oneThird = 1.0 / 3.0;
x = oneThird + oneThird + oneThird;
```

We would expect x to contain the value 1.0, but it probably doesn't. The first assignment statement stores an *approximation* of 1/3 into oneThird, perhaps 0.333333. The second statement stores a value like 0.999999 into x. If we now ask the computer to compare x with 1.0, the comparison yields false.

Instead of testing floating-point numbers for equality, we test for *near* equality. To do so, we compute the difference between the two numbers and test to see if the result is less than some maximum allowable difference. For example, we often use comparisons like this:

```
fabs(r - s) < 0.00001
```

where fabs is the floating-point absolute value function from the C++ standard library. The expression fabs(r - s) computes the absolute value of the difference between two float variables r and s. If the difference is less than 0.00001, the two numbers are close enough to call them equal. We discuss this problem with floating-point accuracy in more detail in Chapter 10.

5.3 The If Statement

Now that we've seen how to write logical expressions, let's use them to alter the normal flow of control in a program. The *If statement* is the fundamental control structure that allows branches in the flow of control. With it, we can ask a question and choose a course of action: *If* a certain condition exists, *then* perform one action, *else* perform a different action.

The If-Then-Else Form

In C++, the If statement comes in two forms: the *If-Then-Else* form and the *If-Then* form. Let's look first at the If-Then-Else. Here is its syntax template:

IfStatement (the If-Then-Else form)

```
if   ( Expression )
        Statement1A
else
        Statement1B
```

The expression in parentheses can be of any simple data type. Almost without exception, this will be a logical (Boolean) expression; if not, its value is implicitly coerced to type bool. At run time, the computer evaluates the expression. If the value is true, the computer executes Statement1A. If the value of the expression is false, Statement1B is executed. Statement1A often is called the *then-clause;* Statement1B, the *else-clause.*

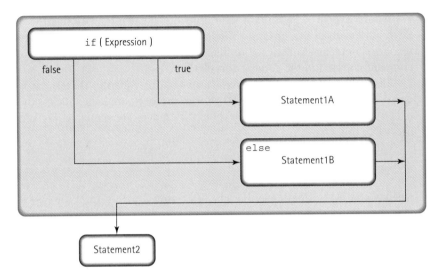

Figure 5–3   *If-Then-Else Flow of Control*

Figure 5–3 illustrates the flow of control of the If-Then-Else. In the figure, Statement2 is the next statement in the program after the entire If statement.

Notice that a C++ If statement uses the reserved words `if` and `else` but does not include the word *then*. Still, we use the term *If-Then-Else* because it corresponds to how we say things in English: "*If* something is true, *then* do this, *else* do that."

The code fragment below shows how to write an If statement in a program. Observe the indentation of the then-clause and the else-clause, which makes the statement easier to read. And notice the placement of the statement following the If statement.

```
if (hours <= 40.0)
    pay = rate * hours;
else
    pay = rate * (40.0 + (hours - 40.0) * 1.5);
cout << pay;
```

In terms of instructions to the computer, the above code fragment says, "If `hours` is less than or equal to 40.0, compute the regular pay and then go on to execute the output statement. But if `hours` is greater than 40, compute the regular pay and the overtime pay, and then go on to execute the output statement." Figure 5–4 shows the flow of control of this If statement.

If-Then-Else often is used to check the validity of input. For example, before we ask the computer to divide by a data value, we should be sure that the value is not zero. (Even computers can't divide something by zero. If you try, most computers halt the

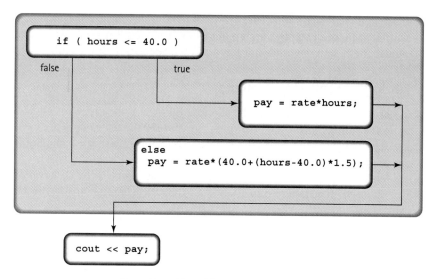

Figure 5–4 *Flow of Control for Calculating Pay*

execution of your program.) If the divisor is zero, our program should print out an error message. Here's the code:

```
if (divisor != 0)
    result = dividend / divisor;
else
    cout << "Division by zero is not allowed." << endl;
```

As another example of an If-Then-Else, suppose we want to determine where in a string variable the first occurrence (if any) of the letter *A* is located. The following code outputs the result of the search:

```
string myString;
string::size_type pos;
        ⋮
pos = myString.find('A');
if (pos == string::npos)
    cout << "No 'A' was found" << endl;
else
    cout << "An 'A' was found in position " << pos << endl;
```

Before we look any further at If statements, take another look at the syntax template for the If-Then-Else. According to the template, there is no semicolon at the end of an If statement. In all of the program fragments above—the worker's pay, division-by-zero, and string search examples—there seems to be a semicolon at the end of each If statement. However, the semicolons belong to the statements in the else-clauses in those examples; assignment statements end in semicolons, as do output statements. The If statement doesn't have its own semicolon at the end.

Blocks (Compound Statements)

In our division-by-zero example, suppose that when the divisor is equal to zero we want to do *two* things: print the error message *and* set the variable named `result` equal to a special value like 9999. We would need two statements in the same branch, but the syntax template seems to limit us to one.

What we really want to do is turn the else-clause into a *sequence* of statements. This is easy. Remember from Chapter 2 that the compiler treats the block (compound statement)

```
{
    ⋮
}
```

like a single statement. If you put a { } pair around the sequence of statements you want in a branch of the If statement, the sequence of statements becomes a single block. For example:

```
if (divisor != 0)
    result = dividend / divisor;
else
{
    cout << "Division by zero is not allowed." << endl;
    result = 9999;
}
```

If the value of `divisor` is 0, the computer both prints the error message and sets the value of `result` to 9999 before continuing with whatever statement follows the If statement.

Blocks can be used in both branches of an If-Then-Else. For example:

```
if (divisor != 0)
{
    result = dividend / divisor;
    cout << "Division performed." << endl;
}
else
{
    cout << "Division by zero is not allowed." << endl;
    result = 9999;
}
```

When you use blocks in an If statement, there's a rule of C++ syntax to remember: *Never use a semicolon after the right brace of a block.* Semicolons are used only to terminate simple statements such as assignment statements, input statements, and output statements. If you look at the examples above, you won't see a semicolon after the right brace that signals the end of each block.

The If-Then Form

Sometimes you run into a situation where you want to say, "*If* a certain condition exists, *then* perform some action; otherwise, don't do anything." In other words, you want the computer to skip a sequence of instructions if a certain condition isn't met. You could do this by leaving the `else` branch empty, using only the null statement:

```
if (a <= b)
    c = 20;
else
    ;
```

Better yet, you can simply leave off the `else` part. The resulting statement is the If-Then form of the If statement. This is its syntax template:

IfStatement (the If-Then form)

```
if    ( Expression )
         Statement
```

Here's an example of an If-Then. Notice the indentation and the placement of the statement that follows the If-Then.

```
if (age < 18)
    cout << "Not an eligible ";
cout << "voter." << endl;
```

This statement means that if `age` is less than 18, first print "Not an eligible " and then print "voter." If `age` is not less than 18, skip the first output statement and go directly to print "voter."

Like the two branches in an If-Then-Else, the one branch in an If-Then can be a block. For example, let's say you are writing a program to compute income taxes. One of the lines on the tax form reads "Subtract line 23 from line 17 and enter result on line

24; if result is less than zero, enter zero and check box 24A." You can use an If-Then to do this in C++:

```
result = line17 - line23;
if (result < 0.0)
{
    cout << "Check box 24A" << endl;
    result = 0.0;
}
line24 = result;
```

This code does exactly what the tax form says it should. It computes the result of subtracting line 23 from line 17. Then it looks to see if `result` is less than 0. If it is, the fragment prints a message telling the user to check box 24A and then sets `result` to 0. Finally, the calculated result (or 0, if the result is less than 0) is stored into a variable named `line24`.

What happens if we leave out the left and right braces in the code fragment above? Let's look at it:

```
result = line17 - line23;          // Incorrect version
if (result < 0.0)
    cout << "Check box 24A" << endl;
    result = 0.0;
line24 = result;
```

Despite the way we have indented the code, the compiler takes the then-clause to be a single statement—the output statement. If `result` is less than 0, the computer executes the output statement, then sets `result` to 0, and then stores `result` into `line24`. So far, so good. But if `result` is initially greater than or equal to 0, the computer skips the then-clause and proceeds to the statement following the If statement—the assignment statement that sets `result` to 0. The unhappy outcome is that `result` ends up as 0 no matter what its initial value was! The moral here is not to rely on indentation alone; you can't fool the compiler. If you want a compound statement for a then- or else-clause, you must include the left and right braces.

A Common Mistake

Earlier we warned against confusing the = operator and the == operator. Here is an example of a mistake that every C++ programmer is guaranteed to make at least once in his or her career:

```
cin >> n;
if (n = 3)                         // Wrong
    cout << "n equals 3";
else
    cout << "n doesn't equal 3";
```

This code segment *always* prints out

```
n equals 3
```

no matter what was input for n.

Here is the reason: We've used the wrong operator in the If test. The expression n = 3 is not a logical expression; it's called an *assignment expression.* (If an assignment is written as a separate statement ending with a semicolon, it's an assignment *statement.*) An assignment expression has a *value* (above, it's 3) and a *side effect* (storing 3 into n). In the If statement of our example, the computer finds the value of the tested expression to be 3. Because 3 is a nonzero value and thus is coerced to true, the then-clause is executed, no matter what the value of n is. Worse yet, the side effect of the assignment expression is to store 3 into n, destroying what was there.

Our intention is not to focus on assignment expressions; we discuss their use later in the book. What's important now is that you see the effect of using = when you meant to use ==. The program compiles correctly but runs incorrectly. When debugging a faulty program, always look at your If statements to see whether you've made this particular mistake.

5.4 Nested If Statements

There are no restrictions on what the statements in an If can be. Therefore, an If within an If is OK. In fact, an If within an If within an If is legal. The only limitation here is that people cannot follow a structure that is too involved, and readability is one of the marks of a good program.

When we place an If within an If, we are creating a *nested control structure.* Control structures nest much like mixing bowls do, with smaller ones tucked inside larger ones. Here's an example, written in pseudocode:

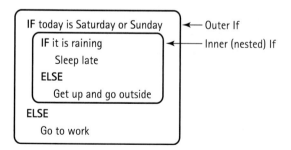

In general, any problem that involves a *multiway branch* (more than two alternative courses of action) can be coded using nested If statements. For example, to print out the name of a month given its number, we could use a sequence of If statements (unnested):

```
if (month == 1)
    cout << "January";
```

```
if (month == 2)
    cout << "February";
if (month == 3)
    cout << "March";
  ⋮
if (month == 12)
    cout << "December";
```

But the equivalent nested If structure,

```
if (month == 1)
    cout << "January";
else
    if (month == 2)              // Nested If
        cout << "February";
    else
        if (month == 3)              // Nested If
            cout << "March";
        else
            if (month == 4)              // Nested If
              ⋮
```

is more efficient because it makes fewer comparisons. The first version—the sequence of independent If statements—always tests every condition (all 12 of them), even if the first one is satisfied. In contrast, the nested If solution skips all remaining comparisons after one alternative has been selected.

In the last example, notice how the indentation of the then- and else-clauses causes the statements to move continually to the right. Instead, we can use a special indentation style with deeply nested If-Then-Else statements to indicate that the complex structure is just choosing one of a set of alternatives. This general multiway branch is known as an *If-Then-Else-If* control structure:

```
if (month == 1)
    cout << "January";
else if (month == 2)              // Nested If
    cout << "February";
else if (month == 3)              // Nested If
    cout << "March";
else if (month == 4)              // Nested If
    ⋮
else
    cout << "December";
```

This style prevents the indentation from marching continuously to the right. But, more important, it visually conveys the idea that we are using a 12-way branch based on the variable month.

It's important to note one difference between the sequence of If statements and the nested If: More than one alternative can be taken by the sequence of Ifs, but the nested If can select only one. To see why this is important, consider the analogy of filling out a questionnaire. Some questions are like a sequence of If statements, asking you to circle all the items in a list that apply to you (such as all your hobbies). Other questions ask you to circle only one item in a list (your age group, for example) and are thus like a nested If structure. Both kinds of questions occur in programming problems. Being able to recognize which type of question is being asked permits you to immediately select the appropriate control structure.

Another particularly helpful use of the nested If is when you want to select from a series of consecutive ranges of values. For example, suppose that we want to print out an appropriate activity for the outdoor temperature, given the following table.

Activity	Temperature
Swimming	Temperature > 85
Tennis	70 < temperature ≤ 85
Golf	32 < temperature ≤ 70
Skiing	0 < temperature ≤ 32
Dancing	Temperature ≤ 0

At first glance, you may be tempted to write a separate If statement for each range of temperatures. On closer examination, however, it is clear that these If conditions are interdependent. That is, if one of the statements is executed, none of the others should be executed. We really are selecting one alternative from a set of possibilities—just the sort of situation in which we can use a nested If structure as a multiway branch.

When the ranges are consecutive, we can take advantage of that fact to make our code more efficient. We arrange the branches in consecutive order by range. Then, if a particular branch has been reached, we know that the preceding ranges have been eliminated from consideration. Thus, the If expressions must compare the temperature to only the lowest value of each range. Look at the following Activity program.

```cpp
//*************************************************************************
// Activity program
// This program outputs an appropriate activity
// for a given temperature
//*************************************************************************
#include <iostream>

using namespace std;

int main()
{
```

```
    int temperature;      // The outside temperature

    // Read and echo temperature

    cout << "Enter the outside temperature:" << endl;
    cin >> temperature;
    cout << "The current temperature is " << temperature << endl;

    // Print activity

    cout << "The recommended activity is ";
    if (temperature > 85)
        cout << "swimming." << endl;
    else if (temperature > 70)
        cout << "tennis." << endl;
    else if (temperature > 32)
        cout << "golf." << endl;
    else if (temperature > 0)
        cout << "skiing." << endl;
    else
        cout << "dancing." << endl;

    return 0;
}
```

Note that if the ranges aren't consecutive, then we must test the data value against both the highest and lowest value of each range.

The Dangling else

When If statements are nested, you may find yourself confused about the `if-else` pairings. That is, to which `if` does an `else` belong? For example, suppose that if a student's average is below 60, we want to print "Failing"; if it is at least 60 but less than 70, we want to print "Passing but marginal"; and if it is 70 or greater, we don't want to print anything.

We code this information with an If-Then-Else nested within an If-Then:

```
if (average < 70.0)
    if (average < 60.0)
        cout << "Failing";
    else
        cout << "Passing but marginal";
```

How do we know to which `if` the `else` belongs? Here is the rule that the C++ compiler follows: In the absence of braces, an `else` is always paired with the closest preceding `if` that doesn't already have an `else` paired with it. We indented the code to reflect this pairing.

Suppose we write the fragment like this:

```
if (average >= 60.0)        // Incorrect version
    if (average < 70.0)
        cout << "Passing but marginal";
else
    cout << "Failing";
```

Here we want the `else` branch attached to the outer If statement, not the inner, so we indent the code as you see it. But indentation does not affect the execution of the code. Even though the `else` aligns with the first `if`, the compiler pairs it with the second `if`. An `else` that follows a nested If-Then is called a *dangling else*. It doesn't logically belong with the nested If but is attached to it by the compiler.

To attach the `else` to the first `if`, not the second, you can turn the outer then-clause into a block:

```
if (average >= 60.0)        // Correct version
{
    if (average < 70.0)
        cout << "Passing but marginal";
}
else
    cout << "Failing";
```

The { } pair indicates that the inner If statement is complete, so the `else` must belong to the outer `if`.

5.5   Testing the State of an I/O Stream

In Chapter 4, we talked about the concept of input and output streams in C++. We introduced the classes `istream`, `ostream`, `ifstream`, and `ofstream`. We said that any of the following can cause an input stream to enter the fail state:

- Invalid input data
- An attempt to read beyond the end of a file
- An attempt to open a nonexistent file for input

C++ provides a way to check whether a stream is in the fail state. In a logical expression, you simply use the name of the stream object (such as `cin`) as if it were a Boolean variable:

```
if (cin)
    ⋮

if ( !inFile )
    ⋮
```

> **Testing the state of a stream** The act of using a C++ stream object in a logical expression as if it were a Boolean variable; the result is `true` if the last I/O operation on that stream succeeded, and `false` otherwise.

When you do this, you are said to be **testing the state of the stream**. The result of the test is either `true` (meaning the last I/O operation on that stream succeeded) or `false` (meaning the last I/O operation failed).

Conceptually, you want to think of a stream object in a logical expression as being a Boolean variable with a value `true` (the stream state is OK) or `false` (the state isn't OK).

In an If statement, the way you phrase the logical expression depends on what you want the then-clause to do. The statement

```
if (inFile)
    ⋮
```

executes the then-clause if the last I/O operation on `inFile` succeeded. The statement

```
if ( !inFile )
    ⋮
```

executes the then-clause if `inFile` is in the fail state. (And remember that once a stream is in the fail state, it remains so. Any further I/O operations on that stream are null operations.)

Here's an example that shows how to check whether an input file was opened successfully:

```
//*****************************************************************
// StreamState program
// This program demonstrates testing the state of a stream
//*****************************************************************
#include <iostream>
#include <fstream>     // For file I/O

using namespace std;

int main()
{
    int      height;
    int      width;
    ifstream inFile;

    inFile.open("measures.dat");       // Attempt to open input file
    if ( !inFile )                     // Was it opened?
    {
        cout << "Can't open the input file.";  // No--print message
        return 1;                               // Terminate program
    }
```

```
        inFile >> height >> width;
        cout << "For a height of " << height << endl
             << "and a width of " << width << endl
             << "the area is " << height * width << endl;
        return 0;
}
```

In this program, we begin by attempting to open the disk file `measures.dat` for input. Immediately, we check to see whether the attempt succeeded. If it was successful, the value of the expression `!inFile` in the If statement is `false` and the then-clause is skipped. The program proceeds to read data from the file and then perform a computation. It concludes by executing the statement

```
return 0;
```

With this statement, the `main` function returns control to the computer's operating system. Recall that the function value returned by `main` is known as the exit status. The value 0 signifies normal completion of the program. Any other value (typically 1, 2, 3, ...) means that something went wrong.

Let's trace through the program again, assuming we weren't able to open the input file. Upon return from the `open` function, the stream `inFile` is in the fail state. In the If statement, the value of the expression `!inFile` is `true`. Thus, the then-clause is executed. The program prints an error message to the user and then terminates, returning an exit status of 1 to inform the operating system of an abnormal termination of the program. (Our choice of the value 1 for the exit status is purely arbitrary. System programmers sometimes use several different values in a program to signal different reasons for program termination. But most people just use the value 1.)

Whenever you open a data file for input, be sure to test the stream state before proceeding. If you forget to, and the computer cannot open the file, your program quietly continues executing and ignores any input operations on the file.

Programming Example

BMI Calculator

PROBLEM The Body Mass Index (BMI) computes a ratio of your weight and height, as a way to determine an appropriate weight. The formula for non-metric values is:

BMI = weight * 703 / height^2

Here is the most commonly used interpretation:

BMI	Interpretation
< 20	Underweight
20–25	Normal
26–30	Overweight
over 30	Obese

Write a program that calculates the BMI given a weight and height and prints out an appropriate message.

INPUT The input should be two `float` values: weight and height.

OUTPUT
Prompts for the input values
A message based on the BMI

DISCUSSION To calculate the BMI, you read in the weight and height and plug them into the formula. To square the height, just multiply height by itself.

BMI = weight * 703 / (height * height)

If you were calculating this by hand, you would probably notice if the weight or height were negative and question it. If the semantics of your data imply that the values should be nonnegative, then your program should test to be sure that they are. The program should test each value and use a Boolean variable to report the results. Here is the main module for this algorithm.

Main	Level 0

```
Get Data
Test data
IF data are OK
    Calculate BMI
    Print message indicating status
ELSE
    Print "Invalid data; weight and height must be positive."
```

Which of these steps require(s) expansion? *Get data*, *Test data*, and *Print message indicating status* all require multiple statements in order to solve their particular subproblem. On the other hand, we can translate *Print "Invalid Data: ..."* directly into a C++ output statement. What about the step *CalculateBMI*? We can write it as a single C++ statement, but there's another level of detail that we must fill in—the actual formula to be used. Because the formula is at a lower level of detail than the rest of the main module, we choose to expand *CalculateBMI* as a level 1 module.

Get Data	Level 1

```
Prompt for weight
Read weight
Prompt for height
Read height
```

Test Data

```
IF weight < 0 OR  height < 0
    Set dataAreOK to false
ELSE
    Set dataAreOK to true
```

Calculate BMI

```
Set bodyMassIndex to weight * 703 / (height * height)
```

Print Message Indicating Status

The problem doesn't say exactly what the message should be, other than reporting the status. Why not jazz up the output a little by printing an appropriate message along with the status.

Status	Message
Underweight	Have a milk shake.
Normal	Have a glass of milk.
Overweight	Have a glass of iced tea.
Obese	See your doctor.

```
Print "Your body mass index is ", bodyMassIndex,  '.'
Print "Interpretation and instructions."
IF bodyMassIndex <20
    Print "Underweight: Have a milk shake."
ELSE IF bodyMassIndex <= 25
    Print "Normal: Have a glass of milk."
ELSE IF bodyMassIndex <= 30
    Print "Overweight: Have a glass of iced tea."
ELSE
    Print "Obese: See your doctor."
```

Module Structure Chart

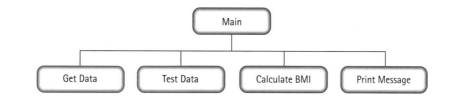

Constants

Name	Value	Function
BMI_CONSTANT	703	Formula constant

Variables

Name	Data Type	Description
weight	float	Weight in pounds
height	float	Height in inches
bodyMassIndex	float	Body mass index
dataAreOK	bool	Reports if data are ok

```cpp
//*****************************************************************
// BMI Program
// This program calculates the body mass index (BMI) given a weight
// in pounds and a height in inches and prints a health message
// based on the BMI. Input in English measures.
//*****************************************************************

#include <iostream>

using namespace std;

int main()
{
    const int BMI_CONSTANT = 703;     // Constant in non-metric formula
    float weight;                     // Weight in weight
    float height;                     // Height in height
    float bodyMassIndex;              // Appropriate BMI
    bool dataAreOK;                   // True if data are non-negative

    // Prompt for and input weight and height
    cout << "Enter your weight in pounds. " << endl;
    cin >> weight;
    cout << "Enter your height in inches. " << endl;
    cin >> height;
```

```
// Test Data
if (weight < 0 || height < 0)
    dataAreOK = false;
else
    dataAreOK = true;

if (dataAreOK)
{
    // Calculate body mass index

    bodyMassIndex = weight * BMI_CONSTANT / (height * height);

    // Print message indicating status

    cout << "Your body mass index is " << bodyMassIndex
        << ". " << endl;
    cout << "Interpretation and instructions. " << endl;
    if (bodyMassIndex < 20)
        cout << "Underweight: Have a milk shake." << endl;
    else if (bodyMassIndex <= 25)
        cout << "Normal: Have a glass of milk."  << endl;
    else if (bodyMassIndex <=  30)
        cout << "Overweight: Have a glass of iced tea."  << endl;
    else
        cout << "Obese: See your doctor." << endl;
}
else
    cout << "Invalid data; weight and height must be positive."
        << endl;
return 0;
}
```

Here are screen shots with both good and bad data.

```
C:\PPSC++\BMI\BMI.exe                                      _ □ x
Enter your weight in pounds.
124
Enter your height in inches.
63.5
Your body mass index is 21.6187.
Interpretation and instructions.
Normal: Have a glass of milk.
```

Testing and Debugging

In Chapter 1, we discussed the problem-solving and implementation phases of computer programming. Testing is an integral part of both phases. Here, we test both phases of the process used to develop the BMI program. Testing in the problem-solving phase is done after the solution is developed but before it is implemented. In the implementation phase, we test after the algorithm is translated into a program, and again after the program has compiled successfully. The compilation itself constitutes another stage of testing that is performed automatically.

Testing in the Problem-Solving Phase: The Algorithm Walk-Through

To test during the problem-solving phase, we do a *walk-through* of the algorithm. For each module in the functional decomposition, we establish an assertion called a precondition and another called a postcondition. A precondition is an assertion that must be true before a module is executed in order for the module to execute correctly. A postcondition is an assertion that should be true after the module has executed, if it has done its job correctly. To test a module, we "walk through" the algorithmic steps to confirm that they produce the required postcondition, given the stated precondition.

Precondition An assertion that must be true before a module begins executing.

Postcondition An assertion that should be true after a module has executed.

Our algorithm has five modules: the main module, Get Data, Test Data, Calculate BMI, and Print Message Indicating Status. Usually there is no precondition for a main module. Our main module's postcondition is that it outputs the correct results, given the correct input. More specifically, the postcondition for the main module is:

- The computer has input two real values into `weight` and `height`.
- If the input is invalid, an error message has been printed; otherwise, the body mass index has been calculated and an appropriate message has been printed based on the result.

Because Get Data is the first module executed in the algorithm and because it does not assume anything about the contents of the variables it is about to manipulate, it has no precondition. Its postcondition is that it has input two real values into `weight` and `height`.

The precondition for module Test Data is that `weight` and `height` have been assigned meaningful values. Its postcondition is that `dataAreOK` contains `true` if the values in `weight` and `height` are nonnegative; otherwise, `dataAreOK` contains `false`.

The precondition for module Calculate BMI is that `weight` and `height` contain meaningful values. Its postcondition is that the variable named `bodyMassIndex` contains the evaluation of the BMI formula (weight * 703 / (height * height)).

The precondition for module Print Message Indicating Status is that `bodyMassIndex` contains the result of evaluating the BMI formula. Its postcondition is that appropriate documentation and the value in `bodyMassIndex` have been printed, along with the messages: "Underweight: Have a milk shake." if the BMI value is less than 20; "Normal: Have a glass of milk." if the value is less than or equal to 25; "Overweight: Have a glass of ice tea." if the value is less than or equal to 30; and "Obese: See your doctor." if the value is greater than 30.

Below the module preconditions and postconditions are summarized in tabular form. In the table, we use *AND* with its usual meaning in an assertion—the logical AND operation. Also, a phrase like "`someVariable` is assigned" is an abbreviated way of asserting that `someVariable` has already been assigned a meaningful value.

Module	Precondition	Postcondition
Main	—	Two float values have been input AND if the input is valid, the BMI formula is calculated and the value is printed with an appropriate message; otherwise, an error message has been printed.
Get Data	—	`weight` and `height` have been input
Test Data	`weight` and `height` are assigned values	`dataAreOK` contains `true` if `weight` and `height` are nonnegative; otherwise, `dataAreOK` contains `false`.
Calculate BMI	`weight` and `height` are assigned values	`bodyMassIndex` contains the evaluation of the BMI formula.
Print Message Indicating Status	`bodyMassIndex` contains the evaluation of the BMI formula	The value of `bodyMassIndex` has been printed, along with a message interpreting the value.

Performing the Algorithm Walk-Through   Now that we've established the preconditions and postconditions, we walk through the main module. At this point, we are concerned only with the steps in the main module, so for now we assume that each lower-level module executes correctly. At each step, we must determine the current conditions. If the step is a reference to another module, we must verify that the precondition of that module is met by the current conditions.

We begin with the first statement in the main module. Get Data does not have a precondition, and we assume that Get Data satisfies its postcondition that it correctly inputs two real values into `weight` and `height`.

The precondition for module Test Data is that `weight` and `height` are assigned values. This must be the case if Get Data's postcondition is true. Again, because we are concerned only with the step at level 0, we assume that Test Data satisfies its postcondition that `dataAreOK` contains `true` or `false`, depending on the input values.

Next, the If statement checks to see if `dataAreOK` is `true`. If it is, the algorithm performs the then-clause. Assuming that Calculate BMI correctly evaluates the BMI formula and that Print Message Indicating Status prints the result and the appropriate message (remember, we're assuming that the lower-level modules are correct for now), then the If statement's then-clause is correct. If the value in `dataAreOK` is `false`, the algorithm performs the else-clause and prints an error message.

We now have verified that the main (level 0) module is correct, assuming the level 1 modules are correct. The next step is to examine each module at level 1 and answer this question: If the level 2 modules (if any) are assumed to be correct, does this level 1 module do what it is supposed to do? We simply repeat the walk-through process for each module, starting with its particular precondition. In this example, there are no level 2 modules, so the level 1 modules must be complete.

Get Data correctly reads in two values—`weight` and `height`—thereby satisfying its postcondition. (The next refinement is to code this instruction in C++. Whether it is coded correctly or not is *not* an issue in this phase; we deal with the code when we perform testing in the implementation phase.)

Test Data checks to see if both variables contain nonnegative values. The If condition correctly uses OR operators to combine the relational expressions so that if either of them are `true`, the then-clause is executed. It thus assigns `false` to `dataAreOK` if either of the numbers are negative; otherwise, it assigns `true`. The module therefore satisfies its postcondition.

Calculate BMI evaluates the BMI formula: weight * 703 / (height * height). The required postcondition therefore is true. But what if the value of height is 0? Oh, dear! We checked that the inputs are nonnegative, but forgot that height is used as a divisor and thus cannot be 0. We'll need to fix this problem before we release this program for general use.

Print Message Indicating Status outputs the value in `bodyMassIndex` with appropriate documentation. It then compares the result to the standards and prints the appropriate interpretation. "Underweight: Have a milk shake." is printed if the value is less than 20, "Normal: Have a glass of milk." if the value is less than or equal to 25, "Overweight: Have a glass of ice tea." if the value is less than or equal to 30, and "Obese: See your doctor." if the value is greater than 30. Thus, the module satisfies its postcondition.

Once we've completed the algorithm walk-through, we have to correct any discrepancies and repeat the process. When we know that the modules do what they are supposed to do, we start translating the algorithm into our programming language.

A standard postcondition for any program is that the user has been notified of invalid data. You should *validate* every input value for which any restrictions apply. A data-validation If statement tests an input value and outputs an error message if the value is not acceptable. (We validated the data when we tested for negative scores in the BMI program.) The best place to validate data is immediately after it is input. To satisfy the data-validation postcondition, the algorithm also should test the input values to ensure that they aren't too large or too small.

Testing in the Implementation Phase

Now that we've talked about testing in the problem-solving phase, we turn to testing in the implementation phase. In this phase, you need to test at several points.

Code Walk-Through   After the code is written, you should go over it line by line to be sure that you've faithfully reproduced the algorithm—a process known as a *code walk-through*. In a team programming situation, you ask other team members to walk through the algorithm and code with you, to double-check the design and code.

Execution Trace   You also should take some actual values and hand-calculate what the output should be by doing an *execution trace* (or *hand trace*). When the program is executed, you can use these same values as input and check the results.

The computer is a very literal device—it does exactly what we tell it to do, which may or may not be what we want it to do. We try to make sure that a program does what we want by tracing the execution of the statements.

We use a nonsense program below to demonstrate the technique. We keep track of the values of the program variables on the right-hand side. Variables with undefined values are indicated with a dash. When a variable is assigned a value, that value is listed in the appropriate column.

Statement	Value of		
	a	b	c
`const int x = 5;`			
`int main()`			
`{`			
`    int a, b, c;`	—	—	—
`    b = 1;`	—	1	—
`    c = x + b;`	—	1	6
`    a = x + 4;`	9	1	6
`    a = c;`	6	1	6
`    b = c;`	6	6	6
`    a = a + b + c;`	18	6	6
`    c = c % x;`	18	6	1
`    c = c * a;`	18	6	18
`    a = a % b;`	0	6	18
`    cout << a << b << c;`	0	6	18
`    return 0;`	0	6	18
`}`			

Now that you've seen how the technique works, let's apply it to the BMI program. We list only the executable statement portion here. The input values are 124 and 63.5.

The then-clause of the first If statement is not executed for these input data, so we do not fill in any of the variable columns to its right. The then-clause of the second If statement is executed, and thus, the else-clause is not. The else-clause of the third If statement is executed, which is another If statement. The then-clause is executed here, leaving the rest of the code unexecuted.

Statement	weight	height	BMI	dataIsOK
`cout << "Enter your weight in pounds. " << endl;`	—	—	—	—
`cin >> weight;`	124	—	—	—
`cout << "Enter your height in inches. " << endl;`	124	—	—	—
`cin >> height;`	124	63.5	—	—
`if (weight < 0 || height < 0)`	124	63.5	—	—
`    dataAreOK = false;`				
`else`				
`    dataAreOK = true;`	124	63.5	—	true
`if ( dataAreOK)`	124	63.5	—	true
`{`				
`    bodyMassIndex = weight * BMI_CONSTANT /`				
`        (height * height);`	124	63.5	21.087	true
`    cout << "Your body mass index is "`				
`        << bodyMassIndex << ". " << endl;`	124	63.5	21.087	true
`    cout << "Interpretation and instructions. "`				
`        << endl;`	124	63.5	21.087	true
`    if (bodyMassIndex < 20)`	124	63.5	21.087	true
`        cout <<"Underweight: Have a milk shake."`				
`            << endl;`				
`    else if (bodyMassIndex <= 25)`	124	63.5	21.087	true
`        cout << "Normal: Have a glass of milk."`				
`            << endl;`	124	63.5	21.087	true
`    else if (bodyMassIndex <= 30)`				
`        cout <<`				
`            "Overweight: Have a glass of ice tea."`				
`                << endl;`				
`    else`				
`        cout << "Obese: See your doctor."`				
`            << endl;`				
`}`				
`else`				
`    cout << "Invalid data; weight "`				
`        << "and height must be positive."`				
`        << endl;`				
`return 0;`	124	63.5	21.087	true

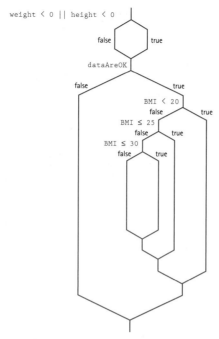

Figure 5–5   *Branching Structure for BMI Program*

When a program contains branches, it's a good idea to retrace its execution with different input data so that each branch is traced at least once. In the next section, we describe how to develop data sets that test each of a program's branches.

Testing Selection Control Structures   To test a program with branches, we need to execute each branch at least once and verify the results. For example, in the BMI program there are five If-Then-Else statements (see Figure 5–5). We need a series of data sets to test the different branches. For example, the following sets of input values for `weight` and `height` cause all of the branches to be executed:

Data Set	Weight in Pounds	Height in Inches	Status
1	110.0	67.5	Underweight
2	120.0	63.0	Normal
3	145.0	62.0	Overweight
4	176.6	60.0	Obese
5	-100	65.0	Error message

Figure 5–6 shows the flow of control through the branching structure of the BMI program for each of these data sets. Every branch in the program is executed at least

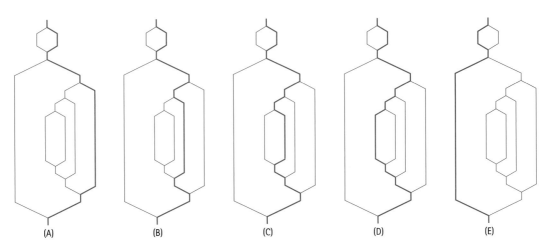

Figure 5–6   *Flow of Control Through BMI Program for Each of Five Data Sets*

once through this series of test runs; eliminating any of the test data sets would leave at least one branch untested. This series of data sets provides what is called *minimum complete coverage* of the program's branching structure.

The approach to testing that we've used here is called *code coverage* because the test data are designed by looking at the code of the program. Another approach to testing, *data coverage*, attempts to test as many allowable data values as possible without regard to the program code. Complete data coverage is as impractical as complete code coverage for many programs.

Often, testing is a combination of these two strategies. Instead of trying every possible data value (data coverage), we examine the code (code coverage) and look for ranges of values for which processing is identical. Then we test the values at the boundaries and, sometimes, a value in the middle of each range. For example, a simple condition such as

```
alpha < 0
```

divides the integers into two ranges:

1. `INT_MIN` through `-1`
2. `0` through `INT_MAX`

Thus, we should test the four values `INT_MIN`, `-1`, `0`, and `INT_MAX`. A compound condition such as

```
alpha >= 0 && alpha <= 100
```

divides the integers into three ranges:

1. `INT_MIN` through `-1`

2. 0 through 100

3. 101 through INT_MAX

Thus, we have six values to test. In addition, to verify that the relational operators are correct, we should test for values of 1 (> 0) and 99 (< 100).

Conditional branches are only one factor in developing a testing strategy. We consider more of these factors in later chapters.

Tests Performed Automatically During Compilation and Execution

Once a program is coded and test data has been prepared, it is ready for compiling. The compiler has two responsibilities: to report any errors and (if there are no errors) to translate the program into object code.

Errors can be syntactic or semantic. The compiler finds syntactic errors. For example, the compiler warns you when reserved words are misspelled, identifiers are undeclared, semicolons are missing, and operand types are mismatched. But it won't find all of your typing errors. If you type > instead of < , you won't get an error message; instead, you get erroneous results when you test the program. It's up to you to design a test plan and carefully check the code to detect errors of this type.

Semantic errors (also called *logic errors*) are mistakes that give you the wrong answer. They are more difficult to locate than syntactic errors and usually surface when a program is executing. C++ detects only the most obvious semantic errors—those that result in an invalid operation (dividing by zero, for example). Although semantic errors sometimes are caused by typing errors, they are more often a product of a faulty algorithm design. The lack of checking whether height is 0 that we found in the algorithm walk-through for the BMI problem is a typical semantic error.

By walking through the algorithm and the code, tracing the execution of the program, and developing a thorough test strategy, you should be able to avoid, or at least quickly locate, semantic errors in your programs.

Testing and Debugging Hints

1. C++ has three pairs of operators that are similar in appearance but very different in effect: == and =, && and &, and || and |. Double-check all of your logical expressions to be sure you're using the "equals-equals," "and-and," and "or-or" operators.

2. If you use extra parentheses for clarity, be sure that the opening and closing parentheses match up. To verify that parentheses are properly paired, start with the innermost pair and draw a line connecting them. Do the same for the others, working your way out to the outermost pair. For example,

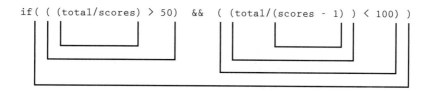

Here is a quick way to tell whether you have an equal number of opening and closing parentheses. The scheme uses a single number (the "magic number"), whose value initially is 0. Scan the expression from left to right. At each opening parenthesis, add 1 to the magic number; at each closing parenthesis, subtract 1. At the final closing parenthesis, the magic number should be 0. For example,

```
if (((total/scores) > 50) && ((total/(scores - 1)) < 100))
    0   123              2   1    23      4           32     10
```

3. Don't use =< to mean "less than or equal to"; only the symbol <= works. Likewise, => is invalid for "greater than or equal to"; you must use >= for this operation.

4. In an If statement, remember to use a { } pair if the then-clause or else-clause is a sequence of statements. And be sure not to put a semicolon after the right brace.

5. Echo print all input data. By doing so, you know that your input values are what they are supposed to be.

6. Test for bad data. If a data value must be positive, use an If statement to test the value. If the value is negative or 0, an error message should be printed; otherwise, processing should continue. For example, the following code segment tests whether three test scores are less than 0 or greater than 100.

```
dataOK = true;
if (test1 < 0 || test2 < 0 || test3 < 0)
{
    cout << "Invalid Data:  Score(s) less than zero." << endl;
    dataOK = false;
}
if (test1 > 100 || test2 > 100 || test3 > 100)
{
    cout << "Invalid Data:  Score(s) greater than 100." << endl;
    dataOK = false;
}
```

These If statements test the limits of reasonable scores, and the rest of the program continues only if the data values are reasonable.

7. Take some sample values and try them by hand as we did for the BMI program. (There's more on this method in Chapter 6.)

8. If your program reads data from an input file, it should verify that the file was opened successfully. Immediately after the call to the open function, an If statement should test the state of the file stream.

9. If your program produces an answer that does not agree with a value you've calculated by hand, try these suggestions:

a. Redo your arithmetic.

b. Recheck your input data.

c. Carefully go over the section of code that does the calculation. If you're in doubt about the order in which the operations are performed, insert clarifying parentheses.

d. Check for integer overflow. The value of an `int` variable may have exceeded `INT_MAX` in the middle of a calculation. Some systems give an error message when this happens, but most do not.

e. Check the conditions in branching statements to be sure that the correct branch is taken under all circumstances.

Summary

Using logical expressions is a way of asking questions while a program is running. The program evaluates each logical expression, producing the value `true` if the expression is true or the value `false` if the expression is not true.

The If statement allows you to take different paths through a program based on the value of a logical expression. The If-Then-Else is used to choose between two courses of action; the If-Then is used to choose whether or not to take a particular course of action. The branches of an If-Then or If-Then-Else can be any statement, simple or compound. They can even be other If statements.

The algorithm walk-through requires us to define a precondition and a postcondition for each module in an algorithm. Then we need to verify that those assertions are true at the beginning and end of each module. By testing our design in the problem-solving phase, we can eliminate errors that can be more difficult to detect in the implementation phase.

An execution trace is a way of finding program errors once we've entered the implementation phase. It's a good idea to trace a program before you run it, so that you have some sample results against which to check the program's output.

Quick Check

1. What are the two values that are the basis for Boolean logic? (p. 156)
2. What does a branch allow the computer to do? (pp. 154–155)
3. What purpose does a nested branch serve? (pp. 171–173)
4. What does a precondition of a module tell us? (pp. 182–183)
5. Write a Boolean expression that is true when the value of the variable `temperature` is greater than 32. (pp. 157–159)
6. Write a Boolean expression that is true when the value of variable `temperature` is in the range of 33 to 211 degrees, and the `bool` variable `fahrenheit` is true. (pp. 160–162)
7. Write an If-Then-Else statement that uses the test from question 5 to output either "`Above freezing.`" or "`Freezing or below.`" (pp. 166–168)
8. Write an If-Then statement that outputs "In range." when the Boolean expression in question 6 is true. (pp. 169–170)

9. Write nested If statements to print messages indicating whether a temperature is below freezing, freezing, above freezing but not boiling, or boiling and above. (pp. 171–174)
10. When tracing a program by hand we write out a table. What do we put in the columns of the table, and what do the rows represent? (pp. 185–186)
11. If a program never seems to take one branch of an If statement, how would you go about debugging it? (pp. 187–189)

Answers

1. True and false. 2. It allows the computer to choose between alternative courses of action, depending on a test of certain conditions. 3. It allows the computer to select among any number of alternative courses of action. 4. A precondition tells us precisely what conditions must exist upon entry to a module for the module to be able to execute correctly. 5. `temperature > 32`
6. `temperature > 32 && temperature < 212 && fahrenheit`
7.
```
if (temperature > 32)
    cout << "Above freezing.";
else
    cout << "Freezing or below.";
```
8.
```
if (temperature > 32 && temperature < 212 && fahrenheit)
    cout << "In range.";
```
9.
```
if (temperature < 32)
    cout << "Below freezing.";
else if (temperature == 32)
    cout << "Freezing.";
else if (temperature < 212)
    cout << "Above freezing and below boiling.";
else
    cout << "Boiling and above.";
```
10. The columns are the values of the variables, and the rows correspond to the result of executing each statement during the trace. 11. Try different inputs to be sure that there is a problem, then check that the conditional test is written correctly. Working backward from there, check to see that each variable in the test is correctly assigned a value. Verify that all of the preconditions of each related module are satisfied before it executes.

Exam Preparation Exercises

1. Define the term "flow of control."
2. The values `true` and `false` are keywords in C++. True or false?
3. The "equals or greater" operator in C++ is written =>. True or false?
4. Why is it that `'A' < 'B'` and `'a' < 'b'` are both `true`, but `'a' < 'B'` is `false`?
5. If `int1` has the value 12, `int2` has the value 18, and `int3` has the value 21, what is the result of each of the following Boolean expressions?
   a. `int1 < int2 && int2 < int3`
   b. `int1 < int3 || int3 < int2`
   c. `int1 <= int2 - 6`
   d. `int2 <= int1 + 5 || int3 >= int2 + 5`

   e. `!(int1 < 30)`

   f. `!(int2 == int1 && int3 == int1)`

   g. `!(int1 > 25) && !(int2 < 17)`

6. If `string1` has the value `"miniscule"`, `string2` has the value `"minimum"`, and `string3` has the value `"miniature"`, what is the result of each of the following expressions?

   a. `string1 > string2`

   b. `string1 > string2 && string2 > string3`

   c. `string1.substr(0, 4) == string2.substr(0, 4)`

   d. `string1 > "maximum"`

   e. `string3.substr(0, 4) == "mini" || string1 == string2`

   f. `string3.length() > string1.length() && string1 > string3`

   g. `!((string1.substr(8, 1) == string3.substr(8, 1)) &&`
      `string1.length() == 9)`

7. Why won't the following expression result in a division-by-zero error when `someInt` has the value 0?

```
someInt != 0 && 5/someInt > 10
```

8. The `bool` operators have lower precedence than the arithmetic operators, with the exception of the `!` operator, which has the same precedence as unary minus. True or false?

9. We enclose the logical expression in an If statement in parentheses only to make the code more readable. C++ doesn't require the parentheses. True or false?

10. What does the following If statement do when the value in `someInt` is 77?

```
if (someInt <= 44) || (someInt - 37 < 40)
    cout << "The data is within range.";
else
    cout << "The data doesn't make sense.";
```

11. What does the following If statement do when the value in `string1` is `"The"`?

```
if (string1.length() == 3 && string1.substr(0, 1) = "T")
    cout << "The word may be \"The\"";
else
{
    string1 = "The";
    cout << "The word is now \"The\"";
}
```

12. What does the following If statement do when the value in `float1` is `3.15`?

```
if (fabs(float1 - 3.14) < 0.00000001)
{
    cout << "The area of the circle of radius 6.0 is
            approximately:"
        << endl;
    cout << 6.0 * 6.0 * float1;
}
```

13. Why does the following If statement always output `"false"` regardless of the value in `someInt`?

```
if (someInt = 0)
    cout << "true";
else
    cout << "false";
```

14. What is output by the following code segment when `score` has the value 85?

```
if (score < 50)
    cout << "Failing";
else if (score < 60)
    cout << "Below average";
else if (score < 70)
    cout << "Average";
else if (score < 80)
    cout << "Above average";
else if (score < 90)
    cout << "Very good";
else if (score < 100)
    cout << "Excellent";
```

15. What is output by the following code segment when `score` has the value 85?

```
if (score < 50)
    cout << "Failing";
if (score < 60)
    cout << "Below average";
if (score < 70)
    cout << "Average";
if (score < 80)
    cout << "Above average";
if (score < 90)
    cout << "Very good";
if (score < 100)
    cout << "Excellent";
```

16. How do you fix a nested If statement that has a dangling else?
17. How would you write a Boolean expression in an If statement if you want the statement's Then branch to execute when file `inData` is in the fail state?
18. Is there any limit to how deeply we can nest If statements?

Programming Warm-Up Exercises

1. Write a Boolean expression that is true when the `bool` variable `moon` has the value "`blue`" or the value "`Blue`".

2. Write a Boolean expression that is true when both `inFile1` and `inFile2` are in the fail state.

3. Write a branching statement that reads into a string variable called `someString`, from a file called `inFile` if the file is not in the fail state.

4. Write a branching statement that tests whether one date comes before another. The dates are stored as integers representing the month, day, and year. The variables for the two dates are thus called `month1`, `day1`, `year1`, `month2`, `day2`, and `year2`. The statement should output an appropriate message depending on the outcome of the test. For example:

```
12/21/01 comes before 1/27/05
```

or

```
7/14/04 does not come before 7/14/04
```

5. Change the branching statement that you wrote for Exercise 4 so that when the first date doesn't come before the second, it sets the first date equal to the second date in addition to printing the message.

6. Write a Boolean expression that is `true` when either of the `bool` variables `bool1` or `bool2` is true, but is `false` whenever both of them are `true` or neither of them is `true`.

7. Write a branching statement that tests whether `score` is in the range of 0 to 100, and outputs an error message if it is not within that range.

8. Change the branching statement that you wrote for Exercise 7 so that when `score` is in the proper range, it adds `score` to a running total variable called `scoreTotal`, and increments a counter called `scoreCount`.

9. Write a code segment that reads an `int` value from each of two files, `infile1` and `infile2`, and if neither file is in the fail state, it writes the lesser value of the two to a file called `outfile`, and reads another value from the file that had the lesser value. If either of the files is in the fail state, then the value from the one that is not in the fail state is written to `outfile`. If both files are in the fail state, then an error message is output to `cout`. The `int` values can be input into variables `value1` and `value2`.

10. Change the following series of If-Then statements into a nested If-Else-If structure.

```
if (score > 100)
    cout << "Duffer.";
if (score <= 100 && score > 80)
    cout << "Weekend regular.";
if (score <= 80 && score > 72)
    cout << "Competitive player.";
if (score <= 72 && score > 68)
    cout << "Turn pro!";
if (score <= 68)
    cout << "Time to go on tour!";
```

11. Write an If structure that outputs the least of three values, count1, count2, and count3. If there is more than one variable with the lowest value, then output the value as many times as it is found in those variables.

12. The following program segment is not supposed to print anything, yet it outputs the first error message, "Error in maximum: 100". What's wrong, and how would you correct it? Why doesn't it output both error messages?

```
maximum = 75;
minimum = 25;
if (maximum = 100)
    cout << "Error in maximum: " << maximum << endl;
if (minimum = 0)
    cout << "Error in minimum: " << minimum << endl;
```

13. Write an If statement that takes the square root of the variable area only when its value is nonnegative. Otherwise the statement should set area equal to its absolute value and then take the square root of the new value. The result should be assigned to the variable root.

Programming Problems

1. Use functional decomposition to write a C++ program that inputs a letter and outputs the corresponding International Civil Aviation Organization alphabet word (these are the words that pilots use when they need to spell something out over a noisy radio channel). The alphabet is as follows:

A   Alpha
B   Bravo
C   Charlie
D   Delta
E   Echo
F   Foxtrot
G   Golf
H   Hotel
I   India
J   Juliet
K   Kilo
L   Lima
M   Mike
N   November
O   Oscar
P   Papa
Q   Quebec
R   Romeo
S   Sierra

T   Tango
U   Uniform
V   Victor
W   Whiskey
X   X-ray
Y   Yankee
Z   Zulu

Be sure to use proper formatting and appropriate comments in your code. Provide appropriate prompts to the user. The output should be labeled clearly and formatted neatly.

2. Use functional decomposition to write a C++ program that asks the user to enter their weight and the name of a planet. The program then outputs how much the user would weigh on that planet. The following table gives the factor by which the weight must be multiplied for each planet. The program should output an error message if the user doesn't type a correct planet name. The prompt and the error message should make it clear to the user how a planet name must be entered. Be sure to use proper formatting and appropriate comments in your code. The output should be clearly labeled and neatly formatted.

Mercury	0.4155
Venus	0.8975
Earth	1.0
Moon	0.166
Mars	0.3507
Jupiter	2.5374
Saturn	1.0677
Uranus	0.8947
Neptune	1.1794
Pluto	0.0899

3. Use functional decomposition to write a C++ program that takes a number in the range of 1 to 12 as input, and outputs the corresponding month of the year, where 1 is January, and so on. The program should output an error message if the number entered is not in the required range. The prompt and the error message should make it clear to the user how a month number must be entered. Be sure to use proper formatting and appropriate comments in your code. The output should be labeled clearly and formatted neatly.

4. Use functional decomposition to write a C++ program that takes a number in the range of 0 to 6 and a second number in the range of 1 to 366 as input. The first number represents the day of the week on which the year begins, where 0 is Sunday, and so on. The second number indicates the day of the year. The program then outputs the name of the day of the week corresponding to the day of the year. The number of the day of the week can be computed as follows:

(start day + day of year − 1) % 7

The program should output an error message if the numbers entered are not in the required ranges. The prompt and the error message should make it clear to the user how the numbers must be entered. Be sure to use proper formatting and appropriate comments in your code. The output should be labeled clearly and formatted neatly.

5. Use functional decomposition to write a C++ program that takes a number in the range of 1 to 365 as input. The number represents the day of the year. The program then outputs the name of the month (assume the year is not a leap year). You can do this by comparing the day of the year to the number of days in the year that precede the start of each month. For example, 59 days precede March, which has 31 days. So if the day of the year is in the range of 60 through 91, then your program would output March. The program should output an error message if the number entered is not in the required range. The prompt and the error message should make it clear to the user how the number must be entered. Be sure to use proper formatting and appropriate comments in your code. The output should be labeled clearly and formatted neatly.

6. Use functional decomposition to write a C++ program that takes as input three numbers representing the number of pins knocked down by a bowler in three throws. The rules of bowling are that if the first throw is a strike (all ten pins knocked down), then the score is equal to those 10 points plus the number knocked down in the next two throws. The maximum score (three strikes) is thus thirty. If the first throw knocks down fewer than ten pins, but the second throw knocks down the remainder of the ten pins (a spare), then the score is those 10 points plus the number of pins knocked down on the third throw. If the first two throws fail to knock down all of the pins (a blow), then the score is just the total number of pins knocked down in the first two throws. Your program should output the computed score, and also should check for erroneous input. For example, a throw may be in the range of 0 through 10 pins, and the total of the first two throws must be less than or equal to 10, except when the first throw is a strike. Be sure to use proper formatting and appropriate comments in your code. The output should be labeled clearly and formatted neatly, and the error messages should be informative.

7. Use functional decomposition to write a C++ program that computes a dance competition score. There are four judges who mark the dancers in the range of 0 to 10, and the overall score is the average of the three highest scores (the lowest score is excluded). Your program should output an error message, instead of the average, if any of the scores are not in the correct range. Be sure to use proper formatting and appropriate comments in your code. The output should be labeled clearly and formatted neatly, and the error message should indicate clearly which score was invalid.

8. Use functional decomposition to write a C++ program that determines the median of three input numbers. The median is the middle number when the three are arranged in order. However, the user can input the values in any order, so your program must determine which value is between the other two. For example, if the user enters:

```
41.52 27.18 96.03
```

then the program would output:

```
The median of 41.52, 27.18, and 96.03 is 41.52.
```

Once you have the three-number case working, extend the program to handle five numbers. Be sure to use proper formatting and appropriate comments in your code. The output should be labeled clearly and formatted neatly.

Programming Example Follow-Up

1. How might you go about choosing values for weight and height so that the BMI values of 20, 25, and 30 might be tested?
2. Change the program so that the BMI is rounded. Choose appropriate cases to test the end conditions. Implement your test plan.
3. Rewrite this program to take metric values for weight and height. Go on the Internet to find the correct formula.
4. Change the original program so that the height is entered in feet and inches. Prompt for and enter them separately.
5. A negative input value for weight or height was considered an error condition in the BMI program. Are there other values for weight or height that should be considered error conditions? Explain.

Looping

Knowledge Goals

- *To understand the flow of control in a loop.*
- *To understand the differences between count-controlled, event-controlled, and flag-controlled loops.*
- *To understand counting and summing operations within a loop.*
- *To know how to choose the correct type of loop for a given problem.*

Skill Goals

To be able to:

- *Construct syntactically correct While loops.*
- *Construct count-controlled, event-controlled, and flag-controlled loops using the While statement.*
- *Use the end-of-file condition to control the input of data.*
- *Construct counting and summing loops with a While statement.*
- *Construct nested While loops.*
- *Choose data sets that test a looping program comprehensively.*

In Chapter 5, we saw that the If statement is one way of making the order of execution of statements different from their physical order. Looping control structures are another. A **loop** executes the same statement (simple or compound) over and over, as long as a condition or set of conditions is satisfied.

In this chapter, we discuss different kinds of loops and how they are constructed using the While statement. We also discuss *nested loops* (loops that contain other loops).

> **Loop**   A control structure that causes a statement or group of statements to be executed repeatedly.

6.1 The While Statement

The While statement, like the If statement, tests a condition. Here is the syntax template for the While statement:

WhileStatement

```
while ( Expression )
    Statement
```

and this is an example of one:

```
while (inputVal != 25)
    cin >> inputVal;
```

The While statement is a looping control structure. The statement to be executed each time through the loop is called the *body* of the loop. In the example above, the body of the loop is the input statement that reads in a value for `inputVal`.

Just like the condition in an If statement, the condition in a While statement can be an expression of any simple data type. Nearly always, it is a logical (Boolean) expression; if not, its value is implicitly coerced to type `bool`. The While statement says, "If

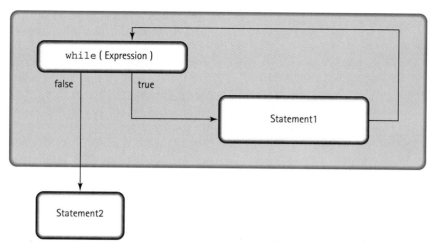

Figure 6–1   *While Statement Flow of Control*

the value of the expression is `true`, execute the body and then go back and test the expression again. If the expression's value is `false`, skip the body." The loop body is thus executed over and over as long as the expression is `true` when it is tested. When the expression is `false`, the program skips the body and execution continues at the statement immediately following the loop. Of course, if the expression is `false` to begin with, the body is not even executed. Figure 6–1 shows the flow of control of the While statement, where Statement1 is the body of the loop and Statement2 is the statement following the loop.

The body of a loop can be a compound statement (block), which allows us to execute any group of statements repeatedly. Most often we use While loops in the following form:

```
while (Expression)
{
    ⋮
}
```

In this structure, if the expression is `true`, the entire sequence of statements in the block is executed, and then the expression is checked again. If it is still `true`, the statements are executed again. The cycle continues until the expression becomes `false`.

6.2 Phases of Loop Execution

The body of a loop is executed in several phases:

- The moment that the flow of control reaches the first statement inside the loop body is the **loop entry**.

Loop entry   The point at which the flow of control reaches the first statement inside a loop.

Iteration   An individual pass through, or repetition of, the body of a loop.

Loop test   The point at which the While expression is evaluated and the decision is made either to begin a new iteration or skip to the statement immediately following the loop.

Loop exit   The point at which the repetition of the loop body ends and control passes to the first statement following the loop.

Termination condition   The condition that causes a loop to be exited.

- Each time the body of a loop is executed, a pass is made through the loop. This pass is called an **iteration**.
- Before each iteration, control is transferred to the **loop test** at the beginning of the loop.
- When the last iteration is complete and the flow of control has passed to the first statement following the loop, the program has **exited the loop**. The condition that causes a loop to be exited is the **termination condition**. In the case of a While loop, the termination condition is that the While expression becomes `false`.

Notice that the loop exit occurs only at one point: when the loop test is performed. Even though the termination condition may become satisfied midway through the execution of the loop, the current iteration is completed before the computer checks the While expression again.

The concept of looping is fundamental to programming. In this chapter, we spend some time looking at typical kinds of loops and ways of implementing them with the While statement. These looping situations come up again and again when you are analyzing problems and designing algorithms.

6.3 Loops Using the While Statement

Count-controlled loop   A loop that executes a specified number of times.

Event-controlled loop   A loop that terminates when something happens inside the loop body to signal that the loop should be exited.

In solving problems, you will come across two major types of loops: **count-controlled loops**, which repeat a specified number of times, and **event-controlled loops**, which repeat until something happens within the loop.

Count-Controlled Loops

A count-controlled loop uses a variable we call the *loop control variable* in the loop test. Before we enter a count-controlled loop, we have to *initialize* (set the initial value of) the loop control variable and then test it. Then, as part of each iteration of the loop, we must *increment* (increase by 1) the loop control variable. Here's an example in a program that repeatedly outputs "Hello!" on the screen:

```
//*******************************************************************
// Hello program
// This program demonstrates a count-controlled loop
//*******************************************************************
#include <iostream>

using namespace std;
```

```
int main()
{
    int loopCount;    // Loop control variable

    loopCount = 1;                    // Initialization
    while (loopCount <= 10)           // Test
    {
        cout << "Hello!" << endl;
        loopCount = loopCount ++;     // Incrementation
    }
    return 0;
}
```

In the Hello program, loopCount is the loop control variable. It is set to 1 before loop entry. The While statement tests the expression

```
loopCount <= 10
```

and executes the loop body as long as the expression is true. Inside the loop body, the main action we want to be repeated is the output statement. The last statement in the loop body increments loopCount by adding 1 to it. Variables that are used this way are called *counters*. In the Hello program, loopCount is incremented with each iteration of the loop—we use it to count the iterations. The loop control variable of a count-controlled loop is always a counter.

When designing loops, it is the programmer's responsibility to see that the condition to be tested is set correctly (initialized) before the While statement begins. The programmer also must make sure that the condition changes within the loop so that it eventually becomes false; otherwise, the loop is never exited.

A loop that never exits is called an *infinite loop* because, in theory, the loop executes forever. In the code above, omitting the incrementation of loopCount at the bottom of the loop leads to an infinite loop; the While expression is always true because the value of loopCount is forever 1. If your program goes on running for much longer than you expect it to, chances are that you've created an infinite loop. You may have to issue an operating system command to stop the program.

Event-Controlled Loops

There are several kinds of event-controlled loops. We look at two of the most common here: sentinel-controlled and end-of-file-controlled. In both of these loops, the termination condition depends on some event occurring while the loop body is executing.

Sentinel-Controlled Loops   Loops often are used to read in and process long lists of data. Each time the loop body is executed, a new piece of data is read and processed. Often a special data value, called a *sentinel* or *trailer value*, is used to signal the program that there is no more data to be processed. Looping continues as long as the data value read is *not* the sentinel; the loop stops when the program recognizes the sentinel. In other words, reading the sentinel value is the event that controls the looping process.

A sentinel value must be something that never shows up in the normal input to a program. For example, if a program reads calendar dates, we could use February 31 as a sentinel value:

```
cin >> month >> day;        // Get a date--priming read
while ( !(month == 2 && day == 31) )
{
    ⋮                                     // Process it
    cin >> month >> day;                  // Get the next date
}
```

This segment reads the first data set prior to entering the loop (we refer to this as a priming read); if it is not the sentinel, it gets processed. At the end of the loop, the next data set is read in, and we go back to the beginning of the loop. If the new data set is not the sentinel, it gets processed just like the first. When the sentinel value is read, the While expression becomes `false` and the loop exits (*without* processing the sentinel).

Many times the problem dictates the value of the sentinel. For example, if the problem does not allow data values of 0, then the sentinel value should be 0. When you process `char` data one line of input at a time, the newline character (`'\n'`) often serves as the sentinel. Here's a program that reads and prints all of the characters from one line of an input file:

```
//************************************************************
// EchoLine program
// This program reads and echoes the characters from one line
// of an input file
//************************************************************
#include <iostream>
#include <fstream>                      // For file I/O

using namespace std;

int main()
{
    char     inChar;                    // An input character
    ifstream inFile;                    // Data file

    inFile.open("text.dat");            // Attempt to open input file
    if ( !inFile )                      // Was it opened?
    {
        cout << "Can't open the input file.";  // No--print message
```

```
        return 1;                    // Terminate program
    }

    inFile.get(inChar);              // Get first character
    while (inChar != '\n')
    {
        cout << inChar;              // Echo it
        inFile.get(inChar);          // Get next character
    }
    cout << endl;
    return 0;
}
```

(Notice that for this particular task we use the get function, not the >> operator, to input a character. Remember that the >> operator skips whitespace characters—including blanks and newlines—to find the next data value in the input stream. In this program, we want to input *every* character, even a blank and especially the newline character.)

What happens if you forget to enter the sentinel value? In an interactive program, the loop executes again, prompting for input. At that point, you can enter the sentinel value. If the input to the program is from a file, once all the data has been read from the file, the loop body is executed again. However, there isn't any data left—because the computer has reached the end of the file—so the file stream enters the fail state. In the next section, we describe a way to use the end-of-file situation as an alternative to using a sentinel.

Before we go on, we mention an issue that is related not to the design of loops but to C++ language usage. In Chapter 5, we talked about the common mistake of using the assignment operator (=) instead of the relational operator (==) in an If condition. This same mistake can happen when you write While statements. See what happens when we use the wrong operator in the previous example:

```
cin >> dataValue >> sentinel;
while (sentinel = 1)                 // Whoops
{
    ⋮
    cin >> dataValue >> sentinel;
}
```

This mistake creates an infinite loop. The While expression is now an assignment expression, not a relational expression. The expression's value is 1 (interpreted in the loop test as true because it's nonzero), and its side effect is to store the value 1 into sentinel, replacing the value that was just input into the variable. Because the While expression is always true, the loop never stops.

End-of-File-Controlled Loops After a program has read the last piece of data from an input file, the computer is at the end of the file (EOF, for short). At this moment, the stream state is all right. But if we try to input even one more data value, the stream goes into the fail state. We can use this fact to our advantage. To write a loop that inputs an unknown number of data items, we can use the failure of the input stream as a form of sentinel.

In Chapter 5, we described how to test the state of an I/O stream. In a logical expression, we use the name of the stream as though it were a Boolean variable:

```
if (inFile)
    ⋮
```

In a test like this, the result is `true` if the most recent I/O operation succeeded, or `false` if it failed. In a While statement, testing the state of a stream works the same way. Suppose we have a data file containing integer values. If `inData` is the name of the file stream in our program, here's a loop that reads and echoes all of the data values in the file:

```
inData >> intVal;              // Get first value
while (inData)                 // While the input succeeded ...
{
    cout << intVal << endl;    // Echo it
    inData >> intVal;          // Get next value
}
```

Let's trace this code, assuming there are three values in the file: 10, 20, and 30. The priming read inputs the value 10. The While condition is `true` because the input succeeded. Therefore, the computer executes the loop body. First the body prints out the value 10, and then it inputs the second data value, 20. Looping back to the loop test, the expression `inData` is `true` because the input succeeded. The body executes again, printing the value 20 and reading the value 30 from the file. Looping back to the test, the expression is `true`. Even though we are at the end of the file, the stream state is still OK—the previous input operation succeeded. The body executes a third time, printing the value 30 and executing the input statement. This time, the input statement fails; we're trying to read beyond the end of the file. The stream `inData` enters the fail state. Looping back to the loop test, the value of the expression is `false` and we exit the loop.

When we write EOF-controlled loops like the one above, we are expecting that the end of the file is the reason for stream failure. But keep in mind that *any* input error causes stream failure. The above loop terminates, for example, if input fails because of invalid characters in the input data. This fact emphasizes again the importance of echo printing. It helps us verify that all the data was read correctly before the EOF was encountered.

Is it possible to use an EOF-controlled loop when we read from the standard input device (via the `cin` stream) instead of a data file? On many systems, yes. For example, with the UNIX operating system, you can type Ctrl-D (that is, you hold down the Ctrl key and tap the D key) to signify end-of-file during interactive input.

Looping Subtasks

We have been looking at ways to use loops to affect the flow of control in programs. But looping by itself does nothing. The loop body must perform a task in order for the loop to accomplish something. In this section, we look at three tasks—counting, summing, and keeping track of a previous value—that often are used in loops.

Counting A common task in a loop is to keep track of the number of times the loop has been executed. For example, the following program fragment reads and counts input characters until it comes to a period. (inChar is of type char; count is of type int.) The loop in this example has a counter variable, but the loop is not a count-controlled loop because the variable is not being used as a loop control variable.

```
count = 0;                   // Initialize counter
cin.get(inChar);             // Read the first character
while (inChar != '.')
{
    count++;                 // Increment counter
    cin.get(inChar);         // Get the next character
}
```

After the loop is finished, count contains one less than the number of characters read. That is, it counts the number of characters up to, but not including, the sentinel value (the period). Notice that if a period is the first character, the loop body is not entered and count contains a 0, as it should. We use a priming read here because the loop is sentinel-controlled.

The counter variable in this example is called an **iteration counter** because its value equals the number of iterations through the loop.

> **Iteration counter** A counter variable that is incremented with each iteration of a loop.

According to our definition, the loop control variable of a count-controlled loop is an iteration counter. However, as you've just seen, not all iteration counters are loop control variables.

Summing Another common looping task is to sum a set of data values. Notice in the following example that the summing operation is written the same way, regardless of how the loop is controlled.

```
sum = 0;                     // Initialize the sum
count = 1;
while (count <= 10)
{
    cin >> number;           // Input a value
    sum = sum + number;      // Add the value to sum
    count++;
}
```

We initialize sum to 0 before the loop starts so that the first time the loop body executes, the statement

```
sum = sum + number;
```

adds the current value of sum (0) to number to form the new value of sum. After the entire code fragment has executed, sum contains the total of the ten values read, count contains 11, and number contains the last value read.

Keeping Track of a Previous Value   Sometimes we want to remember the previous value of a variable. Suppose we want to write a program that counts the number of not-equal operators (!=) in a file that contains a C++ program. We can do so by simply counting the number of times an exclamation mark (!) followed by an equal sign (=) appears in the input. One way in which to do this is to read the input file one character at a time, keeping track of the two most recent characters, the current value and the previous value. In each iteration of the loop, a new current value is read and the old current value becomes the previous value. When EOF is reached, the loop is finished. Here's a program that counts not-equal operators in this way:

```
//*******************************************************************
// NotEqualCount program
// This program counts the occurrences of "!=" in a data file
//*******************************************************************
#include <iostream>
#include <fstream>              // For file I/O

using namespace std;

int main()
{
    int      count;            // Number of != operators
    char     prevChar;         // Last character read
    char     currChar;         // Character read in this loop iteration
    ifstream inFile;           // Data file

    inFile.open("myfile.dat");           // Attempt to open input file
    if ( !inFile )                       // Was it opened?
    {
        cout << "** Can't open input file **"  // No--print message
            << endl;
        return 1;              // Terminate program
    }
    count = 0;                 // Initialize counter
    inFile.get(prevChar);      // Initialize previous value
    inFile.get(currChar);      // Initialize current value
```

```
    while (inFile)              // While previous input succeeded ...
    {
        if (currChar == '=' && // Test for event
            prevChar == '!')
            count++;           // Increment counter
        prevChar = currChar;   // Replace previous value
                               //   with current value
        inFile.get(currChar);  // Get next value
    }
    cout << count << " != operators were found." << endl;
    return 0;
}
```

The counter in this example is an **event counter**;
it is initialized to 0 and incremented only
when a certain event occurs. The counter in
the previous example was an *iteration
counter;* it was initialized to 1 and incremented during each iteration of the loop.

> **Event counter** A variable that is incremented each time a particular event occurs.

Study this loop carefully. It's going to come in handy. There are many problems in
which you must keep track of the last value read in addition to the current value.

6.4 How to Design Loops

It's one thing to understand how a loop works when you look at it and something else
again to design a loop that solves a given problem. In this section, we look at how to
design loops. We can divide the design process into two tasks: designing the control
flow and designing the processing that takes place in the loop. We can in turn break
each task into three phases: the task itself, initialization, and update. It's also important
to specify the state of the program when it exits the loop.

There are seven different points to consider in designing a loop:

1. What is the condition that ends the loop?
2. How should the condition be initialized?
3. How should the condition be updated?
4. What is the process being repeated?
5. How should the process be initialized?
6. How should the process be updated?
7. What is the state of the program on exiting the loop?

We use these questions as a checklist. The first three help us design the parts of the
loop that control its execution. The next three help us design the processing within the
loop. The last question reminds us to make sure that the loop exits in an appropriate
manner.

Designing the Flow of Control

The most important step in loop design is deciding what should make the loop stop. So here is our first question:

- What is the condition that ends the loop?

This question usually can be answered through a close examination of the problem statement. The following table lists some examples.

Key Phrase in Problem Statement	Termination Condition
"Sum 365 temperatures"	The loop ends when a counter reaches 365 (count-controlled loop).
"Process all the data in the file"	The loop ends when EOF occurs (EOF-controlled loop).
"Process until ten odd integers have been read"	The loop ends when ten odd numbers have been input (event counter).
"The end of the data is indicated by a negative test score"	The loop ends when a negative input value is encountered (sentinel-controlled loop).

Now we ask the next two questions:

- How should the condition be initialized?
- How should the condition be updated?

The answers to these questions depend on the type of termination condition.

For count-controlled loops that use an iteration counter, these are the answers to the questions:

- Initialize the iteration counter to 1.
- Increment the iteration counter at the end of each iteration.

For count-controlled loops that use an event counter, these are the answers to the questions:

- Initialize the event counter to 0.
- Increment the event counter each time the event occurs.

For sentinel-controlled loops, we answer our questions this way:

- Open the file, if necessary, and input a value before entering the loop (priming read).
- Input a new value for processing at the end of each iteration.

EOF-controlled loops require the same initialization as sentinel-controlled loops. Updating the loop condition means the loop must keep reading data.

Designing the Process Within the Loop

Next, we fill in the details of the process. In designing the process, we first must decide what we want a single iteration to do. Assume for a moment that the process is going to execute only once. What tasks must the process perform?

- What is the process being repeated?

To answer this question, we have to take another look at the problem statement. The definition of the problem may require the process to sum up data values or to keep a count of data values that satisfy some test. For example:

Count the number of integers in the file `howMany`.

This statement tells us that the process to be repeated is a counting operation.

After we've determined the operations to be performed if the process is executed only once, we design the parts of the process that are necessary for it to be repeated correctly. We often have to add some steps to take into account the fact that the loop executes more than once. This part of the design typically involves initializing certain variables before the loop and then reinitializing or updating them before each subsequent iteration.

- How should the process be initialized?
- How should the process be updated?

For example, if the process within a loop requires that several different counts and sums be performed, each must have its own statements to initialize variables, increment counting variables, or add values to sums. Just deal with each counting or summing operation by itself—that is, first write the initialization statement, and then write the incrementing or summing statement. After you've done this for one operation, you go on to the next.

The Loop Exit

Now we have to consider the consequences of our design and double-check its validity.

- What is the state of the program on exiting the loop?

For example, suppose we've used an event counter and that later processing depends on the number of events. It's important to be sure (with an algorithm walk-through) that the value left in the counter is the exact number of events—that it is not off by 1.

Designing correct loops depends as much on experience as it does on the application of design methodology. At this point, you may want to read through the Problem-Solving Case Study at the end of the chapter to see how the loop design process is applied to a real problem.

6.5 Nested Logic

In Chapter 5, we described nested If statements. It's also possible to nest While statements. Both While and If statements contain statements and are, themselves, statements. So the body of a While statement or the branch of an If statement can contain other While and If statements. By nesting, we can create complex control structures.

Suppose we want to extend our code for counting commas on one line, repeating it for all the lines in a file. We put an EOF-controlled loop around it:

```
cin.get(inChar);               // Initialize outer loop
while (cin)                    // Outer loop test
{
    commaCount = 0;            // Initialize inner loop
                               //    (Priming read is taken care of
                               //    by outer loop's priming read)
    while (inChar != '\n')     // Inner loop test
    {
        if (inChar == ',')
            commaCount++;
        cin.get(inChar);       // Update inner termination condition
    }
    cout << commaCount << endl;
    cin.get(inChar);           // Update outer termination condition
}
```

In this code, notice that we have omitted the priming read for the inner loop. The priming read for the outer loop has already "primed the pump." It would be a mistake to include another priming read just before the inner loop; the character read by the outer priming read would be destroyed before we could test it.

Let's examine the general pattern of a simple nested loop. The dots represent places where the processing and update may take place in the outer loop.

```
Initialize outer loop
while ( Outer loop condition )
{

        ⋮

    Initialize inner loop
    while ( Inner loop condition )
    {
        Inner loop processing and update
    }

        ⋮

}
```

Notice that each loop has its own initialization, test, and update. It's possible for an outer loop to do no processing other than to execute the inner loop repeatedly. On the other hand, the inner loop might be just a small part of the processing done by the outer loop; there could be many statements preceding or following the inner loop.

Let's look at another example. For nested count-controlled loops, the pattern looks like this (where outCount is the counter for the outer loop, inCount is the counter for the inner loop, and limit1 and limit2 are the number of times each loop should be executed):

```
outCount = 1;                        // Initialize outer loop counter
while (outCount <= limit1)
{
    :
    inCount = 1;                     // Initialize inner loop counter
    while (inCount <= limit2)
    {
        :
        inCount++;                   // Increment inner loop counter
    }
    :
    outCount++;                      // Increment outer loop counter
}
```

Here, both the inner and outer loops are count-controlled loops, but the pattern can be used with any combination of loops.

Designing Nested Loops

To design a nested loop, we begin with the outer loop. The process being repeated includes the nested loop as one of its steps. Because that step is more complex than a single statement, our functional decomposition methodology tells us to make it a separate module. We can come back to it later and design the nested loop just as we would any other loop.

Of course, nested loops themselves can contain nested loops (called *doubly nested loops*), which can contain nested loops (*triply nested loops*), and so on. You can use this design process for any number of levels of nesting. The trick is to defer details by using the functional decomposition methodology—that is, focus on the outermost loop first and treat each new level of nested loop as a module within the loop that contains it.

It's also possible for the process within a loop to include more than one loop. For example, here's an algorithm that reads and prints people's names from a file, omitting the middle name in the output:

```
Read and print first name (ends with a comma)
WHILE NOT EOF
    Read and discard characters from middle name (ends with a comma)
    Read and print last name (ends at newline)
    Output newline
    Read and print first name (ends with a comma)
```

The steps for reading the first name, middle name, and last name require us to design three separate loops. All of these loops are sentinel-controlled.

This kind of complex control structure would be difficult to read if written out in full. There are simply too many variables, conditions, and steps to remember at one time. In the next two chapters, we examine the control structure that allows us to break programs down into more manageable chunks—the subprogram.

As a final note about nested loops, it is important to keep in mind that the time it takes the computer to execute a deeply nested loop will be proportional to the product of the number of iterations at each level of the nested structure. For example, if we nest loops that count from 1 to 1000, five levels deep, the innermost loop body will execute 1,000,000,000,000,000 times. Such a loop would take over a week to execute on a typical computer.

Programming Example

Recording Studio Design

PROBLEM   You've gone to work for a consulting firm that specializes in converting existing rooms into recording studios. They have asked you to write a program that inputs a set of loudness measurements for a room and prints out basic statistics. The measurements are made by playing a series of 12 different tones, and recording the readings from a sound level meter onto a file. The meter readings range from 50 to 126 decibels (a measure of loudness). Your program, however, is to output the measurements relative to the first tone—that is, to show how much each individual reading differs from the first. After all the data have been read, the program is to print out the highest and lowest readings.

INPUT   Twelve real numbers, representing the meter readings, on file "acoustic.dat".

OUTPUT   The 12 input values (echo print) and their values relative to the first reading. At the end of the program, the actual value, relative value, and sequence number of both the highest reading and the lowest.

DISCUSSION   This is easy to do by hand. We simply scan the list, subtracting the first value from each value in the list. As we scan the list, we also keep track of which value from the list is the highest and which is the lowest.

How do we translate this process into an algorithm? Let's take a closer look at what we are doing. To find the largest number in a list, we compare the first and second numbers and remember the larger one. Then, we compare that number with the third one, remembering the larger number. We repeat the process for all of the numbers, and the one we remember at the end is the largest. We use the same process to find the smallest number, only we remember the smaller number instead of the larger one. Consider a sample data set:

Reading Number	Actual Reading	Relative Reading
1	86.0	0.0
2	86.5	0.5
3	88.0	2.0
4	83.5	−2.5
5	88.3	2.3
6	89.6	3.6
7	80.1	−5.9
8	84.0	−2.0
9	86.7	0.7
10	79.3	−6.7
11	74.0	−12.0
12	73.5	−12.5

The maximum reading was number 6 at 89.6 decibels. The lowest was reading 12 at 73.5 decibels.

"Scan the list" in our by-hand algorithm translates into a loop. Now that we understand the process, let's design the looping algorithm using our checklist.

1. *What is the condition that ends the loop?* Because there are exactly 12 values in a set of readings, we use a counter to control the loop. When it exceeds 12, the loop exits.

2. *How should the condition be initialized?* The first value will be input before the loop, because it is a special case — it is the value that is subtracted from all the other values to get their relative values. Also, its relative value is automatically 0.0. Thus, the first iteration of the loop gets the second value, so the counter will start at 2.

3. *How should the condition be updated?* The counter should be incremented at the end of each iteration.

4. *What is the process being repeated?* The process reads a value, echo prints it, subtracts the first value from the new value, prints the result, and checks to see if the new value should replace the current high or low value.

5. *How should the process be initialized?* The first number must be read in. Its relative value is automatically printed as 0.0. It is the initial high and low, and it also is saved as the base reading. The sequence number for both the high and low values will be set to 1 and their relative values will be 0.0.

6. *How should the process be updated?* In each iteration, a new current reading is input. If the current reading is greater than high, it replaces the current high. If current is lower than the current low, then it becomes the new low. We also must save the reading number of the highest and lowest values, and their relative values.

7. *What is the state of the program on exiting the loop?* Twelve readings have been input and echo printed together with twelve relative values. The loop control variable equals 13. high contains the greatest value read, highNumber the number of that value, and highRelative the relative

value for that reading; low contains the lowest value, lowNumber holds the number of that reading, and lowRelative has the corresponding relative value.

ASSUMPTIONS   At least 12 real numbers will be input, and all will be within the proper range.

```cpp
//*************************************************************
// Acoustic Program
// This program inputs 12 sound-level readings, taken in a room
// at different frequencies.  The first reading is used as a
// base value.  For each reading, a value relative to the base is
// calculated and printed.  The program ends by printing the
// highest reading and the lowest reading.
//*************************************************************

#include <iostream>
#include <fstream>
#include <iomanip>

using namespace std;

int main()
{
    // Declare variables
    float baseValue;            // First reading
    float current;              // Input during each iteration
    float relative;             // Current minus base value
    float high;                 // Highest value input
    float highRelative;         // High minus base value
    float low;                  // Lowest value input
    float lowRelative;          // Low minus base value
    int highNumber;             // Sequence number of high
    int lowNumber;              // Sequence number of lowest
    int readingNumber;          // Sequence number of current reading

    // Declare and open input file
    ifstream inData;                        // Input file of readings
    inData.open("acoustic.dat");
    if ( !inData )                          // Did input file open correctly?
    {   // no
        cout << "Can't open input file." << endl;
        return 1;                           // Terminate program
    }

    // Initialize variables and output
    readingNumber = 1;
```

```
relative = 0.0;
cout << setw(14) << "Reading Number" << setw(15)
     << "Actual Reading << setw(18) << "Relative Reading"
     << endl;

inData >> baseValue;                    // Input base value

// Write first line of output
cout << fixed << showpoint << setprecision(2) << setw(7)
     << readingNumber << setw(19) << baseValue << setw(15)
     << relative << endl;

// Initialize process
high = baseValue;
highNumber = 1;
highRelative = 0.0;
low = baseValue;
lowNumber = 1;
lowRelative = 0.0;
readingNumber = 2;                      // Initialize loop ending

while (readingNumber <= 12)
{
    inData >> current;                  // Input new reading
    relative = current - baseValue;     // Calculate new relative
    cout << setw(7) << readingNumber << setw(19) << current
         << setw(15) << relative << endl;

    if (current > high)                 // Check for new high
    {
        high = current;
        highNumber = readingNumber;
        highRelative = relative;
    }

  if (current < low)                    // Check for new low
  {
      low = current;
      lowNumber = readingNumber;
      lowRelative = relative;
  }
  readingNumber++;          // Increment reading number

}
```

```
// Print high and low readings
cout << endl;
cout << "Highest reading number is " << highNumber << endl;
cout << "Highest reading is "  << high << endl;
cout << "Highest relative value is " << highRelative << endl;
cout << endl;
cout << "Lowest reading number is " << lowNumber << endl;
cout << "Lowest reading is " << low << endl;
cout << "Lowest relative value is " << lowRelative << endl;

inData.close();
return 0;
}
```

Here is a screen shot of the output.

```
C:\PPSC++\Acoustic\Acoustic.exe                           _ □ x
Reading Number  Actual Reading   Relative Reading
           1            86.00              0.00
           2            86.50              0.50
           3            88.00              2.00
           4            83.50             -2.50
           5            88.30              2.30
           6            89.60              3.60
           7            80.10             -5.90
           8            84.00             -2.00
           9            86.70              0.70
          10            79.30             -6.70
          11            74.00            -12.00
          12            73.50            -12.50

Highest reading number is 6
Highest reading is 89.60
Highest relative value is 3.60

Lowest reading number is 12
Lowest reading is 73.50
Lowest relative value is -12.50
```

Now that you have written the program, you call the president of the consulting firm and fax her the results. After studying the results, she is silent for a moment and says "Oh. Right." "I'm sorry," she says, "but I told you to keep track of the wrong value. We're not interested in the lowest value, but in the lowest *dip in the readings*. You see, the last value is almost always the lowest because it's the lowest tone, and we know that most rooms respond poorly to bass notes. There's nothing we can do about that. But the lowest dip in the readings often occurs with a higher tone and that's usually a sign of a problem that we can fix. Can you change the program to output the lowest dip?" You confirm that a dip is a reading followed by a higher reading.

Now you have to figure out how to recognize a dip in the readings. You draw some graphs with random squiggles on them and pick out the lowest dips by hand. Then you make up some data sets that would generate the graphs. You find that a dip is usually a series of decreasing values followed by increasing values. But it also can be just a series of equal values followed by greater values. The bottom of a dip is merely the lowest value before values start increasing. You know how to keep track of a lowest value, but how do you tell if it is followed by a greater value?

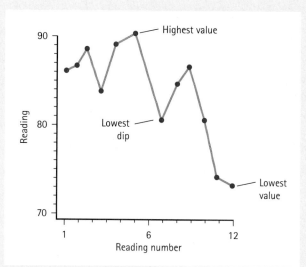

The answer is that you check it after the next value is input. That is, when you read in a new value, you check to see if the preceding value was lower. If it was, then you check to see if it was the lowest value input so far. You've seen the algorithm for keeping track of a previous value, and now you just have to add it to the program.

Now we can return to the checklist and see what must change. The control of the loop stays the same, only the process changes. Thus, we can skip the first three questions.

4. *What is the process being repeated?* It is the same as before, except where we check for the lowest value. Instead, we first check whether the preceding value is less than the current value. If it is, then we check to see if preceding should replace the lowest value so far. In replacing the lowest value, we must assign readingNumber minus one to lowNumber, because the dip occurred with the previous reading. We also could keep track of the previous value of readingNumber, but it is easier to calculate it.

5. *How should the process be initialized?* The change here is that we must initialize preceding. We can set it equal to the first value. We also have to initialize the precedingRelative value to 0.0.

6. *How should the process be updated?* We add steps to set preceding equal to current at the end of the loop, and to saveRelative in precedingRelative for use in the next iteration.

7. *What is the state of the program on exiting the loop?* At this point, preceding holds the last value input and precedingRelative holds the last relative value computed; low holds the value of the lowest dip, lowNumber contains the reading number of the lowest dip, and lowRelative is the difference between the lowest dip and the first value.

Here's the new version of the program.

```
//*******************************************************************
// Acoustic Program
// This program inputs 12 sound-level readings, taken in a room
// at different frequencies.  The first reading is used as a base
// value.  For each reading, a value relative to the base is
```

```
// calculated and printed.  The program ends by printing the
// lowest dip in the readings, where a dip is defined as a reading
// followed by a higher reading
//********************************************************************

#include <iostream>
#include <fstream>
#include <iomanip>

using namespace std;

int main()
{
    // Declare variables
    float baseValue;            // First reading
    float preceding;            // Reading preceding current
    float precedingRelative;    // Relative preceding current
    float current;              // Input during each iteration
    float relative;             // Current minus base value
    float high;                 // Highest value input
    float highRelative;         // High minus base value
    float low;                  // Lowest dip in the readings
    float lowRelative;          // Relative value of low
    int highNumber;             // Sequence number of high
    int lowNumber;              // Sequence number of lowest dip
    int readingNumber;          // Sequence number of current reading

    // Declare and open input file
    ifstream inData;                            // Input file of readings
    inData.open("acoustic.dat");
    if ( !inData )              // Did input file open correctly?
    {   // no
        cout << "Can't open input file." << endl;
        return 1;                   // Terminate program
    }

    // Initialize variables and output
    cout << setw(14) << "Reading Number" << setw(15)
         << "Actual Reading" << setw(18) << "Relative Reading"
         << endl;
    inData >> baseValue;
    preceding = baseValue;
    precedingRelative = 0.0;
    highNumber = 1;
    lowNumber = 1;
    high = baseValue;
```

```cpp
    low = baseValue;
    highRelative = 0.0;
    lowRelative = 0.0;
    readingNumber = 1;
    relative = 0.0;

    // Write first line of output
    cout << fixed << showpoint << setprecision(2) << setw(7)
         << readingNumber << setw(19)
         << baseValue << setw(15) << relative << endl;

    readingNumber = 2;                     // Initialize loop end
    while (readingNumber <= 12)
    {
        inData >> current;                 // Input new reading
        relative = current - baseValue;    // Calculate new relative
        cout << setw(7) << readingNumber << setw(19) << current
             << setw(15) << relative << endl;

        if (current > high)                // Check for new high
        {
            high = current;
            highNumber = readingNumber;
            highRelative = relative;
        }

        if (current > preceding)           // Check for new low
        {
            if (preceding < low)
            {
                low = preceding;
                lowNumber = readingNumber - 1;
                lowRelative = precedingRelative;
            }
        }
        preceding = current;
        precedingRelative = relative;
        readingNumber++;
    }

    // Print high and low readings
    cout << endl;
    cout << "Highest reading number is " << highNumber << endl;
    cout << "Highest reading is "  << high << endl;
    cout << "Highest relative value is " << highRelative << endl;
    cout << endl;
```

```
        cout << "Lowest dip is number " << lowNumber << endl;
        cout << "Lowest dip reading is " << low << endl;
        cout << "Lowest relative dip is " << lowRelative << endl;

        inData.close();
        return 0;
}
```

Here is the output screen.

```
C:\PPSC++\Acoustic\Acoustic.exe                              _ □ ×
Reading Number Actual Reading  Relative Reading
        1              86.00            0.00
        2              86.50            0.50
        3              88.00            2.00
        4              83.50           -2.50
        5              88.30            2.30
        6              89.60            3.60
        7              80.10           -5.90
        8              84.00           -2.00
        9              86.70            0.70
       10              79.30           -6.70
       11              74.00          -12.00
       12              73.50          -12.50

Highest reading number is 6
Highest reading is 89.60
Highest relative value is 3.60

Lowest dip is number 7
Lowest dip reading is 80.10
Lowest relative dip is -5.90
```

Testing and Debugging

Loop-Testing Strategy

Even if a loop has been properly designed and verified, it is still important to test it rigorously because the chance of an error creeping in during the implementation phase is always present. Because loops allow us to input many data sets in one run, and because each iteration may be affected by preceding ones, the test data for a looping program is usually more extensive than for a program with just sequential or branching statements. To test a loop thoroughly, we must check for the proper execution of both a single iteration and multiple iterations.

Remember that a loop has seven parts (corresponding to the seven questions in our checklist). A test strategy must test each part. Although all seven parts aren't implemented separately in every loop, the checklist reminds us that some loop operations serve multiple purposes, each of which should be tested. For example, the incrementing statement in a count-controlled loop may be updating both the process and the ending condition, so it's important to verify that it performs both actions properly with respect to the rest of the loop.

To test a loop, we try to devise data sets that could cause the variables to go out of range or leave the files in improper states that violate either the loop postcondition (an assertion that must be true immediately after loop exit) or the postcondition of the module containing the loop.

It's also good practice to test a loop for four special cases: (1) when the loop is skipped entirely, (2) when the loop body is executed just once, (3) when the loop executes some normal number of times, and (4) when the loop fails to exit.

Statements following a loop often depend on its processing. If a loop can be skipped, those statements may not execute correctly. If it's possible to execute a single iteration of a loop, the results can show whether the body performs correctly in the absence of the effects of previous iterations, which can be very helpful when you're trying to isolate the source of an error. Obviously, it's important to test a loop under normal conditions, with a wide variety of inputs. If possible, you should test the loop with real data in addition to mock data sets. Count-controlled loops should be tested to be sure they execute exactly the right number of times. And finally, if there is any chance that a loop might never exit, your test data should try to make that happen.

Testing and Debugging Hints

1. Plan your test data carefully to test all sections of a program.

2. Beware of infinite loops, in which the expression in the While statement never becomes `false`. The symptom: the program doesn't stop. If you are on a system that monitors the execution time of a program, you may see a message such as "TIME LIMIT EXCEEDED."

   If you have created an infinite loop, check your logic and the syntax of your loops. Be sure there's no semicolon immediately after the right parenthesis of the While condition:

```
while (Expression);          // Wrong
   Statement
```

This semicolon causes an infinite loop in most cases; the compiler thinks the loop body is the null statement (the do-nothing statement composed only of a semicolon). In a count-controlled loop, make sure the loop control variable is incremented within the loop. In a flag-controlled loop, make sure the flag eventually changes.

And, as always, watch for the = versus == problem in While conditions as well as in If conditions. The line

```
while (someVar = 5)       // Wrong (should be ==)
```

produces an infinite loop. The value of the assignment (not relational) expression is always 5, which is interpreted as `true`.

3. Check the loop termination condition carefully and be sure that something in the loop causes it to be met. Watch closely for values that cause one iteration too many or too few (the "off-by–1" syndrome).

4. Remember to use the `get` function rather than the `>>` operator in loops that are controlled by detection of a newline character.

5. Perform an algorithm walk-through to verify that all of the appropriate preconditions and postconditions occur in the right places.

6. Trace the execution of the loop by hand with a code walk-through. Simulate the first few passes and the last few passes very carefully to see how the loop really behaves.

7. Use a *debugger* if your system provides one. A debugger is a program that runs your program in "slow motion," allowing you to execute one instruction at a time and to examine the contents of variables as they change. If you haven't already done so, check to see if a debugger is available on your system.

8. If all else fails, use *debug output statements*—output statements inserted into a program to help debug it. They output messages that indicate the flow of execution in the program or report the values of variables at certain points in the program.

    For example, if you want to know the value of variable `beta` at a certain point in a program, you could insert this statement:

```
cout << "beta = " << beta << endl;
```

    If this output statement is in a loop, you will get as many values of `beta` output as there are iterations of the body of the loop.

    After you have debugged your program, you can remove the debug output statements or just precede them with `//` so that they'll be treated as comments. (This practice is referred to as *commenting out* a piece of code.) You can remove the double slashes if you need to use the statements again.

9. An ounce of prevention is worth a pound of debugging. Use the checklist questions to design your loop correctly at the outset. It may seem like extra work, but it pays off in the long run.

Summary

The While statement is a looping construct that allows the program to repeat a statement as long as the value of an expression is `true`. When the value of the expression becomes `false`, the body of the loop is skipped and execution continues with the first statement following the loop.

With the While statement, you can construct several types of loops that you will use again and again. These types of loops fall into two categories: count-controlled loops and event-controlled loops.

In a count-controlled loop, the loop body is repeated a specified number of times. Event-controlled loops continue executing until something inside the body signals that the looping process should stop. Event-controlled loops include those that test for a sentinel value in the data or for end-of-file. Sentinel-controlled loops are input loops that use a special data value as a signal to stop reading. EOF-controlled loops are loops that continue to input (and process) data values until there is no more data.

A counter is a variable that is used for counting. It may be the loop control variable in a count-controlled loop, an iteration counter in a counting loop, or an event counter that counts the number of times a particular condition occurs in a loop. Summing is a looping operation that keeps a running total of certain values.

When you design a loop, there are seven points to consider: how the termination condition is initialized, tested, and updated; how the process in the loop is initialized, performed, and updated; and the state of the program upon exiting the loop. By answering the checklist questions, you can bring each of these points into focus.

To design a nested loop structure, begin with the outermost loop. When you get to where the inner loop must appear, make it a separate module and come back to its design later.

The process of testing a loop is based on the answers to the checklist questions and the patterns the loop might encounter (for example, executing a single iteration, multiple iterations, an infinite number of iterations, or no iterations at all).

Quick Check

1. What are the four phases of loop execution? (pp. 203–204)
2. How is a count-controlled loop like an event-controlled loop, and how are they different? (pp. 204–208)
3. Does averaging a set of values that are input by a loop involve summing, counting, or both? (pp. 209–211)
4. What type of loop would you use to read a file of drivers' license numbers until a specific number is input? (pp. 211–212)
5. Write a While statement that exits when the int variable count is greater than 10, or the Boolean flag found is true. (pp. 202–203)
6. Write the initialization and update portions of the loop in Exercise 5. The variable found becomes true when the int variable inData contains zero. The count starts at one and is incremented in each iteration. (pp. 211–214)
7. Add a test for end-of-file on cin to the loop in Exercise 6, and add statements to the loop that perform a priming read and an updating read of inData from cin. (pp. 207–208)
8. Add initialization and update operations to the loop in Exercise 7 that cause it to count the occurrences of the value 1 that are input to variable inData, and to sum all of the values read into inData. (pp. 209–210)
9. How would you extend the loop from Exercise 8 so that it would be repeated in its entirety five times? (pp. 214–216)
10. How would you test a looping program that reads hourly temperatures from a file and outputs the daily average? (pp. 224–225)

Answers

1. Entry, iteration, test, exit.   2. They both test for the exit condition at the start of each iteration, but the number of iterations is not predetermined for an event-controlled loop.   3. Both.   4. An event-controlled loop. (The events would be the input of the number, or reaching end-of-file).   5.
```
while (count <= 10 && !found)
```
6.
```
count = 1;
found = false;
while (count <= 10 && !found)
{
    count++;
    found = inData == 0;
}
```
7.
```
count = 1;
found = false;
cin >> inData;
while (count <= 10 && !found && cin)
{
    count++;
    found = inData == 0;
    cin >> inData;
}
```
8.
```
onesCount = 0;
sum = 0;
count = 1;
found = false;
cin >> inData;
while (count <= 10 && !found && cin)
{
    if (inData == 1)
        onesCount++;
    sum = sum + inData;
    count++;
    found = inData == 0;
    cin >> inData;
}
```
9. Nest it within a counting loop that counts from 1 to 5.   10. Run the program with an empty file, a file with 24 input values, a file with fewer than 24 input values, and a file with more than 24 input values. Test the program with 24 input values all the same, and with 24 values that differ so that omitting any of them results in an average that's different from the average of all 24.

Exam Preparation Exercises

1. The While statement exits when the termination condition becomes true. True or false?
2. The body of the While statement is always executed at least once. True or false?
3. Using a block as the body of the While statement enables us to place any number of statements within a loop. True or false?

4. Match the following list of terms with the definitions given below.
   a. Loop entry.
   b. Iteration.
   c. Loop test.
   d. Loop exit.
   e. Termination condition.
   f. Count-controlled loop.
   g. Event-controlled loop.
   h. Iteration counter.
   i. Event counter.
      i. A loop that executes a specified number of times.
      ii. When the flow of control reaches the first statement inside a loop.
      iii. A variable that is incremented each time a particular condition is encountered.
      iv. When the decision is made whether to begin a new iteration or to exit.
      v. A loop that exits when a specific condition is encountered.
      vi. The condition that causes the loop to exit.
      vii. A variable that is incremented with each iteration of a loop.
      viii. When control passes to the statement following the loop.
      ix. An individual pass through a loop.

5. How many times does the following loop execute, and what is its output?

```
count = 1;
while (count <= 12)
{
    cout << count << endl;
    count++;
}
```

6. How many times does the following loop execute, and what is its output?

```
count = 0;
while (count <= 11)
{
    cout << count << ", ";
    count++;
}
```

7. How many times does the following loop execute, and what is its output?

```
count = 1;
while (count < 13)
{
    cout << "$" << count << ".00" << endl;
    count++;
}
```

8. What does the following nested loop structure output?

```
count = 1;
while (count <= 11)
{
    innerCount = 1
    while (innerCount <= (12 - count) / 2)
    {
        cout << " ";
        innerCount++;
    }
    innerCount = 1;
    while (innerCount <= count)
    {
        cout << "@";
        innerCount++;
    }
    cout << endl;
    count++;
}
```

9. What does the following nested loop structure output?

```
count = 1;
while (count <= 10)
{
    innerCount = 1;
    while (innerCount <= 10)
    {
        cout << setw(5) << count * innercount;
        innerCount++;
    }
    cout << endl;
    count++;
}
```

10. The following loop is supposed to sum all of the input values on file `indata`. What's wrong with it? Change the code so that it works correctly.

```
sum = 0;
indata >> number;
while (indata)
{
    indata >> number;
    sum = sum + number;
}
```

11. What sentinel value would you choose for a program that reads names as strings?

12. The following code segment is supposed to write out the odd numbers from 1 to 19. What does it actually output? Change the code to work correctly.

```
number = 1;
while (number < 10)
{
    number++;
    cout << number * 2 - 1 << " ";
}
```

13. Priming reads aren't necessary when a loop is controlled by a sentinel value. True or false?

14. What are the seven questions that must be answered in order to design a loop?

15. The following code segment is supposed to output the average of the five numbers on each input line, for all of the lines in the file. Instead, it simply outputs the sum of all of the numbers in the file. What's wrong with the code segment? Change the code to work correctly.

```
sum = 0;
while (indata)
{
    count = 1;
    while (count <= 5 && indata)
    {
        cin >> number;
        sum = sum + number;
    }
    cout << sum / count << endl;
}
```

Programming Warm-Up Exercises

1. Write a code segment using a While loop that outputs the numbers from –10 to 10.

2. Write a code segment using a While loop that sums the integers, counting up from 1, and stops when the sum is greater than 10,000, printing out the integer that was most recently added to the sum.

3. Write a looping code segment that inputs up to 20 integer scores from file indata, and outputs their average. If the file contains fewer than 20 scores, the segment should still output the correct average. If the file contains more than 20 scores, the additional numbers should be ignored. Be sure to consider what happens if the file is empty.

4. Write a code segment that reads lines of text from file chapter6, and outputs the number of lines in the file that contain the string "code segment".

5. Write a code segment that reads a string from `cin`. The string should be one of, `"Yes"`, `"No"`, `"yes"`, or `"no"`. If it is not, the user should be prompted to input an appropriate response, and the process should repeat. Once a valid response is received, the `bool` variable `yes` should be assigned `true` if the response is `"Yes"` or `"yes"` and `false` if the response is `"No"` or `"no"`.

6. Write a code segment that prints the days of a month in calendar format. The day of the week on which the month begins is represented by an `int` variable `startDay`. When `startDay` is zero, the month begins on a Sunday. The `int` variable `days` contains the number of days in the month. Print a heading with the days of the week as the first line of output. The day numbers should neatly align under these column headings.

7. We could extend the code from Exercise 6 to print a calendar for a year by nesting it within a loop that repeats the code twelve times.

   a. What formula would you use to compute the new start day for the next month?

   b. What additional information would you need to print the calendar for each month?

8. Write a code segment that reads all of the characters on file `textData`, and then outputs the percentage of the characters that are the letter "z".

9. Change the code segment in Exercise 8 so that it stops reading either at the end of the file or after 10,000 characters have been input.

10. Write a code segment that outputs the Fibonacci numbers that are less than 30,000. Each Fibonacci number is the sum of its two predecessors. The first two Fibonacci numbers are 1 and 1. Thus, the sequence begins with:

    1, 1, 2, 3, 5, 8, 13, 21, 34, ...

    Output each number on a separate line.

11. Modify the code segment in Exercise 10 so that it also outputs the position of the Fibonacci number in the sequence. For example:

1	1
2	1
3	2
4	3
5	5
6	8
7	13

12. Write a code segment that inputs an integer from `cin`, and then outputs a row of that many stars on `cout`.

13. How did you answer the checklist questions for Exercise 12?

14. Change the code segment for Exercise 12 to read a series of numbers from file indata, and print a row of stars on cout for each number read. (You can think of this as printing a bar graph of a data file.)

15. What test data would you use to test the code segment in Exercise 14?

Programming Problems

1. Design and write a C++ program that inputs a series of 24 hourly temperatures from a file, and outputs a bar chart (using stars) of the temperatures for the day. The temperature should be printed to the left of the corresponding bar, and there should be a heading that gives the scale of the chart. The range of temperatures should be from –30 to 120. Because it is hard to display 150 characters on the screen, you should have each star represent a range of 3 degrees. That way, the bars will be at most 50 characters wide. Here is a partial example, showing the heading, the output for a negative temperature, and the output for various positive temperatures. Note how the temperatures are rounded to the appropriate number of stars.

```
Temperatures for 24 hours:
     -30            0          30         60         90         120
  -20        *******|
   0                |
   1                |
   2                |*
   3                |*
   4                |*
   5                |**
  10                |***
  50                |*****************
 100                |******************************
```

Use meaningful variable names, proper indentation, and appropriate comments. Thoroughly test the program using your own data sets.

2. The standard deviation of a set of data values gives us a sense of the dispersion of values within their range. For example, a set of test scores with a small standard deviation indicates that most people's scores were very close to the average score. Some instructors thus use the standard deviation as a way of determining the range of values to assign a particular grade.

   Design and write a C++ program that reads a set of scores from the file scores.dat, and outputs their mean and standard deviation on cout. The formula for the standard deviation is

$$s = \sqrt{\frac{n \sum_{i=1}^{n} x_i^2 - \left(\sum_{i=1}^{n} x_i \right)^2}{n(n-1)}}$$

where n is the number of values and x_i represents the individual values. Thus, to compute the standard deviation, you must sum the squares of the individual values, and also square the sum of the values. All of this reading and summing can be done with a single loop, after which the mean and standard deviation of the scores are computed. Be sure to properly label the output. Use meaningful variable names, proper indentation, and appropriate comments. Thoroughly test the program using your own data sets.

3. You are burning some music CDs for a party. You've arranged a list of songs in the order in which you want to play them. However, you would like to maximize your use of space on the CD, which holds 80 minutes of music. So, you want to figure out the total time for a group of songs and see how well they fit. Write a design and a C++ program to help you do this. The data are on file songs.dat. The time is entered as seconds. For example, if a song takes 7 minutes and 42 seconds to play, the data entered for that song would be

462

After all the data has been read, the application should print a message indicating the time remaining on the CD.

The output should be in the form of a table with columns and headings written on a file. For example,

Song Number	Song Time Minutes	Seconds	Total Time Minutes	Seconds
------	-------	-------	-------	-------
1	5	10	5	10
2	7	42	12	52
5	4	19	17	11
3	4	33	21	44
4	10	27	32	11
6	8	55	41	6
7	5	0	46	6

There are 33 minutes and 54 seconds of space left on the 80 minute CD.

Note that the output converts the input from seconds to minutes and seconds. Use meaningful variable names, proper indentation, and appropriate comments. Thoroughly test the program using your own data sets.

4. A palindrome is a phrase that reads the same both forwards and backwards. Write a C++ program that reads a line from cin, prints its characters in reverse

order on `cout`, and then pronounces judgment on whether the input line is a palindrome. For example, here are two sample runs of the program:

```
Enter string: able was I ere I saw elba
able was I ere I saw elba

is a palindrome.

Enter string: madam I'm adam
mada m'I madam

is not a palindrome
```

Hint: use the substr function within a loop to extract and print the characters one-by-one from the string, starting at the end of the string, and at the same time, extract the corresponding character starting at the beginning of the string to compare with it.

Use a prompting message, meaningful variable names, proper indentation, and appropriate comments. Thoroughly test the program using your own data sets.

5. You're working for a company that's building an email list from files of mail messages. They would like you to write a program that reads a file called `mail.dat`, and that outputs every string containing the @ sign to file `addresses.dat`. For the purpose of this project, a string is defined as it is by the C++ stream reader—a contiguous sequence of non-whitespace characters. Given the data:

```
From:   sharon@marzipan.edu
Date: Wed, 13 Aug 2003 17:12:33 EDT
Subject: Re: hi
To:   john@meringue.com

John,

Dave's email is dave_smith@icing.org.

ttyl,

sharon
```

Then the program would output on file `addresses.dat`:

```
sharon@marzipan.edu
john@meringue.com
dave_smith@icing.org.
```

Use meaningful variable names, proper indentation, and appropriate comments. Thoroughly test the program using your own data sets.

Programming Example Follow-Up

1. The first version of program Acoustic remembers the reading number of the highest reading. If there are multiple readings with the same value, it remembers only the first one. Change the program so that it remembers the last of these values instead. Hint: you only need to add one character to the program.

2. The second version of program Acoustic keeps track of the lowest dip in the readings. If there are two dips that are equal, it remembers the first one. Change the program so that it remembers the last one.

3. Does the loop in program Acoustic use a priming read?

4. What type of loop, event-controlled or count-controlled, is used in program Acoustic?

5. The problem states that the readings are on a file. They equally could well have been entered from the keyboard. Change the revised program so that the values are entered in real time.

6. How might you determine whether it is better to enter data from a file or from the keyboard?

Functions

Knowledge Goals

- ■ *To know how functions can be used to reflect the structure of a functional decomposition.*
- ■ *To understand the difference between value and reference parameters.*
- ■ *To know how to use arguments and parameters.*

Skill Goals

To be able to:

- ■ *Write a module of your own design as a void function.*
- ■ *Design the parameter list for each module of a functional decomposition.*
- ■ *Code a program using functions.*
- ■ *Define and use local variables correctly.*
- ■ *Write a program that uses multiple calls to a single function.*

You have been using C++ functions since we introduced standard library routines such as `sqrt` and `abs` in Chapter 3. So far, we have not considered how the programmer can create his or her own functions other than `main`. That is the topic of this chapter and the next.

You might wonder why we waited until now to look at user-defined subprograms. The reason, and the major purpose for using subprograms, is that we write our own value-returning functions and void functions to help organize and simplify larger programs. Until now, our programs have been relatively small and simple, so we didn't need to write subprograms. Now, we are ready to introduce subprograms so that we can begin writing larger and more complex programs.

7.1 Functional Decomposition with Void Functions

As a brief refresher, let's review the two kinds of subprograms with which the C++ language works: value-returning functions and void functions. In this chapter, we concentrate exclusively on creating our own void functions. In Chapter 8, we examine how to write value-returning functions.

From the early chapters on, you have been designing your programs as collections of modules. Many of these modules are naturally implemented as *user-defined void functions*. We now look at how to turn the modules in your algorithms into user-defined void functions.

Writing Modules as Void Functions

It is quite simple to turn a module into a void function in C++. Basically, a void function looks like the `main` function except that the function heading uses `void` rather than `int` as the data type of the function. Additionally, the body of a void function does not contain a statement like

```
return 0;
```

as does `main`. A void function does not return a function value to its caller.

Let's look at a program using void functions. A friend of yours is returning from a long trip, and you want to write a program that prints the following message:

```
* * * * * * * * * * * * *
* * * * * * * * * * * * *
Welcome Home!
* * * * * * * * * * * * *
* * * * * * * * * * * * *
* * * * * * * * * * * * *
* * * * * * * * * * * * *
```

Here is a design for the program.

Main	Level 0

> Print two lines of asterisks
> Print "Welcome Home!"
> Print four lines of asterisks

Print 2 Lines	Level 1

> Print "**************"
> Print "**************"

Print 4 Lines	

> Print "**************"
> Print "**************"
> Print "**************"
> Print "**************"

If we write the two first-level modules as void functions, the `main` function is simply

```
int main()
{
    Print2Lines();
    cout << "Welcome Home!" << endl;
    Print4Lines();
    return 0;
}
```

Notice how similar this code is to the main module of our functional decomposition. It contains two function calls—one to a function named `Print2Lines` and another to a function named `Print4Lines`. Both of these functions have empty argument lists.

The following code should look familiar to you, but look carefully at the function heading.

```
void Print2Lines()                              // Function heading
{
    cout << "***************" << endl;
    cout << "***************" << endl;
}
```

This segment is a *function definition*. A function definition is the code that extends from the function heading to the end of the block that is the body of the function. The function heading begins with the word `void`, signaling the compiler that this is not a value-returning function. The body of the function executes some ordinary statements and does *not* finish with a `return` statement to return a function value.

Now look again at the function heading. Just like any other identifier in C++, the name of a function cannot include blanks, even though our paper-and-pencil module names do. Following the function name is an empty argument list—that is, there is nothing between the parentheses. Later we see what goes inside the parentheses if a function uses arguments. Now let's put `main` and the other two functions together to form a complete program.

```
//*********************************************************************
// Welcome program
// This program prints a "Welcome Home" message
//*********************************************************************
#include <iostream>

using namespace std;

void Print2Lines();                             // Function prototypes
void Print4Lines();

int main()
{
    Print2Lines();                              // Function call
    cout << " Welcome Home!" << endl;
    Print4Lines();                              // Function call
    return 0;
}


//*********************************************************************

void Print2Lines()                              // Function heading
```

```
// This function prints two lines of asterisks

{
    cout << "***************" << endl;
    cout << "***************" << endl;
}


//*********************************************************************

void Print4Lines()                              // Function heading

// This function prints four lines of asterisks

{
    cout << "***************" << endl;
    cout << "***************" << endl;
    cout << "***************" << endl;
    cout << "***************" << endl;
}
```

C++ function definitions can appear in any order. We could have chosen to place the main function last instead of first, but C++ programmers typically put main first and any supporting functions after it.

In the Welcome program, the two statements just before the main function are called *function prototypes*. These declarations are necessary because of the C++ rule requiring you to declare an identifier before you can use it. Our main function uses the identifiers Print2Lines and Print4Lines, but the definitions of those functions don't appear until later. We must supply the function prototypes to inform the compiler in advance that Print2Lines and Print4Lines are the names of functions, that they do not return function values, and that they have no arguments. We say more about function prototypes later in the chapter.

Because the Welcome program is so simple to begin with, it may seem more complicated with its modules written as functions. However, it is clear that it much more closely resembles our functional decomposition. This is especially true of the main function. As our programs grow to include many modules nested several levels deep, the ability to read a program in the same manner as a functional decomposition aids greatly in the development and debugging process.

7.2 An Overview of User-Defined Functions

Now that we've seen an example of how a program is written with functions, let's look briefly and informally at some of the more important points of function construction and use.

Flow of Control in Function Calls

When the program is executed, control begins at the first statement in the main function. When a function call is encountered, control is passed to the first statement in that function's body. The statements in the function are executed. After the last one is executed, control returns to the point immediately following the function call. Because function calls alter the logical order of execution, functions are considered control structures.

In the Welcome program, execution begins with the first executable statement in the main function (the call to Print2Lines). When Print2Lines is called, control passes to its first statement and subsequent statements in its body. After the last statement in Print2Lines has executed, control returns to the main function at the point following the call (the output statement that prints "Welcome Home!").

Function Parameters

Looking at the Welcome program, you can see that Print2Lines and Print4Lines are very similar functions. They differ only in the number of lines that they print. Do we really need two different functions in this program? Maybe we should write only one function that prints *any* number of lines, where the "any number of lines" is passed as an argument by the caller (main). Here is a second version of the program, which uses only one function to do the printing. We call it NewWelcome.

```cpp
//*******************************************************************
// NewWelcome program
// This program prints a "Welcome Home" message
//*******************************************************************
#include <iostream>

using namespace std;

void PrintLines( int );                        // Function prototype

int main()
{
    PrintLines(2);
    cout << " Welcome Home!" << endl;
    PrintLines(4);
    return 0;
}
//*******************************************************************

void PrintLines( int numLines )

// This function prints lines of asterisks, where
// numLines specifies how many lines to print
```

```
{
    int count;        // Loop control variable

    count = 1;
    while (count <= numLines)
    {
        cout << "***************" << endl;
        count++;
    }
}
```

In the function heading of `PrintLines`, you see some code between the parentheses that looks like a variable declaration. This is a *parameter declaration*. The items listed in the call to a function are the **arguments**. The variables declared in the function heading are the **parameters**.

> **Argument** A variable or expression listed in a call to a function; also called *actual argument* or *actual parameter*.
>
> **Parameter** A variable declared in a function heading; also called *formal argument* or *formal parameter*.

In the NewWelcome program, the arguments in the two function calls are the constants 2 and 4, and the parameter in the `PrintLines` function is named `numLines`. The `main` function first calls `PrintLines` with an argument of 2. When control is turned over to `PrintLines`, the parameter `numLines` is initialized to 2. Within `PrintLines`, the count-controlled loop executes twice and the function returns. The second time `PrintLines` is called, the parameter `numLines` is initialized to the value of the argument, 4. The loop executes four times, after which the function returns.

The NewWelcome program brings up a second major reason for using functions—namely, a function can be called from many places in the `main` function (or from other functions). Use of multiple calls can save a great deal of effort in coding many problem solutions.

If more than one argument is passed to a function, the arguments and parameters are matched by their relative positions in the two lists. For example, if you want `PrintLines` to print lines consisting of any selected character, not only asterisks, you might rewrite the function so that its heading is

```
void PrintLines( int   numLines,
                 char whichChar )
```

and a call to the function might look like this:

```
PrintLines(3, '#');
```

The first argument, 3, is matched with `numLines` because `numLines` is the first parameter. Likewise, the second argument, '#', is matched with the second parameter, `whichChar`.

7.3 Syntax and Semantics of Void Functions

Function Call (Invocation)

> **Function call (to a void function)** A statement that transfers control to a void function. In C++, this statement is the name of the function, followed by a list of arguments.

To call (or invoke) a void function, we use its name as a statement, with the arguments in parentheses following the name. A function call in a program results in the execution of the body of the called function. This is the syntax template of a function call to a void function:

FunctionCall (to a void function)

```
FunctionName ( ArgumentList ) ;
```

According to the syntax template for a function call, the argument list is optional. A function is not required to have arguments. However, as the syntax template also shows, the parentheses are required even if the argument list is empty.

If there are two or more arguments in the argument list, you must separate them with commas. Here is the syntax template for ArgumentList:

ArgumentList

```
Expression , Expression . . .
```

When a function call is executed, the arguments are passed to the parameters according to their positions, left to right, and control is then transferred to the first executable statement in the function body. When the last statement in the function has executed, control returns to the point from which the function was called.

Function Declarations and Definitions

In C++, you must declare every identifier before it can be used. In the case of functions, a function's declaration must physically precede any function call.

A function declaration announces to the compiler the name of the function, the data type of the function's return value (either `void` or a data type like `int` or `float`), and the data types of the parameters it uses. The NewWelcome program shows a total of three function declarations. The first declaration (the statement labeled "Function prototype") does not include the body of the function. The remaining two declarations—for `main` and `PrintLines`—include bodies for the functions.

In C++ terminology, a function declaration that omits the body is called a **function prototype**, and a declaration that does include the body is a **function definition**.

> **Function prototype** A function declaration without the body of the function.
>
> **Function definition** A function declaration that includes the body of the function.

The rule throughout C++ is that you can declare an item as many times as you wish, but you can define it only once. In the NewWelcome program, we could include many function prototypes for `PrintLines` (though we'd have no reason to), but only one function definition is allowed.

Function Prototypes We have said that the definition of the `main` function usually appears first in a program, followed by the definitions of all other functions. To satisfy the requirement that identifiers be declared before they are used, C++ programmers typically place all function prototypes near the top of the program, before the definition of `main`.

A function prototype (known as a *forward declaration* in some languages) specifies in advance the data type of the function value to be returned (or the word `void`) and the data types of the parameters. A prototype for a void function has the following form:

FunctionPrototype (for a void function)

```
void FunctionName ( ParameterList );
```

As you can see in the syntax template, no body is included for the function, and a semicolon terminates the declaration. The parameter list is optional, to allow for parameterless functions. If the parameter list is present, it has the following form:

ParameterList (in a function prototype)

```
Datatype & VariableName , DataType & VariableName ...
```

The ampersand (&) attached to the name of a data type is optional and has a special significance that we cover later in the chapter.

In a function prototype, the parameter list must specify the data types of the parameters, but their names are optional. You could write either

```
void DoSomething( int, float );
```

or

```
void DoSomething( int velocity, float angle );
```

Sometimes it's useful for documentation purposes to supply names for the parameters, but the compiler ignores them.

Function Definitions   You learned in Chapter 2 that a function definition consists of two parts: the function heading and the function body, which is syntactically a block (compound statement). Here's the syntax template for a function definition, specifically, for a void function:

FunctionDefinition (for a void function)

```
void FunctionName ( ParameterList )
{
      Statement
         ⋮

}
```

Notice that the function heading does *not* end in a semicolon the way a function prototype does. It is a common syntax error to put a semicolon at the end of the line.

The syntax of the parameter list differs slightly from that of a function prototype in that you *must* specify the names of all the parameters. Also, it's our style preference (but not a language requirement) to declare each parameter on a separate line:

ParameterList (in a function definition)

```
Datatype & VariableName ,
Datatype & VariableName
   ⋮
```

Local Variables

Because a function body is a block, any function—not only the `main` function—can include variable declarations within its body. These variables are called local variables because they are accessible only within the block in which they are declared. As far as the calling code is concerned, they don't exist. If you tried to print the contents of a local variable from another function, a compile-time error such as "UNDECLARED IDENTIFIER" would occur.

Local variable   A variable declared within a block and not accessible outside of that block.

In contrast to local variables, variables declared outside of all the functions in a program are called *global variables*. We return to the topic of global variables in Chapter 8.

Local variables occupy memory space only while the function is executing. At the moment the function is called, memory space is created for its local variables. When the function returns, its local variables are destroyed.* Therefore, every time the function is

---

*We'll see an exception to this rule in the next chapter.

called, its local variables start out with their values undefined. Because every call to a function is independent of every other call to that same function, you must initialize the local variables within the function itself. And because local variables are destroyed when the function returns, you cannot use them to store values between calls to the function.

The following code segment illustrates each of the parts of the function declaration and calling mechanism that we have discussed.

```cpp
#include <iostream>

using namespace std;

void TryThis( int, int, float );       // Function prototype

int main()                             // Function definition
{
    int   int1;                        // Variables local to main
    int   int2;
    float someFloat;
    ⋮
    TryThis(int1, int2, someFloat);    // Function call with three
                                       //   arguments
    ⋮
}

void TryThis( int   param1,            // Function definition with
              int   param2,            //   three parameters
              float param3 )
{
    int   i;                           // Variables local to TryThis
    float x;
    ⋮
}
```

The Return Statement

The main function uses the statement

```cpp
return 0;
```

to return the value 0 (or 1 or some other value) to its caller, the operating system. Every value-returning function must return its function value this way.

A void function does not return a function value. Control returns from the function when it "falls off" the end of the body–that is, after the final statement has executed. As you saw in the NewWelcome program, the PrintLines function simply prints some lines of asterisks and then returns.

Alternatively, there is a second form of the Return statement. It looks like this:

```cpp
return;
```

This statement is valid *only* for void functions. It can appear anywhere in the body of the function; it causes control to exit the function immediately and return to the caller.

Naming Void Functions

When you choose a name for a void function, keep in mind how calls to it will look. A call is written as a statement; therefore, it should sound like a command or an instruction to the computer. For this reason, it is a good idea to choose a name that is an imperative verb or has an imperative verb as part of it. For example,

```
PrintLines(3);
```

Header Files

From the very beginning, we have been using #include directives that request the C++ preprocessor to insert the contents of header files into our programs:

```
#include <iostream>
#include <cmath>        // For sqrt() and fabs()
#include <fstream>      // For file I/O
#include <climits>      // For INT_MAX and INT_MIN
```

Exactly what do these header files contain?

It turns out that there is nothing magical about header files. Their contents are nothing more than a series of C++ declarations. There are declarations of items such as named constants (INT_MAX, INT_MIN), classes (istream, ostream, string), and objects (cin, cout). But most of the items in a header file are function prototypes.

Suppose that your program needs to use the library function sqrt in a statement like this:

```
y = sqrt(x);
```

Every identifier must be declared before it can be used. If you forget to #include the header file cmath, the compiler gives you an "UNDECLARED IDENTIFIER" error message. The file cmath contains function prototypes for sqrt and other math-oriented library functions. With this header file included in your program, the compiler not only knows that the identifier sqrt is the name of a function but it also can verify that your function call is correct with respect to the number of arguments and their data types.

Header files save you the trouble of writing all of the library function prototypes yourself at the beginning of your program. With just one line–the #include directive– you cause the preprocessor to go out and find the header file and insert the prototypes into your program. In later chapters, we see how to create our own header files that contain declarations specific to our programs.

7.4 Parameters

When a function is executed, it uses the arguments given to it in the function call. How is this done? The answer to this question depends on the nature of the parameters. C++ supports two kinds of parameters: **value parameters** and **reference parameters**. With a value parameter, which is declared without an ampersand (&) at the end of the data type

> **Value parameter** A parameter that receives a copy of the value of the corresponding argument.
>
> **Reference parameter** A parameter that receives the location (memory address) of the caller's argument.

name, the function receives a copy of the argument's value. With a reference parameter, which is declared by adding an ampersand to the data type name, the function receives the location (memory address) of the caller's argument. Before we examine in detail the difference between these two kinds of parameters, let's look at an example of a function heading with a mixture of reference and value parameter declarations.

```
void Example( int&  param1,      // A reference parameter
              int    param2,      // A value parameter
              float  param3 )     // Another value parameter
```

With simple data types–int, char, float, and so on–a value parameter is the default (assumed) kind of parameter. In other words, if you don't do anything special (add an ampersand), a parameter is assumed to be a value parameter. To specify a reference parameter, you have to go out of your way to do something extra (attach an ampersand).

Let's look at both kinds of parameters, starting with value parameters.

Value Parameters

In the NewWelcome program, the PrintLines function heading is

```
void PrintLines( int numLines )
```

The parameter numLines is a value parameter because its data type name doesn't end in &. If the function is called using an argument lineCount,

```
PrintLines(lineCount);
```

then the parameter numLines receives a copy of the value of lineCount. At this moment, there are two copies of the data—one in the argument lineCount and one in the parameter numLines. If a statement inside the PrintLines function were to change the value of numLines, this change would not affect the argument lineCount (remember, there are two copies of the data). Using value parameters thus helps us avoid unintentional changes to arguments.

Because value parameters are passed copies of their arguments, anything that has a value may be passed to a value parameter. This includes constants, variables, and even arbitrarily complicated expressions. For the PrintLines function, the following function calls are all valid:

```
PrintLines(3);
PrintLines(lineCount);
PrintLines(2 * abs(10 - someInt));
```

There must be the same number of arguments in a function call as there are parameters in the function heading.* Also, each argument should have the same data type as the parameter in the same position. Notice how each parameter in the following example is matched to the argument in the same position (the data type of each argument below is what you would assume from its name):

Function heading: void ShowMatch(float num1, int num2, char letter)

Function call: ShowMatch(floatVariable, intVariable, charVariable);

If the matched items are not of the same data type, implicit type coercion takes place. For example, if a parameter is of type int, an argument that is a float expression is coerced to an int value before it is passed to the function. As usual in C++, you can avoid unintended type coercion by using an explicit type cast or, better yet, by not mixing data types at all.

When a function returns, the contents of its value parameters are destroyed, along with the contents of its local variables. The difference between value parameters and local variables is that the values of local variables are undefined when a function starts to execute, whereas value parameters are automatically initialized to the values of the corresponding arguments.

Because the contents of value parameters are destroyed when the function returns, they cannot be used to return information to the calling code. What if we *do* want to

*This statement is not the whole truth. C++ has a special language feature—*default parameters*—that lets you call a function with fewer arguments than parameters. We do not cover default parameters in this book.

return information by modifying the caller's arguments? We must use the second kind of parameter available in C++: reference parameters. Let's look at these now.

Reference Parameters

A reference parameter is one that you declare by attaching an ampersand to the name of its data type. It is called a reference parameter because the called function can refer to the corresponding argument directly. Specifically, the function is allowed to inspect *and modify* the caller's argument.

When a function is invoked using a reference parameter, it is the *location* (memory address) of the argument, not its value, that is passed to the function. There is only one copy of the information, and it is used by both the caller and the called function. When a function is called, the argument and the parameter become synonyms for the same location in memory. Whatever value is left by the called function in this location is the value that the caller will find there. Therefore, you must be careful when using a reference parameter because any change made to it affects the argument in the calling code.

The following table summarizes the usage of arguments and parameters.

Item	Usage
Argument	Appears in a function *call*. The corresponding parameter may be either a reference or a value parameter.
Value parameter	Appears in a function *heading*. Receives a *copy* of the value of the corresponding argument.
Reference parameter	Appears in a function *heading*. Receives the *address* of the corresponding argument.

Matching Arguments with Parameters

Earlier we said that with reference parameters, the argument and the parameter become synonyms for the same memory location. When a function returns control to its caller, the link between the argument and the parameter is broken. They are synonymous only during a particular call to the function. The only evidence that a matchup between the two ever occurred is that the contents of the argument may have changed (see Figure 7–1).

Only a variable can be passed as an argument to a reference parameter because a function can assign a new value to the argument. (In contrast, remember that an arbitrarily complicated expression can be passed to a value parameter.) Suppose that we have a function with the following heading:

```
void DoThis( float val,      // Value parameter
             int&  count )    // Reference parameter
```

When flow of control is in the main function,
temperature can be accessed as shown by the arrow.

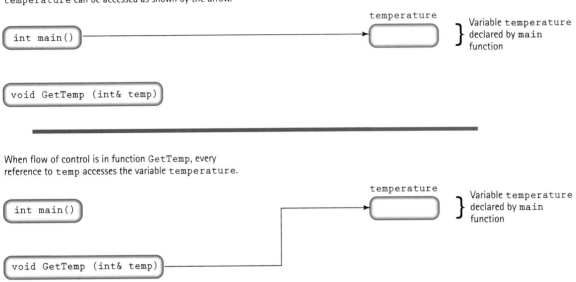

Figure 7–1   *Using a Reference Parameter to Access an Argument*

Then the following function calls are all valid.

```
DoThis(someFloat, someInt);
DoThis(9.83, intCounter);
DoThis(4.9 * sqrt(y), myInt);
```

In the DoThis function, the first parameter is a value parameter, so any expression is allowed as the argument. The second parameter is a reference parameter, so the argument *must* be a variable name. The statement

```
DoThis(y, 3);
```

generates a compile-time error because the second argument isn't a variable name. Earlier we said the syntax template for an argument list is

ArgumentList

Expression , Expression . . .

But you must keep in mind that Expression is restricted to a variable name if the corresponding parameter is a reference parameter.

There is another important difference between value and reference parameters when it comes to matching arguments with parameters. With value parameters, we said that implicit type coercion occurs if the matched items have different data types (the value of the argument is coerced, if possible, to the data type of the parameter). In contrast, with reference parameters, the matched items *must* have exactly the same data type.

The following table summarizes the appropriate forms of arguments.

Parameter	Argument
Value parameter	A variable, constant, or arbitrary expression (type coercion may take place)
Reference parameter	A variable *only*, of exactly the same data type as the parameter

Theoretical Foundations

Argument-Passing Mechanisms

There are three major ways of passing arguments to and from subprograms. C++ supports only two of these mechanisms; however, it's useful to know about all three in case you have occasion to use them in another language.

C++ reference parameters employ a mechanism called *pass by address* or *pass by location*. A memory address is passed to the function. Another name for this is *pass by reference* because the function can refer directly to the caller's variable that is specified in the argument list.

C++ value parameters are an example of *pass by value*. The function receives a copy of the value of the caller's argument. Passing by value can be less efficient than passing by address because the value of an argument may occupy many memory locations (as we see in Chapter 11), whereas an address usually occupies only a single location. For the simple data types `int`, `char`, `bool`, and `float`, the efficiency of either mechanism is about the same.

A third method of passing arguments is called *pass by name*. The argument is passed to the function as a character string that must be interpreted by special runtime support software (called a *thunk*) supplied by the compiler. For example, if the name of a variable is passed to a function, the run-time interpreter looks up the name of the argument in a table of declarations to find the address of the variable. Passing by name can have unexpected results. If an argument has the same spelling as a local variable in the function, the function will refer to the local version of the variable instead of the variable in the calling code.

(continued) ▼

Argument-Passing Mechanisms

Some versions of passing by name allow an expression or even a code segment to be passed to a function. Each time the function refers to the parameter, an interpreter performs the action specified by the parameter. An interpreter is similar to a compiler and nearly as complex. Thus, passing by name is the least efficient of the three argument-passing mechanisms. Passing by name is supported by the ALGOL and LISP programming languages, but not by C++.

There are two different ways of matching arguments with parameters, although C++ supports only one of them. Most programming languages, C++ among them, match arguments and parameters by their relative positions in the argument and parameter lists. This is called *positional matching*, *relative matching*, or *implicit matching*. A few languages, such as Ada, also support *explicit* or *named matching*. In explicit matching, the argument list specifies the name of the parameter to be associated with each argument. Explicit matching allows arguments to be written in any order in the function call. The real advantage is that each call documents precisely which values are being passed to which parameters.

7.5 Designing Functions

We've looked at some examples of functions and defined the syntax of function prototypes and function definitions. But how do we design functions? First, we need to be more specific about what functions do. We've said that they allow us to organize our programs more like our functional decompositions, but what really is the advantage of doing that?

The body of a function is like any other segment of code, except that it is contained in a separate block within the program. Isolating a segment of code in a separate block means that its implementation details can be "hidden" from view. As long as you know how to call a function and what its purpose is, you can use it without looking at the code inside the function body. For example, you don't know how the code for a library function like sqrt is written (its implementation is hidden from view), yet you still can use it effectively.

The specification of what a function does and how it is invoked defines its interface (see Figure 7–2). By hiding a module implementation, or encapsulating the module, we can make changes to it without changing the main function, as long as the interface remains the same. For example, you might rewrite the body of a function using a more efficient algorithm.

Interface A connecting link at a shared boundary that permits independent systems to meet and act on or communicate with each other. Also, the formal description of the purpose of a subprogram and the mechanism for communicating with it.

Encapsulation Hiding a module implementation in a separate block with a formally specified interface.

Heading: `void PrintActivity ( int temp )`
Precondition: `temp` is a temperature value in a valid range
Postcondition: A message has been printed indicating an
appropriate activity given temperature `temp`

Implementation

Figure 7–2   *Function Interface (Visible) and Implementation (Hidden)*

Encapsulation is what we do in the functional decomposition process when we post-pone the solution of a difficult subproblem. We write down its purpose, its precondition and postcondition, and what information it takes and returns, and then we write the rest of our design as if the subproblem had already been solved. We could hand this interface specification to someone else, and that person could develop a function for us that solves the subproblem. We needn't be concerned about how it works, as long as it conforms to the interface specification. Interfaces and encapsulation are the basis for *team programming*, in which a group of programmers work together to solve a large problem.

Thus, designing a function can (and should) be divided into two tasks: designing the interface and designing the implementation. We already know how to design an implementation—it is a segment of code that corresponds to an algorithm. To design the interface, we focus on the *what*, not the *how*. We must define the behavior of the function (what it does) and the mechanism for communicating with it.

You already know how to specify formally the behavior of a function. Because a function corresponds to a module, its behavior is defined by the precondition and post-condition of the module. All that remains is to define the mechanism for communicating with the function. To do so, make a list of the following items:

1. *Incoming values* that the function receives from the caller.

2. *Outgoing values* that the function produces and returns to the caller.

3. *Incoming/outgoing values*—values the caller has that the function changes (receives and returns).

Now decide which identifiers inside the module match the values in this list. These identifiers become the variables in the parameter list for the function. Then the parameters are declared in the function heading. All other variables that the function needs are local and must be declared within the body of the function. This process is repeated for all the modules at each level.

Let's look more closely at designing the interface. First we examine function preconditions and postconditions. After that, we consider in more detail the notion of incoming, outgoing, and incoming/outgoing parameters.

Writing Assertions as Program Comments

We have been writing module preconditions and postconditions as informal, English-language assertions. From now on, we include preconditions and postconditions as comments to document the interfaces of C++ functions. Here's an example:

```
void PrintAverage( float sum,
                   int   count )

// Precondition:
//     sum is assigned  &&  count > 0
// Postcondition:
//     The average sum/count has been output on one line

{
    cout << "Average is " << sum / float(count) << endl;
}
```

The precondition is an assertion describing everything that the function requires to be true at the moment the caller invokes the function. The postcondition describes the state of the program at the moment the function finishes executing.

You can think of the precondition and postcondition as a contract. The contract states that if the precondition is true at function entry, then the postcondition must be true at function exit. The *caller* is responsible for ensuring the precondition, and the *function code* must ensure the postcondition. If the caller fails to satisfy its part of the contract (the precondition), the contract is off; the function cannot guarantee that the postcondition will be true.

Above, the precondition warns the caller to make sure that sum has been assigned a meaningful value and to be sure that count is positive. If this precondition is true, the function guarantees it will satisfy the postcondition. If count isn't positive when PrintAverage is invoked, the effect of the function is undefined. (For example, if count equals 0, the postcondition surely isn't satisfied—the program crashes!)

Sometimes the caller doesn't need to satisfy any precondition before calling a function. In this case, the precondition can be written as the value true or simply omitted. In the following example, no precondition is necessary:

```
void Get2Ints( int& int1,
               int& int2 )

// Postcondition:
//     User has been prompted to enter two integers
//  && int1 == first input value
//  && int2 == second input value

{
    cout << "Please enter two integers: ";
    cin >> int1 >> int2;
}
```

In assertions written as C++ comments, we use either && or AND to denote the logical AND operator, either || or OR to denote a logical OR, either ! or NOT to denote a logical NOT, and == to denote "equals." (Notice that we do *not* use = to denote "equals." Even when we write program comments, we want to keep C++'s == operator distinct from the assignment operator.)

There is one final notation we use when we express assertions as program comments. Preconditions implicitly refer to values of variables at the moment the function is invoked. Postconditions implicitly refer to values at the moment the function returns. But sometimes you need to write a postcondition that refers to parameter values that existed at the moment the function was invoked. To signify "at the time of entry to the function," we attach the symbol @entry to the end of the variable name. Below is an example of the use of this notation. The Swap function exchanges, or swaps, the contents of its two parameters.

```
void Swap( int& firstInt,
           int& secondInt )

// Precondition:
//     firstInt and secondInt are assigned
// Postcondition:
//     firstInt == secondInt@entry
//  && secondInt == firstInt@entry

{
    int temporaryInt;

    temporaryInt = firstInt;
    firstInt = secondInt;
    secondInt = temporaryInt;
}
```

Documenting the Direction of Data Flow

Another helpful piece of documentation in a function interface is the direction of **data flow** for each parameter in the parameter list. Data flow is the flow of information between the function and its caller. We said earlier that each parameter can be classified as an *incoming* parameter, an *outgoing* parameter, or an *incoming/outgoing* parameter. (Some programmers refer to these as *input* parameters, *output* parameters, and *input/output* parameters.)

Data flow The flow of information from the calling code to a function and from the function back to the calling code.

For an incoming parameter, the direction of data flow is one-way—into the function. The function inspects and uses the current value of the parameter but does not modify it. In the function heading, we attach the comment

```
/* in */
```

to the declaration of the parameter. Here is the `PrintAverage` function with comments added to the parameter declarations:

```
void PrintAverage( /* in */ float sum,
                   /* in */ int   count )

// Precondition:
//     sum is assigned  &&  count > 0
// Postcondition:
//     The average sum/count has been output on one line

{
    cout << "Average is " << sum / float(count) << endl;
}
```

Passing by value is appropriate for each parameter that is incoming only. As you can see in the function body, `PrintAverage` does not modify the values of the parameters `sum` and `count`. It merely uses their current values. The direction of data flow is one-way—into the function.

The data flow for an outgoing parameter is one-way—out of the function. The function produces a new value for the parameter without using the old value in any way. The comment `/* out */` identifies an outgoing parameter. Here we've added comments to the `Get2Ints` function heading:

```
void Get2Ints( /* out */ int& int1,
               /* out */ int& int2 )
```

Passing by reference must be used for an outgoing parameter. If you look back at the body of `Get2Ints`, you'll see that the function stores new values into the two variables (by means of the input statement), replacing whatever values they originally contained.

Finally, the data flow for an incoming/outgoing parameter is two-way—into and out of the function. The function uses the old value and also produces a new value for the parameter. We use `/* inout */` to document this two-way direction of data flow. Here is an example of a function that uses two parameters, one of them incoming only and the other one incoming/outgoing:

```
void Calc( /* in */    int  alpha,
           /* inout */ int& beta  )

// Precondition:
//     alpha and beta are assigned
// Postcondition:
//     beta == beta@entry * 7 - alpha
```

```
{
    beta = beta * 7 - alpha;
}
```

This function first inspects the incoming value of `beta` so that it can evaluate the expression to the right of the equal sign. Then it stores a new value into `beta` by using the assignment operation. The data flow for `beta` is therefore considered a two-way flow of information. A pass by value is appropriate for `alpha` (it's incoming only), but a pass by reference is required for `beta` (it's an incoming/outgoing parameter).

Formatting Function Headings

From here on, we follow a specific style when coding our function headings. Comments appear next to the parameters to explain how each parameter is used. Also, embedded comments indicate which of the three data flow categories each parameter belongs to (In, Out, or Inout).

```
void Print( /* in */     float val,     // Value to be printed
            /* inout */ int&  count )   // Number of lines printed
                                        //   so far
```

We use comments in the form of rows of asterisks (or dashes or some other character) before and after a function to make the function stand out from the surrounding code. Each function also has its own block of introductory comments, just like those at the start of a program, as well as its precondition and postcondition.

It's important to put as much care into documenting each function as you would into the documentation at the beginning of a program.

The following table summarizes the correspondence between a parameter's data flow and the appropriate argument-passing mechanism.

Data Flow for a Parameter	Argument-Passing Mechanism
Incoming	Pass by value
Outgoing	Pass by reference
Incoming/outgoing	Pass by reference

There are exceptions to the guidelines in this table. C++ requires that I/O stream objects be passed by reference because of the way streams and files are implemented. We encounter another exception in Chapter 12.

Programming Example

Total Cost of Mortgage

PROBLEM In Chapter 3, you wrote a mortgage calculator. This exercise got you to thinking. All ads from cars to appliances to furniture to houses state that you pay "only so much a month." How much are you really paying for a house or any product bought on the installment plan? You decide to embed your calculator in a program that tells you how much you actually are paying for whatever you are financing. Since you now know about loops, you decide to do the processing within a loop, so that the user can see how a change in the interest rate or length of the contract can affect what you are actually paying.

INPUT At the end of Chapter 4, Case Study Follow Up Exercise 5 had you change your calculator program to allow the user to input the various values. These values are input to this program.

> Total loan amount (float)
> Yearly interest rate (float)
> Number of years (integer)

OUTPUT The input values are echo printed in a table that also shows the amount actually paid over the term of the loan.

DISCUSSION This program is a simple event-controlled loop, within which the user is prompted to input the loan amount, the interest rate, and the number of years. You decide to use a sentinel-controlled loop here, with a negative value for the loan amount as the sentinel. This decision requires that you use a priming read, reading the first loan amount outside the loop and the following loan amounts at the end of the loop.

Here is an implementation of the program in which each module is weritten as a C++ function.

```
//*************************************************************
// Mortgage Payment Tables program
// This program prints a table showing loan amount, interest rate,
// length of loan, monthly payments, and total cost of a mortgage.
//*************************************************************

#include <iostream>
#include <cmath>
#include <iomanip>
#include <fstream>

using namespace std;

// Function prototypes
void PrintHeading(ofstream&);
void DeterminePayment(float, int, float, float&);
void PrintResults(ofstream&, float, int, float, float);
```

```cpp
int main()
{
    // Input variables
    float loanAmount;
    float yearlyInterest;
    int numberOfYears;
    float payment;

    // Declare and open output file
    ofstream dataOut;
    dataOut.open("mortgage.out");
    if ( !dataOut )
    { // no
        cout << "Can't open output file." << endl;
        return 1;
    }

    PrintHeading(dataOut);

    // Prompt for and read loan amount
    cout << "Input the total loan amount; "
         << "a negative value stops processing." << endl;
    cin >> loanAmount;

    // Loop calculating monthly payments
    while (loanAmount >= 0.0)
    {
        // Prompt for and read interest rate and number of years.
        cout << "Input the interest rate." << endl;
        cin >> yearlyInterest;
        cout << "Enter the number of years for the loan" << endl;
        cin >> numberOfYears;

        DeterminePayment(loanAmount, numberOfYears, yearlyInterest,
            payment);
        PrintResults(dataOut, loanAmount, numberOfYears,
            yearlyInterest, payment);
        // Prompt for and read loan amount
        cout << "Input the total loan amount; "
             << "a negative value stops processing."  << endl;
        cin >> loanAmount;
    }

    dataOut.close();
    return 0;
}
```

```
//************************************************************


void DeterminePayment
    ( /* in */ float loanAmount,      // Loan amount
      /* in */ int numberOfYears,     // Term of loan
      /* in */ float yearlyInterest,  // Interest rate
      /* inout */ float& payment )     // Monthly payment


// Calculates the monthly payment for a loan amount using the
// formula for compound interest.
// Precondition:
//     Arguments have been assigned values
// Postcondition:
//     payment contains the monthly payment as calculated by the
//     compound interest formula

{
    // local variables
    float monthlyRate;
    int numberOfPayments;

    monthlyRate = yearlyInterest / 1200;
    numberOfPayments = numberOfYears * 12;
    payment = (loanAmount * pow(1 + monthlyRate, numberOfPayments)
              * monthlyRate) /
              (pow(1 + monthlyRate, numberOfPayments) - 1);
}


//************************************************************


void PrintResults( /* inout */ ofstream& dataOut,    // Output file
                   /* in */     float loanAmount,     // Loan amount
                   /* in */     int numberOfYears,    // Term of loan
                   /* in */     float yearlyInterest, // Interest rate
                   /* in */     float payment )       // Payment


// Prints the loan amount, number of years, yearly interest rate,
// and payment amount on file dataOut
// Precondition:
//     File dataOut has been opened successfully &&
//     All arguments have been assigned values
// Postcondition:
//     Loan amount, number of years, yearly interest rate, and
//     payment have been printed on dataOut with proper
//     documentation.
```

```
{
    dataOut << fixed << setprecision(2) << setw(12) << loanAmount
            << setw(12) << numberOfYears << setw(12)
            << yearlyInterest << setw(15) << payment
            << setw(12) << numberOfYears*12*payment << endl;
}


//*********************************************************************


void PrintHeading( /* inout */ ofstream& dataOut )  // Output file

// Prints the heading on file dataOut for each column in the table.
// Precondition:
//    File dataOut has been opened successfully
// Postcondition:
//    "Loan Amount", "No. Years", "Interest Rate", "Payment",
//    "Total Paid" have been written on file dataOut

{
    dataOut << fixed << setprecision(2) << setw(12) << "Loan Amount"
            << setw(12) << "No. Years" << setw(15)
            << "Interest Rate" << setw(12) << "Payment"
            << setw(12) << "Total Paid" << endl;
}
```

Here is a sample run and the output.

```
C:\PPSC++\Mortgage\MortgageTables.exe                                    _ □ ×
Input the total loan amount; a negative value stops processing.
100000.00
Input the interest rate.
4.99
Enter the number of years for the loan
5
Input the total loan amount; a negative value stops processing.
3000.00
Input the interest rate.
18.0
Enter the number of years for the loan
2
Input the total loan amount; a negative value stops processing.
45000.00
Input the interest rate.
2.9
Enter the number of years for the loan
5
Input the total loan amount; a negative value stops processing.
-1
```

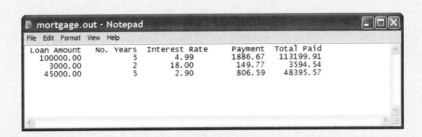

Testing There are three numeric inputs to this program. A negative loan amount ends the processing. The sample run used a variety of values for the loan amount, interest, and length of term. Case Study Follow Up Exercise 2 asks you to examine what happens if the interest and/or number of years is zero or negative.

Testing and Debugging

The parameters declared by a function and the arguments that are passed to the function by the caller must satisfy the interface to the function. Errors that occur with the use of functions often are due to an incorrect use of the interface between the calling code and the called function.

One source of errors is mismatched argument lists and parameter lists. The C++ compiler ensures that the lists have the same number of items and that they are compatible in type. It's the programmer's responsibility, however, to verify that each argument list contains the correct items. This is a matter of comparing the parameter declarations to the argument list in every call to the function. This job is much easier if the function heading gives each parameter a distinct name and describes its purpose in a comment. You can avoid mistakes in writing an argument list by using descriptive variable names in the calling code to suggest exactly what information is being passed to the function.

Another source of error is the failure to ensure that the precondition for a function is met before it is called. For example, if a function assumes that the input file is not at EOF when it is called, then the calling code must ensure that this is true before making the call to the function. If a function behaves incorrectly, review its precondition, then trace the program execution up to the point of the call to verify the precondition. You can waste a lot of time trying to locate an error in a correct function when the error is really in the part of the program prior to the call.

If the arguments match the parameters and the precondition is correctly established, then the source of the error is most likely in the function itself. Trace the function to verify that it transforms the precondition into the proper postcondition. Check that all local variables are initialized properly. Parameters that are supposed to return data to the caller must be declared as reference parameters (with an & symbol attached to the data type name).

An important technique for debugging a function is to use your system's debugger program, if one is available, to step through the execution of the function. If a debugger is not available, you can insert debug output statements to print the values of the arguments immediately before and after calls to the function. It also may help to print the values of all local variables at the end of the function. This information provides a snapshot of the function (a picture of its status at a particular moment in time) at its two most critical points, which is useful in verifying hand traces.

To test a function thoroughly, you must arrange the incoming values so that the precondition is pushed to its limits; then the postcondition must be verified. For example, if a function requires a parameter to be within a certain range, try calling the function with values in the middle of that range and at its extremes.

The assert Library Function

We have discussed how function preconditions and postconditions are useful for debugging (by checking that the precondition of each function is true prior to a function call, and by verifying that each function correctly transforms the precondition into the postcondition) and for testing (by pushing the precondition to its limits and even violating it). To state the preconditions and postconditions for our functions, we've been writing the assertions as program comments:

```
// Precondition:
//     studentCount > 0
```

All comments, of course, are ignored by the compiler. They are not executable statements; they are for humans to examine.

On the other hand, the C++ standard library gives us a way in which to write *executable assertions*. Through the header file cassert, the library provides a void function named assert. This function takes a logical (Boolean) expression as an argument and halts the program if the expression is false. Here's an example:

```
#include <cassert>
    ⋮
assert(studentCount > 0);
average = sumOfScores / studentCount;
```

The argument to the assert function must be a valid C++ logical expression. If its value is true, nothing happens; execution continues on to the next statement. If its value is false, execution of the program terminates immediately with a message stating (a) the assertion as it appears in the argument list, (b) the name of the file containing the program source code, and (c) the line number in the program. In the example above, if the value of studentCount is less than or equal to 0, the program halts after printing a message like this:

```
Assertion failed: studentCount > 0, file myprog.cpp, line 48
```

(This message is potentially confusing. It doesn't mean that studentCount *is* greater than 0. In fact, it's just the opposite. The message tells you that the assertion studentCount > 0 is *false*.)

Executable assertions have a profound advantage over assertions expressed as comments: the effect of a false assertion is highly visible (the program terminates with an error message). The `assert` function is therefore valuable in software testing. A program under development might be filled with calls to the `assert` function to help identify where errors are occurring. If an assertion is false, the error message gives the precise line number of the failed assertion.

Additionally, there is a way to "remove" the assertions without really removing them. If you use the preprocessor directive #define NDEBUG before including the header file `cassert`, like this:

```
#define NDEBUG
#include <cassert>
    ⋮
```

then all calls to the `assert` function are ignored when you run the program. (NDEBUG stands for "No debug," and a #define directive is a preprocessor feature that we don't discuss right now.) After program testing and debugging, programmers often like to "turn off" debugging statements yet leave them physically present in the source code in case they might need the statements later. Inserting the line #define NDEBUG turns off assertion checking without having to remove the assertions.

As useful as the `assert` function is, it has two limitations. First, the argument to the function must be expressed as a C++ logical expression. We can turn a comment such as

```
//  0.0 <= yearlyInterest && numberOfYears <= 30
```

into an executable assertion with the statement

```
assert(0.0 <= yearlyInterest && numberOfYears <= 30);
```

But there is no easy way to turn the comment

```
//  The file contains a loan amount,
//   interest rate, and number of years
```

into a C++ logical expression.

The second limitation is that the `assert` function is appropriate only for testing a program that is under development. A production program (one that has been completed and released to the public) must be robust and must furnish helpful error messages to the user of the program. You can imagine how baffled a user would be if the program suddenly quit and displayed an error message such as

```
Assertion failed: sysRes <= resCount, file newproj.cpp, line 298
```

Despite these limitations, you should consider using the `assert` function as a regular tool for testing and debugging your programs.

Testing and Debugging Hints

1. Follow documentation guidelines carefully when writing functions (see Appendix E). As your programs become more complex and therefore prone to errors, it becomes increasingly important to adhere to documentation and formatting standards. Even if the function name seems to reflect the process being done, describe that process in comments. Include comments stating the function precondition (if any) and postcondition to make the function interface complete. Use comments to explain the purposes of all parameters and local variables whose roles are not obvious.

2. Provide a function prototype near the top of your program for each function you've written. Make sure that the prototype and its corresponding function heading are an *exact* match (except for the absence of parameter names in the prototype).

3. Be sure to put a semicolon at the end of a function prototype. But do *not* put a semicolon at the end of the function heading in a function definition. Because function prototypes look so much like function headings, it's common to get one of them wrong.

4. Be sure the parameter list gives the data type of each parameter.

5. Use value parameters unless a result is to be returned through a parameter. Reference parameters can change the contents of the caller's argument; value parameters cannot.

6. In a parameter list, be sure the data type of each reference parameter ends with an ampersand (&). Without the ampersand, the parameter is a value parameter.

7. Make sure that the argument list of every function call matches the parameter list in number and order of items, and be very careful with their data types. The compiler will trap any mismatch in the number of arguments. But if there is a mismatch in data types, there may be no compile-time error. Specifically, with a pass by value, a type mismatch can lead to implicit type coercion rather than a compile-time error.

8. Remember that an argument matching a reference parameter *must* be a variable, whereas an argument matching a value parameter can be any expression that supplies a value of the same data type (except as noted above in Hint 7).

9. Become familiar with *all* the tools available to you when you're trying to locate the sources of errors—the algorithm walk-through, hand tracing, the system's debugger program, the `assert` function, and debug output statements.

Summary

C++ allows us to write programs in modules expressed as functions. The structure of a program, therefore, can parallel its functional decomposition even when the program is complicated. To make your main function look exactly like level 0 of your functional decomposition, simply write each lower-level module as a function. The main function then executes these other functions in logical sequence.

Functions communicate by means of two lists: the parameter list (which specifies the data type of each identifier) in the function heading, and the argument list in the calling code. The items in these lists must agree in number and position, and they should agree in data type.

Part of the functional decomposition process involves determining what data must be received by a lower-level module and what information must be returned from it. The names of these data items, together with the precondition and postcondition of a module, define its interface. The names of the data items become the parameter list, and the module name becomes the name of the function. With void functions, a call to the function is accomplished by writing the function's name as a statement, enclosing the appropriate arguments in parentheses.

C++ has two kinds of parameters: reference and value. Reference parameters have data types ending in & in the parameter list, whereas value parameters do not. Parameters that return values from a function must be reference parameters. All others should be value parameters. This minimizes the risk of errors, because only a copy of the value of an argument is passed to a value parameter, and thus the argument is protected from change.

In addition to the variables declared in its parameter list, a function may have local variables declared within it. These variables are accessible only within the block in which they are declared. Local variables must be initialized each time the function containing them is called because their values are destroyed when the function returns.

You may call functions from more than one place in a program. The positional matching mechanism allows the use of different variables as arguments to the same function. Multiple calls to a function, from different places and with different arguments, can simplify greatly the coding of many complex programs.

Quick Check

1. What elements of a functional decomposition correspond to functions in C++? (p. 238)
2. What character do we use to indicate a reference parameter, and where does it appear in the parameter's declaration? (pp. 249, 251–253)
3. Where do arguments appear and where do parameters appear? (pp. 251–253)
4. You are writing a function to return the first name from a string containing a full name. How many parameters does the function have, and which of them are reference and which are value parameters? (pp. 254–259)
5. What kind of parameter would you use for an incoming value from an argument? For an outgoing value? For a value that comes in, is changed, and returns to the argument? (pp. 254–259)

6. Where do declarations of functions that are called by `main` appear in the program, with respect to `main`? (pp. 244–246)
7. What parts of a program can access a local variable declared within a function's block? (pp. 246–247)
8. If the same function appears in multiple places in a functional decomposition, how do you convert it into code in a program? (p. 243)

Answers

1. Modules   2. The `&` character appears at the end of the type name of the parameter.   3. Arguments appear in function calls and parameters appear in function headings.   4. It should have two parameters, one for each string. The full name parameter should be a value parameter, and the first name parameter should be a reference parameter.   5. Incoming values use value parameters. Values that return to the argument (`out` or `inout`) must be passed through reference parameters.   6. They must be declared before they are used, so they appear before `main`. However, the declaration may simply be a function prototype and the actual definition can then appear anywhere.   7. Only the statements within the block, following the declaration.   8. You code it once, placing it, or its prototype before any reference to it in the rest of the program, and call it from each place in the program that corresponds to its appearance in the functional decomposition.

Exam Preparation Exercises

1. What three things distinguish a `void` function from `main`?
2. A function prototype must specify the name of a function and the name and type of each of its parameters. True or false?
3. When and to where does control return from a `void` function?
4. Match the following terms with the definitions given below.
   a. Argument
   b. Parameter
   c. Function call
   d. Function prototype
   e. Function definition
   f. Local variable
   g. Value parameter
   h. Reference parameter
      i. A function declaration without a body.
      ii. A parameter that receives a copy of the argument's value.
      iii. A variable declared in a function heading.
      iv. A function declaration with a body.
      v. A variable or expression listed in a call to a function.
      vi. A statement that transfers control to a function.
      vii. A parameter that receives the location of the argument.
      viii. A variable declared within a block.

5. In the following function heading, which parameters are value parameters and which are reference parameters?

```
void ExamPrep (string& name, int age, float& salary,
char level)
```

6. If a function has six parameters, how many arguments must be in a call to the function?

7. What happens if a function assigns a new value to a value parameter? What happens if it assigns a new value to a reference parameter?

8. What's wrong with this function prototype?

```
void ExamPrep (phone& int, name string, age& int)
```

9. Arguments can appear in any order as long as they have the correct types and C++ will figure out the correspondence. True or false?

10. Define encapsulation.

11. For which direction(s) of data flow do you use reference parameters?

12. What is wrong with the following function?

```
void Square (int& x)
{
    x = x * x;
    return 0;
}
```

13. What is wrong with the following function?

```
void Power (int x, int y)
{
    int result;
    result = 1;
    while (y > 0)
    {
        result = result * x;
        y--;
    }
}
```

14. What is wrong with the following function?

```
void Power (int x, int y, int result)
{
    result = 1;
    while (y > 0)
    {
        result = result * x;
        y--;
    }
}
```

15. What is wrong with the following function?

```
void Power (int& x, int& y, int& result)
{
    result = 1;
    while (y > 0)
    {
        result = result * x;
        y--;
    }
}
```

16. A local variable can be referenced anywhere within the block in which it is declared. True or false?
17. Functions can be called from other functions in addition to `main`. True or false?
18. What would be the precondition for a function that reads a file of integers and returns their mean?

Programming Warm-Up Exercises

1. Write the heading for a void function called `Max` that has three `int` parameters, `num1`, `num2`, and `greatest`. The first two parameters receive data from the caller, and `greatest` returns a value. Document the data flow of the parameters with appropriate comments.
2. Write the function prototype for the function in Exercise 1.
3. Write the function definition of the function in Exercise 1 so that it returns the greatest of the two input parameters.
4. Write the heading for a void function called `GetLeast` that takes an `ifstream` parameter called `infile` as an input parameter that is changed, and that has a an `int` parameter called `lowest` that returns a value. Document the data flow of the parameters with appropriate comments.
5. Write the function prototype for the function in Exercise 4.
6. Write the function definition for the function in Exercise 4 so that it reads all of `infile` as a series of `int` values and returns the lowest integer input from `infile`.
7. Add comments to the preceding function definition that state its precondition and postcondition.
8. Write the heading for a function called `Reverse` that takes two string parameters. In the second parameter, the function returns a string that is the character-by-character reverse of the string in the first parameter. The parameters are called `original` and `lanigiro`. Document the data flow of the parameters with appropriate comments.
9. Write the function prototype for the function in Exercise 8.
10. Write the function definition for the function in Exercise 8.
11. Add comments to the preceding function definition that state its precondition and postcondition.

12. Write a void function, `LowerCount`, that reads a line from `cin`, and returns an `int` (`count`) containing the number of lowercase letters in the line. In Appendix C you will find the description of function `islower`, which returns `true` if its `char` parameter is a lowercase character. Document the data flow of the parameters with appropriate comments.

13. Add comments to the function definition that you wrote for Exercise 12 that state its precondition and postcondition.

14. Write a `void` function, `GetNonemptyLine`, that takes an `ifstream` (`infile`) as an in/out parameter, and reads lines from the file until it finds a line that contains characters. It should then return the line via a `string` parameter called `line`. Document the data flow of the parameters with appropriate comments.

15. Write a `void` function, `SkipToEmptyLine`, that takes an `ifstream` (`infile`) as an in/out parameter, and which reads lines from the file until it finds a line that contains no characters. It should then return the number of lines skipped via a `int` parameter called `skipped`. Document the data flow of the parameters with appropriate comments.

16. Write a `void` function, `TimeAdd`, that takes parameters representing two times in days, hours, and minutes, and adds them to get a new time. Each part of the time is an `int`, and hours range from 0 to 23, while minutes range from 0 to 59. There is no limit on the range of days. We assume that the time to be added is positive. The values in the parameters representing the first time are replaced by the result of adding the two times. Here is an example call in which 3 days, 17 hours, 49 minutes is added to 12 days, 22 hours, and 14 minutes.

```
days = 12;
hours = 22;
minutes = 14;
TimeAdd(days, hours, minutes, 3, 17, 49)
```

After the call, the values in the variables are:

```
days = 16
hours = 16
minutes = 3
```

Document the data flow of the parameters with appropriate comments.

17. Extend function `TimeAdd` in Exercise 16 to include seconds.

18. Write a void function, `SeasonPrint`, that takes `int` parameters representing a month and a day and outputs to `cout` the name of the season. For the purposes of this exercise, Spring begins on March 21, Summer begins June 21, Fall begins September 21, and Winter begins December 21. Note that the year begins and ends during Winter. The function can assume that the values in the `month` and `day` parameters have been validated before it is called. Document the data flow of the parameters with appropriate comments.

Programming Problems

1. Rewrite the program from Programming Problem 1 of Chapter 6 using functions. The program is to print a bar chart of the hourly temperatures for one day, given the data on a file. You should have a function to print the chart's heading, and another function that prints the bar of stars for a given temperature value. Note that the second function does not print the value to the left of the bar graph. The main program coordinates the process of inputting values, and calling these functions as necessary.

   Now that your programs are becoming more complex, it is even more important for you to use proper indentation and style, meaningful identifiers, and appropriate comments.

2. You're working for a company that lays ceramic floor tile, and they need a program that estimates the number of boxes of tile for a job. A job is estimated by taking the dimensions of each room in feet and inches, and converting these dimensions into a multiple of the tile size (rounding up any partial multiple) before multiplying to get the number of tiles for the room. A box contains 20 tiles, so the total number needed should be divided by 20 and rounded up to get the number of boxes. The tiles are assumed to be square.

   The program should initially prompt the user for the size of the tile in inches, and the number of rooms to be input. It should then input the dimensions for each room, and output the tiles needed for that room. After the last room is input, the program also should output the total number of tiles needed, the number of boxes needed, and how many extra tiles will be left over.

   Here is an example of how a run might appear:

```
Enter number of rooms: 2
Enter size of tile in inches: 12
Enter room width (feet and inches, separated by a space): 17 4
Enter room length (feet and inches, separated by a space): 9 3
Room requires 180 tiles.
Enter room width (feet and inches, separated by a space): 11 6
Enter room length (feet and inches, separated by a space): 11 9
Room requires 144 tiles.
Total tiles required is 324.
Number of boxes needed is 17.
There will be 16 extra tiles.
```

Use functional decomposition to solve this problem, and code the solution using functions wherever it makes sense to do so. Your program should check for invalid data such as non-positive dimensions, number of rooms less than one, number of inches greater than 11, and so on. It should prompt for corrected input whenever invalid input is detected. Now that your programs are becoming more complex, it is even more important for you to use proper indentation and style, meaningful identifiers, and appropriate comments.

3. Programming Problem 6 in Chapter 4 asked you to write a program to compute the score for one frame in an a game of tenpin bowling. Here you will extend this algorithm to compute the score for an entire game for one player. A game consists of 10 frames, but the tenth frame has some special cases that were not described in Chapter 4.

A frame is played by first setting up the 10 pins. The player then rolls the ball to knock them down. If all 10 are knocked down on the first throw, it is called a strike, and the frame is over. If fewer than 10 are knocked down on the first throw, the number knocked down is recorded and the player gets a second throw. If the remaining pins are all knocked down on the second throw, it is called a spare. The frame ends after the second throw, even if there are pins left standing. If the second throw fails to knock all of the pins down, then the number that it knocked down is recorded, and the score for the frame is just the number of pins knocked down by the two throws. However, in the case of a strike or a spare, the score for the frame depends on throws in the next frame and possibly the frame after that.

If the frame is a strike then the score is equal to 10 points plus the number of pins knocked down in the next two throws. Thus, the maximum score for a frame is thirty, which occurs when the frame is a strike and the two following frames are also strikes. If the frame is a spare, then the score is those 10 points plus the number of pins knocked down on the next throw.

The last frame is played somewhat differently. If the player gets a strike, then he or she gets two more throws so that the score for the strike can be computed. Similarly, if it is a spare, then one extra throw is given. If the first two throws fail to knock down all of the pins then the score for the last frame is just the number knocked down, and there is no extra throw. Here is an example of how the I/O might appear for the start of a run:

```
Enter throw for frame 1: 10
Strike!
Enter throw for frame 2: 7
Enter throw for frame 2: 3
Spare!
Score for frame 1 is 20. Total is 20.
Enter throw for frame 3: 5
Score for frame 2 is 15. Total is 35.
Enter throw for frame 3: 2
Score for frame 3 is 7. Total is 42.
Enter score for frame 4: 12
Input error. Please enter number of pins in range of 0 to 10.
Enter score for frame 4:
```

Your program should input the number of pins knocked down by each throw, and output the score for each frame as it is computed. The program must recognize when a frame has ended (either due to a strike or a second throw). The program also should check for erroneous input. For example, a throw may be in the range of 0 through 10 pins, and the total of the two throws in any of the first nine frames must be less than or equal to 10. Use functional decomposition to solve this problem and code the solution using functions as appropriate. Be sure to use proper formatting and appropriate comments in your code. The output should be clearly labeled and neatly formatted, and the error messages should be informative.

4. Write a simple telephone directory program in C++ that looks up phone numbers in a file containing a list of names and phone numbers. The user should be prompted to enter a first and last name, and the program then outputs the corresponding number, or indicates that the name isn't in the directory. After each lookup, the program should ask the user whether they want to look up another number, and then either repeat the process or exit the program. The data on the file should be organized so that each line contains a first name, a last name, and a phone number, separated by blanks. You can return to the beginning of the file by closing it and opening it again.

   Use functional decomposition to solve the problem and code the solution using functions as appropriate. Be sure to use proper formatting and appropriate comments in your code. The output should be clearly labeled and neatly formatted, and the error messages should be informative.

5. Extend the program in Problem 4 to look up addresses also. Change the file format so that the name and phone number appear on one line, and the address appears on the following line for each entry. The program should ask the user whether they want to look up a phone number, an address, or both, then perform the lookup and output the requested information. The program should recognize an invalid request and prompt the user to enter the request again. As in Problem 4, the program should allow the user to keep entering queries until they indicate that they are done.

6. Programming Problem 1 in Chapter 4 asked you to write a program that inputs a letter and outputs the corresponding word in the International Civil Aviation Organization phonetic alphabet. This problem asks you to turn that program into a function, and use it to convert a string input by the user into the series of words that would be used to spell it out phonetically. For example:

```
Enter string: program
Phonetic version is: Papa Romeo Oscar Golf Romeo Alpha Mike
```

For ease of reference, the ICAO alphabet is repeated here from Chapter 4:

A   Alpha
B   Bravo
C   Charlie
D   Delta
E   Echo
F   Foxtrot
G   Golf
H   Hotel
I   India

J	Juliet
K	Kilo
L	Lima
M	Mike
N	November
O	Oscar
P	Papa
Q	Quebec
R	Romeo
S	Sierra
T	Tango
U	Uniform
V	Victor
W	Whiskey
X	X-ray
Y	Yankee
Z	Zulu

Be sure to use proper formatting and appropriate comments in your code. Provide appropriate prompts to the user. The output should be clearly labeled and neatly formatted.

7. You've been asked to write a program to grade a multiple-choice exam. The exam has 20 questions, each answered with a letter in the range of 'a' through 'f'. The data are stored on a file (exams.dat) where the first line is the key, consisting of a string of 20 characters. The remaining lines on the file are exam answers, and consist of a student ID number, a space, and a string of 20 characters. The program should read the key, then read each exam and output the ID number and score to file scores.dat. Erroneous input should result in an error message. For example, given the data:

```
abcdefabcdefabcdefab
1234567 abcdefabcdefabcdefab
9876543 abddefbbbdefcbcdefac
5554446 abcdefabcdefabcdef
4445556 abcdefabcdefabcdefabcd
3332221 abcdefghijklmnopqrst
```

The program would output on scores.dat:

```
1234567   20
9876543   15
5554446   Too few answers
4445556   Too many answers
3332221   Invalid answers
```

Use functional decomposition to solve the problem and code the solution using functions as appropriate. Be sure to use proper formatting and appropriate comments in your code. The output should be neatly formatted, and the error messages should be informative.

Programming Example Follow-Up

1. Revise the code for the case study program implementing the input modules as functions. Compare the two programs. Which do you find easier to read?
2. Experiment with the mortgage program by using the following input values:

Loan Amount	100000.00
Number of years	0
Interest rate	0
Loan Amount	50000.00
Number of months	−1
Interest rate	−1

   Describe what happens.
3. Add error checking to the Mortgage program to take care of the problems that surfaced in Exercise 2.
4. Add a column to the output of the Mortgage program that shows how much interest has been paid.

Scope, Lifetime, and More on Functions

Knowledge Goals

- To know what a global reference is.
- To understand and be able to avoid unwanted side effects.
- To know when to use a value-returning function.

Skill Goals

To be able to:

- Determine which variables in a program are local.
- Determine which variables are accessible in a given block.
- Determine the lifetime of each variable in a program.
- Design and code a value-returning function for a specified task.
- Invoke a value-returning function properly.

As programs get larger and more complicated, the number of identifiers in a program increases. We invent function names, variable names, constant identifiers, and so on. Some of these identifiers we declare inside blocks. Other identifiers—function names, for example—we declare outside of any block. This chapter examines the C++ rules by which a function may access identifiers that are declared outside its own block. Using these rules, we return to the discussion of interface design that we began in Chapter 7.

Finally, we look at the second kind of subprogram provided by C++: the *value-returning function*. A value-returning function returns a single result—the function value—to the expression from which it was called. In this chapter, you learn how to write such functions.

8.1 Scope of Identifiers

As we saw in Chapter 7, local variables are those declared inside a block, such as the body of a function. Recall that local variables cannot be accessed outside the block that contains them. The same access rule applies to declarations of named constants: Local constants may be accessed only in the block in which they are declared.

Any block, not only a function body, can contain variable and constant declarations. For example, this If statement contains a block that declares a local variable n:

```
if (alpha > 3)
{
    int n;

    cin >> n;
    beta = beta + n;
}
```

As with any local variable, n cannot be accessed by any statement outside the block containing its declaration.

If we listed all the places from which an identifier could be accessed legally, we would describe that identifier's **scope of visibility** or **scope of access**, often just called its **scope**.

Scope The region of program code where it is legal to reference (use) an identifier.

C++ defines several categories of scope for any identifier. We begin by describing three of these categories.

1. *Class scope.* This term refers to the data type called a *class*, which we introduced briefly in Chapter 4. We postpone a detailed discussion of class scope until Chapter 11.

2. *Local scope.* The scope of an identifier declared inside a block extends from the point of declaration to the end of that block.

3. *Global scope.* The scope of an identifier declared outside all functions and classes extends from the point of declaration to the end of the entire file containing the program code.

C++ function names have global scope. (There is an exception to this rule, which we discuss in Chapter 11 when we examine C++ classes.) Once a function name has been declared, the function can be invoked by any other function in the rest of the program. In C++, there is no such thing as a local function—that is, you cannot nest a function definition inside another function definition.

Global variables and constants are those declared outside all functions. When a function declares a local identifier with the same name as a global identifier, the local identifier takes precedence within the function. This principle is called name precedence or name hiding.

> **Name precedence** The precedence that a local identifier in a function has over a global identifier with the same name in any references that the function makes to that identifier; also called *name hiding*.

Here's an example that uses both local and global declarations:

```cpp
#include <iostream>

using namespace std;

void SomeFunc( float );

const int a = 17;           // A global constant
int b;                      // A global variable
int c;                      // Another global variable

int main()
{
    b = 4;                  // Assignment to global b
    c = 6;                  // Assignment to global c
    SomeFunc(42.8);
    return 0;
}
```

```
void SomeFunc( float c )          // Prevents access to global c
{
    float b;                      // Prevents access to global b

    b = 2.3;                      // Assignment to local b
    cout << "a = " << a;          // Output global a (17)
    cout << " b = " << b;         // Output local b (2.3)
    cout << " c = " << c;         // Output local c (42.8)
}
```

In this example, function SomeFunc accesses global constant a but declares its own local variable b and parameter c. Thus, the output would be

```
a = 17 b = 2.3 c = 42.8
```

Local variable b takes precedence over global variable b, effectively hiding global b from the statements in function SomeFunc. Parameter c also blocks access to global variable c from within the function. Function parameters act just like local variables in this respect; that is, parameters have local scope.

Scope Rules

When you write C++ programs, you rarely declare global variables. There are negative aspects to using global variables, which we discuss later. But when a situation crops up in which you have a compelling need for global variables, it pays to know how C++ handles these declarations. The rules for accessing identifiers that aren't declared locally are called **scope rules.**

In addition to local and global access, the C++ scope rules define what happens when blocks are nested within other blocks. Anything declared in a block that contains a nested block is **nonlocal** to the inner block. (Global identifiers are nonlocal with respect to all blocks in the program.) If a block accesses any identifier declared outside its own block, it is a *nonlocal access.*

Scope rules The rules that determine where in the program an identifier may be accessed, given the point where that identifier is declared.

Nonlocal identifier With respect to a given block, any identifier declared outside that block.

Here are the detailed scope rules, excluding class scope and certain language features we have not yet discussed:

1. A function name has global scope. Function definitions cannot be nested within function definitions.

2. The scope of a function parameter is identical to the scope of a local variable declared in the outermost block of the function body.

3. The scope of a global variable or constant extends from its declaration to the end of the file, except as noted in Rule 5.

4. The scope of a local variable or constant extends from its declaration to the end of the block in which it is declared. This scope includes any nested blocks, except as noted in Rule 5.

5. The scope of an identifier does not include any nested block that contains a locally declared identifier with the same name (local identifiers have name precedence).

Here is a sample program that demonstrates C++ scope rules. To simplify the example, only the declarations and headings are spelled out. Note how the While-loop body labeled Block3, located within function Block2, contains its own local variable declarations.

```
// ScopeRules program

#include <iostream>

using namespace std;

void Block1( int, char& );
void Block2();

int  a1;          // One global variable
char a2;          // Another global variable

int main()
{
    ⋮
}

//****************************************************************

void Block1( int   a1,          // Prevents access to global a1
             char& b2 )         // Has same scope as c1 and d2
{
    int c1;        // A variable local to Block1
    int d2;        // Another variable local to Block1
      ⋮
}

//****************************************************************

void Block2()
{
    int a1;        // Prevents access to global a1
    int b2;        // Local to Block2; no conflict with b2 in Block1
```

```
while ( ...)
{                   // Block3
    int c1;         // Local to Block3; no conflict with c1 in Block1
    int b2;         // Prevents nonlocal access to b2 in Block2; no
                    //  conflict with b2 in Block1
      ⋮
}
}
```

Let's look at the ScopeRules program in terms of the blocks it defines and see just what these rules mean. Figure 8–1 shows the headings and declarations in the Scope-Rules program with the scopes of visibility indicated by boxes.

Figure 8–1   *Scope Diagram for ScopeRules Program*

Anything inside a box can refer to anything in a larger surrounding box, but outside-in references aren't allowed. Thus, a statement in Block3 could access any identifier declared in Block2 or any global variable. A statement in Block3 could not access identifiers declared in Block1 because it would have to enter the Block1 box from outside.

Notice that the parameters for a function are inside the function's box, but the function name itself is outside. If the name of the function were inside the box, no function could call another function. This demonstrates merely that function names are globally accessible.

Imagine the boxes in Figure 8–1 as rooms with walls made of two-way mirrors, with the reflective side facing out and the see-through side facing in. If you stood in the room for Block3, you would be able to see out through all the surrounding rooms to the declarations of the global variables (and anything between). You would not be able to see into any other rooms (such as Block1), however, because their mirrored outer surfaces would block your view. Because of this analogy, the term *visible* is often used in describing a scope of access. For example, variable a2 is visible throughout the program, meaning that it can be accessed from anywhere in the program.

Figure 8–1 does not tell the whole story; it represents only scope rules 1 through 4. We also must keep rule 5 in mind. Variable a1 is declared in three different places in the ScopeRules program. Because of name precedence, Block2 and Block3 access the a1 declared in Block2 rather than the global a1. Similarly, the scope of the variable b2 declared in Block2 does *not* include the "hole" created by Block3, because Block3 declares its own variable b2.

Name precedence is implemented by the compiler as follows. When an expression refers to an identifier, the compiler first checks the local declarations. If the identifier isn't local, the compiler works its way outward through each level of nesting until it finds an identifier with the same name. There it stops. If there is an identifier with the same name declared at a level even further out, it is never reached. If the compiler reaches the global declarations (including identifiers inserted by #include directives) and still can't find the identifier, an error message such as "UNDECLARED IDENTIFIER" is issued.

Such a message most likely indicates a misspelling or an incorrect capitalization, or it could mean that the identifier was not declared before the reference to it or was not declared at all. It may also indicate, however, that the blocks are nested so that the identifier's scope doesn't include the reference.

Variable Declarations and Definitions

In Chapter 7, you learned that C++ terminology distinguishes between a function declaration and a function definition. C++ applies the same terminology to variable declarations. A variable declaration becomes a variable definition if it also reserves memory for the variable. All of the variable declarations we have used from the beginning have been variable definitions. What would a variable declaration look like if it were *not* also a definition?

In the previous chapter, we talked about the concept of a multifile program, a program that physically occupies several files containing individual pieces of the program.

C++ has a reserved word `extern` that lets you reference a global variable located in another file. A "normal" declaration such as

```
int someInt;
```

causes the compiler to reserve a memory location for `someInt`. On the other hand, the declaration

```
extern int someInt;
```

is known as an *external declaration*. It states that `someInt` is a global variable located in another file and that no storage should be reserved for it here. System header files such as `iostream` contain external declarations so that user programs can access important variables defined in system files. For example, `iostream` includes declarations like these:

```
extern istream cin;
extern ostream cout;
```

These declarations allow you to reference `cin` and `cout` as global variables in your program, but the variable definitions are located in another file supplied by the C++ system.

In C++ terminology, the statement

```
extern int someInt;
```

is a declaration but not a definition of `someInt`. It associates a variable name with a data type so that the compiler can perform type checking. But the statement

```
int someInt;
```

is both a declaration and a definition of `someInt`. It is a definition because it reserves memory for `someInt`. In C++, you can declare a variable or a function many times, but there can be only one definition.

Except in situations in which it's important to distinguish between declarations and definitions of variables, we'll continue to use the more general phrase *variable declaration* instead of the more specific *variable definition*.

Namespaces

For some time, we have been including the following `using` directive in our programs:

```
using namespace std;
```

What exactly is a namespace? As a general concept, *namespace* is another word for *scope*. However, as a specific C++ language feature, a namespace is a mechanism by which the programmer can create a named scope. For example, the standard header file cstdlib contains function prototypes for several library functions, one of which is the absolute value function, abs. The declarations are contained within a *namespace definition* as follows:

```
// In header file cstdlib:

namespace std
{
    ⋮
    int abs( int );
    ⋮
}
```

A namespace definition consists of the word namespace, then an identifier of the programmer's choice, and then the *namespace body* between braces. Identifiers declared within the namespace body are said to have *namespace scope*. Such identifiers cannot be accessed outside the body except by using one of three methods.

The first method, introduced in Chapter 2, is to use a qualified name: the name of the namespace, followed by the scope resolution operator (::), followed by the desired identifier. Here is an example:

```
#include <cstdlib>

int main()
{
    int alpha;
    int beta;
     ⋮
    alpha = std::abs(beta);     // A qualified name
     ⋮
}
```

The general idea is to inform the compiler that we are referring to the abs declared in the std namespace, not some other abs (such as a global function named abs that we might have written ourselves).

The second method is to use a statement called a *using declaration* as follows:

```
#include <cstdlib>

int main()
{
    int alpha;
    int beta;
    using std::abs;    // A using declaration
```

```
    ⋮
    alpha = abs(beta);
    ⋮
}
```

This `using` declaration allows the identifier `abs` to be used throughout the body of `main` as a synonym for the longer `std::abs`.

The third method—one with which we are familiar—is to use a `using` directive (not to be confused with a `using` declaration).

```
#include <cstdlib>

int main()
{
    int alpha;
    int beta;
    using namespace std;    // A using directive
    ⋮

    alpha = abs(beta);
    ⋮
}
```

With a `using` directive, *all* identifiers from the specified namespace are accessible, but only in the scope in which the `using` directive appears. Above, the `using` directive is in local scope (it's within a block), so identifiers from the `std` namespace are accessible only within `main`. On the other hand, if we put the `using` directive outside all functions (as we have been doing), like this:

```
#include <cstdlib>

using namespace std;

int main()
{
    ⋮
}
```

then the `using` directive is in global scope; consequently, identifiers from the `std` namespace are accessible globally.

Placing a `using` directive in global scope can be a convenience. For example, all of the functions we write can refer to identifiers such as `abs`, `cin`, and `cout` without our having to insert a `using` directive locally in each function. However, global `using` directives are considered a bad idea when creating large, multifile programs. Programmers often make use of several libraries, not just the C++ standard library, when developing complex software. Two or more libraries may, just by coincidence, use the same identifier for completely different purposes. If global `using` directives are employed, *name clashes* (multiple definitions of the same identifier) can occur because all the identifiers have been brought into global scope. (C++ programmers refer to this as "polluting the global namespace.") Over the next several chapters, we continue to use global `using` directives for the `std` namespace because our programs are relatively small and therefore name clashes aren't likely.

Given the concept of namespace scope, we refine our description of C++ scope categories as follows.

1. *Class scope.* This term refers to the data type called a *class*. We postpone a detailed discussion of class scope until Chapter 11.

2. *Local scope.* The scope of an identifier declared inside a block extends from the point of declaration to the end of that block. Also, the scope of a function parameter (formal parameter) extends from the point of declaration to the end of the block that is the body of the function.

3. *Namespace scope.* The scope of an identifier declared in a namespace definition extends from the point of declaration to the end of the namespace body, *and* its scope includes the scope of a `using` directive specifying that namespace.

4. *Global* (or *global namespace*) *scope.* The scope of an identifier declared outside all namespaces, functions, and classes extends from the point of declaration to the end of the entire file containing the program code.

Note that these are general descriptions of scope categories and not scope rules. The descriptions do not account for name hiding (the redefinition of an identifier within a nested block).

8.2 Lifetime of a Variable

A concept related to but separate from the scope of a variable is its lifetime—the period of time during program execution when an identifier actually has memory allocated to it. We have said that storage for local variables is created (allocated) at the moment control enters a function. Then the variables are "alive" while the function is executing, and finally the storage is destroyed (deallocated) when the function exits. In contrast, the life-

> **Lifetime** The period of time during program execution when an identifier has memory allocated to it.
>
> **Automatic variable** A variable for which memory is allocated and deallocated when control enters and exits the block in which it is declared.
>
> **Static variable** A variable for which memory remains allocated throughout the execution of the entire program.

time of a global variable is the same as the lifetime of the entire program. Memory is allocated only once, when the program begins executing, and is deallocated only when the entire program terminates. Observe that scope is a *compile-time* issue, but lifetime is a *run-time* issue.

In C++, an automatic variable is one whose storage is allocated at block entry and deallocated at block exit. A static variable is one whose storage remains allocated for the duration of the entire program. All global variables are static variables. By default, variables declared within a block are automatic variables. However, you can use the reserved word `static` when you declare a local variable. If you do so, the variable is a static variable and its lifetime persists from function call to function call:

```
void SomeFunc()
{
    float   someFloat;      // Destroyed when function exits
    static int someInt;     // Retains its value from call to call
      ⋮
}
```

It is usually better to declare a local variable as `static` than to use a global variable. Like a global variable, its memory remains allocated throughout the lifetime of the entire program. But unlike a global variable, its local scope prevents other functions in the program from tinkering with it.

Initializations in Declarations

One of the most common things we do in programs is first declare a variable and then, in a separate statement, assign an initial value to the variable. Here's a typical example:

```
int sum;

sum = 0;
```

C++ allows you to combine these two statements into one. The result is known as an *initialization in a declaration*. Here we initialize `sum` in its declaration:

```
int sum = 0;
```

In a declaration, the expression that specifies the initial value is called an *initializer*. Above, the initializer is the constant 0.

An automatic variable is initialized to the specified value each time control enters the block:

```
void SomeFunc( int someParam )
{
    int i = 0;                  // Initialized each time
    int n = 2 * someParam + 3;  // Initialized each time
      ⋮
}
```

In contrast, initialization of a static variable (either a global variable or a local variable explicitly declared `static`) occurs once only, the first time control reaches its declaration. Here's an example in which two local static variables are initialized only once (the first time the function is called):

```
void AnotherFunc( int param )
{
    static char ch = 'A';        // Initialized once only
    static int  m  = param + 1;  // Initialized once only
      ⋮
}
```

Although an initialization gives a variable an initial value, it is perfectly acceptable to reassign it another value during program execution.

8.3   Interface Design

We return now to the issue of interface design, which we first discussed in Chapter 7. Recall that the data flow through a function interface can take three forms: incoming only, outgoing only, and incoming/outgoing. Any item that can be classified as purely incoming should be coded as a value parameter. Items in the remaining two categories (outgoing and incoming/outgoing) must be reference parameters; the only way the function can deposit results into the caller's arguments is to have the addresses of those arguments. For emphasis, we repeat the following table from Chapter 7.

Data Flow for a Parameter	Argument-Passing Mechanism
Incoming	Pass by value
Outgoing	Pass by reference
Incoming/outgoing	Pass by reference

Sometimes it is tempting to skip the interface design step when writing a function, letting it communicate with other functions by referencing global variables. Don't! Without the interface design step, you would actually be creating a poorly structured and undocumented interface. Except in well-justified circumstances, the use of global variables is a poor programming practice that can lead to program errors. These errors are extremely hard to locate and usually take the form of unwanted side effects.

Side Effects

Suppose you made a call to the sqrt library function in your program:

```
y = sqrt(x);
```

You expect the call to sqrt to do one thing only: compute the square root of the variable x. You'd be surprised if sqrt also changed the value of your variable x because

Side effect Any effect of one function on another that is not a part of the explicitly defined interface between them.

`sqrt`, by definition, does not make such changes. This would be an example of an unexpected and unwanted side effect.

Side effects are sometimes caused by a combination of reference parameters and careless coding in a function. Perhaps an assignment statement in the function stores a temporary result into one of the reference parameters, accidentally changing the value of an argument back in the calling code. As we mentioned before, using value parameters avoids this type of side effect by preventing the change from reaching the argument.

Side effects also can occur when a function accesses a global variable. An error in the function might cause the value of a global variable to be changed in an unexpected way, causing an error in other functions that access that variable.

The symptoms of a side-effect error are misleading because the trouble shows up in one part of the program when it really is caused by something in another part. To avoid such errors, the only external effect that a function should have is to transfer information through the well-structured interface of the parameter list (see Figure 8–2). If functions access nonlocal variables *only* through their parameter lists, and if all incoming-only parameters are value parameters, then each function is essentially isolated from other parts of the program and side effects cannot occur.

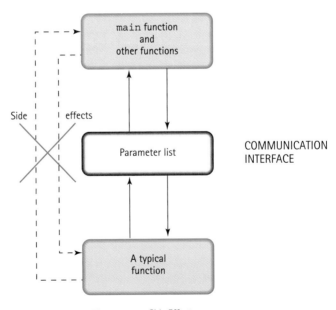

Figure 8–2 *Side Effects*

When a function is free of side effects, we can treat it as an independent module and reuse it in other programs. It is hazardous or impossible to reuse functions with side effects.

Global Constants

Contrary to what you might think, it is acceptable to reference named constants globally. Because the values of global constants cannot be changed while the program is running, no side effects can occur.

There are two advantages to referencing constants globally: ease of change, and consistency. If you need to change the value of a constant, it's easier to change only one global declaration than to change a local declaration in every function. By declaring a constant in only one place, we also ensure that all parts of the program use exactly the same value.

This is not to say that you should declare *all* constants globally. If a constant is needed in only one function, then it makes sense to declare it locally within that function.

8.4 Value-Returning Functions

In Chapter 7 and the first part of this chapter, we have been writing our own void functions. We now look at the second kind of subprogram in C++, the value-returning function. You already know several value-returning functions supplied by the C++ standard library: `sqrt`, `abs`, `fabs`, and others. From the caller's perspective, the main difference between void functions and value-returning functions is the way in which they are called. A call to a void function is a complete statement; a call to a value-returning function is part of an expression.

From a design perspective, value-returning functions are used when there is only one result returned by a function and that result is to be used directly in an expression. For example, suppose we are writing a program that calculates a prorated refund of tuition for students who withdraw in the middle of a semester. The amount to be refunded is the total tuition times the remaining fraction of the semester (the number of days remaining divided by the total number of days in the semester). The people who use the program want to be able to enter the dates on which the semester begins and ends and the date of withdrawal, and they want the program to calculate the fraction of the semester that remains.

Because each semester at this particular school begins and ends within one calendar year, we can calculate the number of days in a period by determining the day number of each date and subtracting the starting day number from the ending day number. The day number is the number associated with each day of the year if you count sequentially from January 1. December 31 has the day number 365, except in leap years, when it is 366.

Let's look at the function definition for Day. Don't worry about how Day works; for now, you should concentrate on its syntax and structure.

```
int Day( /* in */ int month,          // Month number, 1 - 12
         /* in */ int dayOfMonth,      // Day of month, 1 - 31
         /* in */ int year         )   // Year. For example, 2001

// This function computes the day number within a year, given
// the date. It accounts correctly for leap years. The
// calculation is based on the fact that months average 30 days
// in length. Thus, (month - 1) * 30 is roughly the number of
// days in the year at the start of any month. A correction
// factor is used to account for cases where the average is
// incorrect and for leap years. The day of the month is then
// added to produce the day number

// Precondition:
//     1 <= month <= 12
//  && dayOfMonth is in valid range for the month
//  && year is assigned
// Postcondition:
//     Return value is day number in the range 1 - 365
//                     (or 1 - 366 for a leap year)

{
    int correction = 0;   // Correction factor to account for leap
                          //    year and months of different lengths

    // Test for leap year

    if (year % 4 == 0 && (year % 100 != 0 || year % 400 == 0))
        if (month >= 3)          // If date is after February 29
            correction = 1;      //    then add one for leap year

    // Correct for different-length months

    if (month == 3)
        correction = correction - 1;
    else if (month == 2 || month == 6 || month == 7)
        correction = correction + 1;
    else if (month == 8)
        correction = correction + 2;
    else if (month == 9 || month == 10)
        correction = correction + 3;
    else if (month == 11 || month == 12)
```

```
        correction = correction + 4;
    return (month - 1) * 30 + correction + dayOfMonth;
}
```

The first thing to note is that the function definition looks like a void function, except for the fact that the heading begins with the data type `int` instead of the word `void`. The second thing to observe is the Return statement at the end, which includes an integer expression between the word `return` and the semicolon.

> **Function value type**   The data type of the result value returned by a function.

A value-returning function returns one value, not through a parameter but by means of a Return statement. The data type at the beginning of the heading declares the type of value that the function returns. This data type is called the *function type*, although a more precise term is **function value type** (or *function return type* or *function result type*).

The last statement in the `Day` function evaluates the expression

```
(month - 1) * 30 + correction + dayOfMonth
```

and returns the result as the function value.

You now have seen two forms of the Return statement. The form

```
return;
```

is valid *only* in void functions. It causes control to exit the function immediately and return to the caller. The second form is

```
return Expression;
```

This form is valid *only* in a value-returning function. It returns control to the caller, sending back the value of Expression as the function value. (If the data type of Expression is different from the declared function type, its value is coerced to the correct type.)

In Chapter 7, we presented a syntax template for the function definition of a void function. We now update the syntax template to cover both void functions and value-returning functions:

FunctionDefinition

```
DataType FunctionName ( ParameterList )
{
    Statement
       ⋮
}
```

If DataType is the word `void`, the function is a void function; otherwise, it is a value-returning function. Notice from the shading in the syntax template that DataType is optional. If you omit the data type of a function, `int` is assumed. We mention this point only because you sometimes encounter programs where DataType is missing from the function heading. Many programmers do not consider this practice to be good programming style.

The parameter list for a value-returning function has exactly the same form as for a void function: a list of parameter declarations, separated by commas. Also, a function prototype for a value-returning function looks just like the prototype for a void function except that it begins with a data type instead of `void`.

Let's look at another example of value-returning function. The C++ standard library provides a power function, `pow`, that raises a floating-point number to a floating-point power. The library does not supply a power function for `int` values, so let's build one of our own. The function receives two integers, x and n (where $n \geq 0$), and computes x^n. We use a simple approach, multiplying repeatedly by x. Because the number of iterations is known in advance, a count-controlled loop is appropriate. The loop counts down to 0 from the initial value of n. For each iteration of the loop, x is multiplied by the previous product.

```
int Power( /* in */ int x,      // Base number
           /* in */ int n )     // Power to raise base to

// This function computes x to the n power

// Precondition:
//     x is assigned  &&  n >= 0  &&  (x to the n) <= INT_MAX
// Postcondition:
//     Return value is x to the n power

{
    int result;      // Holds intermediate powers of x

    result = 1;
    while (n > 0)
    {
        result = result * x;
        n--;
    }
    return result;
}
```

Boolean Functions

Value-returning functions are not restricted to returning numerical results. We can also use them, for example, to evaluate a condition and return a Boolean result. Boolean functions can be useful when a branch or loop depends on some complex condition. Rather than code the condition directly into the If or While statement, we can call a Boolean function to form the controlling expression.

The C++ standard library provides a number of helpful functions that let you test the contents of char variables. To use them, you #include the header file cctype. Here are some of the available functions; Appendix C contains a more complete list.

Header File	Function	Function Type	Function Value
`<cctype>`	`isalpha(ch)`	int	Nonzero, if ch is a letter ('A'–'Z', 'a'–'z'); 0, otherwise
`<cctype>`	`isalnum(ch)`	int	Nonzero, if ch is a letter or a digit ('A'–'Z', 'a'–'z', '0'–'9'); 0, otherwise
`<cctype>`	`isdigit(ch)`	int	Nonzero, if ch is a digit ('0'–'9'); 0, otherwise
`<cctype>`	`islower(ch)`	int	Nonzero, if ch is a lowercase letter ('a'–'z'); 0, otherwise
`<cctype>`	`isspace(ch)`	int	Nonzero, if ch is a whitespace character (blank, newline, tab, carriage return, form feed); 0, otherwise
`<cctype>`	`isupper(ch)`	int	Nonzero, if ch is an uppercase letter ('A'–'Z'); 0, otherwise

Although they return int values, the "is..." functions behave like Boolean functions. They return an int value that is nonzero (coerced to true in an If or While condition) or 0 (coerced to false in an If or While condition). These functions are convenient to use and make programs more readable. For example, the test

```
if (isalnum(inputChar))
```

is easier to read and less prone to error than if you coded the test the long way:

```
if (inputChar >= 'A' && inputChar <= 'Z' ||
    inputChar >= 'a' && inputChar <= 'z' ||
    inputChar >= '0' && inputChar <= '9'    )
```

In fact, this complicated logical expression doesn't work correctly on some machines. We'll see why when we examine character data in Chapter 10.

Naming Value-Returning Functions

In Chapter 7, we said that it's good style to use imperative verbs when naming void functions. With a value-returning function, the function call represents a value within an expression. Things that represent values, such as variables and value-returning functions, are best given names that are nouns or, occasionally, adjectives. Names that suggest values rather than actions are `Square-Root`, `Cube`, `Factorial`, `StudentCount`, `SumOfSquares`, and `SocialSecurityNum`. As you see, they are all nouns or noun phrases.

Boolean value-returning functions (and variables) are often named using adjectives or phrases beginning with *Is*. Here are a few examples:

```
while (Valid(m, n))
if (Odd(n))
if (IsTriangle(s1, s2, s3))
```

Interface Design and Side Effects

The interface to a value-returning function is designed in much the same way as the interface to a void function. We simply write down a list of what the function needs and what it must return. Because value-returning functions return only one value, there is only one item labeled "outgoing" in the list: the function return value. Everything else in the list is labeled "incoming," and there aren't any "incoming/outgoing" parameters.

Returning more than one value from a value-returning function (by modifying the caller's arguments) is a side effect and should be avoided. If your interface design calls for multiple values to be returned, then you should use a void function instead of a value-returning function.

A rule of thumb is never to use reference parameters in the parameter list of a value-returning function, but to use value parameters exclusively. An exception is the case in which an I/O stream object is passed to a value-returning function. Remember that C++ allows a stream object to be passed only to a reference parameter. Within a value-returning function, the only operation that should be performed is testing the state of the stream (for EOF or I/O errors). A value-returning function should not perform input or output operations. Such operations are considered to be side effects of the function.

When to Use Value-Returning Functions

There aren't any formal rules for determining when to use a void function and when to use a value-returning function, but here are some guidelines:

1. If the module must return more than one value or modify any of the caller's arguments, do not use a value-returning function.

2. If the module must perform I/O, do not use a value-returning function. (This guideline is not universally agreed upon.)

3. If there is only one value returned from the module and it is a Boolean value, a value-returning function is appropriate.

4. If there is only one value returned and that value is to be used immediately in an expression, a value-returning function is appropriate.

5. When in doubt, use a void function. You can recode any value-returning function as a void function by adding an extra outgoing parameter to carry back the computed result.

6. If both a void function and a value-returning function are acceptable, use the one you feel more comfortable implementing.

Value-returning functions were included in C++ to provide a way of simulating the mathematical concept of a function. The C++ standard library supplies a set of commonly used mathematical functions through the header file cmath. A list of these appears in Appendix C.

Background Information

Ignoring a Function Value

The C++ language lets you ignore the value returned by a value-returning function. For example, you could write the following statement in your program without any complaint from the compiler:

```
sqrt(x);
```

When this statement is executed, the value returned by sqrt is promptly discarded. This function call has absolutely no effect except to waste the computer's time by calculating a value that is never used.

Clearly, the above call to sqrt is a mistake. No programmer would write that statement intentionally. But C++ programmers occasionally write value-returning functions in a way that allows the caller to ignore the function value. Such a function is sort of a hybrid between a void function and a value-returning function.

In this book, we don't write hybrid functions. We prefer to keep the concept of a void function distinct from a value-returning function. But there are two reasons why every C++ programmer should know about the topic of ignoring a function value. First, if you accidentally call a value-returning function as if it were a void function, the compiler won't prevent you from making the mistake. Second, you sometimes encounter this style of coding in other people's programs and in the C++ standard library. Several of the library functions are technically value-returning functions, but the function value is used merely to return something of secondary importance such as a status value.

Programming Example

Health Profile

PROBLEM   Your grandmother has just come back from the doctor's office and is confused about all the numbers that were used to evaluate her health. In looking over the report they gave your grandmother, you realize that there could be a market for a program to explain this information to medical patients.

Before you can state the input and output from this program, you need to do some research on the Web. You find that there are two important parts to a cholesterol reading: HDL (good) and LDL (bad). The ratio of the two is also important. You find several references that provide interpretations for a range of input values. The interpretation of your weight is dependent on the ratio of your weight to your size as represented by the body mass index (BMI). Great, you already have a program to calculate the BMI! Blood pressure is made up of two values: systolic and diastolic. When talking about blood pressure, the readings are usually given as "something" over "something," such as 120/80. The first value is the systolic pressure, and the second value is the diastolic pressure. Now, you have enough information to determine the input for your program.

INPUT   Patient's name, HDL, LDL, weight in pounds, height in inches, systolic pressure, and diastolic pressure.

OUTPUT   Patient's name and an interpretation of the cholesterol, weight, and blood pressure readings are written on file "Profile."

DISCUSSION   The decomposition of this problem into tasks is very straightforward. The data values are prompted for, entered, and evaluated. The only question is whether to enter the data all at once and evaluate it or have each evaluation module enter its own data. The principle of information hiding suggests that we embed the data gathering within the functions that evaluate the data.

Here are the interpretations you found on the Internet concerning cholesterol.

HDL	Interpretation
< 40	Too low
>= 40 and < 60	Is okay
>= 60	Excellent

LDL	Interpretation
< 100	Optimal
>=100 and < 130	Near optimal
>=130 and < 160	Borderline high
>=160 and < 190	High
>= 190	Very high

Fortunately, you already have a BMI calculator that can simply be turned into a function (with the food suggestions removed). What about blood pressure readings? Again, here is what you found on the Internet concerning blood pressure readings.

Systolic	Interpretation
< 120	Optimal
< 130	Normal
< 140	Normal high
< 160	Stage 1 hypertension
< 180	Stage 2 hypertension
>= 180	Stage 3 hypertension

Diastolic	Interpretation
< 80	Optimal
< 85	Normal
< 90	High normal
< 100	Stage 1 hypertension
< 110	Stage 2 hypertension
>= 110	Stage 3 hypertension

The algorithm for Evaluate BMI is in Chapter 5, and Evaluate Blood Pressure is identical in form, so we leave the writing of its design as Programming Example Follow-Up Exercise 1.

Here is the program that implements the problem solution:

```
//********************************************************************
// Profile Program
// This program inputs a name, weight, height, blood pressure
// readings, and cholesterol values.  Appropriate health messages
// are written for each of the input values on file healthProfile.
// To save space, we omit from each function the precondition
// comments that document the assumptions made about valid input
// parameter data. These would be included in a program intended
// for actual use.
//********************************************************************

#include <fstream>
#include <iostream>
#include <string>

using namespace std;

// Function prototypes
string Name();
void EvaluateCholesterol( ofstream& healthProfile, string name);
void EvaluateBMI( ofstream& healthProfile, string name);
void EvaluateBloodPressure( ofstream& healthProfile, string name);
```

```
int main()
{
    // Declare and open the output file
    ofstream healthProfile;
    healthProfile.open("Profile");
    if ( !healthProfile )
    { // No
        cout << "Can't open output file." << endl;
        return 1;
    }
    string name;
    name = Name();

    // Write patient's name on output file
    healthProfile << "Patient's name " << name << endl;

    // Evaluate the patient's statistics
    EvaluateCholesterol(healthProfile, name);
    EvaluateBMI(healthProfile, name);
    EvaluateBloodPressure(healthProfile, name);
    healthProfile << endl;

    healthProfile.close();
    return 0;
}

//**********************************************************************

string Name()

// Name function
// This function inputs a name and returns it in first,
// middle initial, and last order
// Postcondition:
//      Return value is the string composed of the first name,
//      blank, middle initial, period, blank, last name

{
    // Declare the patient's name
    string firstName;
    string lastName;
    char middleInitial;

    // Prompt for and enter the patient's name
    cout << "Enter the patient's first name: ";
    cin >> firstName;
    cout << "Enter the patient's last name: ";
```

```
        cin >> lastName;
        cout << "Enter the patient's middle initial: ";
        cin >> middleInitial;
        return firstName + ' '  + middleInitial + ". " + lastName;
}


//*********************************************************************

void EvaluateCholesterol
    ( /* inout */ ofstream& healthProfile,    // Output file
      /* in */     string name )              // Patient's name

// This function inputs HDL (good cholesterol) and LDL (bad
// cholesterol) and prints out a health message based on their
// values on file healthProfile.
// Precondition:
//     Output file has been successfully opened
// Postcondition:
//     Appropriate health messages for the input values of
//     HDL, LDL, and their ratio have been printed on file
//     healthProfile.

{
    int HDL;
    int LDL;

    // Prompt for and enter HDL and LDL
    cout << "Enter HDL for " << name << ": ";
    cin >> HDL;
    cout << "Enter LDL for " << name << ": ";
    cin >> LDL;
    float ratio = LDL/HDL;     // Calculate ratio of LDL to HDL

    healthProfile << "Cholesterol Profile " << endl;
    // Print message based on HDL value
    if (HDL < 40)
        healthProfile << "    HDL is too low" << endl;
    else if (HDL < 60)
        healthProfile << "    HDL is okay" << endl;
    else
        healthProfile << "    HDL is excellent" << endl;
    // Print message based on LDL value
    if (LDL < 100)
        healthProfile << "    LDL is optimal" << endl;
    else if (LDL < 130)
```

```
            healthProfile << "    LDL is near optimal" << endl;
        else if (LDL < 160)
            healthProfile << "    LDL is borderline high" << endl;
        else if (LDL < 190)
            healthProfile << "    LDL is high" << endl;
        else
            healthProfile << "    LDL is very high" << endl;

        if (ratio < 3.22)
            healthProfile << "    Ratio of LDL to HDL is good"
                          << endl;
        else
            healthProfile << "    Ratio of LDL to HDL is not good"
                          << endl;
}


//*********************************************************************


void EvaluateBMI
    ( /* inout */ ofstream& healthProfile,    // Output file
      /* in */    string name )               // Patient's name

// This function inputs weight in pounds and height in inches and
// calculates the body mass index (BMI prints a health message
// based on the BMI. Input in English weights
// Precondition:
//     Output file has been successfully opened
// Postcondition:
//     Appropriate health messages for the BMI based on input values
//     of weight and height have been printed on file healthProfile

{
    const int BMI_CONSTANT = 703; // Constant in English formula
    float pounds;
    float inches;

    // Enter the patient's weight and height
    cout << "Enter the weight in pounds for " << name << ": ";
    cin >> pounds;
    cout << "Enter the height in inches for " << name << ": ";
    cin >> inches;
    float bodyMassIndex = pounds * BMI_CONSTANT / (inches * inches);
    healthProfile << "Body Mass Index Profile" << endl;
```

```
        // Print bodyMassIndex
        healthProfile << "   Body mass index is " << bodyMassIndex
                      << ". " << endl;
        healthProfile << "   Interpretation of BMI " << endl;

        // Print interpretation of BMI
        if (bodyMassIndex <20)
            healthProfile << "   Underweight: BMI is too low"
                          << endl;
        else if (bodyMassIndex <=25)
            healthProfile << "   Normal: BMI is average"  << endl;
        else if (bodyMassIndex <= 30)
            healthProfile << "   Overweight: BMI is too high"
                          << endl;
        else
            healthProfile << "   Obese: BMI is dangerously high"
                          << endl;
}


//*****************************************************************


void EvaluateBloodPressure
    ( /* inout */ ofstream& healthProfile,    // Output file
      /* in */     string name )              // Patient's name

// This function gets blood pressure readings (systolic/diastolic)
// and prints out a  health message based on their values
// on file healthProfile
// Precondition:
//     Output file has been successfully opened
// Postcondition:
//     Appropriate health messages for the blood pressure readings,
//     based on input values of systolic and diastolic pressure have
//     been printed on file healthProfile

{
    // Declare the blood pressure readings
    int systolic;
    int diastolic;

    // Enter the patient's blood pressure readings
    cout << "Enter the systolic blood pressure reading for"
         << name << ": ";
    cin >> systolic;
```

```cpp
    cout << "Enter the diastolic blood pressure reading for "
         << name << ": ";
    cin >> diastolic;
    // Print interpretation of systolic reading
    healthProfile << "Blood Pressure Profile " << endl;
    if (systolic < 120)
        healthProfile << "   Systolic reading is optimal" << endl;
    else if (systolic < 130)
        healthProfile << "   Systolic reading is normal" << endl;
    else if (systolic < 140)
        healthProfile << "   Systolic reading is high normal"
                      << endl;
    else if (systolic < 160)
        healthProfile <<
            "   Systolic indicates hypertension Stage 1" << endl;
    else if (systolic < 180)
        healthProfile <<
            "   Systolic indicates hypertension Stage 2" << endl;
    else
        healthProfile <<
            "   Systolic indicates hypertension Stage 3" << endl;

    // Print interpretation of diastolic reading
    if (diastolic < 80)
        healthProfile << "   Diastolic reading is optimal" << endl;
    else if (diastolic < 85)
        healthProfile << "   Diastolic reading is normal" << endl;
    else if (diastolic < 90)
        healthProfile << "   Diastolic reading is high normal"
                      << endl;
    else if (diastolic < 100)
        healthProfile <<
            "   Diastolic indicates hypertension Stage 1" << endl;
    else if (diastolic < 110)
        healthProfile <<
            "   Diastolic indicates hypertension Stage 2" << endl;
    else
        healthProfile <<
            "   Diastolic indicates hypertension Stage 3" << endl;
}
```

Here is sample input and output.

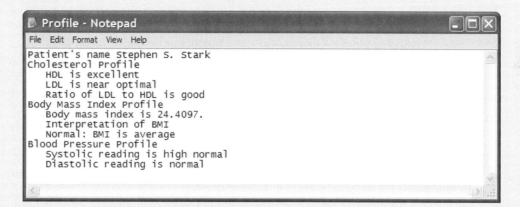

TESTING There are nine inputs to this program: two strings and a character in `Name`, two integer values in `EvaluateChelesterol`, two floating point values in `EvaluateBMI`, and two integer values in `EvaluateBloodPressure`. The code in `Name` duplicates the code in program `Name` in Chapter 4, so we can assume that it is correct. Each of the other functions needs to be checked separately, choosing values that occur at the break points in the If statements of each function.

We have not included any data validation in this case study because the values are input from a patient's chart. Although the values can be assumed to be correct on the chart, we cannot assume that they are input correctly. Programming Example Follow-Up Exercise 3 asks you to add data validation to this program.

Testing and Debugging

One of the advantages of a modular design is that you can test it long before the code has been written for all of the modules. If we test each module individually, then we can assemble the modules into a complete program with much greater confidence that the program is correct. In this section, we introduce a technique for testing a module separately.

Stubs and Drivers

Suppose you were given the code for a module and your job was to test it. How would you test a single module by itself? First of all, it must be called by something (unless it is the `main` function). Second, it may have calls to other modules that aren't available to you. To test the module, you must fill in these missing links.

When a module contains calls to other modules, we can write dummy functions called **stubs** to satisfy those calls.

A stub usually consists of an output statement that prints a message such as "Function such-and-such just got called." Even though the stub is a dummy, it allows us to determine whether the function is called at the right time by the `main` function or another function.

> **Stub** A dummy function that assists in testing part of a program. A stub has the same name and interface as a function that actually would be called by the part of the program being tested, but it is usually much simpler.
>
> **Driver** A simple main function that is used to call a function being tested. The use of a driver permits direct control of the testing process.

A stub also can be used to print the set of values that are passed to it; this tells us whether or not the module being tested is supplying the correct information. Sometimes a stub assigns new values to its reference parameters to simulate data being read or results being computed in order to give the calling module something on which to keep working. Because we can choose the values that are returned by the stub, we have better control over the conditions of the test run.

In addition to supplying a stub for each call within the module, you must provide a dummy program—a **driver**—to call the module itself. A driver program contains the bare minimum of code required to call the module being tested.

By surrounding a module with a driver and stubs, you gain complete control of the conditions under which it executes. This allows you to test different situations and combinations that may reveal errors.

Testing and Debugging Hints

1. Make sure that variables used as arguments to a function are declared in the block where the function call is made.

2. Carefully define the precondition, postcondition, and parameter list to eliminate side effects. Variables used only in a function should be declared as local variables. *Do not* use global variables in your programs. (Exception: It is acceptable to reference `cin` and `cout` globally.)

3. If the compiler displays a message such as "UNDECLARED IDENTIFIER," check that the identifier isn't misspelled (and that it is, in fact, declared), that the identifier is declared before it is referenced, and that the scope of the identifier includes the reference to it.

4. If you intend to use a local name that is the same as a nonlocal name, a misspelling in the local declaration will wreak havoc. The C++ compiler won't complain, but will cause every reference to the local name to go to the nonlocal name instead.

5. Remember that the same identifier cannot be used in both the parameter list and the outermost local declarations of a function.

6. With a value-returning function, be sure the function heading and prototype begin with the correct data type for the function return value.

7. With a value-returning function, don't forget to use a statement

`return` Expression;

to return the function value. Make sure the expression is of the correct type, or implicit type coercion will occur.

8. Remember that a call to a value-returning function is part of an expression, whereas a call to a void function is a separate statement. (C++ softens this distinction, however, by letting you call a value-returning function as if it were a void function, ignoring the return value. Be careful here.)

9. In general, don't use reference parameters in the parameter list of a value-returning function. A reference parameter must be used, however, when an I/O stream object is passed as a parameter.

10. If necessary, use your system's debugger (or use debug output statements) to indicate when a function is called and if it is executing correctly. The values of the arguments can be displayed immediately before the call to the function (to show the incoming values) and immediately after (to show the outgoing values). You also may want to display the values of local variables in the function itself to indicate what happens each time it is called.

Summary

The scope of an identifier refers to the parts of the program in which it is visible. C++ function names have global scope, as do the names of variables and constants that are declared outside all functions and namespaces. Variables and constants declared within a block have local scope; they are not visible outside the block. The parameters of a function have the same scope as local variables declared in the outermost block of the function.

With rare exceptions, it is not considered good practice to declare global variables and reference them directly from within a function. All communication between the modules of a program should be through the argument and parameter lists (and via the function value sent back by a value-returning function). The use of global constants, on the other hand, is considered to be an acceptable programming practice because it adds consistency and makes a program easier to change while avoiding the pitfalls of side effects. Well-designed and well-documented functions that are free of side effects can often be reused in other programs. Many programmers keep a library of functions that they use repeatedly.

The lifetime of a variable is the period of time during program execution when memory is allocated to it. Global variables have static lifetime (memory remains allocated for the duration of the program's execution). By default, local variables have automatic lifetime (memory is allocated and deallocated at block entry and block exit). A local variable may be given static lifetime by using the word `static` in its declaration. This variable has the lifetime of a global variable but the scope of a local variable.

C++ allows a variable to be initialized in its declaration. For a static variable, the initialization occurs once only—when control first reaches its declaration. An automatic variable is initialized each time control reaches the declaration.

C++ provides two kinds of subprograms, void functions and value-returning functions, for us to use. A value-returning function is called from within an expression and returns a single result that is used in the evaluation of the expression. For the function value to be returned, the last statement executed by the function must be a Return statement containing an expression of the appropriate data type.

All the scope rules, as well as the rules about reference and value parameters, apply to both void functions and value-returning functions. It is considered poor programming practice, however, to use reference parameters in a value-returning function definition. Doing so increases the potential for unintended side effects. (An exception is when I/O stream objects are passed as parameters. Other exceptions are noted in later chapters.)

We can use stubs and drivers to test functions in isolation from the rest of a program. They are particularly useful in the context of team-programming projects.

Quick Check

1. If a function references a variable that is not declared in its block or its parameter list, is the reference global or local? (pp. 280–285)
2. How do references to global variables contribute to the potential for unwanted side effects? (pp. 291–293)
3. If a module has three /* in */ parameters and one /* out */ parameter, should it be implemented by a void or a value-returning function? (p. 298)
4. A program has two functions, Quick1 and Quick2. The program itself declares variables check and qc. Function Quick1 declares variables called quest and qc. Function Quick2 declares one variable called quest and a static variable called forever. Which of these variables are local? (pp. 280–285)
5. In Quick Check question 4, which variables are accessible within function Quick1? (pp. 280–285)
6. In Quick Check question 4, what is the lifetime of each of the six variables? (pp. 289–291)
7. What distinguishes a value-returning function from a void function? (pp. 293–297)
8. Given the following function heading, how would you write a call to it that will pass it the value 98.6 and assign the result to the variable fever? (pp. 293–299)

```
bool TempCheck (/* in */ float temp)
```

Answers
1. Global.   2. They enable a function to affect the state of the program through a means other than the well-defined interface of the parameter list.   3. A value-returning function.   4. Variables

declared within the functions are local. In Quick1, quest and qc. In Quick2, quest and for-ever. 5. check, quest, and the locally-declared qc. 6. check and qc in the program, together with forever, are static. The variables in Quick1, and the variable quest in Quick2 are automatic. 7. Using a type-name in place of void, and using a return statement to pass a value back to the caller. 8. fever = TempCheck(98.6);

Exam Preparation Exercises

1. A function parameter is local to the entire block that is the body of the function. True or false?
2. A reference parameter has the same scope as a global variable. True or false?
3. A global variable can be referenced anywhere within the program. True or false?
4. Function names have global scope. True or false?
5. Match the following terms with the definitions given below.
   a. Scope
   b. Name precedence
   c. Scope rules
   d. Nonlocal identifier
   e. Lifetime
   f. Automatic variable
   g. Static variable
   h. Side effect
       i. The semantics that specify where we can reference nonlocal identifiers.
       ii. A variable for which memory is allocated for the duration of the program.
       iii. When one function affects another in a manner that isn't defined by their interface.
       iv. The precedence that a local identifier has over a global identifier with the same name.
       v. The region of program code where it is legal to reference an identifier.
       vi. A variable that has memory allocated at block entry and deallocated at block exit.
       vii. An identifier declared outside of the current block.
       viii. The period in which an identifier has memory allocated to it.
6. Identify the side effect in the following function.

```
int ExamPrep (int param1, int& param2)
{
    if (param2 = param1)
        return param2;
    else if (param2 > param1)
        return param1;
    else
        return param1 * param2;
}
```

7. Identify the side effect in the following program (which uses poor style for naming variables).

```cpp
#include <iostream>

using namespace std;

string a;
int w;

bool GetYesOrNo();

int main ()
{
    cout << "Enter name:";
    cin >> a;
    w = 0;
    cout << "Are there weight data?";
    if (GetYesOrNo());
    {
        cout << "Enter weight:";
        cin >> w;
    }
    cout << "Name is " << a << "  weight is " << w << endl;
}

bool GetYesOrNo()
{
    cout << "Enter yes or no: ";
    cin >> a;
    return a == "yes";
}
```

8. What is the scope of a namespace that is specified in a using directive outside of all functions?

9. What is the scope of the `std` namespace in the following code?

```cpp
// Include directives and function prototypes here

int main()
{
    using namespace std;
    // Rest of main body is here
}
// Function definitions are here
```

10. What is the lifetime of each of the following?
    a. A global variable.
    b. A local variable in a function.
    c. A local, static variable in a function.
11. Rewrite the following declaration and initialization as a single statement.

```
float pi;
pi = 3.14159265;
```

12. If a local, static variable is initialized in its declaration within a function, when does the variable get initialized and how often?
13. If a local, non-static variable is initialized in its declaration within a function, when does the variable get initialized and how often?
14. A value-returning function can have just one `return` statement. True or false?
15. What's wrong with the following function?

```
bool Greater (int a, int b)
{
    if (a > b)
        return true;
}
```

16. What's wrong with the following function?

```
int Average (int a, int b, int c)
{
    return (a + b + c)/3.0;
}
```

17. What's wrong with the following function?

```
void Maximum (int a, int b, int& max)
{
    if (a > b)
        max = a;
    else
        max = b;
    return max;
}
```

18. Using a reference parameter in a value-returning function makes what kind of programming error more likely?

Programming Warm-Up Exercises

1. The following program is written in a very poor style that uses global variables instead of parameters and arguments, resulting in unwanted side effects. Rewrite it using good style.

```
#include <iostream>
using namespace std;
int Power ();
int pow;
int x;
int result;
int main ()
{
cout << "Enter power: ";
cin >> pow;
cout << "Enter value to be raised to power: ";
cin >> x;
cout << Power(x, pow);
}
int Power()
{
result = 1;
while (pow > 0)
{
result = result * x;
pow--;
}
return result;
}
```

2. Write the heading for a `bool` function `Equals` that has two /* in */ `float` parameters, x and y.

3. Write the function prototype for the function in Exercise 2.

4. Write a body for the function in Exercise 2 that compares x and y, returning `true` if their difference is less than 0.00000001, and `false` otherwise.

5. Write the heading and function prototype for a float function called ConeVolume that takes two /* in */ float parameters, radius and height.

6. Write the body for the function heading in Exercise 5. The body computes the volume of a cone using the following formula.

$$\frac{1}{3}\pi \times radius^2 \times height$$

7. Rewrite `void` function described in Programming Warm-Up Exercises 4 and 6 in Chapter 7 as a value-returning function. The function is called `GetLeast` and it takes an `ifstream` parameter called `infile` as an input parameter that is changed. It returns an `int` value that is the lowest value read from the file.

8. Rewrite the `void` function called `Reverse` described in Programming Warm-Up Exercises 8 and 10 in Chapter 7 as a value-returning function. It should take a `string` parameter as input. The function returns a string that is the character-

by-character reverse of the string in the parameter. The parameter is called `original`.

9. Rewrite the void function, `LowerCount` described in Programming Warm-Up Exercise 12 of Chapter 7 as a value-returning function. The function reads a line from `cin`, and returns an `int` containing the number of lowercase letters in the line. In Appendix C you will find the description of function `islower`, which returns `true` if its `char` parameter is a lowercase character.

10. Write a value-returning `float` function called `SquareKm` that takes two `float` parameters, length and width, and the return value is in square kilometers. The parameters are the length and width of an area in miles. The conversion factor for kilometers from miles is 1.6.

11. Write a value-returning `bool` function called `Exhausted` that takes an `int` parameter called `filmRolls`. The function keeps track of how many rolls of film have been processed by the chemistry in a photo-processing machine. When the total number of rolls exceeds 1000, it returns `true`. Each time it is called, the value in the parameter is added to the total. When the total exceeds 1000, the variable containing the total is reset to zero before the function returns, under the assumption that the exhausted chemistry will be replaced before more rolls are processed.

12. Write a value returning `string` function called `MonthAbbrev` that takes an `int` value as a parameter. The parameter, `month`, represents the number of the month. The function returns a string containing the three-letter abbreviation for the corresponding month number. Assume that the month number is in the range of 1 to 12.

13. Modify the function in Exercise 12 to handle month numbers that are not in the valid range by returning the string `"Inv"`.

14. Write a value-returning `float` function called `RunningAvg` that takes a `float` variable, `value`, as its input and returns the running average of all the values that have been passed to the function since the program first called it.

Programming Problems

1. You are working on a project that requires climate data for a location. The maximum daily change in barometric pressure is one aspect of climate that your company needs. You have a file (`barometric.dat`) with hourly barometer readings taken over the course of a year. Each line of the file contains the readings for a single day, separated by blanks. Each reading is expressed in inches of mercury, so it is a decimal number ranging from about 28.00 to 32.00. For each line of data, you need to determine the maximum and minimum reading, and output the difference between those readings to file `differences.dat`. Each output value should be on a separate line of the file. Once the file has been read, the program also should output the greatest and least difference for the year on `cout`. Develop the program using functional decomposition, and use proper style and documentation in your code. Your program should make appropriate use of value-returning functions in solving this problem.

2. Extend the program in Problem 1 so that it also outputs the maximum and minimum barometric reading for each day on file `differences.dat`, and then outputs the maximum and minimum reading for the year on `cout` at the end of the run.

3. You're working for a lumber company, and they would like a program that calculates the cost of lumber for an order. The company sells pine, fir, cedar, maple, and oak lumber. Lumber is priced by board feet. One board foot equals one square foot, one inch thick. The price per board foot is given in the following table:

Pine	0.89
Fir	1.09
Cedar	2.26
Maple	4.50
Oak	3.10

The lumber is sold in different dimensions (specified in inches of width and height, and feet of length) that need to be converted to board feet. For example, a 2 × 4 × 8 piece is 2 inches wide, 4 inches high, and 8 feet long, and is equivalent to 5.333 board feet. An entry from the user will be in the form of a letter and four integer numbers. The integers are: number of pieces, width, height, and length. The letter will be one of P, F, C, M, O (corresponding to the five kinds of wood) or T, meaning Total. When the letter is T, there are no integers following it on the line. The program should print out the price for each entry, and print the total after T is entered. Here is an example run:

Enter item: P 10 2 4 8
10 2×4×8 Pine, cost: $47.47
Enter item: M 1 1 12 8
1 1×12×8 Maple, cost: $36.00
Enter item: T
Total cost: $83.47

Develop the program using functional decomposition, and use proper style and documentation in your code. Your program should make appropriate use of value-returning functions in solving this problem. Be sure that the user prompts are clear, and that the output is labeled appropriately.

4. Write a program that determines the day of the week for a given date. You can invent your own complex algorithm that takes into account the special leap year rules, and changes in calendars, but this is a case where it makes sense to look for things that are familiar. Who else might need to compute values from dates over a wide span of time? Historians work with dates, but generally don't compute from them. Astronomers, however, need to know the difference in time between orbital events in the solar system that span hundreds of years. Consulting an astronomy text, you will find that there is a standard way of representing

a date, called the Julian Day Number (JDN). This is the number of days that have elapsed since January 1, 4713 BC. Given the JDN for a date, there is a simple formula that tells the day of the week:

```
DayOfWeek = (JDN + 1) % 7
```

The result is in the range of 0 to 6, with 0 representing Sunday.

The only remaining problem is how to compute the JDN, which is not so simple. The algorithm computes several intermediate results that are added together to give the JDN. We look at the computation of each of these three intermediate values in turn.

If the date comes from the Gregorian calendar (later than October 15, 1582), then compute intRes1 with the following formula, otherwise let intRes1 be zero.

```
intRes1 = 2 - year / 100 + year / 400        (integer division)
```

The second intermediate result is computed as follows:

```
intRes2 = int(365.25 * Year)
```

We compute the third intermediate value with this formula:

```
intRes3 = int(30.6001 * (month + 1))
```

Finally, the JDN is computed this way:

```
JDN = intRes1 + intRes2 + intRes3 + day + 1720994.5
```

Your program should make appropriate use of value-returning functions in solving this problem. These formulas require nine significant digits; you may have to use the integer type long and the floating-point type double. Your program should prompt appropriately for input of the date, and properly label the output. Use proper coding style with comments to document the algorithm as needed.

5. Reusing functions from Problem 4 as appropriate, write a C++ program that computes the number of days between two dates. If your design for Problem 4 used good functional decomposition, this should be a trivial program to write. You merely need to input two dates, convert them to their JDNs, and take the difference of the JDNs.

Your program should make appropriate use of value-returning functions in solving this problem. These formulas require nine significant digits; you may have to use the integer type long and the floating-point type double. Your program should prompt appropriately for input of the date, and properly label the output. Use proper coding style with comments to document the algorithm as needed.

Programming Example Follow-Up

1. Write the algorithm for the EvaluateBloodPressure module.
2. Write a driver and test function `EvaluateBloodPressure`, making sure that every branch is taken.
3. Add a Boolean function to the three Evaluate modules, which is true if the data are ok and false otherwise. Test the input within each module for negative or zero input values, which should be considered errors. If an error occurs, state in which module it occurs and set the error flag.
4. Rewrite the main program to test this flag after each call and exit the program if an error occurs.

Additional Control Structures

Knowledge Goals

- *To know how to choose the most appropriate looping statement for a given problem.*
- *To understand the purpose of the Break and Continue statements.*

Skill Goals

To be able to:

- *Write a Switch statement for a multiway branching problem.*
- *Write a Do-While statement and contrast it with a While statement.*
- *Write a For statement to implement a count-controlled loop.*

In the preceding chapters, we introduced C++ statements for sequence, selection, loop, and subprogram structures. In some cases, we introduced more than one way of implementing these structures. For example, selection may be implemented by an If-Then structure or an If-Then-Else structure. The If-Then is sufficient to implement any selection structure, but C++ provides the If-Then-Else for convenience because the two-way branch is frequently used in programming.

This chapter introduces five new statements that are also nonessential to, but nonetheless convenient for, programming. One, the Switch statement, makes it easier to write selection structures that have many branches. Two new looping statements, For and Do-While, make it easier to program certain types of loops. The other two statements, Break and Continue, are control statements that are used as part of larger looping and selection structures.

9.1 The Switch Statement

The Switch statement is a selection control structure for multiway branches, similar to nested If statements. The value of the **switch expression**—an expression whose value is matched with a label attached to a branch—determines which one of the branches is executed. For example, look at the following statement:

Switch expression The expression whose value determines which switch label is selected. It cannot be a floating-point or string expression.

```
switch (letter)
{
    case 'X' : Statement1;
               break;
    case 'L' :
    case 'M' : Statement2;
               break;
    case 'S' : Statement3;
               break;
    default  : Statement4;
}
Statement5;
```

In this example, `letter` is the switch expression. The statement means "If `letter` is 'X', execute Statement1 and break out of the Switch statement, continuing with Statement5. If `letter` is 'L' or 'M', execute Statement2 and continue with Statement5. If `letter` is 'S', execute Statement3 and continue with Statement5. If `letter` is none of the characters mentioned, execute Statement4 and continue with Statement5." The Break statement causes an immediate exit from the Switch statement. We'll see shortly what happens if we omit the Break statements.

The syntax template for the Switch statement is

SwitchStatement

```
switch ( IntegralOrEnumExpression )
{
    SwitchLabel ... Statement
            ⋮
}
```

IntegralOrEnumExpression is an expression of integral type—char, short, int, long, bool—or of enum type (we discuss enum in the next chapter). The optional SwitchLabel in front of a statement is either a *case label* or a *default label:*

SwitchLabel

```
⎰ case ConstantExpression :
⎱ default :
```

In a case label, ConstantExpression is an integral or enum expression whose operands must be literal or named constants. The following are examples of constant integral expressions (where CLASS_SIZE is a named constant of type int):

```
3
CLASS_SIZE
'A'
2 * CLASS_SIZE + 1
```

The data type of ConstantExpression is coerced, if necessary, to match the type of the switch expression.

In our opening example that tests the value of letter, the following are the case labels:

```
case 'X' :
case 'L' :
case 'M' :
case 'S' :
```

As that example shows, a single statement may be preceded by more than one case label. Each case value may appear only once in a given Switch statement. If a value appears more than once, a syntax error results. Also, there can be only one default label in a Switch statement.

The flow of control through a Switch statement goes like this. First, the switch expression is evaluated. If this value matches one of the values in a case label, control branches to the statement following that case label. From there, control proceeds sequentially until either a Break statement or the end of the Switch statement is encountered. If the value of the switch expression doesn't match any case value, then one of two things happens. If there is a default label, control branches to the statement following that label. If there is no default label, all statements within the Switch are skipped and control simply proceeds to the statement following the entire Switch statement.

The following Switch statement prints an appropriate comment based on a student's grade (grade is of type char):

```
switch (grade)
{
    case 'A' :
    case 'B' : cout << "Good Work";
               break;
    case 'C' : cout << "Average Work";
               break;
    case 'D' :
    case 'F' : cout << "Poor Work";
               numberInTrouble++;
               break;          // Unnecessary, but a good habit
}
```

Notice that the final Break statement is unnecessary. But programmers often include it anyway. One reason is that it's easier to insert another case label at the end if a Break statement is already present.

If grade does not contain one of the specified characters, none of the statements within the Switch is executed. Unless a precondition of the Switch statement is that grade is definitely one of 'A', 'B', 'C', 'D', or 'F', it would be wise to include a default label to account for an invalid grade:

```
switch (grade)
{
    case 'A' :
    case 'B' : cout << "Good Work";
               break;
    case 'C' : cout << "Average Work";
               break;
    case 'D' :
    case 'F' : cout << "Poor Work";
               numberInTrouble++;
               break;
    default  : cout << grade << " is not a valid letter grade.";
               break;
}
```

A Switch statement with a Break statement after each case alternative behaves exactly like an If-Then-Else-If control structure. For example, our Switch statement is equivalent to the following code:

```
if (grade == 'A' || grade == 'B')
    cout << "Good Work";
else if (grade == 'C')
    cout << "Average Work";
else if (grade == 'D' || grade == 'F')
{
    cout << "Poor Work";
    numberInTrouble++;
}
else
    cout << grade << " is not a valid letter grade.";
```

Finally, we said we would look at what happens if you omit the Break statements inside a Switch statement. Let's rewrite our letter grade example without the Break statements:

```
switch (grade)     // Wrong version
{
    case 'A' :
    case 'B' : cout << "Good Work";
    case 'C' : cout << "Average Work";
    case 'D' :
    case 'F' : cout << "Poor Work";
             numberInTrouble++;
    default  : cout << grade << " is not a valid letter grade.";
}
```

If grade happens to be 'H', control branches to the statement at the default label and the output is

```
H is not a valid letter grade.
```

Unfortunately, this case alternative is the only one that works correctly. If grade is 'A', the resulting output is this:

```
Good WorkAverage WorkPoor WorkA is not a valid letter grade.
```

Remember that after a branch is taken to a specific case label, control proceeds sequentially until either a Break statement or the end of the Switch statement is encountered. Forgetting a Break statement in a case alternative is a very common source of errors in C++ programs.

9.2 The Do-While Statement

The Do-While statement is a looping control structure in which the loop condition is tested at the end (bottom) of the loop. This format guarantees that the loop body executes at least once.

The statement

```
do
{
        Statement1;
        Statement2;
        ⋮
        StatementN;
} while (Expression);
```

means "Execute the statements between do and while as long as Expression has the value true at the end of the loop."

Let's compare a While loop and a Do-While loop that do the same task: They find the first period in a file of data. Assume that there is at least one period in the file.

While Solution

```
dataFile >> inputChar;
while (inputChar != '.')
    dataFile >> inputChar;
```

Do-While Solution

```
do
    dataFile >> inputChar;
while (inputChar != '.');
```

The While solution requires a priming read so that inputChar has a value before the loop is entered. This isn't required for the Do-While solution because the input statement within the loop is executed before the loop condition is evaluated.

Let's look at another example. Suppose a program needs to read a person's age interactively. The program requires that the age be positive. The following loops ensure that the input value is positive before the program proceeds any further.

While Solution

```
cout << "Enter your age: ";
cin >> age;
while (age <= 0)
{
    cout << "Your age must be positive." << endl;
    cout << "Enter your age: ";
```

```
    cin >> age;
}
```

Do-While Solution

```
do
{
    cout << "Enter your age: ";
    cin >> age;
    if (age <= 0)
        cout << "Your age must be positive." << endl;
} while (age <= 0);
```

Notice that the Do-While solution does not require the prompt and input steps to appear twice—once before the loop and once within it—but it does test the input value twice.

We can also use the Do-While to implement a count-controlled loop *if* we know in advance that the loop body should always execute at least once. Below are two versions of a loop to sum the integers from 1 through n.

While Solution

```
sum = 0;
counter = 1;
while (counter <= n)
{
    sum = sum + counter;
    counter++;
}
```

Do-While Solution

```
sum = 0;
counter = 1;
do
{
    sum = sum + counter;
    counter++;
} while (counter <= n);
```

If n is a positive number, both of these versions are equivalent. But if n is 0 or negative, the two loops give different results. In the While version, the final value of sum is 0 because the loop body is never entered. In the Do-While version, the final value of sum is 1 because the body executes once and *then* the loop test is made.

Because the While statement tests the condition before executing the body of the loop, it is called a *pretest loop*. The Do-While statement does the opposite and thus is known as a *posttest loop*. Figure 9–1 compares the flow of control in the While and Do-While loops.

After we look at two other new looping constructs, we offer some guidelines for determining when to use each type of loop.

9.3 The For Statement

The For statement is designed to simplify the writing of count-controlled loops. The following statement prints out the integers from 1 through n:

```
for (count = 1; count <= n; count++)
    cout << count << endl;
```

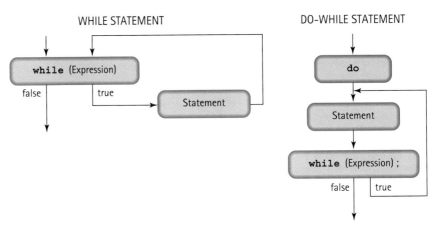

Figure 9–1   *Flow of Control: While and Do-While*

This For statement means "Initialize the loop control variable `count` to 1. While `count` is less than or equal to n, execute the output statement and increment `count` by 1. Stop the loop after `count` has been incremented to n + 1."

In C++, a For statement is merely a compact notation for a While loop. In fact, the compiler essentially translates a For statement into an equivalent While loop as follows:

```
for  ( count = 1 ;  count <= n ;  count++ )
     cout << count << endl;


         count = 1;
         while (count <= n)
         {
             cout << count << endl;
             count++;
         }
```

The syntax template for a For statement is

ForStatement

```
for  (InitStatement Expression1 ;  Expression2 )
     Statement
```

Expression1 is the While condition. InitStatement is a statement that always ends in a semicolon. Therefore, there is always a semicolon before Expression1.

Most often, a For statement is written such that InitStatement initializes a loop control variable and Expression2 increments or decrements the loop control variable. Here are two loops that execute the same number of times (50):

```
for (loopCount = 1; loopCount <= 50; loopCount++)
    ⋮

for (loopCount = 50; loopCount >= 1; loopCount--)
    ⋮
```

Just like While loops, Do-While and For loops may be nested. For example, the nested For structure

```
for (lastNum = 1; lastNum <= 7; lastNum++)
{
    for (numToPrint = 1; numToPrint <= lastNum; numToPrint++)
        cout << numToPrint;
    cout << endl;
}
```

prints the following triangle of numbers.

```
1
12
123
1234
12345
123456
1234567
```

Here is a program that contains both a For statement and a Switch statement. It analyzes the first 100 characters read from the standard input device and reports how many of the characters were letters, periods, question marks, and exclamation marks. For the first category (letters), we use the library function isalpha, one of the "is..." functions we described in Chapter 8. To conserve space, we have omitted the interface documentation for the functions.

```
//*********************************************************************
// CharCounts program
// This program counts the number of letters, periods, question
// marks, and exclamation marks found in the first 100 input
// characters
// Assumption: Input consists of at least 100 characters
//*********************************************************************
#include <iostream>
```

```cpp
#include <cctype>        // For isalpha()

using namespace std;

void IncrementCounter( char, int&, int&, int&, int& );
void PrintCounters( int, int, int, int );

int main()
{
    char inChar;              // Current input character
    int  loopCount;           // Loop control variable
    int  letterCount = 0;     // Number of letters
    int  periodCount = 0;     // Number of periods
    int  questCount = 0;      // Number of question marks
    int  exclamCount = 0;     // Number of exclamation marks

    cout << "Enter your text:" << endl;
    for (loopCount = 1; loopCount <= 100; loopCount++)
    {
        cin.get(inChar);
        IncrementCounter(inChar, letterCount, periodCount,
                         questCount, exclamCount);
    }
    PrintCounters(letterCount, periodCount, questCount,
                  exclamCount);
    return 0;
}

//*******************************************************************

void IncrementCounter( /* in */     char ch,
                       /* inout */ int& letterCount,
                       /* inout */ int& periodCount,
                       /* inout */ int& questCount,
                       /* inout */ int& exclamCount )
{
    if (isalpha(ch))
        letterCount++;
    else
        switch (ch)
        {
            case '.' : periodCount++;
                       break;
            case '?' : questCount++;
                       break;
```

```
            case '!' : exclamCount++;
                       break;
            default  : ;              // Unnecessary, but OK
        }
}


//**********************************************************************

void PrintCounters( /* in */ int letterCount,
                    /* in */ int periodCount,
                    /* in */ int questCount,
                    /* in */ int exclamCount )
{
    cout << endl;
    cout << "Input contained" << endl
         << letterCount << " letters" << endl
         << periodCount << " periods" << endl
         << questCount << " question marks" << endl
         << exclamCount << " exclamation marks" << endl;
}
```

9.4 The Break and Continue Statements

The Break statement, which we introduced with the Switch statement, is also used with loops. A Break statement causes an immediate exit from the innermost Switch, While, Do-While, or For statement in which it appears. Notice the word *innermost*. If break is in a loop that is nested inside another loop, control exits the inner loop but not the outer.

One of the more common ways of using break with loops is to set up an infinite loop and use If tests to exit the loop. Suppose we want to input ten pairs of integers, performing data validation and computing the square root of the sum of each pair. For data validation, assume that the first number of each pair must be less than 100 and the second must be greater than 50. Also, after each input, we want to test the state of the stream for EOF. Here's a loop using Break statements to accomplish the task:

```
loopCount = 1;
while (true)
{
    cin >> num1;
    if ( !cin || num1 >= 100)
        break;
    cin >> num2;
    if ( !cin || num2 <= 50)
        break;
    cout << sqrt(float(num1 + num2)) << endl;
```

```
        loopCount++;
        if (loopCount > 10)
            break;
}
```

Note that we could have used a For loop to count from 1 to 10, breaking out of it as necessary. However, this loop is both count-controlled and event-controlled, so we prefer to use a While loop.

The above loop contains three distinct exit points. Some people vigorously oppose this style of programming, as it violates the single-entry, single-exit philosophy we discussed with regard to multiple returns from a function. Is there any advantage to using an infinite loop in conjunction with break? To answer this question, let's rewrite the loop without using Break statements. The loop must terminate when num1 is invalid or num2 is invalid or loopCount exceeds 10. We'll use Boolean flags to signal invalid data in the While condition:

```
num1Valid = true;
num2Valid = true;
loopCount = 1;
while (num1Valid && num2Valid && loopCount <= 10)
{
    cin >> num1;
    if ( !cin || num1 >= 100)
        num1Valid = false;
    else
    {
        cin >> num2;
        if ( !cin || num2 <= 50)
            num2Valid = false;
        else
        {
            cout << sqrt(float(num1 + num2)) << endl;
            loopCount++;
        }
    }
}
```

One could argue that the first version is easier to follow and understand than this second version. The primary task of the loop body—computing the square root of the sum of the numbers—is more prominent in the first version. In the second version, the computation is obscured by being buried within nested Ifs. The second version also has a more complicated control flow.

The disadvantage of using `break` with loops is that it can become a crutch for those who are too impatient to think carefully about loop design. It's easy to overuse (and abuse) the technique. Here's an example, printing the integers 1 through 5:

```
i = 1;
while (true)
{
    cout << i;
    if (i == 5)
        break;
    i++;
}
```

There is no real justification for setting up the loop this way. Conceptually, it is a pure count-controlled loop, and a simple For loop does the job:

```
for (i = 1; i <= 5; i++)
    cout << i;
```

The For loop is easier to understand and is less prone to error.

A good rule of thumb is: Use `break` within loops only as a last resort. Specifically, use it only to avoid baffling combinations of multiple Boolean flags and nested Ifs.

Another statement that alters the flow of control in a C++ program is the Continue statement. This statement, valid only in loops, terminates the current loop iteration (but not the entire loop). It causes an immediate branch to the bottom of the loop—skipping the rest of the statements in the loop body—in preparation for the next iteration. Here is an example of a reading loop in which we want to process only the positive numbers in an input file:

```
for (dataCount = 1; dataCount <= 500; dataCount++)
{
    dataFile >> inputVal;
    if (inputVal <= 0)
        continue;
    cout << inputVal;
        :
}
```

If `inputVal` is less than or equal to 0, control branches to the bottom of the loop. Then, as with any For loop, the computer increments `dataCount` and performs the loop test before going on to the next iteration.

The Continue statement is not used often, but we present it for completeness (and because you may run across it in other people's programs). Its primary purpose is to avoid obscuring the main process of the loop by indenting the process within an If statement. For example, the above code would be written without a Continue statement as follows:

```
for (dataCount = 1; dataCount <= 500; dataCount++)
{
    dataFile >> inputVal;
    if (inputVal > 0)
    {
        cout << inputVal;
          ⋮
    }
}
```

Be sure to note the difference between `continue` and `break`. The Continue statement means "Abandon the current iteration of the loop, and go on to the next iteration." The Break statement means "Exit the entire loop immediately."

9.5 Guidelines for Choosing a Looping Statement

Here are some guidelines to help you decide when to use each of the three looping statements (While, Do-While, and For).

1. If the loop is a simple count-controlled loop, the For statement is a natural. Concentrating the three loop control actions—initialize, test, and increment/decrement—into one location (the heading of the For statement) reduces the chances of forgetting to include one of them.

2. If the loop is an event-controlled loop whose body should execute at least once, a Do-While statement is appropriate.

3. If the loop is an event-controlled loop and nothing is known about the first execution, use a While (or perhaps a For) statement.

4. When in doubt, use a While statement.

5. An infinite loop with Break statements sometimes clarifies the code but more often reflects an undisciplined loop design. Use it only after careful consideration of While, Do-While, and For.

Programming Example

The Rich Uncle

PROBLEM   Your rich uncle has just died, and in his desk you find two wills. One of them, dated several months ago, leaves you and your relatives a substantial part of his fortune; the other, dated last week, gives it all to his next-door neighbor. Being suspicious that the second will is a forgery, you decide to write a program to analyze writing style and thus compare the wills. The program reads and categorizes each character. When the entire file has been read, it prints a summary table showing the percentage of uppercase letters, lowercase letters, decimal digits, blanks, and end-of-sentence punctuation marks in the data file. The names of the input and output files are read from the keyboard. The name of the input file should be printed on the output.

INPUT   Text on a file whose name is read from the keyboard.

OUTPUT   A table giving the name of each category and what percentage of the total the category represents on the file whose name is read from the keyboard.

DISCUSSION   Doing this task by hand would be tedious but quite straightforward. You would set up five places to make hash marks, one for each of the categories of symbols to be counted. You would then read the text character by character, determine in which category to put each character, and make a hash mark in the appropriate place.

You can look at a character and tell immediately which category to mark. You can simulate "looking" with an If statement with branches for the uppercase letters, the lowercase letters, the digits, a blank, and end-of-sentence punctuation marks. An uppercase letter is defined as one between 'A' and 'Z' inclusive; a lowercase letter is defined as one between 'a' and 'z' inclusive. *But wait:* Before you start writing algorithms to recognize these categories, shouldn't you look in the library to see if they already exist? Sure enough, header file `<cctype>` contains functions to recognize uppercase letters, lowercase letters, and digits.

There is a function that recognizes white space. Will that do for counting blanks? Function `isspace` returns true if the character is a blank, newline, tab, carriage return, or form feed. The problem specifies a count of the number of blanks. A newline might function as the end of a word like a blank, but the problem doesn't ask for the number of words; it asks for the number of blanks.

There is a function to recognize punctuation, but not end-of-sentence punctuation. The problem doesn't state what end-of-sentence marks are. What kinds of sentences are there? Regular sentences, ending in a period; questions, ending in a question mark; and exclamations, ending in an exclamation mark.

At this point you realize that the instructions do not indicate whether the percentages are to be taken of the total number of characters read, including those that do not fit any of the categories, or of the total number of characters that fall into the five categories. You decide to assume that all characters should be counted. Thus, you add an ELSE branch to the module that increments the counters, so that it will increment a counter for all characters that do not fall into one of the five categories. This assumption needs to be added to the program.

ASSUMPTIONS   File is not empty, all characters should be counted.

Here is the program:

```
//*********************************************************************
// Rich Uncle Program
// A table is printed to show the percentage of characters in the
// file that belong to five categories: uppercase characters,
// lowercase characters, decimal digits, blanks, and
// end-of-sentence punctuation marks
// Assumptions: Input file is not empty and percentages are based
// on total number of characters in the file
// To save space, we omit from each function the precondition
// comments that document the assumptions made about valid input
// parameter data. These would be included in a program intended
// for actual use
//*********************************************************************

#include <fstream>
#include <iostream>
#include <iomanip>
#include <cctype>

using namespace std;

// Function prototypes
void OpenFiles(ifstream&, ofstream&);
void IncrementCounter(char, int&, int&, int&, int&, int&, int&);
void PrintTable(ofstream& table, int, int, int, int, int, int);

int main()
{
    // Prepare files for reading and writing
    ifstream text;
    ofstream table;
    char character;

    // Declare and initialize counters
    int uppercaseCounter = 0;           // Number of uppercase letters
    int lowercaseCounter = 0;           // Number of lowercase letters
    int blankCounter = 0;               // Number of blanks
    int digitCounter = 0;               // Number of digits
    int punctuationCounter = 0;         // Number of end '.', '?', '!'
    int allElseCounter = 0;             // Remaining characters

    OpenFiles(text, table);
    if ( !text || !table)
    {
        cout << "Files did not open successfully." << endl;
```

```
            return 1;
        }
    text.get(character);              // Input one character
    do
    { // Process each character
            IncrementCounter(character, uppercaseCounter,
            lowercaseCounter, blankCounter, digitCounter,
            punctuationCounter, allElseCounter);
        text.get(character);
    } while (text);

    PrintTable(table, uppercaseCounter, lowercaseCounter,
        blankCounter, digitCounter, punctuationCounter,
        allElseCounter);

    text.close();
    table.close();
    return 0;
}


//*********************************************************************

void IncrementCounter(
    /* in */     char character),       // Character being examined
    /* inout */ int& uppercaseCounter,   // Uppercase letters
    /* inout */ int& lowercaseCounter,   // Lowercase letters
    /* inout */ int& blankCounter,       // Blanks
    /* inout */ int& digitCounter,       // Digits
    /* inout */ int& punctuationCounter, // '.', '?', '!'
    /* inout */ int& allElseCounter )    // Everything else

// Function IncrementCounter examines character and increments the
// appropriate counter
// Postondition:
//     The category to which the character belongs has been
//     incremented

{
    if (isupper(character))
        uppercaseCounter++;
    else if (islower(character))
        lowercaseCounter++;
    else if (character == ' ')
        blankCounter++;
```

```
        else if (isdigit(character))
            digitCounter++;
        else if ((character == '.') || (character == '?') ||
                (character == '!'))
            punctuationCounter++;
        else
            allElseCounter++;
}


//******************************************************************


void PrintTable(
        /* inout */ ofstream& table,           // Output file
        /* in */ int uppercaseCounter,         // Uppercase letters
        /* in */ int lowercaseCounter,         // Lowercase letters
        /* in */ int blankCounter,             // Blanks
        /* in */ int digitCounter,             // Digits
        /* in */ int punctuationCounter,       // '.', '?', '!'
        /* in */ int allElseCounter )          // Everything else

// Function PrintTable prints the percentages represented by each
// of the five categories
// Postcondition:
//     The output has been written on file table, appropriately
//     labeled

{
    // Calculate total number of characters
    float total = uppercaseCounter + lowercaseCounter
        + blankCounter + digitCounter + punctuationCounter
        + allElseCounter;

    // Write output on stream table
    table << fixed << setprecision(3)
          << "Percentage of uppercase characters: "
          << uppercaseCounter / total * 100 << endl;
    table << fixed << setprecision(3)
          << "Percentage of lowercase characters: "
          << lowercaseCounter / total * 100 << endl;
    table << fixed << setprecision(3) << "Percentage of blanks: "
          << blankCounter / total * 100 << endl;
    table << fixed << setprecision(3) << "Percentage of digits: "
          << digitCounter / total * 100 << endl;
```

```
    table << fixed << setprecision(3)
         << "Percentage of end-of-sentence "
         << "punctuation " << punctuationCounter / total * 100
         << endl;
}


//********************************************************************

void OpenFiles( /* inout */ ifstream& text,    // Input file
                /* inout */ ofstream& table ) // Output file
// Function OpenFiles reads in the names of the input file and the
// output file and opens them for processing.
// Postcondition:
//     Files have been opened AND the input file name has been
//     written on the output file
{
    string inFileName;      // User specified input file name
    string outFileName;     // User specified output file name
    cout << "Enter the name of the file to be processed" << endl;

    cin >> inFileName;
    text.open(inFileName.c_str());

    cout << "Enter the name of the output file" << endl;
    cin >> outFileName;
    table.open(outFileName.c_str());

    // Write label on output file
    table << "Analysis of characters on input file " << inFileName
         << endl;
}
```

TESTING   To be tested thoroughly, the Rich Uncle program must be run with all possible combinations of the categories of characters being counted. Listed below is the minimum set of cases that must be tested.

1. All the categories of characters are present.

2. Four of the categories are present; one is not. (This alone will require five test runs.)

3. Only characters that fall into one of the five categories are present.

4. Other characters are present.

The output listed below was run on a file of over 4,000 characters. (No, it isn't a will, but it is sufficient for testing.)

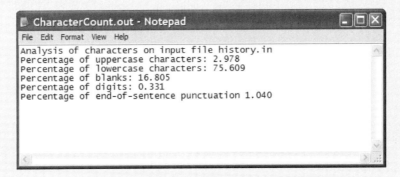

Testing and Debugging

The same testing techniques we used with While loops apply to Do-While and For loops. There are, however, a few additional considerations with these loops.

The body of a Do-While loop always executes at least once. Thus, you should try data sets that show the result of executing a Do-While loop the minimal number of times.

With a data-dependent For loop, it is important to test for proper results when the loop executes zero times. This occurs when the starting value is greater than the ending value (or less than the ending value if the loop control variable is being decremented).

When a program contains a Switch statement, you should test it with enough different data sets to ensure that each branch is selected and executed correctly. You should also test the program with a switch expression whose value is not in any of the case labels.

Testing and Debugging Hints

1. In a Switch statement, make sure there is a Break statement at the end of each case alternative. Otherwise, control "falls through" to the code in the next case alternative.

2. Case labels in a Switch statement are made up of values, not variables. They may, however, include named constants and expressions involving only constants.

3. A switch expression cannot be a floating-point or string expression, and case constants cannot be floating-point or string constants.

4. If there is a possibility that the value of the switch expression might not match one of the case constants, you should provide a `default` alternative. In fact, it is a good practice to always include a `default` alternative.

5. Double-check long Switch statements to make sure that you haven't omitted any branches.

6. The Do-While loop is a posttest loop. If there is a possibility that the loop body should be skipped entirely, use a While statement or a For statement.

7. The For statement heading (the first line) always has three pieces within the parentheses. Most often, the first piece initializes a loop control variable, the second piece tests the variable, and the third piece increments or decrements the variable. The three pieces must be separated by semicolons. Any of the pieces can be omitted, but the semicolons still must be present.

8. With nested control structures, the Break statement can exit only one level of nesting—the innermost Switch or loop in which the `break` is located.

Summary

The Switch statement is a multiway selection statement. It allows the program to choose among a set of branches. A Switch containing Break statements can always be simulated by an If-Then-Else-If structure. If a Switch can be used, however, it often makes the code easier to read and understand. A Switch statement cannot be used with floating-point or string values in the case labels.

The Do-While is a general-purpose looping statement. It is like the While loop except that its test occurs at the end of the loop, guaranteeing at least one execution of the loop body. As with a While loop, a Do-While continues as long as the loop condition is `true`. A Do-While is convenient for loops that test input values and repeat if the input is not correct.

The For statement is also a general-purpose looping statement, but its most common use is to implement count-controlled loops. The initialization, testing, and incrementation (or decrementation) of the loop control variable are centralized in one location, the first line of the For statement.

The For, Do-While, and Switch statements are the ice cream and cake of C++. We can live without them if we absolutely must, but they are very nice to have.

Quick Check

1. If a problem calls for a pure count-controlled loop, would you use a While, a Do-While, or a For statement to implement the loop? (pp. 332–333)
2. When it is executed within a loop, to where does a Break statement transfer control? Where does control proceed from a Continue statement? (pp. 329–332)
3. In converting an If-Else-If multiway branching structure to a Switch statement, what part of the Switch is used to implement the final Else branch of the If-Else-If? (pp. 320–323)
4. Which looping statement always executes its body at least once? (pp. 324–325)
5. Write a For statement that counts from –10 to 10. (pp. 325–329)

Answers

1. A For statement. 2. The Break statement immediately exits the loop. The Continue statement sends control to the end of the loop.   3. The `default` branch.   4. Do-While.   5. `for (int count = -10; count <= 10; count++)`

Exam Preparation Exercises

1. A switch expression may be of type `bool`, `char`, `int`, or `long`, but not of type `float`. True or false?
2. A variable declared in the initialization statement of a For loop has global scope. True of false?
3. Any While loop can be directly rewritten as a Do-While merely by changing the statement syntax and moving the exit condition to the end of the loop. True or false?
4. A Break statement is not allowed in a For loop, but a Continue statement is. True or false?
5. Which of the looping statements in C++ are pretest loops and which are posttest loops?
6. What happens when you forget to include the Break statements in a Switch statement?
7. If you omit all of the clauses within a For loop (`for ( ; ; )`), what would be the condition in an equivalent While loop?
8. How many times is the inner loop body executed in the following nested loop?

```
for (int x = 1; x <= 10; x++)
  for (int y = 1; y <= 10; y++)
    for (int z = 1; z <= 10; z++)
      cout << x + y + z;
```

9. Which looping statement would you choose for a problem in which the decision to repeat a process depends on an event, and the event cannot occur until the process is executed at least once?
10. Which looping statement would you choose for a problem in which the decision to repeat the process depends on an iteration counter and on the state of an input file, and the process may be skipped if the file is empty?
11. What is output by the following code segment if `wood` contains `'O'`?

```
switch (wood)
{
  case 'P' : cout << "Pine";
  case 'F' : cout << "Fir";
  case 'C' : cout << "Cedar";
  case 'O' : cout << "Oak";
  case 'M' : cout << "Maple";
  default  : cout << "Error";
}
```

12. What is output by the following code segment if `month` contains `8`?

```
switch (month)
{
  case 1 : cout << "January"; break;
  case 2 : cout << "February"; break;
  case 3 : cout << "March"; break;
  case 4 : cout << "April"; break;
  case 5 : cout << "May"; break;
  case 6 : cout << "June"; break;
  case 7 : cout << "July"; break;
  case 8 : cout << "August"; break;
  case 9 : cout << "September"; break;
  case 10 : cout << "October"; break;
  case 11 : cout << "November"; break;
  case 12 : cout << "December"; break;
  default : cout << "Error";
}
```

13. What is output by the following code segment?

```
outCount = -1;
do
{
  inCount = 3;
  do
  {
    cout << outCount + inCount << endl;
    inCount --
  } while (inCount > 0);
  outCount++;
} while (outCount < 2);
```

14. What is output by the following code segment?

```
for (int outCount = -1; outCount < 2; outCount++)
  for (int inCount = 3; inCount > 0; inCount--)
    cout << outCount + inCount << endl;
```

15. Rewrite the code segment in Exercise 14 using While loops.
16. What is printed by the following code segment?

```
for (int count = 1; count <= 4; count++)
  switch (count)
  {
    case 4 : cout << " cow?"; break;
    case 2 : cout << " now"; break;
    case 1 : cout << "How"; break;
    case 3 : cout << " brown"; break;
  }
```

17. Write a single simple statement that has the same effect on `cout` as the code segment in Exercise 16.
18. What does the following code segment (which is written in poor style) output?

```
count = 1;
for ( ; ; count++)
  if (count < 3)
    cout << count;
  else
    break;
```

Programming Warm-Up Exercises

1. Write a Switch statement that outputs the day of the week to `cout` according to the `int` value in `day` that ranges from 0 to 6, with 0 being Sunday.
2. Extend the Switch statement in Exercise 1 so that it outputs `"Error"` if the value in `day` is not in the range of 0 through 6.
3. Rewrite the Switch statement in Exercise 2 so that it is within a value-returning function that returns the string with the day of the week, given `day` as its parameter.
4. Write a For loop that uses the function written in Exercise 3 to output the days of the week, each on a separate line, starting from Saturday and working backward to Sunday.
5. Change the For loop in Exercise 4 so that it outputs the days of the week in forward order, starting on Wednesday and going through Tuesday.
6. Write a Do-While loop that prompts for and inputs a user entry of "Y" or "N". If the user fails to enter a correct value, the loop outputs an error message and then repeats the request for them to enter the value.
7. Write a value-returning function that takes an integer parameter and returns an integer result. The function adds up the positive integers, starting at one, until the sum equals or exceeds the value in the parameter, and it then returns the last integer added to the sum. Use a Do-While loop to do the summing.
8. Write a nested For loop that prints out a multiplication table for the integers 1 through 10.
9. Write a nested For loop that prints a filled right triangle of stars, one star on the first line, two on the next, and so on, up to the tenth line having ten stars.
10. Rewrite the nested loop in Exercise 9 with Do-While loops.
11. Rewrite the nested loop in Exercise 9 with While loops.
12. Write a void function, using For loops, that prints a hollow rectangle of stars whose width and height are specified by two `int` parameters. The top and bottom of the rectangle is a solid row of stars, each row between the top and bottom consists of a star, then *width-2* spaces, and another star.
13. Write a nested For loop that outputs the hours and minutes in the period from 3:15 to 7:30.

14. Extend the loop in Exercise 13 to also output seconds.
15. How many lines do the loops in Exercises 13 and 14 output?

Programming Problems

1. Programming Problem 6 in Chapter 7 asked you to write a program that inputs a string and outputs the corresponding words in the International Civil Aviation Organization that would be used to spell it out phonetically. For example:

```
Enter string: program
Phonetic version is: Papa Romeo Oscar Golf Romeo Alpha Mike
```

Rewrite the function in this program that returns the word corresponding to a specified letter, using a Switch statement instead of an If structure. For ease of reference, the ICAO alphabet from Chapter 7 is repeated here:

A   Alpha
B   Bravo
C   Charlie
D   Delta
E   Echo
F   Foxtrot
G   Golf
H   Hotel
I   India
J   Juliet
K   Kilo
L   Lima
M   Mike
N   November
O   Oscar
P   Papa
Q   Quebec
R   Romeo
S   Sierra
T   Tango
U   Uniform
V   Victor
W   Whiskey
X   X-ray
Y   Yankee
Z   Zulu

Be sure to use proper formatting and appropriate comments in your code. Provide appropriate prompts to the user. The output should be clearly labeled and neatly formatted.

2. Programming Problem 2 in Chapter 4 asked you write a C++ program that asks the user to enter their weight and the name of a planet. The program was then to output how much the user would weigh on that planet. Rewrite that program so that the selection of the factor to use in computing the weight is made with a Switch statement instead of an If structure. The computation should be done in a value-returning function and called from `main`.

For ease of reference, the information for the original problem is repeated here. The following table gives the factor by which the weight must be multiplied for each planet. The program should output an error message if the user doesn't type a correct planet name. The prompt and the error message should make it clear to the user how a planet name must be entered. Be sure to use proper formatting and appropriate comments in your code. The output should be clearly labeled and neatly formatted.

Mercury	0.4155
Venus	0.8975
Earth	1.0
Moon	0.166
Mars	0.3507
Jupiter	2.5374
Saturn	1.0677
Uranus	0.8947
Neptune	1.1794
Pluto	0.0899

3. You are working for a company that has traveling salespeople. The salespeople call in their sales to a fulfillment desk, where the sales are all entered into a file. Each sale is recorded as one line on the file `sales.dat` as a salesperson ID number, an item number, and a quantity, all separated by blanks. There are 10 salespeople, with ID's of 1 through 10. The company sells eight different products, with ID's of 7 through 14 (some older products have been discontinued). The unit prices of the products are:

Product Number	Unit Price
7	345.00
8	853.00
9	471.00
10	933.00
11	721.00
12	663.00
13	507.00
14	259.00

You have been asked to write a program that reads in the sales file, and generates a separate file for each salesperson containing just their sales. Each line from the sales file is copied to the appropriate salesperson file (`salespers1.dat` through `salespers10.dat`), with the salesperson ID omitted. The total for the sale (quantity times unit price) is appended to the record. At the end of processing, the total sales for each salesperson should be output with informative labels to `cout`. Use functional decomposition to design the program. Be sure that the program handles invalid ID numbers. If a salesperson ID is invalid, write out an error message to cout. If a product number is invalid, write the error message to the salesperson's file and don't compute a total for that sale. There should be ample opportunity to use Switch statements and value-returning functions in this application.

4. Write a number-guessing game in which the computer selects a random number in the range of 0 to 100, and the user gets up to 20 attempts to guess it. At the end of each game, the user should be told whether they won or lost, and then be asked whether they want to play again. When the user quits, the program should output the total number of wins and losses. To make the game more interesting, the program should vary the wording of the messages that it outputs for winning, for losing, and for asking for another game. Make up 10 different messages for each of these cases, and use random numbers to choose among them. See Appendix C.7 for information on the C++ random number generator functions. This application should provide a good opportunity for you to use a Do-While statement and Switch statements. Use functional decomposition to solve the problem, write your C++ code using good style and documenting comments, and have fun thinking up some messages that will surprise the user.

5. Write a functional decomposition and a C++ program that reads a time in numeric form and prints it in English. The time is input as hours and minutes, separated by a space. Hours are specified in 24-hour time (15 is 3 PM), but the output should be in 12-hour AM/PM form. Note that noon and midnight are special cases. Here are some examples:

Enter time: 12 00
Noon

Enter time: 0 00
Midnight

Enter time: 6 44
Six forty four AM

Enter time: 18 11
Six eleven PM

Write your C++ code using good style and documenting comments. This application should provide you with ample opportunity to use Switch statements.

6. Extend the program in Problem 5 so that it asks the user if he or she wants to enter another time, and then repeats the process until the response to the question is "no". You should be able to code this easily using a Do-While statement.

Programming Example Follow-Up

1. What changes would be necessary in the Rich Uncle program if uppercase letters and lowercase letters were to be counted as members of the same category?

2. You decide that you are interested in counting the number of words in the text. How might you estimate this number?

3. Given that you can calculate the number of words in the text, how can you calculate the average word length?

4. Can you think of any other characteristics of a person's writing style that you might be able to measure?

Simple Data Types: Built-In and User-Defined

Knowledge Goals

- To know all of the simple data types provided by the C++ language.
- To be familiar with specialized C++ operators and expressions.
- To understand the difference between external and internal representations of character data.
- To understand how floating-point numbers are represented in the computer.
- To understand how the limited numeric precision of the computer can affect calculations.
- To understand the concepts of type promotion and type demotion.

Skill Goals

To be able to:

- Select the most appropriate simple data type for a given variable.
- Declare and use an enumeration type.
- Use the For and Switch statements with user-defined enumeration types.
- Distinguish a named user-defined type from an anonymous user-defined type.
- Create a user-written header file.

Until now, we have worked primarily with the data types `int`, `char`, `bool`, and `float`. These four data types are adequate for solving a wide variety of problems. But certain programs need other kinds of data. In this chapter, we take a closer look at all of the simple data types that are part of the C++ language. As part of this look, we discuss the limitations of the computer in doing calculations. We examine how these limitations can cause numerical errors and how to avoid such errors.

There are times when even the built-in data types cannot adequately represent all the data in a program. C++ has several mechanisms for creating *user-defined* data types; that is, we can define new data types ourselves. This chapter introduces one of these mechanisms, the enumeration type. In subsequent chapters, we introduce additional user-defined data types.

10.1 Built-In Simple Types

In Chapter 2, we defined a data type as a specific set of data values (which we call the *domain*) along with a set of operations on those values. For the `int` type, the domain is the set of whole numbers from `INT_MIN` through `INT_MAX`, and the allowable operations we have seen so far are +, -, *, /, %, ++, --, and the relational and logical operations. The domain of the `float` type is the set of all real numbers that a particular computer is capable of representing, and the operations are the same as those for the `int` type except that modulus (%) is excluded. For the `bool` type, the domain is the set consisting of the two values `true` and `false`, and the allowable operations are the logical (!, &&, ||) and relational operations. The `char` type, though used primarily to manipulate character data, is classified as an integral type because it uses integers in memory to stand for characters. Later in the chapter we see how this works.

The `int`, `char`, `bool`, and `float` types have a property in common. The domain of each type is made up of indivisible, or atomic, data values. Data types with this property are called **simple** (or **atomic**) **data types**. When we say that a value is atomic, we mean that it has no component parts that can be accessed individually. For example, a single character of type `char` is atomic, but the string "Good Morning" is not (it is composed of 12 individual characters).

> **Simple (atomic) data type**   A data type in which each value is atomic (indivisible).

Another way of describing a simple type is to say that only one value can be associated with a variable of that type. In contrast, a *structured type* is one in which an entire collection of values is associated with a single variable of that type. For example, a `string` object represents a collection of characters that are given a single name. Beginning in Chapter 11, we look at structured types.

Figure 10-1 displays the simple types that are built into the C++ language.

In this figure, one of the types—enum—is not actually a single data type in the sense that `int` and `float` are data types. Instead, it is a mechanism with which we can define our own simple data types. We look at `enum` later in the chapter.

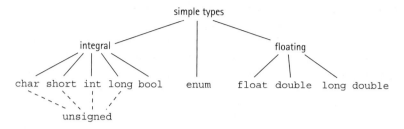

Figure 10-1 *C++ Simple Types*

The integral types char, short, int, and long represent nothing more than integers of different sizes. Similarly, the floating-point types float, double, and long double simply refer to floating-point numbers of different sizes. What do we mean by *sizes*?

In C++, sizes are measured in multiples of the size of a char. By definition, the size of a char is 1. On most—but not all—computers, the 1 means one byte. (Recall from Chapter 1 that a byte is a group of eight consecutive bits [1s or 0s].)

Let's use the notation *sizeof*(SomeType) to denote the size of a value of type Some-Type. Then, by definition, *sizeof*(char) = 1. Other than char, the sizes of data objects in C++ are machine dependent. On one machine, it might be the case that

sizeof(char) = 1
sizeof(short) = 2
sizeof(int) = 4
sizeof(long) = 8

On another machine, the sizes might be as follows:

sizeof(char) = 1
sizeof(short) = 2
sizeof(int) = 2
sizeof(long) = 4

Despite these variations, the C++ language guarantees that the following statements are true:

- 1 = *sizeof*(char) ≤ *sizeof*(short) ≤ *sizeof*(int) ≤ *sizeof*(long).
- 1 ≤ *sizeof*(bool) ≤ *sizeof*(long).
- *sizeof*(float) ≤ *sizeof*(double) ≤ *sizeof*(long double).
- A char is at least 8 bits.
- A short is at least 16 bits.
- A long is at least 32 bits.

> **Range of values** The interval within which values of a numeric type must fall, specified in terms of the largest and smallest allowable values.

For numeric data, the size of a data object determines its **range of values**. Let's look in more detail at the sizes, ranges of values, and literal constants for each of the built-in types.

Integral Types

Before looking at how the sizes of integral types affect their possible values, we remind you that the reserved word `unsigned` may precede the name of certain integral types— `unsigned char`, `unsigned short`, `unsigned int`, `unsigned long`. Values of these types are nonnegative integers with values from 0 through some machine-dependent maximum value. Although we rarely use unsigned types in this book, we include them in this discussion for thoroughness.

Ranges of Values   The following table displays sample ranges of values for the `char`, `short`, `int`, and `long` data types and their `unsigned` variations.

Type	Size in Bytes*	Minimum Value*	Maximum Value*
char	1	–128	127
unsigned char	1	0	255
short	2	–32,768	32,767
unsigned short	2	0	65,535
int	2	–32,768	32,767
unsigned int	2	0	65,535
long	4	–2,147,483,648	2,147,483,647
unsigned long	4	0	4,294,967,295

* These values are for one particular machine. Your machine's values may be different.

C++ systems provide the header file `climits`, from which you can determine the maximum and minimum values for your machine. This header file defines the constants `CHAR_MAX` and `CHAR_MIN`, `SHRT_MAX` and `SHRT_MIN`, `INT_MAX` and `INT_MIN`, and `LONG_MAX` and `LONG_MIN`. The unsigned types have a minimum value of 0 and maximum values defined by `UCHAR_MAX`, `USHRT_MAX`, `UINT_MAX`, and `ULONG_MAX`. To find out the values specific to your computer, you could print them out like this:

```
#include <climits>
using namespace std;
    ⋮
cout << "Max. long = " << LONG_MAX << endl;
cout << "Min. long = " << LONG_MIN << endl;
    ⋮
```

Literal Constants   In C++, integer constants can be specified in three different number bases: decimal (base 10), octal (base 8), and hexadecimal (base 16). The uses of octal and hexadecimal values are outside the scope of this book.

The following table shows examples of integer constants in C++. Notice that an L or a U (either uppercase or lowercase) can be added to the end of a constant to signify long or unsigned, respectively.

Constant	Type	Remarks
1658	int	Decimal (base–10) integer.
03172	int	Octal (base–8) integer. Begins with 0 (zero). Decimal equivalent is 1658.
0x67A	int	Hexadecimal (base–16) integer. Begins with 0 (zero), then either x or X. Decimal equivalent is 1658.
65535U	unsigned int	Unsigned constants end in U or u.
421L	long	Explicit long constant. Ends in L or l.
53100	long	Implicit long constant, assuming the machine's maximum int is, say, 32767.
389123487UL	unsigned long	Unsigned long constants end in UL or LU in any combination of uppercase and lowercase letters.

Notice that this table presents only numeric constants for the integral types. We discuss char constants later in a separate section.

Floating-Point Types

Ranges of Values   Below is a table that gives sample ranges of values for the three floating-point types, float, double, and long double. In this table we show, for each type, the maximum positive value and the minimum positive value (a tiny fraction that is very close to 0). Negative numbers have the same range but the opposite sign. Ranges of values are expressed in exponential (scientific) notation, where 3.4E+38 means 3.4×10^{38}.

Type	Size in Bytes*	Minimum Positive Value*	Maximum Positive Value*
float	4	3.4E–38	3.4E+38
double	8	1.7E–308	1.7E+308
long double	10	3.4E–4932	1.1E+4932

*These values are for one particular machine. Your machine's values may be different.

The standard header file `cfloat` defines the constants `FLT_MAX` and `FLT_MIN`, `DBL_MAX` and `DBL_MIN`, and `LDBL_MAX` and `LDBL_MIN`. To determine the ranges of values for your machine, you could write a short program that prints out these constants.

Literal Constants   When you use a floating-point constant such as 5.8 in a C++ program, its type is assumed to be `double` (double precision). If you store the value into a `float` variable, the computer coerces its type from `double` to `float` (single precision). If you insist on a constant being of type `float` rather than `double`, you can append an F or an f at the end of the constant. Similarly, a suffix of L or 1 signifies a `long double` constant. Here are some examples of floating-point constants in C++:

Constant	Type	Remarks
6.83	double	By default, floating-point constants are of type `double`.
6.83F	float	Explicit `float` constants end in F or f.
6.83L	long double	Explicit `long double` constants end in L or 1.
4.35E-9	double	Exponential notation, meaning 4.35×10^{-9}.

10.2 Additional C++ Operators

C++ has a rich, sometimes bewildering, variety of operators that allow you to manipulate values of the simple data types. Operators you have learned about so far include the assignment operator (=), the arithmetic operators (+, -, *, /, %), the increment and decrement operators (++, --), the relational operators (==, !=, <, <=, >, >=), and the logical operators (!, &&, ||). In certain cases, a pair of parentheses is also considered to be an operator—namely, the function call operator,

```
ComputeSum(x, y);
```

and the type cast operator,

```
y = float(someInt);
```

C++ also has many specialized operators that are seldom found in other programming languages. Here is a table of these additional operators. As you inspect the table, don't panic—a quick scan will do.

Operator	Remarks
Combined assignment operators	
+= Add and assign	
-= Subtract and assign	
*= Multiply and assign	
/= Divide and assign	
Increment and decrement operators	
++ Pre-increment	Example: ++someVar
++ Post-increment	Example: someVar++
- - Pre-decrement	Example: - -someVar
- - Post-decrement	Example: someVar- -
Bitwise operators	Integer operands only
<< Left shift	
>> Right shift	
& Bitwise AND	
| Bitwise OR	
^ Bitwise EXCLUSIVE OR	
~ Complement (invert all bits)	
More combined assignment operators	Integer operands only
%= Modulus and assign	
<<= Shift left and assign	
>>= Shift right and assign	
&= Bitwise AND and assign	
|= Bitwise OR and assign	
^= Bitwise EXCLUSIVE OR and assign	
Other operators	
() Cast	
sizeof Size of operand in bytes	Form: sizeof Expr or sizeof(Type)
? : Conditional operator	Form: Expr1 ? Expr2 : Expr3

The operators in this table, along with those you already know, comprise most—but not all—of the C++ operators. We introduce a few more operators in later chapters as the need arises.

Assignment Operators and Assignment Expressions

C++ has several assignment operators. The equal sign (=) is the basic assignment operator. When combined with its two operands, it forms an assignment expression (*not* an assignment statement). In C++, any expression becomes an expression statement when it is terminated by a semicolon.

> **Assignment expression**   A C++ expression with (1) a value and (2) the side effect of storing the expression value into a memory location.
>
> **Expression statement**   A statement formed by appending a semicolon to an expression.

Because an assignment is an expression, not a statement, you can use it anywhere an expression is allowed. Here is a statement that stores the value 20 into firstInt, the value 30 into secondInt, and the value 35 into thirdInt:

```
thirdInt = (secondInt = (firstInt = 20) + 10) + 5;
```

Some C++ programmers use this style of coding, but others find it hard to read and error-prone.

In Chapter 5, we cautioned against the mistake of using the = operator in place of the == operator:

```
if (alpha = 12)   // Wrong
    ⋮
else
    ⋮
```

The condition in the If statement is an assignment expression, not a relational expression. The value of the expression is 12 (interpreted in the If condition as true), so the else-clause is never executed. Worse yet, the side effect of the assignment expression is to store 12 into alpha, destroying its previous contents.

In addition to the = operator, C++ has several combined assignment operators (+=, *=, and the others listed in our table of operators). These operators have the following semantics:

Statement	Equivalent Statement
i += 5;	i = i + 5;
pivotPoint *= n + 3;	pivotPoint = pivotPoint * (n + 3);

The combined assignment operators are another example of "ice cream and cake." They are sometimes convenient for writing a line of code more compactly, but you can do just fine without them.

Increment and Decrement Operators

The increment and decrement operators (++ and - -) operate only on variables, not on constants or arbitrary expressions. Suppose a variable someInt contains the value 3.

The expression ++someInt denotes preincrementation. The side effect of incrementing someInt occurs first, so the resulting value of the expression is 4. In contrast, the expression someInt++ denotes post-incrementation. The value of the expression is 3, and *then* the side effect of incrementing someInt takes place. The following code illustrates the difference between pre- and post-incrementation:

```
int1 = 14;
int2 = ++int1;
// Increments int1 then assigns 15 to int2

int1 = 14;
int2 = int1++;
// Assigns 14 to int2, then increments int1
```

Using side effects in the middle of larger expressions is always a bit dangerous. It's easy to make semantic errors, and the code may be confusing to read. Look at this example:

```
a = (b = c++) * --d / (e += f++);
```

Some people make a game of seeing how much they can do in the fewest keystrokes possible. But they should remember that serious software development requires writing code that other programmers can read and understand. Overuse of side effects hinders this goal. By far the most common use of ++ and -- is to do the incrementation or decrementation as a separate expression statement:

```
count++;
```

Here, the value of the expression is unused, but we get the desired side effect of incrementing count.

Bitwise Operators

The bitwise operators listed in the operator table (<<, >>, &, |, and so forth) are used for manipulating individual bits within a memory cell. This book does not explore the use of these operators; the topic of bit-level operations is most often covered in a course on computer organization and assembly language programming. However, we point out two things about the bitwise operators.

First, the built-in operators << and >> are the left shift and right shift operators, respectively. The header file iostream uses an advanced C++ technique called *operator overloading* to give additional meanings to these two operators. Thus, if the first (left-hand) operand denotes an output stream, then it is an output operation. If the first operand is an integer variable, it is a left shift operation.

Second, we repeat our caution from Chapter 5: Do not confuse the && and || operators with the & and | operators. The statement

```
if (i == 3 & j == 4)    // Wrong
    k = 20;
```

is syntactically correct because & is a valid operator. The program containing this statement compiles correctly but executes incorrectly. Although we do not examine what the bitwise AND and OR operators do, just be careful to use the relational operators && and || in your logical expressions.

The Cast Operation

You have seen that C++ is very liberal about letting the programmer mix data types. Instead of relying on implicit type coercion, we have recommended using an explicit type cast to show that the type conversion is intentional:

```
intVar = int(floatVar);
```

In C++, the cast operation comes in two forms:

```
intVar = int(floatVar);     // Functional notation
intVar = (int) floatVar;    // Prefix notation. Parentheses required
```

The first form is called functional notation because it looks like a function call. It isn't really a function call (there is no subprogram named int), but it has the appearance of a function call. The second form, prefix notation is the only form available in the C language; C++ added the functional notation.

Although most C++ programmers use the functional notation for the cast operation, there is one restriction on its use. The data type name must be a single identifier. If the type name consists of more than one identifier, you *must* use prefix notation. For example,

```
myVar = unsigned int(someFloat);     // No
myVar = (unsigned int) someFloat;    // Yes
```

The sizeof Operator

The sizeof operator is a unary operator that yields the size, in bytes, of its operand. The operand can be a variable name, as in

```
sizeof someInt
```

or the operand can be the name of a data type, enclosed in parentheses:

```
sizeof(float)
```

You could find out the sizes of a data type on your machine by using code like this:

```
cout << "Size of a short is " << sizeof(short) << endl;
```

The ?: Operator

The last operator in our operator table is the ?: operator, sometimes called the conditional operator. It is a ternary (three-operand) operator with the following syntax:

ConditionalExpression

Expression1 ? Expression2 : Expression3

The computer evaluates Expression1. If the value is true, then the value of the entire expression is Expression2; otherwise, the value of the entire expression is Expression3. We do not use this unusual operator further in this text. It is mentioned here so that you will be familiar with it should you ever encounter it in a program.

Operator Precedence

Below is a summary of operator precedence for the C++ operators we have encountered so far, excluding the bitwise operators. (Appendix B contains the complete list.) In the table, the operators are grouped by precedence level, and a horizontal line separates each precedence level from the next-lower level.

Precedence (highest to lowest)		
Operator	Associativity	Remarks
( )	Left to right	Function call and function-style cast
++ --	Right to left	++ and -- as postfix operators
++ -- ! Unary + Unary -	Right to left	++ and -- as prefix operators
(cast) sizeof	Right to left	
* / %	Left to right	
+ -	Left to right	
< <= > >=	Left to right	
== !=	Left to right	
&&	Left to right	
||	Left to right	
?:	Right to left	
= += -= *= /=	Right to left	

The column labeled *Associativity* describes grouping order. Within a precedence level, most operators group from left to right. For example,

```
a - b + c
```

means

```
(a - b) + c
```

and not

```
a - (b + c)
```

Certain operators, though, group from right to left—specifically, the unary operators, the assignment operators, and the ? : operator. Look at the assignment operators, for example. The expression

```
sum = count = 0
```

means

```
sum = (count = 0)
```

This associativity makes sense because the assignment operation is naturally a right-to-left operation.

A word of caution: Although operator precedence and associativity dictate the *grouping* of operators with their operands, C++ does not define the *order* in which subexpressions are evaluated. Therefore, using side effects in expressions requires extra care. For example, if i currently contains 5, the statement

```
j = ++i + i;
```

stores either 11 or 12 into j, depending on the particular compiler being used. Let's see why. There are three operators in the expression statement above: =, ++, and +. The ++ operator has the highest precedence, so it operates just on i, not the expression i + i. The addition operator has higher precedence than the assignment operator, giving implicit parentheses as follows:

```
j = (++i + i);
```

So far, so good. But now we ask this question: In the addition operation, is the left operand or the right operand evaluated first? The C++ language doesn't dictate the order. If a compiler generates code to evaluate the left operand first, the result is 6 + 6, or 12. Another compiler might generate code to evaluate the right operand first, yielding 6 + 5, or 11. To be assured of left-to-right evaluation in this example, you should force the ordering with two separate statements:

```
++i;
j = i + i;
```

The moral here is that if you use multiple side effects in expressions, you increase the risk of unexpected or inconsistent results. For the newcomer to C++, it's better to avoid unnecessary side effects altogether.

10.3 Working with Character Data

We have been using `char` variables to store character data, such as the character 'A' or 'e' or '+':

```
char someChar;
   ⋮
someChar = 'A';
```

However, because `char` is defined to be an integral type and `sizeof(char)` equals 1, we also can use a `char` variable to store a small (usually one-byte) integer constant. For example,

```
char counter;
   ⋮
counter = 3;
```

On computers with a very limited amount of memory space, programmers sometimes use the `char` type to save memory when they are working with small integers.

A natural question to ask is, How does the computer know the difference between integer data and character data when the data is sitting in a memory cell? The answer is, The computer *can't* tell the difference! To explain this surprising fact, we must look more closely at how character data is stored in a computer.

Character Sets

Each computer uses a particular character set, the set of all possible characters with which it is capable of working. Two character sets widely in use today are the ASCII character set and the EBCDIC character set. ASCII is used by the vast majority of all computers, whereas EBCDIC is found primarily on IBM mainframe computers. ASCII consists of 128 different characters, and EBCDIC has 256 characters. Appendix D shows the characters that are available in these two character sets.

A more recently developed character set called *Unicode* allows many more distinct characters than either ASCII or EBCDIC. Unicode was invented primarily to accommodate the larger alphabets and symbols of various international human languages. In C++, the data type `wchar_t` rather than `char` is used for Unicode characters. In fact, `wchar_t` can be used for other, possibly infrequently used, "wide character" sets in addition to Unicode. In this book, we do not examine Unicode or the `wchar_t` type. We continue to focus our attention on the `char` type and the ASCII and EBCDIC character sets.

Whichever character set is being used, each character has an **external representation**—the way it looks on an I/O device like a printer—and an **internal representation**—the way it is stored inside the computer's memory unit. If you use the `char` constant 'A' in a C++ program, its external representation is the letter *A*. That is, if you print it out you see an *A*, as you would expect. Its internal representation, though, is an integer value. The 128 ASCII characters have internal representations 0 through 127; the EBCDIC characters, 0 through 255. For example, the ASCII table in Appendix D shows that the character 'A' has internal representation 65, and the character 'b' has internal representation 98.

External representation The printable (character) form of a data value.

Internal representation The form in which a data value is stored inside the memory unit.

Let's look again at the statement

```
someChar = 'A';
```

Assuming our machine uses the ASCII character set, the compiler translates the constant 'A' into the integer 65. We could also have written the statement as

```
someChar = 65;
```

Both statements have exactly the same effect—that of storing 65 into `someChar`. However, the second version is *not* recommended. It is not as understandable as the first version, and it is nonportable (the program won't work correctly on a machine that uses EBCDIC, which uses a different internal representation—193—for 'A').

Earlier we mentioned that the computer cannot tell the difference between character and integer data in memory. Both are stored internally as integers. However, when we perform I/O operations, the computer does the right thing—it uses the external representation that corresponds to the data type of the expression being printed.

C++ `char` Constants

In C++, `char` constants come in two different forms. The first form, which we have been using regularly, is a single printable character enclosed by apostrophes (single quotes):

```
'A'    '8'    ')'    '+'
```

Notice that we said *printable* character. Character sets include both printable characters and *control characters* (or *nonprintable characters*). Control characters are not meant to be printed but are used to control the screen, printer, and other hardware devices. If you look at the ASCII character table, you see that the printable characters are those with integer values 32–126. The remaining characters (with values 0–31 and 127) are non-printable control characters.

To accommodate control characters, C++ provides a second form of `char` constant: the *escape sequence*. An escape sequence is one or more characters preceded by a back-slash (\). You are familiar with the escape sequence \n, which represents the newline character. Here is the complete description of the two forms of `char` constant in C++:

1. A single printable character—except an apostrophe (') or backslash (\)—enclosed by apostrophes.

2. One of the following escape sequences, enclosed by apostrophes:

\n	Newline (Line feed in ASCII)
\t	Horizontal tab
\v	Vertical tab
\b	Backspace
\r	Carriage return
\f	Form feed
\a	Alert (a bell or beep)
\\	Backslash
\'	Single quote (apostrophe)
\"	Double quote (quotation mark)
\0	Null character (all 0 bits)
\ddd	Octal equivalent (one, two, or three octal digits specifying the integer value of the desired character)
\xddd	Hexadecimal equivalent (one or more hexadecimal digits specifying the integer value of the desired character)

Even though an escape sequence is written as two or more characters, each escape sequence represents a single character in the character set.

Note that you can use an escape sequence within a string just as you can use any printable character within a string. The statement

```
cout << "\aWhoops!\n";
```

beeps the beeper, displays Whoops!, and terminates the output line. The statement

```
cout << "She said \"Hi\"";
```

outputs She said "Hi" and does not terminate the output line.

Programming Techniques

What kinds of things can we do with character data in a program? The possibilities are endless and depend, of course, on the particular problem we are solving. But several techniques are so widely used that it's worth taking a look at them.

Comparing Characters   In previous chapters, you have seen examples of comparing characters for equality. We have used tests such as

```
if (ch == 'a')
```

and

```
while (inputChar != '\n')
```

Characters also can be compared by using <, <=, >, and >=. For example, if the variable `firstLetter` contains the first letter of a person's last name, we can test to see if the last name starts with *A* through *H* by using this test:

```
if (firstLetter >= 'A' && firstLetter <= 'H')
```

On one level of thought, a test like this is reasonable if you think of < as meaning "comes before" in the character set and > as meaning "comes after." On another level, the test makes even more sense when you consider that the underlying representation of a character is an integer number. The machine literally compares the two integer values using the mathematical meaning of less than or greater than.

When you write a logical expression to check whether a character lies within a certain range of values, you sometimes have to keep in mind the character set your machine uses. A test like

```
if (ch >= 'a' && ch <= 'z')
```

works correctly on machines that use ASCII, because the lowercase letters occupy 26 consecutive positions in the character set. In EBCDIC, however, there is a gap between the lowercase letters *i* and *j* that includes nonprintable characters, and there is another gap between *r* and *s*. A better approach is to take advantage of the "is. . ." functions supplied by the standard library through the header file `cctype`. If you replace the above If test with this one:

```
if (islower(ch))
```

then your program is more portable; the test works correctly on any machine, regardless of its character set. It's a good idea to become well acquainted with these character-testing library functions (Appendix C). They can save you time and help you to write more portable programs.

Converting Digit Characters to Integers   Suppose you want to convert a digit that is read in character form to its numeric equivalent. Because the digit characters '0' through '9' are consecutive in both the ASCII and EBCDIC character sets, subtracting '0' from any digit in character form gives the digit in numeric form:

```
'0' - '0' = 0
'1' - '0' = 1
'2' - '0' = 2
   ⋮
```

Why would you want to do this? Recall that when the extraction operator (>>) reads data into an `int` variable, the input stream fails if an invalid character is encountered. (And once the stream has failed, no further input will succeed). Suppose you're writing a program that prompts an inexperienced user to enter a number from 1 through 5. If the input variable is of type `int` and the user accidentally types a letter of the alphabet, the program is in trouble. To defend against this possibility, you might read the user's response as a character and convert it to a number, performing error checking along the way. Here's a code segment that demonstrates the technique:

```cpp
#include <cctype>    // For isdigit()
using namespace std;
    ⋮
void GetResponse( /* out */ int& response )

// Postcondition:
//     User has been prompted to enter a digit from 1
//     through 5 (repeatedly, and with error messages,
//     if data is invalid)
//  && 1 <= response <= 5

{
    char inChar;
    bool badData = false;

    do
    {
        cout << "Enter a number from 1 through 5: ";
        cin >> inChar;
        if ( !isdigit(inChar) )
            badData = true;                 // It's not a digit
        else
        {
            response = int(inChar - '0');
            if (response < 1 || response > 5)
                badData = true;             // It's a digit, but
        }                                   // it's out of range
        if (badData)
            cout << "Please try again." << endl;
    } while (badData);
}
```

Converting to Lowercase and Uppercase When working with character data, you sometimes find that you need to convert a lowercase letter to uppercase, or vice versa. Fortunately, the programming technique required to do these conversions is easy—a simple call to a library function is all it takes. Through the header file cctype, the standard library provides not only the "is..." functions we have discussed, but also two value-returning functions named toupper and tolower. Here are their descriptions:

Header File	Function	Function Type	Function Value
<cctype>	toupper(ch)	char*	Uppercase equivalent of ch, if ch is a lowercase letter; ch, otherwise
<cctype>	tolower(ch)	char	Lowercase equivalent of ch, if ch is an uppercase letter; ch, otherwise

*Technically, both the argument and the return value are of type int. But conceptually, the functions operate on character data.

Notice that the value returned by each function is just the original character if the condition is not met. For example, tolower('M') returns the character 'm', whereas tolower('+') returns '+'.

A common use of these two functions is to let the user respond to certain input prompts by using either uppercase or lowercase letters. For example, if you want to allow either *Y* or *y* for a "Yes" response from the user, and either *N* or *n* for "No," you might do this:

```
#include <cctype>    // For toupper()
using namespace std;
    ⋮
cout << "Enter Y or N: ";
cin >> inputChar;
if (toupper(inputChar) == 'Y')
{
    ⋮
}
else if (toupper(inputChar) == 'N')
{
    ⋮
}
else
    PrintErrorMsg();
```

Accessing Characters Within a String In the last section, we gave the outline of a code segment that prompts the user for a "Yes" or "No" response. The code accepted a response of 'Y' or 'N' in uppercase or lowercase letters. If a problem requires the user to type the entire word *Yes* or *No* in any combination of uppercase and lowercase letters, the code becomes more complicated. Reading the user's response as a string into a `string` object named `inputStr`, we would need a lengthy If-Then-Else-If structure to compare `inputStr` to "yes", "Yes", "yEs", "yeS", and so on.

As an alternative, let's inspect only the first character of the input string, comparing it with 'Y', 'y', 'N', or 'n', and then ignore the rest of the string. The `string` class allows you to access an individual character in a string by giving its position number in square brackets:

```
StringObject [ Position ]
```

Within a string, the first character is at position 0, the second is at position 1, and so forth. Therefore, the value of Position must be greater than or equal to 0 and less than or equal to the string length minus 1. For example, if `inputStr` is a `string` object and `ch` is a `char` variable, the statement

```
ch = inputStr[2];
```

accesses the character at position 2 of the string (the third character) and copies it into `ch`.

Now we can sketch out the code for reading a "Yes" or "No" response, checking only the first letter of that response.

```
string inputStr;
    ⋮
cout << "Enter Yes or No: ";
cin >> inputStr;
if (toupper(inputStr[0]) == 'Y')
{
    ⋮
}
else if (toupper(inputStr[0]) == 'N')
{
    ⋮
}
else
    PrintErrorMsg();
```

Here is another example of accessing characters within a string. The following program asks the user to type the name of a month and then outputs how many days there are in that month. The input can be in either uppercase or lowercase characters, and the program allows approximate input. For example, the inputs February, FEBRUARY, fEbRu, feb, fe, f, and fyz34x are all interpreted as February because that is the only month that begins with *f*. However, the input Ma is rejected because it could represent either March or May. To conserve space, we have omitted the interface documentation for the DaysInMonth function in this program.

```cpp
//*******************************************************************
// NumDays program
// This program repeatedly prompts for a month and outputs the
// number of days in that month. Approximate input is allowed: only
// the characters needed to determine the month are examined
//*******************************************************************
#include <iostream>
#include <cctype>        // For toupper()
#include <string>        // For string type

using namespace std;

string DaysInMonth( string );

int main()
{
    string month;      // User's input value

    do
    {
        cout << "Name of the month (or q to quit) : ";
        cin >> month;
        if (month != "q")
            cout << "No. of days in " << month << " is "
                 << DaysInMonth(month) << endl;
    } while (month != "q");
    return 0;
}

//*******************************************************************

string DaysInMonth( /* in */ string month )
{
    string::size_type i;                        // Loop control variable
    string badData = "** Invalid month **"; // Bad data message

    // Convert to all uppercase
```

```
for (i = 0; i < month.length(); i++)
    month[i] = toupper(month[i]);

// Make sure length is at least 3 for upcoming tests

month = month + "   ";

// Examine first character, then others if needed

switch (month[0])
{
    case 'J' : if (month[1] == 'A' ||      // January
                   month[2] == 'L'  )      // July
                   return "31";
               else if (month[2] == 'N')   // June
                   return "30";
               else
                   return badData;
    case 'F' : return "28 or 29";          // February
    case 'M' : if (month[2] == 'R' ||      // March
                   month[2] == 'Y'  )      // May
                   return "31";
               else
                   return badData;
    case 'A' : if (month[1] == 'P')        // April
                   return "30";
               else if (month[1] == 'U')   // August
                   return "31";
               else
                   return badData;
    case 'S' :                             // September
    case 'N' : return "30";                // November
    case 'O' :                             // October
    case 'D' : return "31";                // December
    default  : return badData;
}
}
```

10.4 More on Floating-Point Numbers

We have used floating-point numbers off and on since we introduced them in Chapter 2, but we have not examined them in depth. Floating-point numbers have special properties when used on the computer. Thus far, we've almost ignored these properties, but now it's time to consider them in detail.

Representation of Floating-Point Numbers

Let's assume we have a computer in which each memory location is the same size and is divided into a sign plus five decimal digits. When a variable or constant is defined, the location assigned to it consists of five digits and a sign. When an `int` variable or constant is defined, the interpretation of the number stored in that place is straightforward. When a `float` variable or constant is defined, the number stored there has both a whole number part and a fractional part, so it must be coded to represent both parts.

Let's see what such coded numbers might look like. The range of whole numbers we can represent with five digits is −99,999 through +99,999:

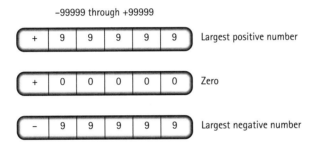

-99999 through +99999

+ 9 9 9 9 9   Largest positive number

+ 0 0 0 0 0   Zero

− 9 9 9 9 9   Largest negative number

Precision   The maximum number of significant digits.

Our **precision** (the number of digits we can represent) is five digits, and each number within that range can be represented exactly.

What happens if we allow one of those digits (the leftmost one, for example) to represent an exponent?

+ 8 2 3 4 5

↑

Exponent

Then +82345 represents the number $+2345 \times 10^8$. The range of numbers we now can represent is much larger:

-9999×10^9 through 9999×10^9

or

−9,999,000,000,000 through +9,999,000,000,000

However, our precision is now only four digits; that is, only four-digit numbers can be represented exactly in our system. What happens to numbers with more digits? The four leftmost digits are represented correctly, and the rightmost digits, or least significant

NUMBER	POWER OF TEN NOTATION	CODED REPRESENTATION	VALUE

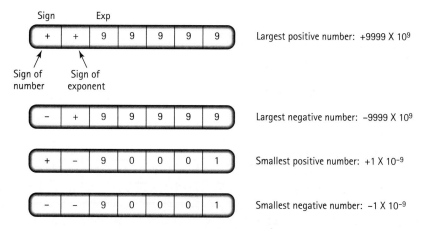

Figure 10-2   *Coding Using Positive Exponents*

digits, are lost (assumed to be 0). Figure 10–2 shows what happens. Note that 1,000,000 can be represented exactly but $-4,932,416$ cannot, because our coding scheme limits us to four **significant digits**.

> **Significant digits**   Those digits from the first nonzero digit on the left to the last nonzero digit on the right (plus any 0 digits that are exact).

To extend our coding scheme to represent floating-point numbers, we must be able to represent negative exponents. Examples are

$$7394 \times 10^{-2} = 73.94$$

and

$$22 \times 10^{-4} = .0022$$

Because our scheme does not include a sign for the exponent, let's change it slightly. The existing sign becomes the sign of the exponent, and we add a sign to the far left to represent the sign of the number itself (see Figure 10–3).

Figure 10–3   *Coding Using Positive and Negative Exponents*

All the numbers between -9999×10^9 and 9999×10^9 can now be represented accurately to four digits. Adding negative exponents to our scheme allows us to represent fractional numbers as small as 1×10^{-9}.

Figure 10–4 shows how we would encode some floating-point numbers. Note that our precision is still only four digits. The numbers 0.1032, -5.406, and 1,000,000 can be represented exactly. The number 476.0321, however, with seven significant digits, is represented as 476.0; the *321* cannot be represented.

Arithmetic with Floating-Point Numbers

When we use integer arithmetic, our results are exact. Floating-point arithmetic, however, is seldom exact. To understand why, let's add the three floating-point numbers x, y, and z using our coding scheme.

First, we add x to y and then we add z to the result. Next, we perform the operations in a different order, adding y to z, and then adding x to that result. The associative law of arithmetic says that the two answers should be the same—but are they? Let's use the following values for x, y, and z:

$$x = -1324 \times 10^3 \quad y = 1325 \times 10^3 \quad z = 5424 \times 10^0$$

Here is the result of adding z to the sum of x and y:

$$
\begin{array}{ll}
\text{(x)} & -1324 \times 10^3 \\
\text{(y)} & \underline{1325 \times 10^3} \\
& 1 \times 10^3 \quad = \quad 1000 \times 10^0
\end{array}
$$

NUMBER	POWER OF TEN NOTATION	Sign		Exp					VALUE
0.1032	$+1032 \times 10^{-4}$	+	–	4	1	0	3	2	0.1032
-5.4060	-5406×10^{-3}	–	–	3	5	4	0	6	-5.406
-0.003	-3000×10^{-6}	–	–	6	3	0	0	0	-0.0030
476.0321	$+4760 \times 10^{-1}$	+	–	1	4	7	6	0	476.0
1,000,000	$+1000 \times 10^3$	+	+	3	1	0	0	0	1,000,000

Figure 10–4 *Coding of Some Floating-Point Numbers*

(x+y)   1000 × 10⁰
(z)   5424 × 10⁰
          ─────────────
          6424 × 10⁰   ← (x+y)+z

Now here is the result of adding x to the sum of y and z:

(y)   1325000 × 10⁰
(z)   5424 × 10⁰
        ─────────────
        1330424 × 10⁰   = 1330 × 10³ (truncated to four digits)

(y+z)   1330 × 10³
(x)   −1324 × 10³
         ─────────────
            6 × 10³   = 6000 × 10⁰ ← x + (y + z)

These two answers are the same in the thousands place but are different thereafter. The error behind this discrepancy is called **representational error.**

Because of representational errors, it is unwise to use a floating-point variable as a loop control variable. Because precision may be lost in calculations involving floating-point numbers, it is difficult to predict when (or even *if*) a loop control variable of type `float` (or `double` or `long double`) will equal the termination value. A count-controlled loop with a floating-point control variable can behave unpredictably.

> **Representational error** Arithmetic error that occurs when the precision of the true result of an arithmetic operation is greater than the precision of the machine.

Also because of representational errors, you should never compare floating-point numbers for exact equality. Rarely are two floating-point numbers exactly equal, and thus you should compare them only for near equality. If the difference between the two numbers is less than some acceptable small value, you can consider them equal for the purposes of the given problem.

Underflow and Overflow In addition to representational errors, there are two other problems to watch out for in floating-point arithmetic: *underflow* and *overflow*.

Underflow is the condition that arises when the value of a calculation is too small to be represented. Going back to our decimal representation, let's look at a calculation involving small numbers:

$$
\begin{array}{r}
4210 \times 10^{-8} \\
\times\ 2000 \times 10^{-8} \\
\hline
8420000 \times 10^{-16} = 8420 \times 10^{-13}
\end{array}
$$

This value cannot be represented in our scheme because the exponent -13 is too small. Our minimum is -9. One way to resolve the problem is to set the result of the calculation to 0.0. Obviously, any answer depending on this calculation will not be exact.

Overflow is a more serious problem because there is no logical recourse when it occurs. For example, the result of the calculation

$$\begin{array}{r} 9999 \times 10^9 \\ \times\ 1000 \times 10^9 \\ \hline 9999000 \times 10^{18} = 9999 \times 10^{21} \end{array}$$

cannot be stored, so what should we do? To be consistent with our response to underflow, we could set the result to 9999×10^9 (the maximum representable value in this case). Yet this seems intuitively wrong. The alternative is to stop with an error message.

C++ does not define what should happen in the case of overflow or underflow. Different implementations of C++ solve the problem in different ways. You might try to cause an overflow with your system and see what happens. Some systems may print a run-time error message such as "FLOATING POINT OVERFLOW." On other systems, you may get the largest number that can be represented.

Although we are discussing problems with floating-point numbers, integer numbers also can overflow both negatively and positively. Most implementations of C++ ignore integer overflow. To see how your system handles the situation, you should try adding 1 to INT_MAX and −1 to INT_MIN. On most systems, adding 1 to INT_MAX sets the result to INT_MIN, a negative number.

Choosing a Numeric Data Type

A first encounter with all the numeric data types of C++ may leave you feeling overwhelmed. To help in choosing among them, here are some guidelines:

1. In general, int is preferable.

   As a rule, you should use floating-point types *only* when absolutely necessary—that is, when you definitely need fractional values. Not only is floating-point arithmetic subject to representational errors, it also is significantly slower than integer arithmetic on most computers.

   For ordinary integer data, use int instead of char or short. It's easy to make overflow errors with these smaller data types. (For character data, though, the char type is appropriate.)

2. Use long only if the range of int values on your machine is too restrictive.
3. Use double and long double only if you need enormously large or small numbers, or if your machine's float values do not carry enough digits of precision.
4. Avoid the unsigned forms of integral types.

By following these guidelines, you'll find that the simple types you use most often are int and float, along with char for character data and bool for Boolean data. Only rarely do you need the longer and shorter variations of these fundamental types.

10.5 User-Defined Simple Types

The concept of a data type is fundamental to all of the widely used programming languages. One of the strengths of the C++ language is that it allows programmers to create new data types, tailored to meet the needs of a particular program. Much of the remainder of this book is about user-defined data types. In this section, we examine how to create our own simple types.

The Typedef Statement

The *Typedef statement* allows you to introduce a new name for an existing type. Its syntax template is

TypedefStatement

```
typedef ExistingTypeName NewTypeName ;
```

The Typedef statement provides a very limited way of defining our own data types. In fact, Typedef does not create a new data type at all: It merely creates an additional name for an existing data type. Despite the fact that Typedef cannot truly create a new data type, it is a valuable tool for writing self-documenting programs.

Names of user-defined types obey the same scope rules that apply to identifiers in general. Most types are defined globally, although it is reasonable to define a new type within a subprogram if that is the only place it is used. The guidelines that determine where a named constant should be defined apply also to data types.

Enumeration Types

C++ allows the user to define a new simple type by listing (enumerating) the literal values that make up the domain of the type. These literal values must be *identifiers*, not numbers. The identifiers are separated by commas, and the list is enclosed in braces. Data types defined in this way are called **enumeration types**. Here's an example:

> **Enumeration type** A user-defined data type whose domain is an ordered set of literal values expressed as identifiers.

```
enum Days {SUN, MON, TUE, WED, THU, FRI, SAT};
```

This declaration creates a new data type named `Days`. Whereas Typedef merely creates a synonym for an existing type, an enumeration type like `Days` is truly a new type and is distinct from any existing type.

The values in the `Days` type—SUN, MON, TUE, and so forth—are called **enumerators**. The enumerators are *ordered*, in the sense that

> **Enumerator** One of the values in the domain of an enumeration type.

SUN < MON < TUE ... < FRI < SAT. Applying relational operators to enumerators is like applying them to characters: The relation that is tested is whether an enumerator "comes before" or "comes after" in the ordering of the data type.

Values in an enumeration type are represented internally as integers. By default, the first enumerator has the integer value 0, the second has the value 1, and so forth. Our declaration of the Days enumeration type is similar to the following set of declarations:

```
typedef int Days;
const int SUN = 0;
const int MON = 1;
const int TUE = 2;
   ⋮
const int SAT = 6;
```

If there is some reason that you want different internal representations for the enumerators, you can specify them explicitly like this:

```
enum Days {SUN = 4, MON = 18, TUE = 9, ...   };
```

There is rarely any reason to assign specific values to enumerators. With the Days type, we are interested in the days of the week, not in the way the machine stores them internally. We do not discuss this feature any further, although you may occasionally see it in C++ programs.

Notice the style we use to capitalize enumerators. Because enumerators are, in essence, named constants, we capitalize the entire identifier. This is purely a style choice. Many C++ programmers use both uppercase and lowercase letters when they invent names for the enumerators.

The identifiers used as enumerators must follow the rules for any C++ identifier. For example,

```
enum Vowel {'A', 'E', 'I', 'O', 'U'};    // Error
```

is not legal because the items are not identifiers. The declaration

```
enum Places {1st, 2nd, 3rd};    // Error
```

is not legal because identifiers cannot begin with digits. In the declarations

```
enum Starch {CORN, RICE, POTATO, BEAN};
enum Grain {WHEAT, CORN, RYE, BARLEY, SORGHUM};    // Error
```

type Starch and type Grain are legal individually, but together they are not. Identifiers in the same scope must be unique. CORN cannot be defined twice.

Suppose you are writing a program for a veterinary clinic. The program must keep track of different kinds of animals. The following enumeration type might be used for this purpose.

Type identifier   Literal values in the domain
        ↓
```
enum Animals {RODENT, CAT, DOG, BIRD, REPTILE, HORSE, BOVINE, SHEEP};
```

```
Animals inPatient;
Animals outPatient;
```
} Creation of two variables of type `Animals`

`RODENT` is a literal, one of the values in the data type `Animals`. Be sure you understand that `RODENT` is not a variable name. Instead, `RODENT` is one of the values that can be stored into the variables `inPatient` and `outPatient`. Let's look at the kinds of operations we might want to perform on variables of enumeration types.

Assignment   The assignment statement

```
inPatient = DOG;
```

does not assign to `inPatient` the character string "DOG", nor the contents of a variable named `DOG`. It assigns the *value* `DOG`, which is one of the values in the domain of the data type `Animals`.

Assignment is a valid operation, as long as the value being stored is of type `Animals`. Both of the statements

```
inPatient = DOG;
outPatient = inPatient;
```

are acceptable. Each expression on the right-hand side is of type `Animals`—`DOG` is a literal of type `Animals`, and `inPatient` is a variable of type `Animals`. Although we know that the underlying representation of `DOG` is the integer 2, the compiler prevents us from using this assignment:

```
inPatient = 2;    // Not allowed
```

Here is the precise rule:

> *Implicit type coercion is defined from an enumeration type to an integral type but not from an integral type to an enumeration type.*

Applying this rule to the statements

```
someInt = DOG;      // Valid
inPatient = 2;      // Error
```

we see that the first statement stores 2 into `someInt` (because of implicit type coercion), but the second produces a compile-time error. The restriction against storing an integer value into a variable of type `Animals` is to keep you from accidentally storing an out-of-range value:

```
inPatient = 65;     // Error
```

Incrementation   Suppose that you want to "increment" the value in `inPatient` so that it becomes the next value in the domain:

```
inPatient = inPatient + 1;    // Error
```

This statement is illegal for the following reason. The right-hand side is OK because implicit type coercion lets you add `inPatient` to 1; the result is an `int` value. But the assignment operation is not valid because you can't store an `int` value into `inPatient`. The statement

```
inPatient++;    // Error
```

is also invalid because the compiler considers it to have the same semantics as the assignment statement above. However, you can escape the type coercion rule by using an *explicit* type conversion—a type cast—as follows:

```
inPatient = Animals(inPatient + 1);    // Correct
```

When you use the type cast, the compiler assumes that you know what you are doing and allows it.

Comparison   The most common operation performed on values of enumeration types is comparison. When you compare two values, their ordering is determined by the order in which you listed the enumerators in the type declaration. For instance, the expression

```
inPatient <= BIRD
```

has the value `true` if `inPatient` contains the value `RODENT`, `CAT`, `DOG`, or `BIRD`.

You can also use values of an enumeration type in a Switch statement. Because `RODENT`, `CAT`, and so on are literals, they can appear in case labels:

```
switch (inPatient)
{
```

```
    case RODENT  :
    case CAT     :
    case DOG     :
    case BIRD    : cout << "Cage ward";
                     break;

    case REPTILE : cout << "Terrarium ward";
                     break;
    case HORSE   :
    case BOVINE  :
    case SHEEP   : cout << "Barn";
}
```

Input and Output   Stream I/O is defined only for the basic built-in types (`int`, `float`, and so on), not for user-defined enumeration types. Values of enumeration types must be input or output indirectly.

To input values, one strategy is to read a string that spells one of the constants in the enumeration type. The idea is to input the string and translate it to one of the literals in the enumeration type by looking at only as many letters as are necessary to determine what it is.

For example, the veterinary clinic program could read the kind of animal as a string, then assign one of the values of type `Animals` to that patient. *Cat, dog, horse,* and *sheep* can be determined by their first letter. *Bovine, bird, rodent,* and *reptile* cannot be determined until the second letter is examined. The following program fragment reads in a string representing an animal name and converts it to one of the values in type `Animals`.

```
#include <cctype>    // For toupper()
#include <string>    // For string type
    :
string animalName;
    :
cin >> animalName;
switch (toupper(animalName[0]))
{
    case 'R' : if (toupper(animalName[1]) == 'O')
                    inPatient = RODENT;
               else
                    inPatient = REPTILE;
               break;
    case 'C' : inPatient = CAT;
               break;
    case 'D' : inPatient = DOG;
```

```
                        break;
        case 'B' : if (toupper(animalName[1]) == 'I')
                        inPatient = BIRD;
                   else
                        inPatient = BOVINE;
                   break;
        case 'H' : inPatient = HORSE;
                   break;
        default  : inPatient = SHEEP;
}
```

Enumeration type values cannot be printed directly either. Printing is done by using a Switch statement that prints a character string corresponding to the value.

```
switch (inPatient)
{
    case RODENT  : cout << "Rodent";
                   break;
    case CAT     : cout << "Cat";
                   break;
    case DOG     : cout << "Dog";
                   break;
    case BIRD    : cout << "Bird";
                   break;
    case REPTILE : cout << "Reptile";
                   break;
    case HORSE   : cout << "Horse";
                   break;
    case BOVINE  : cout << "Bovine";
                   break;
    case SHEEP   : cout << "Sheep";
}
```

You might ask, Why not use just a pair of letters or an integer number as a code to represent each animal in a program? The answer is that we use enumeration types to make our programs more readable; they are another way to make the code more self-documenting.

Returning a Function Value   We have been using value-returning functions to compute and return values of built-in types such as int, float, and char:

```
int Factorial( int );
float CargoMoment( int );
```

C++ allows a function return value to be of *any* data type—built-in or user-defined—except an array (a data type we examine in later chapters).

Named and Anonymous Data Types

The enumeration types we have looked at, `Animals` and `Days`, are called **named types** because their declarations included names for the types. Variables of these new data types are declared separately using the type identifiers `Animals` and `Days`.

C++ also lets us introduce a new type directly in a variable declaration. Instead of the declarations

> **Named type** A user-defined type whose declaration includes a type identifier that gives a name to the type.

```
enum CoinType {NICKEL, DIME, QUARTER, HALF_DOLLAR};
enum StatusType {OK, OUT_OF_STOCK, BACK_ORDERED};

CoinType    change;
StatusType status;
```

we could write

```
enum {NICKEL, DIME, QUARTER, HALF_DOLLAR} change;
enum {OK, OUT_OF_STOCK, BACK_ORDERED} status;
```

A new type declared in a variable declaration is called an **anonymous type** because it does not have a name—that is, it does not have a type identifier associated with it.

> **Anonymous type** A type that does not have an associated type identifier.

If we can create a data type in a variable declaration, why bother with a separate type declaration that creates a named type? Named types, like named constants, make a program more readable, more understandable, and easier to modify. Also, declaring a type and declaring a variable of that type are two distinct concepts; it is best to keep them separate.

User-Written Header Files

As you create your own user-defined data types, you often find that a data type can be useful in more than one program. For example, you may be working on several programs that need an enumeration type consisting of the names of the 12 months of the year. Instead of typing the statement

```
enum Months
{
    JANUARY, FEBRUARY, MARCH, APRIL, MAY, JUNE,
    JULY, AUGUST, SEPTEMBER, OCTOBER, NOVEMBER, DECEMBER
};
```

at the beginning of every program that uses the `Months` type, you can put this statement into a separate file named, say, `months.h`. Then you use `months.h` just as you use

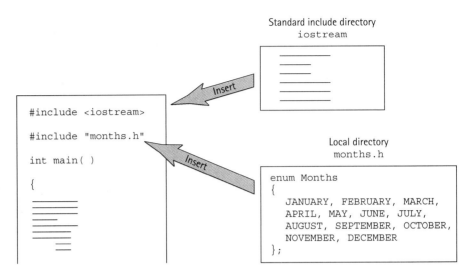

Figure 10-5 *Including Header Files*

system-supplied header files such as `iostream` and `cmath`. By using an #include directive, you ask the C++ preprocessor to insert the contents of the file physically into your program. (Although many C++ systems use the filename extension `.h` [or no extension at all] to denote header files, other systems use extensions such as `.hpp` or `.hxx`.)

When you enclose the name of a header file in angle brackets, as in

#include <iostream>

the preprocessor looks for the file in the standard *include directory,* a directory that contains all the header files supplied by the C++ system. On the other hand, you can enclose the name of a header file in double quotes, like this:

#include "months.h"

In this case, the preprocessor looks for the file in the programmer's current directory. This mechanism allows us to write our own header files that contain type declarations and constant declarations. We can use a simple #include directive instead of retyping the declarations in every program that needs them (see Figure 10-5.)

10.6 More on Type Coercion

As you have learned over the course of several chapters, C++ performs implicit type coercion whenever values of different data types are used in the following:

1. Arithmetic and relational expressions
2. Assignment operations
3. Argument passing

4. Return of the function value from a value-returning function

For item 1—mixed type expressions—the C++ compiler follows one set of rules for type coercion. For items 2, 3, and 4, the compiler follows a second set of rules. Let's examine each of these two rules.

Type Coercion in Arithmetic and Relational Expressions

Suppose that an arithmetic expression consists of one operator and two operands—for example, `3.4*sum` or `var1/var2`. If the two operands are of different data types, then one of them is temporarily **promoted** (or **widened**) to match the data type of the other. To understand exactly what promotion means, let's look at the rule for type coercion in an arithmetic expression.*

> **Promotion (widening)**   The conversion of a value from a "lower" type to a "higher" type according to a programming language's precedence of data types.

Step 1:   Each `char`, `short`, `bool`, or enumeration value is promoted (widened) to `int`. If both operands are now `int`, the result is an `int` expression.

Step 2:   If step 1 still leaves a mixed type expression, the following precedence of types is used:

lowest $\longrightarrow$ highest

`int, unsigned int, long, unsigned long, float, double, long double`

The value of the operand of "lower" type is promoted to that of the "higher" type, and the result is an expression of that type.

A simple example is the expression `someFloat+2`. This expression has no `char`, `short`, `bool`, or enumeration values in it, so step 1 still leaves a mixed type expression. In step 2, `int` is a "lower" type than `float`, so the value 2 is coerced temporarily to the `float` value, say, 2.0. Then the addition takes place, and the type of the entire expression is `float`.

This description of type coercion also holds for relational expressions such as

`someInt <= someFloat`

The value of `someInt` is temporarily coerced to floating-point representation before the comparison takes place. The only difference between arithmetic expressions and relational expressions is that the resulting type of a relational expression is always `bool`—the value `true` or `false`.

---

*The rule we give for type coercion is a simplified version of the rule found in the C++ language definition. The complete rule has more to say about unsigned types, which we don't use in this book.

Type Coercion in Assignments, Argument Passing, and Return of a Function Value

In general, promotion of a value from one type to another does not cause loss of information. On the other hand, **demotion** (or **narrowing**) of data values can potentially cause loss of information.

Consider an assignment operation

$$v = e$$

> **Demotion (narrowing)** The conversion of a value from a "higher" type to a "lower" type according to a programming language's precedence of data types. Demotion may cause loss of information.

where v is a variable and e is an expression. Regarding the data types of v and e, there are three possibilities:

1. If the types of v and e are the same, no type coercion is necessary.

2. If the type of v is "higher" than that of e (using the type precedence we explained with promotion), then the value of e is promoted to v's type before being stored into v.

3. If the type of v is "lower" than that of e, the value of e is demoted to v's type before being stored into v.

Demotion, which you can think of as shrinking a value, may cause loss of information:

- Demotion from a longer integral type to a shorter integral type (such as `long` to `int`) results in discarding the leftmost (most significant) bits in the binary number representation. The result may be a drastically different number.
- Demotion from a floating-point type to an integral type causes truncation of the fractional part (and an undefined result if the whole-number part will not fit into the destination variable). The result of truncating a negative number is machine dependent.
- Demotion from a longer floating-point type to a shorter floating-point type (such as `double` to `float`) may result in a loss of digits of precision.

Our description of type coercion in an assignment operation also holds for argument passing (the mapping of arguments onto parameters) and for returning a function value with a Return statement. For example, assume that `INT_MAX` on your machine is 32767 and that you have the following function:

```
void DoSomething( int n )
{
    ⋮
}
```

If the function is called with the statement

```
DoSomething(50000);
```

then the value 50000 (which is implicitly of type `long` because it is larger than `INT_MAX`) is demoted to a completely different, smaller value that fits into an `int` location. In a similar fashion, execution of the function

```
int SomeFunc( float x )
{
    ⋮
    return 70000;
}
```

causes demotion of the value 70000 to a smaller `int` value because `int` is the declared type of the function return value.

Programming Example
Stylistical Analysis of Text

PROBLEM   The Rich Uncle problem in Chapter 9 intrigued you, so you decide to enhance the program. Rather than calculating percentages of groups of characters, you will just show counts. You also will determine the average word length and the average sentence length. Because you have just learned about enumerated types and Switch statements, you decide to redo the design using these constructs.

DISCUSSION   The Programming Example Follow-Up exercise answers in Chapter 9 suggest that the number of new lines, punctuation marks, and blanks give a good approximation to the number of words. However, if any of these characters appear consecutively, only the first should be counted as an end-of-word symbol. You can use a Boolean variable endOfWord that is set to true when an end-of-word symbol is found. The word counter should only be incremented when endOfWord is false, after which endOfWord is set to true. When an alphanumeric character is read, endOfWord is set to false.

INPUT   Text on the file whose name is read from the keyboard.

OUTPUT   A table giving the file whose name is read from the keyboard, showing the following values.

Total number of alphanumeric characters
Number of uppercase letters
Number of lowercase letters
Number of digits
Number of characters ignored
Number of words
Number of sentences
Average word length
Average sentence length

The Open Files function in the Rich Uncle program can be used directly. In fact, only the Process Character module needs to be decomposed, although the Print Table module will be changed somewhat.

PROCESS CHARACTER   In the Rich Uncle program you used an If statement to determine to which category a character belongs. In this program you will use a Switch statement with case labels of an enumerated type. The categories are uppercase, lowercase, digits, end-of-word, end-of-sentence, and ignore.

enum Features {UPPER, LOWER, DIGIT, EOW, EOS, IGNORE};

This module is where the endOfWord switch must be set. It should be set to false when it is declared and set to true when an end-of-word symbol is found and reset to false when an alphanumeric character is found. In order for this process to work properly, endOfWord must be marked as a static variable. A static variable is a local variable that maintains its value from invocation to invocation.

A Switch statement can be used in the else branch that handles special characters, because characters can be used as case labels.

As you develop the algorithm, you realize that the end-of-sentence markers are also end-of-word markers! Yet, you also want to keep the counts separate. You decide to take care of this problem when you print the results by adding the number of sentences to the number of words.

Here is the program:

```
//***********************************************************
// Style Program
// A stylistic analysis of the following features of text is
// computed:
//    number of words
//    average word length
//    number of sentences
//    average sentence length
//    number of uppercase letters
//    number of lowercase letters
//    number of digits
// To save space, we omit from each function the precondition
// comments that document the assumptions made about valid input
// parameter data. These would be included in a program intended
// for actual use
//***********************************************************

#include <fstream>
#include <iostream>
#include <iomanip>
#include <cctype>

using namespace std;

enum Features {UPPER, LOWER, DIGIT, IGNORE, EOW, EOS};
```

```cpp
// Function prototypes
void OpenFiles(ifstream&, ofstream&);
Features Decode(char character);
void ProcessCharacter(char, int&, int&, int&, int&, int&, int&);
void PrintTable(ofstream& table, int, int, int, int, int, int);

int main()
{
    // Prepare files for reading and writing
    ifstream text;
    ofstream table;
    OpenFiles(text, table);
    if (!text || !table )
    {
        cout << "Files did not open successfully." << endl;
        return 1;
    }

    char character;                    // Input character

    // Declare and initialize counters
    int uppercaseCounter = 0;
    int lowercaseCounter = 0;
    int digitCounter = 0;
    int wordCounter = 0;
    int sentenceCounter = 0;
    int ignoreCounter = 0;


    text.get(character);               // Input one character
    do
    { // Process each character
        ProcessCharacter(character, uppercaseCounter,
            lowercaseCounter, digitCounter, sentenceCounter,
            wordCounter, ignoreCounter);
        text.get(character);           // Input one character
    } while (text);

    PrintTable(table, uppercaseCounter, lowercaseCounter,
        digitCounter, sentenceCounter, wordCounter, ignoreCounter);
    text.close();
    table.close();
    return 0;
}
```

```
//*******************************************************************

Features Decode( /* in */ char character )  // Character decoded

// Function Decode examines the character and returns its type
// Postcondition:
//     Return value is the enumerated type to which character
//     belongs

{
    if (isupper(character))
        return UPPER;
    else if (islower(character))
        return LOWER;
    else if (isdigit(character))
        return DIGIT;
    else
        switch  (character)
        {
            case '.'  :
            case '?'  :
            case '!'  :  return EOS;

            case ' '  :
            case ','  :
            case ';'  :
            case ':'  :
            case '\n' :  return EOW;

        }
    return IGNORE;
}


//*******************************************************************

void OpenFiles( /* inout */ ifstream& text,   // Input file
                /* inout */ ofstream& table ) // Output file

// Function OpenFiles reads in the names of the input file and the
// output file and opens them for processing; input file name is
// written on the output file
// Postcondition:
//     Files have been opened AND the input file name has been
//     written on the output file
```

```cpp
{
    string inFileName;
    string outFileName;
    cout << "Enter the name of the file to be processed" << endl;
    cin >> inFileName;
    text.open(inFileName.c_str());
    cout << "Enter the name of the output file" << endl;
    cin >> outFileName;
    table.open(outFileName.c_str());
    table << "Analysis of characters on input file " << inFileName
          << endl << endl;
}


//*********************************************************************

void PrintTable
    ( /* inout */ ofstream& table,        // Output file
      /* in */ int uppercaseCounter,      // Uppercase letters
      /* in */ int lowercaseCounter,      // Lowercase letters
      /* in */ int digitCounter,          // Digits
      /* in */ int sentenceCounter,       // '.', '?', '!'
      /* in */ int wordCounter,           // Words
      /* in */ int ignoreCounter )        // Everything else

// Function PrintTable prints the percentages represented by each
// of the five categories
// Postcondition:
//     The output has been written on file table, appropriately
//     labeled

{
    int totalAlphaNum;
    totalAlphaNum = uppercaseCounter + lowercaseCounter
        + digitCounter;

    // Print results on file table
    table << "Total number of alphanumeric characters: "
          << totalAlphaNum << endl;
    table << "Number of uppercase letters: " << uppercaseCounter
          << endl;
    table << "Number of lowercase letters: " << lowercaseCounter
          << endl;
    table << "Number of digits: " << digitCounter << endl;
    table << "Number of characters ignored: " << ignoreCounter
          << endl;
```

```cpp
    // Add number of end-of-sentence markers to the word count
    wordCounter = wordCounter + sentenceCounter;

    // Write rest of results on file table
    table << "Number of Words: " <<  wordCounter << endl;
    table << "Number of Sentences: " << sentenceCounter << endl;
    table << "Average word length: " << fixed << setprecision(2)
          << float(totalAlphaNum)/ wordCounter  << endl;
    table << "Average sentence length: " << fixed << setprecision(2)
          << float(wordCounter) / sentenceCounter << endl;

}


//******************************************************************

void ProcessCharacter
     ( /* in  */    char character,        // Character to be
                                           // processed
       /* inout */ int& uppercaseCounter,  // Uppercase letters
       /* inout */ int& lowercaseCounter,  // Lowercase letters
       /* inout */ int& digitCounter,      // Digits
       /* inout */ int& sentenceCounter,   // '.', '?', '!'
       /* inout */ int& wordCounter,       // Words
       /* inout */ int& ignoreCounter )    // Everything else

// Function ProcessCharacter examines character and increments the
// appropriate counter.
// Postcondition:
//     The category to which the character belongs has been
//     incremented

{
    static bool endOfWord = false;

    switch (Decode(character))
    {
        case UPPER :  uppercaseCounter++;
                      endOfWord = false;
                      break;
        case LOWER :  lowercaseCounter++;
                      endOfWord = false;
                      break;
        case DIGIT :  digitCounter++;
                      endOfWord = false;
                      break;
```

```
    case EOW    :   if (!endOfWord)
                    {
                        wordCounter++;
                        endOfWord = true;
                    }
                    break;
    case EOS    :   sentenceCounter++;
                    break;
    case IGNORE:    ignoreCounter++;
                    break;
    }
}
```

TESTING   Let's take a sample of text, calculate the statistics by hand, and compare the results with the output from the program.

Input

The Abacus (which appeared in the sixteenth century) was the first calculator. In the middle of the seventeenth century Blaise Pascal, a French mathematician, built and sold gear-driven mechanical machines which performed whole number addition and subtraction. (Yes, the language Pascal is named for him.)

Later in the seventeenth century a German mathematician Gottfried Wilhelm von Leibniz built the first mechanical device designed to do all four whole number operations: addition, subtraction, multiplication and division. The state of mechanical gears and levers at that time was such that the Leibniz machine was not very reliable.

Output from the program:

```
temp3.out - Notepad
File  Edit  Format  View  Help

Analysis of characters on input file tempHis.in

Total number of alphanumeric characters: 527
Number of uppercase letters: 15
Number of lowercase letters: 512
Number of digits: 0
Number of characters ignored: 5
Number of words: 96
Number of sentences: 5
Average word length: 5.489
Average sentence length: 19.2
```

The number of words, average word length, and average sentence length is wrong. You recount the number of words and again come up with 96. You took care of the case where end-of-sentence markers end words by adding the number of sentences to the number of words. But `endOfWord` wasn't set when end-of-sentence markers were found. You correct the problem in function `ProcessCharacter` like this:

```
case EOS    :   sentenceCounter++;
                endOfWord = true;
                break;
```

You rerun the program and get this output.

```
temp5.out - Notepad
File  Edit  Format  View  Help

Analysis of characters on input file tempHis.in

Total number of alphanumeric characters: 527
Number of uppercase letters: 15
Number of lowercase letters: 512
Number of digits: 0
Number of characters ignored: 5
Number of words: 95
Number of Sentences: 5
Average word length: 5.55
Average sentence length: 19.00
```

The number of words is still off by one. Now you see it. You counted "gear-driven" as two words; the program counts it as one. You are asked to examine a solution to this problem in the Programming Example Follow-Up Exercises.

Testing and Debugging

Floating-Point Data

When a problem requires the use of floating-point numbers that are extremely large, small, or precise, it is important to keep in mind the limitations of the particular system you are using. When testing a program that performs floating-point calculations, determine the acceptable margin of error beforehand, and then design your test data to try to push the program beyond those limits. Carefully check the accuracy of the computed results. (Remember that when you hand-calculate the correct results, a pocket calculator may have *less* precision than your computer system.) If the program produces acceptable results when given worst-case data, it probably performs correctly on typical data.

Coping with Input Errors

Several times in this book, we've had our programs test for invalid data and write an error message. Writing an error message is certainly necessary, but it is only the first step. We must also decide what the program should do next. The problem itself and the severity of the error should determine what action is taken in any error condition. The approach taken also depends on whether or not the program is being run interactively.

In a program that reads its data only from an input file, there is no interaction with the person who entered the data. The program, therefore, should try to adjust for the bad data items, if at all possible.

If the invalid data item is not essential, the program can skip it and continue; for example, if a program averaging test grades encounters a negative test score, it could simply skip the negative score. If an educated guess can be made about the probable value of the bad data, it can be set to that value before being processed. In either event, a message should be written stating that an invalid data item was encountered and outlining the steps that were taken. Such messages form an *exception report*.

If the data item is essential and no guess is possible, processing should be terminated. A message should be written to the user with as much information as possible about the invalid data item.

In an interactive environment, the program can prompt the user to supply another value. The program should indicate to the user what is wrong with the original data. Another possibility is to write out a list of actions and ask the user to choose among them.

These suggestions on how to handle bad data assume that the program recognizes bad data values. There are two approaches to error detection: passive and active. Passive error detection leaves it to the system to detect errors. This may seem easier, but the programmer relinquishes control of processing when an error occurs. An example of passive error detection is the system's division-by-zero error.

Active error detection means having the program check for possible errors and determine an appropriate action if an error occurs. An example of active error detection would be to read a value and use an If statement to see if the value is 0 before dividing it into another number.

Testing and Debugging Hints

1. Avoid using unnecessary side effects in expressions. The test

```
if ((x = y) < z)
    ⋮
```

is less clear and more prone to error than the equivalent sequence of statements

```
x = y;
if (y < z)
    ⋮
```

Also, if you accidentally omit the parentheses around the assignment operation, like this:

```
if (x = y < z)
```

then, according to C++ operator precedence, x is *not* assigned the value of y. It is assigned the value 1 or 0 (the coerced value of the Boolean result of the relational expression y < z).

2. Programs that rely on a particular machine's character set may not run correctly on another machine. Check to see what character-handling functions are supplied by the standard library. Functions such as `tolower`, `toupper`, `isalpha`, and `iscntrl` automatically account for the character set being used.

3. Don't directly compare floating-point values for equality. Instead, check them for near equality. The tolerance for near equality depends on the particular problem you are solving.

4. Use integers if you are dealing with whole numbers only. Any integer can be represented exactly by the computer, as long as it is within the machine's allowable range of values. Also, integer arithmetic is faster than floating-point arithmetic on most machines.

5. Be aware of representational, cancellation, overflow, and underflow errors. If possible, try to arrange calculations in your program to keep floating-point numbers from becoming too large or too small.

6. If your program increases the value of a positive integer and the result suddenly becomes a negative number, you should suspect integer overflow. On most computers, adding 1 to `INT_MAX` yields `INT_MIN`, a negative number.

7. Except when you really need to, avoid mixing data types in expressions, assignment operations, argument passing, and the return of a function value. If you must mix types, explicit type casts can prevent unwelcome surprises caused by implicit type coercion.

8. Consider using enumeration types to make your programs more readable, understandable, and modifiable.

9. Avoid anonymous data typing. Give each user-defined type a name.

10. Enumeration type values cannot be input or output directly.

11. Type demotion can lead to decreased precision or corruption of data.

Summary

A data type is a set of values (the domain) along with the operations that can be applied to those values. Simple data types are data types whose values are atomic (indivisible).

The integral types in C++ are char, short, int, long, and bool. The most commonly used integral types are int and char. The char type can be used for storing small (usually one-byte) numeric integers or, more often, for storing character data. Character data includes both printable and nonprintable characters. Nonprintable characters—those that control the behavior of hardware devices—are expressed in C++ as escape sequences such as \n. Each character is represented internally as a nonnegative integer according to the particular character set (such as ASCII or EBCDIC) that a computer uses.

The floating-point types built into the C++ language are `float`, `double`, and `long double`. Floating-point numbers are represented in the computer with a mantissa and an exponent. This representation permits numbers that are much larger or much smaller than those that can be represented with the integral types. Floating-point representation also allows us to perform calculations on numbers with fractional parts.

However, there are drawbacks to using floating-point numbers in arithmetic calculations. Representational errors, for example, can affect the accuracy of a program's computations. When using floating-point numbers, keep in mind that if two numbers are vastly different from each other in size, adding or subtracting them can produce the wrong answer. Remember, also, that the computer has a limited range of numbers that it can represent. If a program tries to compute a value that is too large or too small, an error message may result when the program executes.

C++ allows the programmer to define additional data types. The Typedef statement is a simple mechanism for renaming an existing type, although the result is not truly a new data type. An enumeration type, created by listing the identifiers that make up the domain, is a new data type that is distinct from any existing type. Values of an enumeration type may be assigned, compared in relational expressions, used as case labels in a Switch statement, passed as arguments, and returned as function values. Enumeration types are extremely useful in the writing of clear, self-documenting programs.

Quick Check

1. Is `bool` considered an integral type or an enum type? (pp. 348–350)
2. What is the difference between the `&&` operator and the `&` operator? (pp. 352–353)
3. How do we represent nonprintable characters as literals in a C++ program? (pp. 360–361)
4. If we were to enlarge the exponent portion of a floating-point representation, what part of the representation would shrink, and what would be the effect of this change? (pp. 367–372)
5. What do we call the error that results when the precision of a calculation is greater than what the precision of the computer can support? (pp. 367–372)
6. If we assign an `int` to a `long`, is the type conversion a promotion or a demotion? (pp. 381–383)
7. Would you use an `int` or a `long` to represent a social security number? (pp. 350–352)
8. Write an enumeration type definition for the four seasons. (pp. 370–378)
9. Write a For loop heading that iterates through the Seasons type defined in Quick Check question 8. (pp. 370–378)
10. Can an anonymous user-defined type be a parameter in a function? (p. 379)

11. In an include directive, how is the file name of a header file in the current direc-tory written differently from the name of a header file in the standard include directory? (pp. 379–380)

Answers

1. It is an integral type. 2. && is a logical AND of a pair of `bool` values, while & is a bitwise AND of a pair of integral values. 3. Using escape sequences, or by using their integer values. 4. The mantissa would shrink. The change would increase the range of the representation but decrease its precision. 5. Representational error. 6. A promotion. 7. A `long`, unless the system supports 64-bit `int` values. 8. `enum Seasons {SPRING, SUMMER, WINTER, AUTUMN};`

9.
```
for (quarter = SPRING;
     quarter <= AUTUMN;
     quarter = Seasons(quarter + 1))
```

10. No. 11. It is enclosed in quotes rather than angle braces.

Exam Preparation Exercises

1. All of the integral types in C++ can be signed or unsigned. True or false?
2. The difference between an assignment expression and an assignment statement is a semicolon. True or false?
3. The sizeof operator can be used to determine whether a machine's `int` type is 32 or 64 bits long. True or false?
4. Floating point numbers are seldom exactly equal. True or false?
5. The values of enumerator types must be written in uppercase letters. True or false?
6. What are the five integral types in C++?
7. What happens if the leading digit of an integer literal is a zero? What if the zero is followed by an X?
8. Which group of C++ operators has the lowest precedence of all?
9. What is the difference in effect of writing `count++` versus `++count`?
10. In what situation is it necessary to use prefix notation for the cast operation instead of functional notation?
11. What functions could you use to simplify the following expression?

    `(reply == 'N' || reply == 'n' || reply == 'Y' || reply == 'y')`

12. If `string` variable `name` contains "Abigail", what does the expression `name[3]` equal?
13. If a computer has a floating point type with five digits of decimal precision, and a one-digit exponent, what would be the result of adding 3.8281×10^4 and 2.4531×10^0?
14. Explain the difference between relative and absolute error in comparing two floating point numbers for equality.

15. What is wrong with the following pair of enumeration type declarations?

```
enum Colors {RED, ORANGE, YELLOW, GREEN, BLUE, INDIGO, VIOLET};
enum Flowers{ROSE, DAFFODIL, LILY, VIOLET, COSMOS, ORCHID};
```

16. Given the declaration of Colors in Exercise 15, what is the value of the expression (YELLOW + 1)?

17. Given the code segment:

```
enum Flowers{ROSE, DAFFODIL, LILY, VIOLET, COSMOS, ORCHID};
Flowers choice;
choice = LILY;
choice++;
```

Why does the compiler give an invalid type error message for the last line?

18. Why is it impossible to use an anonymous type with a function parameter?

Programming Warm-Up Exercises

1. Write the integer value 5
   a. as a literal of type `int`
   b. as a literal of type `long`
   c. as a literal of type `unsigned long`
   d. in base 8 (octal)
   e. in base 16 (hexadecimal)
2. Write the floating point value 3.14159265
   a. as a literal of type float
   b. as a literal of type double
   c. as a literal of type long double
   d. as a literal of type double using an exponent of 0.
3. Write assignment expression statements that do the following:
   a. add 7 to the variable `days`
   b. multiply the value in variable `radius` by 6.2831853
   c. subtract 40 from variable `workHours`
   d. divide variable `average` by variable `count`
4. Write an expression whose result is the number of bits in a value of type `long`.
5. Use the C++ precedence rules to remove any unnecessary parentheses from the following expressions:
   a. `((a * b) + (c * d))`
   b. `((a * b) / (c * d))`
   c. `((a + b) + ((c / (d + e)) * f))`
   d. `(((a + b) / (c + d)) * (e + f))`
   e. `((-a + b) <= (c * d)) && ((a + b) >= (c - d))`
6. Write a code segment that inputs a character, and if it is a numeric character, converts it to an int value.

7. Write a For loop that scans through a string called `inLine`, counting the occurrences of the character `'e'`.

8. Write a value-returning function with a nested Switch statement that returns the number corresponding to a month name that is supplied via a string parameter. The month name may be in uppercase or lowercase, or a mixture.

9. Write an If statement that adds 12 to `hour` if the first letter in string `ampm` is a `'P'` or a `'p'`.

10. Write an expression that returns `true` if the float variable `balance` is equal to `audit` with an absolute error of 0.001 or less.

11. Write an expression that returns `true` if the float variable `year` is equal to `epoch` within 0.00001% of the value in `epoch`. (Think carefully here.)

12. Declare an enumeration type consisting of the nine planets in their order by distance from the Sun (Mercury first, Pluto last).

13. Write a value-returning function that converts the name of a planet given as a `string` parameter to a value of the enumeration type declared in Exercise 12. If the string isn't a proper planet name, return EARTH.

14. Write a value-returning function that converts a planet of the enumeration type declared in Exercise 12 into the corresponding string. The planet is an input parameter and the string is returned by the function. If the input is not a valid planet, return `"Error"`.

15. Write a For statement that prints out the names of the planets in order, using the enumeration type declared in Exercise 12, and the function declared in Exercise 14.

Programming Problems

1. Programming Problem 2 in Chapter 4 asked you write a C++ program that asks the user to enter their weight and the name of a planet. In Chapter 9, Programming Problem 2 asked you to rewrite the program using a Switch statement. Now, rewrite the program so it uses an enumerated type to represent the planet. If you did Programming Warm-Up Exercises 12 through 15, this rewrite should be quite easy.

   For ease of reference, the information for the original problem is repeated here. The following table gives the factor by which the weight must be multiplied for each planet. The program should output an error message if the user doesn't type a correct planet name. The prompt and the error message should make it clear to the user how a planet name must be entered. Be sure to use proper formatting and appropriate comments in your code. The output should be clearly labeled and neatly formatted.

Mercury	0.4155
Venus	0.8975
Earth	1.0
Moon	0.166
Mars	0.3507

Jupiter	2.5374
Saturn	1.0677
Uranus	0.8947
Neptune	1.1794
Pluto	0.0899

2. Programming Problem 3 in Chapter 9 asked you to write a program that generates sales-report files for a set of traveling salespeople. There, we used an integer in the range of 1 through 10 to represent ID numbers for the salespeople. Rewrite the program so that it uses an enumeration type whose values are the names of the salespeople (you can make up the names). The sales file format should replace the salesperson ID number with a string that is the person's last name, so that a line of the file contains a name, an item number, and a quantity. For convenience, the other information concerning the problem is repeated here.

The company sells eight different products, with ID's of 7 through 14 (some older products have been discontinued). The unit prices of the products are:

Product Number	Unit Price
7	345.00
8	853.00
9	471.00
10	933.00
11	721.00
12	663.00
13	507.00
14	259.00

The program reads in the sales file, and generates a separate file for each salesperson containing just his or her sales. Each line from the sales file is copied to the appropriate salesperson file, with the salesperson name omitted. The file names should be the name of the salesperson with .dat appended (you may have to adjust names that don't work as filenames on your computer, such as hyphenated names or names with apostrophes). The total for the sale (quantity times unit price) is appended to the record. At the end of processing, the total sales for each salesperson should be output with informative labels to cout. Use functional decomposition to design the program. Be sure that the program handles invalid salesperson names. If a salesperson name is invalid, write out an error message to cout. If a product number is invalid, write the error message to the salesperson's file and don't compute a total for the sale.

3. You are taking a geology class and the professor wants you to write a program to help students learn the periods of geologic time. The program should let the user enter a range of prehistoric dates (in millions of years), and then output the periods that are included in that range. Each time this is done, the user is asked if they want to continue. The goal of the exercise is for the student to try to figure out when each period began, so that he or she can make a chart of geologic

time. Within the program, represent the periods with an enumeration type made up of their names. You will probably want to create a function that determines the period corresponding to a date, and another that returns the string corresponding to each identifier in the enumeration. Then you can use a For loop to output the series of periods in the range. The periods of geologic time are:

Period Name	Starting Date (millions of years)
Quaternary	2.5
Tertiary	65
Cretaceous	136
Jurassic	192
Triassic	225
Permian	280
Carboniferous	345
Devonian	395
Silurian	435
Ordovician	500
Cambrian	570
Precambrian	4500 or earlier

Use functional decomposition to solve the problem. Be sure to use good coding style and documenting comments. The prompts and error messages that are output should be clear and informative.

4. The educational program that you wrote for Problem 4 was a big success. The geology professor wants you to write another program to help teach geologic time. In this program, the computer picks a date in geologic time and presents it to the student. The student guesses which period corresponds to the date. The student is allowed to continue guessing until he or she gets the right answer. Then the program asks the student whether he or she wants to try again, and repeats the process if the answer is "yes." You should again use an enumeration type consisting of the names of the periods. In this case, you'll probably want to make a function that returns the period corresponding to a string containing the name of a period (the program should work with any style of capitalization of the names). You also may want a function that returns the period for a given date.

Use functional design to solve the problem. Be sure to use good coding style and documenting comments. The prompts, and error messages that are output should be clear and informative. You may want to add some interest to the program by keeping track of the number of guesses taken by the user, and offering differing levels of praise and encouragement depending on how well the user is doing.

5. Write a C++ program that determines the largest number for which your computer can represent its factorial exactly using the `long double` type. The facto-

rial is the product of all numbers from one to the given number. For example, ten factorial (written 10!) is:

1 * 2 * 3 * 4 * 5 * 6 * 7 * 8 * 9 * 10 = 3628800

As you can see, the factorial grows to be a large number very quickly. Your program should keep multiplying the prior factorial by the next integer, then subtract one and check whether the difference between the factorial and the factorial minus one is less than one—an error tolerance. When the maximum precision of the type is reached, and least significant digits are truncated to allow the most significant digits of the product to be stored, then subtracting one should have no effect on the value. Because floating point representations may not be exact, however, the expression

```
abs((number - 1) - number)
```

may not exactly equal 1. That's why you need to include a small error tolerance in the comparison.

Use functional decomposition to solve the problem. Code the program using good style and documenting comments. To keep the user informed of progress, you may wish to output all of the intermediate factorial values. The greatest number and its factorial should be clearly labeled as such.

Programming Example Follow-Up

1. In the Style program, modules ProcessCharacter and PrintTable take six counters as parameters, making a very long parameter list. Could this have been handled any other way?
2. How could you determine whether a hyphen should be counted as an end-of-word symbol or a break in the word due to spacing?
3. Implement the change outlined in your answer to Exercise 2.
4. endOfWord is reset to false every time an alphanumeric character is read. Thus, it is being set to itself over and over again. Can you think of a scheme that would allow you to set it only once?
5. Should error detection be added to program Style? Explain.

Structured Types, Data Abstraction, and Classes

Knowledge Goals

- *To understand the general concept of a C++ union type.*
- *To understand the difference between specification and implementation of an abstract data type.*
- *To understand how encapsulation and information hiding are enforced by the C++ compiler.*

Skill Goals

To be able to:

- *Declare a* `struct` *(record) data type, a data structure whose components may be heterogeneous.*
- *Access a member of a* `struct` *variable.*
- *Define a hierarchical record structure.*
- *Access values stored in a hierarchical record.*
- *Declare a C++* `class` *type.*
- *Declare class objects, given the declaration of a* `class` *type.*
- *Write client code that invokes class member functions.*
- *Implement class member functions.*
- *Organize the code for a C++ class into two files: the specification (*`.h`*) file and the implementation file.*
- *Write a C++ class constructor.*

In this chapter, we expand the definition of a data type to include structured types, which represent collections of components that are referred to by a single name. We begin with a discussion of structured types in general and then examine two structured types provided by the C++ language: the struct and the union.

Next, we introduce the concept of *data abstraction,* the separation of a data type's logical properties from its implementation. Data abstraction is important because it allows us to create data types not otherwise available in a programming language.

In this chapter, we examine *abstract data types* in depth and introduce the C++ language feature for creating abstract data types: the *class.* We conclude with an example that demonstrates data abstraction, abstract data types, and C++ classes.

11.1 Structured Data Types

A **structured data type** is one in which each value is a *collection* of component items. The entire collection is given a single name, yet each component can still be accessed indi-

> **Structured data type**   A data type in which each value is a collection of components and whose organization is characterized by the method used to access individual components. The allowable operations on a structured data type include the storage and retrieval of individual components.

vidually. An example of a structured data type in C++ is the string class. When you declare a variable of type string, it represents an entire collection of characters. But each of the components in the string can be accessed individually.

A structured type gathers together a set of component values and usually imposes a specific arrangement on them (see Figure 11–1). The method used to access the individual components of a structured type depends on how the components are arranged. As we discuss various ways of structuring data, we look at the corresponding access mechanisms.

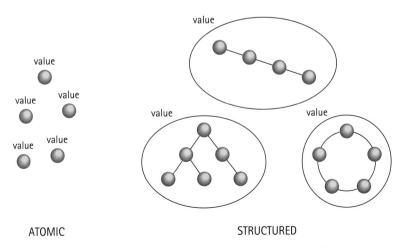

ATOMIC

STRUCTURED

Figure 11–1   *Atomic (Simple) and Structured Data Types*

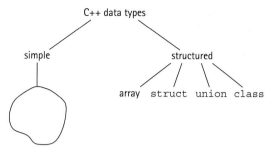

Figure 11–2   *C++ Structured Types*

Figure 11-2 shows the structured types available in C++. In this chapter, we examine the `struct`, `union`, and `class` types. Array data types are the topic of Chapter 12.

11.2 Records (Structs)

In computer science, a **record** is a heterogeneous structured data type. By *heterogeneous*, we mean that the individual components of a record can be of different data types. Each component of a record is called a **field** of the record, and each field is given a name called the *field name*. C++ uses its own terminology with records. A record is called a **structure**, the fields of a record are called **members** of the structure, and each member has a *member name*.*

Record (structure, in C++)   A structured data type with a fixed number of components that are accessed by name. The components may be heterogeneous (of different types).

Field (member, in C++)   A component of a record.

In C++, record data types are most commonly declared according to the following syntax:

StructDeclaration

```
struct TypeName
{
    MemberList
};
```

---

*Technically, a C++ `struct` is almost identical to the `class` type that we introduce later in this chapter. However, in C a `struct` has the properties of a record, and most C++ programmers continue to use the `struct` in its traditional role of directly representing a record. In this book we retain this standard practice.

where TypeName is an identifier giving a name to the data type, and MemberList is defined as

MemberList

```
DataType MemberName ;
DataType MemberName ;
        ⋮
```

The reserved word `struct` is an abbreviation for *structure*. Because the word *structure* has many other meanings in computer science, we'll use *struct* or *record* to avoid any possible confusion about what we are referring to.

You probably recognize the syntax of a member list as being nearly identical to a series of variable declarations. Be careful: A `struct` declaration is a type declaration, and we still must declare variables of this type for any memory locations to be associated with the member names. As an example, let's use a struct to describe a student in a class. We want to store the first and last names, the overall grade point average prior to this class, the grade on programming assignments, the grade on quizzes, the final exam grade, and the final course grade.

```
// Type declarations

enum GradeType {A, B, C, D, F};

struct StudentRec
{
    string      firstName;
    string      lastName;
    float       gpa;            // Grade point average
    int         programGrade;   // Assume 0..400
    int         quizGrade;      // Assume 0..300
    int         finalExam;      // Assume 0..300
    GradeType courseGrade;
};

// Variable declarations

StudentRec firstStudent;
StudentRec student;
int        grade;
```

Notice, both in this example and in the syntax template, that a `struct` declaration ends with a semicolon. By now, you have learned not to put a semicolon after the right brace of a compound statement (block). However, the member list in a `struct` declaration is not considered to be a compound statement; the braces are simply required syntax in the declaration. A `struct` declaration, like all C++ declaration statements, must end with a semicolon.

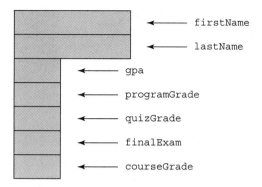

Figure 11–3   *Pattern for a Struct*

firstName, lastName, gpa, programGrade, quizGrade, finalExam, and courseGrade are member names within the struct type StudentRec. These member names make up the member list. Note that each member name is given a type. Also, member names must be unique within a struct type, just as variable names must be unique within a block.

firstName and lastName are of type string. gpa is a float member. program-Grade, quizGrade, and finalExam are int members. courseGrade is of an enumeration data type made up of the grades A through D and F.

None of these struct members are associated with memory locations until we declare a variable of the StudentRec type. StudentRec is merely a pattern for a struct (see Figure 11-3). The variables firstStudent and student are variables of type StudentRec.

Accessing Individual Components

To access an individual member of a struct variable, you give the name of the variable, followed by a dot (period), and then the member name. This expression is called a **member selector**. The syntax template is

> **Member selector** The expression used to access components of a struct variable. It is formed by using the struct variable name and the member name, separated by a dot (period).

MemberSelector

StructVariable . MemberName

This syntax for selecting individual components of a struct is often called *dot notation*. To access the grade point average of firstStudent, we would write

firstStudent.gpa

To access the final exam score of student, we would write

student.finalExam

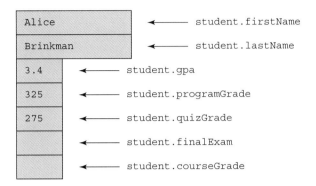

Figure 11-4 *Struct Variable* student *with Member Selectors*

The component of a struct accessed by the member selector is treated just like any other variable of the same type. It may be used in an assignment statement, passed as an argument, and so on. Figure 11-4 shows the struct variable student with the member selector for each member. In this example, we assume that some processing has already taken place, so values are stored in some of the components.

Let's demonstrate the use of these member selectors. Using our student variable, the following code segment reads in a final exam grade; adds up the program grade, the quiz grade, and the final exam grade; and then assigns a letter grade to the result.

```
cin >> student.finalExam;
grade = student.finalExam + student.programGrade +
        student.quizGrade;
if (grade >= 900)
    student.courseGrade = A;
else if (grade >= 800)
    student.courseGrade = B;
else  .
      .
      .
```

Aggregate Operations on Structs

In addition to accessing individual components of a struct variable, we can in some cases use **aggregate operations**. An aggregate operation is one that manipulates the struct as an entire unit.

The following table summarizes the aggregate operations that are allowed on struct variables.

> **Aggregate operation** An operation on a data structure as a whole, as opposed to an operation on an individual component of the data structure.

Aggregate Operation	Allowed on Structs?
I/O	No
Assignment	Yes
Arithmetic	No
Comparison	No
Argument passage	Yes, by value or by reference
Return as a function's return value	Yes

According to the table, one struct variable can be assigned to another. However, both variables must be declared to be of the same type. For example, given the declarations

```
StudentRec student;
StudentRec anotherStudent;
```

the statement

```
anotherStudent = student;
```

copies the entire contents of the struct variable `student` to the variable `anotherStudent`, member by member.

On the other hand, aggregate arithmetic operations and comparisons are not allowed (primarily because they wouldn't make sense). Furthermore, aggregate I/O is not permitted. We must input or output a struct variable one member at a time:

```
cin >> student.firstName;
cin >> student.lastName;
⋮
```

According to the table, an entire struct can be passed as an argument, either by value or by reference, and a struct can be returned as the value of a value-returning function. Let's define a function that takes a `StudentRec` variable as a parameter.

The task of this function is to determine if a student's grade in a course is consistent with his or her overall grade point average (GPA). We define *consistent* to mean that the course grade corresponds correctly to the rounded GPA. The GPA is calculated on a four-point scale, where A is 4, B is 3, C is 2, D is 1, and F is 0. For example, if the rounded GPA is 4 and the course grade is A, then the function returns `true`. If the rounded GPA is 4 and the course grade is not A, then the function returns `false`.

The `Consistent` function is coded below. The parameter `aStudent`, a struct variable of type `StudentRec`, is passed by value.

```
bool Consistent( /* in */ StudentRec aStudent )
```

```
// Precondition:
//      0.0 <= aStudent.gpa <= 4.0
// Postcondition:
//      Function value == true, if the course grade is consistent
//                                 with the overall GPA
//                      == false, otherwise

{
    int roundedGPA = int(aStudent.gpa + 0.5);

    switch (roundedGPA)
    {
        case 0: return (aStudent.courseGrade == F);
        case 1: return (aStudent.courseGrade == D);
        case 2: return (aStudent.courseGrade == C);
        case 3: return (aStudent.courseGrade == B);
        case 4: return (aStudent.courseGrade == A);
    }
}
```

Hierarchical Records

A component of a record can be another record. Records whose components are themselves records are called hierarchical records.

Hierarchical record   A record in which at least one of the components is itself a record.

Let's look at an example in which a hierarchical structure is appropriate. A small machine shop keeps information about each of its machines. There is descriptive information, such as the identification number, a description of the machine, the purchase date, and the cost. Statistical information is also kept, such as the number of down days, the failure rate, and the date of last service. What is a reasonable way of representing all this information?

We can divide the information into two groups: information that changes and information that does not. There are also two dates to be kept: date of purchase and date of last service. These observations suggest use of a record describing a date, a record describing the statistical data, and an overall record containing the other two as components. The following type declarations reflect this structure.

```
struct Date
{
    int month;  // Assume 1..12
    int day;    // Assume 1..31
    int year;   // Assume 1900..2050
};
```

```
struct Statistics
{
    float     failRate;
    Date      lastServiced;
    int       downDays;
};
struct MachineRec
{
    int            idNumber;
    string         description;
    Statistics     history;
    Date           purchaseDate;
    float          cost;
};
```

```
MachineRec machine;
```

The contents of a machine record are now much more obvious. Two of the components of the `struct` type `MachineRec` are themselves structs: `purchaseDate` is of `struct` type `Date`, and `history` is of `struct` type `Statistics`. One of the components of `struct` type `Statistics` is a struct of type `Date`.

How do we access the components of a hierarchical structure such as this one? We build the accessing expressions (member selectors) for the members of the embedded structs from left to right, beginning with the struct variable name. Here are some expressions and the components they access:

Expression	Component Accessed
`machine.purchaseDate`	`Date` struct variable
`machine.purchaseDate.month`	`month` member of a `Date` struct variable
`machine.purchaseDate.year`	`year` member of a `Date` struct variable
`machine.history.lastServiced.year`	`year` member of a `Date` struct variable contained in a struct of type `Statistics`

Figure 11–5 is a pictorial representation of `machine` with values. Look carefully at how each component is accessed.

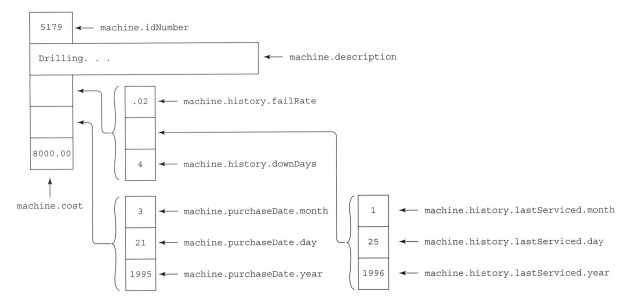

Figure 11-5   *Hierarchical Records in* machine *Variable*

11.3 Unions

In Figure 11-2, we presented a diagram showing the four structured types available in C++. We have discussed struct types and now look briefly at *union* types.

In C++, a union is defined to be a struct that holds only one of its members at a time during program execution. Here is a declaration of a union type and a union variable:

```
union WeightType
{
    long  wtInOunces;
    int   wtInPounds;
    float wtInTons;
};


WeightType weight;
```

The syntax for declaring a union type is identical to the syntax that we showed earlier for the struct type, except that the word union is substituted for struct.

At run time, the memory space allocated to the variable weight does *not* include room for three distinct components. Instead, weight can contain only one of the following: *either* a long value *or* an int value *or* a float value. The assumption is that the program will never need a weight in ounces, a weight in pounds, and a weight in tons simultaneously while executing. The purpose of a union is to conserve memory by forcing several values to use the same memory space, one at a time.

It's quite reasonable to argue that a union is not a data structure at all. It does not represent a collection of values; it represents only a single value from among several *potential* values. On the other hand, unions are grouped together with the structured types because of their similarity to structs.

There is much more to be said about unions, including subtle issues related to their declaration and usage. However, these issues are more appropriate in an advanced study of data structures and systems programming. We have introduced unions only to present a complete picture of the structured types provided by C++ and to acquaint you with the general idea in case you encounter unions in other C++ programs.

11.4 Data Abstraction

As the software we develop becomes more complex, we design algorithms and data structures in parallel. We progress from the logical or abstract data structure envisioned at the top level through the refinement process until we reach the concrete coding in C++.

Pushing the implementation details of a data type to a lower level separates the logical description from the implementation. The separation of the logical properties of a data type from its implementation details is called **data abstraction**, which is a goal of effective programming and the foundation upon which abstract data types are built. (We explore the concept of abstract data types in the next section.)

> **Data abstraction** The separation of a data type's logical properties from its implementation.

Eventually, all the logical properties must be defined in terms of concrete data types and routines written to manipulate them. If the implementation is properly designed, we can use the same routines to manipulate the structure in a wide variety of applications. For example, if we have a routine to compare dates, we can use that routine to compare dates representing days on which equipment was bought or maintained, or dates representing people's birthdays. The concept of designing a low-level structure and writing routines to manipulate it is the basis for C++ `class` types, which we examine later in the chapter.

11.5 Abstract Data Types

We live in a complex world. Throughout the course of each day, we are constantly bombarded with information, facts, and details. To cope with complexity, the human mind engages in *abstraction*—the act of separating the essential qualities of an idea or object from the details of how it works or is composed.

With abstraction, we focus on the *what*, not the *how*. For example, our understanding of automobiles is largely based on abstraction. Most of us know *what* the engine does (it propels the car), but fewer of us know—or want to know—precisely *how* the engine works internally. Abstraction allows us to discuss, think about, and use automobiles without having to know everything about how they work.

In the world of software design, it is now recognized that abstraction is an absolute necessity for managing immense, complex software projects. In introductory computer science courses, programs are usually small (perhaps 50 to 200 lines of code) and understandable in their entirety by one person. However, large commercial software products composed of hundreds of thousands—even millions—of lines of code cannot be designed, understood, or tested thoroughly without using abstraction in various forms. To manage complexity, software developers regularly use two important abstraction techniques: control abstraction and data abstraction.

Control abstraction is the separation of the logical properties of an action from its implementation. We engage in control abstraction whenever we write a function that reduces a complicated algorithm to an abstract action performed by a function call. By invoking a library function, as in the expression

```
4.6 + sqrt(x)
```

we depend only on the function's *specification,* a written description of what it does. We can use the function without having to know its *implementation* (the algorithms that accomplish the result). By invoking the sqrt function, our program is less complex because all the details involved in computing square roots are absent.

Abstraction techniques also apply to data. Every data type consists of a set of values (the domain) along with a collection of allowable operations on those values. In the preceding section, we described data abstraction as the separation of a data type's logical properties from its implementation details. Data abstraction comes into play when we need a data type that is not built into the programming language. We can define the new data type as an **abstract data type (ADT)**, concentrating only on its logical properties and deferring the details of its implementation.

> **Abstract data type** A data type whose properties (domain and operations) are specified independently of any particular implementation.

As with control abstraction, an abstract data type has both a specification (the *what*) and an implementation (the *how*). The specification of an ADT describes the characteristics of the data values as well as the behavior of each of the operations on those values. The user of the ADT needs to understand only the specification, not the implementation, in order to use it. Here's a very informal specification of an ADT, one that might be useful for representing time in a program.

Below is the specification of another.

TYPE
    Time
DOMAIN
    Each Time value is a time of day in the form of hours, minutes, and seconds.
OPERATIONS
    Set the time.
    Print the time.
    Increment the time by one second.
    Compare two times for equality.
    Determine if one time is "less than" (comes before) another.

Notice the complete absence of implementation details. We have not mentioned how the data might actually be stored in a program or how the operations might be implemented. Concealing the implementation details reduces complexity for the user and also shields the user from changes in the implementation.

The specification of an ADT defines abstract data values and abstract operations for the user. Ultimately, of course, the ADT must be implemented in program code. To implement an ADT, the programmer must do two things:

1. Choose a concrete **data representation** of the abstract data, using data types that already exist.

2. Implement each of the allowable operations in terms of program instructions.

> **Data representation** The concrete form of data used to represent the abstract values of an abstract data type.

To implement the Time ADT, we might use three `int` variables for the data representation—one for the hours, one for the minutes, and one for the seconds. Or we might use three strings as the data representation. The specification of the ADT does not confine us to any particular data representation. As long as we satisfy the specification, we are free to choose among alternative data representations and their associated algorithms. Our choice may be based on time efficiency (the speed at which the algorithms execute), space efficiency (the economical use of memory space), or simplicity and readability of the algorithms. Over time, you will acquire knowledge and experience that help you decide which implementation is best for a particular context.

Categories of Abstract Data Type Operations

In general, the basic operations associated with an abstract data type fall into three categories: constructors, transformers, and observers.

An operation that creates a new instance of an ADT (such as a list) is a constructor. Operations that insert an item into a list and delete an item from a list are transformers. An operation that takes one list and appends it to the end of a second list is also a transformer.

A Boolean function that returns `true` if a list is empty and `false` if it contains any components is an example of an observer. A Boolean function that tests to see if a certain value is in the list is another observer.

Some operations are combinations of observers and constructors. An operation that takes two lists and merges them into a (new) third list is both an observer (of the two existing lists) and a constructor (of the third list).

In addition to the three basic categories of ADT operations, a fourth category is sometimes defined: iterators.

An example of an iterator is an operation that returns the first item in a list when it is called initially and returns the next one with each successive call.

> **Constructor** An operation that creates a new instance (variable) of an ADT.
>
> **Transformer** An operation that builds a new value of the ADT, given one or more previous values of the type.
>
> **Observer** An operation that allows us to observe the state of an instance of an ADT without changing it.
>
> **Iterator** An operation that allows us to process—one at a time—all the components in an instance of an ADT.

11.6 C++ Classes

In previous chapters, we have treated data values as passive quantities to be acted upon by functions. In Chapter 10, we viewed category counters as passive data, and we implemented operations as functions that took their values as parameters. Similarly, earlier in this chapter we treated a student record as a passive quantity, using a struct as the data representation and implementing the operation Consistent as a function receiving a struct as a parameter (see Figure 11-6).

This separation of operations and data does not correspond very well with the notion of an abstract data type. After all, an ADT consists of *both* data values and operations on those values. It is preferable to view an ADT as defining an *active* data structure—one that combines both data and operations into a single, cohesive unit (see Figure 11-7). C++ supports this view by providing a built-in structured type known as a class.

> **Class**   A structured type in a programming language that is used to represent an abstract data type.

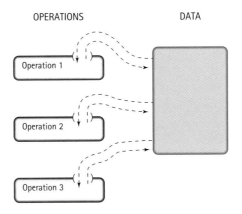

Figure 11-6   *Data and Operations as Separate Entities*

Figure 11-7   *Data and Operations Bound into a Single Unit*

A class is a structured type provided specifically for representing abstract data types. A class is similar to a struct but is nearly always designed so that its components (**class members**) include not only data but also

> **Class member**   A component of a class. Class members may be either data or functions.

functions that manipulate that data.* Here is a C++ class declaration corresponding to the Time ADT that we defined in the previous section:

```
class Time
{
public:
    void Set( int, int, int );
    void Increment();
    void Write() const;
    bool Equal( Time ) const;
    bool LessThan( Time ) const;
private:
    int hrs;
    int mins;
    int secs;
};
```

(For now, you should ignore the word `const` appearing in some of the function prototypes. We explain this use of `const` later in the chapter.)

The `Time` class has eight members—five member functions (`Set`, `Increment`, `Write`, `Equal`, `LessThan`) and three member variables (`hrs`, `mins`, `secs`). As you might guess, the three member variables form the concrete data representation for the Time ADT. The five member functions correspond to the operations we listed for the Time ADT: set the time (to the hours, minutes, and seconds passed as arguments to the `Set` function), increment the time by one second, print the time, compare two times for equality, and determine if one time is less than another. Although the `Equal` function compares two `Time` variables for equality, its parameter list has only one parameter—a `Time` variable. Similarly, the `LessThan` function has only one parameter, even though it compares two times. We'll see the reason later.

Like a `struct` declaration, the declaration of `Time` defines a data type but does not create variables of the type. Class variables (more often referred to as **class objects** or **class instances**) are created by using ordinary variable declarations:

> **Class object (class instance)**   A variable of a `class` type.

```
Time startTime;
Time endTime;
```

_____

As we noted earlier, in C++ a `struct` is almost identical to a `class`. But because of its heritage from the C `struct` construct, most programmers use `class` to implement an ADT, and limit their use of `struct` to applications where a record is needed that has no associated operations.

> **Client**   Software that declares and manipulates objects of a particular class.

Any software that declares and manipulates Time objects is called a client of the class.

As you look at the preceding declaration of the Time class, you can see the reserved words public and private, each followed by a colon. Data and/or functions declared between the words public and private constitute the public interface; clients can access these class members directly. Class members declared after the word private are considered private information and are inaccessible to clients. If client code attempts to access a private item, the compiler signals an error.

Private class members can be accessed only by the class's member functions. In the Time class, the private variables hrs, mins, and secs can be accessed only by the member functions Set, Increment, Write, Equal, and LessThan, not by client code. This separation of class members into private and public parts is a hallmark of ADT design. To preserve the properties of an ADT correctly, an instance of the ADT should be manipulated *only* through the operations that form the public interface. We have more to say about this issue later in the chapter.

Classes, Class Objects, and Class Members

It is important to restate that a class is a type, not a data object. Like any type, a class is a pattern from which you create (or *instantiate*) many objects of that type. Think of a type as a cookie cutter and objects of that type as the cookies.

The declarations

```
Time time1;
Time time2;
```

create two objects of the Time class: time1 and time2. Each object has its own copies of hrs, mins, and secs, the private data members of the class. At a given moment during program execution, time1's copies of hrs, mins, and secs might contain the values 5, 30, and 10; and time2's copies might contain the values 17, 58, and 2. Figure 11–8 is a visual image of the class objects time1 and time2.

(In truth, the C++ compiler does not waste memory by placing duplicate copies of a member function—say, Increment—into both time1 and time2. The compiler generates just one physical copy of Increment, and any class object executes this one copy of the function. Nevertheless, the diagram in Figure 11–8 is a good mental picture of two different class objects.)

Be sure you are clear about the difference between the terms *class object* and *class member*. Figure 11–8 depicts two objects of the Time class, and each object has eight members.

Built-in Operations on Class Objects

C++ treats structs and classes differently from built-in types. Most of the built-in operations do not apply to structs or classes. You cannot use the + operator to add two Time objects, nor can you use the == operator to compare two Time objects for equality.

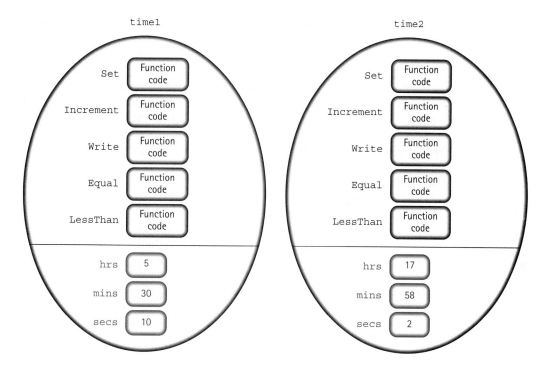

Figure 11–8 *Conceptual View of Two Class Objects*

Two built-in operations that are valid for struct and class objects are member selection (.) and assignment (=). As with structs, you select an individual member of a class by using dot notation. That is, you write the name of the class object, then a dot, then the member name. The statement

```
time1.Increment();
```

invokes the Increment function for the time1 object, presumably to add one second to the time stored in time1. The other built-in operation, assignment, performs aggregate assignment of one class object to another with the following semantics: If x and y are objects of the same class, then the assignment x = y copies the data members of y into x. Below is a fragment of client code that demonstrates member selection and assignment.

```
Time time1;
Time time2;
int  inputHrs;
int  inputMins;
int  inputSecs;
```

```
time1.Set(5, 20, 0);
// Assert: time1 corresponds to 5:20:0

cout << "Enter hours, minutes, seconds: ";
cin >> inputHrs >> inputMins >> inputSecs;
time2.Set(inputHrs, inputMins, inputSecs);

if (time1.LessThan(time2))
    DoSomething();

time2 = time1;                          // Member-by-member assignment
time2.Write();
// Assert: 5:20:0 has been output
```

Earlier we remarked that the Equal and LessThan functions have only one parameter each, even though they are comparing two Time objects. In the If statement of the code segment above, we are comparing time1 and time2. Because LessThan is a class member function, we invoke it by giving the name of a class object (time1), then a dot, then the function name (LessThan). Only one item remains unspecified: the class object with which time1 should be compared (time2). Therefore, the LessThan function requires only one parameter, not two. Here is another way of explaining it: If a class member function represents a binary (two-operand) operation, the first operand appears to the left of the dot operator, and the second operand is in the parameter list.

In addition to member selection and assignment, a few other built-in operators are valid for class objects and structs. These operators are used for manipulating memory addresses, and we defer discussing them until later in the book. For now, think of . and = as the only valid built-in operators.

From the very beginning, you have been working with C++ classes in a particular context: input and output. The standard header file iostream contains the declarations of two classes—istream and ostream—that manage a program's I/O. The C++ standard library declares cin and cout to be objects of these classes:

```
istream cin;
ostream cout;
```

The istream class has many member functions, two of which—the get function and the ignore function—you already have seen in statements like these:

```
cin.get(someChar);
cin.ignore(200, '\n');
```

As with any C++ class object, we use dot notation to select a particular member function to invoke.

You also have used C++ classes when performing file I/O. The header file `fstream` contains declarations for the `ifstream` and `ofstream` classes.

We do not examine in detail the `istream`, `ostream`, `ifstream`, and `ofstream` classes and all of their member functions. What is important to recognize is that classes and objects are fundamental to all I/O activity in a C++ program.

Class Scope

We said earlier that member names must be unique within a struct. Additionally, in Chapter 8 we mentioned four kinds of scope in C++: local scope, global scope, namespace scope, and *class scope*. Class scope applies to the member names within structs, unions, and classes. To say that a member name has class scope means that the name is bound to that class (or struct or union). If the same identifier happens to be declared outside the class, the two identifiers are unrelated. Let's look at an example.

The `Time` class has a member function named `Write`. In the same program, another class (say, `SomeClass`) could also have a member function named `Write`. Furthermore, the program might have a global `Write` function that is completely unrelated to any classes. If the program has statements like

```
Time        checkInTime;
SomeClass someObject;
int        n;
  ⋮
checkInTime.Write();
someObject.Write();
Write(n);
```

then the C++ compiler has no trouble distinguishing among the three `Write` functions. In the first two function calls, the dot notation denotes class member selection. The first statement invokes the `Write` function of the `Time` class, and the second statement invokes the `Write` function of the `SomeClass` class. The final statement does not use dot notation, so the compiler knows that the function being called is the global `Write` function.

Information Hiding

Conceptually, a class object has an invisible wall around it. This wall, called the **abstraction barrier**, protects private data and functions from being accessed by client code. The barrier also prohibits the class object from directly accessing data and functions outside the object. This barrier is a critical characteristic of classes and abstract data types.

Abstraction barrier The invisible wall around a class object that encapsulates implementation details. The wall can be breached only through the public interface.

For a class object to share information with the outside world (that is, with clients), there must be a gap in the abstraction barrier. This gap is the public interface—the class

Black box   An electrical or mechanical device whose inner workings are hidden from view.

Information hiding   The encapsulation and hiding of implementation details to keep the user of an abstraction from depending on or incorrectly manipulating these details.

members declared to be public. The only way that a client can manipulate the internals of the class object is indirectly—through the operations in the public interface. Engineers have a similar concept called a **black box**. A black box is a module or device whose inner workings are hidden from view. The user of the black box depends only on the written specification of *what* it does, not on *how* it does it. The user connects wires to the interface and assumes that the module works correctly by satisfying the specification (see Figure 11–9).

In software design, the black box concept is referred to as **information hiding**. Information hiding protects the user of a class from having to know all the details of its implementation. Information hiding also assures the class's implementor that the user cannot directly access any private code or data and compromise the correctness of the implementation.

You have been introduced to encapsulation and information hiding before. In Chapter 7, we discussed the possibility of hiding a function's implementation in a separate file. In this chapter, you'll see how to hide the implementations of class member functions by placing them in files that are separate from the client code.

The creator of a C++ class is free to choose which members are private and which are public. However, making data members public (as in a struct) allows the client to inspect and modify the data directly. Because information hiding is so fundamental to data abstraction, most classes exhibit a typical pattern: The private part contains data, and the public part contains the functions that manipulate the data.

The Time class exemplifies this organization. The data members hrs, mins, and secs are private, so the compiler prohibits a client from accessing these members directly.

If it is acceptable to let the client *inspect* (but not modify) private data members, a class might provide observer functions. The Time class has three such functions: Write,

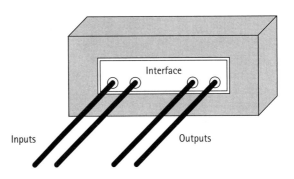

Figure 11–9   *A Black Box*

Equal, and LessThan. Because these observer functions are not intended to modify the private data, they are declared with the word const following the parameter list:

```
void Write() const;
bool Equal( Time ) const;
bool LessThan( Time ) const;
```

C++ refers to these functions as const *member functions*. Within the body of a const member function, a compile-time error occurs if any statement tries to modify a private data member. Although not required by the language, it is good practice to declare as const those member functions that do not modify private data.

11.7 Specification and Implementation Files

An abstract data type consists of two parts: a specification and an implementation. The specification describes the behavior of the data type without reference to its implementation. The implementation creates an abstraction barrier by hiding the concrete data representation as well as the code for the operations.

The Time class declaration serves as the specification of Time. This declaration presents the public interface to the user in the form of function prototypes. To implement the Time class, we must provide function definitions (declarations with bodies) for all the member functions.

In C++, it is customary (though not required) to package the class declaration and the class implementation into separate files. One file—the *specification file*—is a header (.h) file containing only the class declaration. The second file—the *implementation file*—contains the function definitions for the class member functions. Let's look first at the specification file.

The Specification File

Below is the specification file for the Time class. On our computer system, we have named the file Time.h. The class declaration is the same as we presented earlier, with one important exception: We include function preconditions and postconditions to specify the semantics of the member functions as unambiguously as possible for the user of the class.

```
//*******************************************************************
// SPECIFICATION FILE (Time.h)
// This file gives the specification
// of a Time abstract data type
//*******************************************************************

class Time
{
public:
```

```
void Set( /* in */ int hours,
          /* in */ int minutes,
          /* in */ int seconds );
    // Precondition:
    //     0 <= hours <= 23  &&  0 <= minutes <= 59
    //  && 0 <= seconds <= 59
    // Postcondition:
    //     Time is set according to the incoming parameters
    // NOTE:
    //     This function MUST be called prior to
    //     any of the other member functions

void Increment();
    // Precondition:
    //     The Set function has been invoked at least once
    // Postcondition:
    //     Time has been advanced by one second, with
    //     23:59:59 wrapping around to 0:0:0

void Write() const;
    // Precondition:
    //     The Set function has been invoked at least once
    // Postcondition:
    //     Time has been output in the form HH:MM:SS

bool Equal( /* in */ Time otherTime ) const;
    // Precondition:
    //     The Set function has been invoked at least once
    //     for both this time and otherTime
    // Postcondition:
    //     Function value == true, if this time equals otherTime
    //                    == false, otherwise

bool LessThan( /* in */ Time otherTime ) const;
    // Precondition:
    //     The Set function has been invoked at least once
    //     for both this time and otherTime
    //  && This time and otherTime represent times in the
    //     same day
    // Postcondition:
    //     Function value == true, if this time is earlier
    //                             in the day than otherTime
    //                    == false, otherwise
```

```
private:
    int hrs;
    int mins;
    int secs;
};
```

Notice the preconditions for the `Increment`, `Write`, `Equal`, and `LessThan` functions. It is the responsibility of the client to set the time before incrementing, printing, or testing it. If the client fails to set the time, the effect of each of these functions is undefined.

In principle, a specification file should not reveal any implementation details to the user of the class. The file should specify *what* each member function does without disclosing how it does it. However, as you can see in the class declaration, there is one implementation detail that is visible to the user: the concrete data representation of our ADT that is listed in the private part. However, the data representation is still considered hidden information in the sense that the compiler prohibits client code from accessing the data directly.

The Implementation File

The specification (`.h`) file for the `Time` class contains only the class declaration. The implementation file must provide the function definitions for all the class member functions. In the opening comments of the implementation file below, we document the file name as `Time.cpp`.

We recommend that you first skim the C++ code below, not being too concerned about the new language features such as prefixing the name of each function with the symbols

```
Time::
```

Immediately following the program code, we explain the new features.

```
//*******************************************************************
// IMPLEMENTATION FILE (Time.cpp)
// This file implements the Time member functions
//*******************************************************************
#include "Time.h"
#include <iostream>

using namespace std;

// Private members of class:
//      int hrs;
//      int mins;
//      int secs;
```

```cpp
//******************************************************************

void Time::Set( /* in */ int hours,
                /* in */ int minutes,
                /* in */ int seconds )

// Precondition:
//      0 <= hours <= 23   &&   0 <= minutes <= 59
//   && 0 <= seconds <= 59
// Postcondition:
//      hrs == hours  &&  mins == minutes  &&  secs == seconds
// NOTE:
//      This function MUST be called prior to
//      any of the other member functions

{
    hrs = hours;
    mins = minutes;
    secs = seconds;
}


//******************************************************************

void Time::Increment()

// Precondition:
//      The Set function has been invoked at least once
// Postcondition:
//      Time has been advanced by one second, with
//      23:59:59 wrapping around to 0:0:0

{
    secs++;
    if (secs > 59)
    {
        secs = 0;
        mins++;
        if (mins > 59)
        {
            mins = 0;
            hrs++;
            if (hrs > 23)
                hrs = 0;
        }
    }
}
```

```
//*******************************************************************

void Time::Write() const

// Precondition:
//      The Set function has been invoked at least once
// Postcondition:
//      Time has been output in the form HH:MM:SS

{
    if (hrs < 10)
        cout << '0';
    cout << hrs << ':';
    if (mins < 10)
        cout << '0';
    cout << mins << ':';
    if (secs < 10)
        cout << '0';
    cout << secs;
}


//*******************************************************************

bool Time::Equal( /* in */ Time otherTime ) const

// Precondition:
//      The Set function has been invoked at least once
//      for both this time and otherTime
// Postcondition:
//      Function value == true, if this time equals otherTime
//                     == false, otherwise

{
    return (hrs == otherTime.hrs && mins == otherTime.mins &&
            secs == otherTime.secs);
}


//*******************************************************************

bool Time::LessThan( /* in */ Time otherTime ) const

// Precondition:
//      The Set function has been invoked at least once
//      for both this time and otherTime
//   && This time and otherTime represent times in the
```

```
//      same day
// Postcondition:
//      Function value == true, if this time is earlier
//                              in the day than otherTime
//                 == false, otherwise
{
    return (hrs < otherTime.hrs ||
            hrs == otherTime.hrs && mins < otherTime.mins ||
            hrs == otherTime.hrs && mins == otherTime.mins
                            && secs < otherTime.secs);
}
```

This implementation file demonstrates several important points.

1. The file begins with the preprocessor directive

```
#include "Time.h"
```

Both the implementation file and the client code must #include the specification file. Figure 11-10 pictures this shared access to the specification file. This sharing guarantees that all declarations related to an abstraction are consistent. That is, both client.cpp and Time.cpp must reference the same declaration of the Time class located in Time.h.

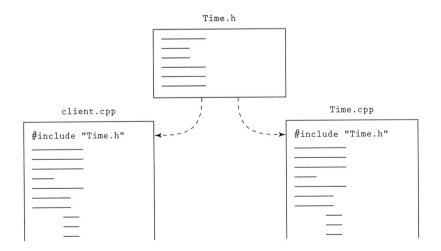

Figure 11-10   *Shared Access to a Specification File*

2. Near the top of the implementation file we have included a comment that restates the private members of the `Time` class.

```
// Private members of class:
//      int hrs;
//      int mins;
//      int secs;
```

This comment reminds the reader that any references to these identifiers are references to the private class members.

3. In the heading of each function definition, the name of the member function is prefixed by the class name (`Time`) and the C++ scope resolution operator (`::`). As we discussed earlier, it is possible for several different classes to have member functions with the same name, say, `Write`. In addition, there may be a global `Write` function that is not a member of any class. The scope resolution operator eliminates any uncertainty about which particular function is being defined.

4. Although clients of a class must use the dot operator to refer to class members (for example, `startTime.Write()`), members of a class refer to each other directly without using dot notation. Looking at the bodies of the `Set` and `Increment` functions, you can see that the statements refer directly to the member variables `hrs`, `mins`, and `secs` without using the dot operator.

   An exception to this rule occurs when a member function manipulates two or more class objects. Consider the `Equal` function. Suppose that the client code has two class objects, `startTime` and `endTime`, and uses the statement

```
if (startTime.Equal(endTime))
    ⋮
```

At execution time, the `startTime` object is the object for which the `Equal` function is invoked. In the body of the `Equal` function, the relational expression

```
hrs == otherTime.hrs
```

refers to class members of two different class objects. The unadorned identifier `hrs` refers to the `hrs` member of the class object for which the function is invoked (that is, `startTime`). The expression `otherTime.hrs` refers to the `hrs` member of the class object that is passed to the parameter, `otherTime`, as a function argument: `endTime`.

5. `Write`, `Equal`, and `LessThan` are observer functions; they do not modify the private data of the class. Because we have declared these to be `const` member functions, the compiler prevents them from assigning new values to the private data.

Compiling and Linking a Multifile Program

In earlier chapters, we have referred to the concept of a multifile program—a program divided up into several files containing source code. In C++, it is possible to compile each of these files separately and at different times. The compiler translates each source code file into an object code file. Figure 11–11 shows a multifile program consisting of the source code files `myprog.cpp`, `file2.cpp`, and `file3.cpp`. We can compile each of these files independently, yielding object code files `myprog.obj`, `file2.obj`, and `file3.obj`. Although each `.obj` file contains machine language code, it is not yet in executable form. The system's linker program brings the object code together to form an executable program file.

Returning to our `Time` class, let's assume we have used the system's editor to create the `Time.h` and `Time.cpp` files. Now we can compile `Time.cpp` into object code. If we are working at the operating system's command line, we use a command similar to the following:

```
cc -c Time.cpp
```

In this example, we assume that `cc` is the name of a command that invokes either the C++ compiler or the linker or both, depending on various options given on the command line. The command-line option `-c` means, on many systems, "compile but do not link." In other words, this command produces an object code file, say, `Time.obj`, but does not attempt to link this file with any other file.

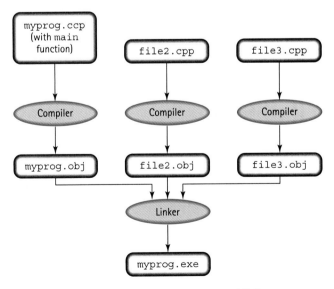

Figure 11–11   *Separate Compilation and Linking*

A programmer wishing to use the `Time` class will write code that #`includes` the file `Time.h`, then declares and uses `Time` objects:

```
#include "Time.h"
  ⋮
Time appointment;

appointment.Set(15, 30, 0);
appointment.Write();
  ⋮
```

If this client code is in a file named `diary.cpp`, an operating system command like

```
cc diary.cpp Time.obj
```

compiles the client program into object code, links this object code with `Time.obj`, and produces an executable program (see Figure 11–12).

The mechanics of compiling, linking, and executing vary from one computer system to another. But on any system, the overall process is the same: You compile the individual source code files into object code, link the object files into an executable program, then execute the program.

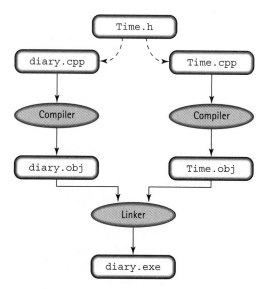

Figure 11–12   *Linking with the `Time` Implementation File*

11.8 Guaranteed Initialization with Class Constructors

The Time class we have been discussing has a weakness. It depends on the client to invoke the Set function before calling any other member function. For example, the Increment function's precondition is

```
// Precondition:
//     The Set function has been invoked at least once
```

If the client fails to invoke the Set function first, this precondition is false and the contract between the client and the function implementation is broken. Because classes nearly always encapsulate data, the creator of a class should not rely on the user to initialize the data. If the user forgets to do so, unpleasant results may occur.

C++ provides a mechanism, called a *class constructor,* to guarantee the initialization of a class object. A constructor is a member function that is implicitly invoked whenever a class object is created.

A constructor function has an unusual name: the name of the class itself. Let's change the Time class by adding two class constructors:

```
class Time
{
public:
    void Set( int, int, int );
    void Increment();
    void Write() const;
    bool Equal( Time ) const;
    bool LessThan( Time ) const;
    Time( int, int, int );          // Constructor
    Time();                          // Constructor
private:
    int hrs;
    int mins;
    int secs;
};
```

This class declaration includes two constructors, differentiated by their parameter lists. The first has three int parameters, which, as we will see, are used to initialize the private data when a class object is created. The second constructor is parameterless and initializes the time to some default value, such as 00:00:00. A parameterless constructor is known in C++ as a *default constructor.*

Constructor declarations are unique in two ways. First, as we have mentioned, the name of the function is the same as the name of the class. Second, the data type of the function is omitted. The reason is that a constructor cannot return a function value. Its purpose is only to initialize a class object's private data.

In the implementation file, the function definitions for the two `Time` constructors might look like the following:

```
//*******************************************************************

Time::Time( /* in */ int initHrs,
            /* in */ int initMins,
            /* in */ int initSecs )
// Constructor

// Precondition:
//     0 <= initHrs <= 23  &&  0 <= initMins <= 59
//  && 0 <= initSecs <= 59
// Postcondition:
//     hrs == initHrs  &&  mins == initMins  &&  secs == initSecs

{
    hrs = initHrs;
    mins = initMins;
    secs = initSecs;
}


//*******************************************************************

Time::Time()

// Default constructor

// Postcondition:
//     hrs == 0  &&  mins == 0  &&  secs == 0

{
    hrs = 0;
    mins = 0;
    secs = 0;
}
```

Invoking a Constructor

Although a constructor is a member of a class, it is never invoked using dot notation. A constructor is automatically invoked whenever a class object is created. The client declaration

```
Time lectureTime(10, 30, 0);
```

includes an argument list to the right of the name of the class object being declared. When this declaration is encountered at execution time, the first (parameterized) constructor is automatically invoked, initializing the private data of lectureTime to the time 10:30:00. The client declaration

```
Time startTime;
```

has no argument list after the identifier startTime. The default (parameterless) constructor is implicitly invoked, initializing startTime's private data to the time 00:00:00.

Remember that a declaration in C++ is a genuine statement and can appear anywhere among executable statements. Placing declarations among executable statements is extremely useful when creating class objects whose initial values are not known until execution time. Here's an example:

```
cout << "Enter appointment time in hours, minutes, and seconds: ";
cin >> hours >> minutes >> seconds;

Time appointmentTime(hours, minutes, seconds);

cout << "The appointment time is ";
appointmentTime.Write();
    ⋮
```

Revised Specification and Implementation Files for Time

By including constructors for the Time class, we are sure that each class object is initialized before any subsequent calls to the class member functions. As a result, we can delete from the Time specification file the warning to call Set before calling any other member functions. Also, we can remove all of the function preconditions that require Set to be called previously. Here is the revised Time specification file:

```
//****************************************************************
// SPECIFICATION FILE (Time.h)
// This file gives the specification
// of a Time abstract data type
//****************************************************************

class Time
{
public:
    void Set( /* in */ int hours,
              /* in */ int minutes,
              /* in */ int seconds );
        // Precondition:
        //      0 <= hours <= 23  &&  0 <= minutes <= 59
```

```
        //   && 0 <= seconds <= 59
        // Postcondition:
        //      Time is set according to the incoming parameters

    void Increment();
        // Postcondition:
        //      Time has been advanced by one second, with
        //      23:59:59 wrapping around to 00:00:00

    void Write() const;
        // Postcondition:
        //      Time has been output in the form HH:MM:SS

    bool Equal( /* in */ Time otherTime ) const;
        // Postcondition:
        //      Function value == true, if this time equals otherTime
        //                     == false, otherwise

    bool LessThan( /* in */ Time otherTime ) const;
        // Precondition:
        //      This time and otherTime represent times in the
        //      same day
        // Postcondition:
        //      Function value == true, if this time is earlier
        //                              in the day than otherTime
        //                     == false, otherwise

    Time( /* in */ int initHrs,
          /* in */ int initMins,
          /* in */ int initSecs );
        // Precondition:
        //      0 <= initHrs <= 23  &&  0 <= initMins <= 59
        //   && 0 <= initSecs <= 59
        // Postcondition:
        //      Class object is constructed
        //   && Time is set according to the incoming parameters

    Time();
        // Postcondition:
        //      Class object is constructed  &&  Time is 00:00:00
private:
    int hrs;
    int mins;
    int secs;
};
```

To save space, we do not include the revised implementation file here. The only changes are as follows:

1. The inclusion of the function definitions for the two class constructors, which we presented earlier.

2. The deletion of all function preconditions stating that the Set function must be invoked previously.

At this point, you may wonder whether we need the Set function at all. After all, both the Set function and the parameterized constructor seem to do the same thing—set the time according to values passed as arguments—and the implementations of the two functions are essentially identical. The difference is that Set can be invoked for an existing class object whenever and as often as we wish, whereas the parameterized constructor is invoked once only—at the moment a class object is created. Therefore, we retain the Set function to provide maximum flexibility to clients of the class.

The following is a complete client program that invokes all of the Time member functions. Observe that the main function begins by creating two Time objects, one by using the parameterized constructor and the other by using the default constructor. The program's output is shown below the program.

```cpp
//*****************************************************************
// TimeClient program
// This is a very simple client of the Time class
//*****************************************************************
#include <iostream>
#include "Time.h"    // For Time class

using namespace std;

int main()
{
    Time time1(5, 30, 0);
    Time time2;
    int  loopCount;

    cout << "time1: ";
    time1.Write();
    cout << "  time2: ";
    time2.Write();
    cout << endl;
    if (time1.Equal(time2))
        cout << "Times are equal" << endl;
    else
        cout << "Times are NOT equal" << endl;

    time2 = time1;
    cout << "time1: ";
```

```
    time1.Write();
    cout << "  time2: ";
    time2.Write();
    cout << endl;

    if (time1.Equal(time2))
        cout << "Times are equal" << endl;
    else
        cout << "Times are NOT equal" << endl;

    time2.Increment();
    cout << "New time2: ";
    time2.Write();
    cout << endl;

    if (time1.LessThan(time2))
        cout << "time1 is less than time2" << endl;
    else
        cout << "time1 is NOT less than time2" << endl;

    if (time2.LessThan(time1))
        cout << "time2 is less than time1" << endl;
    else
        cout << "time2 is NOT less than time1" << endl;

    time1.Set(23, 59, 55);
    cout << "Incrementing time1 from 23:59:55:" << endl;
    for (loopCount = 1; loopCount <= 10; loopCount++)
    {
        time1.Write();
        cout << ' ';
        time1.Increment();
    }
    cout << endl;
    return 0;
}
```

The output from executing the TimeClient program is as follows.

```
time1: 05:30:00  time2: 00:00:00
Times are NOT equal
time1: 05:30:00  time2: 05:30:00
Times are equal
New time2: 05:30:01
time1 is less than time2
```

```
time2 is NOT less than time1
Incrementing time1 from 23:59:55:
23:59:55 23:59:56 23:59:57 23:59:58 23:59:59 00:00:00 00:00:01
00:00:02 00:00:03 00:00:04
```

Guidelines for Using Class Constructors

The class is an essential language feature for creating abstract data types in C++. The class mechanism is a powerful design tool, but along with this power come rules for using classes correctly.

C++ has some very intricate rules about using constructors, many of which relate to language features we have not yet discussed. Below are some guidelines that are pertinent at this point.

1. A constructor cannot return a function value, so the function is declared without a return value type.

2. A class may provide several constructors. When a class object is declared, the compiler chooses the appropriate constructor according to the number and data types of the arguments to the constructor.

3. Arguments to a constructor are passed by placing the argument list immediately after the name of the class object being declared:

   ```
   SomeClass anObject(arg1, arg2);
   ```

4. If a class object is declared without an argument list, as in the statement

   ```
   SomeClass anObject;
   ```

   then the effect depends upon what constructors (if any) the class provides.

   If the class has no constructors at all, memory is allocated for anObject but its private data members are in an uninitialized state.

   If the class does have constructors, then the default (parameterless) constructor is invoked if there is one. If the class has constructors but no default constructor, a syntax error occurs.

Before leaving the topic of constructors, we give you a brief preview of another special member function supported by C++: the *class destructor*. Just as a constructor is implicitly invoked when a class object is created, a destructor is implicitly invoked when a class object is destroyed—for example, when control leaves the block in which a local object is declared. A class destructor is named the same as a constructor except that the first character is a tilde (~):

```
class SomeClass
{
public:
    ⋮
    SomeClass();       // Constructor
    ~SomeClass();      // Destructor
private:
    ⋮
};
```

Programming Example

Abstract Data Type Name

In Chapter 4, we displayed a name in different formats. In Chapter 8, the Health Profile program used a name. Adding a name to the BMI and the Mortgage programs would make sense. Names are often necessary pieces of information. Let's stop this duplication of effort and do the job once and for all—let's write the code to support a name as an abstract data type.

The format for this case study is a little different. Because we are developing only one software component—an ADT—and not a complete program, we omit the Input and Output sections. Instead, we include two sections entitled Specification of the ADT and Implementation of the ADT.

PROBLEM   Design and implement an abstract data type to represent a name. Make the domain and operations general enough to be used in any program that needs to keep track of a name. The informal specification of the ADT is given below.

TYPE
>Name

DOMAIN
>Each Name is a name in the form of first name, middle name, and last name.

OPERATIONS
>Construct a Name instance
>Set a name
>Read a name
>Inspect the first name
>Inspect the middle name
>Inspect the last name
>Inspect the middle initial
>Compare two names for "before," "same," and "after"

Where did these operations come from? From experience. Note that there is no operation to output the name in any particular format. Because we are allowing the user to inspect the parts of the name, the user can combine the parts to suit the user's purpose.

DISCUSSION   We create the Name ADT in two stages: specification, followed by implementation. The result of the first stage is a C++ specification (.h) file containing the declaration of a `Name` class. This file must describe for the user the precise semantics of each ADT operation. The informal specification given above would be unacceptable to the user of the ADT. The descriptions of the operations are too imprecise and ambiguous to be helpful to the user.

The second stage—implementation—requires us to (a) choose a concrete data representation for a name, and (b) implement each of the operations as a C++ function definition. The result is a C++ implementation file containing these function definitions.

SPECIFICATION OF THE ADT   The domain of our ADT is the set of all names made up of a first, middle, and last name. To represent the Name ADT as program code, we use a C++ class named

Name. The ADT operations become public member functions of the class. Let's now specify the operations more carefully.

Construct a new Name instance   For this operation, we use a C++ default constructor. The constructor for Time sets the hours, seconds, and minutes to zeros. Blanks would be the logical equivalent for class Name.

Set the name   The client must supply three arguments for this operation: first, middle, and last. Although we haven't yet determined a concrete data representation for a name, we must decide what data types the client should use for these arguments. The logical choice is for each value to be represented by a string. After thinking about it, we realize that this operation could be coded as a parameterized constructor. However, what if we want to change a name (set it) after it has already been constructed? Let's provide two operations that take the three parts of the name as parameters: one as a constructor and one as a void function.

Read a name   This operation prompts for and reads the three parts of the name from the standard input device.

Inspect the name's first, middle, and last names   All three of these operations are observer operations. They give the client access, indirectly, to the private data. In the Name class, we represent these operations as value-returning member functions with the following prototypes:

```
string first();
string middle();
string last();
```

Why do we need these observer operations? Why not simply let the data representation of the name be public instead of private so that the client can access the values directly? The answer is that the client should be allowed to inspect *but not modify* these values. If the data were public, a client could change the data, thereby compromising the integrity of an instance.

Inspect the middle initial   This operation requires that the first letter of the middle name be extracted and returned. In Chapter 4, we accessed the middle initial as a one-character string. Should we return it as a string here or as a char variable? It really doesn't matter as long as we are consistent in our code and in our documentation. Let's make this function a char function, just to provide a different example.

Compare two names   This operation compares two names and determines whether the first one comes before the second one, they are the same, or the first one comes after the second one. To indicate the result of the comparison, we define an enumeration type with three values:

enum RelationType {BEFORE, SAME, AFTER};

Then we can code the comparison operation as a class member function that returns a value of type RelationType. Here is the function prototype:

```
RelationType ComparedTo( /* in */ Name otherName ) const;
```

Because this is a class member function, the name being compared to otherName is the class object for which the member function is invoked. For example, the following client code tests whether name1 comes before name2.

```
Name name1;
Name name2;
  :
if (name1.ComparedTo(name2) == BEFORE)
  DoSomething();
```

We are now almost ready to write the C++ specification file for our Name class. However, the class declaration requires us to include the private part—the private variables that are the concrete data representation of the ADT. Choosing a concrete data representation properly belongs in the ADT implementation phase, not the specification phase. But, to satisfy the C++ class declaration requirement, we now choose a data representation. The simplest representation for a name is three string values—one each for the first, middle, and last. Here, then, is the specification file containing the Name class declaration (along with the declaration of the RelationType enumeration type).

```
//******************************************************************
// SPECIFICATION FILE (Name.h)
// This file gives the specification of the Name abstract
// data type. There are two constructors: one takes the first,
// middle, and last name as parameters and the second sets first,
// middle, and last to blanks
//******************************************************************

#include <iostream>
#include <string>

using namespace std;

enum RelationType{BEFORE, SAME, AFTER};

class Name
{
public:
    Name();
        // Default constructor
        // Postcondition:
        //      first, middle, and last have been set to blanks

    Name( /* in */ string firstName,
          /* in */ string middleName,
          /* in */ string lastName );
        // Parameterized constructor
        // Postcondition:
        //      first is firstName AND middle is middleName AND
        //      last is lastName
```

```
        void SetName( /* in */ string firstName,
                      /* in */ string middleName,
                      /* in */ string lastName );
    // Postcondition:
    //     first is firstName AND middle is middleName AND
    //     last is lastName

        void ReadName();
    // Postcondition:
    //     Name is prompted for and read from the standard input
    //     device

        string FirstName() const;
    // Postcondition:
    //     Return value is this person's first name

        string LastName() const;
    // Postcondition:
    //     Return value is this person's last name

        string MiddleName() const;
    // Postcondition:
    //     Return value is this person's middle name

        char MiddleInitial() const;
    // Postcondition:
    //     Return value is this person's middle initial

        RelationType ComparedTo( /* in */ Name otherName ) const;
    // Postcondition:
    //     Return value is
    //          BEFORE, if this name comes before otherName
    //          SAME, if this name and otherName are the same
    //          AFTER, if this name is after otherName

private:
    string first;           // Person's first name
    string last;            // Person's last name
    string middle;          // Person's middle name
};
```

IMPLEMENTATION OF THE ADT   We have already chosen a concrete data representation for a name, shown in the specification file as the string variables first, middle, and last. Now we must implement each class member function, placing the function definitions into a C++ implementation file named Name.cpp.

Here is the implementation file that contains function definitions for all of the ADT operations:

```cpp
//****************************************************************
// IMPLEMENTATION FILE (Name.cpp)
// The file implements the Name member functions
//****************************************************************

#include "Name.h"
#include <iostream>

Name::Name()

// Default constructor
// Postcondition:
//    first, middle, and last have been set to blanks

{
    first = " ";
    middle = " ";
    last = " ";
}

//****************************************************************

Name::Name( /* in */ string firstName,     // First name
            /* in */ string middleName,    // Middle name
            /* in */ string lastName )     // Last name

// Parameterized constructor
// Postcondition:
//     firstName has been stored in first; middleName has been
//     stored in middle; lastName has been stored in last

{
    first = firstName;                      // Assign parameters
    last = lastName;
    middle = middleName;
}

//****************************************************************

void Name::SetName( /* in */ string firstName,    // First name
                    /* in */ string middleName,   // Middle name
                    /* in */ string lastName )    // Last name
```

```
// Postcondition:
//      firstName has been stored in first; middleName has been
//      stored in middle; lastName has been stored in last

{
  first = firstName;                        // Assign parameters
  last = lastName;
  middle = middleName;
}

//********************************************************************

void Name::ReadName()

// Postcondition:
//      Name  prompted for and read from the standard input device

{
    cout << "Enter first name: ";    // Prompt for first name
    cin >> first;                    // Get first name
    cout << "Enter middle name: ";   // Prompt for middle name
    cin >> middle;                   // Get middle name
    cout << "Enter last name: ";     // Prompt for last name
    cin >> last;                     // Get last name
}

//********************************************************************

string Name::FirstName() const

// Postcondition:
//    Return value is first

{
    return first;
}

//********************************************************************

string Name::LastName() const

// Postcondition:
//    Return value is last
```

```
{
    return last;
}


//******************************************************************

string Name::MiddleName() const

// Postcondition:
//    Return value is middle

{
    return middle;
}



//******************************************************************

char Name::MiddleInitial() const

// Postcondition:
//    Return value is middle initial

{
    return middle[0];
}

//******************************************************************

RelationType Name::ComparedTo( /* in */ Name otherName ) const

// Precondition:
//     Input parameter contains a valid name
// Postcondition:
//     Return value is
//          BEFORE, if this name comes before otherName
//          SAME, if this name and otherName are the same
//          AFTER, if this name is after otherName
{
    if (last < otherName.last)
        return BEFORE;
    else if (otherName.last < last)
        return AFTER;
    else if (first < otherName.first)
```

```
        return BEFORE;
    else if (otherName.first < first)
        return AFTER;
    else if (middle < otherName.middle)
        return BEFORE;
    else if (otherName.middle < middle)
        return AFTER;
    else
        return SAME;
}
```

A name is a logical entity for which we now have developed an implementation. We have designed and implemented a name ADT that we (or any programmer) can use whenever we have a name as part of our program data. If we discover in the future that additional operations on a name would be useful, we can implement, test, and add them to our set of name operations.

We have said that data abstraction is an important principle of software design. What we have done here is an example of data abstraction. From now on, when a problem needs a name, we can stop our decomposition at the logical level. We do not need to worry about implementing a name each time.

Testing and Debugging

Testing and debugging a C++ class amounts to testing and debugging each member function of the class. All of the techniques you have learned about—algorithm walk-throughs, code walk-throughs, hand traces, test drivers, verification of preconditions and postconditions, the system debugger, and debug outputs—may be brought into play.

Consider how we might test this chapter's Time class. Here is the class declaration, abbreviated by leaving out the function preconditions and postconditions:

```
class Time
{
public:
    void Set( /* in */ int hours,
              /* in */ int minutes,
              /* in */ int seconds );
        // Precondition: ...
        // Postcondition: ...

    void Increment();
        // Postcondition: ...
```

```
    void Write() const;
        // Postcondition: ...

    bool Equal( /* in */ Time otherTime ) const;
        // Postcondition: ...

    bool LessThan( /* in */ Time otherTime ) const;
        // Precondition: ...
        // Postcondition: ...

    Time( /* in */ int initHrs,
          /* in */ int initMins,
          /* in */ int initSecs );
        // Precondition: ...
        // Postcondition: ...

    Time();
        // Postcondition: ...
private:
    int hrs;
    int mins;
    int secs;
};
```

To test this class fully, we must test each of the member functions. Let's step through the process of testing just one of them: the Increment function.

When we implemented the Increment function, we presumably started with a pseudocode algorithm, performed an algorithm walk-through, and translated the pseudocode into the following C++ function:

```
void Time::Increment()

// Postcondition:
//     Time has been advanced by one second, with
//     23:59:59 wrapping around to 00:00:00

{
    secs++;
    if (secs > 59)
    {
        secs = 0;
        mins++;
        if (mins > 59)
        {
```

```
            mins = 0;
            hrs++;
            if (hrs > 23)
                hrs = 0;
        }
    }
}
```

Now we perform a code walk-through, verifying that the C++ code faithfully matches the pseudocode algorithm. At this point (or earlier, during the algorithm walk-through), we do a hand trace to confirm that the logic is correct.

For the hand trace we should pick values of hrs, mins, and secs that ensure code coverage. To execute every path through the control flow, we need cases in which the following conditions occur:

1. The first If condition is false.
2. The first If condition is true and the second is false.
3. The first If condition is true, the second is true, and the third is false.
4. The first If condition is true, the second is true, and the third is true.

Below is a table displaying values of hrs, mins, and secs that correspond to these four cases. For each case we also write down what we hope will be the values of the variables after executing the algorithm.

	Initial Values			Expected Results		
Case	hrs	mins	secs	hrs	mins	secs
1	10	5	30	10	5	31
2	4	6	59	4	7	0
3	13	59	59	14	0	0
4	23	59	59	0	0	0

Using the initial values for each case, a hand trace of the code confirms that the algorithm produces the desired results.

Finally, we write a test driver for the Increment function, just to be sure that our understanding of the algorithm logic is the same as the computer's! Here is a possible test driver:

```
#include <iostream>
#include "Time.h"

using namespace std;
```

```cpp
int main()
{
    Time time;
    int      hours;
    int      minutes;
    int      seconds;

    cout << "Enter a time (use hours < 0 to quit): ";
    cin >> hours >> minutes >> seconds;
    while (hours >= 0)
    {
        time.Set(hours, minutes, seconds);
        time.Increment();
        cout << "Incremented time is ";
        time.Write();
        cout << endl;
        cout << "Enter a time (use hours < 0 to quit): ";
        cin >> hours >> minutes >> seconds;
    }
    return 0;
}
```

Now we compile the test driver and Time.cpp, link the two object files, and execute the program. For input data, we supply at least the four test cases discussed earlier. The program's output should match the desired results. Now that we have tested the Increment function, we can apply the same steps to the remaining class member functions.

If a class has been well tested and there are errors when client code uses the class, always check the member function preconditions. You can waste many hours trying to debug a class member function when, in fact, the function is correct. The error may lie in the client code.

Testing and Debugging Hints

1. The declarations of struct and class types must end with semicolons.

2. Be sure to specify the full member selector when referencing a component of a struct variable or class object.

3. Avoid using anonymous struct types.

4. Regarding semicolons, the declarations and definitions of class member functions are treated the same as any C++ function. The member function prototype, located in the class declaration, ends with a semicolon. The function heading—the part of the function definition preceding the body—does not end with a semicolon.

5. When implementing a class member function, don't forget to prefix the function name with the name of the class and the scope resolution operator (::).

```
void Time::Increment()
{
    ⋮
}
```

6. For now, the only built-in operations that we apply to struct variables and class objects are member selection (.) and assignment (=). To perform other operations, such as comparing two struct variables or class objects, you must access the components individually (in the case of struct variables) or write class member functions (in the case of class objects).

7. If a class member function inspects but does not modify the private data, it is a good idea to make it a const member function.

8. A class member function does not use dot notation to access private members of the class object for which the function is invoked. In contrast, a member function *must* use dot notation to access the private members of a class object that is passed to it as an argument.

9. To avoid errors caused by uninitialized data, it is good practice to always include a class constructor when designing a class.

10. A class constructor is declared without a return value type and cannot return a function value.

11. If a client of a class has errors that seem to be related to the class, start by checking the preconditions of the class member functions. The errors may be in the client, not the class.

Summary

In addition to being able to create user-defined atomic data types, we can create structured data types. In a structured data type, a name is given to an entire group of components. With many structured types, the group can be accessed as a whole, or each individual component can be accessed separately.

The record is a data structure for grouping together heterogeneous data—data items that are of different types. Individual components of a record are accessed by name. In C++, records are referred to as *structures* or as *structs*. We can use a struct variable to refer to the struct as a whole, or we can use a member selector to access any individual member (component) of the struct. Entire structs of the same type may be assigned directly to each other, passed as arguments, or returned as function return values. Comparison of structs, however, must be done member by member. Reading and writing of structs must also be done member by member.

Data abstraction is a powerful technique for reducing the complexity and increasing the reliability of programs. Separating the properties of a data type from the details of its implementation frees the user of the type from having to write code that depends on a particular implementation of the type. This separation also assures the implementor of the type that client code cannot accidentally compromise a correct implementation.

An abstract data type (ADT) is a type whose specification is separate from its implementation. The specification announces the abstract properties of the type. The implementation consists of (a) a concrete data representation and (b) the implementations of the ADT operations. In C++, an ADT can be realized by using the class mechanism. Class members can be designated as public or private. Most commonly, the private members are the concrete data representation of the ADT, and the public members are the functions corresponding to the ADT operations.

Among the public member functions of a class, the programmer often includes one or more class constructors—functions that are invoked automatically whenever a class object is created.

Separate compilation of program units is central to the separation of specification from implementation. The declaration of a C++ class is typically placed in a specification (.h) file, and the implementations of the class member functions reside in another file: the implementation file. The client code is compiled separately from the class implementation file, and the two resulting object code files are linked together to form an executable file. Through separate compilation, the user of an ADT can treat the ADT as an off-the-shelf component without ever seeing how it is implemented.

Quick Check

1. How does a C++ union conserve memory space? (pp. 410–411)
2. How do we create an implementation from a specification for an abstract data type? (pp. 411–413)
3. How does the use of a specification file help to provide encapsulation and information hiding for a class? (pp. 421–423)
4. What is contained between the braces of a struct definition? (pp. 403–405)
5. What operator is used as the member selector of a struct? (pp. 405–406)
6. What do we call a data structure that is implemented by a struct that contains other struct types? (pp. 408–410)
7. How would you write an expression to access the hour member of a struct that is itself a member, called time, of a struct variable called date? (pp. 408–410)
8. The members of a struct, like a class, can include variables, constants, and functions. What default attribute of a member differs between a class and a struct? (pp. 414–419)
9. Write the declaration of a class object, called today, of class Date. (pp. 414–419)
10. How would you call member function GetDay (which takes no parameters) of an object called Today of class Date? (pp. 414–419)
11. Where does the :: scope resolution operator appear in a member function definition within an implementation file? (pp. 423–427)

12. Which file, specification or implementation, omits member function bodies? (pp. 421–423)
13. What distinguishes a class constructor from other member functions? (pp. 430–436)

Answers

1. By allowing a type to have values of different types at different times, avoiding the need to allocate storage for all of the different types at once.   2. By choosing a data representation, and then writing out the operations for the ADT with program instructions.   3. It enables client code to see the formal interface to the class, but none of the implementation details that the creator of the class wishes to hide.   4. A list of the members of the `struct`.   5. The dot (period).   6. A hierarchical record. 7. `date.time.hour`   8. Classes default to private members, structs default to public members. 9. `Date today;`   10. `today.GetDay();`   11. In the heading, between the name of the class and the name of the function.   12. The specification file.   13. Its name is identical to the name of the class, and it is neither void nor does it have a return value type.

Exam Preparation Exercises

1. A `struct` cannot have another `struct` as a member. True or false?
2. A `union` is a `struct` that can hold just one of its members at a time. True or false?
3. Class scope applies to classes, structs, and unions. True or false?
4. Dot notation is used only by class clients to refer to members. Other class members do not need to use dot notation. True or false?
5. Given the following declarations,

```
struct Name
{
   string first;
   string middle;
   string last;
};


Name yourName;
Name myName;
```

What are the contents of the two `Name` variables after each of the following statements, assuming they are executed in the order listed?
a. `yourName.first = "George";`
b. `yourName.last = "Smith";`
c. `myName = yourName;`
d. `myName.middle = "Nathaniel";`
e. `yourName.middle = myName.middle[0] + ".";`

6. What are the three aggregate operations allowed on structs?
7. How does a union differ from an enumeration type?

8. Given the declaration of the Name type in Exercise 5, and the following declarations:

```
struct studentRecord
{
    Name studentName;
    Name teacherName;
    int gradeNumber;
    string grades;
}
```

```
studentRecord sally;
```

a. How would you assign the name Sally Ellen Strong to the `studentName` field of variable `sally`?

b. How would you assign the grade number 7 to that field of `sally`?

c. How would you assign the fourth letter from the `grades` field to char variable `spring`?

9. What happens when a struct is passed as an argument to a value parameter of a function? How does this differ from passing it to a reference parameter?

10. Given the following union declaration:

```
union GradeUnion
{
    char gradeLetter;
    int gradeNumber;
}
```

```
GradeUnion grade;
```

What does each of the following statements do, assuming they are executed in the order shown?

a. `cin >> grade.gradeLetter;`

b. `if (grade.gradeLetter >= 'A' && grade.gradeLetter <= 'D')`

c. `grade.gradeNumber =   4 - int(grade.gradeLetter - 'A');`

11. What are the two major properties of an abstract data type that are defined in its specification?

12. How does the data representation differ from the domain of an abstract data type?

13. By default, are class members public or private?

14. Given an object, called `current`, of class `Time`: How would you write the call to its void member function, called `plus`, that adds an integer number of minutes to the current time? The number of minutes to add is in variable `period`.

15. Which kind of operation, constructor, observer, transformer, or iterator is implemented by a function that is declared as `const`?

16. A class may have multiple constructors, all with the same name. How does the compiler decide which one to call?

17. A class called `Calendar` has a default constructor and a constructor that accepts an integer value specifying the year. How would you invoke each of these for an object called `primary`? Use the current year as the argument to the second constructor.

18. How is the name of a class destructor distinguished from a constructor?

Programming Warm-Up Exercises

1. Declare a `struct` type, `Time`, that represents an amount of time, consisting of minutes and seconds.

2. Write statements that assign the time 6 minutes and 54 seconds to a variable, `someTime`, of type `Time`, as declared in Exercise 1.

3. Declare a `struct` type, `Song`, that represents a song entry in an MP-3 library. It should have fields for title, album, artist, playing time in minutes and seconds (use the type declared in Exercise 1), and music category. The music category is represented by an enumeration type called `Category`.

4. Write statements to declare a variable called `mySong` of type `Song`, and assign it a set of values. For the playing time, use the variable `someTime` declared in Exercise 2. Make up values for the other fields. Assume that the enumeration type `Category` includes any song category that you wish to use.

5. Write a statement to output the playing time from `mySong`, as declared in Exercise 4, in the format `mm:ss`.

6. Write a declaration of a `union` type called `Temporal` that can hold a time represented as a string, as an integer, or as a value of type `Time`, as declared in Exercise 1.

7. Write the declaration of a variable called `shift` of type `Temporal`, as declared in Exercise 6, and a statement that assigns the value of `someTime`, as declared in Exercise 2, to `shift`.

8. Programming Problems 3 and 4 in Chapter 10 asked you to develop educational programs for teaching the periods of geologic time. Now that you know how to write classes, you can turn the Period ADT into a class. Write a specification file for the `Period` class that has a private field that's an enumeration type, representing the names of the periods. It should have functions that return the period as a string, that return the period as an `int`, that return the starting date of the period, and that increment the period to the next most recent period (if the period is already `QUATERNARY`, the increment operation should do nothing). It should have a default constructor that sets the period to `PRECAMBRIAN`, and a constructor with a parameter of the enumeration type to allow the user to create a Period object containing any period. For ease of reference, the table of the time periods is repeated here from Chapter 10. Be sure to use appropriate documenting comments.

Period Name	Starting Date (millions of years)
Quaternary	2.5
Tertiary	65
Cretaceous	136

Jurassic	192
Triassic	225
Permian	280
Carboniferous	345
Devonian	395
Silurian	435
Ordovician	500
Cambrian	570
Precambrian	4500 or earlier

9. Using the `Period` class as specified in Exercise 8, write a For statement that iterates through the periods of geologic time from earliest to most recent, writing out the name of the period and its starting date.

10. Write the function definitions of the two constructors for the `Period` class as specified in Exercise 8.

11. Write the function definition for the `ToInt` observer of the `Period` class specified in Exercise 8.

12. What would the filename be for the file containing the specification of the `Period` class in Exercise 8?

13. Write the `include` directive that would appear near the beginning of the `Period` class implementation file to include the specification file for the `Period` class as described in Exercise 8.

14. Because of floating point representational errors, monetary amounts that need to be exact should not be stored in floating point types. Code the specification for a class that represents an amount of money as dollars and cents. It should have a default constructor that creates an object with zero dollars and zero cents, an observer for dollars, an observer for cents, and an observer that returns the amount as a float. It also should have transformers that add and subtract other values of class `Money`. Be sure to use appropriate documenting comments.

15. Write the function definitions of the two constructors for the `Money` class as specified in Exercise 14.

16. What would be the filename for the file containing the specification of the `Money` class in Exercise 14?

17. Write the `include` directive that would appear near the beginning of the `Money` class implementation file to include the specification file for the `Money` class as described in Exercise 14.

18. Write the function definitions for the observer in the `Money` class of Exercise 14 that returns the values as a float.

Programming Problems

1. Programming Problem 3 in Chapter 10 asked you to develop an educational program to teach about geologic time. Rewrite that program using a class to implement an ADT representing a period of geologic time. If you did Programming Warm-Up Exercises 8 through 13, this will be a relatively easy rewrite. The program should let the user enter a range of prehistoric dates (in millions of years),

and then output the periods that are included in that range. Each time this is done, the user is asked if they want to continue. The goal of the exercise is for the student to try to figure out when each period began, so that he or she can make a chart of geologic time. See Programming Warm-Up Exercise 8 for a list of the geologic time periods and their starting dates.

2. Programming Problem 4 in Chapter 10 asked you to write a second educational program for learning about geologic time. Rewrite that program using a class to implement an ADT representing a period of geologic time. If you did Programming Warm-Up Exercises 8 through 13, then you've already done some of this rewrite. The ADT in those exercises needs to be enhanced with a constructor that takes a string as an argument and converts the string to the corresponding `Period` value (the constructor should work with any style of capitalization of the period names). In this program, the computer picks a date in geologic time and presents it to the student. The student guesses which period corresponds to the date. The student is allowed to continue guessing until he or she gets the right answer. Then the program asks the student whether he or she wants to try again, and repeats the process if the answer is "yes". You also may want to write a function that returns the period for a given date, however, this does not need to be part of the class.

3. In several chapters since Chapter 4, we have included Programming Problems that ask you to develop or rewrite a program that outputs the user's weight on different planets. Our goal in doing this has been for you to see how the same program can be implemented in different ways. Here we would like you to rewrite the program using a class to represent the planet and its gravity. The class should include a constructor that allows a planet to be specified with a string, using any capitalization (if the string is not a planet name, then Earth should be assumed). The default constructor for the class will create an object representing Earth. The class has an observer operator that takes a weight on Earth as an argument and returns the weight on the planet. It should have a second observer that returns the name of the planet as a string with proper capitalization.

For ease of reference, the information for the original problem is repeated here. The following table gives the factor by which the weight must be multiplied for each planet. The program should output an error message if the user doesn't type a correct planet name. The prompt and the error message should make it clear to the user how a planet name must be entered. Be sure to use proper formatting and appropriate comments in your code. The output should be clearly labeled and neatly formatted.

Mercury	0.4155
Venus	0.8975
Earth	1.0
Moon	0.166
Mars	0.3507
Jupiter	2.5374
Saturn	1.0677

Uranus	0.8947
Neptune	1.1794
Pluto	0.0899

4. Design, implement, and test a `class` that represents an amount of time in minutes and seconds. The class should provide a constructor that sets the time to a specified number of minutes and seconds. The default constructor should create an object for a time of zero minutes and zero seconds. The class should provide observers that return the minutes and the seconds separately, and an observer that returns the total time in seconds (minutes × 60 + seconds). Boolean comparison observers should be provided that test whether two times are equal, one is greater than the other, or one is less than the other. Transformers should be provided that add one time to another, and that subtract one time from another. The class should not allow negative time (subtraction of more time than is currently stored should result in a time of 0:00).

5. Design, implement and test a class that represents a song on a CD or in an MP-3 library. If you did Programming Warm-Up Exercises 3 through 5, you already know how to represent a song as a `struct`. The goal here is to make the ADT an encapsulated `class`. It should have members for title, album, artist, playing time in minutes and seconds (if you've done Problem 4, you can use that class here), and music category. The music category is represented by an enumeration type called `Category`. Make up an enumeration of your favorite categories. The class should have a constructor that allows all of the data members to be set, and a default constructor that sets them all to appropriate empty values. It should have an observer operation for each data member, and an observer that returns all of the data for the song as a string. An observer that compares two songs for equality also should be developed. Transformers should be provided to allow each data value to be changed.

6. Design, implement and test a class that represents a phone number. The number should be represented by a country code, an area code, a number, and a type. The first three can be integers. The type member is an enumeration of HOME, OFFICE, FAX, CELL, PAGER. The class should provide a default constructor that sets all of the integer values to zero and the type to HOME. A constructor that enables all of the values to be set also should be provided. You also should provide a constructor that takes just the number and type as arguments, and sets the country and area codes to those of your location. The class will have observers that enable each data member to be retrieved, and transformers that allow each data member to be changed. An additional observer should be provided that compares two phone numbers for equality.

Programming Example Follow-Up

1. Classify each of the seven member functions of the `Name` class as a constructor, a transformer, or an observer operation.
2. Write a test plan for testing the `ComparedTo` function of the `Name` class.
3. Write a driver to implement your test plan for the `ComparedTo` function.

4. What happens if the client enters an initial when prompted for the middle name? What happens if the client enters an initial followed by a period when prompted for the middle name?

5. Enhance the `Name` class with a title field and an observer function to return its value. Should the title be used in the `ComparedTo` function? Explain your answer.

Arrays

Goals

Knowledge Goals

- *To understand the structure of a one-dimensional array.*
- *To know how to use a one-dimensional array in solving a problem.*
- *To understand the structure of arrays of records and class objects.*
- *To know how index values can be made to have semantic content.*
- *To understand the structure of a two-dimensional array.*
- *To understand the structure of a multidimensional array.*

Skill Goals

To be able to:

- *Declare a one-dimensional array, with and without initialization.*
- *Perform fundamental operations on one-dimensional arrays.*
- *Apply subarray processing to a one-dimensional array.*
- *Declare a two-dimensional array.*
- *Perform fundamental operations on a two-dimensional array.*
- *Use arrays as parameters and arguments.*
- *Declare and process a multi-dimensional array.*

In many problems, a data structure has so many components that it is difficult to process them if each one must have a unique member name. An *array*—the fourth of the structured data types supported by C++—is a data type that allows us to represent data of this kind with ease.

In this chapter, we examine array data types as provided by the C++ language; in Chapter 13, we show how to combine classes and arrays to implement an ADT such as a list.

12.1 One-Dimensional Arrays

If we wanted to input 1000 integer values and print them in reverse order, we could write a program of this form:

```
//***************************
// ReverseNumbers program
//***************************
#include <iostream>

using namespace std;

int main()
{
    int value0;
    int value1;
    int value2;
      ⋮
    int value999;

    cin >> value0;
    cin >> value1;
    cin >> value2;
      ⋮
    cin >> value999;

    cout << value999 << endl;
    cout << value998 << endl;
    cout << value997 << endl;
      ⋮
    cout << value0 << endl;
    return 0;
}
```

This program is over 3000 lines long, and we have to use 1000 separate variables. Note that all the variables have the same name except for an appended number that distinguishes them. Wouldn't it be convenient if we could put the number into a counter variable and use For loops to go from 0 through 999, and then from 999 back down to 0? For example, if the counter variable were `number`, we could replace the 2000 original input/output statements with the following four lines of code (we enclose `number` in brackets to set it apart from `value`):

```
for (number = 0; number < 1000; number++)
    cin >> value[number];
for (number = 999; number >= 0; number--)
    cout << value[number] << endl;
```

This code fragment is correct in C++ *if* we declare `value` to be a *one-dimensional array,* which is a collection of variables—all of the same type—in which the first part of each variable name is the same, and the last part is an *index value* enclosed in square brackets. In our example, the value stored in `number` is called the *index.*

The declaration of a one-dimensional array requires that you declare the size of the array. To do so, you indicate within brackets the number of components in the array:

```
int value[1000];
```

This declaration creates an array with 1000 components, all of type `int`. The first component has index value 0, the second component has index value 1, and the last component has index value 999.

Here is the complete ReverseNumbers program, using array notation. This is certainly much shorter than our first version of the program.

```
//***************************
// ReverseNumbers program
//***************************
#include <iostream>

using namespace std;

int main()
{
    int value[1000];
    int number;

    for (number = 0; number < 1000; number++)
        cin >> value[number];
    for (number = 999; number >= 0; number--)
        cout << value[number] << endl;
    return 0;
}
```

As a data structure, an array differs from a struct or class in two fundamental ways:

1. An array is a *homogeneous* data structure (all components are of the same data type), whereas structs and classes are heterogeneous types (their components may be of different types).

2. A component of an array is accessed by its *position* in the structure, whereas a component of a struct or class is accessed by an identifier (the member name).

Let's now define arrays formally and look at the rules for accessing individual components.

Declaring Arrays

A **one-dimensional array** is a structured collection of components (often called *array elements*) that can be accessed individually by specifying the position of a component with a single index value. (Later in the chapter, we introduce multidimensional arrays, which are arrays that have more than one index value.)

One-dimensional array   A structured collection of components, all of the same type, that is given a single name. Each component (array element) is accessed by an index that indicates the component's position within the collection.

Here is a syntax template describing the simplest form of a one-dimensional array declaration:

ArrayDeclaration

```
DataType  ArrayName [ ConstIntExpression ] ;
```

In the syntax template, DataType describes what is stored in each component of the array. Array components may be of almost any type, but for now we limit our discussion to atomic components. ConstIntExpression is an integer expression composed only of literal or named constants. This expression, which specifies the number of components in the array, must have a value greater than 0. If the value is n, the range of index values is 0 through $n - 1$, not 1 through n. For example, the declarations

```
float angle[4];
int   testScore[10];
```

create the arrays shown in Figure 12-1. The `angle` array has four components, each capable of holding one `float` value. The `testScore` array has a total of ten components, all of type `int`.

Accessing Individual Components

To access an individual array component, we write the array name, followed by an expression enclosed in square brackets. The expression specifies which component to

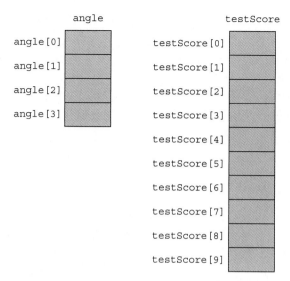

Figure 12–1 *angle* and *testScore* Arrays

access. It may be as simple as a constant or a variable name or as complex as a combination of variables, operators, and function calls. Whatever the form of the expression, it must result in an integer value. Index expressions can be of type char, short, int, long, or bool because these are all integral types. Additionally, values of enumeration types can be used as index expressions, with an enumeration value implicitly coerced to an integer.

The simplest form of index expression is a constant. Using our angle array, the sequence of assignment statements

```
angle[0] = 4.93;
angle[1] = -15.2;
angle[2] = 0.5;
angle[3] = 1.67;
```

fills the array components one at a time (see Figure 12–2).

Each array component—angle[2], for instance—can be treated exactly the same as any simple variable of type float. For example, we can do the following to the individual component angle[2]:

```
angle[2] = 9.6;              Assign it a value.
cin >> angle[2];             Read a value into it.
cout << angle[2];            Write its contents.
y = sqrt(angle[2]);          Pass it as an argument.
x = 6.8 * angle[2] + 7.5;    Use it in an arithmetic expression.
```

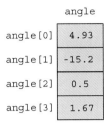

Figure 12–2 *angle Array with Values*

Let's look at index expressions that are more complicated than constants. Suppose we declare a 1000-element array of int values with the statement

```
int value[1000];
```

and execute the following two statements.

```
value[counter] = 5;
if (value[number+1] % 10 != 0)
    ⋮
```

In the first statement, 5 is stored into an array component. If counter is 0, 5 is stored into the first component of the array. If counter is 1, 5 is stored into the second place in the array, and so forth.

In the second statement, the expression number+1 selects an array component. The specific array component accessed is divided by 10 and checked to see if the remainder is nonzero. If number+1 is 0, we are testing the value in the first component; if number+1 is 1, we are testing the second place; and so on. Figure 12–3 shows the index expression as a constant, a variable, and a more complex expression.

Out-of-Bounds Array Indexes

Given the declaration

```
float alpha[100];
```

the valid range of index values is 0 through 99. What happens if we execute the statement

```
alpha[i] = 62.4;
```

when i is less than 0 or when i is greater than 99? The result is that a memory location outside the array is accessed. C++ does not check for invalid (out-of-bounds) array indexes either at compile time or at run

Out-of-bounds array index An index value that, in C++, is either less than 0 or greater than the array size minus 1.

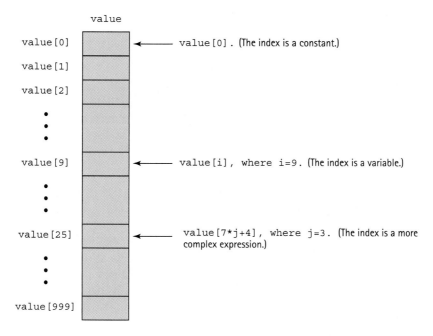

value

value[0]   ←———— value[0] . (The index is a constant.)

value[1]

value[2]

⋮

value[9]   ←———— value[i], where i=9. (The index is a variable.)

⋮

value[25]   ←———— value[7*j+4], where j=3. (The index is a more complex expression.)

⋮

value[999]

Figure 12–3   *An Index as a Constant, a Variable, and an Arbitrary Expression*

time. If i happens to be 100 in the statement above, the computer stores 62.4 into the next memory location past the end of the array, destroying whatever value was contained there. It is entirely the programmer's responsibility to make sure that an array index does not step off either end of the array.

Array-processing algorithms often use For loops to step through the array elements one at a time. Here is a loop to zero out our 100-element alpha array (i is an int variable):

```
for (i = 0; i < 100; i++)
    alpha[i] = 0.0;
```

We could also write the first line as

```
for (i = 0; i <= 99; i++)
```

However, C++ programmers commonly use the first version so that the number in the loop test (100) is the same as the array size. With this pattern, it is important to remember to test for *less-than*, not less-than-or-equal.

Initializing Arrays in Declarations

You learned in Chapter 8 that C++ allows you to initialize a variable in its declaration:

```
int delta = 25;
```

The value 25 is called an initializer. You also can initialize an array in its declaration, using a special syntax for the initializer. You specify a list of initial values for the array elements, separate them with commas, and enclose the list within braces:

```
int age[5] = {23, 10, 16, 37, 12};
```

In this declaration, `age[0]` is initialized to 23, `age[1]` is initialized to 10, and so on. There must be at least one initial value between the braces. If you specify too many initial values, you get a syntax error message. If you specify too few, the remaining array elements are initialized to zero.

Arrays follow the same rule as simple variables about the time(s) at which initialization occurs. A static array (one that is either global or declared as `static` within a block) is initialized once only, when control reaches its declaration. An automatic array (one that is local and not declared as `static`) is reinitialized each time control reaches its declaration.

An interesting feature of C++ is that you are allowed to omit the size of an array when you initialize it in a declaration:

```
float temperature[] = {0.0, 112.37, 98.6};
```

The compiler figures out the size of the array (here, 3) according to how many initial values are listed. In general, this feature is not particularly useful. In Chapter 13, though, we'll see that it can be convenient for initializing certain kinds of `char` arrays called C strings.

Examples of Declaring and Accessing Arrays

We now look in detail at some specific examples of declaring and accessing arrays. Here are some declarations that a program might use to analyze occupancy rates in an apartment building:

```
const int BUILDING_SIZE = 350;    // Number of apartments

int occupants[BUILDING_SIZE];     // occupants[i] is the number of
                                  //   occupants in apartment i
int totalOccupants;               // Total number of occupants
int counter;                      // Loop control and index variable
```

`occupants` is a 350-element array of integers (see Figure 12-4). `occupants[0] = 3` if the first apartment has three occupants; `occupants[1] = 5` if the second apartment has

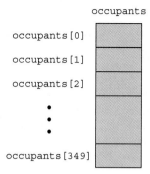

Figure 12–4 *occupants Array*

five occupants; and so on. If values have been stored into the array, then the following code totals the number of occupants in the building.

```
totalOccupants = 0;
for (counter = 0; counter < BUILDING_SIZE; counter++)
    totalOccupants = totalOccupants + occupants[counter];
```

The first time through the loop, `counter` is 0. We add the contents of `totalOccupants` (that is, 0) to the contents of `occupants[0]`, storing the result into `totalOccupants`. Next, `counter` becomes 1 and the loop test occurs. The second loop iteration adds the contents of `totalOccupants` to the contents of `occupants[1]`, storing the result into `totalOccupants`. Now `counter` becomes 2 and the loop test is made. Eventually, the loop adds the contents of `occupants[349]` to the sum and increments `counter` to 350. At this point, the loop condition is false, and control exits the loop.

Note how we used the named constant `BUILDING_SIZE` in both the array declaration and the For loop. When constants are used in this manner, changes are easy to make. If the number of apartments changes from 350 to 400, we need to change only one line: the `const` declaration of `BUILDING_SIZE`. If we had used the literal value 350 in place of `BUILDING_SIZE`, we would need to update several of the statements in the code above, and probably many more throughout the rest of the program.

The following is a complete program that uses the `occupants` array. The program fills the array with occupant data read from an input file and then lets the user interactively look up the number of occupants in a specific apartment.

```
//***************************************************************
// Apartment program
// This program allows a building owner to look up how many
// occupants are in a given apartment
// Note: This program is missing code to check for user input errors
//***************************************************************
```

```
#include <iostream>
#include <fstream>                    // For file I/O

using namespace std;

const int BUILDING_SIZE = 350;    // Number of apartments

int main()
{
    int occupants[BUILDING_SIZE]; // occupants[i] is the number of
                                  //    occupants in apartment i
    int totalOccupants;           // Total number of occupants
    int counter;                  // Loop control and index variable
    int apt;                      // An apartment number
    ifstream inFile;              // File of occupant data (one
                                  //    integer per apartment)

    inFile.open("apt.dat");
    totalOccupants = 0;
    for (counter = 0; counter < BUILDING_SIZE; counter++)
    {
        inFile >> occupants[counter];
        totalOccupants = totalOccupants + occupants[counter];
    }
    cout << "No. of apts. is " << BUILDING_SIZE << endl
         << "Total no. of occupants is " << totalOccupants << endl;

    cout << "Begin apt. lookup..." << endl;
    do
    {
        cout << "Apt. number (1 through " << BUILDING_SIZE
             << ", or 0 to quit): ";
        cin >> apt;
        if (apt > 0)
            cout << "Apt. " << apt << " has " << occupants[apt-1]
                 << " occupants" << endl;
    } while (apt > 0);
    return 0;
}
```

Look closely at the last output statement in the Apartment program. The user enters an apartment number (apt) in the range 1 through BUILDING_SIZE, but the array has indexes 0 through BUILDING_SIZE – 1. Therefore, we must subtract 1 from apt so that we index into the proper place in the array.

Because an array index is an integer value, we access the components by their position in the array—that is, the first, the second, the third, and so on. Using an `int` index is the most common way of thinking about an array. C++, however, provides more flexibility by allowing an index to be of any integral type or enumeration type. (The index expression still must evaluate to an integer in the range from 0 through one less than the array size.) The next example shows an array in which the indexes are values of an enumeration type.

```
enum Drink {ORANGE, COLA, ROOT_BEER, GINGER_ALE, CHERRY, LEMON};

float salesAmt[6]; // Array of 6 floats, to be indexed by Drink type
Drink flavor;      // Variable of the index type
```

`Drink` is an enumeration type in which the enumerators `ORANGE`, `COLA`, ..., `LEMON` have internal representations 0 through 5, respectively. `salesAmt` is a group of six `float` components representing dollar sales figures for each kind of drink (see Figure 12-5). The following code prints the values in the array (see Chapter 10 to review how to increment values of enumeration types in For loops).

```
for (flavor = ORANGE; flavor <= LEMON; flavor = Drink(flavor + 1))
    cout << salesAmt[flavor] << endl;
```

Here is one last example.

```
const int NUM_STUDENTS = 10;

char grade[NUM_STUDENTS]; // Array of 10 student letter grades
int  idNumber;            // Student ID number (0 through 9)
```

The `grade` array is pictured in Figure 12-6. Values are shown in the components, which implies that some processing of the array has already occurred. Following are some simple examples showing how the array might be used.

Figure 12-5 *salesAmt Array*

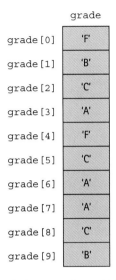

Figure 12-6 *grade Array with Values*

`cin >> grade[2];`	Reads the next nonwhitespace character from the input stream and stores it into the component in `grade` indexed by 2.
`grade[3] = 'A';`	Assigns the character 'A' to the component in `grade` indexed by 3.
`idNumber = 5;`	Assigns 5 to the index variable `idNumber`.
`grade[idNumber] = 'C';`	Assigns the character 'C' to the component of `grade` indexed by `idNumber` (that is, by 5).

`for (idNumber = 0; idNumber < NUM_STUDENTS;`
`    idNumber++)`
`    cout << grade[idNumber];`
	Loops through the `grade` array, printing each component. For this loop, the output would be `FBCAFCAACB`.

`for (idNumber = 0; idNumber < NUM_STUDENTS;`
`    idNumber++)`
`    cout << "Student " << idNumber`
`        << " Grade " << grade[idNumber]`
`        << endl;`
	Loops through `grade`, printing each component in a more readable form.

In the last example, `idNumber` is used as the index, but it also has semantic content—it is the student's identification number. The output would be

```
Student 0 Grade F
Student 1 Grade B
   :
Student 9 Grade B
```

Passing Arrays as Arguments

In Chapter 8, we said that if a variable is passed to a function and it is not to be changed by the function, then the variable should be passed by value instead of by reference. We specifically excluded stream variables (such as those representing data files) from this rule and said that there would be one more exception. Arrays are this exception.

By default, C++ simple variables are always passed by value. To pass a simple variable by reference, you must append an ampersand (&) to the data type name in the function's parameter list:

```
int SomeFunc( float param1,     // Pass-by-value
              char& param2 )    // Pass-by-reference
{
    :
}
```

It is impossible to pass a C++ array by value; arrays are *always* passed by reference. Therefore, you never use & when declaring an array as a parameter. When an array is passed as an argument, its **base address**—the memory address of the first element of the array—is sent to the function. The function then knows where the caller's actual array is located and can access any element of the array.

> **Base address** The memory address of the first element of an array.

Here is a C++ function that will zero out a one-dimensional `float` array of any size:

```
void ZeroOut( /* out */ float arr[],
              /* in */  int   numElements )
{
    int i;

    for (i = 0; i < numElements; i++)
        arr[i] = 0.0;
}
```

In the parameter list, the declaration of `arr` does not include a size within the brackets. If you include a size, the compiler ignores it. The compiler only wants to know that it is a `float` array, not a `float` array of any particular size. Therefore, in the `ZeroOut` function you must include a second parameter—the number of array elements—in order for the For loop to work correctly.

The calling code can invoke the `ZeroOut` function for a `float` array of any size. The following code fragment makes function calls to zero out two arrays of different sizes. Notice how an array parameter is declared in a function prototype.

```
void ZeroOut( float[], int );    // Function prototype
  ⋮
int main()
{
    float velocity[30];
    float refractionAngle[9000];
      ⋮
    ZeroOut(velocity, 30);
    ZeroOut(refractionAngle, 9000);
      ⋮
}
```

With simple variables, passing by value prevents a function from modifying the caller's argument. Although you cannot pass arrays by value in C++, you can still prevent the function from modifying the caller's array. To do so, you use the reserved word const in the declaration of the parameter. Below is a function that copies one int array into another. The first parameter—the destination array—is expected to be modified, but the second array is not.

```
void Copy( /* out */        int destination[],
           /* in */   const int source[],
           /* in */        int size            )
{
    int i;

    for (i = 0; i < size; i++)
        destination[i] = source[i];
}
```

The word const guarantees that any attempt to modify the source array within the Copy function results in a compile-time error.

One final remark about argument passage: It is a common mistake to pass an array *element* to a function when passing the entire array was intended. For example, our ZeroOut function expects the base address of a float array to be sent as the first argument. In the following code fragment, the function call is an error.

```
float velocity[30];
  ⋮
ZeroOut(velocity[30], 30);    // Error
```

First of all, velocity[30] denotes a single array element—one floating-point number—and not an entire array. Furthermore, there is no array element with an index of 30. The indexes for the velocity array run from 0 through 29.

Assertions About Arrays

In assertions written as comments, we often need to refer to a range of array elements:

```
// Assert: alpha[i] through alpha[j] have been printed
```

To specify such ranges, it is more convenient to use an abbreviated notation consisting of two dots:

```
// Assert: alpha[i]..alpha[j] have been printed
```

or, more briefly:

```
// Assert: alpha[i..j] have been printed
```

Note that this dot-dot notation is not valid syntax in C++ language statements. We are talking only about comments in a program.

Using Typedef with Arrays

In Chapter 10, we discussed the Typedef statement as a way of giving an additional name to an existing data type. We can use Typedef to give a name to an array type. Here's an example:

```
typedef float FloatArr[100];
```

This statement says that the type `FloatArr` is the same as the type "100-element array of `float`." (Notice that the array size in brackets comes at the very end of the statement.) We can now declare variables to be of type `FloatArr`:

```
FloatArr angle;
FloatArr velocity;
```

In this book, we don't often use Typedefs to give names to one-dimensional array types. However, when we discuss multidimensional arrays later in the chapter, we'll see that the technique can come in handy.

12.2 Arrays of Records and Objects

Although arrays with atomic components are very common, many applications require a collection of records or class objects. For example, a business needs a list of parts records, and a teacher needs a list of students in a class. Arrays are ideal for these applications. We simply define an array whose components are records or class objects.

Arrays of Records

Let's define a grade book to be a collection of student records as follows:

```
const int MAX_STUDENTS = 150;

enum GradeType {A, B, C, D, F};

struct StudentRec
{
    string      stuName;
    float       gpa;
    int         examScore[4];
    GradeType   courseGrade;
};

StudentRec gradeBook[MAX_STUDENTS];
int        count;
```

This data structure can be visualized as shown in Figure 12–7.

An element of gradeBook is selected by an index. For example, gradeBook[2] is the third component in the array gradeBook. Each component of gradeBook is a

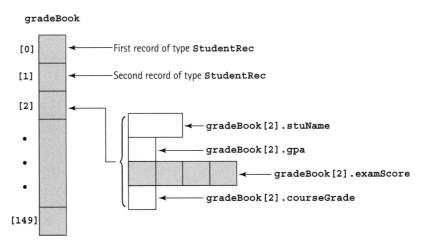

Figure 12–7 *gradeBook Array with Records as Elements*

record of type `StudentRec`. To access the course grade of the third student, we use the following expression:

`gradeBook[2].courseGrade`

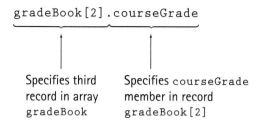

Specifies third record in array `gradeBook`

Specifies `courseGrade` member in record `gradeBook[2]`

The record component `gradeBook[2].examScore` is an array. We can access the individual elements in this component just as we would access the elements of any other array: We give the name of the array followed by the index, which is enclosed in brackets.

`gradeBook[2].examScore[0]`

Specifies third record in array `gradeBook`

Specifies `examScore` member (an array)

Specifies first score in `examScore` member

The following code fragment prints the name of each student in the class:

```
for (count = 0; count < MAX_STUDENTS; count++)
    cout << gradeBook[count].stuName << endl;
```

Arrays of Class Objects

The syntax for declaring and using arrays of class objects is the same as for arrays of structs. Given the `Time` class of Chapter 11, we can maintain a collection of ten appointment times by starting with the declaration

```
Time appointment[10];
```

This statement creates a ten-element array named `appointment`, in which each element is a `TimeType` object. The following statements set the first two appointment times to 8:45:00 and 10:00:00.

```
appointment[0].Set(8, 45, 0);
appointment[1].Set(10, 0, 0);
```

To output all ten appointment times, we would write

```
for (index = 0; index < 10; index++)
{
    appointment[index].Write();
    cout << endl;
}
```

Recall that the `Time` class has two constructors defined for it. One is the default (parameterless) constructor, which sets the time for a newly created object to 00:00:00. The other is a parameterized constructor with which the client code can specify an initial time when the class object is created. How are constructors handled when you declare an array of class objects? Here is the rule in C++:

If a class has at least one constructor, and an array of class objects is declared:

```
SomeClass arr[50];
```

then one of the constructors *must* be the default (parameterless) constructor. This constructor is invoked for each element of the array.

Therefore, with our declaration of the `appointment` array

```
Time appointment[10];
```

the default constructor is called for all ten array elements, setting each time to an initial value of 00:00:00.

12.3 Special Kinds of Array Processing

Two types of array processing occur especially often: using only part of the declared array (a subarray) and using index values that have specific meaning within the problem (indexes with semantic content). We describe both of these methods briefly here and give further examples in the remainder of the chapter.

Subarray Processing

The *size* of an array—the declared number of array components—is established at compile time. We have to declare it to be as big as it would ever need to be. Because the exact number of values to be put into the array often depends on the data itself, however, we may not fill all of the array components with values. The problem is that to avoid processing empty ones, we must keep track of how many components are actually filled.

As values are put into the array, we keep a count of how many components are filled. We then use this count to process only components that have values stored in them. Any remaining places are not processed. For example, if there are 250 students in a class, a program to analyze test grades would set aside 250 locations for the grades. However, some students may be absent on the day of the test. So the number of test grades must be counted, and that number, rather than 250, is used to control the processing of the array.

If the number of data items actually stored in an array is less than its declared size, functions that receive array parameters must also receive the number of data items as a parameter. For example,

```
void Print( /* in */ const char grade[],   // Array for up to
                                            //   250 students
           /* in */        int   numGrades ) // Number of grades
                                            //   actually in array
```

Indexes with Semantic Content

In some problems, an array index has meaning beyond simple position; that is, the index has *semantic content*. An example is the salesAmt array we showed earlier. This array is indexed by a value of enumeration type Drink. The index of a specific sales amount is the kind of soft drink sold; for example, salesAmt[ROOT_BEER] is the dollar sales figure for root beer.

The next section gives additional examples of indexes with semantic content.

12.4 Two-Dimensional Arrays

A one-dimensional array is used to represent items in a list or sequence of values. In many problems, however, the relationships between data items are more complex than a simple list. A **two-dimensional array** is used to represent items in a table with rows and columns, provided each item in the table is of the same data type. A component in a two-dimensional array is accessed by specifying the row and column indexes of the item in the array. This is a familiar task. For example,

> **Two-dimensional array** A collection of components, all of the same type, structured in two dimensions. Each component is accessed by a pair of indexes that represent the component's position in each dimension.

if you want to find a street on a map, you look up the street name on the back of the map to find the coordinates of the street, usually a letter and a number. The letter specifies a column to look on, and the number specifies a row. You find the street where the row and column meet.

Figure 12-8 shows a two-dimensional array with 100 rows and 9 columns. The rows are accessed by an integer ranging from 0 through 99; the columns are accessed

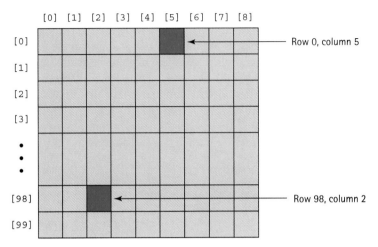

Figure 12–8   *A Two-Dimensional Array*

by an integer ranging from 0 through 8. Each component is accessed by a row-column pair—for example, 0, 5.

A two-dimensional array is declared in exactly the same way as a one-dimensional array, except that sizes must be specified for two dimensions.

```
const int NUM_ROWS = 100;
const int NUM_COLS = 9;
   ⋮
float alpha[NUM_ROWS][NUM_COLS];
```

First dimension   Second dimension

This example declares alpha to be a two-dimensional array, all of whose components are float values. The declaration creates the array that is pictured in Figure 12–8.

To access an individual component of the alpha array, two expressions (one for each dimension) are used to specify its position. Each expression is in its own pair of brackets next to the name of the array:

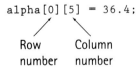

```
alpha[0][5] = 36.4;
```

Row number   Column number

As with one-dimensional arrays, each index expression must result in an integer value.

Figure 12-9 *hiTemp Array*

Let's look now at some examples. Here is the declaration of a two-dimensional array with 364 integer components (52 × 7 = 364):

```
int hiTemp[52][7];
```

hiTemp is an array with 52 rows and 7 columns. Each place in the array (each component) can contain any int value. Our intention is that the array contains high temperatures for each day in a year. Each row represents one of the 52 weeks in a year, and each column represents one of the 7 days in a week. (To keep the example simple, we ignore the fact that there are 365—and sometimes 366—days in a year.) The expression hiTemp[2][6] refers to the int value in the third row (row 2) and the seventh column (column 6). Semantically, hiTemp[2][6] is the temperature for the seventh day of the third week. The code fragment shown in Figure 12-9 would print the temperature values for the third week.

Another representation of the same data might be as follows:

```
enum DayType
{
    MONDAY, TUESDAY, WEDNESDAY, THURSDAY, FRIDAY, SATURDAY, SUNDAY
};

int hiTemp[52][7];
```

Here, hiTemp is declared the same as before, but we can use an expression of type DayType for the column index. hiTemp[2][SUNDAY] corresponds to the same component as hiTemp[2][6] in the first example. (Recall that enumerators such as MONDAY, TUESDAY,... are represented internally as the integers 0, 1, 2, ...) If day is of type DayType and week is of type int, the code fragment shown in Figure 12-10 sets the entire array to 0. (Notice that by using DayType, the temperature values in the array begin with the first Monday of the year, not necessarily with January 1.)

Figure 12–10 *hiTemp Array (Alternate Form)*

Another way of looking at a two-dimensional array is to see it as a structure in which each component has two features. For example, in the following code,

```
enum Colors {RED, ORANGE, YELLOW, GREEN, BLUE, INDIGO, VIOLET};
enum Makes
{
    FORD, TOYOTA, HYUNDAI, JAGUAR, CITROEN, BMW, FIAT, SAAB
};
const int NUM_COLORS = 7;
const int NUM_MAKES = 8;

float crashRating[NUM_COLORS][NUM_MAKES];   // Array of crash
                                            // likelihoods by color
                                            // and make
  ⋮
crashRating[BLUE][JAGUAR] = 0.83;   // Blue Jaguars have a crash
                                    //    likelihood of 0.83
crashRating[RED][FORD] = 0.19;      // Red Fords have a crash
                                    //    likelihood of 0.19
```

the data structure uses one dimension to represent the color and the other to represent the make of automobile. In other words, both indexes have semantic content—a concept we discussed in the previous section.

12.5 Processing Two-Dimensional Arrays

Processing data in a two-dimensional array generally means accessing the array in one of four patterns: randomly, along rows, along columns, or throughout the entire array. Each of these may also involve subarray processing.

The simplest way to access a component is to look directly in a given location. For example, a user enters map coordinates that we use as indexes into an array of street names to access the desired name at those coordinates. This process is referred to as *random access* because the user may enter any set of coordinates at random.

There are many cases in which we might wish to perform an operation on all the elements of a particular row or column in an array. Consider the `hiTemp` array defined previously, in which the rows represent weeks of the year and the columns represent days of the week. If we wanted the average high temperature for a given week, we would sum the values in that row and divide by 7. If we wanted the average for a given day of the week, we would sum the values in that column and divide by 52. The former case is access by row; the latter case is access by column.

Now suppose that we wish to determine the average for the year. We must access every element in the array, sum them, and divide by 364. In this case, the order of access—by row or by column—is not important. (The same is true when we initialize every element of an array to zero.) This is access throughout the array.

There are times when we must access every array element in a particular order, either by rows or by columns. For example, if we wanted the average for every week, we would run through the entire array, taking each row in turn. However, if we wanted the average for each day of the week, we would run through the array a column at a time.

Let's take a closer look at these patterns of access by considering four common examples of array processing.

1. Sum the rows.
2. Sum the columns.
3. Initialize the array to all zeros (or some special value).
4. Print the array.

First, let's define some constants and variables using general identifiers, such as `row` and `col`, rather than problem-dependent identifiers. Then let's look at each algorithm in terms of generalized two-dimensional array processing.

```
const int NUM_ROWS = 50;
const int NUM_COLS = 50;

int arr[NUM_ROWS][NUM_COLS];      // A two-dimensional array
int row;                          // A row index
int col;                          // A column index
int total;                        // A variable for summing
```

Sum the Rows

Suppose we want to sum row number 3 (the fourth row) in the array and print the result. We can do this easily with a For loop:

```
total = 0;
for (col = 0; col < NUM_COLS; col++)
```

```
    total = total + arr[3][col];
cout << "Row sum: " << total << endl;
```

This For loop runs through each column of `arr`, while keeping the row index fixed at 3. Every value in row 3 is added to `total`.

Now suppose we want to sum and print two rows—row 2 and row 3. We can use a nested loop and make the row index a variable:

```
for (row = 2; row < 4; row++)
{
    total = 0;
    for (col = 0; col < NUM_COLS; col++)
        total = total + arr[row][col];
    cout << "Row sum: " << total << endl;
}
```

The outer loop controls the rows, and the inner loop controls the columns. For each value of `row`, every column is processed; then the outer loop moves to the next row. In the first iteration of the outer loop, `row` is held at 2 and `col` goes from 0 through `NUM_COLS-1`. Therefore, the array is accessed in the following order:

```
arr[2][0]    [2][1]    [2][2]    [2][3] ...    [2][NUM_COLS-1]
```

In the second iteration of the outer loop, `row` is incremented to 3, and the array is accessed as follows:

```
arr[3][0]    [3][1]    [3][2]    [3][3] ...    [3][NUM_COLS-1]
```

We can generalize this row processing to run through every row of the array by having the outer loop run from 0 through `NUM_ROWS-1`. However, if we want to access only part of the array (subarray processing), given variables declared as

```
int rowsFilled;    // Data is in 0..rowsFilled-1
int colsFilled;    // Data is in 0..colsFilled-1
```

then we write the code fragment as follows:

```
for (row = 0; row < rowsFilled; row++)
{
    total = 0;
    for (col = 0; col < colsFilled; col++)
        total = total + arr[row][col];
    cout << "Row sum: " << total << endl;
}
```

Figure 12–11 illustrates subarray processing by row.

Figure 12–11   *Partial Array Processing by Row*

Sum the Columns

Suppose we want to sum and print each column. The code to perform this task follows. Again, we have generalized the code to sum only the portion of the array that contains valid data.

```
for (col = 0; col < colsFilled; col++)
{
    total = 0;
    for (row = 0; row < rowsFilled; row++)
        total = total + arr[row][col];
    cout << "Column sum: " << total << endl;
}
```

In this case, the outer loop controls the column, and the inner loop controls the row. All the components in the first column are accessed and summed before the outer loop index changes and the components in the second column are accessed. Figure 12–12 illustrates subarray processing by column.

Initialize the Array

As with one-dimensional arrays, we can initialize a two-dimensional array either by initializing it in its declaration or by using assignment statements. If the array is small, it arr

Figure 12–12   *Partial Array Processing by Column*

is simplest to initialize it in its declaration. To initialize a two-row by three-column array to look like this:

```
14    3   -5
 0   46    7
```

we can use the following declaration.

```
int arr[2][3] =
{
    {14, 3, -5},
    {0, 46, 7}
};
```

In this declaration, the initializer list consists of two items, each of which is itself an initializer list. The first inner initializer list stores 14, 3, and –5 into row 0 of the array; the second stores 0, 46, and 7 into row 1. The use of two initializer lists makes sense if you think of each row of the two-dimensional array as a one-dimensional array of three ints. The first initializer list initializes the first array (the first row), and the second list initializes the second array (the second row). Later in the chapter, we revisit this notion of viewing a two-dimensional array as an array of arrays.

Initializing an array in its declaration is impractical if the array is large. For a 100-row by 100-column array, you don't want to list 10,000 values. If the values are all different, you should store them into a file and input them into the array at run time. If the values are all the same, the usual approach is to use nested For loops and an assignment statement. Here is a general-purpose code segment that zeros out an array with NUM_ROWS rows and NUM_COLS columns:

```
for (row = 0; row < NUM_ROWS; row++)
    for (col = 0; col < NUM_COLS; col++)
        arr[row][col] = 0;
```

In this case, we initialized the array a row at a time, but we could just as easily have run through each column instead. The order doesn't matter as long as we access every element.

Print the Array

If we wish to print out an array with one row per line, then we have another case of row processing:

```
#include <iomanip>    // For setw()
    :
for (row = 0; row < NUM_ROWS; row++)
{
    for (col = 0; col < NUM_COLS; col++)
        cout << setw(15) << arr[row][col];
    cout << endl;
}
```

This code fragment prints the values of the array in columns that are 15 characters wide. As a matter of proper style, this fragment should be preceded by code that prints headings over the columns to identify their contents.

There's no rule that we have to print each row on a line. We could turn the array sideways and print each column on one line simply by exchanging the two For loops. When you are printing a two-dimensional array, you must consider which order of presentation makes the most sense and how the array fits on the page. For example, an array with 6 columns and 100 rows would be best printed as 6 columns, 100 lines long.

Almost all processing of data stored in a two-dimensional array involves either processing by row or processing by column. In most of our examples the index type has been int, but the pattern of operation of the loops is the same no matter what types the indexes are.

The looping patterns for row processing and column processing are so useful that we summarize them below. To make them more general, we use minRow for the first row number and minCol for the first column number. Remember that row processing has the row index in the outer loop, and column processing has the column index in the outer loop.

Row Processing

```
for (row = minRow; row < rowsFilled; row++)
    for (col = minCol; col < colsFilled; col++)
        ⋮               // Whatever processing is required
```

Column Processing

```
for (col = minCol; col < colsFilled; col++)
    for (row = minRow; row < rowsFilled; row++)
        ⋮               // Whatever processing is required
```

12.6 Passing Two-Dimensional Arrays as Arguments

Earlier in the chapter, we said that when one-dimensional arrays are declared as parameters in a function, the size of the array usually is omitted from the square brackets:

```
void SomeFunc( /* inout */ float alpha[],
               /* in */    int   size   )
```

If you include a size in the brackets, the compiler ignores it. As you learned, the base address of the caller's argument (the memory address of the first array element) is passed to the function. The function works for an argument of any size. Because the function cannot know the size of the caller's array, we either pass the size as an argument—as in SomeFunc above—or use a named constant if the function always operates on an array of a certain size.

When a two-dimensional array is passed as an argument, again the base address of the caller's array is sent to the function. But you cannot leave off the sizes of both of the array dimensions. You can omit the size of the first dimension (the number of rows) but not the second (the number of columns). Here is the reason.

In the computer's memory, C++ stores two-dimensional arrays in row order. Thinking of memory as one long line of memory cells, the first row of the array is followed by the second row, which is followed by the third, and so on (see Figure 12–13). To locate beta[1][0] in this figure, a function that receives beta's base address must be able to know that there are four elements in each row—that is, that the array consists of four columns. Therefore, the declaration of a parameter must always state the number of columns:

```
void AnotherFunc( /* inout */ int beta[][4] )
```

Furthermore, the number of columns declared for the parameter must be *exactly* the same as the number of columns in the caller's array. As you can tell from Figure 12–13, if there is any discrepancy in the number of columns, the function will access the wrong array element in memory.

MEMORY

Figure 12–13   *Memory Layout for a Two-Row by Four-Column Array*

Our AnotherFunc function works for a two-dimensional array of any number of rows, as long as it has exactly four columns. In practice, we seldom write programs that use arrays with a varying number of rows but the same number of columns. To avoid problems with mismatches in argument and parameter sizes, it's practical to use a Type-def statement to define a two-dimensional array type and then declare both the argument and the parameter to be of that type. For example, we might make the declarations

```
const int NUM_ROWS = 10;
const int NUM_COLS = 20;
typedef int ArrayType[NUM_ROWS][NUM_COLS];
```

and then write the following general-purpose function that initializes all elements of an array to a specified value:

```
void Initialize( /* out */ ArrayType arr,      // Array to initialize
                 /* in */  int       initVal)  // Initial value
```

```
// Initializes each element of arr to initVal

// Precondition:
//     initVal is assigned
// Postcondition:
//     arr[0..NUM_ROWS-1][0..NUM_COLS-1] == initVal

{
    int row;
    int col;

    for (row = 0; row < NUM_ROWS; row++)
        for (col = 0; col < NUM_COLS; col++)
            arr[row][col] = initVal;
}
```

The calling code could then declare and initialize one or more arrays of type `ArrayType` by making calls to the `Initialize` function. For example,

```
ArrayType delta;
ArrayType gamma;

Initialize(delta, 0);
Initialize(gamma, -1);
   ⋮
```

12.7 Another Way of Defining Two-Dimensional Arrays

We hinted earlier that a two-dimensional array can be viewed as an array of arrays. This view is supported by C++ in the sense that the components of a one-dimensional array do not have to be atomic. The components can themselves be structured—structs, class objects, even arrays. For example, our `hiTemp` array could be declared as follows.

```
typedef int WeekType[7];    // Array type for 7 temperature readings

WeekType hiTemp[52];        // Array of 52 WeekType arrays
```

With this declaration, the 52 components of the `hiTemp` array are one-dimensional arrays of type `WeekType`. In other words, `hiTemp` has two dimensions. We can refer to each row as an entity: `hiTemp[2]` refers to the array of temperatures for week 2. We can also access each individual component of `hiTemp` by specifying both indexes: `hiTemp[2][0]` accesses the temperature on the first day of week 2.

Does it matter which way we declare a two-dimensional array? Not to C++. The choice should be based on readability and understandability. Sometimes the features of the data are shown more clearly if both indexes are specified in a single declaration. At other times, the code is clearer if one dimension is defined first as a one-dimensional array type.

Here is an example of when it is advantageous to define a two-dimensional array as an array of arrays. If the rows have been defined first as a one-dimensional array type, each row can be passed to a function whose parameter is a one-dimensional array of the same type. For example, the following function calculates and returns the maximum value in an array of type WeekType.

```cpp
int Maximum( /* in */ const WeekType data )   // Array to be examined

// Precondition:
//     data[0..6] are assigned
// Postcondition:
//     Function value == maximum value in data[0..6]

{
    int max;        // Temporary max. value
    int index;      // Loop control and index variable

    max = data[0];
    for (index = 1; index < 7; index++)
        if (data[index] > max)
            max = data[index];
    return max;
}
```

Our two-part declaration of hiTemp permits us to call Maximum using a component of hiTemp as follows.

```cpp
highest = Maximum(hiTemp[20]);
```

Row 20 of hiTemp is passed to Maximum, which treats it like any other one-dimensional array of type WeekType (see Figure 12–14). It makes sense to pass the row as an argument because both it and the function parameter are of the same named type, Week-Type.

With hiTemp declared as an array of arrays, we can output the maximum temperature of each week of the year with the following code:

```cpp
cout << " Week   Maximum" << endl
     << "Number Temperature" << endl;
for (week = 0; week < 52; week++)
    cout << setw(6) << week
         << setw(9) << Maximum(hiTemp[week]) << endl;
```

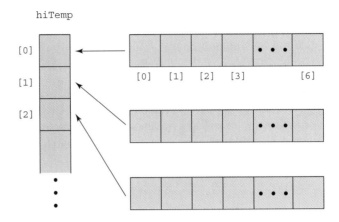

The components of hiTemp
are one-dimensional arrays
of type WeekType.

Figure 12–14   *A One-Dimensional Array of One-Dimensional Arrays*

12.8 Multidimensional Arrays

C++ does not place a limit on the number of dimensions that an array can have. We can generalize our definition of an **array** to cover all cases.

You might have guessed by now that you can have as many dimensions as you want. How many should you have in a particular case? Use as many as there are features that describe the components in the array.

> **Array**   A collection of components, all of the same type, ordered on *N* dimensions (*N* ≥ 1). Each component is accessed by *N* indexes, each of which represents the component's position within that dimension.

Take, for example, a chain of department stores. Monthly sales figures must be kept for each item by store. There are three important pieces of information about each item: the month in which it was sold, the store from which it was purchased, and the item number. We can define an array type to summarize this data as follows:

```
const int NUM_ITEMS = 100;
const int NUM_STORES = 10;

typedef int SalesType[NUM_STORES][12][NUM_ITEMS];

SalesType sales;    // Array of sales figures
int       item;
int       store;
```

```
int       month;
int       numberSold;
int       currentMonth;
```

A graphic representation of the `sales` array is shown in Figure 12–15.

The number of components in `sales` is 12,000 (10 × 12 × 100). If sales figures are available only for January through June, then half the array is empty. If we want to process the data in the array, we must use subarray processing. The following program fragment sums and prints the total number of each item sold this year to date by all stores.

```
for (item = 0; item < NUM_ITEMS; item++)
{
    numberSold = 0;
    for (store = 0; store < NUM_STORES; store++)
        for (month = 0; month <= currentMonth; month++)
            numberSold = numberSold + sales[store][month][item];
    cout << "Item #" << item << " Sales to date = " << numberSold
        << endl;
}
```

Because `item` controls the outer For loop, we are summing each item's sales by `month` and `store`. If we want to find the total sales for each store, we use `store` to control the outer For loop, summing its sales by `month` and `item` with the inner loops.

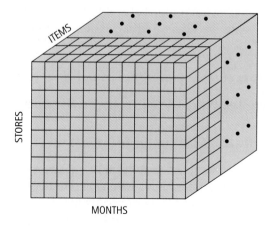

Figure 12–15 *Graphical Representation of `sales` Array*

```
for (store = 0; store < NUM_STORES; store++)
{
    numberSold = 0;
    for (item = 0; item < NUM_ITEMS; item++)
        for (month = 0; month <= currentMonth; month++)
            numberSold = numberSold + sales[store][month][item];
    cout << "Store #" << store << " Sales to date = " << numberSold
        << endl;
}
```

It takes two loops to access each component in a two-dimensional array; it takes three loops to access each component in a three-dimensional array. The task to be accomplished determines which index controls the outer loop, the middle loop, and the inner loop. If we want to calculate monthly sales by store, month controls the outer loop and store controls the middle loop. If we want to calculate monthly sales by item, month controls the outer loop and item controls the middle loop.

If we want to keep track of the departments that sell each item, we can add a fourth dimension.

```
enum Departments {A, B, C, D, E, F, G};
const int NUM_DEPTS = 7;
typedef int SalesType[NUM_STORES][12][NUM_ITEMS][NUM_DEPTS];
```

How would we visualize this new structure? Not very easily! Fortunately, we do not have to visualize a structure in order to use it. If we want the number of sales in store 1 during June for item number 4 in department C, we simply access the array element

```
sales[1][5][4][C]
```

When a multidimensional array is declared as a parameter in a function, C++ requires you to state the sizes of all dimensions except the first. For our four-dimensional version of SalesType, a function heading would look either like this:

```
void DoSomething( /* inout */ int arr[][12][NUM_ITEMS][NUM_DEPTS] )
```

or, better yet, like this:

```
void DoSomething( /* inout */ Sales arr )
```

The second version is the safest (and the most uncluttered to look at). It ensures that the sizes of all dimensions of the parameter match those of the argument exactly. With the first version, the reason that you must declare the sizes of all but the first dimension is the same as we discussed earlier for two-dimensional arrays. Because arrays are stored linearly in memory (one array element after another), the compiler must use this size information to locate correctly an element that lies within the array.

Programming Example

Favorite Rock Group

PROBLEM   At a small college, four campus rock groups have organized a fund-raising project, in which there is going to be a play-off among the groups. Each student gets to vote for his or her favorite and there are two prizes: the best group gets a prize and the class with the best participation gets a prize.

INPUT   An arbitrary number of votes in a file `voteFile`, with each vote represented as a pair of numbers: a class number (1 through 4) and a rock group number (1 through 4); and group names, entered from the keyboard (to be used for printing the output).

OUTPUT   The following three items, written to a file `reportFile`: a tabular report showing how many votes each rock group received in each class, the total number of votes for each rock group, and the total number of votes cast by each class.

DISCUSSION   The data consists of a pair of numbers for each vote. The first number is the class number; the second number is the rock group number.

If we were doing the analysis by hand, our first task would be to go through the data, counting how many people in each class voted for each group. We would probably create a table with classes down the side and rock group names across the top. Each vote would be recorded as a hash mark in the appropriate row and column (see Figure 12–16).

Figure 12–16   *Vote-Counting Table*

When all of the votes had been recorded, a sum of each column would tell us how many votes each group received. A sum of each row would tell us how many people voted in each class.

As is so often the case, we can use this by-hand algorithm directly in our program. We can create a two-dimensional array in which each component is a counter for the number of votes for a particular group in each class; for example, the value indexed by `[2][1]` would be the counter for the votes in class 2 (sophomore) for group 1. Well, not quite. C++ arrays are indexed beginning at 0, so the correct array component would be indexed by `[1][0]`. When we input a class number and group number, we must remember to subtract 1 from each before indexing into the array. Likewise, we must add 1 to an array index that represents a class number or group number before printing it out.

DATA STRUCTURES   A two-dimensional array named `votes`, where the rows represent classes and the columns represent groups.

A one-dimensional array of strings containing the names of the groups, to be used for printing (see Figure 12–17).

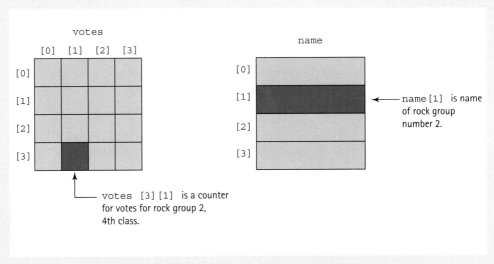

Figure 12–17   *Data Structures for Election Program*

In our discussion we have used the word "class" to represent freshmen, sophomore, junior, or senior. However, we need to be careful. We cannot use the word "class" in our program because it is a reserved word. Let's make the switch here and use the word "level" instead.

Here is the program:

```
//*******************************************************************
// Favorite Rock Group program
// This program reads votes represented by level number and
// rock group number from a data file, calculates the sums per
// level and per rock group, and writes all totals to an
// output file
//*******************************************************************
#include <iostream>
#include <iomanip>      // For setw()
#include <fstream>      // For file I/O
#include <string>       // For string level

using namespace std;

const int NUM_LEVELS = 4;
const int NUM_ROCK_GROUPS = 4;
typedef int VoteArray[NUM_LEVELS][NUM_ROCK_GROUPS];
                            // 2-dimensional array type
                            //   for votes
void GetNames( string[] );
```

```cpp
void OpenFiles( ifstream&, ofstream& );
void WritePerRockGroup( const VoteArray, const string[],
                        ofstream& );
void WritePerLevel( const VoteArray, ofstream& );
void WriteReport( const VoteArray, const string[], ofstream& );
void ZeroVotes( VoteArray );

int main()
{
    string    name[NUM_ROCK_GROUPS];  // Array of rockGroup names
    VoteArray votes;          // Totals for level vs. rockGroups
    int       rockGroup;      // rockGroup number input from voteFile
    int       level;          // level number input from voteFile
    ifstream  voteFile;       // Input file of level, rockGroups
    ofstream  reportFile;     // Output file receiving summaries

    OpenFiles(voteFile, reportFile);
    if ( !voteFile || !reportFile )
    {
        cout << "Files did not open successfully." << endl;
        return 1;
    }


    GetNames(name);
    ZeroVotes(votes);

    // Read and tally votes

    voteFile >> level >> rockGroup;
    while (voteFile)
    {
        votes[level-1][rockGroup-1]++;
        voteFile >> level >> rockGroup;
    }

    // Write results to report file

    WriteReport(votes, name, reportFile);
    WritePerRockGroup(votes, name, reportFile);
    WritePerLevel(votes, reportFile);

    return 0;
}
//*****************************************************************
```

```
void OpenFiles( /* inout */ ifstream& text,
                /* inout */ ofstream& outFile )

// Function OpenFiles reads in the names of the input file and
// the output file and opens them for processing
// Postcondition:
//     Files have been opened AND a label has been written on
//     the output file

{
    string inFileName;
    string outFileName;
    cout << "Enter the name of the file to be processed"
            << endl;
    cin >> inFileName;
    text.open(inFileName.c_str());
    cout << "Enter the name of the output file" << endl;
    cin >> outFileName;
    outFile.open(outFileName.c_str());
    outFile << "Analysis of exams on file " << inFileName
            << endl << endl;
}


//*************************************************************************


void GetNames( /* out */ string name[] )      // Array of rockGroup
                                              //   names
// Reads the rockGroup names from standard input

// Postcondition:
//     The user has been prompted to enter the rockGroup names
//  && name[0..NUM_ROCKGROUPS-1] contain the input names,
//     truncated to 10 characters each

{
    string inputStr;      // An input string
    int    rockGroup;     // Loop counter

    cout << "Enter the names of the rockGroups, one per line,"
            << endl << "in the order they appear on the ballot."
            << endl;
    for (rockGroup = 0; rockGroup < NUM_ROCK_GROUPS; rockGroup++)
    {
        cin >> inputStr;
```

```cpp
        name[rockGroup] = inputStr.substr(0, 10);
    }
}

//*********************************************************************

void ZeroVotes( /* out */ VoteArray votes )   // Array of vote totals

// Zeros out the votes array

// Postcondition:
//     All votes[0..NUM_LEVELS-1][0..NUM_ROCKGROUPS-1] == 0

{
    int level;        // Loop counter
    int rockGroup;    // Loop counter

    for (level = 0; level < NUM_LEVELS; level++)
        for (rockGroup = 0; rockGroup < NUM_ROCK_GROUPS; rockGroup++)
            votes[level][rockGroup] = 0;
}

//*********************************************************************

void WriteReport(
        /* in */      const VoteArray votes,      // Total votes
        /* in */      const string    name[],     // rockGroup names
        /* inout */         ofstream& reportFile ) // Output file

// Writes the vote totals in tabular form to the report file

// Precondition:
//     votes[0..NUM_LEVELS-1][0..NUM_ROCKGROUPS] are assigned
//  && name[0..NUM_ROCKGROUPS-1] are assigned
// Postcondition:
//     The name array has been output across one line, followed by
//     the votes array, one row per line

{
    int level;        // Loop counter
    int rockGroup;    // Loop counter
    // Set up headings
```

```
        reportFile << "            ";
        for (rockGroup = 0; rockGroup < NUM_ROCK_GROUPS; rockGroup++)
            reportFile << setw(12) << name[rockGroup];
        reportFile << endl;

        // Print array by row

        for (level = 0; level < NUM_LEVELS; level++)
        {
            reportFile << "level" << setw(4) << level + 1;
            for (rockGroup = 0; rockGroup < NUM_ROCK_GROUPS; rockGroup++)
                reportFile << setw(12) << votes[level][rockGroup];
            reportFile << endl;
        }
        reportFile << endl;
}


//*********************************************************************


void WritePerRockGroup(
        /* in */      const VoteArray   votes,       // Total votes
        /* in */      const string      name[],      // rockGroup names
        /* inout */        ofstream&    reportFile )  // Output file

// Sums the votes per person and writes the totals to the
// report file

// Precondition:
//     votes[0..NUM_LEVELS-1][0..NUM_ROCKGROUPS] are assigned
//  && name[0..NUM_ROCKGROUPS-1] are assigned
// Postcondition:
//     For each person i, name[i] has been output,
//     followed by the sum
//     votes[0][i] + votes[1][i] + ...  + votes[NUM_LEVELS-1][i]

{
    int level;          // Loop counter
    int rockGroup;      // Loop counter
    int total;          // Total votes for a rockGroup

    for (rockGroup = 0; rockGroup < NUM_ROCK_GROUPS; rockGroup++)
    {
        total = 0;
        // Compute column sum
```

```cpp
        for (level = 0; level < NUM_LEVELS; level++)
            total = total + votes[level][rockGroup];

        reportFile << "Total votes for"
                << setw(10) << name[rockGroup] << ":"
                << setw(3) << total << endl;
    }
    reportFile << endl;
}


//*********************************************************************

void WritePerLevel(
        /* in */      const VoteArray votes,       // Total votes
        /* inout */        ofstream& reportFile )   // Output file

// Sums the votes per level and writes the totals to the
// report file

// Precondition:
//     votes[0..NUM_LEVELS-1][0..NUM_ROCKGROUPS] are assigned
// Postcondition:
//     For each level i, the value i+1 has been output,
//     followed by the sum
//     votes[i][0] + votes[i][1] + ...  + votes[i][NUM_ROCKGROUPS-1]

{
    int level;          // Loop counter
    int rockGroup;      // Loop counter
    int total;          // Total votes for a level

    for (level = 0; level < NUM_LEVELS; level++)
    {
        total = 0;

        // Compute row sum

        for (rockGroup = 0; rockGroup < NUM_ROCK_GROUPS; rockGroup++)
            total = total + votes[level][rockGroup];

        reportFile << "Total votes for level"
                << setw(3) << level + 1 << ':'
                << setw(3) << total << endl;
    }
}
```

TESTING This program was executed with the data listed on the next page. (We list the data in three columns to save space.) The names of the groups entered from the keyboard were Fish, Snake, Sharks, and Leopards. In this data set, there is at least one vote for each group in each class. Case Study Follow-Up Exercise 7 asks you to outline a complete testing strategy for this program.

Input Data

```
1 1      3 1      3 3
1 1      4 3      4 4
1 2      3 4      4 4
1 2      3 2      4 3
1 3      3 3      4 4
1 4      2 1      4 4
2 2      2 3      4 1
2 2      4 3      4 2
2 3      4 4      2 4
2 1      3 2      4 4
```

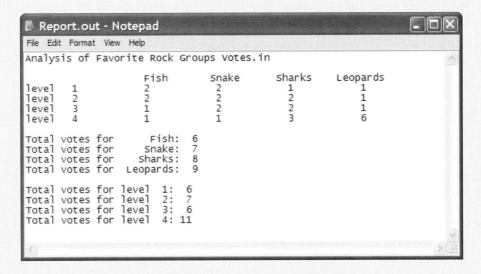

```
Report.out - Notepad
File  Edit  Format  View  Help

Analysis of Favorite Rock Groups Votes.in

                    Fish      Snake     Sharks    Leopards
level    1          2         2         1         1
level    2          2         2         2         1
level    3          1         2         2         1
level    4          1         1         3         6

Total votes for        Fish:  6
Total votes for       Snake:  7
Total votes for      Sharks:  8
Total votes for    Leopards:  9

Total votes for level  1:  6
Total votes for level  2:  7
Total votes for level  3:  6
Total votes for level  4: 11
```

Testing and Debugging

One-Dimensional Arrays

The most common error in processing arrays is an out-of-bounds array index. That is, the program attempts to access a component using an index that is either less than 0 or greater than the array size minus 1. For example, given the declarations

```
char line[100];
int  counter;
```

the following For statement would print the 100 elements of the `line` array and then print a 101st value—the value that resides in memory immediately beyond the end of the array.

```
for (counter = 0; counter <= 100; counter++)
    cout << line[counter];
```

This error is easy to detect because 101 characters get printed instead of 100. The loop test should be `counter < 100`. But you won't always use a simple For statement when accessing arrays. Suppose we read data into the `line` array in another part of the program. Let's use a While statement that reads to the newline character:

```
counter = 0;
cin.get(ch);
while (ch != '\n')
{
    line[counter] = ch;
    counter++;
    cin.get(ch);
}
```

This code seems reasonable enough, but what if the input line has more than 100 characters? After the hundredth character is read and stored into the array, the loop continues to execute with the array index out of bounds. Characters are stored into memory locations past the end of the array, wiping out other data values (or even machine language instructions in the program!).

The moral is: When processing arrays, give special attention to the design of loop termination conditions. Always ask yourself if the loop could possibly keep running after the last array component has been processed.

Whenever an array index goes out of bounds, the first suspicion should be a loop that fails to terminate properly. The second thing to check is any array access involving an index that is based on input data or a calculation. When an array index is input as data, a data validation check is an absolute necessity.

Multidimensional Arrays

Errors with multidimensional arrays usually fall into two major categories: index expressions that are out of order and index range errors.

Suppose we were to expand the rock group program to accommodate ten rock groups and four levels. Let's declare the `votes` array as

```
int votes[4][10];
```

The first dimension represents the levels, and the second represents the rock groups. An example of the first kind of error—incorrect order of the index expressions—would be to print out the `votes` array as follows.

```
for (level = 0; level < 4; level++)
{
    for (rockgroup = 0; rockgroup < 10; rockgroup++)
        cout << setw(4) << votes[rockgroup][level];
    cout << endl;
}
```

The output statement specifies the array indexes in the wrong order. The loops march through the array with the first index ranging from 0 through 9 (instead of 0 through 3) and the second index ranging from 0 through 3 (instead of 0 through 9). The effect of executing this code may vary from system to system. The program may output the wrong array components and continue executing, or the program may crash with a memory access error.

An example of the second kind of error—an incorrect index range in an otherwise correct loop—can be seen in this code:

```
for (level = 0; level < 10; level++)
{
    for (rockgroup = 0; rockgroup < 4; rockgroup++)
        cout << setw(4) << votes[level][rockgroup];
    cout << endl;
}
```

Here, the output statement correctly uses `level` for the first index and `rockgroup` for the second. However, the For statements use incorrect upper limits for the index variables. As with the preceding example, the effect of executing this code is undefined but is certainly wrong. A valuable way to prevent this kind of error is to use named constants instead of the literals 10 and 4. In the programming example, we used NUM_LEVELS and NUM_ROCK_GROUPS. You are much more likely to spot an error (or to avoid making an error in the first place) if you write something like this:

```
for (level = 0; level < NUM_LEVELS; level++)
```

than if you use a literal constant as the upper limit for the index variable.

Testing and Debugging Hints

1. When an individual component of a one-dimensional array is accessed, the index must be within the range 0 through the array size minus 1. Attempting to use an index value outside this range causes your program to access memory locations outside the array.

2. The individual components of an array are themselves variables of the component type. When values are stored into an array, they should either be of the component type or be explicitly converted to the component type; otherwise, implicit type coercion occurs.

3. C++ does not allow aggregate operations on arrays. There is no aggregate assignment, aggregate comparison, aggregate I/O, or aggregate arithmetic. You must write code to do all of these operations, one array element at a time.

4. Omitting the size of a one-dimensional array in its declaration is permitted only in two cases: (1) when an array is declared as a parameter in a function heading and (2) when an array is initialized in its declaration. In all other declarations, you *must* specify the size of the array with a constant integer expression.

5. If an array parameter is incoming-only, declare the parameter as `const` to prevent the function from modifying the caller's argument accidentally.

6. Don't pass an individual array component as an argument when the function expects to receive the base address of an entire array.

7. The size of an array is fixed at compile time, but the number of values actually stored there is determined at run time. Therefore, an array must be declared to be as large as it could ever be for the particular problem. Subarray processing is used to process only the components that have data in them.

8. When functions perform subarray processing on a one-dimensional array, pass both the array name and the number of data items actually stored in the array.

9. With multidimensional arrays, use the proper number of indexes when referencing an array component, and make sure the indexes are in the correct order.

10. In loops that process multidimensional arrays, double-check the upper and lower bounds on each index variable to be sure they are correct for that dimension of the array.

11. When declaring a multidimensional array as a parameter, you must state the sizes of all but the first dimension. Also, these sizes must agree exactly with the sizes of the caller's argument.

12. To eliminate the chances of the size mismatches referred to in item 11, use a Typedef statement to define a multidimensional array type. Declare both the argument and the parameter to be of this type.

Summary

The one-dimensional array is a homogeneous data structure that gives a name to a sequential group of like components. Each component is accessed by its relative position within the group (rather than by name, as in a struct or class), and each component is a variable of the component type. To access a particular component, we give the name of the array and an index that specifies which component of the group we want. The index can be an expression of any integral type, as long as it evaluates to an integer from 0 through the array size minus 1. Array components can be accessed in random order directly, or they can be accessed sequentially by stepping through the index values one at a time.

Two-dimensional arrays are useful for processing information that is represented naturally in tabular form. Processing data in two-dimensional arrays usually takes one of two forms: processing by row or processing by column. An array of arrays, which is useful if rows of the array must be passed as arguments, is an alternative way of defining a two-dimensional array.

A multidimensional array is a collection of like components that are ordered on more than one dimension. Each component is accessed by a set of indexes, one for each dimension, that represents the component's position on the various dimensions. Each index may be thought of as describing a feature of a given array component.

Quick Check

1. Why do we say that an array is a homogeneous data structure? (pp. 458–460)
2. You are solving a problem that requires you to store 24 temperature readings. Which structure would be most appropriate for this: a record, a union, a class or an array? (pp. 458–460)
3. How would you access the 3rd letter in a string data member (called `street`) of a class variable that is the 12th element of an array called `mailList`? (pp. 460–462)
4. Explain how the index of an array of 24 hourly temperature readings has semantic content, if the index is an integer ranging from 0 through 23. (p. 475)
5. How does a two-dimensional array differ syntactically from a one-dimensional array? (pp. 475–478)
6. What aspect of a problem would lead you to consider using a multidimensional array as the representation of its data structure? (pp. 488–490)
7. Write a declaration of an array variable called `temps` that holds 24 values of type `float`. (p. 460)
8. Write a For loop that fills every element of the `temps` array declared in Exercise 7 with the value 32.0. (pp. 462–463)
9. Write a loop that reads values from file `indata` into the `temps` array of Exercise 7, until either end-of-file or 24 values are input. It should keep track of the number of values in the array in an `int` variable called `count`. (pp. 464–468)
10. Write the declaration for a two-dimensional array, called `allTemps`, that holds the 24 hourly readings for each day of a year (up to 366 days). (pp. 475–478)
11. Write a nested For loop that outputs the contents of the `allTemps` array declared in Exercise 7, with the 24 temperatures for a day on a line and 366 lines of days. (pp. 478–484)
12. Write the heading for a function that accepts the `temps` array of Exercise 7 and its length as parameters. Call the function `Quick`, and have it be a `void` function. (pp. 469–470)
13. Write a declaration for a multidimensional array that stores 24 hourly temperatures for each day of a year for a decade. Call the array `decadeTemps`. (pp. 488–490)

Answers

1. Because its elements are all of the same type.   2. An array.   3. `mailList[11].street[2]`
4. The index represents the hour during which the reading was taken, based on a 24-hour clock.
5. It is declared and accessed with two index values instead of one.   6. If the problem has a homogeneous collection of data that is ordered by more than two indexes.

```
7. float temps[24];
8. for (int count = 0; count < 24; count++)
     temps[count] = 32.0;
9. count = 0;
   cin >> inTemp;
   while (indata && count <= 24)
   {
     count++;
     temps[count - 1] = inTemp;
     cin >> inTemp;
   }
10. float allTemps[24][366];
11. for (day = 0; day < 366; day++)
    {
      for (hour = 0; hour < 24; hour++)
        cout << allTemps[hour][day];
      cout << endl;
    }
12. void Quick (/* inout */ float arr[],
                /* in */ int numElements)
13. float decadeTemps[24][366][10]
```

Exam Preparation Exercises

1. The components of an array can be of different types. True or false?
2. Arrays can have any type for their components. True or false?
3. Multidimensional arrays are limited to no more than four dimensions. True or false?
4. In declaring a one-dimensional array, its size must be specified with an integer. True or false?
5. The type of an index expression can be any of the integral types or an enumeration type. True or false?
6. What happens if a program tries to access an array using an index of –1?
7. What aggregate operation(s) are allowed on arrays?
8. To what does the term "base address of an array" refer, and how is it used in a function call?
9. What special type of array can be returned by a value-returning function?
10. If you want to use a nested loop to process a two-dimensional array row-by-row, which dimension's index (row or column) would you increment in the inner loop, and which would you increment in the outer loop?
11. How many elements are there in each of the following arrays?
    a. `int x[27];`
    b. `const int base = 10;`
       `int y[base + 5];`
    c. `int z[100][100][100][100];`
12. What's wrong with the following code segment?

    ```
    int prep[100];
    ```

```
for (int index = 1; index <= 100; index++)
    prep[index] = 0;
```

13. What's wrong with the following code segment?

```
const int limit = 100;
int eprep[limit];
int examp[limit];
for (int index = 0; index < limit; index++)
{
    eprep[index] = 0;
    examp[index] = 0;
}
if (eprep == examp)
    cout << "Equal";
```

14. What's wrong with the following code segment?

```
typedef int Exrep[50];

Exrep Init(/* in */ Exrep); // Prototype
```

15. What's wrong with the following code segment?

```
int prepex[3][4] =
{
    {1, 2, 3},
    {4, 5, 6},
    {7, 8, 9},
    {0, -1, -2}
};
```

16. What's the potential danger in the following code segment?

```
int index;
int value;
int xeperp[100];
cin >> index >> value;
xeperp[index] = value;
```

17. What is the side effect of the following function?

```
int Max (/* in */ int trio[3])
{
    int temp;
    if (trio[0] > trio[1])
    {
        temp = trio[1];
        trio[1] = trio[0];
        trio[0] = temp;
```

```
    }
    if (trio[1] > trio[2])
    {
      temp = trio[2];
      trio[2] = trio[1];
      trio[1] = temp;
    }
    return trio[2];
}
```

18. What does the following code segment output?

```
char pattern[5][5] =
{
    {'*', ' ', '*', ' ', '*'},
    {' ', '*', ' ', '*', ' '},
    {'*', ' ', '*', ' ', '*'},
    {' ', '*', ' ', '*', ' '},
    {'*', ' ', '*', ' ', '*'}
}

for (int outer = 0; outer < 5; outer++)
{
    for (int inner = 1; inner <= 5; inner++)
      cout << pattern[outer][inner % 5];
    cout << endl;
}
```

19. Given the declaration of `pattern` in Exercise 18, what does the following loop output?

```
for (int index = 0; index < 5; index++)
  cout << pattern[index][(index+2) % 5];
```

20. Given the declaration of `pattern` in Exercise 18, what does the following loop output?

```
for (int outer = 0; outer < 5; outer++)
{
    for (int inner = 0; inner < 5; inner++)
      cout << pattern[inner][outer];
    cout << endl;
}
```

21. Given the following declaration:

```
int examPrep [12][15];
```

a. Write a loop to print the first row of the array on one line on `cout`.
b. Write a loop to print the first column of the array on one line on `cout`.

    c. Write a loop to print the first seven rows of the array, each on a single line.

    d. Write a loop to print the entire array backwards and upside down, so that the last line appears first, with last column on the left.

Programming Warm-Up Exercises

1. Write the following declarations.

   a. An array called `topTenList`, of 10 values of type `string`.

   b. An enumeration type of the seven major colors of the spectrum, and a matching array declaration that can be indexed by the spectrum type. The array should be called `colorMix`, and contain values of type `float`.

   c. A two-dimensional array representing the days on a calendar page with up to 6 weeks. Call the array `month`, and declare an enumeration type consisting of the names of the days, that can be used to index the array columns. The weeks should be indexed by an `int`. For the component type of the array, declare a `struct` consisting of an `int` field called `day`, and a `string` field called `activity`.

2. Write a declaration of a named array type, and then declare three arrays of that type. The array type should be called `DataSet`, and the three arrays should be called `input`, `output`, and `working`. Each array should hold five `float` values.

3. Using the `DataSet` type declared in Exercise 2, declare an array of three data sets, called `set`.

4. Using the `set` array declared in Exercise 3, write a nested For loop that initializes all of the values of the three data sets to 0.0.

5. Write a function heading for a function called `Equals` that takes two arrays of the `DataSet` type declared in Exercise 2, and returns a `bool` result. The array parameters should be `const`, as they are input-only parameters to the function.

6. Write the body of the `Equals` function described in Exercise 5. It should return `true` if each element of the first array is equal to its corresponding element in the second array.

7. A gallery needs to keep track of its paintings and photographs. It keeps at most 120 art works on its walls. Each one is described by the following information:

Artist (string)
Title (string)
Medium (oil, watercolor, pastel, acrylic, print, color photo, black and white photo)
Size (struct)
   Height (int)
   Width (int)
Room where it is hung (main, green, blue, north, south, entry, balcony)
Price (float)

Write a declaration for a `struct` that represents a piece of art. Declare `struct` and enumeration types as needed to make up the fields of the `ArtWork` type. Write an additional declaration of a named array type that holds the list of all the art works in the gallery. Lastly, declare an array of this type called `currentList` and an `int` variable `numPieces`. The `numPieces` variable contains the number of pieces represented in the array.

8. Write expressions that retrieve the following values from the array declared in Exercise 7.
   a. The 37th work of art.
   b. The title of the 12th work of art.
   c. The width of the 85th work of art.
   d. The room for the 120th work of art.
   e. The first letter of the artist's name for the 78th work of art.

9. Write a For loop that prints a list of the artist, title, and price for every work in the `currentList` array defined in Exercise 7.

10. Write a code segment that sums the prices of the works in the gallery described in Exercise 7.

11. Write a code segment that outputs the titles of the works in the blue room of the gallery described in Exercise 7.

12. Write a code segment that sums the prices of the oil paintings in the gallery described in Exercise 7 that are larger than 400 square inches in size.

13. A piano is tuned in a scale that is slightly unequal (called a well-tempered scale), rather than a perfectly scientific scale in which each note sounds at twice the frequency of the same note an octave below (called a "just scale"). For this reason, we can't simply calculate the frequency of a note, but must keep it in a table. Declare a two-dimensional array (`scale`) to hold the frequencies of the well-tempered scale. A frequency is represented by a `float` value. The row dimension is indexed by an `int` value representing the octave (there are 8 octaves, numbered 0 through 7), and the other should be indexed by an enumeration type (`Notes`) consisting of the names of the notes. When you write the declaration of the enumeration type, use only sharps (no flats). Thus, the note names of an octave are: C, CSHARP, D, DSHARP, E, F, FSHARP, G, GSHARP, A, ASHARP, and B, in that order.

14. Write a code segment that reads a table of frequencies into the `scale` array declared in Exercise 13 from a file called `frequencies.dat`. The frequency values are arranged one per line on the file.

15. Write a code segment that outputs the frequencies of the notes in the fourth octave of the `scale` array declared in Exercise 13.

16. Write a code segment that outputs the frequencies of all the C notes in the `scale` array declared in Exercise 13.

17. Write a declaration for a four-dimensional array that is indexed by 10 years (0 – 9), 52 weeks (0–51), the 50 states (0–49), and an enumeration type consisting of MAX, MIN, and AVERAGE, called `Type`. The array holds humidity measurements (each component is a `float`).

18. Write a C++ function called `Reset`, that sets all of the components to zero in the array declared in exercise 17.

19. Write a declaration of a `struct` type called `TimePlace` that has three fields, one for each for the first three index values (year, week, state) in the `humidity` array

declared in Exercise 17. `TimePlace` should have a fourth field called `differ-ence`, which is a `float`. Then write a C++ function called `MaxSpread` that takes the `humidity` array as a parameter, and scans through it to find the year, week, and state with the greatest difference in humidity, and returns these values as a `TimePlace` `struct`. If there is more than one week with the greatest difference, then the first one should be returned.

20. Write a code segment that outputs the AVERAGE component of the `humidity` array of Exercise 17, for all the weeks in the last 5 years for the 23rd state.

Programming Problems

1. Write a program to play a game in which you try to sink a fleet of five navy vessels by guessing their locations on a grid. The program uses random numbers to position its ships on a 15 × 15 grid. The ships are of different lengths as follows:

   Frigate: 2 locations
   Tender: 2 locations
   Destroyer: 3 locations
   Cruiser: 3 locations
   Carrier: 4 locations

   The program must pick one square as the starting location, then pick the direction of the ship on the board, and mark off the number of squares in that direction to represent the size of the ship. It must not allow a ship to overlap with another ship, or to run off the board.

   The user enters coordinates in the range of 1 through 15 for the rows and A through O for the columns. The program checks this location, and reports whether it is a hit or a miss. If it is a hit, the program also checks whether the ship has been hit in every location that it occupies. If so, the ship is reported as sunk, and the program identifies which ship it is.

   The user gets 60 shots to attempt to sink the fleet. If the user sinks all of the ships before using all 60 shots, then he or she wins the game. At the end of the game, the program should output the grid, so that the user can see where the ships are located.

2. Programming Warm-Up Exercises 7 to 12 deal with an array representing the inventory for an art gallery. Using the same representation, write a C++ program that reads the gallery's inventory from a file called `art.dat` into the array. Then allow the user to look up the art by specifying any field in the record. As a reminder, here are the fields:

   Artist (string)
   Title (string)
   Medium (oil, watercolor, pastel, acrylic, print, color photo, black and white photo)
   Size (struct)

Height (int)
Width (int)
Room where it is hung (main, green, blue, north, south, entry, balcony)
Price (float)

Thus, the user should be able to specify a field, and a value for that field, and the program returns all works that match. For example, the user may specify Artist and Smithely, and the program will output all of the information concerning every work in the gallery by that artist.

3. Programming Problem 1 in Chapter 9 asked you to write a program that inputs a string and then outputs the corresponding words in the International Civil Aviation Organization alphabet that would be used to spell it out phonetically. For that program, you should have used a large Switch statement. Rewrite that program using an array of strings to hold the words of the alphabet, and index the array by the positions of the letters of the alphabet. By using an index with semantic content, you can avoid the need for the case statement. Be sure that you don't try to index into the array using non-alphabetic characters, as that will result in an out-of-bounds access. For ease of reference, the ICAO alphabet is repeated here from Chapter 9:

A   Alpha
B   Bravo
C   Charlie
D   Delta
E   Echo
F   Foxtrot
G   Golf
H   Hotel
I   India
J   Juliet
K   Kilo
L   Lima
M   Mike
N   November
O   Oscar
P   Papa
Q   Quebec
R   Romeo
S   Sierra
T   Tango
U   Uniform
V   Victor
W   Whiskey
X   X-ray
Y   Yankee
Z   Zulu

Be sure to use proper formatting and appropriate comments in your code. Provide appropriate prompts to the user. The output should be clearly labeled and neatly formatted.

4. Programming Problem 4 in Chapter 6 asked you to write a program to check whether an input line is a palindrome (a word or phrase that is the same backwards and forwards). At that time, we needed to use the substring function to extract individual characters from a string. Because this is a cumbersome way to work with a string, we limited our definition of palindromes to just perfect palindromes—every letter and blank exactly the same in both forward and backward versions. Now that we know how to use arrays, we can expand the definition to ignore blanks, punctuation, and letter case. Thus

```
madam I'm adam
```

becomes

```
madamimadam
```

which is now a palindrome. Write a C++ program that reads a line of input and checks whether it is a palindrome on the basis of this less restrictive definition. Output the reversed line, with all blanks and punctuation removed, and all letters converted to lowercase along with the program's decision.

5. In Chapter 5, Programming Problem 5 asked you to create a class representing a song on a CD or in an MP-3 library. Write a C++ program using that class, which allows the user to specify the name of a data file containing songs (assume there are fewer than 200 songs on the file), and then reads the song data from the file into an array of song objects. The user should then be allowed to enter the name of an artist, and the program will output all of the songs by that artist, along with any other information about the song that is in the array.

Programming Example Follow-Up

1. Rewrite the Favorite Rock Group program using an enumerated type for class (or level). Which code is more readable and self-documenting?
2. Design a complete testing strategy for the Favorite Rock Group program.

Array-Based Lists

Goals

In this chapter, we examine algorithms that build and manipulate data stored as a list in a one-dimensional array. These algorithms are implemented as general-purpose functions that can be modified easily to work with many kinds of lists.

We also consider the *C string*, a special kind of built-in one-dimensional array that is used for storing character strings. We conclude with a case study that uses an array as the main data structure.

13.1 The List as an Abstract Data Type

One use for an array is to store a list of values. A list may contain fewer values than the number of places reserved in the array.

For example, given an array `firstList` with 500 places, only the first `length-1` components might contain valid data. In Figure 13-1, you can see that the *array* goes from `firstList[0]` through `firstList[499]`, but the *list* stored in the array goes from `firstList[0]` through `firstList[length-1]`. The number of places in the array is fixed, but the number of values in the list stored there may vary. The **length** of a list—the number of values currently stored in the list—can vary during the execution of the program.

> **List** A variable-length, linear collection of homogeneous components.
>
> **Length** The number of values currently stored in a list.

Like any data type, a list must have associated with it a set of allowable operations. What kinds of operations would we want to define for a list? Here are some possibilities: create a list, add an item to a list, delete an item from a list, print a list, search a list for a particular value, sort a list into alphabetical or numerical order, and so on. When we define a data type formally—by specifying its properties and the operations that preserve those properties—we are creating an abstract data type (ADT). Now that we are familiar with the idea of using a one-dimensional array to represent a list, we can combine C++ classes and arrays to implement list ADTs.

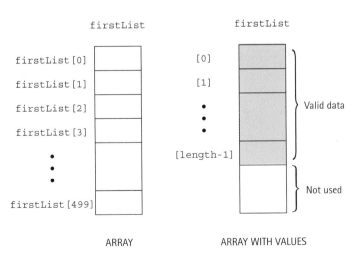

Figure 13-1 *firstList array*

Let's create a general list ADT by (a) allowing the components to be of *any* simple type or of type `string`, (b) defining the maximum length as MAX_LENGTH, a defined constant, and (c) including a wide variety of allowable operations. Here is the specification of the more general list ADT:

TYPE
  List
DOMAIN
  Each instance of type List is a collection of up to MAX_LENGTH components,
     each of type ItemType.
OPERATIONS
  Create an initially empty list.
  Report whether the list is empty (`true` or `false`).
  Report whether the list is full (`true` or `false`).
  Return the current length of the list.
  Insert an item into the list.
  Delete an item from the list.
  Search for a specified item, returning `true` or `false` according to whether the
     item is present in the list.
  Sort the list into ascending order.
  Iterate through the list, returning each item in turn.

We can use a C++ class named `List` to represent the List ADT in our programs. For the concrete data representation, we use two items: a one-dimensional array to hold the list items, and an `int` variable that stores the current length of the list. When we compile the `List` class, we need to supply definitions for MAX_LENGTH and ItemType:

```
const int MAX_LENGTH = [        ];   // Maximum possible number of
                                     //    components needed
typedef [        ] ItemType;         // Type of each component
                                     //    (a simple type or the
                                     //     string class)
```

Here is the specification file for our List ADT. Notice that we use 50 for MAX_LENGTH and `int` for ItemType. Notice also that the abstract operation *Create an initially empty list* is implemented as the class constructor `List()`.

```
//*****************************************************************
// SPECIFICATION FILE (list.h)
// This file gives the specification of a list abstract data type.
// The list components are not assumed to be in order by value.
// To save space, we omit from each function the precondition
// comments that document the assumptions made about valid input
// parameter data. These would be included in a program intended
// for actual use.
//*****************************************************************
```

```
const int MAX_LENGTH =100;      // Maximum possible number of
                                //   components needed
typedef int ItemType;           // Type of each component
                                //   (a simple type or string class)

class List
{
public:
    bool IsEmpty() const;

        // Postcondition:
        //      Return value == true, if list is empty
        //                   == false, otherwise

    bool IsFull() const;

        // Postcondition:
        //      Return value == true, if list is full
        //                   == false, otherwise

    int Length() const;

        // Postcondition:
        //      Return value == length of list

    void Insert( /* in */ ItemType item );

        // Precondition:
        //      NOT IsFull()
        // Postcondition:
        //      item is in list
        //   && Length() == Length()@entry + 1

    void Delete( /* in */ ItemType item );

        // Precondition:
        //      NOT IsEmpty()
        // Postcondition:
        //      IF item is in list at entry
        //          First occurrence of item is no longer in list
        //       && Length() == Length()@entry - 1
        //      ELSE
        //          List is unchanged

    bool IsPresent( /* in */ ItemType item ) const;
```

```
    // Postcondition:
    //      Return value == true, if item is in list
    //                   == false, otherwise

    void Reset();

    // Postcondition:
    //      Iteration is initialized

    ItemType GetNextItem();

    // Precondition:
    //      Iteration has been initialized by call to Reset;
    //      No transformers have been invoked since last call
    // Postcondition:
    //      Return value is the item at the current position
    //      in the list on entry;
    //      If last item has been returned, the next call will
    //      return the first item.

    void SelSort();

    // Postcondition:
    //      List components are in ascending order of value

    List();

    // Constructor
    // Postcondition:
    //      Empty list is created
private:
    int       length;
    int       currentPos;
    ItemType  data[MAX_LENGTH];
};
```

In Chapter 11, we classified ADT operations as constructors, transformers, observers, and iterators. IsEmpty, IsFull, Length, and IsPresent, are observers. Reset, Insert, Delete, and SelSort are transformers. GetNextItem is an iterator. The class constructor is an ADT constructor operation.

The private part of the class declaration shows our data representation of a list: two int variables and an array (see Figure 13–2). However, notice that the preconditions and post-conditions of the member functions mention nothing about an array. The abstraction is a list, not an array. The user of the class is interested only in manipulating lists of items and does not care how we implement a list. If we change to a different data representation (as we do in Chapter 15), neither the public interface nor the client code needs to be changed.

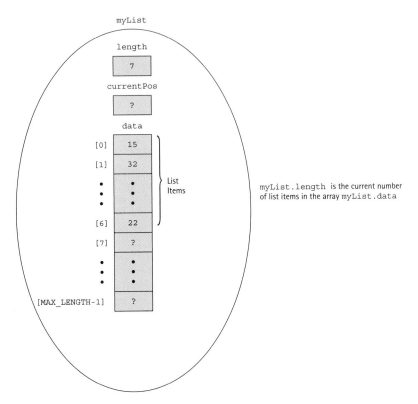

myList

length

7

currentPos

?

data

[0] 15
[1] 32
  •   •
  •   •
  •   •   } List Items
[6] 22
[7] ?
  •   •
  •   •
  •   •
[MAX_LENGTH-1] ?

myList.length is the current number
of list items in the array myList.data

Figure 13-2   *myList, a Class Object of Type* List

Let's look at an example of a client program. A data file contains a weather station's daily maximum temperature readings for one month, one integer value per day. Unfortunately, the temperature sensor is faulty and occasionally registers a temperature of 200 degrees. The following program uses the List class to store the temperature readings, delete any spurious readings of 200 degrees, and output the remaining readings in sorted order. Presumably, the data file contains no more than 31 integers for the month, which should be well under the List class's MAX_LENGTH of 50. However, just in case the file erroneously contains more than MAX_LENGTH values, the reading loop in the following program terminates not only if end-of-file is encountered but also if the list becomes full (IsFull). Another reason to use the IsFull operation in this loop can be found by looking at the function specifications in file list.h—namely, we must guarantee Insert's precondition that the list is not full. Similarly, in the loop that deletes the spurious readings of 200 degrees, we must use the IsEmpty operation to guarantee Delete's precondition that the list is not empty.

```
//***************************************************************
// Temperatures program
// This program inputs one month's temperature readings from a file,
// deletes spurious readings of 200 degrees from a faulty sensor,
```

```cpp
// and outputs the values in sorted order
//****************************************************************
#include <fstream>     // For file I/O
#include "list.h"      // For List class

using namespace std;

int main()
{
    List temps;          // List of temperature readings
    int  oneTemp;        // One temperature reading
    ifstream inData;     // File of temperature readings
    int limit;           // The number of readings
    ofstream outData;    // Output file

    inData.open("temps.dat");
    if ( !inData )
    {
        outData << "Can't open file temps.dat" << endl;
        return 1;
    }

    outData.open("temps.ans");

    // Get temperature readings from file

    inData >> oneTemp;
    while (inData && !temps.IsFull())
    {
        temps.Insert(oneTemp);
        inData >> oneTemp;
    }

    // Output original list

    temps.Reset();                      // Set up for an iteration
    limit = temps.Length();             // Get number of items
    outData << "No. of readings: " << limit << endl;
    outData << "Original list:" << endl;

    for (int count = 0; count < limit; count++)
    {
        oneTemp = temps.GetNextItem();
        outData << oneTemp << endl;
    }
```

```
                    // Discard spurious readings of 200 degrees

        while ( !temps.IsEmpty() && temps.IsPresent(200))
            temps.Delete(200);

        temps.SelSort();                          // Sort list

        // Output sorted list

        temps.Reset();                            // Set up for an iteration
        limit = temps.Length();                   // Get number of items
        outData << "No. of valid readings: " << limit << endl;
        outData << "Sorted list:" << endl;

        for (int count = 0; count < limit; count++)
        {
            oneTemp = temps.GetNextItem();
            outData << oneTemp << endl;
        }
        inData.close();
        outData.close();
        return 0;
    }
```

The following output file is shown in two columns rather than one.

No. of readings: 30	No. of valid readings: 21
Original list:	Sorted list:
70	61
68	65
69	66
68	67
68	68
72	68
200	68
69	68
87	69
200	69
82	69
200	70
200	71

Output file continued:

```
No. of readings: 30          No. of valid readings: 21
Original list:               Sorted list:
81                           72
200                          75
75                           77
78                           78
68                           78
67                           81
200                          82
65                           87
66
200
61
71
200
200
77
78
69
```

We now consider how to implement each of the ADT operations, given that the list items are stored in an array. Before we do so, however, we must distinguish between lists whose components must always be kept in alphabetical or numerical order (*sorted lists*) and lists in which the components are not arranged in any particular order (*unsorted lists*). We begin with unsorted lists.

13.2 Unsorted Lists

Basic Operations

As we discussed in Chapter 11, an ADT is typically implemented in C++ by using a pair of files: the specification file (such as the preceding list.h file) and the implementation file, which contains the implementations of the class member functions. Here is how the implementation file list.cpp starts out:

```
//****************************************************************
// IMPLEMENTATION FILE (list.cpp)
// This file implements the List class member functions
// List representation: a one-dimensional array and a length
//                      variable
//****************************************************************
```

```
#include "list.h"
#include <iostream>

using namespace std;

// Private members of class:
//    int       length;              Length of the list
//    int       currentPos;          Current position during iteration
//    ItemType data[MAX_LENGTH];     Array holding the list
```

Let's look now at the implementations of the basic list operations.

Creating an Empty List   As Figure 13–2 shows, the list exists in the array elements data[0] through data[length-1]. To create an empty list, it is sufficient to set the length member to 0. We do not need to store any special values into the data array to make the list empty, because only those values in data[0] through data[length-1] are processed by the list algorithms.

In the List class, the appropriate place to initialize the list to be empty is the class constructor:

```
List::List()

// Constructor

// Postcondition:
//     length == 0

{
    length = 0;
}
```

One thing you will notice as we go through the List member functions is that the *implementation assertions* (the preconditions and postconditions appearing in the implementation file) are often stated differently from the *abstract assertions* (those located in the specification file). Abstract assertions are written in terms that are meaningful to the user of the ADT; implementation details should not be mentioned. In contrast, implementation assertions can be made more precise by referring directly to variables and algorithms in the implementation code. In the case of the List class constructor, the abstract postcondition is simply that an empty list has been created. On the other hand, the implementation postcondition

```
// Postcondition:
//     length == 0
```

is phrased in terms of our private data representation.

The IsEmpty Operation   This operation returns `true` if the list is empty and `false` if the list is not empty. Using our convention that `length` equals 0 if the list is empty, the implementation of this operation is straightforward.

```
bool List::IsEmpty() const

// Reports whether list is empty

// Postcondition:
//      Return value == true, if length == 0
//                   == false, otherwise

{
    return (length == 0);
}
```

The IsFull Operation   The list is full if there is no more room in the array holding the list items—that is, if the list length equals MAX_LENGTH.

```
bool List::IsFull() const

// Reports whether list is full

// Postcondition:
//      Return value == true, if length == MAX_LENGTH
//                   == false, otherwise

{
    return (length == MAX_LENGTH);
}
```

The Length Operation   This operation simply returns to the client the current length of the list.

```
int List::Length() const

// Returns current length of list

// Postcondition:
//      Return value == length

{
    return length;
}
```

Insertion and Deletion

To devise an algorithm for inserting a new item into the list, we first observe that we are working with an unsorted list and that the values do not have to be maintained in any particular order. Therefore, we can store a new value into the next available position in the array—`data[length]`—and then increment `length`. This algorithm brings up a question: Do we need to check that there is room in the list for the new item? We have two choices. The `Insert` function can test `length` against `MAX_LENGTH` and return an error flag if there isn't any room, or we can let the client code make the test before calling `Insert` (that is, make it a precondition that the list is not full). If you look back at the `List` class declaration in `list.h`, you can see that we have chosen the second approach. The client can use the `IsFull` operation to make sure the precondition is true. If the client fails to satisfy the precondition, the contract between client and function is broken, and the function is not required to satisfy the postcondition.

```
void List::Insert( /* in */ ItemType item )

// Inserts item into the list

// Precondition:
//     length < MAX_LENGTH
// Postcondition:
//     data[length@entry] == item
//  && length == length@entry+1

{
    data[length] = item;
    length++;
}
```

Deleting a component from a list consists of two parts: finding the component and removing it from the list. Before we can write the algorithm, we must know what to do if the component is not there. *Delete* can mean "Delete, if it's there" or "Delete, it *is* there." According to the `List` class declaration in `list.h`, we assume the first meaning; the code for the first definition works for the second as well but is not as efficient. We must start at the beginning of the list and search for the value to be deleted. If we find it, how do we remove it? We take the last value in the list (the one stored in `data[length-1]`), put it where the item to be deleted is located, and then decrement `length`. Moving the last item from its original position is appropriate only for an unsorted list because we don't need to preserve the order of the items in the list.

The definition "Delete, if it's there" requires a searching loop with a compound condition. We examine each component in turn and stop looking when we find the item to be deleted or when we have looked at all the items and know that it is not there.

```
void List::Delete( /* in */ ItemType item )
```

```
// Deletes item from the list, if it is there

// Precondition:
//      length > 0
// Postcondition:
//      IF item is in data array at entry
//          First occurrence of item is no longer in array
//          && length == length@entry - 1
//      ELSE
//          length and data array are unchanged

{
    int index = 0;     // Index variable

    while (index < length && item != data[index])
        index++;

    if (index < length)
    {                                       // Remove item
        data[index] = data[length-1];
        length--;
    }
}
```

To see how the While loop and the subsequent If statement work, let's look at the two possibilities: Either `item` is in the list or it is not. If `item` is in the list, the loop terminates when the expression `index < length` is `true` and the expression `item != data[index]` is `false`. After the loop exit, the If statement finds the expression `index < length` to be `true` and removes the item. On the other hand, if `item` is not in the list, the loop terminates when the expression `index < length` is `false`—that is, when `index` becomes equal to `length`. Subsequently, the If condition is `false`, and the function returns without changing anything.

Sequential Search

In the `Delete` function, the algorithm we used to search for the item to be deleted is known as a *sequential* or *linear search* in an unsorted list. We use the same algorithm to implement the `IsPresent` function of the `List` class.

```
bool List::IsPresent( /* in */ ItemType item ) const

// Searches the list for item, reporting whether it was found

// Postcondition:
//      Return value == true, if item is in data[0..length-1]
//                    == false, otherwise
```

```
{
    int index = 0;      // Index variable

    while (index < length && item != data[index])
        index++;

    return (index < length);
}
```

This algorithm is called a sequential search because we start at the beginning of the list and look at each item in sequence. We stop the search as soon as we find the item we are looking for (or when we reach the end of the list, concluding that the desired item is not present in the list).

We can use this algorithm in any program requiring a list search. In the form shown, it searches a list of ItemType components, provided that ItemType is an integral type or the string class. To use the function with a list of floating-point values, we must modify it so that the While statement tests for near equality rather than exact equality. In the following statement, we assume that EPSILON is defined as a global constant.

```
while (index < length && fabs(item - data[index]) >= EPSILON)
    index++;
```

The sequential search algorithm finds the first occurrence of the searched-for item. How would we modify it to find the last occurrence? We would initialize index to length-1 and decrement index each time through the loop, stopping when we found the item we wanted or when index became −1.

Before we leave this search algorithm, let's introduce a variation that makes the program more efficient, although a little more complex. The While loop contains a compound condition: It stops when it either finds item or reaches the end of the list. We can insert a copy of item into data[length]—that is, into the array component beyond the end of the list—as a sentinel. By doing so, we are guaranteed to find item in the list. Then we can eliminate the condition that checks for the end of the list (index < length) (see Figure 13-3). Eliminating a condition saves the computer the time that would be required to test it. In this case, we save time during every iteration of the loop, so the savings add up quickly. Note, however, that we are gaining efficiency at the expense of space. We must declare the array size to be 1 larger than MAX_LENGTH to hold the sentinel value if the list becomes full. That is, we must change the private part of the class declaration as follows:

```
class List
{
    ⋮
private:
    int       length;
```

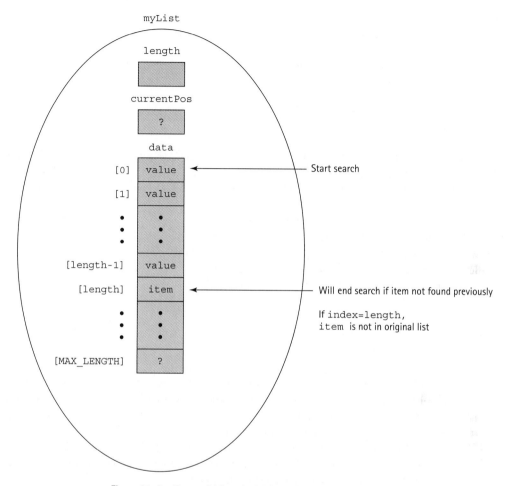

myList

length

currentPos
?

data

[0] value ◄──────── Start search

[1] value

•
•
•

[length-1] value

[length] item ◄──────── Will end search if item not found previously

If index=length,
item is not in original list

[MAX_LENGTH] ?

Figure 13–3 *Sequential Search with Copy of item in data[length]*

```
int      currentPos;
ItemType data[MAX_LENGTH+1];
};
```

Figure 13–3 reflects this change. The last array element shows an index of MAX_LENGTH rather than MAX_LENGTH-1, as in Figure 13–2.

The following function, IsPresent2, implements this new algorithm. After the search loop terminates, the function returns true if index is less than length; otherwise, it returns false.

```
bool List::IsPresent2( /* in */ ItemType item ) const

// Searches the list for item, reporting whether it was found
```

```
// Postcondition:
//     data[0..length-1] are the same as at entry
//  && data[length] is overwritten to aid in the search
//  && Return value == true, if item is in data[0..length-1]
//                  == false, otherwise

{
    int index = 0;                   // Index variable

    data[length] = item;             // Store item at position beyond
                                     //   end of list

    while (item != data[index])
        index++;

    return (index < length);
}
```

Note that the declaration of our List class in the file list.h includes the member function IsPresent but not IsPresent2. We have presented IsPresent2 only to show you an alternative approach to implementing the search operation.

Iterators

Iterators are used with composite types to allow the user to process an entire structure component by component. To give the user access to each item in sequence, we provide two operations: one to initialize the iteration process (analogous to Reset or Open with a file) and one to return a copy of the "next component" each time it is called. The user can then set up a loop that processes each component. We call these operations Reset and GetNextItem. Note that Reset is not an iterator itself, but is an auxiliary transformer that supports the iteration. Another type of iterator is one that takes an operation and applies it to every element in the list.

The Reset function is analogous to the open operation for a file in which the file pointer is positioned at the beginning of the file so that the first input operation accesses the first component of the file. Each successive call to an input operation gets the next item in the file. Therefore, we need a variable that keeps track of the next item to be returned from an iteration. We call that variable currentPos. Reset must initialize currentPos to point to the first item in the list.

The GetNextItem operation is analogous to an input operation; it accesses the next item, the one at currentPos, increments currentPos, and returns the item it accessed. What happens if the last item has been accessed? Let's put currentPos back to the first item. This way, the program may get the wrong answer, but it won't access data outside the list.

Reset

Initialize currentPos to first item

GetNextItem

```
Set item to data[currentPos]
IF  currentPos is length - 1
    Set currentPos to 0
ELSE
    Increment currentPos
Return item
```

currentPos is undefined until it is initialized by Reset. After the first call to GetNextItem, currentPos is the location of the next item to be accessed by GetNextItem. Therefore, to implement this algorithm in an array-based list in C++, currentPos must be initialized to 0. These operations are coded as follows.

```cpp
void List::Reset()
// Post: currentPos has been initialized.
{
    currentPos = 0;
}
```

What would happen if a transformer operation is executed between calls to Get-NextItem? The iteration would be invalid. That is why there is a precondition to prevent this from happening.

```cpp
Itemtype List::GetNextItem()

// Precondition:
//     No transformer has been executed since last
//     call
// Postcondition:
//     Return value is currentPos@entry
//     && current position has been updated
//     If last item has been returned, the next call
//     returns the first item

{
    ItemType item;
    item = data[currentPos];
    if (currentPos == length - 1)
        currentPos = 0;
    else
        currentPos++;
    return item;
}
```

Reset and GetNextItem are designed to be used in a loop in the client program that iterates through all of the items in the list. The precondition in the specifications for GetNextItem protects against trying to access an array element that is not in the list. Look back at the Temperature program. Reset and GetNextItem were used twice: once to print the original list and once to print the corrected sorted list.

Sorting

Although we are implementing an unsorted list ADT, there are times when the user of the List class may want to rearrange the list components into a certain order just before calling the Print function. For example, the user might want to put a list of stock numbers into either ascending or descending order, or the user might want to put a list of words into alphabetical order. Arranging list items into order is a very common operation and is known as sorting.

> **Sorting** Arranging the components of a list into order (for instance, words into alphabetical order or numbers into ascending or descending order).

If you were given a sheet of paper with a column of 20 numbers on it and were asked to write the numbers in ascending order, you would probably do the following:

1. Make a pass through the list, looking for the smallest number.
2. Write it on the paper in a second column.
3. Cross the number off the original list.
4. Repeat the process, always looking for the smallest number remaining in the original list.
5. Stop when all the numbers have been crossed off.

We can implement this algorithm directly in C++, but we need two arrays—one for the original list and a second for the sorted list. If the list is large, we might not have enough memory for two copies of it. Also, how do we "cross off" an array component? We could simulate crossing off a value by replacing it with some dummy value like INT_MAX. That is, we would set the value of the crossed-off variable to something that would not interfere with the processing of the rest of the components. However, a slight variation of our hand-done algorithm allows us to sort the components *in place*. We do not have to use a second array; we can put a value into its proper place in the list by having it swap places with the component currently in that position.

We can state the algorithm as follows. We search for the smallest value in the list and exchange it with the component in the first position in the list. We search for the next-smallest value in the list and exchange it with the component in the second position in the list. This process continues until all the components are in their proper places.

```
FOR count going from 0 through length-2
    Find minimum value in data[count .. length-1]
    Swap minimum value with data[count]
```

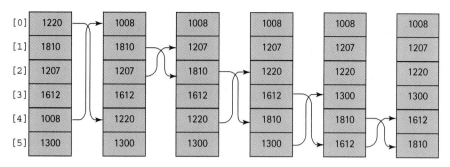

[0]	1220	1008	1008	1008	1008	1008
[1]	1810	1810	1207	1207	1207	1207
[2]	1207	1207	1810	1220	1220	1220
[3]	1612	1612	1612	1612	1300	1300
[4]	1008	1220	1220	1810	1810	1612
[5]	1300	1300	1300	1300	1612	1810

Figure 13–4 *Straight Selection Sort*

Figure 13–4 illustrates how this algorithm works.

Observe that we perform `length-1` passes through the list because `count` runs from 0 through `length-2`. The loop does not need to be executed when `count` equals `length-1` because the last value, `data[length-1]`, is in its proper place after the preceding components have been sorted.

This sort, known as the *straight selection sort,* belongs to a class of sorts called selection sorts. There are many types of sorting algorithms. Selection sorts are characterized by finding the smallest (or largest) value left in the unsorted portion at each iteration and swapping it with the value indexed by the iteration counter. Swapping the contents of two variables requires a temporary variable so that no values are lost (see Figure 13–5).

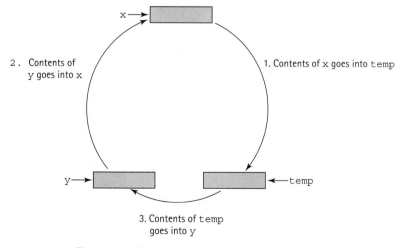

Figure 13–5 *Swapping the Contents of Two Variables, x and y*

Here is the code for the sorting operation of the `List` class:

```
void List::SelSort()

// Sorts list into ascending order

// Postcondition:
//     data array contains the same values as data@entry, rearranged
//     into ascending order

{
   ItemType temp;                // Temporary variable
   int      passCount;           // Loop control variable
   int      searchIndx;          // Loop control variable
   int      minIndx;             // Index of minimum so far

   for (passCount = 0; passCount < length - 1; passCount++)
   {
      minIndx = passCount;

      // Find the index of the smallest component
      // in data[passCount..length-1]

      for (searchIndx = passCount + 1; searchIndx < length;
                                              searchIndx++)

        if (data[searchIndx] < data[minIndx])
           minIndx = searchIndx;

      // Swap data[minIndx] and data[passCount]

      temp = data[minIndx];
      data[minIndx] = data[passCount];
      data[passCount] = temp;
   }
}
```

Note that with each pass through the outer loop, we are looking for the minimum value in the rest of the list (`data[passCount]` through `data[length-1]`). Therefore, `minIndx` is initialized to `passCount` and the inner loop runs from `searchIndx` equal to `passCount+1` through `length-1`. Upon exit from the inner loop, `minIndx` contains the position of the smallest value.

Note that we may swap a component with itself, which occurs if no value in the remaining list is smaller than `data[passCount]`. We could avoid this unnecessary swap by checking to see if `minIndx` is equal to `passCount`. Because this comparison would be made during each iteration of the outer loop, it is more efficient not to check for this possibility and just to swap something with itself occasionally. If the components we are sorting are much more complex than simple numbers, we might reconsider this decision.

This algorithm sorts the components into ascending order. To sort them into descending order, we would scan for the maximum value instead of the minimum value. To do so, we would simply change the relational operator in the inner loop from < to >. Of course, minIndx would no longer be an appropriate identifier and should be changed to maxIndx.

By providing the user of the List class with a sorting operation, we have not turned our unsorted list ADT into a sorted list ADT. The Insert and Delete algorithms we wrote do not preserve ordering by value. Insert places a new item at the end of the list, regardless of its value, and Delete moves the last item to a different position in the list. After SelSort has executed, the list items remain in sorted order only until the next insertion or deletion takes place. We now look at a sorted list ADT in which all the list operations cooperate to preserve the sorted order of the list components.

13.3 Sorted Lists

In the List class, the IsPresent and IsPresent2 algorithms both assume that the list to be searched is unsorted. A drawback to searching an unsorted list is that we must scan the entire list to discover that the search item is not there. Think what it would be like if your city telephone book contained people's names in random rather than alphabetical order. To look up Mary Anthony's phone number, you would have to start with the first name in the phone book and scan sequentially, page after page, until you found it. In the worst case, you might have to examine tens of thousands of names only to find out that Mary's name is not in the book.

Of course, telephone books *are* alphabetized, and the alphabetical ordering makes searching easier. If Mary Anthony's name is not in the book, you discover this fact quickly by starting with the A's and stopping the search as soon as you have passed the place where her name should be.

Let's define a sorted list ADT in which the components always remain in order by value, no matter what operations are applied. Below is the slist.h file that contains the declaration of a SortedList class.

```
//**********************************************************************
// SPECIFICATION FILE (SortedList.h)
// This file gives the specification of a SortedList abstract data
// type. The components are assumed to be in order by value.
// To save space, we omit from each function the precondition
// comments that document the assumptions made about valid input
// parameter data. These would be included in a program intended
// for actual use.
//**********************************************************************
```

```
        const int MAX_LENGTH =100;   // Maximum possible number of
                                     //    components needed
        typedef int ItemType;        // Type of each component
                                     //    (a simple type or string class)

        class SortedList
        {
        public:
            bool IsEmpty() const;

                // Postcondition:
                //      Return value == true, if SortedList is empty
                //                   == false, otherwise

            bool IsFull() const;

                // Postcondition:
                //      Return value == true, if SortedList is full
                //                   == false, otherwise

            int Length() const;

                // Postcondition:
                //      Return value == length of SortedList

            void Insert( /* in */ ItemType& item );

                // Inserts item into the SortedList

                // Precondition:
                //      length < MAX_LENGTH
                //   && data[0..length-1] are in ascending order
                // Postcondition:
                //      item is in the SortedList
                //   && length == length@entry + 1
                //   && data[0..length-1] are in ascending order


            void Delete( /* in */ ItemType item );

                // Precondition:
                //      NOT IsEmpty()
                // Postcondition:
```

```
//        IF item is in SortedSortedList at entry
//           First occurrence of item is no longer
//           in SortedList
//        && Length() == Length()@entry - 1
//        ELSE
//           SortedList is unchanged

bool IsPresent( /* in */ ItemType item ) const;

    // Precondition:
    // Postcondition:
    //     Return value == true, if item is in SortedList
    //                  == false, otherwise

void Reset();

    // Postcondition:
    //     Iteration is initialized

ItemType GetNextItem();

    // Precondition:
    // Iteration has been initialized by call to Reset;
    //     No transformers have been invoked since last call
    // Postcondition:
    //     Returns item at the current position in the
    //     SortedList

SortedList();

    // Constructor
    // Postcondition:
    //     Empty SortedList is created

private:
    int        length;
    int        currentPos;
    ItemType data[MAX_LENGTH];
    void BinSearch( ItemType, bool&, int& ) const;
};
```

How does the declaration of SortedList differ from the declaration of our original List class? Apart from a few changes in the documentation comments, there are only two differences:

1. The SortedList class does not supply a sorting operation to the client. Such an operation is needless, because the list components are assumed to be kept in sorted order at all times.

2. The `SortedList` class has an additional class member in the private part: a `BinSearch` function. This function is an auxiliary ("helper") function that is used only by other class member functions and is inaccessible to clients. We discuss its purpose when we examine the class implementation.

Let's look at what changes, if any, are required in the algorithms for the ADT operations, given that we are now working with a sorted list instead of an unsorted list.

Basic Operations

The algorithms for the class constructor, `IsEmpty`, `IsFull`, `Length`, `Reset` and `GetNextItem` are identical to those in the `List` class. The constructor sets the private data member `length` to 0, `IsEmpty` reports whether `length` equals 0, `IsFull` reports whether `length` equals `MAX_LENGTH`, `Length` returns the value of `length`, and `Print` outputs the list items from first to last.

Insertion

To add a new value to an already sorted list, we could store the new value at `data[length]`, increment `length`, and sort the array again. However, such a solution is *not* an efficient way of solving the problem. Inserting five new items results in five separate sorting operations.

If we were to insert a value by hand into a sorted list, we would write the new value out to the side and draw a line showing where it belongs. To find this position, we start at the top and scan the list until we find a value greater than the one we are inserting. The new value goes in the list just before that point.

We can use a similar process in our `Insert` function. We find the proper place in the list using the by-hand algorithm. Instead of writing the value to the side, we shift all the values larger than the new one down one place to make room for it. The main algorithm is expressed as follows, where `item` is the value being inserted.

```
WHILE place not found AND more places to look
    IF item > current component in list
        Increment current position
    ELSE
        Place found
Shift remainder of list down
Insert item
Increment length
```

Assuming that `index` is the place where `item` is to be inserted, the algorithm for Shift List Down is

```
Set data[length]   = data[length–1]
Set data[length–1] = data[length–2]
      ⋮                    ⋮
Set data[index+1]  = data[index]
```

This algorithm is illustrated in Figure 13–6.

This algorithm is based on how we would accomplish the task by hand. Often, such an adaptation is the best way to solve a problem. However, in this case, further thought reveals a slightly better way. Notice that we search from the front of the list (people always do), and we shift down from the end of the list upward. We can combine the searching and shifting by beginning at the *end* of the list.

If `item` is the new item to be inserted, compare `item` to the value in `data[length-1]`. If `item` is *less*, put `data[length-1]` into `data[length]` and compare `item` to the value in `data[length-2]`. This process continues until you find the

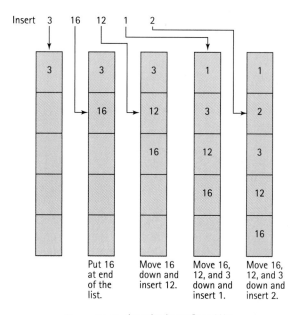

Figure 13–6   *Inserting into a Sorted List*

place where item is greater than or equal to the item in the list. Store item directly below it. Here is the algorithm:

```
Set index = length – 1
WHILE index ≥ 0 AND item < data[index]
    Set data[index + 1] = data[index]
    Decrement index
Set data[index + 1] = item
Increment length
```

What about duplicates? The algorithm continues until an item is found that is less than the one we are inserting. Therefore, the new item is inserted below a duplicate value (if one is there). Here is the code:

```
void SortedList::Insert( /* in */ ItemType item )

// Inserts item into the list

// Precondition:
//      length < MAX_LENGTH
// Postcondition:
//      item is in the list

{
    int index;      // Index and loop control variable

    index = length - 1;
    while (index >= 0 && item < data[index])
    {
        data[index+1] = data[index];
        index--;
    }
    data[index+1] = item;          // Insert item
    length++;
}
```

Notice that this algorithm works even if the list is empty. When the list is empty, length is 0 and the body of the While loop is not entered. So item is stored into data[0], and length is incremented to 1. Does the algorithm work if item is the smallest? The largest? Let's see. If item is the smallest, the loop body is executed length times, and index is −1. Thus, item is stored into position 0, where it belongs. If item is the largest, the loop body is not entered. The value of index is still length − 1, so item is stored into data[length], where it belongs.

This algorithm is the basis for another general-purpose sorting algorithm—an *insertion sort*. In an insertion sort, values are inserted one at a time into a list that was originally empty. An insertion sort is often used when input data must be sorted; each value is put into its proper place as it is read. We use this technique in the Problem-Solving Case Study at the end of this chapter.

Sequential Search

When we search for an item in an unsorted list, we won't discover that the item is missing until we reach the end of the list. If the list is already sorted, we know that an item is missing when we pass the place where it should be in the list. For example, if a list contains the values

7
11
13
76
98
102

and we are looking for 12, we need only compare 12 with 7, 11, and 13 to know that 12 is not in the list.

If the search item is greater than the current list component, we move on to the next component. If the item is equal to the current component, we have found what we are looking for. If the item is less than the current component, then we know that it is not in the list. In either of the last two cases, we stop looking. We can restate this algorithmically with the following code, in which `found` is set to `true` if the search item was found.

```
// Sequential search in a sorted list

index = 0;
while (index < length && item > data[index])
    index++;

found = (index < length && item == data[index]);
```

On average, searching a sorted list in this way takes the same number of iterations to find an item as searching an unsorted list. The advantage of this new algorithm is that we find out sooner if an item is missing. Thus, it is slightly more efficient; however, it works only on a sorted list.

We do not use this algorithm to implement the `SortedList::IsPresent` function. There is a better algorithm, which we look at next.

Binary Search

There is a second search algorithm on a sorted list that is considerably faster both for finding an item and for discovering that an item is missing. This algorithm is called a *binary search*. A binary search is based on the principle of successive approximation.

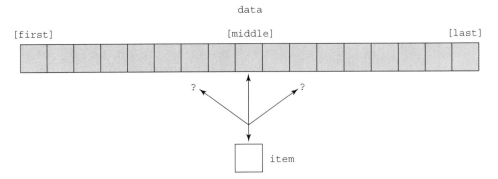

Figure 13-7   *Binary Search*

The algorithm divides the list in half (divides by 2—that's why it's called *binary* search) and decides which half to look in next. Division of the selected portion of the list is repeated until the item is found or it is determined that the item is not in the list.

This method is analogous to the way in which we look up a word in a dictionary. We open the dictionary in the middle and compare the word with one on the page that we turned to. If the word we're looking for comes before this word, we continue our search in the left-hand section of the dictionary. Otherwise, we continue in the right-hand section of the dictionary. We repeat this process until we find the word. If it is not there, we realize that either we have misspelled the word or our dictionary isn't complete.

The algorithm for a binary search is given below. The list of values is in the array data, and the value being looked for is item (see Figure 13-7).

1. Compare item to data[middle]. If item = data[middle], then we have found it. If item < data[middle], then look in the first half of data. If item > data[middle], then look in the second half of data.

2. Redefine data to be the half of data that we search next, and repeat step 1.

3. Stop when we have found item or know it is missing. We know it's missing when there is nowhere else to look and we still have not found it.

This algorithm should make sense. With each comparison, at best, we find the item for which we are searching; at worst, we eliminate half of the remaining list from consideration.

We need to keep track of the first possible place to look (first) and the last possible place to look (last). At any one time, we are looking only in data[first] through data[last]. When the function begins, first is set to 0 and last is set to length-1 to encompass the entire list.

Our three previous search algorithms have been Boolean observer operations. They just answer the question, Is this item in the list? Let's code the binary search as a void function that not only asks if the item is in the list but also asks which one it is (if it's there). To do so, we need to add two parameters to the parameter list: a Boolean flag found (to tell us whether the item is in the list) and an integer variable `position` (to tell us which item it is). If `found` is `false`, `position` is undefined.

```
void SortedList::BinSearch(
      /* in */  ItemType item,              // Item to be found
      /* out */ bool&     found,            // True if item is found
      /* out */ int&      position ) const  // Location if found

// Searches list for item, returning the index
// of item if item was found.

// Precondition:
//      length <= INT_MAX / 2
// Postcondition:
//      IF item is in the list
//          found == true  &&  data[position] contains item
//      ELSE
//          found == false  &&  position is undefined

{
    int first = 0;            // Lower bound on list
    int last = length - 1;    // Upper bound on list
    int middle;               // Middle index

    found = false;
    while (last >= first && !found)
    {
        middle = (first + last) / 2;
        if (item < data[middle])
            // Assert: item is not in data[middle..last]
            last = middle - 1;
        else if (item > data[middle])
            // Assert: item is not in data[first..middle]
            first = middle + 1;
        else
            // Assert: item == data[middle]
            found = true;
    }
    if (found)
        position = middle;
}
```

Should `BinSearch` be a public member of the `SortedList` class? No. The function returns the index of the array element where the item was found. An array index is useless to a client of `SortedList`. The array containing the list items is encapsulated within the private part of the class and is inaccessible to clients. If you review the

SortedList class declaration, you'll see that BinSearch is a *private*, not public, class member. We intend to use it as a helper function when we implement the public operations IsPresent and Delete.

Let's do a code walk-through of the binary search algorithm. The value being searched for is 24. Figure 13–8a shows the values of first, last, and middle during the first iteration. In this iteration, 24 is compared with 103, the value in data[middle]. Because 24 is less than 103, last becomes middle-1 and first stays the same. Figure 13–8b shows the situation during the second iteration. This time, 24 is compared with 72, the value in data[middle]. Because 24 is less than 72, last becomes middle-1 and first again stays the same.

In the third iteration (Figure 13–8c), middle and first are both 0. The value 24 is compared with 12, the value in data[middle]. Because 24 is greater than 12, first becomes middle+1. In the fourth iteration (Figure 13–8d), first, last, and middle are all the same. Again, 24 is compared with the value in data[middle]. Because 24 is less than 64, last becomes middle-1. Now that last is less than first, the process stops; found is false.

The binary search is the most complex algorithm that we have examined so far. The following table shows first, last, middle, and data[middle] for searches of the values 106, 400, and 406, using the same data as in the previous example. Examine the results in this table carefully.

item	first	last	middle	data[middle]	Termination of Loop
106	0	10	5	103	
	6	10	8	200	
	6	7	6	106	found = true
400	0	10	5	103	
	6	10	8	200	
	9	10	9	300	
	10	10	10	400	found = true
406	0	10	5	103	
	6	10	8	200	
	9	10	9	300	
	10	10	10	400	
	11	10			last < first
					found = false

The calculation

```
middle = (first + last) / 2;
```

explains why the function precondition restricts the value of length to INT_MAX/2. If the item being searched for happens to reside in the last position of the list (for exam-

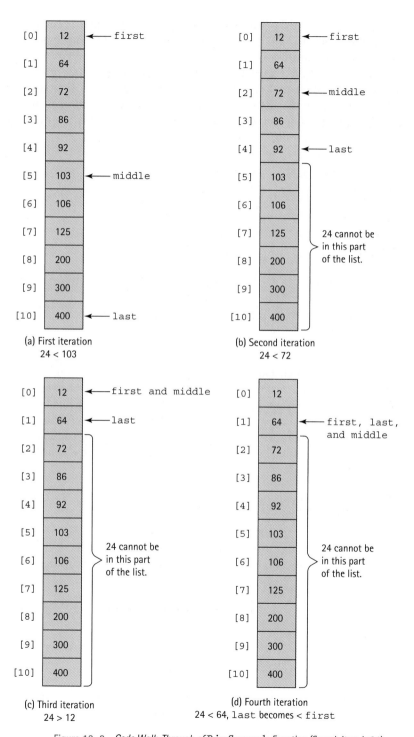

Figure 13–8 *Code Walk-Through of* BinSearch *Function (Search Item Is 24)*

ple, when `item` equals 400 in our sample list), then `first + last` equals `length + length`. If `length` is greater than `INT_MAX/2`, the sum `length + length` would produce an integer overflow.

Notice in the table that whether we searched for 106, 400, or 406, the loop never executed more than four times. It never executes more than four times in a list of 11 components because the list is being cut in half each time through the loop. The table below compares a sequential search and a binary search in terms of the average number of iterations needed to find an item.

	Average Number of Iterations	
Length of List	Sequential Search	Binary Search
10	5.5	2.9
100	50.5	5.8
1000	500.5	9.0
10,000	5000.5	12.4

If the binary search is so much faster, why not use it all the time? It certainly is faster in terms of the number of times through the loop, but more computations are performed within the binary search loop than in the other search algorithms. So if the number of components in the list is small (say, less than 20), the sequential search algorithms are faster because they perform less work at each iteration. As the number of components in the list increases, the binary search algorithm becomes relatively more efficient. Remember, however, that the binary search requires the list to be sorted, and sorting takes time. Keep three factors in mind when you are deciding which search algorithm to use:

1. The length of the list to be searched

2. Whether or not the list is already sorted

3. The number of times the list is to be searched

Given the `BinSearch` function (a private member of the `SortedList` class), it's easy to implement the `IsPresent` function (a public member of the class).

```
bool SortedList::IsPresent( /* in */ ItemType item ) const

// Searches the list for item, reporting whether it was found

// Precondition:
//      length <= INT_MAX / 2
// Postcondition:
//      Return value == true, if item is in data[0..length-1]
//                   == false, otherwise
```

```
{
    bool found;        // True if item is found
    int position;      // Required (but unused) argument for
                       //    the call to BinSearch

    BinSearch(item, found, position);
    return found;
}
```

The body of `IsPresent` calls `BinSearch`, obtaining the result of the search in the variables `found` and `position`. `IsPresent` receives the value of `found` from `BinSearch` and simply passes it on to the client (via the `return` statement). The body of `IsPresent` is not interested in where the item was found, so it ignores the value returned in the `position` argument. Why did we include this third argument when we designed `Bin-Search`? The answer is that the `Delete` operation, which we look at next, calls `Bin-Search` and *does* use the `position` argument.

Deletion

In the `List::Delete` function, we deleted an item by moving up the last component in the list to fill the deleted item's position. Although this algorithm is fine for unsorted lists, it won't work for sorted lists. Moving the last component to an arbitrary position in the list is almost certain to disturb the sorted order of the components. We need a new algorithm for sorted lists.

Let's call `BinSearch` to tell us the position of the item to be deleted. Then we can "squeeze out" the deleted item by shifting up all the remaining array elements by one position:

```
BinSearch(item, found, position)
IF found
      Shift remainder of list up
      Decrement length
```

The algorithm for Shift List Up is

```
Set data[position]    = data[position+1]
Set data[position+1] = data[position+2]
      ⋮                        ⋮
Set data[length–2]    = data[length–1]
```

Here is the coded version of this algorithm:

```
void SortedList::Delete( /* in */ ItemType item )

// Deletes item from the list, if it is there

// Precondition:
//     0 < length <= INT_MAX/2
// Postcondition:
//     IF item is in data array at entry
//          First occurrence of item is no longer in array
//       && length == length@entry - 1
//       && data[0..length-1] are in ascending order
//     ELSE
//        length and data array are unchanged

{
    bool found;       // True if item is found
    int position;     // Position of item, if found
    int index;        // Index and loop control variable

    BinSearch(item, found, position);
    if (found)
    {
        // Shift data[position..length-1] up one position

        for (index = position; index < length - 1; index++)
            data[index] = data[index+1];
        length--;
    }
}
```

Now let's turn our attention to another example of array-based lists—a special kind of array that is useful when working with alphanumeric character data.

13.4 Understanding Character Strings

Ever since Chapter 2, we have been using the `string` class to store and manipulate character strings.

```
string name;

name = "James Smith";
len = name.length();
    ⋮
```

In some contexts, we think of a string as a single unit of data. In other contexts, we treat it as a group of individually accessible characters. As an abstraction, a string is a list of characters that, at any moment in time, has a length associated with it.

Thinking of a string as an ADT, how would we implement the ADT? There are many ways to implement strings. Programmers have specified and implemented their own string classes—the `string` class from the standard library, for instance. And the C++ language has its own built-in notion of a string: the **C string**. In C++, a string constant (or string literal, or literal string) is a sequence of characters enclosed by double quotes:

> **C string** In C and C++, a null-terminated sequence of characters stored in a `char` array.

```
"Hi"
```

A string constant is stored as a `char` array with enough components to hold each specified character plus one more—the *null character*. The null character, which is the first character in both the ASCII and EBCDIC character sets, has internal representation 0. In C++, the escape sequence \0 stands for the null character. When the compiler encounters the string `"Hi"` in a program, it stores the three characters 'H', 'i', and '\0' into a three-element, anonymous (unnamed) `char` array as follows:

Unnamed array

```
[0]   'H'
[1]   'i'
[2]   '\0'
```

The C string is the only kind of C++ array for which there exists an aggregate constant—the string constant. Notice that in a C++ program, the symbols `'A'` denote a single character, whereas the symbols `"A"` denote two: the character 'A' and the null character.*

In addition to C string constants, we can create C string *variables*. To do so, we explicitly declare a `char` array and store into it whatever characters we want to, finishing with the null character. Here's an example:

```
char myStr[8];    // Room for 7 significant characters plus '\0'

myStr[0] = 'H';
myStr[1] = 'i';
myStr[2] = '\0';
```

C string is not an official term used in C++ language manuals. Such manuals typically use the term *string*. However, we use *C string* to distinguish between the general concept of a string and the built-in array representation defined by the C and C++ languages.

In C++, all C strings (constants or variables) are assumed to be null-terminated. This convention is agreed upon by all C++ programmers and standard library functions. The null character serves as a sentinel value; it allows algorithms to locate the end of the string. For example, here is a function that determines the length of any C string, not counting the terminating null character:

```
int StrLength( /* in */ const char str[] )

// Precondition:
//      str holds a null-terminated string
// Postcondition:
//      Function value == number of characters in str (excluding '\0')

{
    int i = 0;   // Index variable

    while (str[i] != '\0')
        i++;
    return i;
}
```

The value of i is the correct value for this function to return. If the array being examined is

then i equals 2 at loop exit. The string length is therefore 2.

The argument to the StrLength function can be a C string variable, as in the function call

```
cout << StrLength(myStr);
```

or it can be a string constant:

```
cout << StrLength("Hello");
```

In the first case, the base address of the `myStr` array is sent to the function, as we discussed in Chapter 12. In the second case, a base address is also sent to the function—the base address of the unnamed array that the compiler has set aside for the string constant.

There is one more thing we should say about our `StrLength` function. A C++ programmer would not actually write this function. The standard library supplies several string-processing functions, one of which is named `strlen` and does exactly what our `StrLength` function does. Later in the chapter, we look at `strlen` and other library functions.

Initializing C Strings

In Chapter 12, we showed how to initialize an array in its declaration by specifying a list of initial values within braces, like this:

```
int delta[5] = {25, -3, 7, 13, 4};
```

To initialize a C string variable in its declaration, you could use the same technique:

```
char message[8] = {'W', 'h', 'o', 'o', 'p', 's', '!', '\0'};
```

However, C++ allows a more convenient way to initialize a C string. You can simply initialize the array by using a string constant:

```
char message[8] = "Whoops!";
```

This shorthand notation is unique to C strings because there is no other kind of array for which there are aggregate constants.

We said in Chapter 12 that you can omit the size of an array when you initialize it in its declaration (in which case, the compiler determines its size). This feature is often used with C strings because it keeps you from having to count the number of characters. For example,

```
char promptMsg[] = "Enter a positive number:";   // Size is 25
char errMsg[] = "Value must be positive.";       // Size is 24
```

Be very careful about one thing: C++ treats initialization (in a declaration) and assignment (in an assignment statement) as two distinct operations. Different rules apply. Remember that array initialization is legal, but aggregate array assignment is not.

```
char myStr[20] = "Hello";   // OK
   ⋮
myStr = "Howdy";            // Not allowed
```

C String Input and Output

In Chapter 12, we emphasized that C++ does not provide aggregate operations on arrays. There is no aggregate assignment, aggregate comparison, or aggregate arithmetic on arrays. We also said that aggregate input/output of arrays is not possible, with one exception. C strings are that exception. Let's look first at output.

To output the contents of an array that is *not* a C string, you aren't allowed to do this:

```
int alpha[100];
   ⋮
cout << alpha;    // Not allowed
```

Instead, you must write a loop and print the array elements one at a time. However, aggregate output of a null-terminated `char` array (that is, a C string) is valid. The C string can be a constant (as we've been doing since Chapter 2):

```
cout << "Results are:";
```

or it can be a variable:

```
char msg[8] = "Welcome";
   ⋮
cout << msg;
```

In both cases, the insertion operator (<<) outputs each character in the array until the null character is found. It is up to you to double-check that the terminating null character is present in the array. If not, the << operator will march through the array and into the rest of memory, printing out bytes until—just by chance—it encounters a byte whose integer value is 0.

To input C strings, we have several options. The first is to use the extraction operator (>>), which behaves exactly the same as with `string` class objects. When reading input characters into a C string variable, the >> operator skips leading whitespace characters and then reads successive characters into the array, stopping at the first trailing whitespace character (which is not consumed, but remains as the first character waiting in the input stream). The >> operator also takes care of adding the null character to the end of the string. For example, assume we have the following code:

```
char firstName[31];    // Room for 30 characters plus '\0'
char lastName[31];

cin >> firstName >> lastName;
```

If the input stream initially looks like this (where □ denotes a blank):

□□John□Smith□□□25

then our input statement stores 'J', 'o', 'h', 'n', and '\0' into `firstName[0]` through `firstName[4]`; stores 'S', 'm', 'i', 't', 'h', and '\0' into `lastName[0]` through `lastName[5]`; and leaves the input stream as

□□□25

The >> operator, however, has two potential drawbacks.

1. If the array isn't large enough to hold the sequence of input characters (and the '\0'), the >> operator will continue to store characters into memory past the end of the array.

2. The >> operator cannot be used to input a string that has blanks within it. (It stops reading as soon as it encounters the first whitespace character.)

To cope with these limitations, we can use a variation of the `get` function, a member of the `istream` class. We have used the `get` function to input a single character, even if it is a whitespace character:

```
cin.get(inputChar);
```

The `get` function also can be used to input C strings, in which case the function call requires two arguments. The first is the array name and the second is an `int` expression.

```
cin.get(myStr, charCount + 1);
```

The `get` function does not skip leading whitespace characters and continues until it either has read `charCount` characters or it reaches the newline character '\n', whichever comes first. It then appends the null character to the end of the string. With the statements

```
char oneLine[81];    // Room for 80 characters plus '\0'
   ⋮
cin.get(oneLine, 81);
```

the `get` function reads and stores an entire input line (to a maximum of 80 characters), embedded blanks and all. If the line has fewer than 80 characters, reading stops at '\n' but does not consume it. The newline character is now the first one waiting in the input stream. To read two consecutive lines worth of strings, it is necessary to consume the newline character:

```
char dummy;
   ⋮
cin.get(string1, 81);
cin.get(dummy);          // Eat newline before next "get"
cin.get(string2, 81);
```

The first function call reads characters up to, but not including, the '\n'. If the input of `dummy` were omitted, then the input of `string2` would read *no* characters because '\n' would immediately be the first character waiting in the stream.

Finally, the `ignore` function—introduced in Chapter 4—can be useful in conjunction with the `get` function. Recall that the statement

```
cin.ignore(200, '\n');
```

says to skip at most 200 input characters but stop if a newline was read. (The newline character *is* consumed by this function.) If a program inputs a long string from the user but only wants to retain the first four characters of the response, here is a way to do it:

```cpp
char response[5];        // Room for 4 characters plus '\0'

cin.get(response, 5);    // Input at most 4 characters
cin.ignore(100, '\n');   // Skip remaining chars up to and
                         //   including '\n'
```

The value 100 in the last statement is arbitrary. Any "large enough" number will do.

Finally, we revisit a topic that came up in Chapter 4. Certain library functions and member functions of system-supplied classes require C strings as arguments. An example is the `ifstream` class member function named `open`. To open a file, we pass the name of the file as a C string, either a constant or a variable:

```cpp
ifstream file1;
ifstream file2;
char     fileName[51];       // Max. 50 characters plus '\0'

file1.open("students.dat");
cin.get(fileName, 51);       // Read at most 50 characters
cin.ignore(100, '\n');       // Skip rest of input line
file2.open(fileName);
```

As discussed in Chapter 4, if our file name is contained in a `string` class object, we still can use the `open` function, *provided* we use the `string` class member function named `c_str` to convert the string to a C string:

```cpp
ifstream inFile;
string   fileName;

cin >> fileName;
inFile.open(fileName.c_str());
```

Comparing these two code segments, you can observe a major advantage of the `string` class over C strings: A string in a `string` class object has unbounded length, whereas the length of a C string is bounded by the array size, which is fixed at compile time.

C String Library Routines

Through the header file `cstring`, the C++ standard library provides a large assortment of C string operations. In this section, we discuss three of these library functions: `strlen`, which returns the length of a string; `strcmp`, which compares two strings using the relations less-than, equal, and greater-than; and `strcpy`, which copies one string to another. Here is a summary of `strlen`, `strcmp`, and `strcpy`:

Header File	Function	Function Value	Effect
`<cstring>`	`strlen(str)`	Integer length of `str` (excluding '\0')	Computes length of `str`
`<cstring>`	`strcmp(str1, str2)`	An integer < 0, if `str1` < `str2` The integer 0, if `str1` = `str2` An integer > 0, if `str1` > `str2`	Compares `str1` and `str2`
`<cstring>`	`strcpy(toStr, fromStr)`	Base address of `toStr` (usually ignored)	Copies `fromStr` (including '\0') to `toStr`, overwriting what was there; `toStr` must be large enough to hold the result

The `strlen` function is similar to the `StrLength` function we wrote earlier. It returns the number of characters in a C string prior to the terminating '\0'. Here's an example of a call to the function:

```
#include <cstring>
   ⋮
char subject[] = "Computer Science";
cout << strlen(subject);    // Prints 16
```

The `strcpy` routine is important because aggregate assignment with the = operator is not allowed on C strings. In the following code fragment, we show the wrong way and the right way to perform a string copy.

```
#include <cstring>
   ⋮
char myStr[100];
   ⋮
myStr = "Abracadabra";           // No
strcpy(myStr, "Abracadabra");    // Yes
```

In `strcpy`'s argument list, the destination string is the one on the left, just as an assignment operation transfers data from right to left. It is the caller's responsibility to make sure that the destination array is large enough to hold the result.

The `strcpy` function is technically a value-returning function; it not only copies one C string to another, but also returns as a function value the base address of the destination array. Programmers nearly always ignore the function value and simply invoke `strcpy` as if it were a void function.

The `strcmp` function is used for comparing two strings. The function receives two C strings as parameters and compares them in *lexicographic* order (the order in which they would appear in a dictionary)—the same ordering used in comparing `string` class objects. Given the function call `strcmp(str1, str2)`, the function returns one of the following int values: a negative integer, if str1 < str2 lexicographically; the value 0, if str1 = str2; or a positive integer, if str1 > str2. The precise values of the negative integer and the positive integer are unspecified. You simply test to see if the result is less than 0, 0, or greater than 0. Here is an example:

```
if (strcmp(str1, str2) < 0)   // If str1 is less than str2 ...
    ⋮
```

We have described only three of the string-handling routines provided by the standard library. These three are the most commonly needed, but there are many more. If you are designing or maintaining programs that use C strings extensively, you should read the documentation on strings for your C++ system.

Programming Example

Calculating Exam Statistics Revisited

PROBLEM You are the grader in your Government class. The teacher has asked you to prepare the following statistics.

    Number of grades
    Average grade
    Lowest grade
    Highest grade
    Number of grades above the average
    Number of grades below the average

INPUT A file whose name is input from the keyboard containing test grades.

OUTPUT A file whose name is input from the keyboard showing the following statistics properly labeled.

DISCUSSION We have just designed and implemented the ADT List. Let's think of this problem in terms of a list of grades. There are the same three separate tasks to be done in this problem, but let's look at them in terms of list operations. We need to average the values in the list, find the maximum and minimum values in the list, and go through the list counting those values above the average and those values below the average. To find the average, we sum the list of grades and divide by the number of grades. We found the minimum and maximum values in a list of numbers in the Design Studio program. The third task involves looking at each grade, comparing it to the average, and incrementing one of two counters.

If all we had to do was find the average and the minimum and maximum grades, we could do the processing at the same time that we read the data values. However, the task of printing the number of grades above and below the average requires that each grade be examined more than once because we don't have the average until all the values have been read. Therefore, we must create a list of the grades so that we can access each one more than once.

We have to examine each grade twice: once to calculate the average, find the minimum value, and find the maximum value and once to compare each grade to the average. We could do all the processing except for the number above and below the average as we initially read the grades. However, it is better style to separate the tasks into separate functions.

DATA STRUCTURES

Simple variables
A list of integer values

Here is the program:

```cpp
//*******************************************************************
// Statistics Program
// This program calculates the average, high score, low score,
// number above the average, and number below the average for
// a file of test scores.  The List ADT is used
// Assumption:  File "testScores" is not empty and does not contain
// more than MAX_GRADES values.
// To save space, we omit from each function the precondition
// comments that document the assumptions made about valid input
// parameter data. These would be included in a program intended
// for actual use.
//*******************************************************************

#include <fstream>
#include <iostream>
#include <iomanip>
#include "list.h"

using namespace std;

// Function Prototypes

void OpenFiles(ifstream& inData, ofstream& outData);
void InputGrades(List& grades, ifstream& inData);
float CalculateAverage(List grades);
int CalculateHighest(List grades);
int CalculateLowest(List grades);
int CalculateAboveAverage(List grades, float average);
int CalculateBelowAverage(List grades, float average);
void PrintResults(ofstream& outData, List grades, float average,
    int highest, int lowest, int aboveAverage, int belowAverage);

int main()
{
    List grades;              // A list of grades

    float average;            // Average grade
    int highest;              // Highest grade
    int lowest;               // Lowest grade
    int aboveAverage;         // Number of grades above the average
    int belowAverage;         // Number of grades below the average

    // Declare and open files
    ifstream inData;
```

```
                            ofstream outData;
                            OpenFiles(inData, outData);

                            // Process grades
                            InputGrades(grades, inData);
                            average = CalculateAverage(grades);
                            highest = CalculateHighest(grades);
                            lowest = CalculateLowest(grades);
                            aboveAverage = CalculateAboveAverage(grades, average);
                            belowAverage = CalculateBelowAverage(grades, average);
                            PrintResults(outData,grades, average, highest, lowest,
                                aboveAverage, belowAverage);

                            inData.close();
                            outData.close();
                            return 0;
                        }


//*********************************************************************

void OpenFiles( /* inout */ ifstream& text,
                /* inout */ ofstream& outFile )

// Function OpenFiles reads in the names of the input file and
// the output file and opens them for processing
// Postcondition:
//      Files have been opened AND a label has been written on the
//      output file
if ( !inData || !outData )
{
    cout << "Files did not open successfully." << endl;
    return 1;
}

{
    string inFileName;
    string outDataName;

    cout << "Enter the name of the file to be processed" << endl;
    cin >> inFileName;
    text.open(inFileName.c_str());

    cout << "Enter the name of the output file" << endl;
    cin >> outDataName;
    outFile.open(outDataName.c_str());
```

```
        // Write label on output
        outFile << "Grade statistics using the List ADT" << endl
                << endl;
    }


    //**********************************************************************


    void InputGrades( /* inout */ List& grades,       // Grade list
                      /* inout */ ifstream& inData ) // Input file

    // Grades are input from file inData and inserted into grades.
    // Precondition:
    //      File is not empty
    // Postcondition:
    //      Each grade in the file has been inserted into list of grades

    {
        int grade;
        // Read grades and put them into the list
        inData >> grade;
        while (inData && !grades.IsFull())
        {
            grades.Insert(grade);
            inData >> grade;
        }
    }


    //**********************************************************************


    float CalculateAverage( /* in */ List grades )

    // This function calculates the average test score
    // Postcondition:
    //      Return value is the average grade

    {
        int sum = 0;
        int limit = grades.Length();         // limit is the number of
                                              // grades
        int grade;

        grades.Reset();                       // Prepare for traversal

        // Add each grade to sum
        for (int index = 0; index < limit; index++)
```

```
        {
            grade = grades.GetNextItem();
            sum = sum + grade;
        }

        return float(sum) / float(limit); // Return average
    }

    //*********************************************************************

    int CalculateHighest( /* in */ List grades ) // List of grades

    // This function calculates the highest grade in the list of
    // grades
    // Postcondition:
    //      Return value is the highest grade

    {
        int limit = grades.Length();        // Number of grades
        int grade;

        grades.Reset();                      // Prepare for iteration
        int maxGrade = 0;

        // Find the maximum grade in the list
        for (int index = 0; index < limit; index++)
        {
            grade = grades.GetNextItem();
            if (grade > maxGrade)
                maxGrade = grade;
        }
        return maxGrade;
    }

    //*********************************************************************

    int CalculateLowest( /* in */ List grades ) // List of grades

    // This function calculates the lowest grade in the list of
    // grades
    // Postcondition:
    //      Return value is the lowest grade

    {
        int limit = grades.Length();        // Number of grades
        int grade;

        grades.Reset();                      // Prepare for iteration
```

```
    int minGrade = 100;

    // Find the miminum grade in the list
    for (int index = 0; index < limit; index++)
    {
        grade = grades.GetNextItem();
        if (grade < minGrade)
            minGrade = grade;
    }
    return minGrade;
}


//******************************************************************

int CalculateAboveAverage
    ( /* in */ List grades,          // List of grades
      /* inout */  float average ) // Average grade

// This function calculates the number of grades above the
// average
// Postcondition:
//     Return value is the number of grades above average

{
    int roundedAverage = (int) (average + 0.5);
    int limit = grades.Length();      // Number of grades
    int grade;
    int number = 0;

    grades.Reset();                        // Prepare for iteration

    // Calculate the number of grades above the average
    for (int index = 0; index < limit; index++)
    {
        grade = grades.GetNextItem();
        if (grade > roundedAverage)
            number++;
    }
    return number;
}


//******************************************************************

int CalculateBelowAverage
    ( /* in */ List grades,           // List of grades
```

```
              /* inout */  float average )  // Average grade

// This function calculates the number of grades below the
// average
// Postcondition:
//     Return value is the number of grades below average

{
    int truncatedAverage = (int) (average);
    int limit = grades.Length();        // Number of grades
    int grade;
    int number = 0;

    grades.Reset();                      // Prepare for iteration

    // Calculate the number of grades below the average
    for (int index = 0; index < limit; index++)
    {
        grade = grades.GetNextItem();
        if (grade < truncatedAverage)
            number++;
    }
    return number;
}

//******************************************************************

void PrintResults( /* inout */ ofstream& outData, // Output file
                   /* in */     List grades,       // Grade list
                   /* in */     float average,     // Average
                   /* in */     int highest,       // Max grade
                   /* in */     int lowest,        // Min grade
                   /* in */     int aboveAverage,  // Number above
                   /* in */     int belowAverage ) // Number below

// Statistics are printed on file outData
// Precondition:
//     Output file has been successfully opened
// Postcondition:
//     Statistics have been written on outData, appropriately
//     labeled

{
    outData << "The number of grades is " << grades.Length()
            << endl;
```

```
    outData << fixed << setprecision(2) << "The average grade is "
            << average << endl;
    outData << "The highest grade is " << highest << endl;
    outData << "The lowest grade is " << lowest << endl;
    outData << "The number of grades above the average is "
            << aboveAverage << endl;
    outData << "The number of grades below the average is "
            << belowAverage << endl;
}
```

TESTING   This implementation is based on a list of values. We must test for cases in which there are no grades, one grade, a few grades, and exactly the maximum number of grades. Here is a run with a few grades.

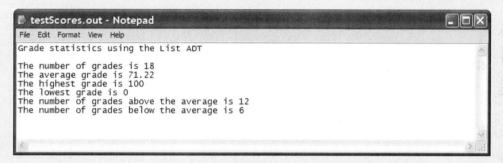

Testing and Debugging

In this chapter, we have discussed, designed, and coded algorithms to construct and manipulate items in a list. In addition to the basic list operations IsFull, IsEmpty, Length, and an iterator pair, the algorithms included three sequential searches, a binary search, insertion into sorted and unsorted lists, deletion from sorted and unsorted lists, and a selection sort. We have already partially tested List::Insert, List::Delete, List::Reset, and List::GetNextItem in conjunction with the case study. The other searching algorithms and the functions SortedList::Insert, SortedList::Delete, and SortedList::SelSort need to be tested. We should test them with lists containing no components, one component, two components, MAX_LENGTH – 1 components, and MAX_LENGTH components.

When we wrote the precondition that the list was not full for operation List::Insert, we indicated that we could handle the problem another way—we could include an error flag in the function's parameter list. The function would call IsFull and set the error flag. The insertion would not take place if the error flag were set to true. Both options are acceptable ways of handling the problem. The important point is that we clearly state whether the calling code or the called function is to check for the error condition. However, it is the calling code that must decide what to do when an error condition occurs. In other words, if errors are handled by means of preconditions, then the user must write the code to guarantee the preconditions. If errors are handled by flags, then the user must write the code to monitor the error flags.

Testing and Debugging Hints

1. Review the Testing and Debugging Hints for Chapter 12. They apply to all one-dimensional arrays, including C strings.

2. Make sure that every C string is terminated with the null character. String constants are automatically null-terminated by the compiler. On input, the >> operator and the `get` function automatically add the null character. If you store characters into a C string individually or manipulate the array in any way, be sure to account for the null character.

3. Remember that C++ treats C string initialization (in a declaration) as different from C string assignment. Initialization is allowed, but assignment is not.

4. Aggregate input/output is allowed for C strings but not for other array types.

5. If you use the >> operator to input into a C string variable, be sure the array is large enough to hold the null character plus the longest sequence of (nonwhitespace) characters in the input stream.

6. With C string input, the >> operator stops at, *but does not consume,* the first trailing whitespace character. Likewise, if the `get` function stops reading early because it encounters a newline character, the newline character is not consumed.

7. When you use the `strcpy` library function, ensure that the destination array is at least as large as the array from which you are copying.

8. General-purpose functions (such as ADT operations) should be tested outside the context of a particular program, using a test driver.

9. Choose test data carefully so that you test all end conditions and some in the middle. End conditions are those that reach the limits of the structure used to store them. For example, in a list, there should be test data in which the number of components is 0, 1, and MAX_LENGTH, as well as between 1 and MAX_LENGTH.

Summary

This chapter has provided practice in working with lists stored in one-dimensional arrays. We have examined algorithms that insert, delete, search, and sort data stored in a list, and we have written functions to implement these algorithms. We can use these functions again and again in different contexts because they are members of general-purpose C++ classes (List and SortedList) that represent list ADTs.

C strings are a special case of char arrays in C++. The last significant character must be followed by a null character to mark the end of the string. C strings are less versatile than a string class. However, it pays to understand how they work because many existing programs in C and C++ use them, and string classes often use C strings as the underlying data representation.

Quick Check

1. What are the three main properties of a list? (pp. 512–518)
2. Where do we insert a new value into a list that isn't sorted? (pp. 519–523)
3. If an item isn't in the list, when does the linear search discover that it is missing? (pp. 523–528)
4. How does a sorted list ADT differ from a list ADT that includes a sort operation? (pp. 531–537)
5. With an insertion sort, what happens to the components that precede the insertion point, and the components that follow it? (pp. 534–537)
6. Where does the binary search algorithm get its name? (pp. 537–543)
7. What two members of a list class are used to represent the data in a list? (pp. 512–513)
8. What are the major steps in deleting a value from a list? (pp. 543–544)
9. What operations in a sorted list are different from the operations in an unsorted list, and how do they differ? (pp. 531–534)
10. How many For loops are there in an implementation of an selection sort? (pp. 528–531)
11. What condition ends a binary search? (pp. 537–538)

Answers
1. It is variable length, linear, and homogenous.   2. At end of the list (assuming the list isn't already full).   3. When it has examined the last element in the list.   4. The components of a sorted list are always kept in order, but the components of a regular list are only sorted after the sort operation executes, until the next insertion or deletion.   5. The components that precede the insertion point remain where they are, and the ones following the insertion point shift over one place to make room.   6. The name comes from its pattern of dividing the area of the search by two on each iteration.   7. A data array containing the specified item type in each component, and a length represented by an `int`.   8. Search for the value, delete the value, shift any succeeding values up one place.   9. There is no sort operation in the sorted list. The insert operation inserts a new value in its proper place rather than at the end of the list. The delete operation shifts the succeeding components up one place, rather than moving the last component into the vacated position. Searching in the sorted list can be done with a binary search rather than a linear search.   10. Two.   11. Either the value is found, or the first and last indexes of the search area are the same and the value has not been found.

Exam Preparation Exercises

1. Why do we say that a list is linear?
2. What do we mean when we say that a list is homogeneous?

3. If the Length operation associated with an *unsorted* list returns 43, and we then call the Delete operation for the list, passing it a value that matches the 21st item in the list:
    a. What is the index of the component that is deleted?
    b. What is the index of the component that takes its place?
    c. What does the Length operation return after the deletion?
    d. How many components in the list change their position as a result of the deletion?

4. If ItemType is float, how do we need to change the following While loop condition, as written in the sequential search, and why do we need to change it?

```
while (index < length && item != data[index])
```

5. The following statements are supposed to swap two values in an array, but they are in the wrong order. Rearrange them into the proper order.

```
data[value2] = temp;
data[value1] = data[value2];
temp = data[value1];
```

6. In a selection sort, what is accomplished by the inner loop each time it executes?

7. If the Length operation associated with a *sorted* list returns 43, and we then call the Delete operation for the list, passing it a value that matches the 21st item in the list:
    a. What is the index of the component that is deleted?
    b. What is the index of the component that takes its place?
    c. What does the Length operation return after the deletion?
    d. How many components in the list change their position as a result of the deletion?

8. On average, a sequential search of a sorted list takes the same number of iterations as searching an unsorted list. True or false?

9. We should use a binary search for large sorted lists, but a sequential search is more efficient when a list has few components. True or false?

10. Why don't we need a separate sorting operation in a sorted-list ADT?

11. A sorted list contains 16 elements, and the binary search operation is called with a value that matches the 12th value in the list. How many iterations does it take for the binary search to find this match?

12. What are the characters stored in the following C string?

```
char exam[4] = "Hop";
```

Programming Warm-Up Exercises

1. Write a C++ Boolean function named Deleted that has three parameters: someItem (of type ItemType as used in this chapter), oldList, and newList (both of type List as defined in this chapter). The function returns true if someItem is found in oldList, but is not present in newList.

2. The `List` type in this chapter allows us to store multiple copies of an item in the list. Sometimes it is useful to have a list in which any given item can appear just once. Change the implementation of the `Insert` function so that it only adds an item to the list if the item is not already there.

3. What is wrong with the following code segment, and what must be changed in type `List` to make it work correctly?

```
List inVals;
for (int count = 1; count <= 100; count++)
{
    cin >> inVal;
    inVals.Insert(inVal);
}
```

4. We would like to add a `DeleteAll` function to the `List` type that deletes all occurrences of an item from a list. Write the code that must be added to the specification file for the type to enable us to add this function.

5. Write the implementation of the `DeleteAll` function as described in Exercise 4.

6. We would like to add a `Replace` function to the `List` type that takes two parameters, `oldItem` and `newItem` of `ItemType`. The function finds `oldItem` in the list, deletes it, and inserts `newItem` in its place. The list is unchanged if `oldItem` is not present in the list. Write the code that must be added to the specification file for the type to enable us to add this function.

7. Write the implementation of the `Replace` function as described in Exercise 6.

8. The `SortedList` type keeps items in ascending order. Which function(s) would need to be changed to make the list keep the items in descending order?

9. Change the implementation of the `BinSearch` function so that it will work with a list that keeps items in descending order.

10. In Exercise 5 you wrote a `DeleteAll` function for the `List` type. Implement a `DeleteAll` function for the `SortedList` type, taking advantage of the fact that all occurrences of the item are stored in adjacent locations in the array. Note that the binary search does not necessarily return the position of the first occurrence of an item; it can return the position of any matching item. Thus, in this case, it may be more efficient to use a linear search to find the start of the matching items. Be sure that your function updates the length of the list as necessary.

11. In Exercise 7 you wrote a `Replace` function for the `List` type that deletes one value and replaces it with another. Reimplement the `Replace` function for the `SortedList` type. Note that in this case, the replacement value needs to be inserted in the proper position in the list to maintain the ordering of the items.

12. Write a code segment that fills a `SortedList` called `inData` with values that are input from a file called `unsorted`.

13. We wish to add a `FilePrint` function to the `SortedList` type. Like the `Print` operation, it outputs the contents of the list in order, but `FilePrint` takes a parameter called `outFile` of type `ofstream`, and writes the values to that file. Write the implementation of this function in the `SortedList` type.

Programming Problems

1. Write a program using the `List` class from this chapter that implements a To-Do list. The items in the list will be strings. The user should be prompted to enter a command (add an item, mark an item as done or partially done, delete an item, and print the list) and data as necessary. Simply storing items in the list is easy, but the List class doesn't directly support the recording of the status of each task. There are different ways that you might want to go about this. One would be to implement a struct or a class that represents an item and its status, and modify the `List` class to work with this struct or class as its item type. Another way would be to keep three lists: Done, Partial, and Undone. When an item is created, it enters the Undone list. When its status is changed, it moves to one of the other lists as appropriate. Choose the approach that you prefer, and implement the application using proper style, effective prompts, and sufficient documentation.

2. Many instructors like to see the distribution of scores on an exam before they assign grades. You're working for an art history professor who has asked you to develop a program that will read all of the scores from an exam and print out a bar chart that shows the distribution. The range of the scores varies from exam to exam, and there are at most 250 students in the class. Use or modify the `SortedList` class from this chapter as necessary to help you do this task. The integer scores are entered into a file called `exams.dat` in random order. Your program's job is to read in the data, sort it, and output a bar chart with one * for each exam that has a particular score. The first bar in the chart should be the highest score, and the last bar in the chart should be the lowest score. Each line of output should start with the score value, followed by the appropriate number of stars. When there is a score value that didn't appear on any exams, just output the value and no stars, then go to the next line.

3. Enhance the program in Problem 2 as follows: The data file now contains a score and a name. Modify the `SortedList` class so that it uses a struct consisting of the score and the name as its fields. The program should input the file data into the modified list. In addition to displaying the bar chart, the program will also output the sorted list to a file called `byscore.dat`.

4. You've gathered lists of e-mail addresses from a variety of sources, and you want to send out a mass mailing to all of the addresses. However, you don't want to send out duplicate messages. All of the e-mail addresses (represented as strings) have been combined on a single file called `rawlist.dat`. You need to write a program that reads them all and discards any that already have been input. Use one of the list classes from this chapter, modifying it as necessary to work with string data, and to deal with up to 1000 items. After all of the data have been read, output the new mailing list to a file called `cleanlist.dat`.

5. You're working for the state vehicle registry, and it just has been discovered that the people who make the license plates have been mistakenly producing occasional duplicates. You have a file (`platesmade.dat`) containing a list of plate numbers, which are recorded as they are made. You need to write a program that reads this file and identifies any duplicates in the list so that notices can be sent out to recall them. The plate numbers, which consists of letters and

numbers, should be stored as strings. Output the duplicates into a file called `recallplates.dat`. Use the `SortedList` class from this chapter to help you in writing this application, modifying it if necessary.

Programming Example Follow-Up

1. Revise the program to combine `CalculateAverage`, `CalculateHighest`, and `CalculateLowest` into one function `Calculate`.
2. Revise the program from Exercise 1 so that `CalculateAboveAverage` and `CalculateBelowAverage` are combined into one function `AboveBelow`.
3. Is it better to have the functions combined or left separate?

Object-Oriented Software Development

Knowledge Goals

- *To know the distinction between structured (procedural) programming and object-oriented programming.*
- *To know the characteristics of an object-oriented language.*
- *To understand the difference between static and dynamic binding of operations to objects.*

Skill Goals

To be able to:

- *Create a new C++ class from an existing class by using inheritance.*
- *Create a new C++ class from an existing class by using composition.*
- *Apply the object-oriented design methodology to solve a problem.*
- *Take an object-oriented design and code it in C++.*

In this chapter, we examine how classes and objects can be used to guide the entire software development process. Although the design phase precedes the implementation phase in the development of software, we reverse the order of presentation in this chapter. We begin with *object-oriented programming,* a topic that includes design but is more about implementation issues. We describe the basic principles, terminology, and programming language features associated with the object-oriented approach. After presenting these fundamental concepts, we look more closely at the design phase—*object-oriented design.*

14.1 Object-Oriented Programming

We introduced object-oriented design (OOD) briefly in Chapter 4. Recall that OOD decomposes a problem into objects—self-contained entities composed of data and operations on the data. The process of implementing an object-oriented design is called **object-oriented programming (OOP)**. The end result is a program that is a collection of interacting objects (see Figure 14–1). In OOD and OOP, data plays a leading role; the primary contribution of algorithms is to implement the operations on objects.

> **Object-oriented programming (OOP)** The use of data abstraction, inheritance, and dynamic binding to construct programs that are collections of interacting objects.

Several programming languages have been created specifically to support OOD and OOP: C++, Java, Smalltalk, Simula, CLOS, Objective-C, Eiffel, Actor, Object-Pascal, recent versions of Turbo Pascal, and others. These languages, called *object-oriented programming languages*, have facilities for

1. Data abstraction
2. Inheritance
3. Dynamic binding

You have already seen that C++ supports data abstraction through the class mechanism. Some non-OOP languages also have facilities for data abstraction. But only OOP languages support the other two concepts—*inheritance* and *dynamic binding.* Before we define these two concepts, we discuss some of the fundamental ideas and terminology of object-oriented programming.

14.2 Objects

In OOP, the term *object* has a very specific meaning: It is a self-contained entity encapsulating data and operations on the data. In other words, an object represents an instance of an ADT. More specifically, an object has an internal *state* (the current values of its private data, called *instance variables*), and it has a set of *methods* (public operations). Methods are the only means by which an object's state can be inspected or modified by another object. An object-oriented program consists of a collection of objects, communicating with one another by *message passing.* If object A wants object B to per-

PROGRAM

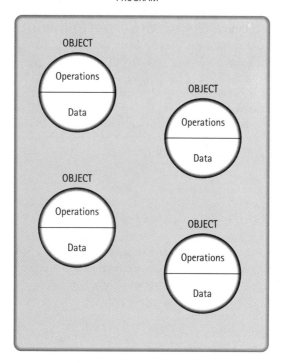

Figure 14–1   *Program Resulting from Object-Oriented Programming*

form some task, object A sends a message containing the name of the object (B, in this case) and the name of the particular method to execute. Object B responds by executing this method in its own way, possibly changing its state and sending messages to other objects as well.

Let's review the Time class that we defined in Chapter 11 to represent the ADT Time, and change it slightly to reflect object-oriented terminology and principles. There were seven operations (called responsibilities in object-oriented terminology): Set, Increment, Write, Equal, LessThan, and two constructors, one that takes hours, minutes, and seconds as parameters, and one that sets the time to zero.

In object-oriented terminology, there are two types of responsibilities (operations): action responsibilities and knowledge responsibilities. All of Time's are actions: They do or calculate something. However, an object needs to be able to report on its own status; that is, each object should have a function that reports the internal state of each appropriate private data variable. Such functions could replace the Write function or supplement it. If the client code can *inspect* the internal state (not *change* it), the code can print the time in a form that is relevant to the problem using the ADT. In this case, let's add these functions rather than replace Write. Operations that return the state of an internal variable are knowledge responsibilities.

Let's make another change in the `Time` class. Let's add a function to prompt for and read the values from the standard input device. Here then are the revised specification and implementation files for class `Time`. We omit the documentation that hasn't changed.

```
//********************************************************************
// SPECIFICATION FILE (Time.h)
// This file gives the specification of a Time ADT with
// action responsibilities and knowledge responsibilities
//********************************************************************

class Time
{
public:
    // Action responsibilities

    void Set( /* in */ int hours,
              /* in */ int minutes,
              /* in */ int seconds );

    void Increment();

    void Write() const;

    bool Equal( /* in */ Time otherTime ) const;

    bool LessThan( /* in */ Time otherTime ) const;

    Time( /* in */ int initHrs,
          /* in */ int initMins,
          /* in */ int initSecs );

    Time();

    void ReadTime();

        // Postcondition:
        //     hours, minutes, and seconds have been prompted for,
        //     read, and set

    // Knowledge responsibilities

    int Hours() const;
```

```
    // Postcondition:
    //      Return value is time

  int Minutes() const;

    // Postcondition:
    //      Return value is minutes

  int Seconds() const;

    // Postcondition:
    //      Return value is seconds


private:
    int hrs;
    int mins;
    int secs;
};
```

Here is the part of the implementation file for class Time that implements the changed functions.

```
//******************************************************************
// IMPLEMENTATION FILE (Time.cpp)
// This file implements the Time member functions
//******************************************************************

#include "Time.h"
#include <iostream>

using namespace std;
  ⋮


//******************************************************************

int Time::Hours() const

// Postcondition:
//      Return value is hrs

{
    return hrs;
}
```

```
//*****************************************************************

int Time::Minutes() const

// Postcondition:
//      Return value is mins

{
    return mins;
}

//*****************************************************************

int Time::Seconds() const

// Postcondition:
//      Return value is seconds

{
    return secs;
}

//*****************************************************************

void Time::ReadTime()

// Postcondition:
//      hours, minutes, and seconds have been prompted for, read,
//      and stored into hrs, mins, and secs

{
    cout << "Enter hours (<= 23): " << endl;
    cin >> hrs;
    cout << "Enter minutes (<= 59): " << endl;
    cin >> mins;
    cout << "Enter seconds (<= 59): " << endl;
    cin >>  secs;
}

//*****************************************************************
```

In C++, we define the properties and behavior of objects by using the class mechanism. Within a program, classes can be related to each other in various ways. The three most common relationships are as follows:

1. Two classes are independent of each other and have nothing in common.

2. Two classes are related by *inheritance.*

3. Two classes are related by *composition.*

The first relationship—none—is not very interesting. Let's look at the other two—inheritance and composition.

14.3 Inheritance

In the world at large, it is often possible to arrange concepts into an *inheritance hierarchy*—a hierarchy in which each concept inherits the properties of the concept immediately above it in the hierarchy. For example, we might classify different kinds of vehicles according to the inheritance hierarchy in Figure 14–2. Moving down the hierarchy, each kind of vehicle is more specialized than its *parent* (and all of its *ancestors*) and is more general than its *child* (and all of its *descendants*). A wheeled vehicle inherits properties common to all vehicles (it holds one or more people and carries them from place to place) but has an additional property that makes it more specialized (it has wheels). A car inherits properties common to all wheeled vehicles but also has additional, more specialized properties (four wheels, an engine, a body, and so forth).

The inheritance relationship can be viewed as an *is-a relationship*. Every two-door car is a car, every car is a wheeled vehicle, and every wheeled vehicle is a vehicle.

OOP languages provide a way of creating inheritance relationships among classes. In these languages, **inheritance** is the mechanism by which one class acquires the properties of another class. You can take an existing class A (called the **base class** or **superclass**) and create from it a new class B (called the **derived class** or **subclass**). The derived class B inherits all the

> **Inheritance**   A mechanism by which one class acquires the properties—the data and operations—of another class.
>
> **Base class (superclass)**   The class being inherited from.
>
> **Derived class (subclass)**   The class that inherits.

properties of its base class A. In particular, the data and operations defined for A are now also defined for B. (Notice the "is-a" relationship—every B is also an A.) The idea,

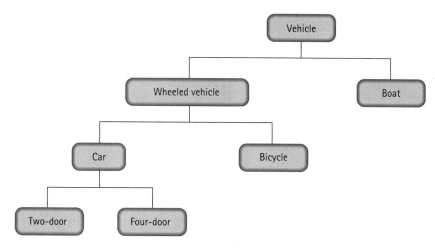

Figure 14–2   *Inheritance Hierarchy*

next, is to specialize class B, usually by adding specific properties to those already inherited from A. Let's look at an example in C++.

Deriving One Class from Another

Suppose that we want to modify the Time class in the last section by adding, as private data, a variable of an enumeration type indicating the (American) time zone—for example, EST for Eastern Standard Time. We'll need to modify the Set function and the class constructors to accommodate a time zone value. And the Write function should print the time in the form

```
12:34:10 CST
```

In C++, as in other OOP languages, there is a quick way in which to add time zone features: Use inheritance. Let's derive a new class from the Time class and then specialize it. This new, extended time class—call it ExtTime—inherits the members of its base class, Time. Here is the declaration of ExtTime:

```
enum ZoneType {EST, CST, MST, PST, EDT, CDT, MDT, PDT};

class ExtTime : public Time
{
public:
    void Set( /* in */ int        hours,
              /* in */ int        minutes,
              /* in */ int        seconds,
              /* in */ ZoneType timeZone );
    void Write() const;
    ZoneType zone();   // Returns the time zone
    ExtTime( /* in */ int        initHrs,      // Constructor
             /* in */ int        initMins,
             /* in */ int        initSecs,
             /* in */ ZoneType initZone );
    ExtTime();                                  // Default constructor,
                                                //   setting time to
                                                //   0:0:0 EST
private:
    ZoneType zone;
};
```

The opening line

```
class ExtTime : public Time
```

states that ExtTime is derived from Time. The reserved word public declares Time to be a *public base class* of ExtTime. This means that all public members of Time (except constructors) are also public members of ExtTime. In other words, Time's member functions Set, Increment, and Write can also be invoked for ExtTime objects.* However, the public part of ExtTime specializes the base class by reimplementing (redefining) the inherited functions Set and Write and by providing its own constructors and a function to return the time zone.

The private part of ExtTime declares that a new private member is added: zone. The private members of ExtTime are therefore hrs, mins, secs (all inherited from Time), and zone. Figure 14–3 pictures the relationship between the ExtTime and Time classes. This diagram shows that each ExtTime object has a Time object as a *subobject*. Every ExtTime is a Time, and more.

In Figure 14–3, you see an arrow between the two ovals labeled Increment. Because Time is a public base class of ExtTime, and because Increment is not redefined by ExtTime, the Increment function available to clients of ExtTime is the same as the one inherited from Time. We use the arrow between the corresponding ovals to indicate this fact. (Notice in the diagram that Time's constructors are operations on Time, not on ExtTime. The ExtTime class must have its own constructors.)

Inheritance and Accessibility

With C++, it is important to understand that inheritance does not imply accessibility. Although a derived class inherits the members of its base class, both private and public, it cannot access the private members of the base class. Figure 14–3 shows the variables hrs, mins, and secs to be encapsulated within the Time class. Neither external client code nor ExtTime member functions can refer to these three variables directly. If a derived class were able to access the private members of its base class, any programmer could derive a class from another and then write code to directly inspect or modify the private data, defeating the benefits of encapsulation and information hiding.

---

*If a class declaration omits the word public and begins as

class DerivedClass : BaseClass

or if it explicitly uses the word private,

class DerivedClass : private BaseClass

then BaseClass is called a *private base class* of DerivedClass. Public members of BaseClass are *not* public members of DerivedClass. That is, clients of DerivedClass cannot invoke BaseClass operations on DerivedClass objects. We do not work with private base classes in this book.

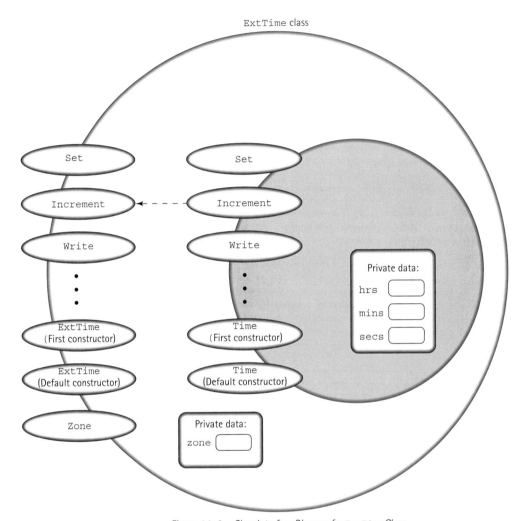

Figure 14–3 *Class Interface Diagram for* ExtTime *Class*

Specification of the ExtTime Class

Below is the fully documented specification of the ExtTime class. Notice that the pre-processor directive

```
#include "time.h"
```

is necessary for the compiler to verify the consistency of the derived class with its base class.

```
//****************************************************************
// SPECIFICATION FILE (exttime.h)
// This file gives the specification of an ExtTime abstract data
// type.  The Time class is a public base class of ExtTime, so
```

```
// public operations of Time are also public operations of ExtTime.
//*****************************************************************
#include "time.h"

enum ZoneType {EST, CST, MST, PST, EDT, CDT, MDT, PDT};

class ExtTime : public Time
{
public:
    void Set( /* in */ int      hours,
              /* in */ int      minutes,
              /* in */ int      seconds,
              /* in */ ZoneType timeZone );
        // Precondition:
        //      0 <= hours <= 23  &&  0 <= minutes <= 59
        //   && 0 <= seconds <= 59  &&  timeZone is assigned
        // Postcondition:
        //      Time is set according to the incoming parameters

    void Write() const;
        // Postcondition:
        //      Time has been output in the form HH:MM:SS ZZZ
        //      where ZZZ is the time zone

    ZoneType Zone () const;
        // Postcondition:
        //      Return value == zone

    ExtTime( /* in */ int      initHrs,
             /* in */ int      initMins,
             /* in */ int      initSecs,
             /* in */ ZoneType initZone );
        // Precondition:
        //      0 <= initHrs <= 23  &&  0 <= initMins <= 59
        //   && 0 <= initSecs <= 59  &&  initZone is assigned
        // Postcondition:
        //      Class object is constructed
        //   && Time is set according to the incoming parameters

    ExtTime();
        // Postcondition:
        //      Class object is constructed
        //   && Time is 0:0:0 Eastern Standard Time
private:
    ZoneType zone;
};
```

With this new class, the programmer can set the time with a time zone (via a class constructor or the redefined `Set` function), output the time with its time zone (via the redefined `Write` function), and increment the time by one second (via the inherited `Increment` function):

```cpp
//*********************************************************************
// TimeDemo program
// This is a very simple client of the ExtTime class
//*********************************************************************
#include <iostream>
#include "exttime.h"    // For ExtTime class

using namespace std;

int main()
{
    ExtTime time1(5, 30, 0, CDT);  // Parameterized constructor used
    ExtTime time2;                 // Default constructor used
    int     loopCount;

    cout << "time1: ";
    time1.Write();
    cout << endl << "time2: ";
    time2.Write();
    cout << endl;

    time2.Set(23, 59, 55, PST);
    cout << "New time2: ";
    time2.Write();
    cout << endl;

    cout << "Incrementing time2:" << endl;
    for (loopCount = 1; loopCount <= 10; loopCount++)
    {
        time2.Write();
        cout << ' ';
        time2.Increment();
    }
    return 0;
}
```

When executed, the TimeDemo program produces the following output.

```
time1: 05:30:00 CDT
time2: 00:00:00 EST
New time2: 23:59:55 PST
```

```
Incrementing time2:
23:59:55 PST 23:59:56 PST 23:59:57 PST 23:59:58 PST 23:59:59 PST
00:00:00 PST 00:00:01 PST 00:00:02 PST 00:00:03 PST 00:00:04 PST
```

Implementation of the ExtTime Class

The implementation of the ExtTime class needs to deal only with the new features that are different from Time. Specifically, we must write code to redefine the Set and Write functions and we must write the two constructors.

With derived classes, constructors are subject to special rules. At run time, the base class constructor is implicitly called first, before the body of the derived class's constructor executes. Additionally, if the base class constructor requires arguments, these arguments must be passed by the derived class's constructor. To see how these rules pertain, let's examine the implementation file exttime.cpp.

```cpp
//******************************************************************
// IMPLEMENTATION FILE (exttime.cpp)
// This file implements the ExtTime member functions.
// The Time class is a public base class of ExtTime
//******************************************************************
#include "exttime.h"
#include <iostream>
#include <string>

using namespace std;

// Additional private members of class:
//      ZoneType zone;


//******************************************************************

ExtTime::ExtTime( /* in */ int      initHrs,
                  /* in */ int      initMins,
                  /* in */ int      initSecs,
                  /* in */ ZoneType initZone )

    : Time(initHrs, initMins, initSecs)

// Constructor

// Precondition:
//      0 <= initHrs <= 23   &&   0 <= initMins <= 59
//      && 0 <= initSecs <= 59   &&   initZone is assigned
// Postcondition:
//      Time is set according to initHrs, initMins, and initSecs
```

```
//      (via call to base class constructor)
//   && zone == initZone

{
    zone = initZone;
}

//**********************************************************************

ExtTime::ExtTime()

// Default constructor

// Postcondition:
//      Time is 0:0:0 (via implicit call to base class's
//      default constructor)
//   && zone == EST

{
    zone = EST;
}

//**********************************************************************

void ExtTime::Set( /* in */ int      hours,
                   /* in */ int      minutes,
                   /* in */ int      seconds,
                   /* in */ ZoneType timeZone )

// Precondition:
//      0 <= hours <= 23   &&   0 <= minutes <= 59
//   && 0 <= seconds <= 59   &&   timeZone is assigned
// Postcondition:
//      Time is set according to hours, minutes, and seconds
//   && zone == timeZone

{
    Time::Set(hours, minutes, seconds);
    zone = timeZone;
}

//**********************************************************************

    ZoneType ExtTime::Zone() const
```

```
    // Postcondition:
    //      Return value == zone

    {
        return zone;
    }

//*****************************************************************

void ExtTime::Write() const

// Postcondition:
//      Time has been output in the form HH:MM:SS ZZZ
//      where ZZZ is the time zone

{
    static string zoneString[8] =
    {
        "EST", "CST", "MST", "PST", "EDT", "CDT", "MDT", "PDT"
    };

    Time::Write();
    cout << ' ' << zoneString[zone];
}
```

In the first constructor in Figure 14–5, notice the syntax by which a constructor passes arguments to its base class constructor:

```
ExtTime::ExtTime( /* in */ int       initHrs,
                  /* in */ int       initMins,
                  /* in */ int       initSecs,
                  /* in */ ZoneType initZone )

    : Time(initHrs, initMins, initSecs)      ←   Constructor initializer

{
    zone = initZone;
}
```

After the parameter list to the ExtTime constructor (but before its body), you insert what is called a *constructor initializer*—a colon and then the name of the base class along with the arguments to *its* constructor. When an ExtTime object is created with a declaration such as

```
ExtTime time1(8, 35, 0, PST);
```

the ExtTime constructor receives four arguments. The first three are simply passed along to the Time class constructor by means of the constructor initializer. After the

`Time` class constructor has executed (creating the base class subobject as shown in Figure 14–3), the body of the `ExtTime` constructor executes, setting `zone` equal to the fourth argument.

The second constructor in the implementation file (the default constructor) does not need a constructor initializer; there are no arguments to pass to the base class's default constructor. When an `ExtTime` object is created with the declaration

```
ExtTime time2;
```

the `ExtTime` class's default constructor first implicitly calls `Time`'s default constructor, after which its body executes, setting `zone` to EST.

Next, look at the `Set` function. This function reimplements the `Set` function inherited from the base class. Consequently, there are two distinct `Set` functions, one a public member of the `Time` class, the other a public member of the `ExtTime` class. Their full names are `Time::Set` and `ExtTime::Set`. The `ExtTime::Set` function begins by "reaching up" into its base class and calling `Time::Set` to set the hours, minutes, and seconds. (Remember that a class derived from `Time` cannot access the private data `hrs`, `mins`, and `secs` directly; these variables are private to the `Time` class.) The function then finishes by assigning a value to `ExtTime`'s private data, the `zone` variable.

The `Write` function uses a similar strategy. It reaches up into its base class and invokes `Time::Write` to output the hours, minutes, and seconds. Then it outputs a string corresponding to the time zone. The `Write` function establishes an array of eight strings and selects the correct string by using `zone` to index into the array. Why is `zoneString` declared to be `static`? Remember that by default, local variables in C++ are automatic variables—that is, memory is allocated for them when the function begins execution and is deallocated when the function returns. With `zoneString` declared as `static`, the array is allocated once only, when the program begins execution, and remains allocated until the program terminates. From function call to function call, the computer does not waste time creating and destroying the array.

Now we can compile the file `exttime.cpp` into an object code file, say, `exttime.obj`. After writing a test driver and compiling it into `test.obj`, we obtain an executable file by linking three object files:

1. `test.obj`
2. `exttime.obj`
3. `time.obj`

We can then test the resulting program.

The remarkable thing about derived classes and inheritance is that modification of the base class is unnecessary. The source code for the implementation of the `Time` class may be unavailable. Yet variations of this ADT can continue to be created without that source code, in ways the creator never even considered. Through classes and inheritance, OOP languages facilitate code reuse. A class such as `Time` can be used as-is in many different contexts, or it can be adapted to a particular context by using inheritance. Inheritance allows us to create *extensible* data abstractions—a derived class typically extends the base class by including additional private data or public operations or both.

Avoiding Multiple Inclusion of Header Files

We saw that the specification file `exttime.h` begins with an `#include` directive to insert the file `time.h`:

```
#include "time.h"

enum ZoneType {EST, CST, MST, PST, EDT, CDT, MDT, PDT};

class ExtTime : public Time
{
    :
};
```

Now think about what happens if a programmer using the `ExtTime` class already has included `time.h` for other purposes, overlooking the fact that `exttime.h` also includes it:

```
#include "time.h"
#include "exttime.h"
```

The preprocessor inserts the file `time.h`, then `exttime.h`, and then `time.h` a second time (because `exttime.h` also includes `time.h`). The result is a compile-time error, because the `Time` class is defined twice.

The widely used solution to this problem is to write `time.h` this way:

```
#ifndef TIME_H
#define TIME_H
class Time
{
    :
};
#endif
```

The lines beginning with "#" are directives to the preprocessor. `TIME_H` (or any identifier you wish to use) is a preprocessor identifier, not a C++ program identifier. In effect, these directives say:

If the preprocessor identifier `TIME_H` is not already defined, then

  1. define `TIME_H` as an identifier known to the preprocessor,

and

  2. let the declaration of the `Time` class pass through to the compiler.

If a subsequent `#include "time.h"` is encountered, the test `#ifndef TIME_H` will fail. The `Time` class declaration will not pass through to the compiler a second time.

14.4 Composition

Earlier we said that two classes typically exhibit one of the following relationships: They are independent of each other, they are related by inheritance, or they are related by composition. Composition (or containment) is the relationship in which the internal data of one class A includes an object of another class B. Stated another way, a B object is contained within an A object.

> **Composition (containment)**   A mechanism by which the internal data (the state) of one class includes an object of another class.

C++ does not have (nor need) any special language notation for composition. You simply declare an object of one class to be one of the data members of another class. Let's look at an example.

Design of an Entry Class

You are developing a program to represent an appointment book. Each day object will be a sorted list of appointment objects. In preparation, you decide to build an Entry ADT with two fields, an object of a Name ADT and an object of a Time ADT. You may need to add more information for an appointment object later, but this gives you a start. Constructing this object should be easy because you already have a `Time` class and a `Name` class. For the purpose of an appointment calendar, you decide to ignore middle name or initial and the seconds in the time. You can always add the middle name later if you need it. Of course, you do need operations that return the name and time to the client program.

The operations can be `NameStr`, which returns a name composed of the first and last name, and `TimeStr`, which returns the hours and minutes with a colon between. Of course, we need constructors. How many? Well, you know that the `Name` class has two constructors, one that takes the parts of the name as parameters and one that reads the name from the standard input device (default). The same thing is true of the `Time` class. Thus, we need a default constructor for `Entry` class, which will call the default constructors for `Name` and `Time`, and a parameterized constructor, which will pass the parameters to `Name`'s and `Time`'s parameterized constructors.

```
//*****************************************************************
// SPECIFICATION FILE (Entry.h)
// This file contains the specification of the Entry ADT,
// which has two contained classes, Name and Time
//*****************************************************************

#include "Time.h"
#include "Name.h"
#include <string>

class Entry
{
```

```
public:
    string NameStr() const;
        // Returns a string made up of first name, blank, last name
        // Postcondition:
        //      Return value is first name of Name object, blank,
        //      and last name of Name object
    string TimeStr() const;
        // Returns a string made up of hour, colon, minutes
        // Postcondition:
        //      Return value is minutes from Time object, colon, and
        //      seconds of Time object
    Entry();
        // Default constructor
        // Postcondition:
        //      Entry object has been constructed

    Entry( (/* in */ string firstName,    // First name
            /* in */ string middleName,    // Middle name
            /* in */ string lastName)      // Last name
            /* in */ int    initHours,     // Hours
            /* in */ int    initMinutes,   // Minutes
            /* in */ int    initSeconds )  // Seconds
        // Parameterized constructor
        // Postcondtion:
        //      Entry object has been constructed with firstName,
        //      middleName, and lastName as arguments to Name
        //      parameterized constructor; Time object
        //      initHours, initMinutes, and initSeconds as arguments
        //      to Time parameterized constructor

private:
    Name name;
    Time time;
}
```

Implementing the member functions Name and Time is easy: They just involve invoking member functions of Name and Time. The specification files for each of these classes provide the interface that the functions must use. An abbreviated version of Name.h is shown below; Time.h has been shown previously in this chapter.

```
// SPECIFICATION FILE (Name.h)
...
enum RelationType{BEFORE, SAME, AFTER};
class Name
```

```
{
public:
    Name();
        // Default constructor
        // Postcondition:
        //      Name is prompted for and read from the standard input
        //      device
    Name( /* in */ string firstName,
          /* in */ string middleName,
          /* in */ string lastName );
        // Parameterized constructor
        // Postcondition:
        //      first is firstName AND middle is middleName AND
        //      last is lastName
    string FirstName() const;
        // Postcondition:
        //      Return value is this person's first name

    string LastName() const;
        // Postcondition:
        //      Return value is this person's last name


    . . .
};
```

Implementing the default class constructors involves invoking the default constructors for the Name object and the Time object. The default Entry constructor has nothing
else to do. Thus, the body of the default constructor for Entry is empty. The parameterized constructor must pass the parameters to the Name and Time constructors. How is
this done? We use the constructor initializer that we described in the last section. Thus,
the parameterized constructor for Entry also has no body.

```
//*****************************************************************
// IMPLEMENTATION FILE (Entry.cpp)
// This file contains the specification of the Entry ADT,
// which has two contained classes, Name and Time
//*****************************************************************

#include "Entry.h"
#include <string>

#include <fstream>
#include <iostream>
using namespace std;
string Entry::NameStr() const
```

```
    // Returns a string made up of first name, blank, last name
    // Postcondition:
    //    Return value is first name of Name object, blank, and
    //    last name of Name object

{

    return (name.FirstName() + ' ' + name.LastName());
}

string Entry::TimeStr() const

    // Returns a string made up of hour, colon, minutes
    // Postcondition:
    //       Return value is minutes from Time object, colon, and
    //       seconds of Time object

{

    return "" + time.Hours() + ":" + time.Minutes();
}

bool Entry::LessThan(Entry entry) const

    // Compares time with entry.time
    // Postcondition:
    //       Return value is true if time is less than entry.time;
    //       false otherwise

{

    return time.LessThan(entry.time);
}

bool Entry::Equal(Entry entry) const

    // Compares time with entry.time
    // Postcondition:
    //       Return value is true if self is equal to entry.time;
    //       false otherwise

{

    return time.Equal(entry.time);
}

Entry::Entry()
```

```
        // Default constructor
        // Postcondition:
        //      Entry object has been constructed
{
}

Entry::Entry( /* in */ string firstName,
              /* in */ string middleName,
              /* in */ string lastName,
              /* in */ int   initHours,
              /* in */ int   initMinutes,
              /* in */ int   initSeconds )

  // Constructor initializers
  : name(firstName, middleName, lastName),
    time(initHours, initMinutes, initSeconds)

      // Parameterized constructor
      // Postcondtion:
      //      Entry object has been constructed with firstName,
      //      middleName, and lastName as arguments to Name
      //      parameterized constructor; initHours, initMinutes,
      //      and initSeconds as arguments to Time parameterized
      //      constructor

{
}
```

Testing: Here is a driver that creates two objects of class Entry and applies the appropriate functions to them.

```
//******************************************************************
// DRIVER for class Entry
// This program tests the constructors and return functions
//******************************************************************

#include <iostream>
#include "Entry.h"

using namespace std;

int main()
{
    Entry entry1("Sally", "Jane", "Smith", 12, 20, 0);
    Entry entry2("Mary", "Beth", "Jones", 10, 30, 0);
```

```
    entry1.ReadEntry();

    cout << "Entry 1: " << entry1.NameStr() << " "
         << entry1.TimeStr() << endl;
    cout << "Entry 2: " << entry2.NameStr() << " "
         << entry2.TimeStr() << endl;
    return 0;
}
```

What? Class Entry doesn't compile? We get the following error message:

```
Error    : illegal operand
EntryEr.cpp line 33   return "" + time.Hours() + ":" +
time.Minutes();
```

What could be wrong with this statement? We just created a string out of a string, an integer value, a colon, and another integer value. We have used concatenation to build stings since Chapter 2. Numbers are converted to strings for output. What's different about this statement? The C++ system automatically converts integers to strings *for output*, but there is no type cast from integers to strings except for output.

In order to create a string including integers, we could write it out to a file and then read it back in as a string. This would work, but it would be extremely time consuming (disk access is over a million times slower than memory access). Fortunately, the designers of the language realized that there might be times when a conversion from integers to strings would be useful. Thus they derived a class called stringstream from class iostream, which allows us to write values to a string as if we were writing them to a file. Because the data is not actually sent to a file but is kept in memory, the conversion is done quickly.

We declare an object of class ostringstream, and use the insertion operator (<<) to send the integers to the object. To get them back as a string, we use the str member function of class ostringstream. Here then is the corrected version of TimeStr, using an object of class ostringstream, followed by the output from the driver.

```
#include <sstream>          // ostringstream
string Entry::TimeStr() const

// Returns a string made up of hour, colon, minutes, colon, seconds
// Postcondition:
//     Return value is minutes from Time object, colon, and
//     seconds of Time object

{
    string outStr;
    ostringstream tempOut;  // Access ostringstream
```

```
    if (time.Hours() < 10)
        tempOut << '0';
    tempOut << time.Hours() << ":";
    if (time.Minutes() < 10)
        tempOut << '0';
    tempOut << time.Minutes() << ":";
    if (time.Seconds() < 10);
        tempOut << '0';
    tempOut << time.Seconds();
    outStr = tempOut.str();
    return outStr;
}
```

Once this function is inserted, the driver produces this output.

Constructor Initializer

We've twice seen the unusual notation—the constructor initializer—inserted between the parameter list and the body of a constructor. The first time was when we implemented the parameterized ExtTime class constructor. There, we used the constructor initializer to pass some of the incoming arguments to the base class constructor. Here, we use a constructor initializer to pass some of the arguments to member objects' (name's and time's) constructors. Whether you are using inheritance or composition, the purpose of a constructor initializer is the same: to pass arguments to another constructor. The only difference is the following: With inheritance, you specify the name of the *base class* prior to the argument list, as follows:

```
ExtTime::ExtTime( /* in */ int      initHrs,
                  /* in */ int      initMins,
                  /* in */ int      initSecs,
                  /* in */ ZoneType initZone )

    : Time(initHrs, initMins, initSecs)
```

With composition, you specify the name of the *member object* prior to the argument list:

```
Entry::Entry( /* in */ string firstName,
              /* in */ string middleName,
              /* in */ string lastName,
              /* in */ int   initHours,
              /* in */ int   initMinutes )
// Constructor initializers
  : name(firstName, middleName, lastName),
    time(initHours, initMinutes)
```

Having discussed both inheritance and composition, we can give a complete description of the order in which constructors are executed:

Given a class X, if X is a derived class, its base class constructor is executed first. Next, constructors for member objects (if any) are executed. Finally, the body of X's constructor is executed.

When an `Entry` object is created, the constructors for its `name` member and its `time` member are first invoked. After the `name` and `time` objects are constructed, the body of `Entry`'s constructor is executed, which in this case is empty.

14.5 Dynamic Binding and Virtual Functions

Early in the chapter, we said that object-oriented programming languages provide language features that support three concepts: data abstraction, inheritance, and dynamic binding. The phrase *dynamic binding* means, more specifically, *dynamic binding of an operation to an object*. To explain this concept, let's begin with an example.

Given the `Time` and `ExtTime` classes of this chapter, the following code creates two class objects and outputs the time represented by each.

```
Time    startTime(8, 30, 0);
ExtTime endTime(10, 45, 0, CST);

startTime.Write();
cout << endl;
endTime.Write();
cout << endl;
```

This code fragment invokes two different `Write` functions, even though the functions appear to have the same name. The first function call invokes the `Write` function of the `Time` class, printing out three values: hours, minutes, and seconds. The second call

> **Static binding**   The compile-time determination of which function to call for a particular object.

invokes the `Write` function of the `ExtTime` class, printing out four values: hours, minutes, seconds, and time zone. In this code fragment, the compiler uses **static (compile-time) binding** of the operation (`Write`) to the appropriate object. The compiler can easily determine which `Write` function to call by checking the data type of the associated object.

In some situations, the compiler cannot determine the type of an object, and the binding of an operation to an object must occur at run time. One situation, which we look at now, involves passing class objects as arguments.

The basic C++ rule for passing class objects as arguments is that the argument and its corresponding parameter must be of identical type. With inheritance, though, C++ relaxes the rule. You may pass an object of a child class *C* to an object of its parent class *P*, but not the other way around—that is, you cannot pass an object of type *P* to an object of type *C*. More generally, you can pass an object of a descendant class to an object of any of its ancestor classes. This rule has a tremendous benefit—it allows us to write a single function that applies to any descendant class instead of writing a different function for each. For example, we could write a fancy `Print` function that takes as an argument an object of type `Time` or any class descended from `Time`:

```
void Print( /* in */ Time someTime )
{
    cout << "*************************" << endl;
    cout << "** The time is ";
    someTime.Write();
    cout << endl;
    cout << "*************************" << endl;
}
```

Given the code fragment

```
Time    startTime(8, 30, 0);
ExtTime endTime(10, 45, 0, CST);

Print(startTime);
Print(endTime);
```

the compiler lets us pass either a `Time` object or an `ExtTime` object to the `Print` function. Unfortunately, the output is not what we would like. When `endTime` is printed, the time zone `CST` is missing from the output. Let's see why.

The Slicing Problem

Our `Print` function uses passing by value for the parameter `someTime`. Passing by value sends a copy of the argument to the parameter. Whenever you pass an object of a child class to an object of its parent class using a pass by value, only the data members they have in common are copied. Remember that a child class is often "larger" than its parent—that is, it contains additional data members. For example, a `Time` object has three data members (`hrs`, `mins`, and `secs`), but an `ExtTime` object has four data members (`hrs`, `mins`, `secs`, and `zone`). When the larger class object is copied to the smaller parameter using a pass by value, the extra data members are discarded or "sliced off." This situation is called the *slicing problem* (see Figure 14–4).

(The slicing problem also occurs with assignment operations. In the statement

```
parentClassObject = childClassObject;
```

only the data members that the two objects have in common are copied. Additional data members contained in `childClassObject` are not copied.)

With passing by reference, the slicing problem does not occur because the *address* of the caller's argument is sent to the function. Let's change the heading of our `Print` function so that `someTime` is a reference parameter:

```
void Print( /* in */ Time& someTime )
```

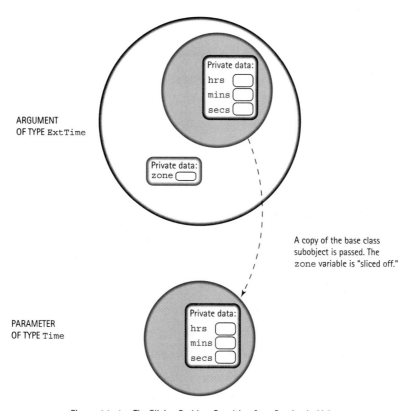

ARGUMENT
OF TYPE `ExtTime`

Private data:
hrs
mins
secs

Private data:
zone

A copy of the base class subobject is passed. The zone variable is "sliced off."

PARAMETER
OF TYPE `Time`

Private data:
hrs
mins
secs

Figure 14–4   *The Slicing Problem Resulting from Passing by Value*

Now when we pass endTime as the argument, its address is sent to the function. Its time zone member is not sliced off because no copying takes place. But to our dismay, the Print function *still* prints only three of endTime's data members—hours, minutes, and seconds.

Within the Print function, the difficulty is that static binding is used in the statement

```
someTime.Write();
```

The compiler must generate machine language code for the Print function at compile time, but the type of the actual argument (Time or ExtTime) isn't known until run time. How can the compiler know which Write function to use—Time::Write or ExtTime::Write? The compiler cannot know, so it uses Time::Write because the parameter someTime is of type Time. Therefore, the Print function always prints just three values—hours, minutes, and seconds—regardless of the type of the argument. Fortunately, C++ provides a very simple solution to our problem: *virtual functions.*

Virtual Functions

Suppose we make one small change to our Time class declaration: We begin the declaration of the Write function with the reserved word virtual.

```
class Time
{
public:
    ⋮
    virtual void Write() const;
    ⋮
private:
    ⋮
};
```

Dynamic binding   The run-time determination of which function to call for a particular object.

Declaring a member function to be virtual instructs the compiler to generate code that guarantees **dynamic** (run-time) **binding** of a function to an object. That is, the determination of which function to call is postponed until run time. (Note that to make Write a virtual function, the word virtual appears in one place only—the Time class declaration. It does not appear in the Write function definition that is located in the time.cpp file, nor does it appear in any descendant class—such as ExtTime—that redefines the Write function.)

Virtual functions work in the following way. If a class object is passed *by reference* to some function, and if the body of that function contains a statement

```
param.MemberFunc( ... );
```

then

1. If `MemberFunc` is not a virtual function, the type of the *parameter* determines which function to call. (Static binding is used.)

2. If `MemberFunc` is a virtual function, the type of the *argument* determines which function to call. (Dynamic binding is used.)

With just one word—`virtual`—the difficulties we encountered with our `Print` function disappear entirely. If we declare `Write` to be a virtual function in the `Time` class, the function

```
void Print( /* in */ Time& someTime )
{
    ⋮
    someTime.Write();
    ⋮
}
```

works correctly for arguments either of type `Time` or of type `ExtTime`. The correct `Write` function (`Time::Write` or `ExtTime::Write`) is invoked because the argument carries the information necessary at run time to choose the appropriate function. Deriving a new and unanticipated class from `Time` presents no complications. If this new class redefines the `Write` function, then our `Print` function still works correctly. Dynamic binding ensures that each object knows how to print itself, and the appropriate version will be invoked. In OOP terminology, `Write` is a **polymorphic operation**—an operation that has multiple meanings depending on the type of the object that responds to it at run time.

> **Polymorphic operation** An operation that has multiple meanings depending on the type of the object to which it is bound at run time.

Here are some things to know about using virtual functions in C++:

1. To obtain dynamic binding, you must use passing by reference when passing a class object to a function. If you use passing by value, the compiler does not use the `virtual` mechanism; instead, member slicing and static binding occur.

2. In the declaration of a virtual function, the word `virtual` appears only in the base class, not in any derived class.

3. If a base class declares a virtual function, it *must* implement that function, even if the body is empty.

4. A derived class is not required to provide its own reimplementation of a virtual function. In this case, the base class's version is used by default.

5. A derived class cannot redefine the function return type of a virtual function.

14.6 Object-Oriented Design

We have looked at language features that let us implement an object-oriented design. Now let's turn to the phase that precedes implementation—OOD itself.

A computer program usually models some real-life activity or concept. A banking program models the real-life activities associated with a bank. A spreadsheet program models a real spreadsheet, a large paper form used by accountants and financial planners. A robotics program models human perception and human motion.

Nearly always, the aspect of the world that we are modeling (the *application domain* or *problem domain*) consists of objects—checking accounts, bank tellers, spreadsheet rows, spreadsheet columns, robot arms, robot legs. The computer program that solves the real-life problem also includes objects (the *solution domain*)—counters, lists, menus, windows, and so forth. OOD is based on the philosophy that programs are easier to write and understand if the major objects in a program correspond closely to the objects in the problem domain.

There are many ways in which to perform object-oriented design. Different authors advocate different techniques. Our purpose is not to choose one particular technique or to present a summary of all the techniques. Rather, our purpose is to describe a three-step process that captures the essence of OOD:

1. Identify the objects and operations.
2. Determine the relationships among objects.
3. Design the driver.

In this section, we do not show a complete example of an object-oriented design. Instead, we describe the important issues involved in each of the three steps.

Step 1: Identify the Objects and Operations

OOD begins by identifying the major objects and the associated operations on those objects. To identify solution-domain objects, a good way to start is to look at the problem domain. More specifically, go to the problem definition and look for important nouns and verbs. The nouns (and noun phrases) may suggest objects; the verbs (and verb phrases) may suggest operations. The nouns-and-verbs technique is only a starting point—it points us to *potential* objects and operations.

Determining which nouns and verbs are significant is one of the most difficult aspects of OOD. There are no cookbook formulas for doing so, and there probably never will be. Not all nouns become objects, and not all verbs become operations. The nouns-and-verbs technique is imperfect, but it does give us a first approximation to a solution.

The solution domain includes not only objects drawn from the problem domain but also *implementation-level* objects. These are objects that do not model the problem domain but are used in building the program itself. Objects such as these are often available in class libraries so that we don't need to design and implement them from scratch each time we need them in different programs.

Step 2: Determine the Relationships Among Objects

After selecting potential objects and operations, the next step is to examine the relationships among the objects. In particular, we want to see whether certain objects might be related either by inheritance or by composition. Inheritance and composition relationships not only pave the way for code reuse—as we emphasized in our discussion of OOP—but also simplify the design and allow us to model the problem domain more accurately.

Step 3: Design the Driver

The final step is to design the driver—the top-level algorithm. In OOD, the driver is the glue that puts the objects (along with their operations) together. When implementing the design in C++, the driver becomes the `main` function.

Notice that structured design *begins* with the design of the top-level algorithm, whereas OOD *ends* with the top-level algorithm. In OOD, most of the control flow has already been designed in steps 1 and 2; the algorithms are located within the operations on objects. As a result, the driver often has very little to do but process user commands or input some data and then delegate tasks to various objects.

14.7 Implementing the Design

In OOD, when we first identify an object, it is an *abstract object*. We do not immediately choose an exact data representation for that object. Similarly, the operations on objects begin as *abstract operations*, because there is no initial attempt to provide algorithms for these operations.

Eventually, we have to implement the objects and operations. For each abstract object, we must

- Choose a suitable data representation.
- Create algorithms for the abstract operations.

To select a data representation for an object, the C++ programmer has three options:

1. Use a built-in data type.
2. Use an existing ADT.
3. Create a new ADT.

For a given object, a good rule of thumb is to consider these three options in the order listed. A built-in type is the most straightforward to use and understand, and operations on these types are already defined by the language. If a built-in type is not adequate to represent an object, you should survey available ADTs in a class library (either the system's or your own) to see if any are a good match for the abstract object. If no suitable ADT exists, you must design and implement a new ADT to represent the object.

Fortunately, even if you must resort to option 3, the mechanisms of inheritance and composition allow you to combine options 2 and 3. When we needed an `ExtTime` class earlier in the chapter, we used inheritance to build on an existing `Time` class. And when we created an `Entry` class, we used composition to include a `Time` object and `Name` object in the private data.

In addition to choosing a data representation for the abstract object, we must implement the abstract operations. With OOD, the algorithms that implement the abstract operations are often short and straightforward. We have seen numerous examples in this chapter in which the code for ADT operations is only a few lines long. But this is not always the case. If an operation is extremely complex, it may be best to treat the operation as a new problem and use functional decomposition on the control flow. In this situation, it is appropriate to apply both functional decomposition and object-oriented methodologies together. Experienced programmers are familiar with both methodologies and use them either independently or in combination with each other. However, the software development community is becoming increasingly convinced that although functional decomposition is important for designing low-level algorithms and operations on ADTs, the future in developing huge software systems lies in OOD and OOP.

Programming Example

Creating an Appointment Calendar

PROBLEM   Create an appointment calendar with the following operations:

> Given a date, insert a time and name pair.
> Given a date, return the day's time and name pairs in order of time.
> Given a date and a time, return true if the time is free, false otherwise.

DISCUSSION   What are the objects in this description? A date, a time, a name, and a collection of time/name pairs for each date. All of the operations begin "Given a date" and involve doing something with name/time pairs. Let's simplify this problem by implementing a list of name/time pairs first. The next step would be to combine the list of name/time pairs with a date to create a day's list of appointments.

We already have a `Name` class, a `Time` class, and an `Entry` class made up of `Name` and `Time` objects. Collection is another name for a list. We have a `List` class. It looks like this problem is simply putting building blocks together, where the building blocks are classes. We can use each of these classes directly except for the `List` class.

The `List` class is a list of `ItemType` objects in which `ItemType` is set by a Typedef statement. In the case study in the last chapter, we used the `List` class to hold a list of integers. Here we have a list of `Entry` objects, which should be ordered by time. That's OK; we have a `SortedList` class we can use. No, it isn't OK. The `SortedList` operations `Insert` and `BinSearch` involve comparing two items using the relational operators. Our `Time` class has comparison operators `Equal` and `LessThan`; the relational operators are not defined on `Time` objects. This means that we must add two functions to class `Entry`: `LessThan` and `Equal`.

While we are enhancing class `Entry`, let's add a `ReadEntry` function to the class. An `Entry` object should have an action responsibility to read values into itself.

Here are the prototypes for the new functions:

```
bool LessThan( Entry entry ) const;

    // Compares time with entry.time
    // Postcondition:
    //     Return value is true if time is less than entry.time;
    //     false otherwise

bool Equal( Entry entry ) const;

    // Compares time with entry.time
    // Postcondition:
    //     Return value is true if time is equal to entry.time;
    //     false otherwise

void ReadEntry();

    // Postcondition:
    //     Values have been read from the keyboard and stored
    //     into name and time
```

Is our current `SortedList` class useless? No; we must rewrite two of the functions using the appropriate comparisons `LessThan` and `Equal` from the `Entry` class, thus specializing the list, but we can use the operations that do not require a comparison as is.

The operations that need to be rewritten are `Insert` and `BinSearch`. What about `Delete`? Our problem doesn't indicate that we need to delete an appointment, but we should anticipate such an operation in the future. However, as `Delete` uses `BinSearch`, it doesn't have to be changed. Note that "item" is of class `Entry`, and our comparisons are on time, so `LessThan` and `Equal` in class `Entry` just call `LessThan` and `Equal` in class `Time`.

The calls to the `SortedList` functions to implement the tasks go into the driver at the moment. When we incorporate what we have done here into the bigger task, the driver will become part of the class that manipulates a day's events.

Most of the work for this program was done elsewhere. We just had to put the pieces together. The `Name` class and the `Time` class had already been tested and were not altered. We have added three new functions to class `Entry`, and changed two functions in class `SortedList`. We need to retest the current version of class `Entry` before we try running the driver. Here is the implementation file for the expanded class Entry, the driver to test it, and the output from the driver.

```cpp
//***********************************************************************
// IMPLEMENTATION FILE (Entry.cpp)
// This file contains the specification of the Entry ADT,
// which has two contained classes, Name and Time
//***********************************************************************

#include "Entry.h"
#include <string>
#include <fstream>
#include <iostream>
#include <sstream>              // ostringstream

using namespace std;

string Entry::NameStr() const

// Returns a string made up of first name, blank, last name
// Postcondition:
//      Return value is first name of Name object, blank, and
//      last name of Name object

{
    return (name.FirstName() + ' ' + name.LastName());
}

string Entry::TimeStr() const

// Returns a string made up of hour, colon, minutes, colon, seconds
// Postcondition:
//      Return value is minutes from Time object, colon, and
//      seconds of Time object

{
    string outStr;
    ostringstream tempOut;  // Access ostringstream class
    if (time.Hours() < 10)
        tempOut << '0';
    tempOut << time.Hours() << ":";
    if (time.Minutes() < 10)
        tempOut << '0';
    tempOut << time.Minutes() << ":";
    if (time.Seconds() < 10)
        tempOut << '0';
```

```
        tempOut << time.Seconds();
        outStr = tempOut.str();
        return outStr;
}


void Entry::ReadEntry()

// Postcondition:
//      Values have been read from the keyboard into name and time.

{
        name.ReadName();
        time.ReadTime();
}


bool Entry::LessThan(Entry entry) const

// Compares time with entry.time
// Postcondition:
//      Return value is true if time is less than entry.time;
//      false otherwise

{
        return time.LessThan(entry.time);
}


bool Entry::Equal(Entry entry) const

// Compares time with entry.time
// Postcondition:
//      Return value is true if self is equal to entry.time;
//      false otherwise

{
        return time.Equal(entry.time);
}


Entry::Entry()

// Default constructor
// Postcondition:
//      Entry object has been constructed
{
}
```

```
Entry::Entry( /* in */ string firstName,
              /* in */ string middleName,
              /* in */ string lastName,
              /* in */ int   initHours,
              /* in */ int   initMinutes,
              /* in */ int   initSeconds )

    // Constructor initializers
    : name(firstName, middleName, lastName),
      time(initHours, initMinutes, initSeconds)

// Parameterized constructor
// Postcondition:
//     Entry object has been constructed with firstName,
//     middleName, and lastName as arguments to Name
//     parameterized constructor; initHours, initMinutes,
//     and initSeconds as arguments to Time parameterized
//     constructor

{
}

//***********************************************************************
// DRIVER for expanded class Entry (File ExpEntryDr.cpp)
// This program tests the constructors and return functions
//***********************************************************************

#include <iostream>
#include "Entry.h"
using namespace std;

int main()
{
    Entry entry1;
    Entry entry2("Mary", "Beth", "Jones", 10, 30, 0);

    entry1.ReadEntry();

    // Testing consructors and ReadEntry
    cout << "Entry 1: " << entry1.NameStr() << " "
        << entry1.TimeStr() << endl;
    cout << "Entry 2: " << entry2.NameStr() << " "
        << entry2.TimeStr() << endl;

    // Testing LessThan
    if (entry1.LessThan(entry2))
```

```cpp
        cout << "Entry 1 is less than Entry 2" << endl;
    else
        cout << "Entry 1 is not less than Entry 2" << endl;
    if (entry2.LessThan(entry1))
        cout << "Entry 2 is less than Entry 1" << endl;
    else
        cout << "Entry 2 is not less than Entry 1" << endl;

    // Testing Equal
    if (entry1.Equal(entry2))
        cout << "Entry 1 equals Entry 2" << endl;
    else
        cout << "Entry 1 does not equal Entry 2" << endl;

    entry1 = entry2;
    cout << "entry1 set to entry2" << endl;
    if (entry1.Equal(entry2))
        cout << "Entry 1 equals Entry 2" << endl;
    else
        cout << "Entry 1 does not equal Entry 2" << endl;

    return 0;
}
```

```
C:\PPSC++\2-22-04\Ch14\EntryTest.exe                        _ □ x
Enter first name: Susy
Enter middle name: Sunshine
Enter last name: Smith
Enter hours (<= 23):
9
Enter minutes (<= 59):
30
Enter seconds (<= 59):
0
Entry 1: Susy Smith 09:30:00
Entry 2: Mary Jones 10:30:00
Entry 1 is less than Entry 2
Entry 2 is not less than Entry 1
Entry 1 does not equal Entry 2
entry1 set to entry2
Entry 1 equals Entry 2
```

Now that the expanded class Entry has been tested, we can continue with the rest of the problem. Here are the implementations of the changed functions in class SortedList.

```cpp
//***************************************************************

void SortedList::Insert( /* in */ ItemType& item )
```

```
// Inserts item into the SortedList

// Precondition:
//     length < MAX_LENGTH
//  && data[0..length-1] are in ascending order
// Postcondition:
//     item is in the SortedList
//  && length == length@entry + 1
//  && data[0..length-1] are in ascending order

{
    int index;    // Index and loop control variable
    index = length - 1;
    while (index >= 0 && item.LessThan(data[index]))
    {
        data[index+1] = data[index];
        index--;
    }
    data[index+1] = item;          // Insert item
    length++;
}

//********************************************************************

void SortedList::BinSearch(
    /* in */  ItemType item,            // Item to be found
    /* out */ bool&    found,           // True if item is found
    /* out */ int&     position ) const // Location if found

// Searches list for item, returning the index of item if item was
// found.

// Precondition:
//     length <= INT_MAX / 2
//  && data[0..length-1] are in ascending order
// Postcondition:
//     IF item is in the list
//         found == true  && data[position] contains item
//     ELSE
//         found == false  &&  position is undefined

{
    int first = 0;           // Lower bound on list
    int last = length - 1;   // Upper bound on list
    int middle;              // Middle index
```

```
        found = false;
        while (last >= first && !found)
        {
            middle = (first + last) / 2;
            if (item.LessThan(data[middle]))
                // Assert: item is not in data[middle..last]
                last = middle - 1;
            else if (data[middle].LessThan(item))
                // Assert: item is not in data[first..middle]
                first = middle + 1;
            else
                // Assert: item == data[middle]
                found = true;
        }
        if (found)
            position = middle;
    }
```

TESTING In order to test the list of class Entry items, we must create a another driver. The driver that incorporates calls to class SortedList is shown below. Entries are read in, inserted into the list, accessed one at a time and printed, compared to another entry, and deleted. The output screen from this driver is shown below the code.

```
//*********************************************************************
// DRIVER for List of Entry class objects
// Four entries are read from the keyboard and inserted into the
// list of entries.  The entries are accessed one at a time and
// printed.  A time that is in the list is checked; a time that is
// not in the list is checked.  An item is deleted and the list is
// printed to show that the item is gone.
//*********************************************************************

#include <iostream>
#include "SortedList.h"
using namespace std;

int main()
{
    int limit;              // Number of items in the list
    Entry nameTime;
    SortedList list;
    for (int count = 1; count <= 3; count++) // Enter data
    {
        nameTime.ReadEntry();
        list.Insert(nameTime);
    }
```

```
        // Prepare and iterate through the list, printing items
        limit = list.Length();
        list.Reset();                            // Prepare for iteration
        for (int count = 0; count < limit; count++)
        {
            nameTime = list.GetNextItem();
            cout << "Name: " << nameTime.NameStr() << " Time: "
                << nameTime.TimeStr() << endl;
        }

        // Item is in the list
        if (list.IsPresent(nameTime))
            cout << nameTime.TimeStr() << " is not free." << endl;
        else
            cout << nameTime.TimeStr() << " is free. " << endl;

        // Item is not in the list
        Entry entry2("Nell", "Boylan", "Dale", 0, 0, 0);
        if (list.IsPresent(entry2))
            cout << entry2.TimeStr() << " is not free." << endl;
        else
            cout << entry2.TimeStr() << " is free. " << endl;

        // Delete and iterate through the list, printing items
        list.Delete(nameTime);
        list.Reset();                            // Prepare for iteration
        limit = list.Length();
        for (int count = 0; count < limit; count++)
        {
            nameTime = list.GetNextItem();
            cout << "Name: " << nameTime.NameStr() << " Time: "
                << nameTime.TimeStr() << endl;
        }
        return 0;
    }
```

```
C:\PPSC++\EntryListTest.exe                                          _ □ ×
Enter first name: Sarah
Enter middle name: Jane
Enter last name: Jones
Enter hours (<= 23):
10
Enter minutes (<= 59):
30
Enter seconds (<= 59):
00
Enter first name: Susan
Enter middle name: Margaret
Enter last name: Smith
Enter hours (<= 23):
9
Enter minutes (<= 59):
30
Enter seconds (<= 59):
00
Enter first name: Judy
Enter middle name: Dale
Enter last name: David
Enter hours (<= 23):
3
Enter minutes (<= 59):
00
Enter seconds (<= 59):
0
Name: Judy David Time: 03:00:00
Name: Susan Smith Time: 09:30:00
Name: Sarah Jones Time: 10:30:00
10:30:00 is not free.
00:00:00 is free.
Name: Judy David Time: 03:00:00
Name: Susan Smith Time: 09:30:00
```

As we keyed in the data for the driver, we realize that we have a problem. Class `Time` represents hours, minutes, and seconds; that is, it represents *active* time. To create or set or read a time, the user must enter hours, minutes, and seconds. There is an operation to increment time by one second. For our appointment calendar, we don't care about seconds or incrementing time by a second. Appointment times are different; they are *static* times. We are only interested in hours and minutes. How do we solve this problem? We could define a derived class and redefine the operations to work only with hours and minutes. However, this isn't the natural use for inheritance. A static time isn't a dynamic time *and more*. Let's just define a class `AptTime`, in which we remove the increment operation and change the other operations to just work with hours and minutes. Do we have to make corresponding changes in class `Entry`? Yes; we need to remove seconds from the constructor and the time string and change the Include statement. We leave the coding and testing of class `AptTime` to the Programming Example Follow-Up Exercises.

Here is the screen shot from the same input, using `AptTime` rather than `Time`. The only difference is that the user is not prompted to enter seconds.

```
C:\PPSC++\EntryListTest.exe                                    _ □ X
Enter first name: Sarah
Enter middle name: Jane
Enter last name: Jones
Enter hours (<= 23):
10
Enter minutes (<= 59):
30
Enter first name: Susan
Enter middle name: Margaret
Enter last name: Smith
Enter hours (<= 23):
9
Enter minutes (<= 59):
30
Enter first name: Judy
Enter middle name: Dale
Enter last name: David
Enter hours (<= 23):
3
Enter minutes (<= 59):
00
Name: Judy David Time: 03:00:00
Name: Susan Smith Time: 09:30:00
Name: Sarah Jones Time: 10:30:00
10:30:00 is not free.
00:00:00 is free.
Name: Judy David Time: 03:00:00
Name: Susan Smith Time: 09:30:00
```

Testing and Debugging

Testing and debugging an object-oriented program is largely a process of testing and debugging the C++ classes on which the program is built. The top-level driver also needs testing, but this testing is usually uncomplicated—OOD tends to result in a simple driver.

To review how to test a C++ class, you should refer back to the Testing and Debugging section of Chapter 11. There we walked through the process of testing each member function of a class. We made the observation that you could write a separate test driver for each member function or you could write just one test driver that tests all of the member functions. The latter approach is recommended only for classes that have a few simple member functions.

When an object-oriented program uses inheritance and composition, the order in which you test the classes is, in a sense, predetermined. If class X is derived from class Y or contains an object of class Y, you cannot test X until you have designed and implemented Y. Thus, it makes sense to test and debug the lower-level class (class Y) before testing class X. This chapter's Programming Example demonstrated this sequence of testing. We tested the lowest level class—the Time class—first. Next, we tested the TimeCard class, which contains a Time object. Finally, we tested the TimeCardList class, which contains an array of TimeCard objects. The general principle is that if class

X is built on class Y (through inheritance or composition), the testing of X is simplified if Y is already tested and is known to behave correctly.

Testing and Debugging Hints

1. Review the Testing and Debugging Hints for Chapter 11. They apply to the design and testing of C++ classes, which are at the heart of OOP.

2. When using inheritance, don't forget to include the word `public` when declaring the derived class:

```
class DerivedClass : public BaseClass
{
    ⋮
};
```

The word `public` makes `BaseClass` a public base class of `DerivedClass`. That is, clients of `DerivedClass` can apply any public `BaseClass` operation (except constructors) to a `DerivedClass` object.

3. The header file containing the declaration of a derived class must `#include` the header file containing the declaration of the base class.

4. Although a derived class inherits the private and public members of its base class, it cannot directly access the inherited private members.

5. If a base class has a constructor, it is invoked before the body of the derived class's constructor is executed. If the base class constructor requires arguments, you must pass these `arguments` using a constructor initializer:

```
DerivedClass::DerivedClass( ... )
      : BaseClass(arg1, arg2)
{
   ⋮
}
```

If you do not include a constructor initializer, the base class's default constructor is invoked.

6. If a class has a member that is an object of another class and this member object's constructor requires arguments, you must pass these arguments using a constructor initializer:

```
SomeClass::SomeClass( ... )
      : memberObject(arg1, arg2)
{
   ⋮
}
```

If there is no constructor initializer, the member object's default constructor is invoked.

7. To obtain dynamic binding of an operation to an object when passing class objects as arguments, you must
   - Pass the object by reference, not by value.
   - Declare the operation to be `virtual` in the base class declaration.

8. If a base class declares a virtual function, it *must* implement that function even if the body is empty.

9. A derived class cannot redefine the function return type of a virtual function.

Summary

Object-oriented design (OOD) decomposes a problem into objects—self-contained entities in which data and operations are bound together. In OOD, data is treated as an active, rather than passive, quantity. Each object is responsible for one part of the solution, and the objects communicate by invoking each other's operations.

OOD begins by identifying potential objects and their operations. Examining objects in the problem domain is a good way to begin the process. The next step is to determine the relationships among the objects using inheritance (to express is-a relationships) and composition (to express has-a relationships). Finally, a driver algorithm is designed to coordinate the overall flow of control.

Object-oriented programming (OOP) is the process of implementing an object-oriented design by using language mechanisms for data abstraction, inheritance, and dynamic binding. Inheritance allows any programmer to take an existing class (the base class) and create a new class (the derived class) that inherits the data and operations of the base class. The derived class then specializes the base class by adding new private data, adding new operations, or reimplementing inherited operations—all without analyzing and modifying the implementation of the base class in any way. Dynamic binding of operations to objects allows objects of many different derived types to respond to a single function name, each in its own way. Together, inheritance and dynamic binding have been shown to reduce dramatically the time and effort required to customize existing ADTs. The result is truly reusable software components whose applications and lifetimes extend beyond those conceived of by the original creator.

Quick Check

1. How do structured programs differ from object-oriented programs in terms of the components that interact with each other to solve a problem? (p. 568)
2. What are the three main facilities that are provided by an object-oriented language that enable object-oriented programming? (p. 568)
3. Is a virtual function bound statically or dynamically? (pp. 591–595)
4. If you have a class called `Phone` and you want to extend it to support a country code, calling the new class `InternationalPhone`, how would you write the class heading for the new subclass? (pp. 573–575)

5. Suppose that in Quick Check 4, you wanted to create `InternationalPhone` as a separate class that contains an instance of `Phone`, rather than making it a subclass of phone. Describe how you would go about doing this. (pp. 584–590)
6. What are the three major steps in designing an object-oriented solution to a problem? (p. 596)
7. Given a design for an object that lists the data that it contains and provides algorithms for the operations that it performs, what C++ construct would you use to represent the object, its data, and its operations? (pp. 568–569)

Answers

1. In a structured program, functions interact with one another and with the data in the program. In an object-oriented program, objects (which bind operations and data together) are the components that interact. 2. Data abstraction, inheritance, and dynamic binding. 3. Dynamically. 4. `class InternationalPhone : public Phone` 5. By placing a member field within `InternationalPhone` that is of class `Phone`. 6. Identify the objects and operations, determine the relationships among the objects, design the driver. 7. The object would be represented by a class. Its data would be represented by member fields of the class. The object's operations would be represented by member functions of the class.

Exam Preparation Exercises

1. Match the following terms with the definitions given below.
   a. Structured program
   b. Object-oriented program
   c. Inheritance
   d. Superclass
   e. Subclass
   f. Composition
   g. Static binding
   h. Dynamic binding
   i. Polymorphic
      i. Determining, at run time, from which class to call a function.
      ii. A class from which properties are acquired.
      iii. A collection of classes designed using abstraction, inheritance, and polymorphism.
      iv. An operation that has different meanings depending on its binding to an object.
      v. Including an object of one class within another class.
      vi. A class that acquires properties from another class.
      vii. Determining, at compile time, from which class to call a function.
      viii. A collection of functions, designed using functional decomposition.
      ix. Acquiring the properties of another class.
2. Structured programming is better suited to developing small programs while object-oriented programming is better for writing large programs. True or false?

3. Inheritance allows us to reuse functions from a base class, and add new functions. But we cannot replace functions in the base class with new implementations. True or false?

4. To solve the slicing problem we use a combination of pass-by-reference and virtual functions? True or false?

5. If we want a function to be virtual, where do we write the keyword? In the base class declaration file, in the base class definition file, in the derived class declaration file, or in the derived class definition file?

6. What C++ language mechanism implements composition?

7. Suppose you have a subclass that contains several data members that are not defined in its superclass. What happens to those data members if you assign an object of the subclass to a variable of the superclass?

8. A client is supplied with the following declaration for a base class and a derived class.

```
class BaseClass
{
public:
    void PrintFields() const;
      ⋮
};


class DerivedClass : BaseClass
{
public:
    void NewFunction();
    DerivedClass( /* in */ int StartValue);
      ⋮
};
```

So, the client writes the following code to call the constructor for an object of type DerivedClass, and then prints the fields in the newly created object.

```
DerivedClass anObject(10);
anObject.PrintFields();
```

But the compiler reports an error for the second statement. What's wrong? How would you fix this problem?

9. Consider the following base and derived class declarations.

```
class BaseClass
{
public:
    void BaseAlpha();
private:
    void BaseBeta();
    float baseField;
};
```

```
class DerivedClass : public BaseClass
{
public:
    void DerivedAlpha();
    void DerivedBeta();
private:
    int derivedField;
};
```

For each class, do the following:

a. List all private data members.

b. List all private data members that the class's member functions can reference directly.

c. List all functions that the class's member functions can invoke.

d. List all member functions that a client of the class may invoke.

10. A class called `DerivedClass` is a subclass of a class called `BaseClass`. `DerivedClass` also has a member field that is an object of class `ComposedClass`.

a. Which class's constructor is called first when an object of class `DerivedClass` is created?

b. Which class's constructor is called last when an object of class `DerivedClass` is created?

11. Why does slicing occur with pass-by-value but not with pass-by-reference when a derived class object is being passed to a parameter of its base class?

12. What's wrong with the following class declarations?

```
class BaseClass
{
public:
    virtual void BaseAlpha();
private:
    float baseField;
};
```

```
class DerivedClass : public BaseClass
{
public:
    virtual void BaseAlpha();
private:
    int derivedField;
};
```

13. Explain the difference between an *is-a* relationship and a *has-a* relationship.

14. When we code a derived class in separate files, which of the following do we do?

a. Include the base class specification and implementation file in both the derived class specification file and its implementation files.

    b. Include the base class specification file in the derived class specification file, and include the base class implementation file in the derived class implementation file.

    c. Include the base class specification file in the derived class specification file.

    d. Include the base class implementation file in the derived class implementation file.

Programming Warm-Up Exercises

1. Given the following declaration for a test score class, write a derived class declaration called `IDScore` that adds an integer student ID number as a private member, and that supplies a constructor that has parameters corresponding to the three member fields, and an observer that returns the ID number.

```
class TestScore
{
public:
    TestScore(/* in */ string name,
              /* in */ int score);
    string GetName() const;
    int GetScore() const;
private:
    string studentName;
    int studentScore;
};
```

2. Write the implementation file for the `TestScore` class in Exercise 1. The constructor just assigns its parameters to the private data members, and the observers simply return the corresponding member.

3. Write the implementation file for the `IDScore` class in Exercise 1. The constructor just assigns its parameters to the private data members, and the observer simply returns the corresponding member.

4. Write the specification file for a class called `Exam` that uses composition to create an array of 100 objects of class `IDScore` as defined in Exercise 1. The class can use the default constructor, and will have a function that assigns an `IDScore` object to a location in the array, given the object and the location as parameters. The class should also have an observer that returns the `IDScore` object at the position specified by its parameter.

5. Write the implementation file for class `Exam` as defined in Exercise 4.

6. The following class represents a telephone number in the United States.

```
// SPECIFICATION FILE (phone.h)

enum PhoneType (HOME, OFFICE, CELL, FAX, PAGE);

class Phone
```

```
{
public:
    Phone( /* in */ int newAreaCode,
           /* in */ int newNumber,
           /* in  */ PhoneType newType);
    void Write () const;
private:
    int areaCode;
    int number;
    PhoneType type;
}
```

Using inheritance, we want to derive an international phone number class, InternPhone, from the Phone class. For this exercise, we assume that the only change necessary is to add a country code (an integer) that identifies the country or region. The public operations of InternPhone are Write, which reimplements the Write function from the base class, and a class constructor that takes four parameters corresponding to the four member fields in the class. Write the class declaration for the InternPhone class.

7. Implement the InternPhone class constructor as described in Exercise 6.

8. Implement the Write function of the InternPhone class as described in Exercise 6.

9. Write a global function WritePhone that takes a single parameter and uses dynamic binding to print either a U.S. phone number (Phone class) or an international phone number (InternPhone class). Make the necessary change(s) in the declaration of the Phone class from Exercise 6 so that WritePhone executes correctly.

10. Given the following declaration for a class that represents a computer in a company's inventory, write a derived class declaration (for a class called InstallRecord) that adds a string field representing the location of the computer, and a field of class SimpleDate that holds the installation date. The new class should provide observers for each of the new fields. It should also reimplement the Write function.

```
class Computer
{
public:
    Computer(
        /* in */ string newName,
        /* in */ string newBrand,
        /* in */ string newModel,
        /* in */ int    newSpeed,
        /* in */ string newSerial,
        /* in */ int    newNumber);
    string GetName() const;
    string GetBrand() const;
```

```
        string GetModel() const;
        int GetSpeed() const;
        string GetSerial() const;
        int GetNumber() const;
        void Write() const;

    private:
        string name;
        string brand;
        string model;
        int speed;
        string serialNumber;
        int inventoryNumber;
    };
```

11. Implement the constructor for the `Computer` class declared in Exercise 10.
12. Implement the constructor for the `InstallRecord` class declared in Exercise 10.
13. Implement the `Write` function for the `Computer` class declared in Exercise 10. It should output each member field on a separate line.
14. Implement the Write function for the `InstallRecord` class declared in Exercise 10. It should output each member field on a separate line. Assume that the `SimpleDate` class provides a `void` function called `Write()` that outputs the date in a standard format.
15. Expand class `ExtTime` by redefining function `ReadTime`.

Programming Problems

1. Use object-oriented programming to develop a game application that simulates a roulette table. The roulette table has 36 numbers (1 to 36) that are arranged in three columns of 12 rows. The first row has the numbers 1 through 3, the second row contains 4 through 6, and so on. There is also a number 0 that is outside of the table of numbers. The numbers in the table are colored red and black (0 is green). The red numbers are 1, 3, 5, 7, 9, 12, 14, 16, 18, 19, 21, 23, 25, 27, 30, 32, 34, 36. The other half of the numbers are black. In a simplified set of rules, players can bet on an individual number (including 0), the red numbers, the black numbers, the even numbers, the odd numbers, the numbers 1 to 18, the numbers 19 to 36, and any of the columns or rows in the table.

   The user should be allowed to enter one of the bets, and the application uses the `rand` function from `<cstdlib>` as the basis for computing the number that would be rolled on the wheel. It then compares this number to the bet, and reports whether it won or lost. The process repeats until the user enters a quit command.

2. Use object-oriented programming to develop an extension to the application of Problem 1. The new application also should allow the user to enter an initial amount of money into an account. In addition to placing a bet, the user specifies an amount to go with the bet. The amount is deducted from the account. Any

winnings are added to the account. The current winnings or losses (difference from the original amount) should be displayed in addition to the value of the account. Winnings are computed as follows:

Single number bets pay 36 times the amount placed
Row bets pay 12 times
Column bets pay 3 times
Odd/Even, Red/Black, High/Low half bets pay 2 times the amount

The user should not be allowed to bet more than is in the account.

3. Use object-oriented programming to develop a game application that plays the children's game of rock, paper, scissors. The user enters a letter, indicating their choice. When a choice is entered, the `rand` function from `<cstdlib>` is used to pick a value in the range of 1 through 3, with 1 corresponding to rock, 2 corresponding to paper, and 3 corresponding to scissors. The computer's choice is compared to the user's choice according to the rules: rock breaks scissors, scissors cut paper, paper covers rock. Choices that match are ties. Output a count of the wins by the user and the computer, and of the ties. The application ends when the user enters an invalid choice.

4. Use object-oriented programming to develop an extension to the application of Problem 3. The new application should accept either the original single letter, or the full words (rock, paper, scissors). The capitalization of the words should not matter. The extended application also should end only when the user enters "q" or "quit" as a choice and should prompt the user for one of the valid choices if an invalid value is entered.

5. Use the `Computer` and `InstallRecord` classes declared in Programming Warm-Up Exercises 10 to 14, together with the `SortedList` class developed in Chapter 13 as the basis for an object-oriented program that keeps track of a company's computer inventory. The company has at most 500 computers. Operations that should be supported are:

Add a new computer to the list.
Delete a computer from the list.
Change the location of a computer.
Print a list of all computers in inventory-number order.
Print a list of all computers in a given location.
Print a list of all computers of a particular brand.
Print a list of all computers installed before a given date.

The application should keep the list sorted by inventory number. It should read an initial list from a file called `original.dat`. At the end of processing, it should write the current data in the list onto a file called `update.dat` in a format that could be read back in by the program as an initial list. You will also need to develop the `SimpleDate` class to the degree necessary to support the application.

Programming Example Follow-Up

1. Implement and test class `AptTime`.
2. It is not appropriate for `AptTime` (a static time) to inherit from `Time` (an active time). Would it be appropriate for an active time to inherit from a static time? Explain.
3. As you look at the output from the driver, you see that the times look strange. 03:00 certainly is technically less than 09:30, but surely the appointment time is 03:00 in the afternoon and should come after 09:30. The time is specified as a 24-hour clock. We could tell the user to enter the times on a 24-hour basis or we could change class `AptTime` to have an additional field that contains PM or AM or we could derive a class from AptTime that has a PM or AM field. Think about this solution and outline what would have to be changed to implement time on a 12-hour clock.
4. Implement your solution to Problem 3.
5. Write a driver and test the new class developed in Problem 4.
6. Substitute the new class from Problem 4 into the driver for the Case Study and rerun that test.

Recursion

Knowledge Goals

■ *To understand the distinction between the base case(s) and the general case in a recursive definition.*

Skill Goals

To be able to:

■ *Write a recursive algorithm for a problem involving only simple variables.*

■ *Write a recursive algorithm for a problem involving structured variables.*

Goals

In C++, any function can call another function. A function can even call itself! When a function calls itself, it is making a **recursive call**. The word *recursive* means "having the characteristic of coming up again, or repeating." In this case, a function call is being repeated by the function itself. Recursion is a powerful technique that can be used in place of iteration (looping).

Recursive solutions are generally less efficient than iterative solutions to the same problem. However, some problems lend themselves to simple, elegant, recursive solutions and are exceedingly cumbersome to solve iteratively. Some programming languages are especially oriented to recursive algorithms—LISP is one of these. C++ lets us take our choice: We can implement both iterative and recursive algorithms.

Our examples are divided into two groups: problems that use only simple variables and problems that use structured variables. If you are studying recursion before reading Chapters 11–12 on structured data types, then cover only the first set of examples and leave the rest until you have completed the chapters on structured data types.

15.1 What Is Recursion?

You may have seen a set of gaily painted Russian dolls that fit inside one another. Inside the first doll is a smaller doll, inside of which is an even smaller doll, inside of which is yet a smaller doll, and so on. A recursive algorithm is like such a set of Russian dolls. It reproduces itself with smaller and smaller examples of itself until a solution is found—that is, until there are no more dolls. The recursive algorithm is implemented by using a function that makes recursive calls to itself.

In Chapter 8, we wrote a function named Power that calculates the result of raising an integer to a positive power. If X is an integer and N is a positive integer, the formula for X^N is

$$x^N = \underbrace{X \times X \times X \times X \times \ldots \times X}_{N \text{ times}}$$

We could also write this formula as

$$x^N = X \times \underbrace{(X \times X \times \ldots \times X)}_{(N-1) \text{ times}}$$

or even as

$$x^N = X \times X \times \underbrace{(X \times X \times \ldots \times X)}_{(N-2) \text{ times}}$$

In fact, we can write the formula most concisely as

$$X^N = X \times X^{N-1}$$

This definition of X^N is a classic recursive definition—that is, a definition given in terms of a smaller version of itself.

X^N is defined in terms of multiplying X times X^{N-1}. How is X^{N-1} defined? Why, as $X \times X^{N-2}$, of course! And X^{N-2} is $X \times X^{N-3}$; X^{N-3} is $X \times X^{N-4}$; and so on. In this example, "in terms of smaller versions of itself" means that the exponent is decremented each time.

When does the process stop? When we have reached a case for which we know the answer without resorting to a recursive definition. In this example, it is the case where N equals 1: X^1 is X. The case (or cases) for which an answer is explicitly known is called the base case. The case for which the solution is expressed in terms of a smaller version of itself is called the recursive or general case. A recursive algorithm is an algorithm that expresses the solution in terms of a call to itself, a recursive call. A recursive algorithm must terminate; that is, it must have a base case.

Figure 15-1 shows a recursive version of the Power function with the base case and the recursive call marked. The function is embedded in a program that reads in a number and an exponent and prints the result.

> **Recursive definition**   A definition in which something is defined in terms of smaller versions of itself.
>
> **Base case**   The case for which the solution can be stated nonrecursively.
>
> **General case**   The case for which the solution is expressed in terms of a smaller version of itself; also known as *recursive case*.
>
> **Recursive algorithm**   A solution that is expressed in terms of (a) smaller instances of itself and (b) a base case.

Figure 15–1   *Power Function*

```
//**********************************************************************
// Exponentiation program
//**********************************************************************
#include <iostream>

using namespace std;

int Power( int, int );

int main()
{
    int number;             // Number that is being raised to power
    int exponent;           // Power the number is being raised to

    cin >> number >> exponent;
```

```
        cout << Power(number, exponent);  ◄─────────── // Nonrecursive call
        return 0;
}


//**************************************************************************

int Power( /* in */ int x,    // Number that is being raised to power
           /* in */ int n )   // Power the number is being raised to

// Computes x to the n power by multiplying x times the result of
// computing x to the n - 1 power

// Precondition:
//     x is assigned  &&  n > 0
// Postcondition:
//     Function value == x raised to the power n
// Note:
//     Large exponents may result in integer overflow

{
    if (n == 1)
        return x;  ◄──────────────────────────── // Base case
    else
        return x * Power(x, n - 1);  ◄─────────── // Recursive call
}
```

Each recursive call to Power can be thought of as creating a completely new copy of the function, each with its own copies of the parameters x and n. The value of x remains the same for each version of Power, but the value of n decreases by 1 for each call until it becomes 1.

Let's trace the execution of this recursive function, with number equal to 2 and exponent equal to 3. We use a new format to trace recursive routines: We number the calls and then discuss what is happening in paragraph form.

Call 1: Power is called by main, with number equal to 2 and exponent equal to 3. Within Power, the parameters x and n are initialized to 2 and 3, respectively. Because n is not equal to 1, Power is called recursively with x and n − 1 as arguments. Execution of Call 1 pauses until an answer is sent back from this recursive call.

Call 2: x is equal to 2 and n is equal to 2. Because n is not equal to 1, the function Power is called again, this time with x and n − 1 as arguments. Execution of Call 2 pauses until an answer is sent back from this recursive call.

Call 3: x is equal to 2 and n is equal to 1. Because n equals 1, the value of x is to be returned. This call to the function has finished executing, and the function return value (which is 2) is passed back to the place in the statement from which the call was made.

Call 2: This call to the function can now complete the statement that contained the recursive call because the recursive call has returned. Call 3's return value (which is 2) is multiplied by x. This call to the function has finished executing, and the function return value (which is 4) is passed back to the place in the statement from which the call was made.

Call 1: This call to the function can now complete the statement that contained the recursive call because the recursive call has returned. Call 2's return value (which is 4) is multiplied by x. This call to the function has finished executing, and the function return value (which is 8) is passed back to the place in the statement from which the call was made. Because the first call (the nonrecursive call in main) has now completed, this is the final value of the function Power.

This trace is summarized in Figure 15–2. Each box represents a call to the Power function. The values for the parameters for that call are shown in each box.

What happens if there is no base case? We have infinite recursion, the recursive equivalent of an infinite loop. For example, if the condition

> **Infinite recursion**   The situation in which a function calls itself over and over endlessly.

```
if (n == 1)
```

were omitted, Power would be called over and over again. Infinite recursion also occurs if Power is called with n less than or equal to 0.

In actuality, recursive calls can't go on forever. Here's the reason. When a function is called, either recursively or nonrecursively, the computer system creates temporary storage for the parameters and the function's (automatic) local variables. This temporary storage is a region of memory called the *run-time stack*. When the function returns, its parameters

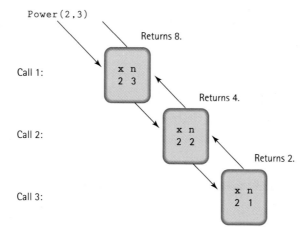

Figure 15–2   *Execution of* Power(2, 3)

and local variables are released from the run-time stack. With infinite recursion, the recursive function calls never return. Each time the function calls itself, a little more of the run-time stack is used to store the new copies of the variables. Eventually, all the memory space on the stack is used. At that point, the program crashes with an error message such as "RUN-TIME STACK OVERFLOW" (or the computer may simply hang).

15.2 Recursive Algorithms with Simple Variables

Let's look at another example: calculating a factorial. The factorial of a number N (written $N!$) is N multiplied by $N - 1$, $N - 2$, $N - 3$, and so on. Another way of expressing factorial is

$$N! = N \times (N - 1)!$$

This expression looks like a recursive definition. $(N - 1)!$ is a smaller instance of $N!$—that is, it takes one less multiplication to calculate $(N - 1)!$ than it does to calculate $N!$ If we can find a base case, we can write a recursive algorithm. Fortunately, we don't have to look too far: $0!$ is defined in mathematics to be 1.

Factorial (In: n)

```
IF n is 0
    Return 1
ELSE
    Return n * Factorial(n – 1)
```

This algorithm can be coded directly as follows.

```
int Factorial ( /* in */ int n )

// Precondition:
//      n >= 0
// Postcondition:
//      Function value == n!
// Note:
//      Large values of n may cause integer overflow

{
    if (n == 0)
        return 1;                            // Base case
    else
        return n * Factorial(n - 1);         // General case
}
```

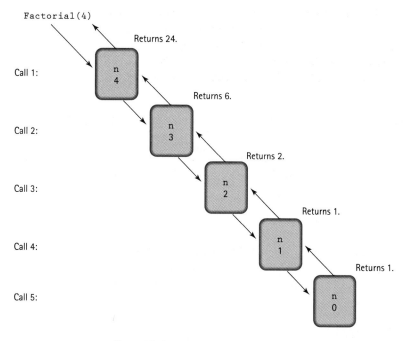

Factorial(4)

Returns 24.

Call 1:

n
4

Returns 6.

Call 2:

n
3

Returns 2.

Call 3:

n
2

Returns 1.

Call 4:

n
1

Returns 1.

Call 5:

n
0

Figure 15–3   *Execution of* Factorial(4)

Figure 15-3 summarizes the execution of the Factorial function with an argument of 4.

Let's organize what we have done in these two solutions into an outline for writing recursive algorithms.

1. Understand the problem. (We threw this in for good measure; it is always the first step.)
2. Determine the base case(s).
3. Determine the recursive case(s).

We have used the factorial and the power algorithms to demonstrate recursion because they are easy to visualize. In practice, one would never want to calculate either of these functions using the recursive solution. In both cases, the iterative solutions are simpler and much more efficient because starting a new iteration of a loop is a faster operation than calling a function. Let's compare the code for the iterative and recursive versions of the factorial problem.

Iterative Solution

```
int Factorial ( /* in */ int n )
{
    int factor;
    int count;

    factor = 1;
    for (count = 2; count <= n; count++)
        factor = factor * count;
    return factor;
}
```

Recursive Solution

```
int Factorial ( /* in */ int n )
{
    if (n == 0)
        return 1;
    else
        return n * Factorial(n - 1);
}
```

The iterative version has two local variables, whereas the recursive version has none. There are usually fewer local variables in a recursive routine than in an iterative routine. Also, the iterative version always has a loop, whereas the recursive version always has a selection statement—either an If or a Switch. A branching structure is the main control structure in a recursive routine. A looping structure is the main control structure in an iterative routine.

In the next section, we examine a more complicated problem—one in which the recursive solution is not immediately apparent.

15.3 Towers of Hanoi

One of your first toys may have been three pegs with colored circles of different diameters. If so, you probably spent countless hours moving the circles from one peg to another. If we put some constraints on how the circles or discs can be moved, we have an adult game called the Towers of Hanoi. When the game begins, all the circles are on the first peg in order by size, with the smallest on the top. The object of the game is to move the circles, one at a time, to the third peg. The catch is that a circle cannot be placed on top of one that is smaller in diameter. The middle peg can be used as an auxiliary peg, but it must be empty at the beginning and at the end of the game.

To get a feel for how this might be done, let's look at some sketches of what the configuration must be at certain points if a solution is possible. We use four circles or discs. The beginning configuration is:

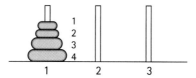

To move the largest circle (circle 4) to peg 3, we must move the three smaller circles to peg 2. Then circle 4 can be moved into its final place:

Let's assume we can do this. Now, to move the next largest circle (circle 3) into place, we must move the two circles on top of it onto an auxiliary peg (peg 1 in this case):

To get circle 2 into place, we must move circle 1 to another peg, freeing circle 2 to be moved to its place on peg 3:

The last circle (circle 1) can now be moved into its final place, and we are finished:

Notice that to free circle 4, we had to move three circles to another peg. To free circle 3, we had to move two circles to another peg. To free circle 2, we had to move one circle to another peg. This sounds like a recursive algorithm: To free the nth circle, we have to move $n - 1$ circles. Each stage can be thought of as beginning again with three pegs, but with one less circle each time. Let's see if we can summarize this process, using n instead of an actual number.

Get N Circles Moved from Peg 1 to Peg 3

Get n – 1 circles moved from peg 1 to peg 2
Move nth circle from peg 1 to peg 3
Get n – 1 circles moved from peg 2 to peg 3

This algorithm certainly sounds simple; surely there must be more. But this really is all there is to it.

Let's write a recursive function that implements this algorithm. We can't actually move discs, of course, but we can print out a message to do so. Notice that the beginning peg, the ending peg, and the auxiliary peg keep changing during the algorithm. To make the algorithm easier to follow, we call the pegs `beginPeg`, `endPeg`, and `auxPeg`. These three pegs, along with the number of circles on the beginning peg, are the parameters of the function.

We have the recursive or general case, but what about a base case? How do we know when to stop the recursive process? The clue is in the expression "Get n circles moved." If we don't have any circles to move, we don't have anything to do. We are finished with that stage. Therefore, when the number of circles equals 0, we do nothing (that is, we simply return).

```
void DoTowers(
    /* in */ int circleCount,    // Number of circles to move
    /* in */ int beginPeg,       // Peg containing circles to move
    /* in */ int auxPeg,         // Peg holding circles temporarily
    /* in */ int endPeg       )  // Peg receiving circles being moved
{
    if (circleCount > 0)
    {
        // Move n - 1 circles from beginning peg to auxiliary peg

        DoTowers(circleCount - 1, beginPeg, endPeg, auxPeg);
        cout << "Move circle from peg " << beginPeg
            << " to peg " << endPeg << endl;

        // Move n - 1 circles from auxiliary peg to ending peg

        DoTowers(circleCount - 1, auxPeg, beginPeg, endPeg);
    }
}
```

It's hard to believe that such a simple algorithm actually works, but we'll prove it to you. Following is a driver program that calls the DoTowers function. Output statements have been added so you can see the values of the arguments with each recursive call. Because there are two recursive calls within the function, we have indicated which recursive statement issued the call.

```cpp
//*******************************************************************
// TestTowers program
// This program, a test driver for the DoTowers function, reads in
// a value from standard input and passes this value to DoTowers
//*******************************************************************
#include <iostream>
#include <iomanip>     // For setw()

using namespace std;

void DoTowers( int, int, int, int );

int main()
{
    int circleCount;     // Number of circles on starting peg

    cout << "Input number of circles: ";
    cin >> circleCount;
    cout << "OUTPUT WITH " << circleCount << " CIRCLES" << endl
         << endl;
    cout << "CALLED FROM  #CIRCLES" << setw(8) << "BEGIN"
         << setw(8) << "AUXIL." << setw(5) << "END"
         << "      INSTRUCTIONS" << endl
         << endl;
    cout << "Original    :";
    DoTowers(circleCount, 1, 2, 3);
    return 0;
}


//*******************************************************************

void DoTowers(
    /* in */ int circleCount,     // Number of circles to move
    /* in */ int beginPeg,        // Peg containing circles to move
    /* in */ int auxPeg,          // Peg holding circles temporarily
    /* in */ int endPeg      )    // Peg receiving circles being moved

// This recursive function moves circleCount circles from beginPeg
// to endPeg.  All but one of the circles are moved from beginPeg
```

```
            // to auxPeg, then the last circle is moved from beginPeg to endPeg,
            // and then the circles are moved from auxPeg to endPeg.
            // The subgoals of moving circles to and from auxPeg are what
            // involve recursion

            // Precondition:
            //     All parameters are assigned  &&  circleCount >= 0
            // Postcondition:
            //     The values of all parameters have been printed
            //  && IF circleCount > 0
            //         circleCount circles have been moved from beginPeg to
            //         endPeg in the manner detailed above
            //     ELSE
            //         No further actions have taken place

        {
            cout << setw(6) << circleCount << setw(9) << beginPeg
                << setw(7) << auxPeg << setw(7) << endPeg << endl;
            if (circleCount > 0)
            {
                cout << "From  first:";
                DoTowers(circleCount - 1, beginPeg, endPeg, auxPeg);
                cout << setw(58) << "Move circle " << circleCount
                    << " from " << beginPeg << " to " << endPeg << endl;
                cout << "From second:";
                DoTowers(circleCount - 1, auxPeg, beginPeg, endPeg);
            }
        }
```

The output from a run with three circles follows. "Original" means that the parameters listed beside it are from the nonrecursive call, which is the first call to DoTowers. "From first" means that the parameters listed are for a call issued from the first recursive statement. "From second" means that the parameters listed are for a call issued from the second recursive statement. Notice that a call cannot be issued from the second recursive statement until the preceding call from the first recursive statement has completed execution.

```
OUTPUT WITH 3 CIRCLES

CALLED FROM  #CIRCLES    BEGIN  AUXIL.  END    INSTRUCTIONS

Original   :    3          1      2     3
From  first:    2          1      3     2
From  first:    1          1      2     3
From  first:    0          1      3     2
                                               Move circle 1 from 1 to 3
```

From second:	0	2	1	3	
					Move circle 2 from 1 to 2
From second:	1	3	1	2	
From first:	0	3	2	1	
					Move circle 1 from 3 to 2
From second:	0	1	3	2	
					Move circle 3 from 1 to 3
From second:	2	2	1	3	
From first:	1	2	3	1	
From first:	0	2	1	3	
					Move circle 1 from 2 to 1
From second:	0	3	2	1	
					Move circle 2 from 2 to 3
From second:	1	1	2	3	
From first:	0	1	3	2	
					Move circle 1 from 1 to 3
From second:	0	2	1	3	

15.4 Recursive Algorithms with Structured Variables

In our definition of a recursive algorithm, we said there were two cases: the recursive or general case, and the base case for which an answer can be expressed nonrecursively. In the general case for all our algorithms so far, an argument was expressed in terms of a smaller value each time. When structured variables are used, the recursive case is often in terms of a smaller structure rather than a smaller value; the base case occurs when there are no values left to process in the structure.

We examine a recursive algorithm for printing the contents of a one-dimensional array of *n* elements to show what we mean.

Print Array

> IF more elements
>   Print the value of the first element
>   Print array of n − 1 elements

The recursive case is to print the values in an array that is one element "smaller"; that is, the size of the array decreases by 1 with each recursive call. The base case is when the size of the array becomes 0—that is, when there are no more elements to print.

Our arguments must include the index of the first element (the one to be printed). How do we know when there are no more elements to print (that is, when the size of the array to be printed is 0)? We know we have printed the last element in the array when the index of the next element to be printed is beyond the index of the last element in the array. Therefore, the index of the last array element must be passed as an argument. We call the indexes `first` and `last`. When `first` is greater than `last`, we are finished. The name of the array is `data`.

```
void Print( /* in */ const int data[],   // Array to be printed
            /* in */          int first,  // Index of first element
            /* in */          int last  ) // Index of last element
{
    if (first <= last)
    {                                            // Recursive case
        cout << data[first] << endl;
        Print(data, first + 1, last);
    }
    // Empty else-clause is the base case
}
```

A code walk-through of the function call

```
Print(data, 0, 4);
```

is shown in Figure 15.4.

Notice that once the deepest call (the call with the highest number) was reached, each of the calls before it returned without doing anything. When no statements are executed after the return from the recursive call to the function, the recursion is known as tail recursion. Tail recursion often indicates that the problem could be solved more easily using iteration. We used the array example because it made the recursive process easy to visualize; in practice, an array should be printed iteratively.

Tail recursion   A recursive algorithm in which no statements are executed after the return from the recursive call.

Figure 15–4 shows the execution of the `Print` function with the values of the parameters for each call. Notice that the array gets smaller with each recursive call (`data[first]` through `data[last]`). If we want to print the array elements in reverse order recursively, all we have to do is interchange the two statements within the If statement.

15.5 Recursion or Iteration?

Recursion and iteration are alternative ways of expressing repetition in a program. When iterative control structures are used, processes are made to repeat by embedding code in a looping structure such as a While, For, or Do-While. In recursion, a process is made to repeat by having a function call itself. A selection statement is used to control the repeated calls.

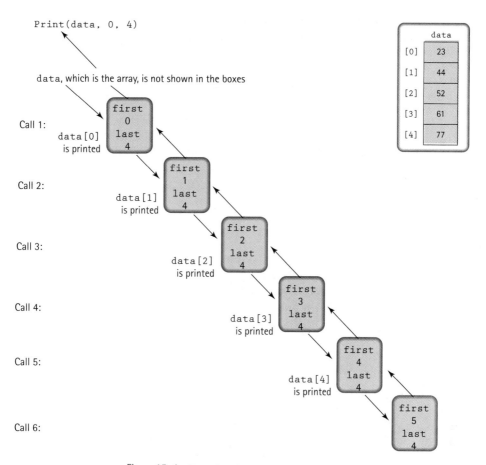

Figure 15–4   *Execution of* Print(data, 0, 4)

Which is better to use—recursion or iteration? There is no simple answer to this question. The choice usually depends on two issues: efficiency and the nature of the problem being solved.

Historically, the quest for efficiency, in terms of both execution speed and memory usage, has favored iteration over recursion. Each time a recursive call is made, the system must allocate stack space for all parameters and (automatic) local variables. The overhead involved in any function call is time-consuming. On early, slow computers with limited memory capacity, recursive algorithms were visibly—sometimes painfully—slower than the iterative versions. However, studies have shown that on modern, fast computers, the overhead of recursion is often so small that the increase in computation time is almost unnoticeable to the user. Except in cases where efficiency is absolutely critical, then, the choice between recursion and iteration more often depends on the second issue—the nature of the problem being solved.

Consider the factorial and power algorithms we discussed earlier in the chapter. In both cases, iterative solutions were obvious and easy to devise. We imposed recursive solutions on these problems only to demonstrate how recursion works. As a rule of thumb, if an iterative solution is more obvious or easier to understand, use it; it will be more efficient. However, there are problems for which the recursive solution is more obvious or easier to devise, such as the Towers of Hanoi problem. (It turns out that the Towers of Hanoi problem is surprisingly difficult to solve using iteration.) Computer science students should be aware of the power of recursion. If the definition of a problem is inherently recursive, then a recursive solution should certainly be considered.

Testing and Debugging

Recursion is a powerful technique when used correctly. Improperly used, recursion can cause errors that are difficult to diagnose. The best way to debug a recursive algorithm is to construct it correctly in the first place. To be realistic, however, we give a few hints about where to look if an error occurs.

Testing and Debugging Hints

1. Be sure there is a base case. If there is no base case, the algorithm continues to issue recursive calls until all memory has been used. Each time the function is called, either recursively or nonrecursively, stack space is allocated for the parameters and automatic local variables. If there is no base case to end the recursive calls, the run-time stack eventually overflows. An error message such as "STACK OVERFLOW" indicates that the base case is missing.

2. Be sure you have not used a While structure. The basic structure in a recursive algorithm is the If statement. There must be at least two cases: the recursive case and the base case. If the base case does nothing, the else-clause is omitted. The selection structure, however, must be there. If a While statement is used in a recursive algorithm, the While statement usually should not contain a recursive call.

3. As with nonrecursive functions, do not reference global variables directly within a recursive function unless you have justification for doing so.

4. Parameters that relate to the size of the problem must be value parameters, not reference parameters. The arguments that relate to the size of the problem are usually expressions. Arbitrary expressions can be passed only to value parameters.

5. Use your system's debugger program (or use debug output statements) to trace a series of recursive calls. Inspecting the values of parameters and local variables often helps to locate errors in a recursive algorithm.

Summary

A recursive algorithm is expressed in terms of a smaller instance of itself. It must include a recursive case, for which the algorithm is expressed in terms of itself, and a base case, for which the algorithm is expressed in nonrecursive terms.

In many recursive problems, the smaller instance refers to a numeric argument that is being reduced with each call. In other problems, the smaller instance refers to the size of the data structure being manipulated. The base case is the one in which the size of the problem (value or structure) reaches a point for which an explicit answer is known.

Quick Check

1. Which case causes a recursive algorithm to end its recursion: the base case or the general case? (pp. 620–624)
2. In writing a recursive algorithm that computes the factorial of N, what would you use as the base case, and what would be the general case? (pp. 624–626)
3. In writing a recursive algorithm that outputs the values in an array, what would you use as the base case, and what would be the general case? (pp. 631–632)

Answers

1. The base case.   2. The base case would be that when N is zero, the result is one. The general case would be that when N is greater than zero, we multiply it by the product of the numbers from 1 to N-1, as returned from a recursive call.   3. The base case would be that if there are no elements remaining, we return. The general case would be that if there are elements remaining, we print the first one, then recurse to print the rest.

Exam Preparation Exercises

1. Recursion is an alternative to:
   a. branching
   b. looping
   c. function invocation
   d. event handing
2. A recursive function can be void or value-returning? True or false?
3. When a function calls itself recursively, its parameters and local variables are saved on the run-time stack until it returns. True or false?
4. Tail recursion occurs when all of the processing happens at the end of the function, after the return from the recursive call. True or false?
5. Given the recursive formula $F(N) = F(N-2)$, with the base case $F(0) = 0$, what are the values of $F(4)$, $F(5)$, and $F(6)$? If any of the values are undefined, say so.
6. Given the recursive formula $F(N) = F(N - 1) * 2$, with the base case $F(0) = 1$, what are the values of $F(3)$, $F(4)$, and $F(5)$? If any of the values are undefined, say so.
7. What happens when a recursive function never encounters a base case?

8. What practical limitation prevents a function from calling itself recursively for-ever?

9. A tail-recursive function would be more efficiently implemented with a loop in most cases. True or false?

10. When you develop a recursive algorithm to operate on a simple variable, what does the general case typically make smaller with each recursive call?
   a. The data type of the variable
   b. The number of times the variable is referenced
   c. The value in the variable

10. When you develop a recursive algorithm to operate on a data structure, what does the general case typically make smaller with each recursive call?
   a. The number of elements in the structure
   b. The number of times the variable is referenced
   c. The distance to the end of the structure

12. Given the following input data:

```
10
20
30
```

what is output by the following program?

```cpp
#include <iostream>

using namespace std;

void Rev();

int main()
{
    Rev();
    return 0;
}

//*******************

void Rev()
{
    int number;
    cin >> number;
    if (cin)
    {
        Rev();
        cout << number << endl;
    }
}
```

13. Repeat Exercise 12, replacing the Rev function with the following version.

```
void Rev()
{
    int number;
    cin >> number;
    if (cin)
    {
        cout << number << endl;
        Rev();
        cout << number << endl;
    }
}
```

14. What is output by the following program?

```
#include <iostream>

using namespace std;

void Rec(string word);

int main()
{
    Rec("abcde");
    return 0;
}

//*******************

void Rec(string word)
{
    if (word.length() > 0)
    {
        cout << word.substr(0, 1);
        Rec(word.substr(1, word.length()-2));
        cout << word.substr(word.length()-1, 1) << endl;
    }
}
```

15. What does the program in Exercise 14 output if the initial call to Rec from main uses "abcdef" as the argument?

Programming Warm-Up Exercises

1. Write a value-returning recursive function that computes the sum of the digits in a given positive int argument. For example, if the argument is 12345, then the function returns 1 + 2 + 3 + 4 + 5 = 15.

2. Write a value-returning recursive function that uses the `DigitSum` function of Exercise 1 to compute the single digit to which the `int` argument's digits ultimately sum. For example, given the argument 999, the `DigitSum` would be 9 + 9 + 9 = 27, but the recursive digit sum would then be 2 + 7 = 9.

3. Write a recursive version of a binary search of a sorted array of int values that are in ascending order. The function's arguments should be the array, the search value, and the maximum and minimum indexes for the array. The function should return the index where the match is found, or else -1.

4. Write a recursive function that asks the user to enter a positive integer number each time it is called, until zero or a negative number is input. The function then outputs the numbers entered in reverse order. If the I/O dialog is the following:

```
Enter positive number, 0 to end: 10
Enter positive number, 0 to end: 20
Enter positive number, 0 to end: 30
Enter positive number, 0 to end: 0
```

the function outputs:

```
30
20
10
```

5. Extend the function of Exercise 4 so that it also outputs a running total of the numbers as they are entered. For example the I/O dialog might be the following:

```
Enter positive number, 0 to end: 10
Total: 10
Enter positive number, 0 to end: 20
Total: 30
Enter positive number, 0 to end: 30
Total: 60
Enter positive number, 0 to end: 0
```

and the function then outputs:

```
30
20
10
```

6. Extend the function of Exercise 5 so that it also outputs a running total as the numbers are printed out in reverse order. For example the I/O dialog might be the following:

```
Enter positive number, 0 to end: 10
Total: 10
Enter positive number, 0 to end: 20
Total: 30
Enter positive number, 0 to end: 30
Total: 60
```

```
Enter positive number, 0 to end: 0
```

and the function then outputs:

```
30 Total: 30
20 Total: 50
10 Total: 60
```

7. Extend the function of Exercise 4 so that it reports the greatest value entered, at the end of its output. If the I/O dialog is the following:

```
Enter positive number, 0 to end: 10
Enter positive number, 0 to end: 20
Enter positive number, 0 to end: 30
Enter positive number, 0 to end: 0
```

the function outputs:

```
30
20
10
The greatest is 30
```

8. Change the function of Exercise 7 so that it outputs the greatest number entered thus far, as the user is entering the data. For example, the I/O dialog might be the following:

```
Enter positive number, 0 to end: 10
Greatest: 10
Enter positive number, 0 to end: 30
Greatest: 30
Enter positive number, 0 to end: 20
Greatest: 30
Enter positive number, 0 to end: 0
```

and the function then outputs:

```
20
30
10
The greatest is 30
```

9. Change the function of Exercise 8 so that it also outputs the greatest number thus far, as it outputs the numbers in reverse order. For example, the I/O dialog might be the following:

```
Enter positive number, 0 to end: 10
Greatest: 10
Enter positive number, 0 to end: 30
Greatest: 30
Enter positive number, 0 to end: 20
```

```
Greatest: 30
Enter positive number, 0 to end: 0
```

and the function then outputs:

```
20 Greatest: 20
30 Greatest: 30
10 Greatest: 30
The greatest is 30
```

Programming Problems

1. The greatest common divisor (GCD) of two positive integers is the largest integer that divides the numbers exactly. For example, the greatest common divisor of 14 and 21 is 7; for 13 and 22 it is 1; and for 45 and 27 it is 9. We can write a recursive formula for finding the GCD, given that the two numbers are called a and b, as:

   GCD(a, b) = a, if b = 0
   GCD(a, b) = GCD(b, a%b), if b > 0

   Implement this recursive formula as a recursive C++ function, and write a driver program that allows you to test it interactively.

2. Write a C++ program to output the binary (base-2) representation of a decimal integer. The algorithm for this conversion is to repeatedly divide the decimal number by 2, until it is zero. Each division produces a remainder of 0 or 1, which becomes a digit in the binary number. For example, if we want the binary representation of decimal 13, we find it with the following series of divisions:

   ```
   13/2 = 6    remainder 1
   6/2 = 3     remainder 0
   3/2 = 1     remainder 1
   1/2 = 0     remainder 1
   ```

   The binary representation of 13 is thus 1101. The only problem with this algorithm is that the first division generates the low-order binary digit, the next division generates the second-order digit, and so on, until the last division produces the high-order digit. Thus, if we output the digits as they are generated, they are in reverse order. You should use recursion to reverse the order of output.

3. Change the program for Problem 2 so that it works for any base up to 10. The user should enter the decimal number and the base, and the program outputs the number in the given base.

4. Write a C++ program using recursion to convert a number in binary (from 1 to 10) to a decimal number. The algorithm for this is that each successive digit in the number is multiplied by the base (two) raised to the power corresponding to its position in the number. The low-order digit is position 0. We sum together all

of these products to get the decimal value. For example, if we have the binary number 111001, we convert it to decimal as follows:

$1 * 2^0 = 1$
$0 * 2^1 = 0$
$0 * 2^2 = 0$
$1 * 2^3 = 8$
$1 * 2^4 = 16$
$1 * 2^5 = 32$

Decimal value = $1 + 0 + 0 + 8 + 16 + 32 = 57$

A recursive formulation of this can extract each digit and compute the corresponding power of the base by which to multiply. Once the base case (the last digit is extracted), the function can sum the products as it returns.

In C++ we can represent a binary number using integers. However, there is a danger—the user can enter an invalid number by typing a digit that's unrepresentable in the base. For example, the number 1011201 is an invalid binary number because 2 isn't allowed in the binary number system. Your program should check for invalid digits as they are extracted, and handle the error in a way that is appropriate (that is, it shouldn't output a numerical result), and provide an informative error message to the user.

5. Modify the program from Problem 4 to work for any number base in the range of 1 through 10. The user should enter a number and a base, and the program outputs the decimal equivalent. If the user enters a digit that is invalid for the base, the program should output an error message, and not display a numerical result.

6. A maze is to be represented by a 12 × 12 array composed of three values: Open, Wall, or Exit. There is one exit from the maze. Write a program to determine whether it is possible to exit the maze from each possible starting point (any open square can be a starting point). You may move vertically or horizontally to any adjacent open square. You may not move to a square containing a wall. The input consists of a series of 12 lines of 12 characters each, representing the contents of each square in the maze. The characters are O, W, or E. Your program should check that there is only one exit. As the data are entered, the program should make a list of all of the starting point coordinates. It can then run through this list, solving the maze for each starting point.

GLOSSARY

Abstract data type A data type whose properties (domain and operations) are specified independently of any particular implementation.

Abstract step A step for which some implementation details remain unspecified.

Abstraction barrier The invisible wall around a class object that encapsulates implementation details. The wall can be breached only through the public interface.

Aggregate operation An operation on a data structure as a whole, as opposed to an operation on an individual component of the data structure.

Algorithm A step-by-step procedure for solving a problem in a finite amount of time.

Anonymous type A type that does not have an associated type identifier.

Argument A variable or expression listed in a call to a function; also called *actual argument* or *actual parameter*.

Argument list A mechanism by which functions communicate with each other.

Arithmetic/logic unit (ALU) The component of the central processing unit that performs arithmetic and logical operations.

Array A collection of components, all of the same type, ordered on N dimensions ($N \geq 1$). Each component is accessed by N indexes, each of which represents the component's position within that dimension.

Assignment expression A C++ expression with (1) a value and (2) the side effect of storing the expression value into a memory location.

Assignment statement A statement that stores the value of an expression into a variable.

Automatic variable A variable for which memory is allocated and deallocated when control enters and exits the block in which it is declared.

Auxiliary storage device A device that stores data in encoded form outside the computer's main memory.

Base address The memory address of the first element of an array.

Base case   The case for which the solution can be stated nonrecursively.

Base class (superclass)   The class being inherited from.

Binary operator   An operator that has two operands.

Black box   An electrical or mechanical device whose inner workings are hidden from view.

C string   In C and C++, a null-terminated sequence of characters stored in a `char` array.

Central processing unit (CPU)   The part of the computer that executes the instructions (program) stored in memory; made up of the arithmetic/logic unit and the control unit.

Class   A structured type in a programming language that is used to represent an abstract data type.

Class member   A component of a class. Class members may be either data or functions.

Class object (class instance)   A variable of a `class` type.

Client   Software that declares and manipulates objects of a particular class.

Compiler   A program that translates a high-level language into machine code.

Composition (containment)   A mechanism by which the internal data (the state) of one class includes an object of another class.

Computer   A programmable device that can store, retrieve, and process data.

Computer program   A sequence of instructions to be performed by a computer.

Computer programming   The process of planning a sequence of steps for a computer to follow.

Concrete step   A step for which the implementation details are fully specified.

Constructor   An operation that creates a new instance (variable) of an ADT.

Control abstraction   The separation of the logical properties of an action from its implementation.

Control structure   A statement used to alter the normally sequential flow of control.

Control unit   The component of the central processing unit that controls the actions of the other components so that instructions (the program) are executed in the correct sequence.

Count-controlled loop   A loop that executes a specified number of times.

Data   Information in a form a computer can use.

Data abstraction   The separation of a data type's logical properties from its implementation.

Data flow   The flow of information from the calling code to a function and from the function back to the calling code.

Data representation   The concrete form of data used to represent the abstract values of an abstract data type.

Data type   A specific set of data values, along with a set of operations on those values.

Declaration   A statement that associates an identifier with a data object, a function, or a data type so that the programmer can refer to that item by name.

Demotion (narrowing)   The conversion of a value from a "higher" type to a "lower" type according to a programming language's precedence of data types. Demotion may cause loss of information.

Derived class (subclass)   The class that inherits.

Direct addressing   Accessing a variable in one step by using the variable name.

Documentation   The written text and comments that make a program easier for others to understand, use, and modify.

Driver   A simple `main` function that is used to call a function being tested. The use of a driver permits direct control of the testing process.

Dynamic binding   The run-time determination of which function to call for a particular object.

Editor   An interactive program used to create and modify source programs or data.

Encapsulation   Hiding a module implementation in a separate block with a formally specified interface.

Enumeration type   A user-defined data type whose domain is an ordered set of literal values expressed as identifiers.

Enumerator   One of the values in the domain of an enumeration type.

Evaluate   To compute a new value by performing a specified set of operations on given values.

Event counter   A variable that is incremented each time a particular event occurs.

Event-controlled loop   A loop that terminates when something happens inside the loop body to signal that the loop should be exited.

Expression   An arrangement of identifiers, literals, and operators that can be evaluated to compute a value of a given type.

Expression statement   A statement formed by appending a semicolon to an expression.

External representation   The printable (character) form of a data value.

Field (member, in C++)   A component of a record.

File   A named area in secondary storage that is used to hold a collection of data; the collection of data itself.

Flow of control   The order in which the computer executes statements in a program.

Function   A subprogram in C++.

Function call (function invocation)   The mechanism that transfers control to a function.

Function call (to a void function)   A statement that transfers control to a void function. In C++, this statement is the name of the function, followed by a list of arguments.

Function definition   A function declaration that includes the body of the function.

Function overloading   The use of the same name for different C++ functions, distinguished from each other by their parameter lists.

Function prototype   A function declaration without the body of the function.

Function value type   The data type of the result value returned by a function.

Functional decomposition   A technique for developing software in which the problem is divided into more easily handled subproblems, the solutions of which create a solution to the overall problem.

Functional equivalence   A property of a module that performs exactly the same operation as the abstract step it defines. A pair of modules are also functionally equivalent to each other when they perform exactly the same operation.

General case The case for which the solution is expressed in terms of a smaller version of itself; also known as *recursive case.*

Generic algorithm An algorithm in which the actions or steps are defined but the data types of the items being manipulated are not.

Hardware The physical components of a computer.

Hierarchical record A record in which at least one of the components is itself a record.

Identifier A name associated with a function or data object and used to refer to that function or data object.

Infinite recursion The situation in which a function calls itself over and over endlessly.

Information Any knowledge that can be communicated.

Information hiding The encapsulation and hiding of implementation details to keep the user of an abstraction from depending on or incorrectly manipulating these details.

Inheritance A mechanism by which one class acquires the properties—the data and operations—of another class.

Input/output (I/O) devices The parts of the computer that accept data to be processed (input) and present the results of that processing (output).

Interactive system A system that allows direct communication between user and computer.

Interface A connecting link at a shared boundary that permits independent systems to meet and act on or communicate with each other. Also, the formal description of the purpose of a subprogram and the mechanism for communicating with it.

Internal representation The form in which a data value is stored inside the memory unit.

Iteration An individual pass through, or repetition of, the body of a loop.

Iteration counter A counter variable that is incremented with each iteration of a loop.

Iterator An operation that allows us to process—one at a time—all the components in an instance of an ADT.

Length The number of values currently stored in a list.

Lifetime The period of time during program execution when an identifier has memory allocated to it.

List A variable-length, linear collection of homogeneous components.

Literal value Any constant value written in a program.

Local variable A variable declared within a block and not accessible outside of that block.

Loop A control structure that causes a statement or group of statements to be executed repeatedly.

Loop entry The point at which the flow of control reaches the first statement inside a loop.

Loop exit The point at which the repetition of the loop body ends and control passes to the first statement following the loop.

Loop test The point at which the While expression is evaluated and the decision is made either to begin a new iteration or skip to the statement immediately following the loop.

Machine language The language, made up of binary-coded instructions, that is used directly by the computer.

Member selector The expression used to access components of a struct or class variable. It is formed by using the struct or class variable name and the member name, separated by a dot (period).

Memory unit Internal data storage in a computer.

Metalanguage A language that is used to write the syntax rules for another language.

Mixed type expression An expression that contains operands of different data types; also called *mixed mode expression.*

Module A self-contained collection of steps that solves a problem or subproblem; can contain both concrete and abstract steps.

Name precedence The precedence that a local identifier in a function has over a global identifier with the same name in any references that the function makes to that identifier; also called *name hiding.*

Named constant (symbolic constant) A location in memory, referenced by an identifier, that contains a data value that cannot be changed.

Named type A user-defined type whose declaration includes a type identifier that gives a name to the type.

Nonlocal identifier With respect to a given block, any identifier declared outside that block.

Object-oriented design (OOD) A technique for developing software in which the solution is expressed in terms of objects—self-contained entities composed of data and operations on that data.

Object-oriented programming (OOP) The use of data abstraction, inheritance, and dynamic binding to construct programs that are collections of interacting objects.

Object program The machine language version of a source program.

Observer An operation that allows us to observe the state of an instance of an ADT without changing it.

One-dimensional array A structured collection of components, all of the same type, that is given a single name. Each component (array element) is accessed by an index that indicates the component's position within the collection.

Operating system A set of programs that manages all of the computer's resources.

Out-of-bounds array index An index value that, in C++, is either less than 0 or greater than the array size minus 1.

Parameter A variable declared in a function heading; also called *formal argument* or *formal parameter.*

Peripheral device An input, output, or auxiliary storage device attached to a computer.

Polymorphic operation An operation that has multiple meanings depending on the type of the object to which it is bound at run time.

Postcondition An assertion that should be true after a module has executed.

Precision The maximum number of significant digits.

Precondition An assertion that must be true before a module begins executing.

Programming Planning or scheduling the performance of a task or an event.

Programming language   A set of rules, symbols, and special words used to construct a computer program.

Promotion (widening)   The conversion of a value from a "lower" type to a "higher" type according to a programming language's precedence of data types.

Range of values   The interval within which values of a numeric type must fall, specified in terms of the largest and smallest allowable values.

Record (structure, in C++)   A structured data type with a fixed number of components that are accessed by name. The components may be heterogeneous (of different types).

Recursive algorithm   A solution that is expressed in terms of (a) smaller instances of itself and (b) a base case.

Recursive call   A function call in which the function being called is the same as the one making the call.

Recursive definition   A definition in which something is defined in terms of smaller versions of itself.

Reference parameter   A parameter that receives the location (memory address) of the caller's argument.

Representational error   Arithmetic error that occurs when the precision of the true result of an arithmetic operation is greater than the precision of the machine.

Reserved word   A word that has special meaning in C++; it cannot be used as a programmer-defined identifier.

Scope   The region of program code where it is legal to reference (use) an identifier.

Scope rules   The rules that determine where in the program an identifier may be accessed, given the point where that identifier is declared.

Self-documenting code   Program code containing meaningful identifiers as well as judiciously used clarifying comments.

Semantics   The set of rules that determines the meaning of instructions written in a programming language.

Short-circuit (conditional) evaluation   Evaluation of a logical expression in left-to-right order with evaluation stopping as soon as the final truth value can be determined.

Side effect   Any effect of one function on another that is not a part of the explicitly defined interface between them.

Significant digits   Those digits from the first nonzero digit on the left to the last nonzero digit on the right (plus any 0 digits that are exact).

Simple (atomic) data type   A data type in which each value is atomic (indivisible).

Software   Computer programs; the set of all programs available on a computer.

Software engineering   The application of traditional engineering methodologies and techniques to the development of software.

Sorting   Arranging the components of a list into order (for instance, words into alphabetical order or numbers into ascending or descending order).

Source program   A program written in a high-level programming language.

Static binding   The compile-time determination of which function to call for a particular object.

Static variable   A variable for which memory remains allocated throughout the execution of the entire program.

Structured data type   A data type in which each value is a collection of components and whose organization is characterized by the method used to access individual components. The allowable operations on a structured data type include the storage and retrieval of individual components.

Structured (procedural) programming   The construction of programs that are collections of interacting functions or procedures.

Stub   A dummy function that assists in testing part of a program. A stub has the same name and interface as a function that actually would be called by the part of the program being tested, but it is usually much simpler.

Switch expression   The expression whose value determines which switch label is selected. It cannot be a floating-point or string expression.

Syntax   The formal rules governing how valid instructions are written in a programming language.

Tail recursion   A recursive algorithm in which no statements are executed after the return from the recursive call.

Termination condition   The condition that causes a loop to be exited.

Test plan   A document that specifies how a program is to be tested.

Test plan implementation   Using the test cases specified in a test plan to verify that a program outputs the predicted results.

Testing the state of a stream   The act of using a C++ stream object in a logical expression as if it were a Boolean variable; the result is `true` if the last I/O operation on that stream succeeded, and `false` otherwise.

Transformer   An operation that builds a new value of the ADT, given one or more previous values of the type.

Two-dimensional array   A collection of components, all of the same type, structured in two dimensions. Each component is accessed by a pair of indexes that represent the component's position in each dimension.

Type casting   The explicit conversion of a value from one data type to another; also called type conversion.

Type coercion   The implicit (automatic) conversion of a value from one data type to another.

Unary operator   An operator that has just one operand.

Value parameter   A parameter that receives a copy of the value of the corresponding argument.

Value-returning function   A function that returns a single value to its caller and is invoked from within an expression.

Variable   A location in memory, referenced by an identifier, that contains a data value that can be changed.

Void function (procedure)   A function that does not return a function value to its caller and is invoked as a separate statement.

Answers to Selected Exercises

Chapter 1   Exam Preparation Exercises

2. Analysis and specification, general solution (algorithm), verify.
4. The analysis and specification step within the problem-solving phase.
6. a. iii, b. i, c. iv, d. ii
8. The control unit directs the actions of the other components in the computer to execute program instruction in the proper order.
10. False. Peripheral devices are external to the CPU and its main memory.

Chapter 1   Programming Warm-Up Exercises

2. Follow separate algorithm for filling glass with water and placing on counter
   If right-handed,
      pick up toothpaste tube in left hand and unscrew cap by turning counter-clockwise
      place toothpaste cap on counter
      transfer toothpaste tube to right hand and pick up toothbrush in left hand, holding it by its handle
      place open end of toothpaste tube against tips of brush bristles and squeeze toothpaste tube just enough to create a 0.5-inch-long extrusion of toothpaste on brush
      pull toothpaste tube away from brush and place tube on counter
      transfer toothbrush to right hand, holding it by its handle
      open mouth and insert brush, placing toothpaste-covered bristles against one tooth
      scrub tooth with brush by moving brush up and down 10 times
      reposition brush to an unscrubbed tooth
      repeat previous two steps until all teeth have been brushed
      spit toothpaste into sink
      put toothbrush in sink

> pick up glass in right hand
> fill mouth with water from glass
> swish water in mouth for five seconds
> spit water from mouth into sink
> repeat previous three steps three times

Otherwise (if left-handed)

> pick up toothpaste tube in right hand and unscrew cap by turning counter-clockwise
> place toothpaste cap on counter
> transfer toothpaste tube to left hand and pick up toothbrush in right hand, holding it by its
>   handle
> place open end of toothpaste tube against tips of brush bristles and squeeze toothpaste tube
>   just enough to create a 0.5-inch-long extrusion of toothpaste on brush
> pull toothpaste tube away from brush and place tube on counter
> transfer toothbrush to left hand, holding it by its handle
> open mouth and insert brush, placing toothpaste-covered bristles against one tooth
> scrub tooth with brush by moving brush up and down 10 times
> reposition brush to an unscrubbed tooth
> repeat previous two steps until all teeth have been brushed
> spit toothpaste into sink
> put toothbrush in sink
> pick up glass in left hand
> fill mouth with water from glass
> swish water in mouth for five seconds
> spit water from mouth into sink
> repeat previous three steps three times

Place glass on counter

Follow separate algorithm for cleaning up after brushing teeth

4. Change step u to:

   u. Repeat step t nine times.

Chapter 2   Exam Preparation Exercises

2. a. vi, b. ix, c. iv, d. v, e. vii, f. ii, g. i, h. x, i. iii, j. viii.

4. The template allows an identifier to begin with a digit. Identifiers can begin with a letter or an underscore, and digits may appear only in the second character position and beyond.

6. True.

8. Note that the second line concatenates two words without a separating space.

```
Four score and
seven years agoour fathers
brought forth on this
continent a new nation...
```

10. By preceding it with a backslash character (\").

12. The // form of comment cannot span more than one line. It also cannot be inserted into the middle of a line of code because everything to the right of // becomes a comment.

14. No. The end1 identifier is a manipulator, and is not a string value.
16. std::cout << "Hello everybody!" << std::endl;
18. By splitting it into pieces that fit on a line, and joining them with the concatenation operator.

Chapter 2   Programming Warm-Up Exercises

2. Note that the \" escape sequence is needed in six places here:

```
cout << "He said, \"How is that possible?\"" << endl
     << "She replied, \"Using manipulators.\"" << endl
     << "\"Of course,\" he exclaimed!" << endl;
```

4.
```
const string FIRST = "Your first name inserted here";
const string LAST = "Your last name inserted here";
// Insert your middle initial in place of A:
const char MIDDLE = 'A';
```

6. PART1 + PART2 + PART1 + PART3
8.
```
#include <iostream>
#include <string>

using namespace std;

const string TITLE = "Rev.";
const char FIRST = 'H';
const char MID 'G';
const char DOT = '.';

int main()
{
    cout << TITLE << FIRST << DOT << MID << DOT
         << " Jones";
}
```

Chapter 3   Exam Preparation Exercises

2. Integer overflow.
4.

	integer / floating	constant / variable
a. const int TRACKS_ON_DISK = 17;	integer	constant
b. float timeOfTrack;	floating	variable
c. const float MAX_TIME_ON_DISK = 74.0;	floating	constant
d. short tracksLeft;	integer	variable
e. float timeLeft;	floating	variable
f. long samplesInTrack;	integer	variable
g. const double SAMPLE_RATE = 262144.5;	floating	constant

6. a. 21, b. 21.6, c. 13.0, d. 18, e. 20, f. 22, g. 18.0.
8. True.
10. The ++ operator.
12. `main` returns an `int` value.
14. False. When used alone they are equivalent, but used within a larger expression, they can give different results (this is explained more in Chapter 10).
16. a. 29
    b. 1
    c. `"ought to start with logic"`
    d. 0
    e. `"log"`
    f. 1
    g. `string::npos`

Chapter 3   Programming Warm-Up Exercises

2. a. `days / 7`
   b. `days % 7`
4. `float(dollars * 100 + quarters * 25 + dimes * 10 +`
   `    nickels * 5 + pennies) / 100.0`
6. a. `3 * X + Y`
   b. `A * A + 2 * B + C`
   c. `((A + B)/(C - D)) * (X / Y)`
   d. `((A * A + 2 * B + C)/D) / (X * Y)`
   e. `sqrt(fabs(A - B))`
   f. `pow(X, -cos(Y))`
8. `startOfMiddle = name.find(' ') + 1;`
10. `cout << setprecision(5) << setw(15) << distance;`
12.
```
//********************************************
// Celsius program
// This program outputs the Celsius temperature
// corresponding to a given Fahrenheit temperature
//********************************************

#include <iostream>

using namespace std;

int main()
{
    const float FAHRENHEIT = 72.0;
    float celsius;

    celsius = 5/9 * (FAHRENHEIT - 32);
    cout << fixed << "Celsius equivalent of Fahrenheit "
```

```
        << FAHRENHEIT << " is " << celsius << " degrees.";
    return 0;
}
```

Chapter 4   Exam Preparation Exercises

2. a. The insertion operator cannot be used with `cin`.
   b. The extraction operator cannot be used with `cout`.
   c. The right operand of the extraction operator must be a variable.
   d. The arguments are in reverse order.
   e. The function name should not have a capital L, and the arguments are reversed.
4. a = 70, b = 80, c = 30, d = 0, e = 20, f = 30.
6. a. `string1 = "January 25, 2005"`
   b. The reading marker is at the start of the next line.
8. It returns \n.
10. Some variation in the answer is acceptable, as long as it is clear that the prompt for the inexperienced user is much more detailed.
    a. `cout << "Enter a date in the format of mm/dd/yyyy."`
          `<< " For example, for October 18, 1989, enter 10/18/1989.";`
    b. `cout << "Enter date, format mm/dd/yyyy.";`
12. `ifstream` and `ofstream`.
14. The correction is to convert the name into a C string.

```
ifstream inData;
string name;

cout << "Enter the name of the file: ");
cin >> name;
infile.open(name.c_str());
```

16. False. The file immediately enters the fail state, and I/O operations on it are simply ignored.
18. The answer can vary, but should at least include vehicle, customer, and agency. A little more thought might add garage, repair shop, contract, and so on.
20. a. no, b. yes, c. yes, d. no, e. no.

Chapter 4   Programming Warm-Up Exercises

2. `cout << "Enter a name in the format: first middle last:";`
   `cin >> first >> middle >> last;`

4.
```
float number1;
float number2;
float number3;
float average;

cout << "Enter the first number and press return: ";
```

```
cin >> number1;
cout << "Enter the second number and press return: ";
cin >> number2;
cout << "Enter the third number and press return: ";
cin >> number3;
average = (number1 + number2 + number3) / 3.0;
cout << "The average is: " << average << endl;
```

6. The names of the variables may differ from those shown here. Instead of using the ignore function to skip a single character, reading into a dummy char variable may also be used.

a.
```
int int1;
char char1;
float float1;

cin >> int1 >> char1 >> float1;
```

b.
```
string string1;
string string2;
int int1;
int int2;

cin >> string1 >> int1 >> string2 >> int2;
```

c.
```
int int1;
int int2;
float float1;

cin >> int1;
cin.ignore(1, ',');
cin >> int2;
cin.ignore(1, ',');
cin >> float1;
```

d.
```
char char1;
char char2;
char char3;
char char4;

cin >> char1;
cin.ignore(1, ' ');
cin >> char2;
cin.ignore(1, ' ');
cin >> char3;
cin.ignore(1, ' ');
cin >> char4;
cin.ignore(1, ' ');
```

e. `float float1;`

```
cin.ignore(1, '$');
cin >> float1;
```

8.
```
#include <fstream>
fstream temps;
temps.open("temperatures.dat");
```

10.
```
#include <iostream>
#include <fstream>


using namespace std;

fstream inData;
fstream outData;
const float PI = 3.14159265;
float radius;
float circumference;
float area;

int main()
{
    inData.open("indata.dat");
    outData.open("outdata.dat");
    inData >> radius;
    circumference = radius * 2 * PI;
    area = radius * radius * PI;
    cout << "For the first circle, the circumference is "
         << circumference << " and the area is " << area << endl;
    outData << radius << " " << circumference << " " << area << endl;
    inData >> radius;
    circumference = radius * 2 * PI;
    area = radius * radius * PI;
    cout << "For the second circle, the circumference is "
         << circumference << " and the area is " << area << endl;
    outData << radius << " " << circumference << " " << area << endl;
}
```

12. `inFile >> int1 >> int2 >> int3;`

14.

Top level:

Write letter
Mail letter

Write letter	Level 2

Write return address and date
Write company address
Write salutation
Write body of letter
Write closing
Sign letter

Mail letter	

Address envelope
Write return address
Attach stamp to envelope
Fold letter in thirds
Insert letter in envelope
Seal envelope
Place envelope in mail box

Chapter 5   Exam Preparation Exercises

2. False. They are predefined constants.
4. Because, in the collating sequence of the character set, the uppercase letters all come before the lowercase letters.
6. a. true
   b. true
   c. true
   d. true
   e. true
   f. false
   g. false
8. True.
10. It outputs `"The data doesn't make sense."`
12. Nothing.
14. It outputs `Very good`
16. Add braces to enclose the If-Then statement.
18. There is no limit, although a human reader finds it difficult to follow too many levels.

Chapter 5   Programming Warm-Up Exercises

```
2. !inFile1 && !inFile2
4. if (year1 < year2 && month1 < month2 && day1 < day2)
        cout << month1 << "/" << day1 << "/" year1
            << " comes before "
```

```
            << month2 << "/" << day2 << "/" << year2;
    else
        cout << month1 << "/" << day1 << "/" year1
            << " does not come before "
            << month2 << "/" << day2 << "/" << year2;
```

6. `bool1 || bool2 && !(bool1 && bool2)`

8.
```
if (score < 0 || score > 100)
    cout << "Score is out of range";
else
{
    scoreTotal = scoreTotal + score;
    scoreCount++;
}
```

10.
```
if (score > 100)
    cout << "Duffer.";
else if (score > 80)
    cout << "Weekend regular.";
else if (score > 72)
    cout << "Competitive player.";
else if (score > 68)
    cout << "Turn pro!";
else
    cout << "Time to go on tour!";
```

12. The conditional tests are using = instead of ==. Both branches have the error, but the second one doesn't output the message because the result of the assignment expression is 0, which is treated as false by the branch.

```
maximum = 75;
minimum = 25;
if (maximum == 100)
    cout << "Error in maximum: " << maximum << endl;
if (minimum == 0)
    cout << "Error in minimum: " << minimum << endl;
```

Chapter 6   Exam Preparation Exercises

2. False.
4. a. ii, b. ix, c. iv, d. viii, e. vi, f. i, g. v, h. vii, i. iii.
6. Twelve times.

   `0, 1, 2, 3, 4, 5, 6, 7, 8, 9, 10, 11,`

8. The output is:

```
        @
       @@
      @@@
     @@@@
    @@@@@
   @@@@@@
  @@@@@@@
 @@@@@@@@
@@@@@@@@@
@@@@@@@@@@
@@@@@@@@@@@
```

10. The code fails to process the first value on the file. The corrected code is:

```
sum = 0;
indata >> number;
while (indata)
{
    sum = sum + number;
    indata >> number;
}
```

12. The output is:

```
3  5  7  9  11  13  15  17  19
```

The corrected code is:

```
number = 0;
while (number < 10)
{
    cout << number * 2 - 1 << " ";
    number++;
}
```

14. What is the condition that ends the loop? How should the condition be initialized? How should the condition be updated? What is the process being repeated? How should the process be initialized? How should the process by updated? What is the state of the program on exiting the loop?

Chapter 6   Programming Warm-Up Exercises

2.
```
count = 1;
sum = 0;
while (sum <= 10000)
{
    sum = sum + count;
```

```
        count++;
    }
    cout << count - 1;
```

4.
```
    count = 0;
    getline(chapter6, line);
    while (chapter6)
    {
        if (line.find("code segment") < string::npos)
          count++;
        getline(chapter6, line);
    }
    cout << "The string was found " << count << " times."
```

6.
```
    cout << "Sun  Mon  Tue  Wed  Thu  Fri  Sat" << endl;
    count = 1;
    while (count <= startDay)  //Print blanks in first week
    {
        cout << "     ";
        count++;
    }
    dayNumber = 1;
    while (dayNumber <= days)  //Print day numbers for month
    {
        while (count <= 7)     //Print for one week in month
        {
            if (dayNumber <= days)
                cout << setw(3) << dayNumber << "  ";
            count++;
            dayNumber++;
        }
        cout << endl;
        count = 1;
    }
```

8.
```
    char oneChar;
    int eCount;
    int charCount;
    eCount = 0;
    textData >> oneChar;
    charCount = 0;
    while (textData)
    {
        charCount++;
        if (oneChar == 'z')
            eCount++;
```

```
            textData >> oneChar;
        }
    cout << "Percentage of letter 'z': "
            << float(eCount) / charCount * 100;
10. first = 1;
    second = 1;
    cout << first << endl << second << endl;
    while (second < 30000)
    {
        next = first + second;
        first = second;
        second = next;
        cout << second << endl;
    }

12. cout << "Enter number of stars: ";
    cin >> number;
    count = 1;
    while (count <= number)
    {
        cout << '*';
        count++;
    )
    cout << endl;

14. indata >> number;
    while (indata)
    {
        count = 1;
        while (count <= number)
        {
            cout << '*';
            count++;
        }
        cout << endl;
        indata >> number;
    }
```

Chapter 7   Exam Preparation Exercises

2. False. The parameter name is optional.
4. a. v, b. iii, c. vi, d. i, e. iv, f. viii, g. ii, h. vii.
6. The call must have six arguments, unless default parameters are used (we do not cover their use in this book, but they are mentioned).

8. The type must come before the name of each parameter instead of after it. The & should be appended to the type instead of to the parameter name. The prototype should end with a semicolon.

10. Hiding a module implementation in a separate block with a formally specified interface.

12. It should not contain a `return` statement.

14. The result is not passed back to the caller—`result` should be a reference parameter instead of a value parameter.

16. False. Like any other variable declaration, it can be accessed only by statements within the block that follows its declaration.

18. That the file contains valid data (only integers), and that it has at least one value (the mean is undefined for an empty data set).

Chapter 7   Programming Warm-Up Exercises

```
2. void Max (int, int, int&);
4. void GetLeast (/* inout */ ifstream& infile,
                  /* out */   int&      lowest)

6. void GetLeast (/* inout */ ifstream& infile,
                  /* out */   int&      lowest)
   {
       int number;
       infile >> number;      // Get a number
       lowest = INT_MAX;      // Initially use greatest int
       while (infile)
       {
           if (number < lowest)
               lowest = number;   // Remember lower number
           infile >> number;      // Get next number
       }
   }

8. void Reverse ( /* in */   string  original,
                  /* out */ string& lanigiro )

10. void Reverse ( /* in */   string  original,
                   /* out */ string& lanigiro )
   {
       int count;
       count = 1;
       lanigiro = "";
       while (count <= original.length())
       {
           lanigiro = lanigiro +
               original.substr(original.length() - count, 1);
           count++;
       }
   )
```

```
12. void LowerCount ( /* out */ int& count)
    {
        char inChar;
        count = 0;
        cin >> inChar;
        while (cin && inChar != '\n')
        {
          if (islower(inChar))
              count++;
          cin >> inChar;
        }
    }

14. void GetNonemptyLine ( /* inout */ ifstream& infile,
                           /* out */    string&   line)
    {
        getline(infile, line);
        while (infile && line == "")
            getline(infile, line);
    }

16. void TimeAdd ( /* inout */ int& days,
                   /* inout */ int& hours,
                   /* inout */ int& minutes,
                   /* in */    int  addDays,
                   /* in */    int  addHours,
                   /* in */    int  addMinutes)
    {
        int extraHour;
        int extraDay;
        minutes = (minutes + addMinutes) % 60;
        extraHour = (minutes + addMinutes) / 60;
        hours = (hours + addHours + extraHour) % 24;
        extraDay = (hours + addHours + extraHour) / 24;
        days = days + addDays + extraDay;
    }

18. void SeasonPrint (/* in */ int month,
                      /* in */ int day)
    {
        if (month == 12 && day >= 21)
            cout << "Winter";
        else if ((month == 9 and day >= 21) || month > 9)
            cout << "Fall";
        else if ((month == 6 and day >= 21) || month > 6)
            cout << "Summer";
```

```
    else if ((month == 3 and day >= 21) || month > 3)
        cout << "Spring";
    else
        cout << "Winter";
}
```

Chapter 8   Exam Preparation Exercises

2. False. It is local to the function's body.
4. True.
6. The combination of `param2` being a reference parameter and the erroneous use of an assignment expression instead of an equality test in the first If statement results in the argument to `param2` being assigned the value in `param1` every time the function is called.
8. The namespace is in global scope.
10. a. Static, b. Automatic, c. Static.
12. It is initialized once, when control first reaches the statement.
14. False.
16. The `return` expression is of type `float`, and the return type of the function is `int`.
18. It makes a side effect error more likely.

Chapter 8   Programming Warm-Up Exercises

```
2. bool Equals (/* in */ float x,
               /* in */ float y)

4. bool Equals (/* in */ float x,
               /* in */ float y)
   {
       return abs(x - y) < 0.00000001;
   }

6. float ConeVolume (/* in */ float radius,
                     /* in */ float height);
   {
       return 1.0/3.0 * 3.14159265 * radius * radius * height;
   }

8. string Reverse (/* in */  string  original)
   {
       string lanigiro;
       int count;
       count = 1;
       lanigiro = "";
       while (count <= original.length())
       {
           lanigiro = lanigiro +
```

```
                    original.substr(original.length() - count, 1);
            count++;
        }
        return lanigiro;
    )
```

10.
```
float SquareKm (/* in */ float length,
                /* in */ float width);
{
    return length * 1.6 * width * 1.6;
}
```

12.
```
string MonthAbbrev (/* in */ int month)
{
    if (month == 12) return "Dec";
    else if (month == 11) return "Nov";
    else if (month == 10) return "Oct";
    else if (month == 9) return "Sep";
    else if (month == 8) return "Aug";
    else if (month == 7) return "Jul";
    else if (month == 6) return "Jun";
    else if (month == 5) return "May";
    else if (month == 4) return "Apr";
    else if (month == 3) return "Mar";
    else if (month == 2) return "Feb";
    else return "Jan";
}
```

14.
```
float RunningAvg (/* in */ float value)
{
    static float total = 0.0;
    static int count = 0;
    total = total + value;
    count++;
    return total/float(count);
}
```

Chapter 9   Exam Preparation Exercises

2. False. It has local scope.
4. False. Both Break and Continue are allowed in any of the looping statements.
6. Control jumps to the `case` matching the `switch` expression, but then proceeds to execute the remaining statements in all of the succeeding `cases`.
8. 1000 times.
10. A While statement would be the best choice.
12. August

14. 2
    1
    0
    3
    2
    1
    4
    3
    2

16. How now brown cow?

18. 12

Chapter 9   Programming Warm-Up Exercises

2.
```cpp
switch (day)
{
    case 0 : cout << "Sunday"; break;
    case 1 : cout << "Monday"; break;
    case 2 : cout << "Tuesday"; break;
    case 3 : cout << "Wednesday"; break;
    case 4 : cout << "Thursday"; break;
    case 5 : cout << "Friday"; break;
    case 6 : cout << "Saturday"; break;
    default: cout << "Error";
}
```

4.
```cpp
for (int day = 6, day >= 0, day--)
    cout << DayOfWeek(day) << endl;
```

6.
```cpp
char response;
do
{
    cout << "Please enter 'Y' or 'N': ";
    cin >> response;
    if (response != 'Y' && response != 'N')
        cout << "Invalid response. ";
} while (response != 'Y' && response != 'N');
```

8.
```cpp
for (int row = 1; row <= 10; row++)
{
    for (int col = 1; col <= 10; col++)
        cout << setw(5) << row * col;
    cout << endl;
}
```

```
10. int line;
    int star;
    line = 1;
    do
    {
        star = 1;
        do
        {
            cout << '*';
            star++;
        } while (star <= line);
        cout << endl;
        line++;
    } while (line <= 10);
12. void Rectangle (/* in */ int height,
                    /* in */ int width)
    {
        for (int col = 1; col <= width; col++)
            cout << '*';
        cout << endl;
        for (int row = 2; row <= height - 1; row++)
        {
            cout << '*';
            for (int col = 2; col < width - 1; col++)
                cout << ' ';
            cout << '*' << endl;
        }
        for (int col = 1; col <= width; col++)
            cout << '*';
        cout << endl;
    }
14. int startHour = 3;
    int endHour = 7;
    int startMin = 15;
    int endMin = 30;
    int beginMin;
    int lastMin;

    for (int hour = startHour; hour <= endHour; hour++)
    {
        if (hour == startHour)
            beginMin = startMin;
        else
            beginMin = 0;
```

```
        if (hour == endHour)
            lastMin = endMin;
        else
            lastMin = 59;

        for (int min = beginMin; min <= lastMin; min++)
            for (int sec = 0; sec <= 59; sec++)
                cout << hour << ':' << min << ':' << sec << endl;
}
```

Chapter 10   Exam Preparation Exercises

2. True.
4. True.
6. `char, short, int, long, bool.`
8. The assignment operators.
10. When the type name is not a single word, as in `unsigned int`.
12. `'g'`
14. Absolute error is a fixed value of allowable error, whereas relative error multiplies the allowable error by one of the values being compared.
16. The value of the expression is 3.
18. Because we must use the same type name for arguments, parameters, and function prototypes. If the type doesn't have a name, we can't use it in this context.

Chapter 10   Programming Warm-Up Exercises

2. a. 3.14159265F
   b. 3.14159265
   c. 3.14159265L
   d. 3.14159265E0
4. `sizeof(long) * 8`
6.
```
cin >> charIn;
if (isdigit( charIn))
  numIn = charIn - '0';
```

8.
```
int MonthNum (/* in */ string month)
{
    switch (tolower(month[0]))
    {
        case 'a': switch (tolower(month[1]))
                {
                    case 'p': return 4;
                    case 'u': return 8;
                    default : return 0;
                }
```

```
            case 'd': return 12;
            case 'f': return 2;
            case 'j': switch (tolower(month[3]))
                          {
                              case 'e': return 6;
                              case 'u': return 1;
                              case 'y': return 7;
                              default : return 0;
                          }
            case 'm': switch (tolower(month[2]))
                          {
                              case 'r': return 3;
                              case 'y': return 5;
                              default : return 0;
                          }
            case 'n': return 11;
            case 'o': return 10;
            case 's': return 9;
            default : return 0;
        }
    }
```

10. `abs(balance - audit) <= 0.001`

12. `enum Planets {MERCURY, VENUS, EARTH, MARS,`
    `               JUPITER, SATURN, URANUS, NEPTUNE, PLUTO};`

14.
```
string PlanetToString (/* in */ Planet sphere)
{
    switch (sphere)
    {
        case MERCURY: return "Mercury";
        case VENUS: return "Venus";
        case EARTH: return "Earth";
        case MARS: return "Mars";
        case JUPITER: return "Jupiter";
        case SATURN: return "Saturn";
        case URANUS: return "Uranus";
        case NEPTUNE: return "Neptune";
        case PLUTO: return "Pluto";
        default : return "Error";
    }
}
```

Chapter 11   Exam Preparation Exercises

2. True.
4. True.
6. Assignment, passing as a parameter, return value from a function.
8. a. `sally.studentName.first = "Sally";`
      `sally.studentName.middle = "Ellen";`
      `sally.studentName.last = "Strong";`

   b. `sally.gradeNumber = 7;`

   c. `spring = sally.grades[3]`

10. a. Makes the type of `grade` be `char`, and inputs a `char` to `grade`.
    b. Compares the value in `grade` to see if it is in the range of `'A'` through `'D'`.
    c. Computes the integer equivalent of the letter grade, changes the type of `grade` to `int`, and assigns the numeric value to it.
12. The data representation is a concrete form of the domain, expressed in terms of structures and types supported by the programming language.
14. `current.plus(period);`
16. By matching the number, order, and types of the arguments with the parameter list.
18. It is written with a tilde before the name.

Chapter 11   Programming Warm-Up Exercises

2. `someTime.minutes = 6;`
   `someTime.seconds = 54;`

4. `Song mySong;`

   `mySong.title = "Long Run for a Collie Dog";`
   `mySong.album = "Timmy's Nightmare"`
   `mySong.artist = "Rebekah MacIntash";`
   `mySong.playTime = someTime;`
   `mySong.type = BLUES;`

6.
```
union Temporal
{
    string asString;
    int asInteger;
    Time asTime;
}
```

8.
```
//*****************************************
// SPECIFICATION FILE (Period)
// This file gives the specification of a
// class for geologic time periods
//*****************************************
```

```
class Period
{
public:
    enum PeriodName { PRECAMBRIAN, CAMBRIAN, ORDOVICIAN,
                      SILURIAN, DEVONIAN, CARBONIFEROUS,
                      PERMIAN, TRIASSIC, JURASSIC,
                      CRETACEOUS, TERTIARY, QUATERNARY};

    Period();
    // Default constructor
    // Creates object with value PRECAMBRIAN

    Period(PeriodName);
    // Constructor
    // Creates object with value specified

    String ToString() const;
    // Observer
    // Returns name of object as a string

    int ToInt() const;
    // Observer
    // Returns value of object as an int, 0 = PRECAMBRIAN

    float StartDate() const;
    // Observer
    // Returns starting date of period in millions of years ago

    void Increment();
    // Transformer
    // Advances value of object to next most recent period
    // Won't advance past QUATERNARY

private:

    PeriodName thisPeriod;

}
```

10.
```
    Period::Period()
    // Default constructor
    // Creates object with value PRECAMBRIAN
    {
        PeriodName = PRECAMBRIAN;
    }
```

```
Period::Period(/* in */ PeriodName aPeriod)
// Constructor
// Creates object with value specified
{
    thisPeriod = aPeriod;
}
```

12. The file would be called `Period.h`.

14.
```
//*****************************************
// SPECIFICATION FILE (Money)
// This file gives the specification of a
// class for representing money as dollars
// and cents using integers.
//*****************************************

class Money
{
public:

    Money();
    // Default constructor
    // Creates object with value $0.00

    Money(int, int);
    // Constructor
    // Creates object with value specified
    // in dollars and cents

    int Dollars() const;
    // Observer
    // Returns dollars portion of object as an int

    int Cents() const;
    // Observer
    // Returns cents portion of object as an int

    float Amount() const;
    // Observer
    // Returns money value as a float

    void Add(Money);
    // Transformer
    // Adds value of money object in parameter
```

```
        void Sub(Money);
        // Transformer
        // Subtracts value of money object in parameter

    private:

        int dollars;
        int cents;
    }
```

16. The file name would be Money.h.
18. `float Money::Amount() const`
    ```
    // Observer
    // Returns money value as a float
    {
        return float(dollars) + float(cents)/100.0;
    }
    ```

Chapter 12   Exam Preparation Exercises

2. True.
4. True.
6. C++ does not report an out-of-bounds access as an error. The program accesses the location preceding the first element of the array, which may be a completely unrelated value in memory.
8. The base address is the memory location of the first element of an array. It is the value that is passed to a reference parameter in a function call.
10. The inner loop would increment the column index, keeping the row constant. The outer loop would increment the row index to move to the next row after each row is processed.
12. The For loop runs from 1 to 100 instead of 0 to 99. The last iteration will assign zero to an out-of-bounds location.
14. Functions cannot return array types.
16. Because the index value is input and then used without any checking, an out-of-bounds array access is likely.
18.
```
*  * *
 *  *
  *  * *
 *  *
  *  * *
```
20.
```
*  *  *
 *  *
*  *  *
 *  *
*  *  *
```

Chapter 12   Programming Warm-Up Exercises

2. ```
typedef float DataSet[5];
DataSet input;
DataSet output;
DataSet working;
```

4. ```
for (int row = 0; row < 3; row++)
    for (int col = 0; col < 5; col++)
        set[row][col] = 0.0;
```

6. ```
bool Equals (/* in */ const DataSet first,
             /* in */ const DataSet second)
{
    for(int index = 0; index < 5; index++)
        if (first[index] != second[index])
            return false;
    // Only reaches end of loop if all are equal
    return true;
}
```

8. a. `currentList[36]`

   b. `currentList[11].title`

   c. `currentList[84].size.width`

   d. `currentList[119].room`

   e. `currentList[77].artist[0]`

10. ```
float total = 0.0;
for (int index = 0; index < numPieces; index++)
    total = total + currentList[index].price;
```

12. ```
float total = 0.0;
for (int index = 0; index < numPieces; index++)
    if(currentList[index].medium == OIL)
        if (currentList[index].size.width *
                currentList[index].size.height > 400)
        total = total + currentList[index].price;
```

14. ```
for (int octave = 0; octave < 8; octave++)
    for (Notes note = A; note <= GSHARP; note = Notes(note  + 1))
        cin >> scale[octave][note];
```

16. ```
for (int octave = 0; octave < 8; octave++)
    cout << scale[octave][C] << endl;
```

18. ```
void Reset (float humidity[10][52][50][3])
{
  for (int year = 0; year < 10; year++)
      for (int week = 0; week < 52; week++)
          for (int state = 0; state < 50; state++)
```

```
                    for (Type type = MAX; type <= AVERAGE;
                        type = Type(type + 1));
                        humidity = 0.0;
    }
```

20. ```
    for (int year = 5; year < 10; year++)
        for (int week = 0; week < 52; week++)
            cout << humidity[year][week][22][AVERAGE] << endl;
    ```

Chapter 13   Exam Preparation Exercises

2. That all of the components have the same type.
4. `while (index < length && fabs(item -data[index]) >= EPSILON)`
   We need to change it because floating point numbers cannot be compared reliably for exact equality.
6. It has identified the smallest value in the portion of the list that remains to be sorted.
8. True.
10. Because the values in a sorted list are always kept in order.
12. `'H'`, `'o'`, `'p'`, and `'\0'`

Chapter 13   Programming Warm-Up Exercises

2. ```
   void List::Insert( /* in */ ItemType item)

   // Inserts item into list without duplication

   {
       if (!IsPresent(item))
       {
           data[length] = item;
           length++;
       }
   }
   ```

4. ```
   void DeleteAll( /* in */ ItemType item);
   // Precondition:
   //      NOT IsEmpty()
   //      && item is assigned
   // Postcondition:
   //      IF item is present in list
   //          All occurrences of item are deleted from list
   //          && Length() ==
   //              Length()@entry - number of occurrences of item
   //      ELSE
   //          List is unchanged
   ```
   ```

6. ```
void Replace(/* in */ ItemType item,
              /* in */ ItemType newItem);
// Precondition:
//   NOT IsEmpty()
//   && oldItem is assigned
//   && newItem is assigned
// Postcondition:
//   IF oldItem is present in list
//   First occurrence of oldItem is replaced by newItem
//   ELSE
//   List is unchanged
```

8. The `Insert` and `BinSearch` functions must be changed to enable descending order. We don't have to change `IsPresent` or `Delete`, because they both use `BinSearch` to locate the item.

10. ```
void SortedList::DeleteAll( /* in */ ItemType item)

// Deletes all occurrences of item from the list

{
    int first;
    int index = 0;
    while (index < length && item != data[index])
        index++;
    first = index;
    while (index < length && item == data[index])
        index++;
    for (int position = index; position < length; position++)
        data[first + position - index] = data[position];
    length = length - (index - first);
}
```

12. ```
SortedList inData;
ifstream unsorted;
ItemType oneItem;

unsorted >> oneItem;
while (unsorted && !inData.IsFull())
{
    inData.Insert(oneItem);
    unsorted >> oneItem;
}
```
```

Chapter 14   Exam Preparation Exercises

2. True.
4. True.
6. Declaration of a class data member to be an object of the class that we want to compose into the new class being defined.
8. The class declaration for `DerivedClass` doesn't specify that it is making the members of `BaseClass` public, so they are not available to the client code. The heading should be changed to:

```
class DerivedClass : public BaseClass
```

10. a. The `BaseClass` constructor is called first.
    b. The `DerivedClass` constructor is called last.
12. The `virtual` designation should be used only with the base class declaration of `BaseAlpha`.
14. c.

Chapter 14   Programming Warm-Up Exercises

2.
```
#include "testscore.h"
#include <iostream>
#include <string>

using namespace std;

TestScore::TestScore(
    /* in */ string name,
    /* in */ int score)
{
    studentName = name;
    studentScore = score;
}

TestScore::string GetName() const
{
    return studentName;
}

TestScore::int GetScore() const
{
    return studentScore;
}
```

4.
```
#include "idscore.h"

class Exam
{
```

```cpp
public:
  SetScore(
      /* in */ int location,
      /* in */ IDScore score );
  IDScore GetScore(
      /* in */ int location ) const;

private:
    IDScore examList[100];
}
```

6.
```cpp
class InternPhone : public Phone
{
public
    InternPhone
        ( /* in */ int newCountry,
          /* in */ int newAreaCode,
          /* in */ int newNumber,
          /* in */ PhoneType newType );
    void Write () const;
private:
    int country;
}
```

8.
```cpp
void InternPhone::Write() const
{
    cout << country;
    Phone::Write();
    cout << endl;
}
```

10.
```cpp
class InstallRecord : public Computer
{
public:
    InstallRecord(
        /* in */ string newName,
        /* in */ string newBrand,
        /* in */ string newModel,
        /* in */ int    newSpeed,
        /* in */ string newSerial,
        /* in */ int    newNumber,
        /* in */ string newLocation,
        /* in */ SimpleDate newDate );
    void Write() const;
```

```
        string getNewLocation();
        SimpleDate getSimpleDate();

    private:
        string location;
        SimpleDate installDate;
    };
```

12.
```
    InstallRecord::InstallRecord(
        /* in */ string newName,
        /* in */ string newBrand,
        /* in */ string newModel,
        /* in */ int    newSpeed,
        /* in */ string newSerial,
        /* in */ int    newNumber,
        /* in */ string newLocation,
        /* in */ SimpleDate newDate )
      : Computer( newName, newBrand, newModel,
                newSpeed, newSerial, newNumber )
    {
        location = newLocation;
        installDate = newDate;
    }
```

14.
```
    void InstallRecord::Write() const;
    {
        Computer::Write();
        cout << location << endl;
        installDate.Write();
    }
```

Chapter 15   Exam Preparation Exercises

2. True.
4. False. Tail recursion occurs when nothing is done after the return from the recursive call.
6. F(3) = 8, F(4) = 16, F(5) = 32.
8. It will run out of space on the run time stack.
10. c. The value in the variable.
12.
```
    30
    20
    10
```

14.
```
    abcc
    d
    e
```

Chapter 15   Programming Warm-Up Exercises

2.
```
int OneDigit (int number)
{
    if (number <= 9)
        return number;
    else
        return OneDigit(DigitSum(number));
}
```

4.
```
void Ex4()
{
    int number;
    cout << "Enter a positive number, 0 to end: ";
    cin >> number;

    if (number != 0)
    {
        cout << number << endl;
        Ex4();
        cout << number << endl;
    }
}
```

6.
```
void Ex6(int sum, int& revSum)
{
    int number;
    cout << "Enter a positive number, 0 to end: ";
    cin >> number;

    if (number != 0)
    {
        cout << "Total: " << sum + number <<endl;
        Ex6(sum + number, revSum);
        revSum = revSum + number;
        cout << number << " Total: " << revSum << endl;
    }
}
```

8.
```
void Ex8(int& greatest)
{
    int number;
    cout << "Enter a positive number, 0 to end: ";
    cin >> number;

    if (number > greatest)
```

```
        greatest = number;

    if (number != 0)
    {
        cout << "Greatest: " << greatest << endl;
        Ex8(greatest);
        cout << number << endl;
    }


}
```

The greatest must be written immediately following the call.

Appendix A Reserved Words

The following identifiers are *reserved words*–identifiers with predefined meanings in the C++ language. The programmer cannot declare them for other uses (for example, variable names) in a C++ program.

and	double	not	this
and_eq	dynamic_cast	not_eq	throw
asm	else	operator	true
auto	enum	or	try
bitand	explicit	or_eq	typedef
bitor	export	private	typeid
bool	extern	protected	typename
break	false	public	union
case	float	register	unsigned
catch	for	reinterpret_cast	using
char	friend	return	virtual
class	goto	short	void
compl	if	signed	volatile
const	inline	sizeof	wchar_t
const_cast	int	static	while
continue	long	static_cast	xor
default	mutable	struct	xor_eq
delete	namespace	switch	
do	new	template	

Appendix B Operator Precedence

The following table summarizes C++ operator precedence. Several operators are not discussed in this book (typeid, the comma operator, ->*, and .*, for instance). For information on these operators, see Stroustrup's *The C++ Programming Language,* Third Edition (Addison-Wesley, 1997).

In the table, the operators are grouped by precedence level (highest to lowest), and a horizontal line separates each precedence level from the next-lower level.

In general, the binary operators group from left to right; the unary operators, from right to left; and the ?: operator, from right to left. Exception: The assignment operators group from right to left.

Precedence (highest to lowest)

Operator	Associativity	Remarks
::	Left to right	Scope resolution (binary)
::	Right to left	Global access (unary)
()	Left to right	Function call and function-style cast
[] -> .	Left to right	
++ --	Right to left	++ and - - as postfix operators
typeid dynamic_cast	Right to left	
static_cast const_cast	Right to left	
reinterpret_cast	Right to left	
++ -- ! Unary + Unary -	Right to left	++ and - - as prefix operators
~ Unary * Unary &	Right to left	
(cast) sizeof new delete	Right to left	
->* .*	Left to right	
* / %	Left to right	
+ -	Left to right	
<< >>	Left to right	
< <= > >=	Left to right	
== !=	Left to right	
&	Left to right	
^	Left to right	
|	Left to right	
&&	Left to right	
||	Left to right	
?:	Right to left	
= += -= *= /= %=	Right to left	
<<= >>= &= |= ^=	Right to left	
throw	Right to left	
,	Left to right	The sequencing operator, not the separator

Appendix C   A Selection of Standard Library Routines

The C++ standard library provides a wealth of data types, functions, and named constants. This appendix details only some of the more widely used library facilities. It is a good idea to consult the manual for your particular system to see what other types, functions, and constants the standard library provides.

This appendix is organized alphabetically according to the header file your program must #include before accessing the listed items. For example, to use a mathematics routine such as sqrt, you would #include the header file cmath as follows:

```
#include <cmath>
using namespace std;
  ⋮
y = sqrt(x);
```

Note that every identifier in the standard library is defined to be in the namespace std. Without the using directive above, you would write

```
y = std::sqrt(x);
```

C.1   The Header File cassert

assert(booleanExpr)
> *Argument:*   A logical (Boolean) expression
> *Effect:*   If the value of booleanExpr is true, execution of the program simply continues. If the value of booleanExpr is false, execution terminates immediately with a message stating the Boolean expression, the name of the file containing the source code, and the line number in the source code.
> *Function return value:* None (a void function)
> *Note:*   If the preprocessor directive #define NDEBUG is placed before the directive #include <cassert>, all assert statements are ignored.

C.2   The Header File cctype

isalnum(ch)
> *Argument:*   A char value ch
> *Function return value:* An int value that is
> - nonzero (true), if ch is a letter or a digit character ('A'–'Z', 'a'–'z', '0'–'9')
> - 0 (false), otherwise

isalpha(ch)
    Argument: A char value ch
    Function return value: An int value that is
- nonzero (true), if ch is a letter ('A'–'Z', 'a'–'z')
- 0 (false), otherwise

iscntrl(ch)
    Argument: A char value ch
    Function return value: An int value that is
- nonzero (true), if ch is a control character (in ASCII, a character with the value 0–31 or 127)
- 0 (false), otherwise

isdigit(ch)
    Argument: A char value ch
    Function return value: An int value that is
- nonzero (true), if ch is a digit character ('0'–'9')
- 0 (false), otherwise

isgraph(ch)
    Argument: A char value ch
    Function return value: An int value that is
- nonzero (true), if ch is a nonblank printable character (in ASCII, '!' through '~')
- 0 (false), otherwise

islower(ch)
    Argument: A char value ch
    Function return value: An int value that is
- nonzero (true), if ch is a lowercase letter ('a'–'z')
- 0 (false), otherwise

isprint(ch)
    Argument: A char value ch
    Function return value: An int value that is
- nonzero (true), if ch is a printable character, including the blank (in ASCII, ' ' through '~')
- 0 (false), otherwise

ispunct(ch)
    Argument: A char value ch
    Function return value: An int value that is
- nonzero (true), if ch is a punctuation character (equivalent to isgraph(ch) && !isalnum(ch))
- 0 (false), otherwise

isspace(ch)
Argument: A `char` value `ch`
Function return value: An `int` value that is
- nonzero (`true`), if `ch` is a whitespace character (blank, newline, tab, carriage return, form feed)
- 0 (`false`), otherwise

isupper(ch)
Argument: A `char` value `ch`
Function return value: An `int` value that is
- nonzero (`true`), if `ch` is an uppercase letter ('A'–'Z')
- 0 (`false`), otherwise

isxdigit(ch)
Argument: A `char` value `ch`
Function return value: An `int` value that is
- nonzero (`true`), if `ch` is a hexadecimal digit ('0'–'9', 'A'–'F', 'a'–'f')
- 0 (`false`), otherwise

tolower(ch)
Argument: A `char` value `ch`
Function return value: A character that is
- the lowercase equivalent of `ch`, if `ch` is an uppercase letter
- ch, otherwise

toupper(ch)
Argument: A `char` value `ch`
Function return value: A character that is
- the uppercase equivalent of `ch`, if `ch` is a lowercase letter
- ch, otherwise

C.3 The Header File `cfloat`

This header file supplies named constants that define the characteristics of floating-point numbers on your particular machine. Among these constants are the following:

FLT_DIG   Approximate number of significant digits in a `float` value on your machine
FLT_MAX   Maximum positive `float` value on your machine
FLT_MIN   Minimum positive `float` value on your machine
DBL_DIG   Approximate number of significant digits in a `double` value on your machine
DBL_MAX   Maximum positive `double` value on your machine
DBL_MIN   Minimum positive `double` value on your machine

LDBL_DIG	Approximate number of significant digits in a `long double` value on your machine
LDBL_MAX	Maximum positive `long double` value on your machine
LDBL_MIN	Minimum positive `long double` value on your machine

C.4 The Header File `climits`

This header file supplies named constants that define the limits of integer values on your particular machine. Among these constants are the following:

CHAR_BITS	Number of bits in a byte on your machine (8, for example)
CHAR_MAX	Maximum `char` value on your machine
CHAR_MIN	Minimum `char` value on your machine
SHRT_MAX	Maximum `short` value on your machine
SHRT_MIN	Minimum `short` value on your machine
INT_MAX	Maximum `int` value on your machine
INT_MIN	Minimum `int` value on your machine
LONG_MAX	Maximum `long` value on your machine
LONG_MIN	Minimum `long` value on your machine
UCHAR_MAX	Maximum `unsigned char` value on your machine
USHRT_MAX	Maximum `unsigned short` value on your machine
UINT_MAX	Maximum `unsigned int` value on your machine
ULONG_MAX	Maximum `unsigned long` value on your machine

C.5 The Header File `cmath`

In the `math` routines listed below, the following notes apply.

1. Error handling for incalculable or out-of-range results is system dependent.

2. All arguments and function return values are technically of type `double` (double-precision floating-point). However, single-precision (`float`) values may be passed to the functions.

`acos(x)`
  Argument: A floating-point expression x, where $-1.0 \le x \le 1.0$
  Function return value: Arc cosine of x, in the range 0.0 through π

`asin(x)`
  Argument: A floating-point expression x, where $-1.0 \le x \le 1.0$
  Function return value: Arc sine of x, in the range $-\pi/2$ through $\pi/2$

`atan(x)`
  Argument: A floating-point expression x
  Function return value: Arc tangent of x, in the range $-\pi/2$ through $\pi/2$

ceil(x)
   Argument: A floating-point expression x
   Function return value: "Ceiling" of x (the smallest whole number $\geq$ x)

cos(angle)
   Argument: A floating-point expression angle, measured in radians
   Function return value: Trigonometric cosine of angle

cosh(x)
   Argument: A floating-point expression x
   Function return value: Hyperbolic cosine of x

exp(x)
   Argument: A floating-point expression x
   Function return value: The value e(2.718...) raised to the power x

fabs(x)
   Argument: A floating-point expression x
   Function return value: Absolute value of x

floor(x)
   Argument: A floating-point expression x
   Function return value: "Floor" of x (the largest whole number $\leq$ x)

log(x)
   Argument: A floating-point expression x, where x > 0.0
   Function return value: Natural logarithm (base e) of x

log10(x)
   Argument: A floating-point expression x, where x > 0.0
   Function return value: Common logarithm (base 10) of x

pow(x, y)
   Arguments: Floating-point expressions x and y. If x = 0.0, y must be positive; if x $\leq$ 0.0, y must be a whole number
   Function return value: x raised to the power y

sin(angle)
   Argument: A floating-point expression angle, measured in radians
   Function return value: Trigonometric sine of angle

sinh(x)
   Argument: A floating-point expression x
   Function return value: Hyperbolic sine of x

sqrt(x)
  Argument: A floating-point expression x, where $x \geq 0.0$
  Function return value: Square root of x

tan(angle)
  Argument: A floating-point expression angle, measured in radians
  Function return value: Trigonometric tangent of angle

tanh(x)
  Argument: A floating-point expression x
  Function return value: Hyperbolic tangent of x

C.6   The Header File cstddef

This header file defines a few system-dependent constants and data types. From this header file, the only item we use in this book is the following symbolic constant:

NULL   The null pointer constant 0

C.7   The Header File cstdlib

abs(i)
  Argument: An int expression i
  Function return value: An int value that is the absolute value of i

atof(str)
  Argument: A C string (null-terminated char array) str representing a floating point number, possibly preceded by whitespace characters and a '+' or '−'
  Function return value: A double value that is the floating-point equivalent of the characters in str
  Note: Conversion stops at the first character in str that is inappropriate for a floating-point number. If no appropriate characters were found, the return value is system dependent.

atoi(str)
  Argument: A C string (null-terminated char array) str representing an integer number, possibly preceded by whitespace characters and a '+' or '−'
  Function return value: An int value that is the integer equivalent of the characters in str

Note: Conversion stops at the first character in `str` that is inappropriate for an integer number. If no appropriate characters were found, the return value is system dependent.

`atol(str)`
  Argument: A C string (null-terminated `char` array) `str` representing a long integer, possibly preceded by whitespace characters and a '+' or '–'

  Function return value: A `long` value that is the long integer equivalent of the characters in `str`

  Note: Conversion stops at the first character in `str` that is inappropriate for a `long` integer number. If no appropriate characters were found, the return value is system dependent.

`exit(exitStatus)`
  Argument: An `int` expression `exitStatus`
  Effect: Program execution terminates immediately with all files properly closed
  Function return value: None (a void function)
  Note: By convention, `exitStatus` is 0 to indicate normal program completion and is nonzero to indicate an abnormal termination.

`labs(i)`
  Argument: A `long` expression i
  Function return value: A `long` value that is the absolute value of i

`rand()`
  Argument: None
  Function return value: A random `int` value in the range 0 through RAND_MAX, a constant defined in `cstdlib` (RAND_MAX is usually the same as INT_MAX)
  Note: See `srand` below.

`srand(seed)`
  Argument: An `int` expression `seed`, where `seed` $\geq$ 0
  Effect: Using `seed`, the random number generator is initialized in preparation for subsequent calls to the `rand` function.
  Function return value: None (a void function)
  Note: If `srand` is not called before the first call to `rand`, a `seed` value of 1 is assumed.

system(str)
Argument:	A C string (null-terminated char array) str representing an operating system command, exactly as it would be typed by a user on the operating system command line
Effect:	The operating system command represented by str is executed.
Function return value:	An int value that is system dependent
Note:	Programmers often ignore the function return value, using the syntax of a void function call rather than a value-returning function call.

C.8   The Header File cstring

The header file cstring (not to be confused with the header file named string) supports manipulation of C strings (null-terminated char arrays).

strcat(toStr, fromStr)
Arguments:	C strings (null-terminated char arrays) toStr and fromStr, where toStr must be large enough to hold the result
Effect:	fromStr, including the null character '\0', is concatenated (joined) to the end of toStr.
Function return value:	The base address of toStr
Note:	Programmers usually ignore the function return value, using the syntax of a void function call rather than a value-returning function call.

strcmp(str1, str2)
Arguments:	C strings (null-terminated char arrays) str1 and str2
Function return value:	An int value < 0, if str1 < str2 lexicographically
	The int value 0, if str1 = str2 lexicographically
	An int value > 0, if str1 > str2 lexicographically

strcpy(toStr, fromStr)
Arguments:	toStr is a char array and fromStr is a C string (null-terminated char array), and toStr must be large enough to hold the result
Effect:	fromStr, including the null character '\0', is copied to toStr, overwriting what was there.
Function return value:	The base address of toStr
Note:	Programmers usually ignore the function return value, using the syntax of a void function call rather than a value-returning function call.

strlen(str)
Argument:	A C string (null-terminated char array) str
Function return value:	An int value ≥ 0 that is the length of str (excluding the '\0')

C.9 The Header File `string`

This header file supplies a programmer-defined data type (specifically, a *class*) named `string`. Associated with the `string` type are a data type `string::size_type` and a named constant `string::npos`, defined as follows:

`string::size_type`   An unsigned integer type related to the number of characters in a string

`string::npos`   The maximum value of type `string::size_type`

There are dozens of functions associated with the `string` type. Below are several of the most important ones. In the descriptions, `s` is assumed to be a variable (an *object*) of type `string`.

`s.c_str()`
   Arguments: None
   Function return value: The base address of a C string (null-terminated `char` array) corresponding to the characters stored in `s`

`s.find(arg)`
   Argument: An expression of type `string` or `char`, or a C string (such as a literal string)
   Function return value: A value of type `string::size_type` that gives the starting position in `s` where `arg` was found. If `arg` was not found, the return value is `string::npos`.
   Note: Positions of characters within a string are numbered starting at 0.

`getline(inStream, s)`
   Arguments: An input stream `inStream` (of type `istream` or `ifstream`) and a `string` object `s`
   Effect: Characters are input from `inStream` and stored into `s` until the newline character is encountered. (The newline character is consumed but not stored into `s`.)
   Function return value: Although the function technically returns a value (which we do not discuss here), programmers usually invoke the function as though it were a void function.

`s.length()`
   Arguments: None
   Function return value: A value of type `string::size_type` that gives the number of characters in the string

`s.size()`
   Arguments: None
   Function return value: The same as `s.length()`

```
s.substr(pos, len)
```
Arguments: Two unsigned integers, `pos` and `len`, representing a position and a length. The value of `pos` must be less than `s.length()`.

Function return value: A temporary `string` object that holds a substring of at most `len` characters, starting at position `pos` of `s`. If `len` is too large, it means "to the end" of the string in `s`.

Note: Positions of characters within a string are numbered starting at 0.

C.10 The Header File `sstream`

This header file supplies various classes derived from `iostream` that enable the user to apply stream-like operations to strings instead of files. In this text, we use only the `ostringstream` class, which enables us to convert numeric types to formatted string values. We can apply the insertion operator (<<) to an `ostringstream` object to append values to it, and then read back its contents in string form, using the `str` member function. In the following, `oss` is an `ostringstream` object.

```
ostringstream()
```
Argument: None
Return value: An empty `osstringstream` object

```
ostringstream(arg)
```
Argument: A string
Return value: An `ostringstream` object initialized to the argument string

```
<<
```
Left argument: An `ostringstream` object
Right argument: An expression that can be converted to a string, including output manipulators.
Return value: An `ostringstream` object
Evaluated: Left to right

```
oss.str()
```
Argument: None
Return value: A string containing whatever has been appended to `oss`

```
oss.str(arg)
```
Argument: A string
Effect: Assigns the value of the argument to `oss`. Using the empty string as the argument effectively sets the content of the `ostringstream` object to be empty.

Appendix D   Character Sets

The following charts show the ordering of characters in two widely used character sets: ASCII (American Standard Code for Information Interchange) and EBCDIC (Extended Binary Coded Decimal Interchange Code). The internal representation for each character is shown in decimal. For example, the letter *A* is represented internally as the integer 65 in ASCII and as 193 in EBCDIC. The space (blank) character is denoted by a "□".

Left Digit(s)	Right Digit				ASCII					
	0	1	2	3	4	5	6	7	8	9
0	NUL	SOH	STX	ETX	EOT	ENQ	ACK	BEL	BS	HT
1	LF	VT	FF	CR	SO	SI	DLE	DC1	DC2	DC3
2	DC4	NAK	SYN	ETB	CAN	EM	SUB	ESC	FS	GS
3	RS	US	□	!	"	#	$	%	&	'
4	(	)	*	+	,	-	.	/	0	1
5	2	3	4	5	6	7	8	9	:	;
6	<	=	>	?	@	A	B	C	D	E
7	F	G	H	I	J	K	L	M	N	O
8	P	Q	R	S	T	U	V	W	X	Y
9	Z	[	\	]	^	_	`	a	b	c
10	d	e	f	g	h	i	j	k	l	m
11	n	o	p	q	r	s	t	u	v	w
12	x	y	z	{			}	~	DEL		

Codes 00–31 and 127 are the following nonprintable control characters:

NUL	Null character	VT	Vertical tab	SYN	Synchronous idle
SOH	Start of header	FF	Form feed	ETB	End of transmitted block
STX	Start of text	CR	Carriage return	CAN	Cancel
ETX	End of text	SO	Shift out	EM	End of medium
EOT	End of transmission	SI	Shift in	SUB	Substitute
ENQ	Enquiry	DLE	Data link escape	ESC	Escape
ACK	Acknowledge	DC1	Device control one	FS	File separator
BEL	Bell character (beep)	DC2	Device control two	GS	Group separator
BS	Back space	DC3	Device control three	RS	Record separator
HT	Horizontal tab	DC4	Device control four	US	Unit separator
LF	Line feed	NAK	Negative acknowledge	DEL	Delete

Left Digit(s)	Right Digit	EBCDIC									
		0	1	2	3	4	5	6	7	8	9
6						□					
7						¢	.	<	(	+	|
8		&									
9		!	$	*	)	;	¬	−	/		
10								^	,	%	_
11		>	?								
12			`	:	#	@	'	=	"		a
13		b	c	d	e	f	g	h	i		
14							j	k	l	m	n
15		o	p	q	r						
16			~	s	t	u	v	w	x	y	z
17									\	{	}
18		[	]								
19					A	B	C	D	E	F	G
20		H	I								J
21		K	L	M	N	O	P	Q	R		
22								S	T	U	V
23		W	X	Y	Z						
24		0	1	2	3	4	5	6	7	8	9

In the EBCDIC table, nonprintable control characters—codes 00-63, 250-255, and those for which empty spaces appear in the chart—are not shown.

Appendix E   Program Style, Formatting, and Documentation

Throughout this text, we encourage the use of good programming style and documentation. Although the programs you write for class assignments may not be looked at by anyone except the person grading your work, outside of class you will write programs that will be used by others.

Useful programs have very long lifetimes, during which they must be modified and updated. When maintenance work must be done, either you or another programmer will have to do it. Good style and documentation are essential if another programmer is to understand and work with your program. You will also discover that after not working with your own program for a few months, you'll be amazed at how many of the details you've forgotten.

E.1   General Guidelines

The style used in the programs and fragments throughout this text provides a good starting point for developing your own style. Our goals in creating this style were to make it simple, consistent, and easy to read.

Style is of benefit only for a human reader of your program—differences in style make no difference to the computer. Good style includes the use of meaningful variable names, comments, and indentation of control structures, all of which help others to understand and work with your program. Perhaps the most important aspect of program style is consistency. If the style within a program is not consistent, then it becomes misleading and confusing.

Sometimes, a particular style is specified for you by your instructor or by the company you work for. When you are modifying someone else's code, you should use his or her style in order to maintain consistency within the program. However, you will also develop your own, personal programming style based on what you've been taught, your own experience, and your personal taste.

E.2   Comments

Comments are extra information included to make a program easier to understand. You should include a comment anywhere the code is difficult to understand. However, don't overcomment. Too many comments in a program can obscure the code and be a source of distraction.

In our style, there are four basic types of comments: headers, declarations, in-line, and sidebar.

Header comments appear at the top of the program and should include your name, the date that the program was written, and its purpose. It is also useful to include sections describing input, output, and assumptions. Think of the header comments as the reader's introduction to your program. Here is an example:

```
// This program computes the sidereal time for a given date and
// solar time.
//
// Written By: Your Name
//
// Date Completed: 4/8/05
//
// Input: A date and time in the form MM DD YYYY HH MM SS
//
// Output: Sidereal time in the form HH MM SS
//
// Assumptions: Solar time is specified for a longitude of 0
//     degrees (GMT, UT, or Z time zone)
```

Header comments should also be included for all user-defined functions (see Chapters 7 and 8).

Declaration comments accompany the constant and variable declarations in the program. Anywhere that an identifier is declared, it is helpful to include a comment that explains its purpose. In programs in the text, declaration comments appear to the right of the identifier being declared. For example:

```
const float E = 2.71828;     // The base of the natural logarithms

float deltaX;                // The difference in the x direction
float deltaY;                // The difference in the y direction
```

Notice that aligning the comments gives the code a neater appearance and is less distracting.

In-line comments are used to break long sections of code into shorter, more comprehensible fragments. These are often the names of modules in your algorithm design, although you may occasionally choose to include other information. It is generally a good idea to surround in-line comments with blank lines to make them stand out. For example:

```
// Prepare file for reading

scoreFile.open("scores.dat");

// Get data

scoreFile >> test1 >> weight1;
scoreFile >> test2 >> weight2;
scoreFile >> test3 >> weight3;

// Print heading


cout << "Test Score   Weight" << endl;
```

Even if comments are not used, blank lines can be inserted wherever there is a logical break in the code that you would like to emphasize.

Sidebar comments appear to the right of executable statements and are used to shed light on the purpose of the statement. Sidebar comments are often just pseudocode statements from the lowest levels of your design. If a complicated C++ statement requires some explanation, the pseudocode statement should be written to the right of the C++ statement. For example:

```
while (file1 && file2)     // While neither file is empty...
{
    ⋮
```

In addition to the four main types of comments that we have discussed, there are some miscellaneous comments that we should mention. After the `main` function, we recommend using a row of asterisks (or dashes or equal signs or ...) in a comment before and after each function to help it to stand out. For example:

```
//****************************************************************

void PrintSecondHeading()
{
    :
}

//****************************************************************
```

In this text, we use C++'s alternative comment form

```
/* Some comment */
```

to document the flow of information for each parameter of a function:

```
void GetData( /* out */ int age,        // Patient's age
              /* out */ int weight )    // Patient's weight
{
    :
}

void Print( /* in */     float val,     // Value to be printed
            /* inout */ int&  count )   // Number of lines printed
                                        //   so far
{
    :
}
```

(Chapter 7 describes the purpose of labeling each parameter as /* in */, /* out */, or /* inout */.)

Programmers sometimes place a comment after the right brace of a block (compound statement) to indicate which control structure the block belongs to:

```
while (num >= 0)
{
    :

    if (num == 25)
    {
        :
    } // if
} // while
```

Attaching comments in this fashion can help to clarify the code and aid in debugging mismatched braces.

E.3   Identifiers

The most important consideration in choosing a name for a data item or function in a program is that the name convey as much information as possible about what the data item is or what the function does. The name should also be readable in the context in which it is used. For example, the following names convey the same information but one is more readable than the other:

```
datOfInvc        invoiceDate
```

Identifiers for types, constants, and variables should be nouns, whereas names of void functions (non-value-returning functions) should be imperative verbs or phrases containing imperative verbs. Because of the way that value-returning functions are invoked, their names should be nouns or occasionally adjectives. Here are some examples:

Variables	address, price, radius, monthNumber
Constants	PI, TAX_RATE, STRING_LENGTH, ARRAY_SIZE
Data types	NameType, CarMakes, RoomLists, Hours
Void functions	GetData, ClearTable, PrintBarChart
Value-returning functions	CubeRoot, Greatest, Color, AreaOf, IsEmpty

Although an identifier may be a series of words, very long identifiers can become quite tedious and can make the program difficult to read.

The best approach to designing an identifier is to try writing out different names until you reach an acceptable compromise—and then write an especially informative declaration comment next to the declaration.

Capitalization is another consideration when choosing an identifier. C++ is a case-sensitive language; that is, uppercase and lowercase letters are distinct. Different programmers use different conventions for capitalizing identifiers. In this text, we begin each variable name with a lowercase letter and capitalize the beginning of each successive English word. We begin each function name and data type name with a capital letter and, again, capitalize the beginning of each successive English word. For named constants, we capitalize the entire identifier, separating successive English words with underscore (_) characters. Keep in mind, however, that C++ reserved words such as main, if, and while are always lowercase letters, and the compiler will not recognize them if you capitalize them differently.

E.4   Formatting Lines and Expressions

C++ allows you to break a long statement in the middle and continue onto the next line. (However, you cannot split a line in the middle of an identifier, a literal constant, or a string.) When you must split a line, it's important to choose a breaking point that is logical and readable. Compare the readability of the following code fragments.

```
cout << "For a radius of " << radius << " the diameter of the cir"
     << "cle is " << diameter << endl;
```

```
cout << "For a radius of " << radius
     << " the diameter of the circle is " << diameter << endl;
```

When you must split an expression across multiple lines, try to end each line with an operator. Also, try to take advantage of any repeating patterns in the expression. For example,

```
meanOfMaxima = (Maximum(set1Value1, set1Value2, set1Value3) +
               Maximum(set2Value1, set2Value2, set2Value3) +
               Maximum(set3Value1, set3Value2, set3Value3)) / 3.0;
```

When writing expressions, also keep in mind that spaces improve readability. Usually you should include one space on either side of the = operator and most other operators. Occasionally, spaces are left out to emphasize the order in which operations are performed. Here are some examples:

```
if (x+y > y+z)
    maximum = x + y;
else
    maximum = y + z;
hypotenuse = sqrt(a*a + b*b);
```

E.5   Indentation

The purpose of indenting statements in a program is to provide visual cues to the reader and to make the program easier to debug. When a program is properly indented, the way the statements are grouped is immediately obvious. Compare the following two program fragments:

```
while (count <= 10)           while (count <= 10)
{                             {
cin >> num;                       cin >> num;
if (num == 0)                     if (num == 0)
{                                 {
count++;                              count++;
num = 1;                              num = 1;
}                                 }
cout << num << endl;              cout << num << endl;
cout << count << endl;           cout << count << endl;
}                             }
```

As a basic rule in this text, each nested or lower-level item is indented by four spaces. Exceptions to this rule are parameter declarations and statements that are split across two or more lines. Indenting by four spaces is a matter of personal preference. Some people prefer to indent by three, five, or even more than five spaces.

In this book, we indent the entire body of a function. Also, in general, any statement that is part of another statement is indented. For example, the If-Then-Else contains two parts, the then-clause and the else-clause. The statements within both clauses are indented four spaces beyond the beginning of the If-Then-Else statement. The If-Then statement is indented like the If-Then-Else, except that there is no else-clause. Here are examples of the If-Then-Else and the If-Then:

```cpp
if (sex == MALE)
{
    maleSalary = maleSalary + salary;
    maleCount++;
}
else
    femaleSalary = femaleSalary + salary;

if (count > 0)
    average = total / count;
```

For nested If-Then-Else statements that form a generalized multiway branch (the If-Then-Else-If, described in Chapter 5), a special style of indentation is used in the text. Here is an example:

```cpp
if (month == JANUARY)
    monthNumber = 1;
else if (month == FEBRUARY)
    monthNumber = 2;
else if (month == MARCH)
    monthNumber = 3;
else if (month == APRIL)
    ⋮
else
    monthNumber = 12;
```

The remaining C++ statements all follow the basic indentation guideline mentioned previously. For reference purposes, here are examples of each.

```cpp
while (count <= 10)
{
    cin >> value;
    sum = sum + value;
    count++;
}

do
{
    GetAnswer(letter);
    PutAnswer(letter);
} while (letter != 'N');

for (count = 1; count <= numSales; count++)
    cout << '*';
```

```
for (count = 10; count >= 1; count--)
{
    inFile >> dataItem;
    outFile << dataItem << ' ' << count << endl;
}

switch (color)
{
    RED     : cout << "Red";
              break;
    ORANGE  : cout << "Orange";
              break;
    YELLOW  : cout << "Yellow";
              break;
    GREEN   :
    BLUE    :
    INDIGO  :
    VIOLET  : cout << "Short visible wavelengths";
              break;
    WHITE   :
    BLACK   : cout << "Not valid colors";
              color = NONE;
}
```

Outstanding New Titles:

Computer Science Illuminated, Second Edition
Nell Dale and John Lewis
ISBN: 0-7637-0799-6
©2004

Programming and Problem Solving with C++, Fourth Edition
Nell Dale and Chip Weems
ISBN: 0-7637-0798-8
©2004

Programming and Problem Solving with Java
Nell Dale, Chip Weems,
and Mark R. Headington
ISBN: 0-7637-0490-3
©2003

C++ Plus Data Structures, Third Edition
Nell Dale
ISBN: 0-7637-0481-4
©2003

Databases Illuminated
Catherine Ricardo
ISBN: 0-7637-3314-8
©2004

Applied Data Structures with C++
Peter Smith
ISBN: 0-7637-2562-5
©2004

Foundations of Algorithms Using Java Pseudocode
Richard Neapolitan and Kumarss Naimipour
ISBN: 0-7637-2129-8
©2004

Foundations of Algorithms Using C++ Pseudocode, Third Edition
Richard Neapolitan and Kumarss Naimipour
ISBN: 0-7637-2387-8
©2004

Artificial Intelligence Illuminated
Ben Coppin
ISBN: 0-7637-3230-3
©2004

Managing Software Projects
Frank Tsui
ISBN: 0-7637-2546-3
©2004

The Essentials of Computer Organization and Architecture
Linda Null and Julia Lobur
ISBN: 0-7637-0444-X
©2003

Readings in CyberEthics, Second Edition
Richard Spinello and Herman Tavani
ISBN: 0-7637-2410-6
©2004

A Complete Guide to C#
David Bishop
ISBN: 0-7637-2249-9
©2004

C#.NET Illuminated
Art Gittleman
ISBN: 0-7637-2593-5
©2005

A First Course in Complex Analysis with Applications
Dennis G. Zill and Patrick Shanahan
ISBN: 0-7637-1437-2
©2003

Discrete Mathematics, Second Edition
James L. Hein
ISBN: 0-7637-2210-3
©2003

http://www.jbpub.com/

**JONES AND BARTLETT
PUBLISHERS**
BOSTON   TORONTO   LONDON   SINGAPORE

1.800.832.0034

Take Your Courses to the Next Level

Turn the page to preview new and forthcoming titles in Computer Science and Math from Jones and Bartlett…

Providing solutions for students and educators in the following disciplines:

- Introductory Computer Science
- Java
- C++
- Databases
- C#
- Data Structures

- Algorithms
- Network Security
- Software Engineering
- Discrete Mathematics
- Engineering Mathematics
- Complex Analysis

Please visit http://computerscience.jbpub.com/ and http://math.jbpub.com/ to learn more about our exciting publishing programs in these disciplines.